KB060452

서울대학교 법학연구소
Medvlla Iurisprudentiae **02**

Corporate Law and Governance
- Collected Papers

김건식

Kon Sik Kim

박영사

서문

이 책은 내가 지난 40년간 영문으로 발표한 논문을 모은 책이다. 원래는 따로 책으로 묶을 만큼 대단한 것도 아니기에 그냥 내버려둘 생각이었다. 그런데 마침 서울대 법학연구소에서 퇴임교수들의 대표적인 논문을 골라 책으로 발간한다는 방침에 따라 내게도 선별을 독촉하는 전화와 이메일을 보내왔다. 이미 기존 논문들을 모은 책을 따로 출간해 온 나로서는 중복을 피할 수 없어 난처했다. 법학연구소 소장을 맡고 계신 정긍식 선생께 내 사정을 말씀드리고 대신 영문논문을 모은 책을 내주실 수 있는지 문의했더니 선뜻 응해주셨다.

이 책에 실린 16편의 논문은 내 40년 연구인생에 걸쳐서 발표된 것이다. 처음 두 편(I-3, IV-3)은 유학시절에 작성한 것이다. 유학을 마치고 강단에 설 때만해도 장차 영문논문을 많이 쓸 수 있을 것으로 기대했다. 그런데 세 번째 영문논문을 발표하기까지는 무려 14년의 세월을 보내야만 했다. 영문으로 박사학위논문을 작성하는데 진이 빠진 탓도 있지만 그 보다는 우리 법에 관한 글을 구태여 영문으로 작성하는 작업의 의미에 대해서 회의를 품었던 탓이 더 크다. 그러나 전반적으로 국제교류가 활성화될 뿐 아니라 특히 내 전문분야인 비교회사법 내지 비교기업지배구조에 대한 국제학계의 관심이 높아감에 따라 그런 회의는 차츰 수그러들게 되었다.

이 책에 실린 논문은 거의 주문생산에 의한 것이다. 학생 때 발표한 두 편과 Stephen Choi교수와 쓴 논문(III-2) 정도가 예외인 셈이다. 국제교류의 빈도가 높아짐에 따라 외국에서 글을 의뢰받는 경우가 늘게 되고 여러 사정상 그것을 거절하기 어려운 경우가 많았다. 그러다 보니 40년 동안 나온 것을 모았다곤 하지만 논문의 압도적 다수가 지난 20년 사이에 발표된 것이고 절반 정도는 지난 10년 사이에 발표된 것이다. 오히려 나이가 들면서 영문논문이 늘게 된 것은 국내 학계에서의 발표요청이 급속히 줄어듦에 따른 결과이기도 하다.

16편의 글들 중에서 6편이 공저한 것이다. 학자들의 공동작업은 우리 법학계에서는 별로 많지 않지만 외국에서는 흔하다. 나로서는 오래 전부터 공동작업을 적극적으로 시도했다. 일을 어떻게 분담하더라도 적어도 혼자서 작업하는 경우보다 훨씬 수고를 덜 수 있다는 점이 큰 매력이다. 실수를 최소화할 수 있을 뿐 아니라 종종 뜻밖의 깨달음을 얻을 수도 있다. 이들 6편의 작업을 하면서도 다소간 차이는 있지만 공저자로부터 많은 도움을 받았다. 이 기회를 빌려 새삼 공동작업에 응해주신 공저자 분들께 감사의 뜻을 표한다.

독자들의 양해를 구해야 할 점도 적지 않다. 이 글들은 오랜 기간에 걸쳐 작성된 것이다 보니 정도의 차이는 있지만 이제 낡아버린 경우가 많다. 또한 비슷한 테마가 다뤄지는 경우에는 다소 중복된 부분도 없지 않다. 그에 못지않게 견디기 어려운 것은 워낙 다양한 출판물에 발표하다보니 스타일이 각양각색이란 것이다. 이런 문제점들을 보완하여 깔끔한 책의 모습을 갖추려면 어마어마한 시간과 노력이 필요할 것이다. 독자들께는 죄송한 말씀이지만 주어진 시간은 한정되고 예정된 작업들은 줄지어 있는 내 현실을 고려할 때 그런 부담을 선택할 수는 없었다. 어차피 체계적인 구조를 갖춘 단행본도 아니니 독자들께서 너그럽게 양해해주시기를 부탁드리는 바이다. 내놓기 부끄러운 논문집이지만 후진들이 이런 정도의 글이라면 나도 한번 써볼 수 있겠다고 발심(發心)을 하는 계기라도 될 수 있다면 다행이겠다.

끝으로 이 책이 나올 수 있도록 도움을 주신 분들께 감사드리고 싶다. 서울대학교 법학전문대학원의 장승화 원장님과 정긍식 소장님의 지원에 감사드린다. 그리고 연보·논저 목록과 대담을 정리해준 송순섭 조교와 편집을 맡아준 박영사의 한두희 대리께 다시 한번 감사드리는 바이다.

2020년 4월 26일
김건식

김건식(金建植) 교수 연보·논저 목록

I. 연 보

생년월일 : 1955년 1월 10일
부 : 김우봉(金又峰)　　모 : 박순임(朴順任)
처 : 윤현숙(尹賢淑)　　자 : 현구(炫九), 현진(炫鎭)
e-mail : konsikim@snu.ac.kr

[학력]

1973. 2.	경기고등학교 졸업
1977. 2.	서울대학교 법과대학 법학사(LL.B.)
1979. 2.	서울대학교 대학원 법학석사(LL.M.)
1980. 6.	Harvard Law School 법학석사(LL.M.)
1985. 6.	University of Washington School of Law 법학박사(J.D.)
1995. 12.	University of Washington School of Law 법학박사(Ph.D.)

[수상]

2012. 4.	황조근정훈장
2015. 2.	무애학술상(무애학술연구재단)
2017. 2.	우수논문상(한중법학회)

[학내경력]

1986. 9.~1988. 9.	서울대학교 법과대학 전임강사
1988. 10.~1993. 3.	서울대학교 법과대학 조교수
1993. 4.~1998. 3.	서울대학교 법과대학 부교수
1998. 4.~2020. 2.	서울대학교 법과대학/법학전문대학원 교수
1994. 6.~1995. 5.	서울대학교 법과대학 학생부학장
2000. 1.~2002. 1.	Journal of Korean Law 초대 편집위원장
2001. 12.~2003. 12.	서울대학교 법학연구소장
2002. 4.~2008. 5.	서울대학교 법학연구소 금융법센터장

| 2003. 9.～2020. 2. | BFL 편집위원장 |
| 2008. 6.～2010. 5. | 서울대학교 법과대학/법학전문대학원 학장/원장 |

[학외경력: 국내]

1992. 1.～1996. 12.	법무부 민사특별법제정특별분과 위원회 위원(집단소송법)
1996. 9.～2001. 2.	금융감독위원회 증권조사심의조정위원
1997. 4.～2008. 5.	한국상장회사협의회 주식업무자문위원
1997. 12.～1999. 12.	법무부 상법개정위원회 및 회사법개정위원회 위원
1998. 3.～2000. 3.	SK텔레콤 주식회사 사외감사
1998. 9.～2004. 1.	재정경제부 금융산업발전심의회 위원
1998. 10.～현재	성보문화재단 이사
2001. 4.～2003. 3.	금융감독위원회 회계감리위원
2004. 3.～2009. 2.	KT 사외이사
2004. 3.～2010. 3.	LG화학 주식회사 사외이사
2008. 7.～2010. 6.	한국법학전문대학원협의회 이사장
2010. 6.～2014. 12.	메트라이프생명보험주식회사 사외이사
2012. 12.～2014. 12.	안전행정부 정보공개위원회 위원장
2013. 3.～2014. 2.	한국상사법학회 회장
2013. 5.～2015. 5.	법무부 정책위원회 위원

[학외경력: 국외]

2002～2005	World Bank (East Asia & Pacific Regional Office), Short Term Consultant
2010～2014	일본 동경대학 법과대학원 자문위원회 위원
2014～2020	Global Corporate Governance Colloquia 이사
2017. 4.	National University of Singapore, Law Faculty, 자문위원 (International Advisory Panel)
2019～현재	European Corporate Governance Institute, Research Member

[해외연구 및 국제교류]

1986. 3.～1986. 6.	University of Washington School of Law, 강사
1990. 7.～1991. 8.	독일 뮌헨대학교 객원연구원(독일 훔볼트재단 연구비 수령)
1995. 8.～1996. 2.	일본 동경대학 대학원 법학정치학연구과, 객원조교수
1997. 1.～1997. 2.	홍콩 City University of Hong Kong, 객원교수
1998. 7.～1999. 7.	Duke Law School (Hong Kong program), 교수

1998. 1.~1998. 2.	Harvard Law School, 객원교수
2000. 7.	Stanford Law School 객원연구원
2001. 9.~2001. 11.	Columbia Law School 객원연구원
2011. 10.	중국인민대학 법학원 객원연구원
2016. 1.~2016. 2.	National University of Singapore, Law Faculty, 객원연구교수(2018. 1.~2018. 2.) (Visiting Research Professor)
2016. 8.~2016. 12.	New York University School of Law, 객원교수(Global Professor)
2019. 1.~2019. 2.	National University of Singapore, Law Faculty, Lionel Sheridan Visiting Professor
2020. 1.	호주 Monash University Law Faculty, 객원연구원

II. 논저 목록

1. 단행본(단독 및 공동)

- 『프랑스상사회사법개설』, 법무부(1988.12) (공저자: 김은기, 윤영신).
- 『무의결권우선주에 관한 연구』, 한국상장회사협의회(1994.11).
- *Chaebol and Corporate Governance in Korea*, 워싱턴 주립대 박사학위 논문(1995.12).
- 『미국증권법』, 홍문사(1996.1).
- 『스왑거래의 법적 연구』, 한국금융연구원(1996.12).
- *International Encyclopaedia of Corporations and Partnerships Monograph "South Korea"*, Kluwer Law International (공저자: Choong-Kee Lee)(1999.10).
- 『미국의 증권규제』, 홍문사(2001.7) (공저자: 송옥렬).
- 『기업회계기준의 법적 지위에 대한 의견』, 한국회계연구원(2003.3) (공저자: 박정훈, 이창희).
- 『증권거래법』 제4판, 두성사(2006.6) (초판: 2000.9; 제2판: 2001.12; 제3판: 2004.5).
- 『21세기 회사법 개정의 논리』, 도서출판 소화(2007.3) (공저자: 송옥렬, 안수현, 윤영신, 정순섭, 최문희, 한기정).
- 『기업지배구조와 법』, 도서출판 소화(2010.3).
- 『회사법연구 I』, 도서출판 소화(2010.9) (2011년 학술원 우수학술도서).
- 『회사법 연구 II』, 도서출판 소화(2010.9) (2011년 학술원 우수학술도서).
- 『자본시장법』 제3판, 두성사(2013.10) (공저자: 정순섭) (초판: 2009.4; 제2판: 2010.9).
- 『주석상법(회사IV)』 제5판(정동윤 편), 한국사법행정학회(2014.12) (공저자: 송종준, 최완진) (제4판: 2003년; 제3판: 1999.2).
- 『회사법』 초판, 박영사(2015.1).
- 『신체계회사법』 제7판, 박영사(2018.2) (공저자: 노혁준, 박준, 송옥렬, 안수현, 윤영신, 최문희) (초판: 2010.3; 제2판: 2010.10; 제3판: 2012.2; 제4판: 2013.2; 제5판: 2014.2; 제6판: 2016.2).
- 『중국회사법』, 박영사(2018.2) (공저자: 김종길, 남옥매, 서의경, 양병찬, 오일환, 장진보, 정영진).
- 『회사법』 제4판, 박영사(2020.2) (공저자: 노혁준, 천경훈) (제3판: 2018.2; 제2판: 2016.3).
- *Corporations and Partnerships-South Korea* (third edition), Kluwer(2019.4) (공저자: Kyung-Hoon Chun, Hyeok-Joon Rho, Ok-Rial Song) (1판: 2014.3; 2판 2015.10).

2. 편집

- 『상사판례연구 I, II, III』, 박영사(1996.11) (공편자: 최기원, 김성태, 목영준, 김용덕, 권순일).
- 『금융거래법강의』, 법문사(1999.3) (공편자: 남효순).
- 『새로운 금융법체제의 모색』, 도서출판 소화(2006.11) (공편자: 정순섭).

- 『지주회사와 법(보정판)』, 도서출판 소화(2008.6) (공편자: 노혁준) (초판: 2005.10).
- *Transforming Corporate Governance in East Asia*, Routledge (2008.7) (공편자: Hideki Kanda, Curtis Milhaupt).
- *German and Asian Perspectives on Company Law*, Mohr Siebeck (2016.12) (공편자: Holger Fleischer, Hideki Kanda, Peter Mülbert).
- *Issues and Challenges in Corporate and Capital Market Law: Germany and East Asia*, Mohr Siebeck (2018.6) (공편자: Holger Fleischer, Hideki Kanda, Peter Mülbert).
- *German and East Asian Perspectives on Corporate and Capital Market Law: Investors versus Companies*, Mohr Siebeck (2019) (공편자: Holger Fleischer, Hideki Kanda, Peter Mülbert).

3. 논문

- "Class Action 소고", 서울대학교 대학원 석사학위논문(1979.2).
- "the Demand on Directors Requirement and the Business Judgment Rule in the Shareholders Derivative Suit", 6 *Journal of Corporation Law* 511-529 (1981.10).
- "미국주식회사법", 한미상사법비교연구(한미상사법비교연구회) (1982.6).
- "관계회사간의 거래와 조세회피", 세무사 1985년 2월호(1985.2).
- "미연방증권법규상 증권의 정의", 대한변호사협회지 1985년 8월호(1985.8).
- "Corporate Governance in Korea", 8 *Journal of Comparative Business and Capital Market Law* 21-37 (1986.10).
- "회사의 정치헌금", 법조 제35권 제2호(1986.10).
- "은행업무와 증권업무의 분리(1)", 서울대학교 법학 제27권 제4호(1986.12).
- "회사법의 구조개혁", 서울대학교 법학 제28권 제1호(1987.4).
- "무의결권주식에 대한 소고", 증권 제52호(1987.7).
- "주식과 의결권 – 차등의결권주식에 대한 논의를 중심으로 –", 『사회과학의 제문제』(임원택 교수 정년기념 논문집), 법문사(1988.3).
- "미국 소비자신용법제의 개관", 서울대학교 법학 제29권 제3·4호(1988.12).
- "리스계약의 운용실태", 민사판례연구 제11집(1989.4).
- "명의개서의 해태와 무상발행신주의 귀속", 판례월보 1989년 4월호(1989.4).
- "기업내용공시의 법적규제 – 적시공시를 중심으로 –", 상장협 제19호(1989.5).
- "비엔나조약의 역사, 현상, 장래", 상사법연구 제7권(1989.12).
- "감사의 제3자에 대한 책임", 민사판례연구 제12집(1990.4).
- "현물출자와 신주인수권", 서울대학교 법학 제31권 제1·2호(1990.8).
- "주식발행을 통한 자금조달과 중소기업", 저스티스 제24권 제1호(1991.6).
- "고객의 주식을 보관하는 증권회사의 의무", 인권과 정의 1991년 12월호(1991.12).
- "소수주주의 보호와 주주의 성실의무", 서울대학교 법학 제32권 제3·4호(1991.12).

- "주주간의 이해상충에 관한 시론", 한림법학포럼 제1호(1992.4).
- "콘체른에서의 소수주주보호", 『기업법의 현대적 과제』(행솔 이태로 교수 화갑기념 논문집), 조세통 람사(1992).
- "리스거래에서 물건인수와 차수증의 발급이 갖는 의미", 인권과 정의 1992년 11월호(1992.11).
- "부존재하는 주주총회결의에 기하여 선임된 대표이사와 거래한 제3자의 보호", 서울대학교 법 학 제34권 제1호(1993.2).
- "불법행위법과 법경제학", 민사판례연구 제15집(1993.4).
- "주주의 직접손해와 간접손해", 서울대학교 법학 제34권 제2호(1993.8).
- "미국회사법상 반대주주의 주식매수청구권", 서울대학교 법학 제34권 제3·4호(1993.12).
- "기업집단과 소수주주보호: 미국회사법을 중심으로", 성곡논총 제25집(1994.6).
- "자기거래와 미국회사법의 절차적 접근방식", 서울대학교 법학 제35권 제1호(1994.6).
- "미국증권법(I)", 증권 제81호(1994.9).
- "미국증권법(II)", 증권 제82호(1995.1).
- "재벌과 소수주주보호", 『한국의 대기업: 누가 소유하며 어떻게 지배되는가?』, 기업구조연구회 (1995.2).
- "미국증권법(III)", 증권 제83호(1995.4).
- "미국의 법률가 양성제도", 서울대학교 법학 제36권 제1호(1995.5).
- "우리나라 기업내용공시제도의 문제점과 개선방안", 상장협 제33호(1996.5).
- "내부통제 메커니즘의 법리적 고찰", 정광선 편, 『21세기 한국기업의 통합체제』(1996.7).
- "주주대표소송의 활성화와 관련된 몇 가지 문제점 – 일본의 경험을 참고로 하여 –", 서울대학교 법학 제37권 제2호(1996.9).
- "지주회사규제의 재검토: 일본에서의 개정론을 중심으로", 권오승 편, 『공정거래법강의』(1996.11).
- "미국의 증권예탁결제제도", 비교사법 제3권 제2호(1996.12).
- "증권회사직원의 이익보장약정과 투자자의 구제", 민사판례연구 제19집(1997.2).
- "상호와 상표의 법적 보호", 정상조 편, 『지적재산권법 강의』, 홍문사(1997.3).
- "개정증권거래법상의 공개매수제도", 인권과 정의 제248호(1997.4).
- "독일의 회사지배와 은행: Mülbert교수의 법률가대회보고서를 중심으로", 서울대학교 법학 제 38권 제1호(1997.5).
- "우리 상법의 성립사적, 비교법적 고찰: 총칙, 상행위편", 『기업과 법』(도암 김교창변호사 화갑기념 논문집), 한국사법행정학회(1997).
- "리스계약", 『민법주해XVI』, 박영사(1997.7).
- "증권판례의 최근 동향", 민사판례연구 제20집(1998.6).
- "금융자산의 증권화", 상사법연구 제17권 제2호(1998.10) (공저자: 이중기).
- "새로운 경영감독체제의 모색", 상장협 제38호(1998.10) (공저자: 윤영신).
- "회사형투자신탁과 투자자보호", 『21세기 상사법의 전개』(하촌 정동윤 선생 화갑기념 논문집), 법문사(1999).

- "이른바 워런트의 도입을 위한 소론", 서울대학교 법학 제40권 제1호(1999.5).
- "인터넷을 통한 증권거래와 증권거래법", 인터넷 증권거래의 법제도적 기반에 관한 연구(정보통신정책연구원 연구보고서) (1999.10).
- "집단적 증권투자의 구조", 인권과 정의 1999년 10월호(1999.10).
- "글로발시대의 자금조달 - 우리 자금조달법제의 국제적 적합성", 국제거래법연구 제8집(1999.12).
- "지배주주의 통제방안: 행동, 구조, 시장", 이선외 편, 『한국 기업지배구조의 현재와 미래』, 미래경영개발연구원(2000.3) (공저자: 정승욱).
- "감사위원회, 어떻게 도입할 것인가", 이선외 편, 『한국 기업지배주주의 현재와 미래』, 미래경영개발연구원(2000.3) (공저자: 윤영신).
- "외부감사인의 부실감사로 인한 손해배상책임", 최기원 외 편, 『상사판례연구IV』, 박영사(2000.4).
- "2000년 개정증권거래법 해설", 최기원 외 편, 『상사판례연구V』, 박영사(2000.4).
- "Controlling the Controlling Shareholders : Conduct, Structure and Market", *Recent Transformations in Korea Law and Society* (Dae-Kyu Yoon ed.), Seoul National University Press (2000.6) (공저자: Seung-Wook Jeong).
- "미국법상 주주의 회계장부열람권", 판례실무연구 IV(2000.9).
- "기업변호사의 역할과 윤리", 서울법대 편, 『법률가의 윤리와 책임』, 박영사(2000.9).
- "금융지주회사의 법적 규제", 권오승 편, 『공정거래법 강의II』, 법문사(2000.11).
- "벤처투자와 법적인프라", 증권법연구 제1권 제1호(2000.12).
- "파생금융상품", 민사판례연구 제23집(2001.2).
- "주식배당과 과제", 서울대학교 법학 제41권 제4호(2001.2) (공저자: 이창희).
- "내부자거래규제의 이론적 기초", 증권학회지 제28집(2001.6).
- "기업지배구조에 관한 최근의 논의에서 무엇을 배울 것인가?", 기업지배구조연구 제1호(2001.12).
- "회사법상 충실의무법리의 재검토", 『(21세기) 한국상사법학의 과제와 전망』(심당 송상현 선생 화갑기념 논문집), 박영사(2002).
- "이사의 배상책임보험", 상장협 제45호(2002.3) (공저자: 최문희).
- "준법감시인제도의 조기정착을 위한 시론", 증권법연구 제3권 제1호(2002.6) (공저자: 안수현).
- "Intermediary Risk in the Indirect Holding System: A Comment From the Perspective of a Civil Law Jurist", 12 *Duke Journal of International and Comparative Law* 335 (2002.10).
- "기업지배구조의 개선과 경쟁: 기업지배구조특별부의 신설을 제안하며", 증권법연구 제3권 제2호(2002.12) (공저자: 스티븐 최).
- "Establishing a New Stock Market for Shareholder Value Oriented Firms in Korea", 3 *Chicago Journal of International Law* (University of Chicago Law School) 277 (2002.12) (공저자: Stephen Choi).
- "채권결제제도의 개혁: 일본의 예를 중심으로", 증권법연구 제4권 제1호(2003.6) (공저자: 김이수).
- "자본제도와 유연한 회사법", 이창희·장승화 편, 『절차적 정의와 법의 지배』, 박영사(2003.6).

- "Revamping Fiduciary Duties in Korea: Does Law Matter to Corporate Govenance", in Curtis Milhaupt ed., *Global Markets, Domestic Institutions*, Columbia University Press (2003.8) (공저자: Joongi Kim).
- "우리 기업지배구조의 전환", 강원법학 제16권(김정후 선생 정년기념 논문집) (2003.8).
- "이사의 주의의무과 경영판단원칙", 민사판례연구 제26집(2004.2).
- "법적 시각에서 본 내부통제", BFL 제4호(2004.3) (공저자: 안수현).
- "금융법통합작업의 추진현황 – 법제화방안을 중심으로", 금융연구 제18권 별책(2004.8) (공저자: 정순섭).
- "내부자거래와 내부정보의 이용", 『상법연구의 향기』(정희철 교수 정년 20년 기념논문집), 인산기념 논집편찬위원회(2004.10).
- "증권의 다양화에 관한 기초적 고찰", 민사판례연구 제27집(2005.2).
- "수익증권 판매회사의 환매의무", BFL 제12호(2005.7).
- "법적 시각에서 본 감사위원회", BFL 제13호(2005.9).
- "지주회사의 운영과 회사법: 총론적 고찰", 『지주회사와 법』, 도서출판 소화(2005.10) (공저자: 노혁준).
- "21세기를 맞는 우리 회사법과 회사법학: 그 한계와 과제", 저스티스 제92호(2006.7).
- "재벌총수의 사익추구행위와 회사법", BFL 제19호(2006.9).
- "금융환경의 변화와 금융규제", 김건식·정순섭 편, 『새로운 금융법체제의 모색』, 도서출판 소화(2006.11) (공저자: 정순섭).
- "韓國における企業統治の轉換", ソフトロー研究 제7호(日本 東京大學) (2006.11) (翻訳: 河南大德).
- "Consolidation of Financial Services Laws in Korea: an Interim Report", *Regulatory Reforms in the Age of Financial Consolidation* (Lee-Jay Cho & Joon-Kyung Kim ed.), KDI Press (2006.12) (공저자: 정순섭).
- "증권거래법상 상장법인 특례규정의 문제점과 개선방안", BFL 제23호(2007.5) (공저자: 최문희).
- "구증권투자신탁업법상 판매회사의 환매의무", BFL 제23호(2007.5).
- "경영자 보수와 기업지배구조", 기업지배구조연구 제33권(2007.7/8).
- "이사의 감시의무와 내부통제", 상사판례연구 제7권, 박영사(2007.7).

- "Transplanting Audit Committees to Korean Soil: A Window into the Evolution of Korean Corporate Governance", 9 *Asian Pacific Law & Policy Journal* 163 (2007.12).
- "The Role of Judges in Corporate Governance: the Korean Experience", *Transforming Corporate Governance in East Asia* (Hideki Kanda *et al.*, eds.), Routledge (2008.7).
- "Corporate Legal Personality and Corporate Loss in Korean Law", *Festschrift für Klaus J. Hopt zum 70. Geburtstag am 24. August 2010: Unternehmen, Markt und Verantwortung*, Walter de Gruyter (2010.8).
- "도산에 임박한 회사와 이사의 의무", 상사법연구 제30권 제3호(2011.11).
- "영국 도산법의 부당거래와 부실기업 이사의 의무", 『기업법·지식재산법의 새로운 지평』(진산 김문환 선생 정년기념 논문집) 제2권, 법문사(2011).

- "Invigorating Shareholder Derivative Actions in South Korea", *The Derivative Action in Asia* (Dan W. Puchiniak *et al.* eds.), Cambridge University Press (2012.7) (공저자: Hyeok-Joon Rho).
- "기업지배구조", 『회사법대계(I)』(2013.2).
- "企業支配構造の変化 – 日本・韓国・中国の経験を素材にして, 會社・金融・法(上) (岩原紳作외 편)", 商事法務(2013.11) (翻訳: 田中佑季).
- "Codification in East Asia: Commercial Law", *Codification in East Asia* (Wen-Yeu Wang ed.), Springer International Publishing (2014.2).
- "Corporate Law and Corporate Law Scholarship in Korea: A Comparative Essay", *Legal Innovations in Asia* (John O. Haley & Toshiko Takenaka eds.), Edward Elgar (2014.10).
- "법인격과 법인격부인원리", BFL 제69호(2015.1).
- "Dynamics of shareholder power in Korea", *Research Handbook on Shareholder Power* (Randall S. Thomas & Jennifer G. Hill eds.), Edward Elgar (2015.8).
- "주주총회 결의하자소송의 하자사유에 관한 입법론적 고찰", 상사법연구 제34권 제3호(2015.11) (공저자: 최문희).
- "삼성물산 합병 사례를 통해 본 우리 기업지배구조의 과제 – 법, 제도, 문화", BFL 제74호(2015.11).
- "중국 국유기업의 민영화 – 중국 기업지배구조의 서론적 고찰", 중국법연구 제28집(2016.5).
- "기업집단과 관계자거래", 상사법연구 제35권 제3호(2016.8).
- "Declining Relevance of Lawsuits on the Validity of Shareholder Resolution in Korea – A Comparative Essay German and Asian Perspectives on Company Law", in Holger Fleischer *et al.* eds., *German and Asian Perspectives on Company Law*, Mohr Siebeck (2016.12) (공저자: Moon-Hee Choi).
- "중국의 기업집단과 관계자거래", 중국법연구 제31집(2017.8).
- "Varieties of Independent Directors in Asia: Divergent Convergence", in Dan W. Puchniak *et al.*, *Independent Directors in Asia: A Historical, Contextual and Comparative Approach* (Cambridge University Press) (2017.11) (공저자: Dan W. Puchniak).
- "자사주식 취득에 대한 회사의 금융지원", 외법논집 제42권 제4호(2018.11).
- "이사회 업무집행에 관한 주주간계약", 비교사법 제26권 제1호(통권84호) (2019.2).
- "Related Party Transactions in East Asia", in Luca Enriques and Tobias Tröger eds., *The Law and Finance of Related Party Transactions* (Cambridge University Press) (2019.6).

4. 서평

- "Robert Charles Clark, Corporate Law", 서울대학교 법학 제28권 제1호(1987.4).

5. 번역

- 역서 -

• 『주식회사법리의 새로운 경향』, 경문사(1983) (공역자: 송상현) (원저: Melvin A. Eisenberg, *The Structure of the Corporation* (1976)).

• 『회사법의 해부』, 도서출판 소화(2014.7) (공역자: 노혁준, 박준, 송옥렬, 안수현, 윤영신, 천경훈, 최문희) (원저: Kraakman et al., *Anatomy of Corporate Law* 2nd ed. 2009 Oxford).

- 논문 및 강연번역 -

• 법현실주의로부터 비판법학까지: 간략한 지성사, 현상과 인식 제11권 제2호(1987.8) (원논문: G. Edward White, "From Realism to Critical Legal Studies: A Truncated Intellectual History," 40 Southwestern Law Journal 819 (1986).

• "EC내부자거래지침과 독일에서의 내부자거래법제정을 위한 몇 가지 고찰", 국제거래법연구 제2집(1993.6) (원논문: Klaus J. Hopt, "EG-Vorgaben und Überlegungen für ein deutsches Insider-Gesetz").

• "증권거래법의 역외적용", 국제거래법연구 제3집(1994.4) (원논문: Misao Tatsuta, "Securities Regulation: Its Extraterritorial Application").

• "UR의 성과: 뉴질랜드의 입장", 국제거래법연구 제4집(1995.5) (원논문: Gordon Anderson, "Agriculture and the Uruguay Round: A New Zealand Perspective").

• "세계화시대의 법학교육", 서울대학교 법학 제37권 제3·4호(1996.12) (원논문: Robert Clark, "How Many Lawyers? - A View Into the 21st Century").

• "세계화하는 기업지배: 형태상의 수렴인가 기능상의 수렴인가", 서울대학교 법학 제38권 제3·4호(1997.12) (원논문: Ronald J. Gilson, "Globalizing Corporate Governance: Convergence of Form or Function").

• "이식된 법제도의 역할과 회사법", 상사법연구 제21권 제3호(2002.10) (원논문: Curtis J. Milhaupt, "The Role of Legal Transplants in Corporate Law").

6. 주요 연구용역보고서

• "우리나라 지주회사금지제도의 평가 및 개선방안", 공정거래위원회 연구용역보고서(1997.9) (공동연구자: 장지상, 최도성).

• "회계사의 손해배상책임", 한국공인회계사회 보고서(1998.5) (공동연구자: 윤진수).

• "경제선진화를 위한 산업조직 개편방안연구I: 재벌문제의 종합적 고찰과 정책대안의 모색", 한국과학문화재단 프로젝트 보고서(2000.8) (공동연구원: 강철규 외 18명).

• "회계기준 및 준칙과 관련 법규와의 조화", 금감원 연구보고서(2001.6) (공동연구원: 정운오, 이창희).

• "불공정거래규제시스템 실효성제고방안", 한국증권거래소 용역보고서(2001.12) (공동연구자: 김화진, 권종호, 안수현).

• "금융분야부패방지대책", 국무조정실 연구용역보고서(2001.12) (공동연구자: 이윤재, 안수현, 최문희, 김

동환, 정재욱).

- "Template for the Report on the Observance of Standards and Codes (ROSC)", Corporate Governance Country Assessment (Republic of Korea), World Bank (2002.3).
- "불공정거래 재재수단의 강화방안", 한국증권법학회(2002.3) (공동연구자: 우영호, 송웅순, 정윤모).
- "상장법인의 배당제도 개선", 투자자보호강화를 위한 증시제도 개선방안, 한국증권법학회(2002.7) (공동연구자: 안수현).
- "공시제도 선진화 방안", 한국증권연구원(2002.9) (공동연구자: 우영호, 정윤모, 김문현, 엄경식, 이준섭).
- "한국증권시장 경쟁력 강화를 위한 증권거래법 개편방안", 한국증권법학회(2002.10) (공동연구자: 강희철, 고창현, 권종호, 김건식, 김상규, 김화진, 송종준, 안수현, 오영근, 이준섭, 이중기, 정순섭, 하규수, Hilgendorf).
- "기업자금조달 활성화를 위한 유가증권제도의 개선방안에 관한 연구", 한국증권거래소 연구프로젝트 보고서(2003.6) (공동연구자: 윤영신, 안수현, 정순섭).
- "기업지배권시장관련 제도개선에 관한 연구", 한국증권거래소 연구용역보고서(2004.8) (공동연구자: 송종준, 송옥렬).
- "증권거래법의 역외적용 및 외국감독기관과의 공조제도 정비방안 연구", 금융감독위원회 연구용역 보고서(2004.10) (공동연구자: 정순섭).
- "금융관계 법률의 체계정비에 관한 연구", 한국증권거래소 연구용역보고서(2004.12) (공동연구자: 노혁준, 심영, 안수현, 윤영신, 이원우, 이중기, 정순섭, 최문희, 한기정).
- "금융상품의 복합화·다양화에 따른 금융소비자 보호장치 강화방안연구", 재정경제부 용역보고서(2006.4) (공동연구자: 정순섭, 최성근).
- "ABS의 진정양도 요건에 관한 연구", 금융감독원 용역보고서(2006.11) (공동연구자: 정순섭).
- "상장법인 특례조항의 문제점과 개선방안", 법무부 용역보고서(2006.12) (공동연구자: 최문희).
- "국제적 기준에 부합하는 합법적 LBO 가이드라인 제정방안", 법무부 연구용역보고서(2011.12) (공동연구자: 송옥렬, 이상원).
- "금융감독 선진화를 위한 감독체계 개편 방안", 국무총리실 용역보고서(2012.10) (공동연구자: 박준, 송옥렬, 조재호, 이원우, 정순섭, 한기정, 김선구).
- "상호주보유와 순환출자개선에 관한 연구", 법무부 용역보고서(2012.12) (공동연구자: 천경훈).

Contents

I. General issues

Codification in East Asia: Commercial Law

Kon Sik Kim

Abstract

In most countries, "commercial law" is well accepted as an independent body of law in the legal community. Commercial law (or, more commonly, parts of commercial law) is being taught in law schools and researched by scholars who specialize it as a distinct subject. Specific areas of law regarded as comprising commercial law, however, vary depending on a country. Bankruptcy law, for example, is a field of commercial law in some countries(e.g., U.S.), but in other countries a separate area of law neighboring civil procedure(e.g., Korea and Japan).

Legislation in the field of commercial law is more diverse. Some countries now have a special code covering general commercial law matters (commercial code). Other countries have a group of individual statutes on specific areas of commercial activities.

Commercial codes of the civil law countries were enacted largely under the influences of French or German codes, which had stemmed from *lex mercatoria* (law merchant) of the medieval times. Common law countries generally do not have a commercial code proper, although they have individual statutes on commercial matters. The U.S. is a notable exception with its famous Uniform Commercial Code. The UCC, however, covers areas of law quite different from those dealt with in commercial codes of civil law jurisdictions.

Commercial codes of civil law countries have been subject to substantial changes in recent years. In countries such as Germany and Japan, the process called "de-codification" has been in progress. Company law, an original component of a continental code, now often constitutes a separate code. Insurance contract law is another example. In other countries (such as France and Korea), however, commercial codes have been expanding to incorporate newly emerging business activities. Faced with these conflicting developments, commercial law scholars have been called to reconsider the identity of commercial law, and of the commercial code, in modern times.

The general report purports to discuss dynamic changes in commercial law legislations occurring in four East Asian jurisdictions - China, Japan, Korea and Taiwan. The four jurisdictions all belong to the civil law family and have been, and still are, closely intertwined with each other, culturally as well as historically. Developments in these jurisdictions, however, show a variety of possibilities in systematizing commercial law rules, providing a rich source for comparative law research.

The four jurisdictions can be divided into two groups, depending on the presence of a commercial code. While Japan and Korea both have its own commercial code, neither China nor Taiwan has one. Although Korea imported its commercial code from Japan half a century ago, the two countries have followed different routes since then. While de-codification has been underway in Japan, the Korean code has been gaining weight with provisions on new business activities. Although Taiwan has no commercial code in a formal sense, its civil code has a number of commercial law provisions. On the other hand, China does not even have a civil code at the moment. It only has a statute for general provisions of civil law, and a growing set of individual civil and commercial statutes. And attempts have been made to enact a civil code and a statute on general provisions of commercial law.

The general report has been largely based on the national reports prepared by the following scholars.

China: Jianbo Lou (Peking University) (C1)

       Xianchu Zhang (University of Hong Kong)(C2)

       Qiao Liu (Xian Jiaotong University) (C3)

Japan: Tomotaka Fujita (University of Tokyo)[1]

Korea: Ok-Rial Song (Seoul National University)

Taiwan: Ming-Jye Huang & Wang-Ruu Tseng (National Taiwan University)

The general report liberally draws on the above reports without citation. As three national reports have been submitted on China, passages relating to China will contain references to relevant reports(for example, (C1: 3))at the end. No original source cited in the individual national report will be cited here. This report proceeds as follows: First, the historical formation of commercial law legislation in the four jurisdictions will be surveyed in chronological order. Second, the structures and contents of commercial law legislation of the four jurisdictions will be compared with each other. Third, some observations will be made on the basis of the East Asian experiences.

---

1) In addition to Professor Fujita's report, the following article by the same author is quite helpful.
Fujita T (2010) General discussion: current status and future of the commercial code's general principles and commercial acts. NBL 935: 7 (in Japanese).

Historical Evolution of Commercial Law Legislation – Vertical Survey

1 European Origin

Commercial codes of the civil law countries emerged largely under the influences of French and German codes. These modern commercial codes trace back to the *lex mercatoria* (law merchant) of the medieval times. The *lex mercatoria* consists of rules and practices adopted by merchants in their trade activities. Merchants relied on specialized merchant courts to solve their disputes quickly and effectively. With the rise of state authority in the 16th century, the *lex mercatoria* was replaced with national commercial laws in Europe. The Rules on Commerce *(Ordonnance sur le commerce)* of 1673 and the Maritime Rules *(Ordonnance de la marine)* of 1681, both pronounced by King Louis XIV of France, are their prime examples. These statutes were a collection of public as well as private law rules applicable to the merchant class. The Rules on Commerce included chapters on accounting, companies, bills of exchange, bankruptcy and commercial jurisdiction.

The French commercial code *(Code de commerce)*, widely recognized as the first modern commercial code in history, was enacted in 1807 after the civil code *(Code civil)* of 1804. At that time, France consciously decided to maintain a separate commercial code and courts to promote commerce.[2] A legacy of the French revolution, the commercial code had been designed to apply to non-merchants as well, as long as they engaged in "commercial acts" *(actes de commerce)*.

The French commercial code of 1807 was influenced by the Rules on Commerce of 1673 both in form and in substance. It may have been due to the fact that the code had been drafted by those practitioners who were familiar with the Rules on Commerce.[3] Now grown to a full-fledged code with 648 provisions, it was originally composed of the following four parts: (1) commerce in general (including negotiable instruments), (2) maritime law, (3) bankruptcy, and (4) commercial court.

The French commercial code exerted a strong influence on subsequent commercial codes. The general German commercial code *(das Allgemeine Deutsche Handelsgesetzbuch*: ADHGB) of 1861, the predecessor of the German commercial code *(das Handelsgesetzbuch*: HGB) of

---

2) Sasaoka M (2010), The commercial code in France. NBL 935: 63 (in Japanese).
3) Sasaoka, supra note 2, 61.

1897, was created under its influence. The ADHGB (and the HGB), however, kept "merchant" as a core concept which determined the scope of its applicability. The ADHGB did not have the parts on bankruptcy and commercial court. The insurance provisions did not exist in the ADHGB and were later adopted in a separate statute. The ADHGB consisted of the general provisions and the following five parts: (1) merchant class, (2) companies, (3) silent partnership, (4) commercial acts, and (5) maritime law. As the ADHGB was enacted in the absence of a universal civil code in Germany, it included provisions on "juridical acts", a key civil law concept.

When Germany was unified under Prussia's leadership in 1871, there was discussion as to whether they should have two separate codes or one combined civil code. In 1881, Switzerland incorporated commercial statutes into its code of obligation(*Obligationenrecht*). Germany, however, took a different course by enacting in 1897 an independent commercial code, the HGB, based on the notion of merchants. The original HGB consisted of the following four parts: (1) merchants, (2) companies and silent partnership, (3) commercial acts, (4) maritime law. In 1937, provisions related to stock company were removed from the HGB to a new stock company act. In 1985, a new part on books and records was added to the HGB to comply with an EU directive.

2 Japan

Among the countries in East Asia, Japan was the first in adopting commercial statutes under the influence of European codes. After the *Meiji* restoration in 1868, Japan was badly in need of a set of modern statutes to deal with the West on an equal footing. Japan first turned to a German jurist named Hermann Rösler, who completed his draft code in 1884. It was composed of the general provisions and the following four parts: (1) commerce in general, (2) maritime law, (3) bankruptcy, and (4) commercial disputes. Although Rösler's draft code was similar to the French code in structure, its substance was under the influence of the ADHGB. After going through a review by a government committee, his draft code was finally passed into law, commonly called the old commercial code in 1890.

Like Rösler's draft code, the old commercial code was similar to the French code in form, consisting of three parts: (1) general provisions, (2) maritime law, and (3) bankruptcy. It was closer to the German code in substance. The old commercial code, however, could not take effect due to political controversies. A primary source of criticism on the old code was the discrepancy between it and then existing business customs. After many twists and turns, the old commercial code came into effect in 1898, but was soon replaced by the new Commercial Code in 1899. Unlike the old code, the new code was prepared by three Japanese scholars, but was still under the influence of the ADHGB.

The new Commercial Code was modeled after the German code in form as well. It was composed of five parts: (1) general provisions, (2) companies, (3) commercial acts, (4) commercial paper, and (5) maritime Law. This format is similar to the HGB, which is composed of four parts, (1) merchants, (2) companies, (3) commercial acts, and (4) maritime law. Like its German counterpart, the new Commercial Code did not have provisions on bankruptcy.

Although efforts had been made to reconcile the code and commercial realities, the discrepancy between the two was obvious from the beginning. Numerous questions were raised regarding the interpretation of the code provisions. Discussion did not cease among practitioners and scholars. Although numerous revisions have been made since its enactment, they were primarily directed at company law. Provisions on commercial papers were later separated from the code into two independent statutes in early 1930s. More recently, the company law provisions were removed from the code to form a new code, the Company Act of 2005. Also, in 2008, insurance provisions in the code were separated from the code to form a new code on insurance law.

3 Korea

When Korea was under Japanese control, Japanese codes were applicable in Korea. Japan's Commercial Code was one of those Japanese codes. Although Korea was liberated from Japan in 1945 and the government was established in 1948, it took almost two decades for Korea to enact its own commercial code. The Commercial Code was enacted in 1962, and came into effect in 1963. The Civil Code was adopted in 1958 and no serious attempt had been made to combine the two codes into one.

Although Koreans wanted to establish its independence in the field of legislation, they could not achieve their aspiration in the field of commercial law at least. The Commercial Code was not substantially different from its Japanese counterpart. It started with the following five parts: (1) general provisions, (2) commercial acts, (3) companies, (4) insurance, and (5) maritime law. While the Japanese code had insurance provisions included in the part for commercial acts, the Korean code had (and still has) a separate part for insurance law. And while Japan had a separate act for companies with limited liability (equivalent of German

GmbH), Korea still has provisions on them in the Commercial Code. Except for these minor differences, the two codes were very close to each other in structure. Of more striking was their similarity in substance. Before Japan and Korea started following different paths in the commercial law legislation around the new millennium, the commercial codes of the two countries were identical in most, if not all, respects.

The similarity still remains especially for the first two parts of the code: parts for (1) general provisions and (2) commercial acts. The Korean code deals with commercial agents in the part for commercial acts while they are covered in the part for general provisions in Japan. Also, the Korean code has a separate chapter for provisions on sale of business, while such provisions are included in the chapter for trade name in Japan.

4 Taiwan

Despite the fact that Taiwan and Korea share a colonial past, Taiwan has followed an entirely different route in the field of commercial law legislation. Taiwan's commercial statutes date back to the Nationalist government in the 1920s. The government at that time made a conscious decision to adopt a unified code rather than two separate codes for civil and commercial law. The decision was justified by the absence of the distinct merchant class in China and "the trend of modern legislation". (T:3).

The example of "modern legislation" embraced by the Nationalist government was the Swiss code of obligations, the first code based on the combined code approach, which was enacted in 1881 and revised in1911. The Nationalist government enacted its Civil Code in 1929. The Civil Code, however, had not been applicable until 1945 in Taiwan as Taiwan had been under Japanese control from 1895 to 1945.

The Civil Code incorporated a number of provisions on "commercial acts" in the chapter on "particular kinds of obligations." Those commercial acts included such matters as running account, managers and commercial agents, storage, transportation, and forwarding agency. These are the ones covered by the commercial codes of Japan and Korea. Interpreting these provisions, practitioners and scholars have been relying on theories developed in Germany and Japan.

Other elements of commercial law with special commercial traits, which could not be accommodated in the civil code, were allocated to individual statutes, such as the Negotiable Instrument Act, the Company Act, the Maritime Act and the Insurance Act, all promulgated in 1929. These special acts were drafted under strong influence of Anglo-American law. The list of such special commercial statutes has been later expanded to include, for example, the Business Registration Act, the Banking Act, and the Securities and Exchange act. No attempt has been made to put so-called "general provisions of commercial law" into a separate chapter or law or to enact a commercial code like the one adopted in Japan and Korea.

5 *China*

(1) Codes in General

When the Communist government was established in 1949 in Mainland China, it completely broke up with the legal system which had existed under the Nationalist government. The need for private law rules hardly existed as the communist government was not keen to foster business activities on the part of the general public. It was only after the economic reform started in the late 1970s that the country started feeling such need.

(2) Laws in the Civil Law Area

China currently does not have a code in the field of private law. Attempts have been made to enact a civil code. After some failed attempts, the government started in 1998 its initiative to enact a civil code and completed a draft code in 2002. The draft code embraced without modification the then existing civil law statutes such as the Contract Law, the Marriage Law, the Adoption Law and the Inheritance Law. As this kind of mechanical compilation of existing statutes was heavily criticized by commentators, the draft code could not pass into law. (C1: 2-3) Instead of a general civil code, China has a set of individual statutes. It includes the Inheritance Law(1985), the General Principles of the Civil Law(1986), the Guarantee Law(1995), the Contract Law(1999), the Adoption Law(1991), the Marriage Law(1980), the Real Property Law(2007), the Tort Liability Law(2009), and the Law on the Application of Law for Foreign-related Civil Relations(2010).[4] Almost all the above-mentioned individual civil statutes in China are supported by relevant judicial interpretations of the Supreme People's Court. Those individual civil law statutes and respective supporting judicial interpretations provide a basis for the codification of civil law in Mainland China. (C1: 4-5)

In the absence of a civil code, the General Principles of the Civil Law(GPCL) serves as a

---

4) Although these codes have been revised relatively frequently, the years of revision have not been indicated for the sake of simplicity. The same applies to other statutes cited herein.

parent law now. The GPCL, consisting of nine chapters and 156 articles, is no equivalent of a book on general principles in a German-style civil code. While it contains provisions (such as those on persons, legal acts and agency) that would typically be included in a book on general principles, the GPCL also contains more specific provisions that would more properly be included in the books on properties, law of obligations, and family law. Moreover, the GPCL has provisions on commercial law matters such as individual commercial households, enterprise legal persons and business joint operation. (C2: 2) The GPCL plays a fundamental role in providing guidelines for dealing with civil and commercial matters in Mainland China. (C1: 5)

In addition to the GPCL, individual civil statutes such as the Contract Law, Real Property Law and Tort Liability Law also govern civil and commercial law matters. The Contract Law consists of 23 chapters and 428 articles. The general provisions of the Contract Law are made up of the first eight chapters—general provisions, formation of the contract, validity of the contract, performance of the contract, modification and assignment of the contract, termination of rights and obligations under the contract, liability for breach of contract and miscellaneous provisions. The specific provisions of the Contract Law, starting from Chap. 9 to Chap. 23, provide for fifteen kinds of classified contracts such as sales and leases. The Contract Law, however, also governs those contracts beyond the scope of the classified contracts. (C1: 5)

Coexistence of numerous statutes in the civil law area generates conflicts and inconsistencies. Scholars still dispute as to the form and substance of the future civil code. (C2: 5-7) At the moment, however, there is no immediate plan on the part of the government to enact a civil code. (C2: 5)

(3) Laws in the Commercial Law Area

Efforts to enact commercial law statutes started with China's decision to move from a planned-economy to a more market-oriented economy. Actually, most individual commercial statutes have been adopted and substantially revised since the decision of the 14th Communist Party of China(CPC) Congress in 1990 to embrace market economy.

At present, there is no commercial code in China. And there is no movement toward codification at the moment. This may be due to the belief that a code is not suitable for a field like commercial law which must respond to changing realities. (C1: 7) Commercial law legislation in China is therefore solely composed of individual statutes and judicial interpretations supporting such statutes. Such individual statutes in China can be roughly divided into tw o groups. One group relates to merchants (or business organizations), and the other relates to various commercial transactions). (C1: 9)

The first group of statutes includes but not limited to: the Sole Proprietorship Law(1999), the Partnership Enterprise Law(1997), the Company Law(1993), Sino-Foreign Equity Joint Venture Law (1978), Sino-Foreign Contractual Joint Venture Law (1988), Wholly Foreign Owned Enterprise Law (1986), the Law on Industrial Enterprises Owned by the Whole People(1988), the Law on Township Enterprises(1996), and the Law on the Peasant Professional Cooperative Organization(2006). In addition, China also has some administrative regulations and administrative rules issued respectively by the State Council or ministries/commissions subject to the State Council defining merchants, such as Provisional Regulations on Private Enterprises(1988), Regulations on Administration of the Individual Industrial and Commercial Household(2011), Regulations on Rural Collectively-owned Enterprise(1990), and Regulations on Urban Collectively-owned Enterprise(1991). (C1: 9-10)

The second group of individual commercial statutes, including but not limited to the Maritime Law(1992), the Insurance Law(1995), the Negotiable Instrument Law(1995), the Securities Law(1998), the Trust Law(2001) and the Enterprise Bankruptcy Law(2006), mainly deals with commercial acts such as marine transportation, the issuance and transactions of securities, acceptance of negotiable instrument, and bankruptcy liquidation. Those statutes, however, contain provisions on the qualification and organizational structure of merchants in specific fields, e.g., securities broker-dealers, insurance companies. (C1: 10)

These commercial statutes are close to their counterparts in Germany or Japan, in particular in terms of legislative framework and terminologies. Some of these statutes, however, are under Anglo-American Influence. The Company Law provides a good example. The Company Law merely recognizes two types of company, i.e. limited liability company and company limited by shares, both coming from the continental law. Also, China originally adopted the German-style board of supervisors to monitor the directors, managers and oth-er officers. At the time of 2005 revision, the concept of independent directors were formally introduced at least for listed companies(Art. 123 of the Company Act) under the influence of Anglo-American law. (C1: 11)

In China, now, commercial matters are governed by the civil statutes including GPCL, the Contract Law and the Tort Liability Law and the group of individual commercial statutes including the Company Law, the Partnership Enterprise Law, the Sole Proprietorship Law, and the Enterprise Bankruptcy Law.

(4) General Provisions of Commercial Law – Shenzhen Regulations

There is not even an equivalent of GPCL in the commercial law area. It has been argued that China needs a law on general principles of commercial law, a counterpart of the GPCL in the civil law area, to make its individual commercial statute work as a unity. Some scholars have published their own drafts of such general principles. More importantly, a kind of such general principles has already been in force since 1999 as local regulations in Shenzhen Special Economic Zone ("the Regulations"). To date the Regulations remain the only effective legislation with general provisions for commercial matters.

The structure of the Regulations is as follows. (C3: 8-9) It has the following eight chapters composed of 65 articles in total.

Chapter 1: General Provisions (legislative purpose, scope of application and fundamental principles of the Regulations)

Chapter 2: Merchants

Chapter 3: Commercial Registration (a total of 18 articles)

Chapter 4: Merchant Names and Transfer of Business (11 articles)

Chapter 5: Commercial Books

Chapter 6: Business Employees (a manager's powers and responsibilities)

Chapter 7: Commercial Agents

Chapter 8: Miscellaneous Articles

The provisions for merchants in Chap. 2, along with related provisions in Chap. 6 (Business Employees) and Chap. 7 (Commercial Agents), reflect an essential feature of a commercial code not found elsewhere in Chinese law. The Regulations are based on the concept of merchant, which is defined in Article 5 as "a natural person, a legal person or any other economic organization lawfully registered for engaging in commercial acts for the purpose of making profits, in his or its own name, and as his or its regular business." This is the first example of statutory definition of merchant. Article 5 also define commercial acts as "acts of merchants in production and operation, the wholesaling and retailing of commodities, the development of science and technology, and the provision of advice and other services to another person." The focus onthe concept of merchant shows the influence of the German HGB on the Regulations.

The weight of the Regulations, however, remains on Chap. 3 (Commercial Registration) and Chap. 4 (Merchant Names and Transfer of Business), which together constitute almost one half of the Regulations. It is the provisions in these two chapters that give to the Regulations an essentially administrative, regulatory character.

(5) Future of Commercial Law Legislation in China

As mentioned earlier, there is no formal plan to unify individual commercial statutes into a commercial code. In the years ahead, Mainland China may move into a code system in which a civil code serves as the parent law for both civil and commercial law and applies to both civil and commercial relations, supplemented by individual commercial statutes. Some scholars argue that there is still a need for general provisions governing commercial matters even in such a system.

Professor Baoshu Wang, a leading commercial law scholar and the leading drafter of the Shenzhen Regulations mentioned above, specifically suggests that such general principles of commercial law shall contain three parts. The first part (the "General Provisions") stipulates the purpose of the law, the scope of application, and basic principles of commercial law. The second part (the "Merchants") defines the concept, qualification and classification of merchants, as well as provisions about commercial register, trade names, business transfer, commercial books, managers and other commercial employees and commercial agents. The third part (the "Commercial Acts") provides the concept and classification of commercial act, commercial agent, commercial lien, commercial guarantee and so on.

The proposed general principles of commercial law, according to Professor Wang, shall play the following two roles, i.e., to lay down principles and a conceptual framework for existing individual commercial statutes, and to provide specific institutions, such as business transfer, commercial books, and so on, which are stipulated concretely neither in civil law nor in individual commercial statutes.

Attempts have been already made to codify civil law. There has been no official movement, however, to adopt such general principles of commercial law. Scholars are also in disagreement as to whether or not China should enact a commercial code. Some scholars argue that separating commercial law from general civil enactments has its merits simply because commercial acts have their own characteristics, such as status of merchants, their business operation for profit and special concerns for safety of transactions. (C2: 7-8) Other scholars argue that in the presence of a civil code there will be no need to adopt a commercial code or general principles of commercial law. (C2: 9) Although the chance of having a comprehensive commercial code seems at this moment to be remote, China is more likely to enact a law on the general principles of commercial law, which may resemble the Regulations in structure. (C3: 13)

Types of Commercial Law Legislation Compared – Horizontal Survey

1 Overview

As the preceding historical survey shows, the four East Asian jurisdictions have been follow-ing divergent routes when it comes to commercial law legislation. Although both Japan and Korea started with a continental commercial code, their codes have been moving in oppo-site directions, especially during the last decade. On the other hand, China and Taiwan are similar to each other in the sense that neither has a commercial code. Instead, the two ju-risdictions have a set of individual commercial statutes. The similarity, however, ends there. While Taiwan sticks with a combined civil code adopted in 1929, China does not even have a civil code. Different directions in which the four jurisdictions have been moving lately will be discussed one by one.

2 Shrinking Commercial Code: Japan

Japan still has a separate Commercial Code as Germany does. The Commercial Code of 1899 originally had five parts: (1) General Provisions, (2) Companies, (3) Commercial Acts, (4) Commercial Paper, and (5) Maritime Law. The Commercial Code has been subject to a process of "de-codification". Arguments in favor of de-codification emerged relatively ear-ly in Japan.[5] Even during the pre-World War II period, it was generally understood that the Commercial Code did not cover every commercial activity. The company with limited liability (equivalent of German GmbH) was covered not in the Commercial Code but in a separate law in 1938. Provisions on notes and on checks were removed from the Commercial Code into new laws, the Act on Notes(1932) and the Act on Checks(1933), respectively.

De-codification has progressed rapidly during the last decade. A critical step in the direc-tion of de-codification was taken in 2005 when the book of company law was removed from the Commercial Code to a new code. This move in particular was noteworthy in many respects. Above all, the structure, if not the substance, of company law rules has been completely reconstructed. Now, a company law scholar of France or Germany will be sur-prised to learn that Japan originally borrowed its company law provisions from Europe. The

---

5) Fujita, supra note 1, at 8.

new Company Act includes the same provisions as in the part on general provisions of the Commercial Code. The general provisions in the Commercial Code have lost its "general" character as they are now applicable only to non-company merchants.

Another important development took place in the field of insurance law. The insurance provisions originally included in the part on commercial acts were removed from the Commercial Code into a separate law in 2008. Yet another phase of de-codification is now in progress in connection with the revision of the Civil Code. An interim report on the revision suggests that a number of provisions included in the part on commercial acts, the chapter on general provisions in particular, be incorporated into the revised Civil Code.[6] Currently, the Commercial Code is composed of the following three parts.

Part I General Provisions (Articles 1 to 32)
    Ch. 1 General provisions
    Ch. 2 Merchants
    Ch. 3 Commercial registration
    Ch. 4 Trade name
    Ch. 5 Books and records
    Ch. 6 Employees with the power of agency
    Ch. 7 Commercial agent
    Ch. 8 Miscellaneous provisions

Part II Commercial Act (Articles 501 to 683)
    Ch. 1 General provisions
    Ch. 2 Sales
    Ch. 3 Running account
    Ch. 4 Silent partnership
    Ch. 5 Trade broker
    Ch. 6 Commission agent
    Ch. 7 Forwarding agent
    Ch. 8 Inland transport
    Ch. 9 Accommodation and storage

---

6) If the plan set forth in the report is implemented the number of provisions in the part on commercial acts will be decreased from 22 to around 10. Fujita, supra note 1, at 9 n.11.

Part III Maritime Law (Arts. 684 to 851)

As shown above, moving along the path of the German HGB, Japan's Commercial Code has been shrinking its coverage. Given this situation, it is not surprising that some people argue for the "break-up" of the Commercial Code. Such a view, however, does not seem to have many supporters yet. It will grow stronger if more provisions (those related to transport, for example) are to be removed from the Commercial Code in future.

3 Expanding Commercial Code: Korea

(1) Civil code

Korea has a separate civil code, which was enacted in 1958. A code with 1,111 provisions, the civil code is primarily based on continental legal concepts principles. The parts on family law and inheritance, on the other hand, reflect existing local customs. The rest of the civil code is similar to the German civil code (BGB). It consists of the following five parts: (1) the General Provisions, (2) the Property, (3)Liabilities and Obligations (including Contracts and Torts), (4) Family and (5) Succession.

(2) Commercial Code

The commercial code currently consists of the following six parts: (1) general provisions, (2) commercial acts, (3) companies, (4) insurance, (5) maritime law, and (6) air transportation. The current codes of Japan and Korea only share the three parts (general provisions, commercial acts and maritime law) with each other. In particular, the parts (1) and (2) above remain still similar to their counterparts in the Japanese code.

Part I General Provisions (Article 1 to 45)

    Ch. 1 General provisions

    Ch. 2 Merchants

    Ch. 3 Employees with the power of agency

    Ch. 4 Trade name

    Ch. 5 Books and records

    Ch. 6 Commercial registration

    Ch. 7 Sale of business (Arts. 16 to 18 of Japanese code)

Part II Commercial Act (Articles 46 to 168-12)

> Ch. 1 General Provisions modify the Civil Code in the context of commercial transactions
>
> Ch. 2 Sales
>
> Ch. 3 Running account
>
> Ch. 4 Silent partnership
>
> Ch. 4-2 Limited liability partnership (2011)
>
> Ch. 5 Commercial agent
>
> Ch. 6 Trade broker
>
> Ch. 7 Commission agent
>
> Ch. 8 Forwarding agent
>
> Ch. 9 Inland Transport
>
> Ch. 10 Accommodation (Arts. 594 to 596 of the Japanese code)
>
> Ch. 11 Storage
>
> Ch. 12 Financial lease (2010)
>
> Ch. 13 Franchise business (2010)
>
> Ch. 14 Factoring (2010)

Except for the recently adopted chapters on financial lease, franchise business, factoring and limited liability partnerships, the two parts of the Korean and Japanese codes largely overlap. The similarity between the two codes no longer exists outside the two parts.

(3) Company Law

The Korean code still maintains a part on company law. Part III (Companies: Articles 169 to 637-2) covers general company law matters. It contains the basic rules applicable to a variety of business forms. The Commercial Code now provides for the following five types of company: the partnership company (*offene Handelsgesellschaft*), the limited partnership company (*Kommanditgesellschaft*), the stock company (*Aktiengesellschaft*), the company with limited liability (*Gesellschaft mit beschränkter Haftung*: GmbH), and the newly adopted limited liability company. The first four types of company originated from the German company statutes, and the limited liability company, newly introduced in 2011, was of American origin.

(4) Insurance and Maritime Law

Part IV of the Commercial Code((Articles 638 to 739) provides a self-sufficient set of rules on insurance contract. The focus of this part is on modifying and complementing contract law principles included in the Civil Code. Rules regulating insurance companies are found in a separate statute.

The remaining two parts of the Commercial Code, Part V(Maritime Law)(Articles 740 to 895) and Part VI(Air Transportation)(Articles 896 to 935), relate to transport law. Korea has not joined the international conventions of sea transport such as the Hague-Visby Convention, the Hamburg Convention, or the recent Amsterdam Convention. Instead, Part V is based on a mixture of several international conventions.

Part VI on air transport was added in 2011. As Korea already ratified the Montreal Convention in 1999, Part VI is applicable only to domestic disputes and international disputes not covered by the Montreal Convention. When Part VI was being discussed in 2008 and 2009, some scholars argued for an independent statute on air transport. This proposal was not adopted, however. It is suspected that the decision was based on a desire on the part of lawmakers to enhance the status of the rules by putting them in the Commercial Code, which looks more prestigious as one of the basic codes in Korea.

From the codification perspective, it should be noted that the Commercial Code now contains all three types of transport law: (1) inland transport (Part II), (2) sea transport (Part V), and (3) air transport (Part VI). Also, a recent proposed draft for rules governing multimodal transport will be added to Part II.

(5) Future of the Commercial Code

In contrast to its Japanese counterpart, Korea's Commercial Code has been expanding, although not to the point of the French commercial code of 2000, which covers such areas as competition and insolvency. Although the size of the Commercial Code is becoming massive, there is no plan or discussion as to how to deal with the growing code. No significant proposal has been made to disband or further expand the current code. For a time being, at least, its structure and contents will be maintained.

4 Combined Code Approach: Taiwan

Taiwan sticks with the Civil Code the Nationalist government enacted in 1929. It does not have a separate commercial code. The Civil Code covers commercial as well as civil matters. The Civil Code is composed of the following five parts: (1) general principles, (2) obligations, (3) property (4) family, and (5) succession.

Although Taiwan's Civil Code was modeled after the Swiss code, it is different from the Swiss code in one significant respect. Although the Swiss code does not contain a part on the general principles of civil law, Taiwan's code has one under the influence of German law. The Civil Code does not have all the commercial law rules found in a commercial code in countries like Korea. It only includes rules on commercial law issues closely related to civil law. Such rules are located in the part on obligations. The part on obligations is divided into two chapters, one on general provisions and the other on "particular kinds of obligations." It is the chapter on particular kinds of obligations that contains the commercial law rules. Rules on commercial matters such as running account, manager and commercial agent, warehousing, carriage and forwarding agency are included there.

The term "merchant" appears in some provisions in the Civil Code (e.g., Articles 127, 29, 950). But there is no definition of the term. Although specific commercial acts such as warehousing and transport are regulated in the Civil Code, the abstract term "commercial act" is not employed by the Commercial Code.

Commercial matters not closely related to civil law are dealt with in individual commercial statutes. These statutes include the Business Registration Act, the Company Act, Maritime Act, the Negotiable Instruments Act and the Insurance Act. Taiwan's Civil Code is thus different from the Swiss code in the sense that it does not have a chapter on company law. Although Taiwan has no separate commercial code, matters included in a commercial code are all covered by individual statutes. In a sense, Taiwan's commercial law legislation is similar to that of Japan in the sense that most commercial matters are handled not by a code, but by individual commercial statutes. If Japan's attempt to move some provisions on commercial acts to the Civil Code proves successful, the similarity between the two systems will be further strengthened.

5 No Code: China

China currently has no civil code, and no commercial code. With no civil code, China differs from Taiwan. The civil and commercial law legislation is composed of a group of individual statutes in China. Almost all the individual statutes are supported by relevant judicial interpretations of the Supreme People's Court.

China is similar to Taiwan, and, to a lesser degree, Japan in the sense that its commercial law legislation largely consists of individual statutes. Statutes on forms of doing business in China are more numerous because of the heavy involvement of public entities in business matters. They include the Sole Proprietorship Law, the Partnership Enterprise Law, the Company Law, Sino-Foreign Equity Joint Venture Law (SFEJVL), Sino-Foreign Contractual Joint Venture Law (SFCJVL), Wholly Foreign Owned Enterprise Law (WFOEL), the Law on Industrial Enterprises Owned by the Whole People, the Law on Township Enterprises, and the Law on the Peasant Professional Cooperative Organization.

In addition to these statutes, there are also administrative regulations and administrative rules generally recognized as constituting law In the broad sense of the word. They include Provisional Regulations on Private Enterprises, Regulations on Administration of the Individual Industrial and Commercial Household, Regulations on Rural Collectively-owned Enterprise, Regulations on Urban Collectively-owned Enterprise, Implementing Regulations for SFEJVL, Detailed Rules for SFCJVL and Detailed Rules for WFOEL.

China also has a group of individual statutes on commercial transactions. They include the Maritime Law, the Insurance Law, the Negotiable Instrument Law, Securities Law, the Trust Law and the Enterprise Bankruptcy Law. Those statutes, however, contain provisions on the qualification and organizational structure of firms involved in specific fields such as securities broker-dealers and insurance companies.

It is unlikely that those individual commercial statutes will be incorporated into a future civil code. None of the draft civil codes including the one proposed by the Legislative Affairs Commission of the SCNPC includes any of the commercial statutes.

As mentioned earlier, China has attempted to enact a civil code before. Such an attempt may well bear fruit in future. If China adopts a civil code, the discrepancy between China's and Taiwan's private law legislation will be decreased. And if China further adopts an act on general principles of commercial law, such discrepancywill further decrease.

6 Summary

The four jurisdictions can be arranged depending on the degree of codification in the area of commercial law. Korea is the country which shows the strongest influence of codification. It has a commercial code which has been expanding. Next to Korea is Japan. Japan still maintains a commercial code, which has been in decline in importance as it has been losing its contents. Taiwan is the third jurisdiction in terms of the degree of codification. It has a civil code at least, although the field of commercial law is covered by a number of individual statutes. The level of codification is lowest in China without even a civil code. The situation may change, however, as China has shown some interest in a civil code and a growing interest in general principles of commercial law.

Some Observations

1 History

Commercial codes, as distinguished from civil codes, emerged in Europe largely as a result of historical accidents. Their origin is different from that of civil codes which trace back to Roman law. Commercial codes originated from a body of customary rules and practices that the merchant class had developed to govern their trade operations. When France, and later Germany, started enacting codes, they put these customary rules into a separate code. The concept of "merchant" occupied the center stage of the ADHGB. Even in the French commercial code, its key concept, commercial acts, derived from those activities merchants had engaged in. Items included in the modern commercial codes mostly originated from medieval Europe.

The commercial code was not a product of logical necessity. This proposition was corroborated by the Swiss Code of Obligations. Switzerland enacted in 1881 just one code which also covered commercial law matters. In 1911, the Swiss Code of Obligations was incorporated into the Civil Code (*Zivilgesetzbuch*) which was enacted in 1907 and remains applicable still now.

It was also by accident that the idea of commercial code had traveled eastward to Japan at the end of the 19th century. After the *Meiji* Restoration in 1868, Japan was in urgent need of a full set of modern statutes in order to interact with the West. From the perspective of receiving laws, continental codes were far more convenient than judge-made common law rules. At that time, Japan regarded Germany as a role model and coincidentally a German law professor, Rösler, was working in Japan for the government as consultant. Moreover, the ADHGB of 1861 was now being applied to the whole German empire. Given the circumstances, it was almost inevitable for the new Commercial Code that was finally enacted in 1897 to have a strong German flavor.

This kind of historical accident was repeated in Korea after it gained independence from Japan in 1945. The newly established Korean government also needed to have its own codes. Sophisticated commercial law scholars who could be mobilized for drafting a new code were few in number. Virtually all the jurists were trained in Japanese law during the colonial period. Although they were aware of the combined civil codes in Europe, it was not a feasible option to digress too far from the existing Japanese code familiar to them. The situation was quite different in 1929 when the Chinese Nationalist government enacted its civil code modeled after the Swiss civil code, the most recent code at the time. Although many of the lawyers of the Nationalist government were under the influence of Japanese legal scholarship[7], the government did not embrace the Japanese model. They continued to keep their combined code even after they moved to Taiwan in 1949. Although Taiwan has no separate commercial code, distinction between civil and commercial laws remains in teaching and research. Taiwanese lawyers rely heavily on German and Japanese legal theories in applying their commercial law provisions.

Among civil law countries, China is unique as it has no full-fledged code modeled after European codes. It has been adopting individual laws as a specific legal need arises. This policy seems understandable given the unique economic system existing in China. China has been evolving since the 1980s from a purely communist system into a "socialist market economy". It was unrealistic to import a European code in its entirety into China. As the viability of a commercial code was in dispute by the 1980s, it may have been wise not to enact a commercial code based on an old concept of merchant.

2 Theory

It seems generally agreed that there is a distinct area of private law which is conceptually separate from a civil law. Widely called commercial (or business) law, this area of law governs business activities from the perspective of private law. Now, a growing number of laws belong to this area of law. It is, however, difficult to find an underlying theory unifying these various laws into an integral body of law. Now, scholars in developed countries do not seem to have much interest in such grand theories.

Any capitalist society needs a body of rules applicable to business activities. Such commercial law rules can be divided into two groups. One group contains rules setting forth solutions different from those of a civil code. Provisions on commercial acts belong to this group of rules. The other group includes rules for transactions and institutions of strong commercial nature not covered by a conventional civil code. Company law and maritime

---

7) Chen T (2010) One hundred years of Taiwanese civil law. Hokkaido law review 61(3): 231-232 (in Japanese).

law are prime examples.

The boundary of commercial law remains in dispute. Unlike this theoretical issue, how to organize such commercial law rules in legislation is essentially a task of technical nature.[8] In implementing this legislative task, we can in theory think of three options. The first option is to have a giant commercial code covering all the rules related to business. The French commercial code of 2000 may be regarded as embodying this model most faithfully. The second option, on the other extreme, is not to have a comprehensive commercial code, but to have a group of laws covering distinct areas of business. If we adopt this piecemeal approach, the first group of commercial law rules mentioned above may be incorporated into a civil code. China and Taiwan may belong to this category.

The remaining option lies in between the two options. A country may have a commercial code and a group of statutes governing individual business law areas. The problem is how to draw a line between the commercial code and the remaining statutes. It is now well understood that the conventional concepts like "merchant" and "commercial act" are not up to the task. Contemporary jurists have come up with no concept persuasive enough to replace them. Although the concept of "enterprise" has been strongly advocated by a small group of scholars, it does not attract much attention these days. This seems to be the situation surrounding the commercial code in Japan and Germany. Although the commercial code has been decreasing in relevance as well as in size, the lawmakers are not eager to take any action.

3 Function

Even in countries with a dwindling commercial code, commercial law scholars seem to have little interest in the commercial code itself. Instead, they seem more occupied with various legal problems arising from the increasingly global marketplace. This is by no means surprising given the technical nature of commercial law legislation.

The picture of commercial law legislation in the four jurisdictions appears rather confusing. Each jurisdiction seems to follow an idiosyncratic route in commercial law legislation. From a functional perspective, however, diversity is not so significant. Shareholder derivative suit, for example, is available in all these jurisdictions regardless of where it is provided for. And, indeed, as China advances its capitalist development, diversity in substance of com-

---

8) Schmidt K(2010), Münchener Kommentar zum Handelsgesetzbuch. 3. Auflage C.H.Beck, Munich. Vorbemerkung zu § 1 Rn 4.

mercial law will further decrease.

If a functional approach continues to prevail in these jurisdictions, the status quo will go on as long as no serious problem arises from a dwindling or expanding commercial code. If the commercial code keeps losing its provisions to other statutes such as the civil code or other individual laws, the commercial code will become hollow. This is what is happening in Japan. But even in Japan, the voice for abolition of the commercial code is not strong. Even though such a view has been asserted since the 1920s, it has relatively few supporters even in academic circles. An argument for abolition may gain momentum when the hollowing of the commercial code further proceeds.

On the contrary, it is intriguing that some commercial law scholars in China advocate the need for a law on general principles of commercial law and a commercial code. According to a Chinese scholar, "[c]odification in China has been viewed as a crucial benchmark of maturity of a legal system, the highest stage of legal systematization and the full display of institutional civilization." (C2: 11) Although contemporary scholars in countries like Japan and Germany do not seem to have much faith in a commercial code, Chinese scholars still seem to keep a scholarly predilection for systemization.

4 Path Dependence

From the perspective of a host country importing laws from other countries, it may be more convenient to import a code than individual statutes. Once a code is imported, however, it is difficult to change. This is the case, even when some provisions turn out incongruous with commercial realities of the host country. They may be just left intact as long as they do not impose any serious burden on the business community. Difficulty of change may be partly due to the ignorance on the part of the host country. It takes substantial time and intellectual energy to fully understand what a provision in the code means and actually functions in the home country. Changing the code is even more difficult as the lawmakers need to make sure that new provisions do not conflict with the existing structure.

It must be noted that path dependence in commercial law legislation may be less strong than in other areas of law. This is primarily due to the nature of commercial law itself. Business activities at the marketplace are bound to change. Countries are under pressure to modify their commercial law to accommodate such changes. As business activities are now taking place across borders, trading countries cannot afford to ignore changes in laws of foreign countries.

When a host country revises an imported code, it often refers to changes made in the home country. A country can attempt an independent revision of the imported code only when its legal scholarship has reached a level high enough to allow such an endeavor. In such a view, vigorous legislative activities recently occurring in Japan may be regarded as demonstrating the maturity of its legal scholarship.

5 Future

A commercial code based on the concept of merchant or commercial act may not have as much appeal as before. In the rapidly changing business environment, piecemeal legislation may be perceived as more appropriate. The idea of codification as a means of organizing complicated rules is not dead, however. When the volume of individual statutes in the area of business law becomes too unwieldy, a need to systematize complicated rules will emerge. This is not surprising given the fact that conventional codes were prepared to "make law more accessible" to the general public.[9] It seems still too early to predict what a new type of commercial code emerging in the 21st century will look like. And, in the four East Asian jurisdictions at least, it will likely take some time to witness such a revolutionary change.

---

9) Watson A (2001), The evolution of western private law. Expanded ed. Johns Hopkins, Baltimore. at 8.

References

Books

SCHMIDT K(2010), MÜNCHENER KOMMENTAR ZUM HANDELSGESETZBUCH. 3.

WATSON A (2001), THE EVOLUTION OF WESTERN PRIVATE LAW. EXPANDED ED.

Articles

Chen T (2010) One hundred years of Taiwanese civil law. Hokkaido law review 61(3): 231-232 (in Japanese)

Fujita T (2010) General discussion: current status and future of the commercial code's general principles and commercial acts. NBL 935: 7 (in Japanese).

Sasaoka M (2010), The commercial code in France. NBL 935: 63 (in Japanese)

Corporate law and corporate law scholarship in Korea: A comparative essay

Kon Sik Kim[1]

I. INTRODUCTION

Korea's stellar economic performance during the last four decades of the 20th century is well known and widely admired. Other segments of Korean society have been moving forward in step with its economic progress. Not only cars and smart phones, but also movies and pop singers symbolize the elevated status of Korea in the global market. Korea's corporate law, however, largely lagged behind the business sector. Its corporate statutes played no significant role until the end of the last century.

The situation, however, changed dramatically as the country fell into a financial crisis in 1997. The crisis was, for better or worse, generally regarded as a consequence of Korea's poor corporate governance. Under pressure from international institutions such as the International Monetary Fund (IMF) and the World Bank, the Korean government embarked on improving corporate governance by, among other things, revamping its corporate statutes. The post-crisis corporate law reforms advanced the relevance of corporate law in the business community, and, in turn, contributed to a rapid growth of corporate law practice. In the process, however, corporate law scholars have played no significant role, as discussed later.[2] On the contrary, corporate law scholarship has been influenced by these developments.

The purpose of this chapter is to review the transformation of corporate law in Korea during the last two decades from a comparative perspective. The term "corporate law" here is used in a broader sense, encompassing the capital market law. During the same period, the corporate statutes have been amended eight times,[3] and a wide range of provisions have

---

1) This chapter draws partly on my previous article published in Korean, titled *"Our Corporate Law and Corporate Legal Scholarship in the 21st Century: Its Limits and Challenges"* JUSTICE No. 92 239–52 (2006). This article is funded by the Seoul National University Law Foundation in 2014.
2) *See infra* Part III(i).

been introduced or amended. This chapter will not purport to describe any individual provision or principle in detail.[4] Instead, this chapter will survey more general features of corporate law and corporate legal scholarship in Korea, with a special emphasis on forces shaping the current statutes.

Korean corporate law has undergone a substantial change since the financial crisis in 1997, which will be reflected in the organization of this chapter. Part II will discuss the status of corporate law and corporate law scholarship prior to the financial crisis. Part III will then survey post-crisis developments related to corporate law. Part IV will examine post-crisis corporate law scholarship. Part V will address challenges of future corporate law reform.

II. PRE-CRISIS CORPORATE LAW AND CORPORATE LAW SCHOLARSHIP

(i) Genesis: Overwhelming Influence of Japanese Law

Although sporadic efforts had been made to introduce a modern legal system even before Korea was colonized by Japan in 1910, it was not until the beginning of Japanese rule that a full-fledged set of modern statutes was applied in Korea. During the colonial period (1910 –1945), the Japanese government applied its own statutes in Korea with some adaptation. Japan's Commercial Code, which contained corporate statutes, was one of those Japanese codes. The Japanese Commercial Code, originally adopted in 1899 and later revised in 1911 and 1938, was heavily influenced by German law.

When the Korean government was established in 1948, one of its initial tasks was to replace

---

3) They were amended in 1995, 1998, 1999, 2001, 2009 (twice), 2011, and 2014.

4) There is now a growing body of literature in English on individual topics of Korean corporate law. Since the crisis, I have published the following papers: *Invigorating Shareholder Derivative Actions in South Korea*, in Dan W. Puchniak et al. eds., THE DERIVATIVE ACTION IN ASIA 189–217 (2012) (with Hyeok-Joon Rho); *Corporate Legal Personality and Corporate Loss in Korean Law*, in Stefan Grundmann et al. eds., UNTERNEHMEN, MARKT UND VERANTWORTUNG (De Gruyter, Festschrift für Klaus J. Hopt zum 70. Geburtstag am 24. August 2010); *The role of judges in corporate governance: the Korean experience*, in Hideki Kanda et al. eds. TRANSFORMING CORPORATE GOVERNANCE IN EAST ASIA (2008); *Transplanting Audit Committees to Korean Soil: A Window into the Evolution of Korean Corporate Governance*, 9 ASIAN-PAC. L. & POL'Y J. 163 (2007); *Revamping Fiduciary Duties in Korea: Does Law Matter to Corporate Governance?*, in Curtis Milhaupt ed., GLOBAL MARKETS, DOMESTIC INSTITUTIONS, 373–99 (2003) (with Joongi Kim); *Establishing a New Stock Market for Shareholder Value Oriented Firms in Korea*, 3 CHI. J. INT'L L. 277 (Fall, 2002) (with Stephen Choi).

the existing Japanese laws with its own laws. Due to the political and social turmoil caused by the Korean War, the legislation project could not proceed as planned. The new Commercial Code came into force only in 1963, almost 20 years after liberation from Japanese control. Although Koreans wanted to reconfirm Korean independence in the field of legislation, they could not achieve their aspiration in the field of commercial law at least. The Commercial Code was not substantially different from its Japanese counterpart. Although Korea and Japan started following different paths in corporate law legislation around the new millennium, their corporate statutes as of 1963 were identical in most, if not all, respects. Like their Japanese counterpart, the new statutes incorporated some elements of US practice. They adopted, for example, the concepts of authorized capital, boards of directors and shareholders derivative suits.

(ii) Irrelevance of Corporate Law

As most of the codes enacted in the early days were modeled after codes of Western countries, a substantial gap existed between law and reality in Korea. Corporate law was no exception. A primary reason for this incongruity may be the reality that the corporate form, appropriate for large, publicly held firms, was adopted by a wide range of firms, even by a sole proprietor with modest capital.

The corporate statutes were of little relevance in Korea's efforts to develop its economy. Their irrelevance may be due to two conceptually distinct but related factors: concentrated ownership and debt financing. In the beginning of the economic growth in the 1960s, firms relied overwhelmingly on debt financing. As founding entrepreneurs did not need to issue shares to outsiders, they could maintain an absolute majority of the shares. As early as the late 1960s, the government began its efforts to foster a capital market and virtually forced major firms to carry out IPOs (Initial Public Offerings). Although the ownership portion of founding entrepreneurs was gradually on the decrease, they still held on average slightly more than 20 percent of the shares in the early 1980s. Their effective control, however, was much stronger than the official figure suggested, due to the widespread practice of "disguised IPO," in which entrepreneurs parked their shares in the accounts of their subordinates or relatives.

The corporate statutes were mainly designed to restrain agency problems arising from the conflicts between managers and shareholders. Most of the statutes were rarely invoked in the presence of a controlling shareholder. Firms were managed in almost complete disregard of corporate formalities. It was customary not to hold a board meeting even in the largest firms. An officer would prepare only the minutes of the board meeting, using the seals deposited by the directors. In smaller firms, even the general shareholders meeting (GSM) was often dispensed with. In such firms, the distinction between the firm itself and the controlling shareholder was often disregarded and the controlling shareholder would sometimes usurp corporate funds for personal purposes. These kinds of irregularities did not receive attention until a formal complaint was filed by a disgruntled shareholder.

(iii) Corporate Law Practice

The irrelevance of corporate law resulted in a small number of corporate law cases. Even in the 1980s, corporate law cases were not only scant but also involved a limited number of fact patterns, such as failure to comply with requirements for a resolution at the GSM. Underdeveloped corporate law deterred the sophistication of local law practice. Until the end of the 1970s, practicing lawyers were basically solo practitioners specializing in litigation. Although a few law firms emerged in the 1970s, they were primarily serving foreign clients doing business in Korea. Even major corporate law disputes were handled by solo practitioners, not law firms. Also, it was quite unusual for a domestic firm to retain a lawyer in the absence of a dispute.

(iv) Corporate Law Scholarship

The irrelevance of corporate law naturally had an effect on the nature of legal scholarship. Especially in the earlier period of economic growth, legal scholars devoted themselves to accurately understanding the foreign concepts. A typical academic paper dealt with a corporate law principle or doctrine, touching upon its foreign origin. Instead of pursuing the principle's actual or potential applications in real life, scholars tended to devote themselves to importing new theories developed in foreign countries. This kind of aloofness on the part of corporate law scholars may be understandable because there were few pressing corporate law issues at that stage. A measure of such aloofness, however, still remains among legal academics to this day.

(v) Growth of Minority Shareholders

With the expansion of economy and the progress of democracy in the late 1980s, the government had to reduce intervention in resource allocation and rely more on market mechanisms. The government made further efforts to develop the capital market and to encourage firms to rely more on equity financing. Firms also felt the need to rely on the capital market. Firms have been expanding rapidly during the 1970s and 1980s, but they could not continue to borrow because their debt equity ratio was already too high and the government's pressure became stronger. Another factor in favor of equity financing was the growth of Korea's capital market. As the growing middle class were seeking investment opportunities other than bank deposits, the capital market was becoming more attractive for large firms as a cheaper source of funds.

As firms started issuing shares, the relative holdings of controlling shareholders were bound to decline. In the 1990s, the portion of controlling shareholders fell to 10 percent on average. The sudden increase of non-voting preferred shares in the late 1980s may be regarded as an attempt by controlling shareholders to bolster their decreasing shares. Far more popular among controlling shareholders was a scheme to use shares held by affiliated firms. By this time, virtually all large firms belonged to a business group, commonly called a chaebol. Controlling shareholders maintained their ultimate control by means of widespread intra-group shareholdings. As shown later, this phenomenon more or less continues to this day, forming the most distinctive feature of Korea's corporate governance.

With the decrease of shares directly owned by the controlling family, the gap between the cash-flow right and the control right grew. This is the classic situation in which conflict between the controlling shareholders and minority shareholders arises. Despite the growing presence of outside investors, the behavior of the controlling family changed little. They exercised absolute control in their business empire. As their cash-flow right dwindled, they now had more incentive to engage in so-called 'tunneling' activities, which aggravated the already poor reputation of chaebol among the general public.

(vi) Lethargy of Corporate Law

It was clear even in the early 1990s that the existing corporate statutes fell short of addressing these changed business realities. Minority shareholders had no effective remedies against tunneling activities of the controlling family. Nevertheless, there was no sign of change in corporate statutes, nor in corporate law scholarship. It was widely known that every chaebol had a single controlling shareholder, often called a "chairman" or chongsu, at the top. Few scholars, however, attempted to do research as to whether or not the existing statutes were adequate to constrain the behavior of the chairman. Nor was there an earnest proposal to stem the possibility of abuse by changing the statutes.

The first major revision of the corporate statutes took place in 1984, more than 20 years after the code was enacted. The 1984 revision strengthened the power of the statutory auditor by empowering him to supervise operational as well as accounting matters. Provisions were introduced to control cross-shareholdings and to allow stock dividends. Carefully following the revisions adopted in Japan, the 1984 revisions were not geared to the challenges of corporate governance facing Korea.

The second opportunity to revamp the corporate statutes came in 1995. By this time, the problem of *chaebol* chairmen had become more acute and the inadequacy of the corporate statutes more obvious. No significant attempt was made, however, to address the problems of *chaebol* in the 1995 revision. Although the 1995 revision did introduce the appraisal remedy for dissenting shareholders, it was already available to shareholders of a listed firm under the then-existing Securities Transaction Law.

(vii) Players in the Corporate Law Revision Process

Why did those corporate law revisions fail to respond to the changing realities? The answer to this question may be related to the actual process of corporate law reform. Corporate law revision was, and still is, carried out by the Ministry of Justice (MOJ), a ministry dominated by prosecutors. Prosecutors were generally not interested in, and had no expertise in, corporate law issues. Although the MOJ recently established a separate section for commercial law matters, only one junior prosecutor is normally assigned for the corporate law revision. As a result, the MOJ has been heavily relying on the corporate law committee dominated by senior law professors. By 1995, corporate governance was a hot topic not just in the US but also in other parts of the world. Even in Korea, a small group of scholars started publishing papers on the subject, but the corporate governance discourse failed to attract attention from those senior academics.

Before the committee embarks on a revision process, the MOJ routinely seeks opinions from various related institutions, most of which are closely aligned with the business interests. In 1995, there was virtually no institution claiming to advocate for the interests of investors in Korea. Neither the ruling party nor the opposition parties were as yet interested in appealing to general investors. So when the academic members of the corporate law committee failed to perceive the perils of the *chaebol* structure, the voice of minority shareholders was completely lost in the legislative process.

Korea thus wasted the last opportunity to reinvigorate its corporate statutes before the financial crisis hit the country in 1997.

III. POST-CRISIS DEVELOPMENTS

(i) Post-crisis Corporate Governance Reforms

The 1997 financial crisis called attention to the importance of corporate law reforms for the first time in Korea. Although the exact cause of the crisis may be hard to determine, it was widely accepted by the general public that poor corporate governance of *chaebol* was a major factor leading the country to the crisis. Indeed, it was in 1997 that the term "corporate governance" was casually used by the media for the first time in Korea. Under pressure from the IMF and the World Bank, Korea had to go through a broad range of reforms, many of them in the area of corporate law. For example, large listed firms are required to fill a majority of board seats with outside directors, and to establish an audit committee, instead of a statutory auditor. Threshold shareholding requirements for the rights of minority shareholders have been substantially relaxed to make it easier for minority shareholders to exercise their rights. Now, for example, a shareholder with 0.01 percent of the shares, not 5 percent under the pre-1998 law, can file a derivative suit against directors.

As discussed later, the corporate statutes have been revised several times after the crisis. The most recent and comprehensive revision was undertaken in 2011. Now, the focus of the 2011 revision was shifted from corporate governance to allowing more leeway to firms in structuring and operating their business enterprises. For example, the scope of securities that firms can issue has been expanded.

As a consequence of the series of law reforms, Korea's corporate law has become closer to that of developed countries such as the US at least in substance. And, at the same time, the relevance of corporate law has been strengthened in the economic community. This has led to dramatic changes in corporate law practice. Two examples of such changes will be introduced here: the rise of court cases and the growth of law firms.

(ii) Rise of Corporate Law Cases

With the democratization of Korea in the late 1980s came the explosion of litigation. Lawsuits increased dramatically. Corporate law cases were no exception. Since the financial crisis, corporate law cases further increased. This trend stands out in a corporate law casebook. The 2013 edition of a leading casebook on corporate law[5] covers 246 Supreme Court decisions altogether. Table 4.2.1 shows the distribution of the decisions by year. The number of decisions announced during the period 2001–2010 is more than the number of the decisions announced during the period 1961–2000.

A similar phenomenon is observed in the field of capital market law. A textbook on capital market law[6] discusses 91 Supreme Court decisions. Table 4.2.2 shows that more than half of them (57 out of 91) were those announced during the period of 2001–2010.

Table 4.2.1 Supreme Court decisions by year: Corporate law

Period	Number of decisions
1960s	2
1970s	16
1980s	28
1990s	52
2001–2010	123
2011–2012	25
Total	246

Table 4.2.2 Supreme Court decisions by year: Capital market law

Period	Number of decisions
1960s	1
1970s	5
1980s	2
1990s	26
2001–2010	57
Total	91

---

5) KON SIK KIM ET AL., CORPORATE LAW (4th ed. 2013).
6) KON SIK KIM & SUNSEOP JUNG, CAPITAL MARKET LAW (2d. ed. 2010).

(iii) Growth of Law Firms

A byproduct of the explosive increase in the number of corporate law disputes is the rapid rise of law firms in Korea. A few small-scale law firms emerged in Korea only in the late 1970s. Kim & Chang, the largest law firm in Korea, had only two founding lawyers until the mid-1970s. The firm had grown to 101 as of November 1997, when the crisis hit Korea. It continued to expand to 483 as of 2013, a more than four-fold expansion during the 15-year period.

Kim & Chang is not the only law firm that grew during the post-crisis period. Table 4.2.3 shows the number of lawyers at the top ten law firms in Korea.

Table 4.2.3 Top 10 Law firms in Korea (March 2013)

Rank	Firm	Number of lawyers
1	Kim & Chang	483
2	Bae, Kim & Lee	298
3	Lee & Ko	296
4	Shin & Kim	249
5	Yoon & Yang	228
6	Yulchon	198
7	Barun	139
8	Logos	98
9	Jipyong & Jisung	97
10	Hwang Mok Park	96

Source: Ministry of Justice, Korea (March 2013)

The number of law firms also increased during the same period. Only a limited number of them had existed up until the end of 1970s. Even in the mid-1990s, when the term "law firm" became known to the general public, there were only four law firms with 50 to 100 lawyers each in Korea. The number of law firms has grown from fewer than 100 in 1996, to 185 in 2000, to 461 in 2009, and to 724 in 2013.[7] The rapid advance of law firms transformed the configuration of Korea's legal profession almost completely. Until the end of

---

7) Sung-Soo Hong, *Growth of Law Firms and Change in Professional Ethics*, Law & Society Vol. 41, 145, 158 (2011) (in Korean): Korean Bar Association Website (http://www.koreanbar.or.kr) (visited on August 28, 2013).

1970s, virtually all the lawyers were solo practitioners specializing in litigation. As of 2013, 13,216 lawyers are now practicing in Korea, 6,146 of them, almost half, are affiliated with law firms.[8]

Although not all the law firm lawyers specialize in corporate law, a significant number of them deal with corporate and capital market law. Even in the late 1980s, corporate law disputes were generally handled by solo practitioners. It is now rare, however, to find a high-profile case not represented by a major law firm.

IV. POST-CRISIS CORPORATE LAW SCHOLARSHIP

(i) Role of Corporate Law Scholars

What kind of role did corporate law scholars play in this transformation of corporate law? Not much. As discussed earlier, the MOJ's corporate law committee has been dominated by law professors. The two pre-crisis revisions in 1984 and 1995, and the original statutes enacted in 1962, were the brainchild of corporate law scholars, not the MOJ and not the National Assembly. In the revisions (1998, 1999, and 2001) immediately following the financial crisis, however, the MOJ adopted a more aggressive posture, putting pressure on the committee's academic members to be more amenable to reform measures.[9]

In order to secure financial support from international institutions such as the IMF and the World Bank, the government made a commitment to take reform measures recommended by them. Thus, the MOJ had no option but to push ahead with promised reforms. Members of the corporate law committee were generally reluctant to adopt many of the reform measures. For example, the proposal to introduce an audit committee was opposed by most members, and by senior legal scholars in particular.[10] Proposals to lower the minimum par from 5000 Won to 100 Won (Art. 329(4))[11] and to eliminate the requirement for the minimum number of incorporators (Art. 288) were also in dispute.

---

8) Korean Bar Association Website (http://www.koreanbar.or.kr) (visited on August 28, 2013).
9) I joined the committee from the 1998 revision.
10) I headed a working committee responsible for drafting provisions related to board committees including an audit committee.
11) Under the current statutes, a corporation may issue even no-par stocks.

Hostility toward these reform measures was widely shared by other members of the legal academy. Why they came to have such a negative view toward the reform measures is not clear. Some of them may have felt uncomfortable with what struck them as a wholesale import of Anglo-American concepts into the corporate statutes. Or, such hostility was possibly due to the prevailing academic mindset of corporate law scholars.

(ii) Lack of Functional Analysis

During the crisis, legal academics were largely unable to come up with their own reform measures to remedy defects of the existing statutes. Impetus and insights for reform came from outside the legal academy. This inability may be at least partly due to the lack of functional analysis in the mainstream corporate legal scholarship.

A functional approach to law aims to develop a menu of solutions for a social problem. Thus, the starting point of a functional analysis is to identify the problem. The next step is to search for effective solutions. This is the stage where comparative law may come to play a role. The last step of this functional analysis is to assess the effectiveness of an adopted solution in addressing the problem. From the functional perspective, the value of a country's corporate law provisions depends not on their theoretical consistency, but on their effectiveness in handling pressing corporate law tasks of the country.

This kind of functional approach, however, has been very weak, if not totally absent, in Korea. The prevalent attitude was to regard corporate law as a system of immutable concepts. Legal scholars tended to focus on solutions rather than problems. Although things are changing now, scholars still tend to pay more attention to the details of an individual legal doctrine than to how it actually affects the problem. For example, a number of papers have been published on the provision on self-dealing (Art. 398), few of them attempt to reveal its limits in addressing problems actually arising from the *chaebol* context.

(iii) Overcoming the Dogmatic Mode of Research

A functional analysis may start from overcoming the conventional mode of research, which was heavily tilted toward dogmatic reasoning. It requires legal scholars to pay more attention to facts rather than concepts. Legal scholars have so far turned away from empirical research. As most of them are not equipped with skills necessary for empirical research, it is too much to expect them to engage in empirical research like their counterparts in the

US. They should be encouraged, however, to take advantage of a growing body of empirical research based on Korean data.

A functional analysis is employed to affect the behavior of corporate actors. In this regard, even a corporate law scholar needs to take an interdisciplinary approach. The law and economics approach to corporate law is now well known among Korean scholars. A small but growing number of young scholars have expertise in finance and accounting. From now on, however, perspectives of other disciplines, such as political science and psychology, will be of help.

So far such an interdisciplinary research has been rare. There are grounds for optimism, however. The first factor is the influence of the corporate law scholarship in the US, which is heavily imbued with a variety of interdisciplinary research. Every year, an increasing number of young Koreans visit leading law schools in the US. When they come back and join the legal academy, they are expected to practice what they have studied in the US. The second factor may take longer to stir up a change. Following Japan, Korea started a US-style law school system in 2009. Unlike in Japan, a majority of incoming students are those who have specialized in non-law subjects such as social sciences and engineering. The new breed of lawyers is expected to have much less difficulty and psychological inhibition in practicing empirical methods in their legal research.

V. CHALLENGES OF CORPORATE LAW REFORM

A functional approach in corporate law will be essential for enhancing the level and relevance of corporate law scholarship in future. Efforts of legal scholars alone will not bring a better corporate law regime, however. There are two sizeable obstacles to corporate law reform. The first is the difficulty of the *chaebol* problem. The second is the political environment. In sum, the first relates to the technical difficulty of coming up with a set of effective solutions, and the second relates to the difficulty of implementing those solutions in the existing political environment.

(i) Difficulty of the Chaebol Problem

The ownership structure of large Korean firms is often characterized as controlling minority shareholder (CMS) structure. A CMS effectively controls the whole business group by

means of extensive inter-company shareholdings. A number of major *chaebol* have converted into a holding company structure. But if both the controlling shareholder of the
holding company and the holding company itself usually hold far less than 50 percent in
the individual firms in the group, the CMS problem remains, although in a less serious
form, in the holding company structure.

Figure 4.2.1 shows the size of internal ownership in the top ten *chaebol* in Korea. Internal
ownership here refers to the sum of shares held by the CMS and those held by member firms.
Figure 4.2.1 shows the three basic features of Korea's CMS structure. First, the CMS's direct
holdings are extremely low, less than one percent in 2012. Second, the CMS exercises absolute control by means of holdings of member firms. Third, despite persistent criticism of
this disparity between the CMS's cash-flow right and the control right, the CMS structure
has remained stable over the last two decades.

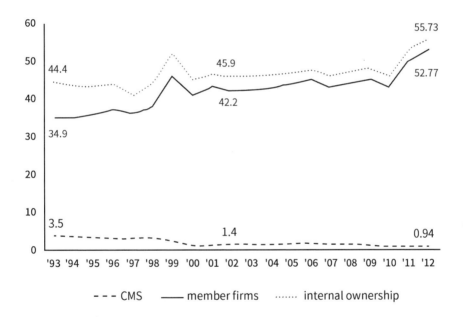

Source: Fair Trade Commission, Press Release, July 2, 2012

Figure 4.2.1 Changes in the size of internal ownership in the top ten chaebol (unit: %)

The CMS structure allows all the member firms to maintain a long-term perspective without too much focus on short-term profits. This aspect is often touted as a principal advantage of the current *chaebol* structure. On the other hand, the CMS structure is prone to
abuse. The most well known example of such abuse is so-called 'tunneling' by the CMS.

In Korea, tunneling is believed to take place on two occasions. First, the CMS engages in tunneling to enable his heirs to accumulate funds for securing control. The CMS has developed a variety of tactics. In the 1990s, a popular tactic was to issue or transfer equity securities to his heirs at low prices. Some CMS were held liable for damages and even went to jail for such tactics. Even Chairman Lee of Samsung narrowly avoided conviction by the 6–5 decision at the Supreme Court a few years ago.

After the danger of issuing equity securities was made clear, the CMS took a more cautious approach. They turned to what Koreans call "concentrated awarding of contracts," a scheme of favoring heirs in awarding contracts. This practice became so widespread that it is difficult to find a *chaebol* that has not engaged in this practice. Although this practice recently gained much notoriety even among the general public, it has not been easy to restrain this practice as a technical matter.

The second instance where a *chaebol* engages in tunneling activities is when it tries to save a distressed member firm. In theory, of course, it is possible for the CMS to let the firm go bankrupt. As a practical matter, however, it has been, and still is, very difficult to cut off such a troubled subsidiary for various reasons: the detrimental effect on the group reputation, sanctions by creditor banks, and dampening employee morale, for example. Even if salvaging the distressed firm can be justified for business reasons, it is very difficult to allocate the financial burden fairly among the member firms. There is a risk that the CMS may be convicted for breach of trust if he is found to have made a wrong decision.[12]

Tunneling can be eliminated if *chaebol* groups are disbanded or intra-group transactions are banned altogether. Neither of the two can be an option at the moment. Korea has not yet found an effective solution for this problem, which does not seem so serious in other developed economies.

(ii) Political Environment

As discussed above, it is technically difficult to get at a set of effective measures for the *chaebol* problem. Even if the legal academy manages to come up with a policy solution, it may be difficult to pursue it depending on the political environment.

The battlefield of corporate governance reform now appears heavily tilted in favor of *chaebol*, which wields influence over major players in Korean society such as politicians, bureau-

---

12) The risk is not just theoretical, but real. A chairman of a Top 10 business group was convicted for these salvaging transactions and sentenced to four years' imprisonment.

crats, mainstream media, and academics. On the contrary, only a small number of in-tellectuals and liberal politicians can be counted as critics of *chaebol*. What can change the balance of power between the two forces is the general public, who feel rather ambivalent about the *chaebol*'s dominance in Korea. Feeling proud of the success of *chaebol* in the global market place, they feel, at the same time, uncomfortable with the abuse of power by the CMS. The mood changes swiftly. Depending on the political mood of the time, a partic-ular reform bill may or may not pass.

Until the mid-1990s, the general public was not interested in corporate law. The corporate statutes were almost entirely left to the discretion of a small number of scholars. As the statutes became more relevant to corporate actors including the CMSs, room for political intervention also grew. Under these circumstances, two types of risk exist with respect to corporate law reform. The first type of risk is that a desirable bill is blocked by political forces. The second type of risk is that an unreasonable bill is passed due to political forces. There are many instances of the first type of risk, which are relatively well known. The sec-ond type of risk is constantly emphasized by the allies of *chaebol*. The second type of risk is also real, and may be quite serious given the difficulty of discovering a set of adequate measures. For the time being, however, the second type of risk is not likely to materialize according to the current political atmosphere.

VI. CONCLUDING REMARKS

Until the 1980s, corporate law in Korea was a rather quiet, and even dull, field of law. With the financial crisis in 1997 as a turning point, corporate law has evolved into an exciting, even creative, field of law. It has been changing from a received system of concepts and doctrines, to a set of solutions designed for problems of the business community. As it gains relevance, however, corporate law has been subject to political pressure. Prior to the financial crisis, corporate law reform had attracted little public attention. A recent corporate law reform bill[13] promoted by the MOJ was discussed in the editorial section of major dai-ly newspapers, and even at the dinner President Park had with business leaders. Political intervention is just a fact of life in a corporate governance reform in developed countries such as the US, Germany, and Japan. As it moves along the road to a developed economy, Korea is becoming similar to other developed countries in this respect as well.

---

13) I did not participate in the drafting process.

Corporate Governance in Korea

Kon Sik Kim*

The 1984 revision of Korea's Commercial Code failed to respond adequately to the issues of structure and governance in large Korean corporations. The managements of such corporations are able to circumvent both legal and market restraints on this conduct and thus act more freely than their U.S. counterparts. If the Korean economy is to continue expanding the government must confront the problem of management accountability or suffer stagnation as foreign and domestic investors seek other markets.

1. Introduction

Large corporations play a central role in modern capitalist societies. Corporate influence extends beyond the economic arena to both political and cultural affairs. Because of this influence, lawyers, economists, and business leaders have carefully studied the structure and governance of business corporations. In the United States, debate on corporate governance among both academics and practitioners[1] led the American Law Institute (ALI) to propose an ambitious first draft of Principles of Corporate Governance[2]. Criticism of the draft was extensive when it came out in 1982[3]. In the more recent drafts[4], the ALI qualified its orig-

---

* Visiting Lecturer in Law, University of Washington; J.D. 1985, University of Washington: LL.M. 1980, Harvard University; LL.M. 1979, LL.B. 1977, Seoul National University, Korea.
1) *See, e.g.,* Commentaries on Corporate Structure and Corporate Governance, The ALI-ABA Symposiums 1977-1978, at 6-8 (D. Schwartz ed. 1979). Many consider the current checks on management, including the accountability of directors and managers to shareholders, to be legally insufficient. *Id.*
2) Principles of Corporate Governance and Structure: Restatement and Recommendations (Tent. Draft No. 1. 1982) [hereinafter cited as ALI Draft No. 1].
3) *See* Business Roundtable, Statement of the Business Roundtable on the American Law Institute's Proposed "Principles of Corporate Governance and Structure: Restatement and Recommendations" (1983); Fischel, *The Corporate Governance Movement,* 35 Vand. L. Rev. 1259 (1982) (disputing the existence of any corporate governance problem and arguing that economic theory dictates the way a firm is organized); Scott, *Corporation Law and the American Law Institute Corporate Governance Project.* 35 Stan. L Rev. 927, 946-47 (1983) (arguing that outside directors and auditors are not necessarily preferable to inside directors and inside auditors and that the ALl disregarded the relevance of economic theory to firm organization).

inal position on many points. The recent revision of Korea's Commercial Code[5], which became effective on September 1, 1984, provides an opportunity to compare corporate governance in Korea with corporate management in the United States. Corporate governance has not been discussed as extensively in Korea as it has in the United States. The 1984 revision is the first statutory change since the Commercial Code was enacted in 1962.

During the past two decades, Korea's economy has expanded rapidly and business corporations have played a decisive role in Korea's economic development[6]. Although the 1984 revision covers more than 150 provisions, it barely addresses the issue of corporate structure and governance. This apparent neglect of corporate governance should not suggest a resolution of corporate governance issues in Korea. Rather, corporate governance eventually will provoke widespread controversy in Korea.

This paper examines the statutory framework of corporate structure and governance in Korea. Providing a background for subsequent discussions, section 2 shows how the shareholding pattern of large corporations in Korea differs from the U.S. pattern. It then briefly discusses the significance of such differences. Section 3 examines how the various statutory mechanisms in Korea are designed to control management behavior and the reasons they fail to work. Finally, section 4 deals with market mechanisms restraining management conduct in Korea.

2. Ownership and Control of Large Corporations in Korea: Its Reality and Significance

2.1. Concentrated Ownership Structure

The Korean Commercial Code permits four types of business organizations: (1) the partnership company, an entity whose members assume unlimited liability for the company's obligations; (2) the limited partnership company, an entity composed of two classes of members, those who assume unlimited liability for the company's obligations, and those who do not assume liability beyond the value of their shares; (3) the private limited liability company, an entity similar to a closed corporate enterprise; and (4) the stock company, the

---

4) Principles of Corporate Governance: Analysis and Recommendations (Tent. Drafts No. 2 & 3, 1984) [hereinafter cited as ALI Draft No. 2 and ALI Draft No. 3, respectively].
5) *Sangbop.* (Commercial Code) Law No. 1000 of 1962, *as revised by* Law No. 3724 of 1984.
6) *See* L. Jones & I. Sakong, Government, Business, and Entrepreneurship in Economic Development: The Korean Case (1980).

equivalent of the publicly held business corporation in the United States.

Korean companies clearly favor the corporate form. Even joint venture corporations, which could operate more efficiently as private limited liability companies, prefer this type of organization[7]. As in Japan, the overwhelming popularity of the corporate form probably results from the "first class" image that such companies project[8].

Most Korean corporations are relatively small[9]. Although a closely held corporation is not necessarily small by definition[10], virtually all corporations below the one billion won line are closely held[11]. Moreover, many of the large corporations above the one billion won line are probably closely held[12]. In addition, available data indicate that the shareholdings in corporations listed on the Korean Stock Exchange are not widely distributed among the public, but heavily concentrated in a small number of people.

The number of corporations listed on the Korean Stock Exchange increased from 66 in 1972 to 334 in 1982[13]. Table 1 indicates that the government goal of wider distribution of equities among the public has been achieved to a marked degree in the period 1972-1982[14]. Concentration of shareholdings nevertheless remains. Table 1 indicates that only 5,011 shareholders of 334 listed corporations hold as much as 54.83% of the total shares. This sharply contrasts with the situation in the United States[15].

---

7) Introduction to the Law and Legal System of Korea 842 (S. Song ed. 1983) [hereinafter cited as S. Song].
8) See Z. Kitagawa, 4 Doing Business in Japan. Pt. VII. § 1.03(1)(c) (1983); see also S. Song. supra note 7, at 842 (noting that in Korean business circles the appellation, private limited liability company, connotes diminutiveness).
9) Cf. P. Kuznets, Economic Growth and Structure in the Republic of Korea 165 (1977) (noting that Korean establishments are small by international standards).
10) See H. Henn & J. Alexander, Laws of Corporations 694-95 (3rd ed. 1983) ("No distinction between the closely held corporation and the public issue corporation can be made according to size.").
11) See S. Song, supra note 7, at 842-45.
12) Id.
13) Korea Stock Exchange, Han'guk chunggwon Koraeso, chusik (stock) (July 1984) at 72-73 (statistics section).
14) Korea Stock Exchange, Chusik (July, 1984), at 8 (statistics section).
15) Because most Korean corporations were highly leveraged, they could not raise the capital needed for rapid economic growth. Government policy, therefore, sought to ameliorate the capital structure by promoting the securities market. Y. Shin, Securities Regulations in Korea 45-50, 100-11 (1983).

Table I   Distribution of equity ownership by shareholding[16]

	End of 1972	End of 1982
Below 100 shares		
Persons	76,096 (73.69%)	158,875 (23.29%)
Shares	1,229,206 (0.58%)	5,947,890 (0.13%)
100-1,000 shares		
Persons	18,526 (17.94%)	276,641 (40.55%)
Shares	5,953,606 (2.79%)	115,365,896 (2.43%)
1,000-10,000 shares		
Persons	6,823 (6.60%)	191,367 (280.05%)
Shares	20,160,664 (9.43%)	649,246,801 (13.65%)
10,000-100,000 shares		
Persons	1,610 (1.55%)	50,281 (0.73%)
Shares	40,545,600 (18.97%)	1,376,152,300 (28.96%)
Over 100,000 shares		
Persons	211 (0.20%)	5,022 (0.73%)
Shares	145,902,380 (68.25%)	2,606,577,365 (54.83%)
Total		
Persons	103,266 (100.00%)	682,175 (100.00%)
Shares	214,791,456 (100.00%)	4,753.290,252 (100.00%)

The actual extent of concentration of shareholdings in Korea, however, may be much greater than table 1 suggests. Most business corporations in Korea are owned by single families[17]. They are reluctant to go public and thus endanger their control over the corporations they themselves have founded[18]. For financing, even the largest corporations heavily rely on domestic or foreign banks, or on private money markets rather than the securities market[19]. The government has pressured corporations to go public to improve the highly leveraged corporate financial structure and to achieve wider distribution among the public of shares in major business institutions. The government has provided various incentives, including favorable tax treatment for publicly held corporations[20]. Moreover, the government has

---

16) *See Voting Rights in Major Corporations: Subcomm. on Reports, Accounting and Management of the Senate Comm. on Governmental Affairs*, 95th Cong., 1st Sess. 8-10 (1981), *cited in* E. Herman, Corporate Control, Corporate Power 102 (1981).
17) *See* Y. Shin, *supra* note 15, at 100.
18) *See id.* at 42.
19) *Id.* at 44.
20) *See Kiopkonggae Chokchinbop* (Act Encouraging Public Offering by Enterprises) Law No. 2420 of 1972; *Chabonsijang Yuksong e Kwanhan Pomnyul* (Capital Market Promotion Act) Law No. 2046 of 1968;

simply ordered selected corporations to go public[21]. In response, a number of leading corporations have either refused to go public or have disguised themselves as public by placing a substantial portion of shares under the names of "close friends, relatives, employees, and occasionally, controlling shareholders of other corporations in a reciprocal arrangement"[22]. Another phenomenon strengthening the actual degree of concentration of equity ownership in Korea is the widespread practice of cross or circular shareholdings among corporations in the same business group. One of the most notable byproducts of rapid economic growth in Korea is the emergence of several giant business conglomerates[23]. At present, most of the largest business corporations in Korea belong to one of these conglomerates. The extensive use of the cross or circular ownership device has contributed to the rapid expansion of these conglomerates. Through this device, controlling persons have been able to expand their holdings without necessarily relinquishing ultimate control. Public concern has finally caused lawmakers to prohibit a subsidiary from acquiring the stock of its parent[24].

These factors suggest the existence of a single controlling family even in large corporations. The head of this family actively manages corporate affairs or at least closely supervises the performance of management. Typically. the entrepreneur who has founded the business group is the source of all power in the group[25].

Thus, one may make a rough distinction among large corporations in Korea and the United States. In large U.S. corporations, ownership and control are separate; management, rather than shareholders, has control over corporate affairs. In contrast, both ownership and control of Korean corporations are in the hands of strong-willed founders. Although these entrepreneurs usually assume the role of chief executives in the corporations, their ultimate power derives not only from their status as top executive officers, but also from their status as controlling shareholders.

Popinsebop (Corporation Tax Act) Law No. 1964 of 1967; Y. Shin, supra note 15, at 45-49, 64-68.

21) Act Encouraging Public Offering by Enterprises, art. 4; see Y. Shin, supra note 15. at 64-66.

22) Y. Shin. supra note 15. at 162. Article 189 of Korea's Securities and Exchange Law prohibits listed corporations from holding the shares of other listed corporations in such a reciprocal arrangement. Chunggwvon Koraehop (Securities and Exchange Law) Law No. 972 of 1962. amended by Law No. 3541 of 1982.

23) See L Jones & I. Sakong. supra note 6. at 258-69.

24) Commercial Code, art. 342.

25) See L. Jones & I. Sakong, supra note 6, at 258-60.

2.2. Significance of the Existence of Owner-managers

The previous subsection concludes that in a typical large corporation in Korea, a single family controls a substantial block of shares and the head of the family is actively engaged in management of the member companies in his business group. Thus, the interests of shareholders and management overlap substantially. Consequently, agency problems are much less acute in Korea than in the United States[26]. Indeed, owner-managers' relentless pursuit of their own interests has contributed to the remarkable growth of the Korean business corporation. Given the current integration of ownership and control, corporate governance seems less important an issue in Korea than in the United States. Without significant agency problems, the most important function of corporate law is the protection of minority rights against the misconduct of controlling shareholders.

It is difficult to predict how this concentrated shareholding pattern of Korean corporations will change. Yet, due to current government policy as well as economic forces, it is clear that the percentage of controlling shareholders' holdings will eventually decline with the passage of time. In order to distribute shares more evenly among the public, the government encourages corporations to rely on equity financing instead of debt financing[27]. The government also discourages banks from further lending to their large corporate borrowers[28]. Because debt financing has lost much of its appeal[29], the inflation rates of the recent years have been low[30]. Moreover, as long as both government policy and the securities laws continue to discourage hostile takeovers and challenges to existing control[31], controlling share-

---

26) Agency problems arise when decision-making agents (management) "do not bear a substantial share of the wealth effects of their decision." Fama & Jensen, *Separation of Ownership and Control.* 26 J. L. & Econ. 301 (1983): *see also* Jensen & Meckling, *Theory of the Firn: Managerial Behavior, Agency Costs and Ownership Structure*, 3 J. Fin. Econ. 305 (1976).

27) *Much to Crow About*, Business Korea. Nov. 1983, at 59-60. Government encouragement includes such policies as permitting corporations to issue shares at market value, rather than par value, and giving corporations flexibility in deciding dividend rates thereby increasing the attractiveness of stock investment. *Id.*

28) *See Big Business Concentration Put Under a New Critical Light.* Business Korea. July 1984. at 51. 54-55 (government has tried to limit bank loans to one borrower to 25% of a bank's net worth): *Dong-A Ilbo.* Aug. 27, 1984, at I *Id..* Aug. 22, 1984, at 2.

29) Since financial institutions' lending rates have been kept below the market rates, those able to obtain institutional credits (in most cases, large corporations) have been subsidized primarily by those depositors who pay inflation taxes. Thus, it is less likely that rational savers would borrow to obtain financial assets and then have to pay inflation taxes. Most, therefore. choose not to hold financial assets. D. Cole & Y. Park. Financial Development in Korea. 1945-1978. at 189-93 (1983).

30) In 1983. wholesale prices rose by only 0.2% and consumer prices by just 3.4%. This trend of price stability is expected to continue in 1984. *High Growth, Low Inflation Seen to Continue Through '85,* Business Korea, June 1984. at 38. 39.

holders may substantially reduce their holdings without risking ultimate control. As the percentage of controlling shareholders' equity interest decreases, however. their interest and that of the corporation may diverge, causing agency problems to develop.

Because government policy and economic forces may take a long time to affect corporate structure, Korea should develop effective statutory mechanisms to control management behavior. However, the statutory scheme must not unduly encumber management's efforts to maximize corporate profits and shareholder gain since these goals are central to the corporation[32].

3. Statutory Mechanisms for Checking Management

The Korean Commercial Code provides that "the business of the company ... shall be executed by the resolution of the board of directors"[33]. In the United States it is generally recognized that management, headed by the chief executive officer, rather than the board, operates the business[34]. In Korea, the "representative director," the functional equivalent of the chairman of the board in the United States, is the supreme authority in the actual operation of the corporate business. Representative directors have authority to perform all acts relating to the corporate business on behalf of the corporation[35]. In Korea, three organizational units are responsible for examining management conduct: (1) the board of directors; (2) "inside auditors": and (3) shareholders. Contrary to the statutory purpose, however, none of these checks can effectively curtail management's power vis-à-vis the minority shareholders.

---

31) *See* Y. Shin. *supra* note 15. at 286-358.
32) *See* ALl Draft No. 2. *supra* note 4, § 2.01.
33) Commercial Code, art. 393.
34) M. Eisenberg, The Structure of the Corporation 139-41 (1976). Thus, a number of modem corporate statutes in the United States provide that the business of a corporation shall be managed by "or under the direction or" a board. See, e.g.. Del. Code Ann., tit. 8. § 141(a) (1983): Cal. Corp. Code. § 300 (West Supp. 1983): Model Bus. Corp. Act, § 35 (1982). ALl Draft No. 2, §3.01 suggests that corporate law provide that the management of the business of a publicly held corporation shall be conducted by or under the supervision of certain senior executives who are designated by the board of directors.
35) Commercial Code. arts. 209, 389(3).

3.1. The Board of Directors

The Code requires a corporation to have at least three directors who are elected at share-holder meetings[36]. Since cumulative voting is unavailable[37], a controlling shareholder may fill all the board positions with his supporters.

Under the Code, the board, or the shareholders, if so provided in the articles of in-corporation, has the power to appoint representative directors[38]. Although the original Code had no provision for the board's power to supervise and to remove representative di-rectors, commentators did not dispute the board's supervisory role[39]. The 1984 amend-ments confirm this view by providing that the board shall supervise the execution of corpo-rate affairs by its directors[40].

In the United States, as it became clear that the board of a large publicly held corporation does not, and, is not, in a position to actually "manage" the corporate business, the over-sight function of the board has moved into the limelight[41]. Nevertheless, there has been wide criticism that, in actuality, the board fails to perform that role[42]. Although the sit-uation in Korea is similar, it is more pronounced. In fact, the oversight function of the board is virtually absent for several practical reasons.

First, the subordination of directors to the representative director renders meaningful super-vision impossible. Although similar criticism has been directed at U.S. corporations[43], the degree of such subordination is much stronger in Korea, since in most cases the controlling shareholder himself or his "right-hand man" serves as representative director. While the board selects the representative director as a legal matter[44], the representative director (or controlling shareholder behind him) selects the board members as a practical matter. The controlling shareholder usually selects directors from among his long-time employees. The

---

36) *Id.* art. 382(1).
37) Unlike several U.S. state laws, Korea's Commercial Code does not provide for cumulative voting. *See. e.g..* Del. Code. Ann.. tit. 8. § 214 (1983): Model Bus. Corp. Act, §33 (1982).
38) Commercial Code, art. 389(1). The board may appoint more than one representative director. *See id.* art. 389(2).
39) H. Chong. *Sangbophak Wollon* I (Principles of Commercial Law) 425, 428 (1980).
40) Commercial Code, art. 393(2).
41) *See, e.g.,* M. Eisenberg, *supra* note 34, at 157-70, American Bar Association. *Corporate Director's Guidebook,* 33 Bus. Law. 1591, 1621 (1978); ALI Draft No. 2. *supra* note 4, § 3.02.
42) *See, e.g..* M. Mace. Directors: Myth and Reality (1971): Mace, *Directors: Myth and Reality - Ten Years Later,* 32 Rutgers L. Rev. 293 (1979).
43) *See* M. Eisenberg, *supra* note 34, at 144-48.
44) Commercial Code, art. 389(1).

loyalty of the candidate to the controlling shareholder is the crucial factor in the selection process. Removable at any time with or without cause at a shareholders meeting[45], a director serves at the pleasure of the controlling shareholder. Consequently, to expect a director to risk his position by defying this shareholder is quite unrealistic.

A second factor that renders board supervision of management ineffective is the near absence of outside directors on the board[46]. Even in large corporations, most directors serve as officers or employees of the corporation they "direct."

A recent survey shows that 92 out of 197 listed corporations have no outside directors on their boards[47]. Thus, under the circumstances, the board may well be compared to a batter who "calls his own strikes." The supervisory function of the board thus remains an illusion. The 1984 amendments merely confirm the board's oversight function, without introducing significant changes. Some Korean commentators have recommended that a majority of the board members should be selected from outside the company[48], but these recommendations have not appealed to the corporate community[49]. Such a response is not surprising, considering that Korean entrepreneurs have been reluctant to allow outsiders to participate in their businesses, even as shareholders.

3.2. Auditors

3.2.1. Inside Auditors

The presence of inside auditors in Korean corporations may justify the exclusion of outside directors on the board. Indeed, the 1984 amendments to the KCC focus on strengthening the power of inside auditors.

Under the Code, a stock corporation must have at least one inside auditor, who may not

---

45) Such removal requires a two-thirds majority vote of the shares represented at a meeting where a majority of the total outstanding shares are represented. A director removed without cause from his office before the expiration of his term of office is entitled to compensation for any damage caused by such removal. *Id.* art. 385(1).

46) For purposes of this article, an independent director is one who does not hold an executive position in the corporation in which he or she serves. According to this definition, outside directors are not necessarily "independent" of management control.

47) Kim, *Sangjanghoesa isahoe wa sangmuhoe ui siltaebunsok* (An Empirical Study of the Board and Executive Committee in Listed Corporations) *in* K. Kim, *Hoesabop ui Chemunje* (Issues in Corporation Law) 296, 303 (1982).

48) *Id.* at 310-12.

49) Neither the recommendations drafted by the Federation of Korean Industries nor those drafted by the Korean Chamber of Commerce has mentioned the term "outside director." *Han'guk Sangsabop Hakhoe* (Korean Commercial Law Society), *Sangbop Kaejong Ui Nonjom* (Issues in Revising the Commercial Code) 261-62. 276-77 (1981).

serve concurrently as a director, a manager, or as any other employee of the corporation[50]. Inside auditors are selected at shareholder meetings[51]. In selecting inside auditors, any shareholder with more than three percent of the total outstanding voting shares may not vote the excess shares[52]. The recent revision extends the term of office for inside auditors from one to two years[53].

Prior to the revision, the responsibilities of inside auditors were generally limited to accounting matters[54]. The amended Code expands the role of inside auditors to cover operational as well as accounting matters by providing that "the inside auditor shall examine the directors' performance"[55]. In addition, inside auditors are jointly and severally liable to the corporation for damages caused by their failure to perform their duties[56]. Such a failure may give rise to a derivative suit[57].

Although the 1984 revision theoretically strengthens the role of the inside auditor, in practice he or she will merely act as a "rubber stamp." This discrepancy between theory and practice exists because the amendments have failed to ensure the independence of the inside auditor.

The Code prohibits the inside auditor from serving concurrently as a director, a manager, or any other employee of the corporation[58]. but the Code requires no more. As long as he or she is not presently maintaining any of those positions, any person may serve as inside auditor, however obvious and strong his or her ties are to management. One may ar-

---

50) Commercial Code, art. 411.
51) *Id.* art. 409(1).
52) *Id.* art. 409(7).
53) More accurately, the term of office of inside auditors extends to the close of the ordinary shareholders' meeting dealing with the last settlement of accounting within two years after taking office. *Id.* art. 410.
54) *Sangbop* (Commercial Code) Law No. 1000 of 1962, *reprinted in* Korean Legal Center, 3 Laws of the Republic of Korea § 8 (4th ed. 1983).
55) 1984 Commercial Code, art. 412(1). The amendments further provide for the following new responsibilities of the inside auditor:
    (1) to call on the directors at any time for a report on the business and to investigate corporate affairs such as financial status, *id.* art. 412(2):
    (2) to attend board meetings and present his opinion, *id.* art. 391-2(l);
    (3) to review directors' proposals and documents submitted at shareholder meetings and to determine whether such proposals/documents comply with the law and articles of incorporation, *id.* art. 413;
    (4) to report to the board of directors if he finds that a director has violated the law or articles of incorporation, *id.* art. 391-2(2);
    (5) to enjoin a director from violating the law or articles of incorporation if such a violation would irreparably harm the corporation, *id.* art. 402;
    (6) to represent the corporation in a suit between the directors and the corporation, *id.* art 394;
    (7) to submit an audit report covering specified matters to directors, *Id.* art. 447-4.
56) *Id.* art. 414(1). If an auditor's failure to perform his duties as an inside auditor is due to bad faith or gross negligence, he or she may be liable to a third party. *Id.* art. 414(2).
57) *Id.* arts. 403-06, 415.
58) *Id.* art. 411.

gue that prohibiting a shareholder with more than three percent of the total outstanding voting shares from voting the excess shares may diminish substantially the influence of the controlling shareholder on the election of inside auditors[59]. The three percent maximum provision, however, may be avoided by secretly distributing the excess shares among relatives or friends[60]. Combined with the inertia and disorganization of small shareholders, this procedural approach is unlikely to enhance the neutrality of inside auditors.

3.2.2. Outside Auditors

The external audit, required under other statutes, may remedy the deficiency of the internal audit system under the Commercial Code. The most important audit is the external audit required by the Law Concerning the External Audit of Stock Corporations (External Audit Law)[61]. Pursuant to the External Audit Law, a corporation with both capital and total assets in excess of 500 million won and 3 billion won, respectively, must have its financial statements audited by an outside auditor[62]. The outside auditor, who must be either a certified public accountant or an accounting firm, has the following duties: (1) to audit the financial statements and submit an audit report to the corporation and the Audit Supervision Committee attached to the Securities Supervisory Board[63]; (2) to report any improper acts committed by a director in performing his duties and any material violations of law or the articles of incorporation[64]; and (3) to attend shareholder meetings upon request of the shareholders and present opinion or answer questions[65]. Outside auditors may be liable to the corporation or third parties for failure to perform their duties, and may be subject to disciplinary measures for violation of the Law[66].

Nonetheless, Korean law provides that "corporations" must appoint the outside auditor[67]. The power to appoint an outside auditor will, therefore, rest in most cases with the board

---

59) *Id.* art. 409(2).
60) *See* Lee, *Kamsachedo ui chemunje* (Problems of the Auditor System). in *Hoesabop ui Hyondaejok Kwaje* (Modern Issues in Corporation Law) 172, 186 (1981).
61) *Chusik Hoesa ui Oebu Kamsa e Kwanhan Pomnyul* (External Audit Law) Law No. 3297 of 1980.
62) *Id.* art. 2. In addition, a corporation that is listed on the stock exchange or raises funds from the public may be subject to an outside audit. Securities and Exchange Law, art. 182.
63) External Audit Law, art. 8. The Securities Supervisory Board is the executive body of the Securities Administration Commission, the Korean equivalent of the Securities and Exchange Commission in the United States. *See generally*, Y. Shin, *supra* note 15, 96-98 (describing the establishment of an institution similar to the SEC in Korea).
64) External Audit Law, art. 10.
65) *Id.* art. 11.
66) *Id.* arts. 16-17
67) *Id.* art. 4.

of directors or, as a practical matter, the representative director[68]. Accordingly, the independence and objectivity of an external audit is clearly questionable.

3.3. Shareholders

3.3.1. General Meeting: Law and Reality

A general meeting of shareholders must be held once a year, but if the corporation has more than one fiscal period a year a meeting must be held once during each period[69]. Usually, the board of directors determines whether to convene a general meeting[70], but shareholders with five percent or more of the total outstanding shares may force the board to call an extraordinary meeting of shareholders[71].

The power of shareholders at the general meeting is limited to the matters provided for in the Code or the articles of incorporation[72]. Ordinarily, matters handled at that meeting include: (1) approval of the balance sheet, the income statement, and the profit or loss disposal statement[73]; and (2) election of directors and inside auditors[74].

Except as otherwise provided in the Code or the articles of incorporation, shareholders representing a majority of the total outstanding shares constitute a quorum, and a majority vote of the shares represented at the meeting is required to pass ordinary resolutions[75]. A two-thirds majority is necessary for matters such as: (1) amendment of the articles of incorporation[76]; (2) transfer of all or a substantial part of the business[77]; (3) removal of directors and inside auditors[78]; and (4) merger, consolidation, or dissolution[79].

Similar to their U.S. counterparts, small shareholders in Korea have little interest in attending shareholder meetings. Most of them are speculators rather than investors[80]. If small

---

68) The Commercial Code powers vested in the shareholders are limited to those enumerated in the Code and articles of incorporation. These powers include the right to appoint only internal auditors at shareholder meetings. *See* Commercial Code, art. 361.
69) *Id.* arts. 365(l), (2). Extraordinary meetings may be held from time to time as necessary. *Id.* art. 365(3).
70) *Id.* art. 362.
71) *Id.* art. 366.
72) *Id.* art. 361.
73) *Id.* art. 449.
74) *Id.* arts. 382(1). 409(1).
75) *Id.* art. 368(l).
76) *Id.* art. 434.
77) *Id.* art. 374.
78) *Id.* arts. 385(1), 415.
79) *Id.* arts. 518. 522.
80) A 1983 survey shows that 57.7% of 300 investors surveyed have transferred stock in less than three months while only 6.9% of these investors have held stock for more than six months. While as many as 30.1% short-term investors are mainly interested in a quick profit from a stock price rise, less than

shareholders do attend meetings, their impact is minimal because a majority of the shares are in the hands of a few controlling shareholders. Consequently. despite the legal illusion of management accountability to shareholders, the reality is that management is accountable only to the largest shareholders. Under such a governance structure shareholder meetings will inevitably serve merely to validate the acts and proposals of management.

3.3.2. Shareholders' Rights Vis-à-vis Directors

3.3.2.1. Shareholders' rights in removing directors.   Shareholders may remove directors at any time, with or without cause, by passing a special resolution at a shareholder meeting[81]. If, despite the director's material misconduct, the resolution fails to pass, then shareholders with five percent or more of the outstanding shares may resort to the courts for judicial removal of the director[82]. The shareholders may apply for a temporary order to deprive the director of his authority and to appoint an acting director[83]. The availability of such a procedure thus provides shareholders with a limited remedy for director mismanagement. The five percent requirement, nonetheless. poses an enormous obstacle to shareholder use of this device in the large publicly held corporation.

3.3.2.2. Inspection rights.   A shareholder may inspect or copy financial statements and audit reports kept at the main office[84]. To gain access to accounting books and records, however, shareholders are required to have at least five percent of the total outstanding shares[85]. Normally, directors must prove the unreasonableness of the shareholders' demand for such inspection in order to avoid it[86], but in publicly held corporations the shareholders carry the burden of proving that their demand is reasonable[87]. Thus, shareholder access to financial information remains limited.

If any doubt arises as to the existence of grave misconduct on the part of directors, shareholders with five percent of the total shares may demand that the court appoint an inspector authorized to investigate corporate affairs and financial status[88]. Nevertheless, be-

---

3% of them are dividend-seeking investors. *Joong-Ang Ilbo*. Jan. 31, 1984, at. 4.
81) Commercial Code, art. 385(1). A director removed without cause before the expiration of his term of office is entitled to compensation for any damage caused by the removal. *Id.*
82) *Id.* art. 385(2).
83) *Id.* art. 407.
84) *Id.* art. 448(2).
85) *Id.* art. 466(1).
86) *Id.* art. 466(2).
87) Capital Market Promotion Act, art. 11-5.
88) Commercial Code, art. 467(1).

cause of this five percent shareholding requirement, small shareholders' ability to gauge management performance is effectively minimized.

3.3.2.3. Fiduciary duties.
Korea has no provision expressly stating the fiduciary duties of management[89]. Since the mandate provisions of the Civil Code[90] are applicable to the relationship between the corporation and directors[91], the latter have the duty of care of a good manager[92], which is functionally equivalent to the fiduciary duty imposed on the director of a U.S. corporation. Moreover, the Commercial Code provides three sets of regulations to prevent directors from breaching their duty as good managers[93].

First, a director who seeks to execute any transaction with the corporation on his own behalf or on behalf of a third person must obtain the board's approval[94]. Although the Code does not expressly provide so. it is generally agreed that such a requirement is limited to those transactions that may cause a conflict of interest between the director and the corporation[95].

Second, a director who intends to effect a transaction that falls within the same line of business as carried on by the corporation must obtain approval of the shareholders[96]. If the director acts on his own behalf, then the corporation may treat the transaction as though it were effected on behalf of the corporation[97]. If he acts on behalf of a third person, then the corporation still may demand any benefit resulting from the transaction[98]. The avaricious director may be liable to the corporation for any damage caused by his conduct and may be removed[99].

The scope of this principle, which purports to prohibit competition with the corporation, is quite limited compared with that of the "corporate opportunity" doctrine in the United States. While the U.S. doctrine precludes corporate fiduciaries from usurping corporate op-

---

89) *But see* Model Bus. Corp. Act §35 (1982).
90) *Minbop* (Civil Code) Law No. 471 of 1958. arts. 680-92.
91) Commercial Code, art. 382(2).
92) Civil Code, art. 681.
93) Commercial Code, art. 398.
94) *Id.* art. 382(2).
95) *See. e.g.,* Kang Tae-yong v. Hanjin Sikpum Kong'op Chusik Hoesa, 73 Ta 955 (Sup. Ct. Jan. 15. 1984) (court applied KCC. art. 398 to such a transaction); Ha Tong-Ho v. Hanil Yogaek Chadongch'a Chusik Hoesa. 80 Ta 828 (Sup. Ct. July 22. 1980) (held transaction without board approval null and void).
96) Commercial Code, art. 397(1). This approval requirement also applies to a director seeking to become a director of another corporation in the same line of business as the first corporation. *Id.*
97) *Id.* art. 397(2).
98) *Id.*
99) Chong, *supra* note 39, at 434.

portunities - "opportunities in which the corporation has a right, property interest, or expectancy, or which in justice should belong to the corporation"[100] - the Korean counterpart adheres to the concept of "line of business," which is only one of a variety of standards traditionally employed by U.S. courts in determining whether an opportunity constitutes a "corporate opportunity"[101].

Third. the amount of director compensation must be determined by a resolution of the shareholders, unless the articles of incorporation provide otherwise[102]. Although not expressly supported by the language of the Code, a shareholders meeting generally sets only the total amount of compensation available to all the directors, while the board apportions a salary to each director[103]. If compensation is not fixed either in the articles of incorporation or by resolution, a court may determine a "reasonable amount" based on relevant facts[104].

While these laws do indeed provide for limited management accountability to shareholders, limited access to corporate records[105] and majority shareholders that are probably the least interested in curbing directors' indiscretions[106], ensure that such laws will be ineffective in enforcing fiduciary duties.

3.3.2.4. Derivative suits.   The Code provides for other mechanisms to enforce the directors' responsibilities as well. The shareholders' derivative suit is the most important of these mechanisms. Shareholders holding five percent of the corporation's outstanding shares may demand that the corporation bring suit to hold directors liable for failing to perform their duties[107]. If the corporation fails to bring suit within thirty days after the demand, then the shareholders may file a derivative suit against the directors[108]. A shareholder holding

---

100) H. Henn & J. Alexander, *supra* note 10, at 632.
101) *See Id.* at 633-34; Brudney & Clark. *A New Look at Corporate Opportunities*, 94 Harv. L Rev. 997, 1006-22 (1981).
102) Commercial Code, art. 388.
103) T. Lee, *Pallye Kyojae Hoesabop* (Casebook on Corporation Law) 433 (2nd ed. 1982).
104) Kim, I-Kon v. Han'guk Hwamul Chadongch'a Chusik Hoesa, 65 Ta 1156 (Sup. Ct. Aug. 31, 1965).
105) *See supra* notes 84-88 and accompanying text.
106) *See supra* notes 17-25 and accompanying text.
107) Commercial Code, art. 403(1).
108) *Id.* art. 403(3). In the United States, both courts and commentators are in sharp disagreement as to whether or not disinterested directors or an "independent" litigation committee should be able to bar a shareholder derivative action on the grounds that the action is not in the best interest of the corporation. *See* ALI Draft No. 1, *supra* note 2, at 295-350. No Korean case addresses this issue. See Takeuchi, *Kabunushi no daihyo sosho* (Shareholders Derivative Actions), *in 3 Hogaku Kyokai Hyakushunen Kinen Rombunshu* (Essays in Celebration of the 100th Anniversary of the Founding of the Jurisprudence Association) 191-94 (1983) for a view that favors shareholder derivative suits without board intervention.

more than five percent of the outstanding stock may also file a derivative suit to enjoin a director who engages in an ultra vires or other illegal act that might cause irreparable harm to the corporation[109].

The derivative suit provisions, however, have been totally ignored in Korea. During the two decades since its adoption, no reported derivative suit exists[110]. This peculiar phenomenon has been attributed to various factors. First, the Commercial Code requires dissenting shareholders to have at least five percent of the corporation's outstanding stock in order to file a derivative suit[111]. This five percent requirement poses an enormous obstacle to a shareholder of a large publicly held corporation[112].

Second, a Korean court has limited discretion to determine whether or not a director breached his or her fiduciary duties. The legality of a director's conduct depends on a relatively simple decision as to whether he or she obtained approval by shareholders or the board rather than on an objective determination as to whether or not that conduct was "fair or reasonable"[113].

Third, shareholders are not generally in a position to collect enough information to win a derivative suit. Disclosure requirements under Korea's securities law are inadequate[114]. More importantly, no discovery system comparable to that in the United States is available in Korea[115].

Finally, a shareholder in Korea has a much weaker economic incentive to bring a derivative suit than his U.S. counterpart. As in the United States. successful shareholders in Korea are entitled to reimbursement by the corporation for a "reasonable amount" of attorney fees incurred in litigating the suit[116]. But the "reasonable amount" must be within the scope of actual fees[117]. In determining the "reasonable amount," Korean courts are reluctant to award damages beyond the "going rate"[118].

While the shareholder derivative suit is a common method of overseeing corporate action

---

109) Commercial Code, art. 402.
110) This situation contrasts with that which exists in the United States; U.S. shareholders commonly file derivative suits. *See* Kim, *The Protection of Minority Shareholders in Korean Public Corporations: A Comparative Study with American Corporation Law*, 9 Korean J. Comp. L. 33, 45-50 (1981).
111) Commercial Code, arts. 402, 403(1).
112) Kim, *supra* note 109, at 47.
113) *See* Model Bus. Corp. Act § 8.30 (1982).
114) Y. Shin, *supra* note 15, at 362-67.
115) *Id.* at 854.
116) Commercial Code, art. 405. For a discussion of U.S. law, see H. Henn & J. Alexander, *supra* note 10, at 1107-14 (1983).
117) Commercial Code, art. 405.
118) S. Song, *supra* note 15, at 854.

in the United States, the five percent shareholding requirement, the lack of discovery, limited judicial discretion, and weak incentives severely limit the derivative suit as an effective mechanism for enforcing corporate directors' responsibility in Korea.

4. Absence of Market Imposed Checks on Management

Three types of market mechanism restrain corporate management: the product market; the financial market; and the market for corporate control[119]. It is unlikely, however, that market pressures in Korea influence manages of large corporations to significantly modify their behavior. Several factors contribute to the minimized impact of market mechanisms on corporate managers in Korea. Many large Korean corporations, for example, dominate their own product markets[120]. The government tightly controls Korea's financial market and business performance has been much less important a factor in bank loan decisions than in the United States[121]. The market for corporate control, regarded as the most important of all the market mechanisms, does not exist in Korea.

Practical reasons prevent hostile takeovers in Korea. Because shares are heavily concentrated in the hands of a small number of controlling shareholders, gaining a majority or controlling block of shares through a tender offer is impossible as a practical matter. Indeed, a major reason for Korean entrepreneurs' opposition to public offerings of their stock has been their fear of losing control. To dispel this fear, the government has provided some statutory safeguards for incumbent management.

Under the Securities and Exchange Law, a shareholder in a corporation listed on the Korean Stock Exchange may not hold shares in excess of the percentage he or she initially held at the time of listing[122]. Subject to a fine, a shareholder violating this prohibition may not vote the excess shares and may have to dispose of them[123]. Some exceptions to this prohibition exist, however. For example, one may acquire shares through a tender offer solicitation or a direct purchase from a shareholder holding more than ten percent[124].

---

119) Eisenberg, *The Modernization of Corporate Law: An Essay for Bill Cary.* 37 U. Miami L. Rev. 187, 203-04 (1983). Free market theorists argue that these three market mechanisms spur management to perform honestly and efficiently for fear of business failure, high financing cost, and takeover, respectively. *Id.*

120) *See* L. Jones & 1. Sakong, *supra* note 6, at 171-75.

121) *See* D. Cole & Y. Park, *supra* note 29, at 284.

122) Securities and Exchange Law, art. 200(1). In calculating the percentage of shareholding, the shares held under the name of certain relatives or other related persons are treated as the shares of the shareholder involved.

123) *Id.* art. 200(3).

These restrictions are much more effective in discouraging shifts in corporate control than the reporting requirement under U.S law[125]. While Korean law flatly prohibits ownership increase beyond the ten percent maximum limit[126], U.S. law merely requires a party acquiring five percent or more of a certain security to report such acquisition and his intentions with respect to the issuer of such security[127]. Given the concentration of shareholdings in a few controlling shareholders in Korea, this ten percent limit imposes an insurmountable obstacle to corporate raiders.

In addition, Korean statutes governing tender offers generally are favourable to the management of the target corporation rather than the tender offeror[128]. As a defensive tactic, the target corporation may campaign to persuade its shareholders not to sell their shares to the offeror[129]. In communicating with its shareholders, the target corporation may not omit a material fact or state a misleading fact[130]. Even if the target company's recommendation is misleading, however, remedies such as amendment orders or stop orders are not available under the present securities statutes. Moreover, unlike U.S. law[131], Korean law does not explicitly require the target corporation to submit information that would aid a shareholder in evaluating the management's recommendation[132]. The Korean securities laws thus remove the most effective curb on corporate management that a minority shareholder possesses - the threat of hostile takeover.

---

124) *Id.* art. 200(2).
125) *See* Securities and Exchange Act of 1934, 15 U.S.C. § 78m(d) (1982).
126) Securities and Exchange Law, art. 200.
127) Securities and Exchange Act of 1934, § 13(d).
128) *See* Y. Shin, *supra* note 15, at 288.
129) Securities and Exchange Law, art. 25; Enforcement Decree for the Securities and Exchange Law, Law No. 818 of 1962, art. 13.
130) Enforcement Decree for the Securities and Exchange Law, art. 130.
131) Securities and Exchange Act of 1934,15 U.S.C. § 78n(d)(4). and Rule 14d-9, 17 C.F.R. § 240.14d-9 (1985) require Schedule 14D-9, 17 C.F.R. § 240.14d-101 (1985) to be filed under similar circumstances.
132) If the target company chooses not to make any recommendation, then it need not disclose any material information regarding the tender offer unless the Securities Administration Committee so orders. Securities and Exchange Law, art. 27.

5. Conclusion

The Korean corporation differs from the U.S. corporation in that ownership and control merge, often in one family or individual. The Korean Commercial Code has attempted to address this problem by providing means for checking management behavior. Unfortunately, the Code is ineffective; rather than changing the existing system, the Code perpetuates the system by requiring checking mechanisms that management can easily manipulate to serve its own ends. Market mechanisms are also unable to restrain corporate management.

The failure of the Code and the market to control corporate managers has not left them completely unrestrained. The government has influenced major financial institutions in their decisions whether or not to grant loans to a particular company[133]. In this manner the government may discipline managers for their poor performance.

To rely on government to discipline managers, however, is undesirable because of the arbitrariness and possibility of corruption. Consequently, Korea presently lacks an effective method for restraining corporate managers and must search for other mechanisms that effectively increase management accountability to minority shareholders.

---

133) D. Cole & Y. Park, *supra* note 29, at 284.

A Civil Law Jurist's Perspective on Intermediary Risk in the Indirect Holding System for Securities: A Comment on Schwarcz & Benjamin

KON SIK KIM*

I. INTRODUCTION

Professors Schwarcz and Benjamin classify the situations in which an intermediary holds securities for investors in their highly stimulating article entitled *Intermediary Risk in the Indirect Holding System for Securities*. The authors identify two situations in which an intermediary holds securities for investors: that in which the intermediary does, and does not, have beneficial rights.[1] The authors seemingly assume that intermediary risk does not arise where the intermediary has no beneficial rights. This point is made explicitly in an article published previously by Professor Schwarcz.[2] In *Intermediary Risk in a Global Economy*, Professor Schwarcz discusses two cases in which the intermediary has no beneficial rights: namely, trust and bail. In civil law countries, however, there is yet another example: the case of the so-called commission agent. A commission agent is a merchant who executes contracts for commission in its own name, on behalf of the customer's account. Securities brokers are the most common example. Securities brokers normally hold securities for their customers. Yet whose claim will prevail if a broker goes bankrupt, the broker's creditors or its customers? In the absence of special statutory provision, one cannot be sure that the latter has priority over the former.[3] Thus, in theory, substantial intermediary risk may exist

---

* Professor of Law, Seoul National University.

1) Steven L. Schwarcz & Joanna Benjamin, *Intermediary Risk in the Indirect Holding System for Securities*, 12 DUKE J. COMP. & INT'L L. 309 (2002).

2) Steven L. Schwarcz, *Intermediary Risk in a Global Economy*, 50 DUKE L.J. 1541, 1566–71 (2001).

3) The Korean Commercial Code specifically indicates that "goods or valuable instruments which have been received by the commission agent from his principal, goods, valuable instruments, or claims acquired through sales and purchases in the commission agency are regarded as the possession of or claims of the principal in the relations between the principal and the commission agent or the latter's creditor." SANGBOP [Commercial Code], Act No. 1000 of 1962, art. 103 (S. Korea). The Japanese Commercial Code has no such provision. SH H (Jap.).

in a jurisdiction with no special provisions on this issue. Schwarcz and Benjamin, however, focus on the situation in which an intermediary transfers an undivided fractional interest in securities to an investor. They emphasize that in some civil law jurisdictions, the investor may not necessarily prevail over the intermediary's general creditors. Thus, the authors propose that such states enact into law a rule clearly indicating that such a transfer constitutes a valid and enforceable transfer, and that the transferee may assert its rights only against the intermediary in privity. I do not object to, and even welcome, the authors' proposal as a general proposition. In the Korean context, however, the authors' proposal may not be relevant.

II. THE INDIRECT HOLDING SYSTEM UNDER THE SECURITIES TRANSACTION ACT

Korea, like other civil law countries such as Germany and Japan, has special provisions on the indirect securities holding and book-entry transfer system. While Germany and Japan have enacted separate acts for those provisions, Korea has incorporated them into the Securities Transaction Act (STA), the primary legislation for regulating securities markets.[4] Under the STA's indirect holding provisions, the intermediary risk discussed by the authors is addressed adequately. Ultimate investors, rather than intervening intermediaries, are regarded as holders of securities, as long as the books are kept properly. The provisions are applicable only to those securities deposited with the Korea Securities Depository (KSD), the only authorized securities depository in Korea. Thus, in theory, the provisions are inapplicable to those securities not deposited with the KSD. In practice, however, there is virtually no instance in which an intermediary fails to deposit with the KSD. Under the STA, brokers are required to deposit investors' securities with the KSD.[5] Other financial firms including banks are under no such duty, but may choose to use the KSD as sub-custodian, which they do consistently. Indeed, financial firms serving as custodians for foreign investors are required to deposit them with the KSD.[6] While institutional investors may deposit their assets directly with the KSD, individual investors must go through their brokers. Brokers must keep a book and list such information as the names and holdings of investors.[7] The

---

4) *Chunggwon Koraebop* [Securities Transaction Act], Act No. 2920 of 1976, arts. 173–178, *translated in* 11 KOREAN LEGIS. RES. INST., STATUTES OF THE REP. OF KOREA 720 (1997).

5) *Id.* art. 44-4.

6) *Chunggwonbup Kamdok Kyujong* [Securities Business Supervision Regulation], art. 7-15 (on file with the Duke Journal of Comparative and International Law).

7) *Chunggwon Koraebop, supra* note 4, art. 174-2, § 1.

KSD must keep its own book for the holdings of depositing institutions and distinguish between their house and customer accounts.[8] As a legal matter, investors registered in the broker's book are regarded as co-owners of the securities.[9] As a practical matter, however, they are treated as owners of the securities equivalent to their co-ownership shares. For example, an investor registered as a beneficial shareholder in the book of an intermediary may exercise most of his shareholder rights directly, although he cannot request the delivery of his share of securities from the KSD. The proposed rule thus will add virtually nothing to the rule existent under the STA. The proposed rule, however, may be useful in countries that lack such provisions.

III. THE SITUATION IN JURISDICTIONS THAT LACK INDIRECT HOLDING PROVISIONS

As Schwarcz and Benjamin discuss, the situation with respect to intermediary risk is unclear in jurisdictions that lack indirect holding provisions. In my opinion, in such jurisdictions, an investor who has acquired from an intermediary an undivided fractional interest in securities should have priority over the intermediary's general creditors. Such a result may frustrate the creditor's expectations, especially if he or she has been misled into thinking that the intermediary is the sole owner of the securities it holds. A creditor is not entitled, however, to rely on the appearance of an intermediary holding securities. Under the Korean Civil Code, for example, transfer of ownership of a physical asset does not necessarily require an actual delivery of the asset in question. Transfer may be made by the transferor's declaration to serve as an immediate possessor of the asset for the transferee.[10] If transfer is completed by this method, those creditors extending credit to the transferor without knowledge of this transfer may be disappointed later. But such a result may be unavoidable, as the parties may achieve the same result by first having the transferor actually deliver the asset to the transferee and then having the transferee deposit it back to the transferor. If transfer by the possession recharacterization method can be made for all the assets of the intermediary, there is no reason why it should not be allowed for a part of the assets. So even in a civil law country, transfer of an undivided fractional interest in securities by the recharacterization possession method should be allowed in the absence of special legislation. In such a case, the transferor

---

8) *Id.* art. 174, § 3.
9) *Id.* art. 174-4, § 1.
10) *Id.* art. 189 (concerning the recharacterization of possession).

and the transferee are deemed to co-own the assets. The transferee can make a claim to the transferor-custodian for delivery of his share of securities.

Why, then, should one need the rule proposed by Schwarcz and Benjamin? When the intermediary directly holds the assets, such a rule may not be necessary.[11] But when the intermediary wishes to transfer a fractional undivided interest in the securities held by a higher-tier intermediary, it is not necessarily clear in civil law countries whether the transfer can be validly completed by the transferring intermediary's notice to the higher-tier holder.[12] Under the conventional view, a property interest may not be transferred without specifying the subject of the interest. The rule proposed by the authors will clarify that transfer of such a fractional undivided interest may be completed without going through the cumbersome process of specification.

IV. PROBLEMS WITH THE CO-OWNERSHIP APPROACH UNDER THE STA

As mentioned earlier, thanks to the indirect holding provisions in the STA, intermediary risk does not matter for investors in Korean securities.[13] But it by no means follows that the co-ownership approach adopted by the STA creates no problems in other respects. First, the co-ownership concept does not correspond well with so called dematerialized securities, as investors' interest in such securities may not be regarded as ownership from the technical legal perspective.[14] Second, the co-ownership approach generates substantial transaction costs in cross-border securities transactions, since it often may be difficult for the parties to identify and comply with the governing laws applicable to the transaction in question. Although unifying conflict-of-laws rules may somewhat reduce the uncertainty involved, unification has its own problems.[15] In that respect, I join many experts in thinking that the "security entitlement" concept adopted in the U.C.C. Article 8 is preferable.

---

11) Of course, it is good to eliminate any uncertainty surrounding this issue.
12) *See, e.g., Kinyūhōiinkai* [Financial Law Board], *Shōken no furikae Kessai ni Kakaru hōsei ni Kansuru chūkan ronten seiri ni tsuite* [Interim Note on Legal Rules Relating to Book-Entry Securities Settlement], at 6 n.13 (Apr. 3, 2000), *available at* http://www.flb.jp/publication06-j.PDF (last visited Feb. 2, 2002).
13) On the other hand, it may matter for those Korean investors who invest in foreign securities.
14) *Chunggwon Koraebop, supra* note 4, however, does not distinguish between certificated and certificateless securities.
15) Schwarcz & Benjamin, *supra* note 1, at 329–30 & nn.66–71.

V. CONCLUSION

The securities entitlement under the U.C.C. Article 8 is a mixture of property and *in personam* rights. It has a property right feature as its holder has priority over the intermediary's general creditors; at the same time, it has an *in personam* feature as its holder can assert his or her right only against the intermediary with whom he or she directly deals. A holder of security entitlements may, however, determine how the voting rights are exercised. In effect, the rights of entitlement holders are not significantly different from those of shareholders under the STA. They differ only at a conceptual level. Importing a foreign concept like security entitlement is not easy, especially because it directly undermines the fundamental division between property and *in personam* rights in traditional civil law. The neat distinction between the two kinds of rights, however, has already been subject to challenge. Although the indirect securities holding system in civil law countries such as Korea, Japan, and Germany has been consistent with the co-ownership approach, the element of possession in the co-ownership of securities is becoming increasingly abstract and artificial. And when we give up the notion of certificate, which is not really essential in the book entry settlement system, we will no longer be able to maintain the concept of ownership, and we will be forced to devise a new concept to represent the interest of lower-tier investors.

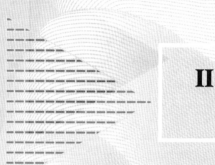

II. Shareholders and corporate organs

Dynamics of shareholder power in Korea*

Kon Sik Kim

INTRODUCTION

Korean society has undergone a transformation during the last fifty years. Developments in the Korean economy are particularly noteworthy. Small family firms which sprouted from the ruins of the Korean War have evolved into giant conglomerates competing in the global marketplace. The shareholder profile of large corporations has changed in the process. Fifty years ago, even the largest firms were essentially family operations without significant outside investors. As of 2012, more than 10 percent of the population (5 million out of 50 million people) invests in the stock market.[1] Despite the staggering growth of the shareholding public, the legal status of shareholders remains largely the same as 50 years ago. Their role and influence, however, has been changing.

The purpose of this chapter is to explore the dynamics of shareholder power in Korea. Shareholder power has attracted much attention recently in connection with the so-called shareholder empowerment debate, which has taken center stage in recent corporate governance discourse in the US. The shareholder empowerment debate, however, fails to draw much attention in Korea. The ubiquity of control shareholders may weaken the need to empower shareholders to stem the potential abuse by strong managers. However, it still seems worthwhile to explore the topic of shareholder power in the context of corporate governance in Korea. Such an endeavor will help in understanding better how shareholder power works in a different corporate governance environment.

Why do we care about shareholder power? It is largely because shareholder power can be viewed as a means to promote shareholder interest, which is widely accepted as an im-

* This chapter is funded by the Seoul National University Law Foundation in 2014.

1) Website of the Korea Exchange (http://www.krx.co.kr/m2/m2_5/m2_5_6/m2_5_6_1/JHPKOR 02005_06_01.jsp).

portant, if not the supreme, goal of corporate governance. The inquiry can then be started from the more fundamental concept of shareholder interest. Inquiries into shareholder interest may be divided into normative and positive ones. A normative study may aim to grapple with the question of whether managers, in running the firm, should pursue shareholder interest only. This debate on shareholder supremacy has recently become more popular (e.g. Stout 2012), partly due to the growing disparity between the rich and the poor. Despite its theoretical appeal, the normative debate is likely to be swayed by political or ideological inclinations. Thus, for practical purposes, it may make more sense to focus on the positive inquiry as to how and to what extent shareholder interest affects the operation of business firms in Korea.

Answering this positive question is not easy either, as it may depend on so many factors. Shareholder power is one of those factors. Other things being equal, stronger shareholder power will more likely promote shareholder interest in practice. This chapter approaches shareholder power from two fronts. First, the chapter will focus on the 'shareholder' part of shareholder power. Influence of shareholder power may vary depending on realities of share ownership such as ownership structure and shareholder profile. Second, the chapter will discuss 'powers' of shareholders in Korea, both in reality as well as on the book.

This chapter proceeds as follows. It will begin with the 'shareholder' part of shareholder power. Section I will briefly survey ownership structure and shareholder profile in Korea. It will then move to the 'power' part of shareholder power. Section II will first explain various shareholder powers available under the Korean Commercial Code, the code that includes corporate statutes. Since what counts in corporate governance is law in reality, not law on the book, section II will also discuss how these powers are exercised in reality. Section III will explore how shareholder interest is reflected in the performance of firms in Korea. Section IV deals with the role of two players who can potentially bring in changes in the practice of corporate governance in Korea. In conclusion, section V will discuss options currently available to policymakers in Korea.

I. REALITIES OF SHARE OWNERSHIP

Before embarking on a discussion of shareholder power, we need to examine who share-holders are. Shareholder behavior may vary depending on the ownership structure and the identity of shareholders (Hill 2010). Each of these two factors will be discussed in turn here.

A. Ownership Structure

Corporate governance in Korea centers around *chaebols*, large business conglomerates that dominate the national economy. The ownership structure of a *chaebol* is often characterized as a controlling minority shareholder (CMS) structure. A patriarch with the title of 'chairman' is the CMS who effectively controls all the member firms of a particular *chaebol* by means of extensive inter-company shareholdings. Composed of numerous pyramidal and circular holdings, *chaebol*'s actual ownership structure is quite complicated. Encouraged by the government policy, many *chaebols* have managed to convert to a simplified holding company structure during the last decade. As the holding company at the top usually holds far less than 50 percent of the shares in operating subsidiaries below, the CMS structure remains intact, albeit in a somewhat mitigated form, in such a *chaebol* adopting a holding company structure.

Figure 24.1 shows the size of internal ownership in the top ten *chaebols* in Korea. Internal ownership here refers to the sum of shares held by the CMS (including his family members) and those held by the member firms. Figure 24.1 shows three basic features of Korea's CMS structure (Kim 2014). First, the CMS's direct holdings in the top ten *chaebols* are extremely low (less than 1 percent in 2012), although the figure for smaller business groups is substantially higher. Second, the CMS can still secure absolute control by means of holdings of other member firms. Third, despite persistent criticism of the disparity between the CMS's cash-flow right and the control right, the CMS structure has remained stable over the last two decades.

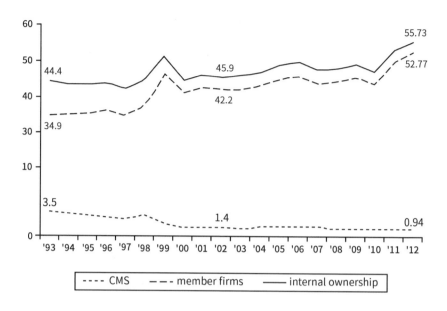

Source: Fair Trade Commission.

Figure 24.1 Size of internal ownership at top 10 chaebols

As the CMS's cash-flow right decreases, he becomes more like a manager. What distinguishes him from professional managers is the degree of entrenchment of his position. Unlike even the most successful professional managers in the US, a CMS in Korea stays on until the end of his biological life and, moreover, turns the whole group over to his heirs. Despite persistent criticism of the general public, this kind of 'dynastic succession' continues to take place in virtually all *chaebols.*

What may be more troubling than this dynastic succession is the exacerbated conflict of interest between the CMS and the rest of the shareholders. As the gap between the cash-flow right and the control right grows, a CMS will naturally have more incentives to engage in so-called tunneling activities conducted to enrich the CMS (or his heirs) at the expense of general shareholders.

B. Shareholder Profile

As Figure 24.1 shows, the CMS directly holds only a small fraction of shares. Who then holds the rest of the shares? Table 24.1 shows changes in shareholdings (in terms of market capitalization) by type of shareholders in the firms listed in the Korea Exchange. According to Table 24.1, the composition of shareholders remained relatively stable during the last decade and displayed three distinct features. First, 'other corporations' remain major shareholders, primarily due to the CMS's dependence on member firms for control. Second, the portion of institutional investors is relatively low, in recent years hovering in the low teens. Third, the size of foreign ownership is quite high, exceeding 30 percent in 2012. The last two factors, institutional investors and foreign investors, will be discussed separately in detail in the following sections.

Table 24.1 Shareholding by type of shareholder (2000–2011) (% of market capitalization)

Year	Government	Institutions	Other corporations	Individuals	Foreigners
2011	2.39	12.97	29.64	24.40	30.60
2010	3.28	13.45	28.01	24.09	31.17
2009	1.71	12.04	21.24	34.57	30.44
2008	2.75	11.69	28.34	29.96	27.25
2007	2.87	19.98	20.96	25.25	30.94
2006	3.93	20.80	18.13	21.98	35.16
2005	3.65	18.56	18.02	22.59	37.17
2004	4.13	17.01	17.95	20.80	40.10
2003	4.58	15.70	18.77	23.29	37.67
2002	6.56	15.28	19.82	25.55	32.79
2001	8.94	15.35	17.12	26.42	32.17
2000	13.20	16.43	19.93	23.47	26.98

Source: Korea Exchange.

C. Institutional Investors and the National Pension Fund

According to Table 24.1, institutional investors account for 12.97 percent of the entire market capitalization as of 2012. Table 24.2 below shows how this 12.97 percent is divided among different types of institutional investors.

Table 24.2 Shareholdings by type of institutional investor (%)

Type of institutional investor	
Securities companies	0.26
Insurance companies	0.59
Collective investment vehicle	6.02
Banks	3.03
Merchant & mutual savings banks	0.16
Pension funds	2.91
Total	12.97

Source: Korea Exchange.

Table 24.3 Shareholdings by type of foreign investor (2010)

Type	
Individual	0.8
Institutions	99.2
Investment fund	48.3
Banks	13.3
Securities companies	2.1
Insurance companies	2.6
Pension & sovereign funds	9.9
Others*	23.0

Note: *Foreign direct investment included.

Source: Financial Supervisory Service (Press Release: April 21, 2011).

It seems helpful to distinguish the National Pension Fund (NPF) from the rest of the institutional investors. The NPF's holdings have been on the increase, although the portion of general institutional investors remains stagnant. As of 2011, the NPF invested 17.81 percent of the total fund (348 trillion won) in the domestic stock market (Lee 2012). According to a plan it announced, the NPF is to increase this figure to more than 20 percent by 2017. As of 2012 the NPF accounts for 5.53 percent of the total stock market capitalization (Lee 2012). If the market capitalization remains 70 percent of the GDP, the average ratio of market capitalization for the period from 2000 to 2010 (Lee 2012), this figure is expected to reach 8.8 percent in 2015.

Already, however, the presence of the NPF in the stock market is causing concern among large listed firms. The number of listed firms in which the NPF holds 5 percent or more has been rapidly on the increase: 85 in 2009, 140 in 2010, 174 in 2011 and 218 in 2012.[2] As of 2012, the NPF holds 9 percent or more in as many as 35 firms, is the largest shareholder in six firms, and is the second largest shareholder in 114 firms (Lee 2012).

D. Foreign Investors

The financial crisis of 1997 triggered the rapid rise in foreign investments in Korea. In May 1998 the government eliminated existing restrictions on foreign investment except for certain industries related to national interest such as telecommunication and mass media. The portion of shareholdings of foreign investors exceeded 40 percent in 2004, and slid back to 30 percent in 2011. As foreign investors generally prefer blue chip stocks, their portion in such firms is even higher. For example, as of October 8, 2013, foreign investors account for 48.99 percent of the shares in Samsung Electronics, 46.11 percent in Hyundai Motors, 54.29 percent in POSCO (a leading steel manufacturer) and 63.99 percent in KB Financial Holdings (a leading financial group), according to the website of the Korea Exchange (www.krx.co.kr).

As Table 24.3 shows, almost all the foreign investors are institutions. Some of these institutional investors, investment funds in particular, are more ready to speak up for shock waves through the business community by attempting to appoint their own nominees to the board of directors. Perhaps the most famous episode was a confrontation that erupted in 2004 between the SK Group, the third largest *chaebol*, and a foreign investor called Sovereign Asset Management Limited (Milhaupt and Pistor 2008).

Under pressure from the business community, the government took a measure in 2005 designed to discourage foreign investors from trying to influence corporate policies. The government required foreign investors to declare their investment purposes in a report that must be filed when their holdings in a listed firm reach 5 percent of the shares (Capital Market and Financial Investment Business Law (Capital Market Law), Art. 147(1), Presidential Decree, Art. 154(1)). The Capital Market Law divides investments into two categories: simple investments and investments with a purpose to exert an influence on the control of the firm. The 'influence on control' in this context is defined very broadly. For example, it is deemed to exist if the foreign investor intends to ask for an increase in dividend (Capital Market Act 147(1), Presidential Decree 154(1)(iv)). If the investor is found

---

2) Data available from the website of the National Pension Service (http://institute.nps.or.kr).

to deviate from the declared purpose, various sanctions including criminal sanctions may be imposed. A foreign investor is thus under pressure to indicate their purpose as involving an interest in control, even when it really has no intention to seek control in a conventional sense. Table 24.4 shows that as of 2009 as many as 60 firms listed on the Primary Market of the Korea Exchange have a foreign investor with an interest in control. The number of foreign investors actually interested in control, however, may be much lower.

II. SHAREHOLDER POWER

I will now turn to the 'power' part of shareholder power, which is a means for shareholders to exert influence. This section will be divided into two parts. In the first part I will discuss various rights of shareholders under the Korean Commercial Code (KCC) (Chun et al. 2014). As is well known, however, rights on the books do not necessarily correspond with rights in reality. Thus, I will explore shareholder rights in reality in the second part.

Table 24.4 Number of listed firms with a foreign investor holding 5% or more

	2007	2008	2009
Management control	67	67	60
Simple investment	223	186	155

Source: Financial Supervisory Service (Press Release: April 15, 2010).

A. Shareholder Rights under the Statutes

A.1. Voting rights

Shareholders enjoy a variety of rights under the KCC, which may be again divided into two groups: voting rights and other rights. A shareholder is in principle entitled to one vote for one share (Art. 369(1)), except for non-voting shares (Art. 344–3). Voting rights are exercised at the general shareholders meeting (GSM). The GSM under the KCC enjoys a broader scope of power than under, say, Delaware law. Under the KCC, the GSM may decide on such matters as are provided for in the KCC or in the Articles of Incorporation (Art. 361). The KCC explicitly subjects a broad range of matters to resolution at the GSM.

For example the GSM is authorized to determine CEO pay (Art. 388),[3] dividends (Art. 462(2)), and the selection of audit committee members in some listed firms (Art. 542(1)). In addition, the GSM's power can be expanded to cover other matters as long as the Articles of Incorporation so stipulate. Indeed, the KCC explicitly allows the firm to empower the GSM to decide on matters such as issuance of new shares (Art. 416) and appointment of representative directors (Art. 389(1)). It is also widely agreed that even in the absence of such an explicit provision in the KCC, it is still possible to expand the GSM's scope of power by inserting an appropriate provision in the Articles of Incorporation.

A.2. Other rights

Aside from voting rights shareholders have a wide range of other rights under the KCC. In order to minimize potential abuse, the KCC imposes on shareholders a shareholding threshold for particular rights, although these thresholds are substantially reduced for listed firms (Art. 542–6). For example, 1 percent shareholding threshold for derivative suits has been reduced to 0.01 percent for listed firms (Art. 542–6(6)). Other rights that are of significance from the perspective of shareholder power include the following.

First, shareholders can take the initiative in introducing resolutions at the GSM. A shareholder with 3 percent of the shares can force the board of directors to convene the GSM (Art. 366(1)) and can have the board include a certain item on the agenda of the GSM (Art. 363–2(1)). The same shareholder of a listed firm can also nominate his or her own outside director candidates at the GSM (Art. 542–8(5)).

Second, shareholders can block a particular corporate action by filing a lawsuit. A prime example of this right is a lawsuit to invalidate a particular corporate action (such as a GSM's resolution (Art. 376(1)) or a merger (Art. 529)), which is available to a shareholder with just one share. Shareholders holding 1 percent of the shares can bring a lawsuit to enjoin an illegal act of a director if the firm may suffer irrevocable damages (Art. 402). Moreover, shareholders holding 3 percent of the shares can seek dismissal of a director by filing a lawsuit when the GSM fails to dismiss the director in spite of his or her unjust or illegal conduct (Art. 385(2)).

Third, shareholders holding 1 percent of the shares can file a derivative lawsuit against wrongdoing directors (including de facto directors) for damages (Arts. 403(1), 401(2)).

Fourth, every shareholder is entitled to dividends in accordance with the number of shares

---

3) In practice, however, only a ceiling on the total amount of compensation of directors is determined at the GSM.

(Art. 464). Dividends are determined in principle by the GSM (Art. 462(2)). If a shareholder is not satisfied with the dividend rate proposed by management, he or she is authorized to make a motion at the GSM to increase the proposed rate.

Fifth, a dissenting shareholder is entitled to an appraisal remedy in some fundamental changes such as sale of business and mergers (Arts. 374–2, 522–3).

Sixth, a shareholder with 3 percent of the shares can gain access to the firm's books and accounts (Art. 466(1)).

B. Shareholder Rights in Reality

B.1. Reality of the GSM

As its scope of power extends to a wide range of matters, the GSM has the potential, in theory, to grow into a venue for shareholder interest. The GSM's role in corporate governance in Korea, however, is as limited as in other developed countries. Some factors are believed to militate against the proper functioning of the GSM. First, the presence of the CMS, who maintains a control block of shares, is probably the most decisive factor. As long as this situation persists, not much action is likely to take place at the GSM.

Second, institutional investors are not enthusiastic about exerting their influence on their portfolio companies (Kang 2012). According to a survey 78 institutional investors cast a dissenting vote only on 70 out of the total 14,697 items (0.48 percent) at GSMs during the first half of 2012 (Kang 2012). While it is true that passivity of institutional investors has been a universal phenomenon and not just confined to Korea (Goto 2014; Hill 2010), activist hedge funds are now playing a growing role in some countries including the US (e.g., Cheffins and Armour 2011; Katelouzou forthcoming). Passivity of institutional investors is more serious in Korea. A multitude of local institutional investors are *chaebol* affiliates themselves and naturally are reluctant to practice shareholder activism on other *chaebol* firms. Even non-*chaebol* institutional investors hesitate to provoke animosity on the part of *chaebol* firms by acting in concert with shareholder activists or foreign investors. Only some foreign institutional investors cast dissenting votes from time to time (Kang 2012).

Third, there are technical barriers which deter shareholders, especially foreign investors, from voting at the GSM. Under the KCC, notice must be sent to each shareholder two weeks in advance of the GSM (Art. 363(1)). On average, shareholders in firms composing the KOSPI (Korea Composite Stock Price Index, which covers 200 listed firms) become aware of the information included in the formal notice 17 days before the GSM (Korea

Corporate Governance Service (no date)). Foreign investors often complain that this two-week period is too short to make a decision and go through their internal compliance procedure. A more cumbersome hurdle may be the extreme concentration of the GSMs on a few particular dates. As an overwhelming majority of firms in Korea adopt the calendar year as their business year, the annual GSMs are mostly held in March. Table 24.5 shows the distribution of the GSMs in 2012 in 190 KOSPI firms adopting the calendar year as the business year. According to Table 24.5, more than 70 percent of the GSMs are concentrated on the third and fourth weeks of March. All the GSMs held in the third week were held on Friday, March 16 and out of 82 GSMs held in the fourth week, 78 were held on Friday, March 23. It is commonly believed that a primary reason for this universal preference for a particular date for the GSM is to minimize the attendance by professional shareholders such as shareholder activists and gadflies. As a result of this practice, however, it is a major challenge for a foreign investor investing in numerous firms to exercise their votes properly.

Table 24.5 Distribution of the GSMs held in March, 2012

	1st week	2nd	3rd	4th	5th	total
No. of firms	7.	6	59	82	36	190
Percentage	3.68	3.16	31.05	43.16	18.95	100

Source: Korea Corporate Governance Service.

B.2. Growing importance of NPF

After the financial crisis in 1997, there were several instances where a few NGO-affiliated activist shareholders, with the support of foreign investors, caused a stir at a GSM by confronting management (Kim and Kim 2001). Recently, however, GSMs have calmed down markedly. A quiet change, however, is now taking place at GSMs. This change, which has more potential significance, has been initiated by the NPF. According to Table 24.6, with the increase in its holdings, the NPF has become more eager to attend GSMs and less hesitant to vote against management proposals. As of 2005, the NPF opposed management in only 38 out of 1,395 items (2.7 percent). The number of items opposed by the NPF increased to 426 out of 2,343 (18.18 percent) as of June 2012 (Kang 2012).

When casting its votes at GSMs, the NPF is required to follow its own internal voting guidelines.[4] The guidelines set out two criteria for its exercise of voting (Lee 2012). A primary principle is to exercise its vote in ways which promote shareholder value in the long-term (Art. 4). A subordinate principle, which may potentially contradict the primary principle, mandates that the NPF take social responsibility factors, such as environment, society and corporate governance into account when exercising voting power (Art. 4–2). Depending on how it interprets these two criteria, the NPF has a potential to unleash a dramatic change in the terrain of corporate governance in Korea.

B.3. Reality of shareholders' other rights

Shareholders almost always exercise their dividend rights. Their other rights granted under the KCC, those not subject to a shareholding threshold, are also often exercised. For example, a dissatisfied shareholder sometimes files a lawsuit to invalidate a shareholder resolution (Art. 376(1)). The shareholders' appraisal right (Art. 374–2) is another example of shareholder power commonly exercised by dissenting shareholders. It is not unusual for a firm to give up a merger because of the firm's financial burden incurred by the exercise of the appraisal right.

As mentioned earlier, many of the significant shareholder rights are subject to substantial shareholding thresholds under the KCC. Although some of these shareholding thresholds are lowered for large listed firms, they normally pose a barrier for shareholders. Table 24.7 shows the number of cases where a shareholder right conditioned on a shareholding threshold has been exercised in a firm listed in the Primary Market of the Korea Exchange. As shown in Table 24.7 such rights are only exercised in less than 2 percent of the total listed firms.

Despite the threshold requirement, however, shareholders have managed to file derivative suits and have won in a small number of cases (Rho and Kim 2012). Compared with foreign investors, who have occasionally come forward to file a lawsuit against a firm or managers, domestic institutional investors including the NPF have so far been totally inactive.

---

4) The Voting Guidelines are available from the website of the National Pension Service (http://institute.nps.or.kr).

Table 24.6 Voting by the NPF

	Portfolio firms	No. of GSMs attended	No. of items voted on	Voting records		
				Yes	No	Abstention
2005	494	317	1,395	1,334	38	23
				95.6%	2.70%	1.7%
2006	535	487	1,878	1,796	70	12
				95.63%	3.73%	0.64%
2007	584	453	1,926	1,830	96	0
				95.02%	4.98%	0.00%
2008	505	514	2,010	1,899	109	2
				94.5%	5.4%	0.10%
2009	581	494	2,003	1,865	132	6
				93.11%	6.59%	0.30%
2010	563	528	2,153	1,979	174	0
				91.92%	8.08%	0.00%
2011	591	556	2,175	2,022	153	0
				92.97%	7.03%	0.00%
2012.6	609	505	2,329	2,004	423	2
				82.50%	17.41%	0.08%

Source: Ministry of Health and Welfare (2012, 8).

Table 24.7 Exercise of shareholder rights conditioned on an ownership threshold

	2007	2008	2009	2010	2011	2012
No. of cases (%)	10 (1.47)	7 (1.02)	4 (0.57)	9 (1.30)	10 (1.50)	14 (1.97)
Firms	678	685	706	690	668	710

Source: Korea Corporate Governance Service, Corporate Governance White Paper 2012, at 93.

C. Evaluation of Shareholder Power: Strong on the Book, Weak in Reality

The scope of shareholder power is relatively broad under the KCC. As mentioned earlier, the GSM is granted wider powers than in the US. Shareholders are equipped with a full array of rights normally available in other developed jurisdictions. In reality, however, shareholders do not take full advantage of these rights. As for voting at the GSM, the presence of the CMS renders the shareholders' voting right less relevant, if not entirely meaningless. As for shareholders' other rights, shareholders often hesitate to exercise them, either because they cannot meet a relevant shareholding threshold or because they do not find it financially worthwhile to exercise such rights.

Weak shareholder power may naturally lead to low dividends. Korean firms have generally been known to pay little dividends. But as they went through the financial crisis in 1997, they started paying more dividends and engaging in more share repurchases. While the total amount of cash dividends paid by the top 30 *chaebols* between 1995 and 1997 was 1.8 trillion won, the amount increased to 4.2 trillion won between 1998 and 2000 (Park 2004). The amount of share repurchases increased more than five times during the same period. According to a survey based on the annual reports of the top 500 firms, listed firms appear less willing to pay dividends than non-listed firms. In 2012 the ratio of dividends against total labor costs was 15.3 percent for listed firms, and 28.2 percent for non-listed firms.5 The apparent reluctance on the part of listed firms to pay dividends may be due to a few factors. First, as the cash-flow right of the CMS is miniscule, the CMS naturally has little incentive to share corporate profits with other shareholders by paying dividends. Second, it appears that market pressure for dividends is still not as strong as, say, in the US, although foreign investors now seem to play a role in applying such pressure.

III. SHAREHOLDER INTEREST: HOW IT AFFECTS FIRM PERFORMANCE

A. Theory

It is occasionally discussed among legal scholars whether and to what extent a mega-firm should (and should be allowed to) pursue non-shareholder interests. Despites its theoretical appeal such discussion rarely leads to any practical outcome. Suffice it to say here that shareholder supremacy as a guiding goal of corporate governance seems to have fewer followers in Korea than in the US.

At the same time, however, it is widely presumed in Korea that in reality firms are managed to maximize the interest of the CMS. Admittedly, the interest of the CMS largely overlaps with that of general shareholders. This point becomes clear when the CMS is confronted with stakeholders, employees in particular. Compared with general shareholders, however, the CMS tends to take a longer-term perspective as he or she normally has no intention to part with control of the firm.

The interest of the CMS diverges with that of general shareholders when it comes to 'tunneling', the term commonly employed to refer to activities carried out to transfer wealth from general shareholders to the CMS (Johnson et al. 2000). Conducted in various ways, tunneling is widely believed to be pervasive in Korea. As of 2012, in as many as five of the ten biggest *chaebols*, the chairman was either convicted for crimes such as breach of trust or held liable for damages for violation of fiduciary duty.

An increased potential for tunneling is probably the most obvious disadvantage of the CMS structure of *chaebol*. On the other hand the *chaebol*'s CMS structure has advantages as well. Stability in top management and the long-term perspective of the CMS may be counted as factors contributing to the phenomenal success of *chaebols* like Samsung and Hyundai Motors. In addition the superior status of *chaebols* in mobilizing resources and political support is frequently cited as an advantage in comparison with stand-alone firms. Research shows that *chaebol* firms face fewer financial constraints thanks to the internal capital market (Shin and Park 1999). It is difficult to tell how this trade-off between the benefits and risks of the *chaebol*'s CMS structure actually turns out.

B. Empirical Evidence

There is now a growing list of empirical studies on the relationship between corporate governance in general and the business performance of Korean firms (e.g. Baek et al. 2004; Black 1998; Joh 2003). These studies generally attempt to inquire into a correlation between a particular element of corporate governance and business performance or firm value. Share ownership structure and identity of shareholders are among those corporate governance features commonly adopted as independent variables in such studies.

C. Share Ownership Structure

The relationship between share ownership structure and firm performance has been a popular topic for empirical research. It is now generally accepted that firm performance first improves with the increase in ownership concentration but eventually declines beyond a certain point (Morck et al. 1988; Thomsen and Pedersen 2000). A study based on panel data for 579 firms in Korea during the period from 2000 to 2006 confirms that a similar hump-shaped relationship exists between ownership structure and firm performance (Lee 2008). The reason for the decline in firm performance beyond a certain point of concentration is believed to be tunneling.

A similar line of studies focuses on the disparity between the cash-flow right and the control right. They find that firm market value increases with the cash-flow ownership of the largest shareholders, but drops with the growth of disparity between the cash-flow right and the control right (Baek et al. 2004; Joh 2003). The same basic relationship is found in public firms in most of East Asia (Claessens et al. 2002).

Regarding the impact of *chaebol* affiliation, academic research findings so far seem largely negative. A study that was published a decade ago found that the value of a *chaebol* firm is lower than that of an independent firm, due to its preference for profit stability (rather than maximization), excessive investment in less profitable businesses and the possibility of supporting troubled affiliate firms (Ferris et al. 2003). According to a more recent study, *chaebol* firms tend to pay smaller dividends (Hwang et al. 2013). Another recent study also confirms that the listed firms with a *chaebol* structure show significant decreases in market valuation and lower dividend rates (Almeida et al. 2011).

D. Identity of Shareholders

D.1. Institutional investors

A group of studies has focused on the identity of shareholders. What attracts most attention seems to be the influence of institutional investors and foreign investors, who in theory have an incentive as well as a capacity to engage in shareholder activism. In the US, it has been suggested that shareholder activism by institutional investors does not have strong positive effects on firm performance (Black 1998; Romano 2001). It was also widely believed that institutional investors, hedge funds in particular, concentrate on short-term results. A more recent work on hedge fund activism, however, suggests that interventions by activist hedge funds positively affect long-term operating performance and do not negatively affect long-term shareholder returns in a targeted firm (Bebchuk et al. 2013).

On the impact of institutional investors in Korea, there is not much empirical research. A recent study based on panel data of 417 listed firms in Korea over the five-year period from 1999 to 2003 tentatively concludes that institutional investors are short-term oriented, despite the absence of negative effect of institutional ownership on R&D investment (Lee 2011).

D.2. Foreign investors

In contrast to the dearth of research on the impact of institutional investors, many researchers have delved into the effect of foreign investors. Several studies suggest that the level of shareholdings by foreign investors is positively related to business performance (Baek et al. 2004). A study has found a positive relationship between foreign share ownership and revenue growth rate (Park 2004). The direction of causality, however, is not clear from the study. Another study finds that foreign investor ownership in Korea has a greater impact on firm value than domestic bank ownership (Choi et al. 2007). On a similar note, firms with larger equity ownership by foreign investors are found to have experienced a smaller drop in share value during the economic crisis (Baek et al. 2004).

It is generally agreed that the level of foreign share ownership is positively related to the level of dividends (Kang et al. 2010). Another study finds that the level of dividends (including share repurchases) is more strongly related to the total holdings of foreign investors holding 5 percent or more (Sul and Kim 2006). A recent study also finds that pay-performance sensitivity is most significant in firms with high foreign ownership (Garner and Kim 2011). The authors assume that pay-performance sensitivity represents an improvement in corporate governance and thus will lead to an increase in firm value (Garner and Kim 2011).

IV. TWO AGENTS OF CHANGE

There are two players that may possibly bring in changes in the practice of corporate governance in Korea. They are the NPF and foreign investors.

A. The NPF

As detailed above, the rapid rise of the NPF in recent years is noteworthy. The NPF may be likened to a double-edged sword, however. If the NPF emphasizes shareholder interest, the CMS will feel pressure to pursue it more aggressively. According to its Voting Guidelines mentioned earlier, the NPF enjoys fairly wide scope for discretion in voting. It has often been stated recently that the NPF should play a more active role in corporate governance matters in large listed firms. In the NPF, the voting decision is made by a committee composed of insiders. Although the NPF is technically separate from the government, most people suspect that the committee is not free from pressure from the government.

An enlarged role for the NPF may bring undesirable consequences. This risk has come to the forefront in a recent episode involving a major financial group, one of the few large firms not dominated by an individual CMS. It was reported that the financial holding company controlling the group had asked the NPF to nominate a candidate before it held the GSM to elect directors. The request, for better or worse, was subsequently withdrawn before the GSM.

There is yet another recent episode that suggests tension resulting from the growing influence of the NPF. In February 2014, the NPF revised its Voting Guidelines. An original proposal included a provision requiring the NPF to oppose appointment of a person to the board of directors if the person has been convicted for misappropriation of corporate assets or breach of trust. The provision was finally dropped due to pressure from the business community.

B. Foreign Investors

As demonstrated earlier, foreign investors have been, and still are, a force restraining the abuse of power by the CMS, especially in larger listed firms. Their influence, however, does not seem as dominant as their combined holdings suggest. First, they have so far shown no strong tendency to act in concert. Second, they must overcome various technical obstacles mentioned earlier to embark on shareholder activism. Third, activist foreign investors must cope with negative publicity intensified by the local media.

One should not take for granted the passivity of foreign investors forever. They will likely take action in two situations. First, they may act when a CMS continues to show poor performance. So far, blue chip *chaebol* firms have generally managed to avoid such an unfortunate situation. Second, an egregious case of tunneling may rouse at least a few foreign investors to action. On several occasions, foreign investors have shown their willingness to act by cooperating with local activist shareholders in filing a derivative lawsuit against wrongdoing owner-managers.

A current dispute involving a *chaebol* and a foreign investor illustrates an inherent vulnerability of the CMS structure. The dispute involves the Hyundai Group, a *chaebol* controlled by a CMS named Ms Hyun, and Schindler Holding, a global firm manufacturing elevators. Schindler now owns more than 20 percent of the shares of Hyundai Elevator (HE), an affiliate of the Hyundai Group. A circular share ownership structure exists among three major affiliates of the Hyundai Group – HE, Hyundai Shipping (HS) and Hyundai Logistics. Faced with hostile takeover risks, HE, a 24 percent shareholder of HS, had to strengthen its control over HS by entering into financial derivative transactions with financial institutions. In effect, the derivative transactions allowed HE to secure a substantial number of votes in return for HE's obligation to pay a hefty fee and to assume downside risks. The dispute arose as HS fell into trouble due to the slump in the global shipping industry. HE's accumulated loss from the transactions amounts to several hundred million dollars, far in excess of its operating profits. In addition to numerous lawsuits for various remedies, Schindler has filed a derivative lawsuit against Ms Hyun and other top executives of HE to stop the derivative transactions and to seek damages. Ms Hyun has tried to justify the whole scheme as an exercise of business judgment. If she loses, it will be extremely difficult for her to keep control over her business group. As Schindler's claim aims at the foundation of the *chaebol*'s CMS structure, the outcome of this dispute may have far-reaching repercussions for the entire business community.

V. CONCLUSION

As long as the CMS remains in power, shareholders' voting rights will be less relevant in Korea. On the other hand, shareholders' other rights, especially their right to file a lawsuit against the firm or managers, will continue to occupy the center stage. Corporate governance reform efforts have so far been concentrated on, among other things, facilitating the exercise of shareholders' other rights. On the other hand, no significant attempt has been made to expand or narrow the scope of power of the GSM. Corporate governance discourse will likely change if the CMS somehow loses control and, as a consequence, becomes indistinguishable from a professional manager. In such a situation a shareholder *disempowerment* debate may emerge in Korea.

At the moment, however, a more pressing issue for policymakers in Korea is how to deal with ubiquitous CMSs and the agency problems caused by them. CMSs have been widely known to engage in tunneling activities. Thanks to the efforts of prosecutors and judges, however, egregious types of tunneling now appear to be held in check. A more controversial aspect of the CMS structure is that a CMS is not replaced, but his or her status is almost without exception inherited by his or her heirs regardless of their competence. Sympathizers of *chaebol* may tout this dynastic feature of the CMS structure as a source of stability in *chaebol* firms. It is not clear what will become of those *chaebol* firms if the CMS structure eventually collapses. At present, even among large listed firms, only a handful of firms have no individual CMS. Commonly called 'ownerless firms', these firms are mostly former government-owned corporations that have been privatized during the last twenty years. With professional managers and a board of directors dominated by outside directors, these firms have enjoyed the highest ratings in terms of corporate governance. In recent years, however, ominous signs have emerged that suggest the intervention of political forces in the internal affairs of these firms. For example, their CEOs tend to be replaced with the change of government and mostly in awkward situations. Also, several of their outside directors are believed to have been appointed due to their political ties. Combined with the growing influence of the NPF, this turn of events causes many observers to be concerned that these ownerless firms are turning into de facto state-owned enterprises.

In contrast to ownerless firms, which regularly go through a political whirlwind whenever there is a regime change, *chaebol* firms appear better positioned to ride political waves. Although the government has been making various requests or demands of *chaebols*, no attempt has yet been made, to the best of my knowledge, to replace the CMS at a *chaebol*, even when the CMS falls into a crisis of confidence such as being convicted for a serious crime. Thus, as long as the current political climate continues, one may safely predict that the CMS structure will remain unchanged at least for a while and that shareholder power will remain largely an issue for academics.

References

Almeida, Heitor, Sang Yong Park, Marti G. Subrahmanyam and Daniel Wolfenzon. 2011. The Structure and Formation of Business Groups: Evidence from Korean Chaebols, *Journal of Financial Economics*, 99: 447–475.

Baek, Jae-Seung, Jun-Koo Kang and Kyung Suh Park. 2004. Corporate Governance and Firm Value: Evidence from the Korean Financial Crisis, *Journal of Financial Economics*, 71: 265–313.

Bainbridge, Stephen M. 2006. Director Primacy and Shareholder Disempowerment, *Harvard Law Review*, 119: 1735–1758.

Bebchuk, Lucian A., Alon Brav and Wei Jiang. 2013. The Long-Term Effects of Hedge Fund Activism (http://papers.ssrn.com/sol3/papers.cfm?abstract_id52291577).

Black, Bernard S. 1998. Shareholder Activism and Corporate Governance in the U.S., in P. Newman, ed., *The New Palgrave Dictionary of Economics and the Law, Vol. III*, London & New York: Palgrave Macmillan.

Black, Bernard S., Woochan Kim, Husung Jang and Kyung Suh Park. 2010. How Corporate Governance Affects Firm Value: Evidence on Channels from Korea (http://ssrn.com/abstract51365945).

Cheffins, Brian R. and John Armour. 2011. The Past, Present and Future of Shareholder Activism by Hedge Funds, *Journal of Corporation Law*, 37: 51–103.

Choi, Jongmoo J., Sae Woon Park and Sean Sehyun Yoo. 2007. The Value of Outside Directors: Evidence from Corporate Governance Reform in Korea, *Journal of Financial and Quantitative Analysis*, 42: 941–962.

Chun, Kyung-Hoon, Kon-Sik Kim, Hyeok-Joon Rho and Ok-Rial Song. 2014. *Corporations and Partnerships – South Korea*, AH Alphen and den Rijn: Kluwer International.

Claessens, Stijn, Simeon Djankov, Joseph P.H. Fan and Larry H.P. Lang. 2002. Disentangling the Incentive and Entrenchment Effects of Large Shareholdings, *Journal of Finance*, 57: 2741–2772.

Ferris, Stephen P., Kenneth A. Kim and Pattanaporn Kitsabunnarat. 2003. The Costs (and Benefits?) of Diversified Business Groups: The Case of Korean Chaebols, *Journal of Banking & Finance*, 27: 251–273.

Garner, Jacqueline L. and Won Yong Kim. 2011. Are Foreign Investors Really Beneficial? Evidence from South Korea (http://ssrn.com/abstract51546782).

Goto, Gen. 2014. Legally 'Strong' Shareholders of Japan, *Michigan Journal of Private Equity & Venture Capital Law*, 3: 125–163.

Hill, Jennifer G. 2010. The Rising Tension between Shareholder and Director Power in the Common Law World, *Corporate Governance: An International Review*, 18: 344–359.

Hwang, Lee-Seok, Hakkon Kim, Kwangwoo Park and Rae Soo Park. 2013. Corporate Governance and

Payout Policy: Evidence from Korean Business Groups (http://ssrn.com/abstract52314723).

Joh, Sung-Wook. 2003. Corporate Governance and Firm Profitability: Evidence from Korea before the Economic Crisis, *Journal of Financial Economics*, 68: 287–322.

Johnson, Simon, Rafael La Porta, Florencio Lopez de Silanes and Andrei Shleifer. 2000. Tunneling, *American Economic Review*, 90: 22–27.

Kang, Jung-Min. 2012. Voting by Institutional Investors in 2012 (Economic Reform Research Institute Report No. 2012–21) (in Korean).

Kang, Shinae, Wonsik Sul and Soojung Kim. 2010. Impact of Foreign Institutional Investors on Dividend Policy in Korea: A Stock Market Perspective, *Journal of Financial Management and Analysis*, 23: 10–26.

Katelouzou, Dionysia. Forthcoming. The Legal Determinants of Shareholder Activism: A Theoretical and Empirical Comparative Analysis.

Kim, Jooyoung and Joongi Kim 2001. Shareholder Activism in Korea: A Review of How PSPD Has Used Legal Measures to Strengthen Korean Corporate Governance, *Journal of Korean Law*, 1: 51–76.

Kim, Kon Sik. 2014. Corporate Law and Corporate Law Scholarship in Korea: A Comparative Essay, in John O. Haley and Toshiko Takenaka, eds, *Legal Innovations in Asia: Judicial Law-Making and the Influence of Comparative Law*, Cheltenham, UK: Edward Elgar Publishing.

Korea Corporate Governance Service, Information related to the General Shareholders Meeting (undated internal memo in Korea).

Lee, Byung-Gi. 2012. Issues and Challenges in the NPF's Duty to Vote and Corporate Governance (Policy Research 2012–11, Korea Economic Research Institute) (in Korean).

Lee, Sanghoon. 2008. Ownership Structure and Financial Performance: Evidence from Panel Data of South Korea (http://ssrn.com/abstract51279919).

Lee, Sanghoon. 2011. Institutional Ownership in Korea – An Empirical Analysis of Panel Data, 13 *Jaimu jongchaik ronjip* (Finance Policy Review) 13: 145–168 (a paper published in English in a Korean academic journal).

Milhaupt, Curtis J. and Katharina Pistor. 2008. *Law and Capitalism*, Chicago and London: University of Chicago Press.

Morck, Randall, Andrei Shleifer and Robert Vishny. 1988. Management Ownership and Market Valuation: An Empirical Analysis, *Journal of Financial Economics*, 20: 295–315.

Park, Young Seog. 2004. Assessing the Impact of Corporate Governance on Productivity and Growth in Korea, in Eduardo T. Gonzalez, ed., *Impact of Corporate Governance on Productivity: Asian Experience*, Tokyo: Asian Productivity Organization, 205–239.

Rho, Hyeok-Joon and Kon Sik Kim. 2012. Invigorating Shareholder Derivative Actions in South Korea, in

Dan W. Puchiniak et al., eds, *The Derivative Action in Asia*, Cambridge: Cambridge University Press, 186–214.

Romano, Roberta. 2001. Less is More: Making Institutional Investor Activism a Valuable Mechanism of Corporate Governance, *Yale Journal on Regulation*, 18: 174–251.

Shin, Hyun-Han and Young Suk Park. 1999. Financing Constraints and Internal Capital Markets: Evidence from Korean Chaebols, *Journal of Corporate Finance*, 5: 169–191.

Stout, Lynn. 2012. *The Shareholder Value Myth*, San Francisco: Berrett-Koehler Publishers, Inc.

Sul, Wonsik and Soojung Kim. 2006. Impact of Foreign Investors on Firm's Dividend Policy, *Journal of Korean Securities Association*, 35(1): 1–40 (in Korean).

Thomsen, Steen and Torben Pedersen. 2000. Ownership Structure and Economic Performance in the Largest European Companies, *Strategic Management Journal*, 21: 689–705.

Varieties of Independent Directors in Asia

A Taxonomy

Dan W. Puchniak and Kon Sik Kim*

I Introduction

At first blush, the rise of the independent director in Asia appears to be a straightforward example of a significant legal transplant from the United States (US) to Asia. A few decades ago, independent directors, which are an American legal invention,[1] were virtually non-existent in Asia.[2] Today, as this book reveals, they are ubiquitous throughout Asia.

* The authors would like to thank the National University of Singapore (NUS) Centre for Asian Legal Studies (CALS) and EW Barker Centre for Law & Business (EWBCLB) for providing funding to support this research. A substantial part of this chapter was shaped during the period when the second author was visiting NUS Law as a Visiting Research Professor at CALS and EWBCLB in 2016. The second author would like to particularly express his gratitude for the generous invitation by CALS and EWBCLB to facilitate this joint research at NUS Law. We would also like to extend our special thanks to Harald Baum for detailed discussions, insights and feedback, which significantly improved earlier draft s of this chapter. In addition, we would like to thank Hitotsubashi University, Tokyo University and the University of Chicago for organising forums to present earlier draft s of this chapter, which were important in its development. In addition, we would like to thank Bruce Aronson, Gen Goto, Souichirou Kozuka, Curtis Milhaupt, Luke Nottage, Zenichi Shishido, Holger Spamann and Umakanth Varottil for valuable feedback and discussions related to earlier draft s of this chapter. Finally, we are grateful to Samantha Tang for her diligent and skilful research assistance, which exceeded our high expectations. As always, any errors remain our own.

1) See Chapter 1 at III for a brief history of the American origins of the independent director.
2) See, for example, Chapter 4 (Japan) at I (Japan's apparent resistance against the adoption of independent directors); Chapter 5 (South Korea) at III.1.b (Korea first enacted statutory requirements for independent directors in 2000); Chapter 6 (China) at II.2 (first Chinese company to adopt independent directors did so in 1993 to comply with the listing rules of the Hong Kong Stock Exchange); Chapter 7 (Taiwan) at II.1 (Taiwan Stock Exchange first enacted listing rules for independent directors in 2002); Chapter 8 (Hong Kong) at II.4 (Hong Kong Stock Exchange first enacted listing rules for independent directors in 1993); Chapter 9 (Singapore) at III.1 (Singapore first enacted statutory requirements for independent directors in 1989); Chapter 10 (India) at III (Securities and Exchange Board of India first enacted listing requirements for independent directors in 2000). See also C. H. Tan, 'Corporate Governance and Independent Directors', *Singapore Academy of Law Journal*, 15 (2003), 355, 365.

Even for those familiar with corporate governance in Asia, the evidence in this book demonstrating the extent to which Asian jurisdictions have promoted and adopted 'independent directors' will likely surprise. A recent report from the leading American proxy advisory firm Institutional Shareholder Services (ISS) claims that over 70 percent of listed companies in China now have a board comprising a majority of 'independent directors' – ranking China far ahead of Australia and the United Kingdom (UK) in terms of its percentage of boards with a majority of 'independent directors'.[3] For over a decade, Singapore has reported that a majority of all of the directors in its listed companies are 'independent', and that 98 per cent of its listed companies comply with the 'independent director' provisions in its 'comply or explain' Code of Corporate Governance – a higher compliance rate than in the UK, where the 'comply or explain' model was invented.[4] In 2000, South Korea made it *mandatory* for all large listed companies to have a board composed of at least half 'independent directors'.[5] Additionally, since 2004, such boards have been required to have a majority of 'independent directors'[6] – which on its face is a stricter requirement than in any major jurisdiction in the European Union, where the regulation of 'independent directors' generally takes the form of non-mandatory recommendations.[7] In 2000, India made it mandatory for publicly listed companies to have a board with at least one-third

---

3) The ISS Report found that approximately 50 per cent of listed companies in Australia and the UK have boards composed of a majority of independent directors. See T. Gopal, 'Japan: A Closer Look at Governance Reforms' (ISS, 2015), available at www.issgovernance.com. No information was provided in this report as to the definition of 'independent directors' used, or the method used to collect the information presented in the report. For further discussion on the report's shortcomings in its classification of China's board architecture, see note 75 below. Email clarification was sought from the author of the report on 2 June 2016, but no response was forthcoming as of the publication of this book.

4) By 2006, 98 per cent of all Singapore-listed companies reported full compliance with the recommendation in Singapore's Code of Corporate Governance that one-third of the board be composed of independent directors, and the majority of directors in listed companies were reportedly independent. See Chapter 9 (Singapore) at I; H. Tjio, *Principles and Practice of Securities Regulation in Singapore*, 2nd edn (LexisNexis, 2011), 326. By contrast, compliance with the recommendation in the UK's 2010 Code of Corporate Governance and 2012 Code of Corporate Governance that at least half of the board be composed of independent non-executive directors for companies listed on the Financial Times Stock Exchange 350 Index ranged from 80 per cent in 2011 to 92 per cent in 2015. See Financial Reporting Council, 'Developments in Corporate Governance and Stewardship 2015' (Financial Reporting Council, 2016), available at www.frc.org.uk; Financial Reporting Council, 'Developments in Corporate Governance and Stewardship 2011: The Impact and Implementation of the UK Corporate Governance and Stewardship Codes' (Financial Reporting Council, 2011), available at www.frc.org.uk. Given that the recommended proportion of independent directors on the board for Singapore and the UK were different (one-third and half respectively), a strict comparison of these compliance rates may not be perfectly accurate, but nevertheless provides a useful guide. For a detailed explanation of the 'comply or explain' model, see Chapter 1 at IV.1.

5) See Chapter 5 (South Korea) at III.1.b.

6) See Chapter 5 (South Korea) at III.1.b.

7) P. L. Davies and K. J. Hopt, 'Boards in Europe: Accountability and Convergence', *American Journal of Comparative Law*, 61 (2013), 301, 319.

'independent directors', and if the board chair is also an executive of the company then the board must be at least half 'independent directors'[8] – which again appears to be a stricter requirement than in most leading Western countries.[9] In as early as 1993, Hong Kong made it mandatory for all listed companies to have a board with at least two 'independent directors', and more recently made it mandatory for at least one-third of such boards to be composed of 'independent directors'.[10] These facts reveal a reality which is the opposite of what conventional wisdom suggests: many of Asia's leading economies have surpassed those in the West in terms of the proportion of 'independent directors' on their corporate boards.[11] In a similar vein, many of the laws and regulations in Asia's leading economies appear to do more to promote or require 'independent directors' on the boards of listed companies than those in many leading Western economies.[12] The reality that most leading listed companies in Asia now have a significant number (or, in fact, in many cases a majority) of 'independent directors' on their board is a striking development that has been largely overlooked.[13]

To be clear, this does not suggest that 'independent directors' have been vigorously promoted and widely adopted in every jurisdiction in Asia. In fact, until recently, a majority of listed companies in Japan had no 'independent directors'[14] and about one-third of listed

---

8) See Chapter 10 (India) at III.

9) Davies and Hopt, 'Boards in Europe'.

10) See Chapter 8 (Hong Kong) at II.1.

11) Conventional wisdom suggests that the boards of Asian companies are often dominated by insiders. See S. Claessens and J. P. H. Fan, 'Corporate Governance in Asia: A Survey', *International Review of Finance*, 3 (2002), 71, 82; C. L. Ahmadjian, 'Corporate Governance and Business Systems in Asia' in G. Redding and M. A. Witt (eds.), The *Oxford Handbook of Asian Business Systems* (Oxford University Press, 2014), 342–343.

12) See Chapter 4 (Japan) at II.1.b–c; Chapter 5 (South Korea) at III; Chapter 6 (China) at III.2; Chapter 7 (Taiwan) at II.1; Chapter 8 (Hong Kong) at II; Chapter 9 (Singapore) at II.4; Chapter 10 (India) at III; Chapter 11 (Australia) at III.

13) As South Korea requires all large listed companies to have their board composed of a majority of independent directors, all large listed Korean companies now have a majority of independent directors on their boards. See Chapter 5 (South Korea) at III.1.b. Another prominent example is in Singapore where all of the directors on the board of Temasek (the holding company for Singapore's Government-Linked Companies), except for the CEO, are non-executive independent directors. In addition, 64.87 per cent of the directors in the 23 listed Government-Linked Companies – which comprise the vast majority of the most prominent listed companies in Singapore – are independent directors. See Chapter 9 (Singapore) at III.3. It is also noteworthy that independent directors constitute at least half of the boards of many of the most prominent Asian companies such as Lenovo (7 out of 11), Samsung (5 out of 9), Tencent (4 out of 8), Sony (9 out of 12), Tata Steel (6 out of 12), Acer Group (4 out of 7) and DBS Group Holdings (7 out of 9). See, for example, Lenovo, 'Corporate Governance: Board of Directors', available at www.lenovo.com; Samsung, 'Board of Directors', available at www.samsung.com; Tencent, 'Board', available at www.tencent.com; Sony, 'Corporate Governance', available at www.sony.com; Tata Steel, 'Board of Directors', available at www.tatasteel.com; Acer Group, 'Corporate Governance', available at www.acer-group.com; DBS Group Holdings, 'Annual Report 2015: Board of Directors', available at www.dbs.com.

companies in Taiwan still have none.[15] Even in Japan and Taiwan, however, recent legal reforms have driven significant increases in the number of 'independent directors' on corporate boards – a trend that appears likely to continue in both countries.[16] In several important[17] but often overlooked developing Asian countries, such as Bangladesh,[18] Indonesia,[19] Malaysia,[20] the Philippines, Thailand and Vietnam,[21] unbeknownst to most comparative corporate governance experts, 'independent directors' have become a mainstay in corporate boardrooms.[22] As such, it is now indisputable that the 'independent director' is a ubiquitous feature of corporate governance throughout Asia – and its rise appears to have no immediate end in sight.[23]

As explained in section II of this chapter, however, the meteoric rise of the 'independent director' in Asia is considerably more complex than it appears. A comparison of the jurisdiction-specific chapters in this book reveals that although the *label* 'independent director' has been transplanted precipitously from the US (in some cases via the UK) throughout Asia, who is labelled an 'independent director' (i.e., the 'form' that independent directors take)[24] and what independent directors do (i.e., the 'function' they perform)[25] in Asia dif-

---

14) G. Goto, 'The Outline for the Companies Act Reform in Japan and Its Implications', *Journal of Japanese Law*, 35 (2013), 13, 19.

15) See Chapter 7 (Taiwan) at II.2.a: 'As of 2014, 66.34 percent of TWSE-listed and OTC-traded companies have independent directors on their boards.'

16) Political and regulatory support for independent directors has driven their gradual adoption by companies in Japan and Taiwan. See Chapter 4 (Japan) at IV; Chapter 7 (Taiwan) at IV.

17) Thailand (67 million), Indonesia (252 million) and the Philippines (100 million) – have an estimated total population of 607 million. See UNData, 'Data', available at data.un.org.

18) Emerging Markets Committee of the International Organization of Securities Commissions, 'Corporate Governance Practices in Emerging Markets' (2007), available at www.iosco.org.

19) M. Prabowo and J. Simpson, 'Independent Directors and Firm Performance in Family Controlled Firms: Evidence from Indonesia', *Asian Pacific Economic Literature*, 25 (2011), 121.

20) H. Ibrahim and F. A. Samad, 'Corporate Governance Mechanisms and Performance of Public-Listed Family-Ownership in Malaysia', *International Journal of Economics and Finance*, 3 (2011), 105.

21) D. Vo and T. Phan, 'Corporate Governance and Firm Performance' (2013), available at www.murdoch.edu.au.

22) For a basic overview of some of the rules regarding independent directors in many Asian jurisdictions, including Indonesia, Malaysia, the Philippines and Thailand, see generally, ACGA, 'Rules and Recommendations on the Number of Independent Directors in Asia' (2010), available at www.acga-asia.org/.

23) Most of the jurisdictions surveyed in this book predict a potential increase in the number of independent directors in their respective jurisdiction. See Chapter 4 (Japan) at IV; Chapter 7 (Taiwan) at IV; Chapter 8 (Hong Kong) at IV; Chapter 9 (Singapore) at V; Chapter 10 (India) at VII.

24) The precise requirements for independence may differ across jurisdictions, which may take the form of a positive definition of independence consisting of a broadly framed standard, or negative definition of independence in the form of a list of disqualifications, or both. See, for example, Chapter 4 (Japan) at II.1 (a broadly-framed standard of independence with a list of disqualifications); Chapter 5 (South Korea) at III.2.b (a list of disqualifications); Chapter 8 (Hong Kong) at II.2 (a broadly-framed standard of independence with a list of situations in which the director's independence is more likely to be questioned).

fer significantly from the American concept of the independent director. To add to the complexity, the form and function of 'independent directors' vary *within Asia* from jurisdiction to jurisdiction.[26] As such, in reality, there are *varieties* of independent directors in Asia – none of which conform to the American concept of the independent director. This challenges the widely-held assumption that 'independent directors' are universally similar[27]

---

25) The primary purpose of the 'American-style' independent director is to monitor management on behalf of dispersed shareholders – as such they are required to be independent from management (but not significant shareholders). See U. Velikonja, 'The Political Economy of Board Independence', *North Carolina Law Review*, 92 (2014), 855, 863–864; B. R. Cheffins, 'The History of Modern U.S Corporate Governance: Introduction' in B. R. Cheffins (ed.), *The History of Modern U.S. Corporate Governance* (Edward Elgar, 2012); J. Gordon, 'The Rise of Independent Directors in the United States, 1950–2005: Of Shareholder Value and Stock Market Prices', *Stanford Law Review*, 59 (2007), 1465.

26) Independent directors in the jurisdictions surveyed in this book may possess idiosyncratic skills that allow them to perform particular roles in their specific jurisdiction. See *infra* III.4 and III.5. See also Chapter 5 (South Korea) at IV.4 (observing the increasing preference in South Korea for appointing former government officials as independent directors, possibly to act as a communication channel between the listed company and the government); Chapter 6 (China) at II.3; Chapter 7 (Taiwan) at II.2.b; Chapter 9 (Singapore) at III.2 and III.3 (opining that independent directors in Singapore family companies are likely to operate as mediators and advisors to family members; also opining the independent directors in Singapore Government-Linked Companies are appointed to fill the managerial-monitoring gap created by Singapore's unique regulatory environment); Chapter 10 (India) at IV.2 (observing that former government officials or politicians are often appointed as independent directors; also noting that academics are often appointed as independent directors in South Korea, China, Taiwan and India respectively). Other commentators have also made similar observations. See, for example, D. W. Puchniak, 'Multiple Faces of Shareholder Power in Asia: Complexity Revealed' in J. Hill and R. Thomas (eds.), *Research Handbook on Shareholder Power* (Edward Elgar, 2015), 514, 525–526 (observing that in Asia's controlling shareholder environment independent directors may be a mechanism for amplifying the block shareholder's controlling power or a signalling device for 'good' corporate governance; also noting that in Japan outside directors have sometimes served to reinforce *keiretsu* and cross-shareholding links, and in China some have suggested that 'independent' directors may be puppets for the government); D. C. Clarke, 'Independent Director in Chinese Corporate Governance', *Delaware Journal of Corporate Law*, 31 (2006), 125, 207–208 (noting that a survey of 500 listed companies in China found that 45 per cent of independent directors were university professors or researchers from institutes, and observing that the common stereotype of independent directors was a well-meaning but ineffectual academic or celebrity appointed for their prestige and possibly to satisfy regulatory requirements).

27) The assumption that independent directors are the same regardless of their jurisdiction of origin is common in much of the leading research in the field. See, for example, B. S. Black et al., 'Corporate Governance Indices and Construct Validity' (ECGI Finance Working Paper No. 483/ 2016, September 2016), 27 Table 2, available at https://papers.ssrn.com/sol3/papers.cfm?abstract_id=2838273; D. Katelouzou and M. Siems, 'Disappearing Paradigms in Shareholder Protection: Leximetric Evidence for 30 Countries, 1990–2013', *Journal of Corporate Law Studies*, 15 (2015), 127; B. S. Black et al., 'Does Corporate Governance Predict Firms' Market Values? Evidence from Korea', *Journal of Law, Economics and Organisation*, 22 (2006), 366. Similar assumptions also appear to have been made in other corporate governance surveys and rankings. See N. A. Chakra et al., 'Doing Business 2017: Equal Opportunity for All' (World Bank, 2016), available at www.doingbusiness.org; N. A. Chakra et al., 'Doing Business 2016: Protecting Minority Investors' (World Bank, 2015), available at www.doingbusiness.org; N. A. Chakra and H. Kaddoura, 'Doing Business 2015: Measuring Business Regulations, Protecting Minority Investors in [Name of Economy]' (World Bank, 2014), available at www.doingbusiness.org; L. A. Bebchuk and A. Hamdani, 'The Elusive Quest for Global Governance Standards', *University of Pennsylvania Law Review*, 157 (2009), 1263, 1302–1304, 1311.

and follow the American concept of the independent director.[28] It also complicates inter jurisdictional comparisons of 'independent directors' within Asia, which is a core objective of this book.

Section III of this chapter attempts to overcome this significant hurdle for comparative analysis by offering an explanation for why distinct varieties of independent directors have emerged throughout Asia. At first blush, this question is perplexing. All of Asia's leading economies claim to have either explicitly adopted or been heavily influenced by the American and/or 'Anglo-American' independent director model.[29] With a common model, one would expect to find a high degree of uniformity among independent directors in Asia – not diverse varieties. However, a comparative analysis of the jurisdiction-specific chapters in this book reveals six principal factors that have driven independent directors in Asia to evolve in a variety of unique jurisdiction-specific ways: (1) shareholder ownership structures; (2) legal origins; (3) types of shareholders; (4) functional substitutes; (5) political economy; and (6) cultural norms. Understanding how these factors have driven distinct varieties of independent directors to emerge and evolve in Asia's leading economies allows us to construct a loose taxonomy of the varieties of independent directors in Asia. This taxonomy provides a useful tool for identifying which inter jurisdictional comparisons are likely to yield significant insights, and which are likely to mislead.

Section IV of this chapter concludes by highlighting how an understanding of the varieties of independent directors in Asia can advance corporate governance practice and contribute to comparative corporate governance theory. The conclusion illuminates the importance of jurisdiction-specific knowledge for accurately understanding the rise and functions of independent directors in Asia. However, while this chapter extracts the important comparative lessons from the jurisdiction-specific chapters in this book, the details in each of the jurisdiction-specific chapters remain essential.

---

28) This is implicit in the literature surveyed at note 27 above, given that it did not occur to any of the authors to explicitly draw a distinction between US-style independent directors and independent directors as an umbrella concept.

29) See Chapter 4 (Japan) at II.1.a; Chapter 5 (South Korea) at II.4; Chapter 6 (China) at II.1; Chapter 7 (Taiwan) at I; Chapter 8 (Hong Kong) at II.4; Chapter 9 (Singapore) at II.3; Chapter 10 (India) at III. The roots of the 'Anglo-American' concept of the independent director are explained below at II.1 and II.2; the 'American' concept of the independent director is explained below at II.3.

II Varieties of Independent Directors in Asia: Diversity Revealed

1 The Myth of the Monolithic 'Anglo-American' Independent Director

Counting the number of 'independent directors' on corporate boards has become a key metric for comparing the quality of corporate governance across countries and companies around the world. Leading corporate governance advisory firms, which influence the allocation of trillions of dollars of global capital, have developed multijurisdictional comparative indices that treat the number of 'independent directors' on corporate boards as a critical factor for measuring 'good' corporate governance.[30] The World Bank uses the requirement for 'independent directors' to be on corporate boards as one of the metrics in its influential 'Ease of Doing Business Index', which ranks the business regulatory environments of 190 economies each year.[31] The number of 'independent directors' on corporate boards is a key variable in several of the most influential corporate governance research indices that drive entire areas of comparative corporate governance scholarship.[32]

All of these influential comparative corporate governance measures make the same assumption: that the term 'independent director' universally refers to people who meet the same criteria and perform the same corporate governance function. Indeed, the assumption that independent directors universally take the same form and perform the same function is the foundation upon which many multijurisdictional policy initiatives and leading academic research that focus on independent directors are built.[33] Obviously, if the criteria for labelling a person an 'independent director' and/or the function that a person labelled as an 'independent director' performs differ significantly from jurisdiction to jurisdiction, then comparing 'independent directors' across jurisdictions is essentially an exercise in comparing 'apples and oranges'.

Based on a comparative analysis of the jurisdiction-specific chapters in this book, it appears that the form and function of independent directors in Asia's leading economies differ sig-

---

30) See, for example, ISS, 'Board Independence at a Glance' (2016), available at www.isscorporatesolutions.com ; MSCI, 'ESG Ratings', available at www.msci.com.

31) See, for example, Chakra et al., 'Doing Business 2017: Equal Opportunity for All'; Chakra et al., 'Doing Business 2016: Protecting Minority Investors'; Chakra and Kaddoura, 'Doing Business 2015: Measuring Business Regulations, Protecting Minority Investors in [Name of Economy]'

32) See, for example, Katelouzou and Siems, 'Disappearing Paradigms in Shareholder Protection', 127; Black et al., 'Does Corporate Governance Predict Firms' Market Values?', 366.

33) See notes 27 and 28 above.

nificantly from the American concept of the independent director. Although there are important similarities in the form and function of 'independent directors' within Asia, there are also significant intra-Asia jurisdictional differences. While intra-Asia comparisons of 'independent directors' may have more utility than Asia–US comparisons, jurisdictional differences in the form and function of independent directors within Asia must also be recognised and accounted for in comparative analyses.

In sum, the comparative evidence in this book reveals that the label 'independent director' masks the reality that the form and function of 'independent directors' in Asia depart significantly from the American concept of the independent director. This monolithic label obscures the reality that jurisdictional differences in the form and function of 'independent directors' within Asia may be significant. Most importantly, the label conceals interesting intra-Asia jurisdictional similarities that provide valuable opportunities for tailored and insightful comparative analyses. The balance of this section of the chapter will explain how 'independent directors' in Asia depart significantly from the American concept of the independent director, as well as highlight important similarities and differences in the form and function of independent directors in leading Asian economies.

2 The Independent Director in Asia: Untangling Its Anglo-American Roots

The genesis of the independent director as a global corporate governance mechanism can be traced to the 1970s in the US.[34] Since then, the primary function of independent directors in American corporate governance has been clear: to monitor management on behalf of dispersed shareholders, who are hindered by collective action problems from monitoring management themselves.[35] This managerial-monitoring function is at the core of the American corporate governance model, which for decades has been focused on solving the primary governance problem in companies with dispersed shareholders: functionally autonomous managers taking advantage of their unchecked power to enrich themselves at the expense of dispersed shareholders.[36]

Despite the fact that independent directors account for the vast majority of directors on American boards, there is still considerable debate about whether American independent directors are effective managerial-monitors.[37] It is, however, uncontroversial that the

---

34) See Chapter 1 at I.2; Chapter 2 at II; Chapter 9 (Singapore) at II.1.
35) Gordon, 'The Rise of Independent Directors in the United States', 1490.
36) See Chapter 9 (Singapore) at II.1; B. R. Cheffins, 'The History of Corporate Governance' in M. Wright et al. (eds.), *Oxford Handbook of Corporate Governance* (Oxford University Press, 2013).

'independent director' in the US was (and still is) designed to function as a corporate governance mechanism primarily to monitor management on behalf of dispersed shareholders.[38] As such, it makes perfect sense that the NYSE and NASDAQ definitions of 'independence' focus on ensuring that independent directors are independent from the managers of the corporation on whose board they sit.[39]

It is also uncontroversial that in the US, independent directors were not (and are not) primarily designed to be a mechanism for monitoring controlling shareholders.[40] On the contrary, at least based on the theory that underlies the American corporate governance model, independent directors become functionally redundant in companies with a controlling shareholder. As the theory goes, in controlled companies, controlling shareholders are fully capable of either monitoring management or managing the company themselves – rendering nugatory the problem of unchecked self-interested managers, which is the primary corporate governance concern in companies with dispersed shareholders that independent directors in the US are designed to fix.[41]

This theory is evident in the NYSE and NASDAQ listing rules, which explicitly exempt companies with a controlling shareholder from the otherwise mandatory requirement that boards of listed companies must have a majority of independent directors.[42] It is also clear that the definition of 'independence' employed in the NYSE and NASDAQ listing rules do not prohibit significant shareholders or those connected with significant shareholders from qualifying as 'independent directors'.[43] Instead, in the US, share ownership by independent directors is often viewed as an effective way to align their interests with dispersed shareholders and incentivise them to monitor management more effectively on behalf of dis-

---

37) See Chapter 1 at III.7; Chapter 2 at II and IV; Chapter 10 (India) at IV.

38) See Chapter 1 at I.2 and III; Chapter 2 at II.

39) § 303A.02, NYSE Listed Company Manual, available at http://nysemanual.nyse.com/lcm; § 5605(a)(2), NASDAQ Listing Rules, available at http://nasdaq.cchwallstreet.com

40) See Chapter 1 at III.4; Gordon, 'The Rise of Independent Directors in the United States', 1508 at n. 168; B. M. Ho, 'Restructuring the Boards of Directors of Public Companies in Hong Kong: Barking up the Wrong Tree', *Singapore Journal of International and Comparative Law*, 1 (1997), 507, 518–524.

41) B. M. Ho, 'Restructuring the Boards of Directors of Public Companies in Hong Kong', 527.

42) Weil, Gotshal & Manges LLP, 'Public Company Advisory Group, Requirements for Public Company Boards: Including IPO Transition Rules' (2013), 2, 13, 15, available at www.weil.com; Wachtell, Lipton, Rosen & Katz, *Compensation Committee Guide* (2014), 3 n. 3, 73, available at www.wlrk.com. See also § 303A.02, NYSE Listed Company Manual; § IM-5615-5, NASDAQ Stock Market Rules.

43) In fact, the NYSE and NASDAQ listing rules go a step further by exempting controlled companies from the requirement that their nomination committee and remuneration committee must be composed entirely of (American-style) independent directors. See US Securities Exchange Commission, 'NASD and NYSE Rulemaking: Relating to Corporate Governance' (Release No. 34-48745, 2003), available at www.sec.gov; Findlaw, 'SEC Approves NYSE and NASDAQ Proposals Relating to Director Independence' (23 March 2006), available at http://corporate.findlaw.com.

persed shareholders.[44]

Given this context, it is unsurprising that in the 1990s, the American concept of the independent director became a core feature of the UK's Combined Code of Corporate Governance (UK Code).[45] It is well recognised that the US and UK share the unique distinction of having a high proportion of listed companies with dispersed shareholders.[46] As such, it is understandable that the original definition of 'independence' in the UK Code focused on ensuring that independent directors were independent from the company's management, without any restriction on significant shareholders qualifying as independent directors – wholly embracing the American managerial-monitoring concept of the independent director.[47] Moreover, the UK provided a corporate governance architecture similar to the US within which its American-style independent directors could function, as the typical UK listed company had (and still has) a one-tier board with sub-committees for nomination, remuneration and audit.

In sum, it is clear that the inaugural UK Code did more than merely transplant the 'independent director' *label* from the US to the UK. It transplanted the form of the American independent director (i.e., directors who are independent from management only) to perform the function of the American independent director (i.e., monitoring management on behalf of dispersed shareholders) into a corporate governance architecture similar to the US (i.e., a one-tier board with committee system). From this perspective, it appears that the American concept of the independent director was indeed transplanted into the inaugural UK Code, arguably creating the concept of the 'Anglo-American' independent director. In this context, UK–US comparisons of the independent director are more akin to 'twins separated at birth' than 'apples and oranges'.

This is not to suggest that the UK independent director has *remained* true to its American origins. The American-style definition of independence in the inaugural UK Code was amended in 2003 to require independent directors to be independent from both the management *and* significant shareholders.[48] The UK also amended its rules in 2014 for electing independent directors in premium-listed companies[49] with controlling shareholders to give

---

44) D. C. Clarke, 'Th ree Concepts of the Independent Director', *Delaware Journal of Corporate Law*, 32 (2007), 73, 91.

45) See Chapter 1 at IV.1; Chapter 9 (Singapore) at II.1.

46) See Chapter 1 at III.6, IV.1.

47) See Chapter 1 at IV.1; Chapter 9 (Singapore) at II.1.

48) Section 1(A.3.1), The Combined Code on Corporate Governance (Financial Reporting Council, 2003), available at www.ecgi.org. This was at the recommendation of D. Higgs, 'Review of the Role and Effectiveness of the Non-Executive Directors' (2003), available at www.ecgi.org.

49) Premium-listed companies are required to comply with UK-specific rules that are higher than the

minority shareholders a non-binding vote over their election – aiming to make independent directors a more effective mechanism for monitoring controlling shareholders.[50] Moreover, since the Global Financial Crisis, the UK has decreased its emphasis on the independence of directors, while the US has moved in the opposite direction.[51] In sum, it appears that the form and function of the UK independent director has evolved away from its US origins.

In addition, longstanding differences in UK–US corporate law and governance suggest that it is likely that independent directors in the UK and US had different functions even at the time of transplantation. The importance US corporate law places on independent directors as gatekeepers for hostile takeovers and derivative actions contrasts sharply with the UK, where independent directors play a peripheral role in such critical matters.[52] The absolute right under UK company law to remove (independent) directors at any time[53] in public companies is diametrically opposed to a history of staggered boards in listed US companies.[54] The mandatory approach of regulating independent directors in the US contrasts sharply with the UK's hallmark 'comply or explain' regulatory regime.[55] Such differences in UK–US corporate law and governance suggest that upon closer examination, even at the time of transplantation, references to an 'Anglo-American' concept of the independent director may have masked important differences. Ultimately, although the core concept of the American independent director – a managerial-monitor director, on a one-tier board, in a company with dispersed shareholders – was transplanted into the inaugural UK Code, it is clear that the UK independent director has evolved in its own way. Moreover, even at the

---

European Union minimum requirements. See London Stock Exchange, 'Listing Regime', available at www.londonstockexchange.com.

50) Where a premium-listed company has a controlling shareholder, the election and reelection of independent directors is subject to approval by the: (1) shareholders as a whole; and (2) independent (i.e., minority) shareholders. If the company fails to obtain the necessary approvals, it may propose a special resolution that: (1) must be voted on within a period of 90 to 120 days from the original vote; and (2) must be approved by the shareholders as a whole. See Listing Rule 9.2.2.AR, 9.2.2.ER and 9.2.2.F; Financial Conduct Authority, 'PS 14/8: Response to CP13/15: Enhancing the Effectiveness of the Listing Regime' (May 2014), available at www.fca.org.uk.

51) See Chapter 2.

52) See Chapter 1 at III.3; Chapter 2 at IV.4.

53) A director may be removed at any time without cause pursuant to an ordinary resolution passed by the company's shareholders: see section 168(1), Companies Act 2006, c. 46 (UK). Similar provisions are present in other jurisdictions: see section 152, Companies Act, 2006, c. 50 (Singapore); section 462, Companies Ordinance, c. 622 (Hong Kong); Art. 339, para. 1 and Art. 341, Company Law, Art No. 86 of July 26, 2005 (Japan).

54) R. Kraakman et al., *The Anatomy of Corporate Law: A Comparative and Functional Approach*, 2nd edn (Oxford University Press, 2009), 60–61.

55) See Chapter 1 at IV.1.

time of transplantation, distinct aspects of UK–US corporate law and governance required UK–US independent directors to perform different functions in different regulatory environments. This realisation does not comport with the widely held assumption of a universal concept of the independent director or even an 'Anglo-American' concept of the independent director.

For at least three reasons, this nuanced understanding of the American concept of the independent director and its evolution in the UK are essential for understanding the rise of the independent director in Asia. First, all of Asia's leading economies claim to have either explicitly adopted or been heavily influenced by the American and/or 'Anglo-American' independent director models.[56] As such, to evaluate these claims and understand their historical roots requires a clear understanding of the history of the independent director in the UK and US. Second, the clear differences that have emerged between the UK–US independent director models suggest that varieties in the form and function of the independent director in Asia should be expected. Indeed, the fact that the UK and US – two common law, English speaking, Western countries, with similar corporate board and shareholder ownership structures – have developed different concepts of the independent director suggests that diversity, rather than uniformity, among independent directors in Asia should be expected; the opposite of what conventional wisdom suggests.[57] Third, differences between UK–US independent directors and the evolution that has occurred in the UK concept suggest that claims that Asian jurisdictions have modelled their systems on the US, UK and/or 'Anglo-American' concept of the independent director should be scrutinised.

3   The Form of Independent Directors in Asia: Decisively Un-American and Surprisingly Diverse

A comparison of the jurisdiction-specific chapters in this book reveals that none of Asia's leading economies (i.e., China, India, Hong Kong, Japan, Singapore, South Korea and Taiwan) have adopted the American concept of the independent director in form and function. In its thinnest conception, the form that 'independent directors' take can be considered to be the object of their independence (i.e., what they are designed to be independent from). Based on this conception, the thinnest form of the American independent

---

56) See Chapter 4 (Japan) at II.1.a; Chapter 5 (South Korea) at II.4; Chapter 6 (China) at II.1; Chapter 7 (Taiwan) at I; Chapter 8 (Hong Kong) at II.4; Chapter 9 (Singapore) at II.3; Chapter 10 (India) at III.
57) For further discussion on convergence in corporate governance, see H. Hansmann and R. Kraakman, 'The End of History for Corporate Law', *Georgetown Law Journal*, 89 (2001), 439; Chapter 13 at II.

director is to be a director who is independent from the company's management – but not from the company's significant shareholders.[58]

Considering the US origins of the independent director and the conventional wisdom that the American concept of the independent director has become a global phenomenon,[59] it is surprising that *none* of Asia's leading economies currently use the American concept of the independent director, even in its thinnest form. Today, independent directors in all of Asia's leading economies are designed to be independent from the company's management *and* significant shareholders.[60] In fact, in China, India, Hong Kong, South Korea and Taiwan it has always been this way (i.e., none of these jurisdictions have ever used the American concept of the independent director, even in its thinnest form).[61]

Japan and Singapore stand out as two leading Asian economies that, at one time in their histories, have utilised or claimed to utilise the American concept of the independent director in its thinnest form. Japan's situation is somewhat complex. In 2002, Japan amended its company law to *ostensibly* provide the option of adopting an 'American-style board' with 'American-style independent directors'.[62] However, upon closer examination, these so-called 'American-style independent directors' were in fact defined in such a way that they were not actually required to be independent from either management or significant shareholders. In reality, these directors were only required to not work for the company or its subsidiaries (i.e., to be 'outside directors').[63] Most importantly, these so-called 'independent directors' were legally permitted to have personal connections with management and/or to be employed by significant shareholders (i.e., they did not even need to satisfy the American concept of the independent director in its thinnest form).[64] Starting in

---

58) See Chapter 1 at I.2 and III.
59) B. R. Cheffins, 'Corporate Governance Reform: Britain as an Exporter' in David Hume Institute, *Hume Papers on Public Policy: Corporate Governance and the Reform of the Company Law* (Edinburgh University Press, 2000); D. C. Langevoort, 'The Human Nature of Corporate Boards: Law, Norms, and the Unintended Consequences of Independence and Accountability', *Georgetown Law Journal*, 89 (2001), 797, 798; see also Chapter 9 (Singapore) at II.
60) See Chapter 4 (Japan) at II.1.a, II.1.b and II.1.c; W. Tanaka, 会社法 [Company Law] (2016), 212–216; Chapter 5 (South Korea) at III.2.b; Chapter 6 (China) at III.3; Chapter 7 (Taiwan) at II.1; Chapter 8 (Hong Kong) at II.2; Chapter 9 (Singapore) at II.3; Chapter 10 (India) at III.
61) See Chapter 5 (South Korea) at III.2.b; Chapter 6 (China) at III.3; Chapter 7 (Taiwan) at II.1; Chapter 8 (Hong Kong) at II.2; Chapter 10 (India) at III.
62) D. W. Puchniak, 'The 2002 Reform of the Management of Large Corporations in Japan: A Race to Somewhere?', *Australian Journal of Asian Law*, 5 (2003), 42; R. J. Gilson and C. J. Milhaupt, 'Choice as Regulatory Reform: The Case of Japanese Corporate Governance', *American Journal of Comparative Law*, 53(2) (2005), 343; P. Lawley, 'Panacea or Placebo? An Empirical Analysis of the Effect of the Japanese Committee System Corporate Governance Law Reform', *Asian-Pacific Law and Policy Journal*, 9 (2007), 105.
63) See Chapter 4 (Japan) at II.1.a.

the late 2000s, the definition of independence was gradually tightened by successive amendments to the Tokyo Stock Exchange listing rules, which required independent directors to be independent from management *and* significant large-block shareholders.[65] Finally, Japan's recently amended Companies Act expanded the definition of 'outside directors' to require them to be independent from corporate management *and* large-block shareholders.[66] Singapore stands out among Asia's leading economies as the only jurisdiction that has enthusiastically embraced the American concept of the independent director, at least in its thinnest form.[67] In 2001, Singapore explicitly designed its independent director to be independent from management, but not from significant shareholders.[68] In 2005, the Singapore government considered seriously a proposal to amend its definition of independence to require independence from management *and* significant shareholders, but this proposal was ultimately rejected.[69] It was not until the latest version of Singapore's Corporate Governance Code went into force in 2015, that its definition of independence was expanded to ostensibly require independence from management *and* significant shareholders.[70] This recent shift in Singapore's approach has moved Asia's most enthusiastic adopter of the American form of the independent director away from it.

A thicker conception of the form that 'independent directors' may take would include the position that 'independent directors' occupy within a jurisdiction's corporate governance architecture and the legal nature of such a position. According to the American concept, 'independent directors' hold positions as directors on one-tier boards with nomination, audit and remuneration committees. These positions are secured by mandatory law, which currently requires independent directors to compose a majority of board members and all board-committee members in listed companies.[71]

An examination of the positions that 'independent directors' occupy in the diverse corporate governance architectures of Asia's leading economies reveals a significant departure from this thicker conception of the form of the American independent director – with

---

64) See Chapter 4 (Japan) at II.1.a.
65) See Chapter 4 (Japan) at II.1.b.
66) See Chapter 4 (Japan) at II.1.c.
67) See Chapter 9 (Singapore) at II.4 and III.1.
68) Corporate Governance Committee, *Consultation Paper* (2000), 5, available at www.mas.gov.sg; Corporate Governance Committee, *Report of the Committee and Code of Corporate Governance* (2001), 8, available at www.acra.gov.sg; see also Chapter 9 (Singapore) at III.1.
69) The Council on Corporate Disclosure and Governance, *Consultation Paper on Proposed Revisions to the Code of Corporate Governance* (2004), 7–9, available at www.acga-asia.org.
70) Code of Corporate Governance, Art. 2.3(e)–(f), 4 n.2 (defining '10% shareholder'), 5 n.6 (defining 'directly associated'); see also Chapter 9 (Singapore) at IV.1.
71) See Chapter 1 at III.4.

China arguably providing the clearest example. All listed companies in China have a 'double board'[72] structure (i.e., a 'management board' composed of shareholder representatives who make management decisions and a 'supervisory board' composed of shareholder and employee representatives who supervise the management board and senior managers).[73] This 'double board' structure has no equivalent in American corporate governance.[74] In turn, the nature of the positions held by 'independent directors' in listed companies in China and the US are different, which is problematic for comparative analyses. Some comparative research considers all of the directors on the supervisory board of a Chinese listed company to be 'independent directors';[75] other comparative research only considers directors on the management board of a Chinese listed company who meet the Chinese definition for independence to be 'independent directors'.[76] This confusion is understandable as the Chinese and American board structures differ substantially and, therefore, the positions that 'independent directors' adopt in each jurisdiction are distinct – with no formal (or functional)[77] equivalence. This makes comparisons difficult and potentially misleading when it is assumed – which is often the case – that the nature of the positions that Chinese and American independent directors occupy are equivalent.[78]

Comparisons of independent directors in Japan and the US confront a similar problem.[79] Japan's new Companies Act allows listed companies to adopt a one-tier board, 'double board'[80]

---

72) For clarity, we refer to the two-tier board in China and Taiwan as a 'double board'. The 'double board' is distinct from the German two-tier board for a number of reasons, especially since China and Taiwan do not permit the supervisory board to appoint the management board. See Chapter 6 (China) at II.2; Chapter 7 (Taiwan) at II.1.

73) Chapter 6 (China) at II.2.

74) The 'double board' structure is derived from the German corporate governance system. See Chapter 1 at IV.3; Chapter 6 (China) at II.2; Chapter 7 (Taiwan) at II.1.

75) This assumption appears to have been made in a report issued by ISS: Gopal, 'Japan: A Closer Look at Governance Reforms'. It is unclear if supervisory board members were deemed to be independent directors for jurisdictions with two-tier boards in 'Exhibit 3: Global Comparison of Board Independence' provided in the report. A distinction should be made between supervisory board members and independent directors, especially in the case of China, where independent directors were introduced to perform the monitoring functions that supervisory board members were unable to provide. See Chapter 6 (China) at II.2. Email clarification was sought from the author of the report on 2 June 2016, but no response was forthcoming as of the publication of this book.

76) Clarke, 'The Independent Director in Chinese Corporate Governance', 150–151; Z. Yuan, 'Independent Directors in China: The Path in Which Direction?', *International Company and Commercial Law Review*, 22 (2011), 352, 354–357.

77) See II.4 below.

78) See note 75 above.

79) An ISS report on Japan's 2014 reform of its independent director regime directly compares the average percentage of board independence in Japan and the US without further elaboration on the material difference between the two regimes: Gopal, 'Japan: A Closer Look at Governance Reforms'.

80) Japan's 'double board' is distinct from the German two-tier board system, as the board of statutory auditors is not allowed to appoint or dismiss directors. A shareholder resolution is required to elect and

or hybrid board – each having distinct types of directorial positions and roles for independent directors.[81] As the vast majority of listed companies in Japan have adopted a 'double board', which is staffed by *kansayaku* (statutory auditors), the independent directors in Japan and the US occupy different types of positions. An influential school of thought suggests that members of Japan's 'supervisory board' (i.e., *kansayaku*) are essentially similar to American independent directors and, therefore, should be counted as such in multijurisdictional comparisons.[82] The more common view, however, is that only members of the 'management board' who meet the Japanese definition for independence should be considered to be 'independent directors'.[83] However, directors on the 'management board' are monitored by the 'supervisory board' staff ed by *kansayaku*, which by definition makes their position and responsibilities distinct in form from American independent directors.[84]

In Taiwan, the company law has recently been amended to require large companies to abandon the 'double board' and adopt a one-tier board by the end of 2017.[85] As such, from 2018, the nature of the position held by independent directors in Taiwan will be broadly comparable to American independent directors, at least in this one aspect. Similarly, listed companies in Hong Kong, India, Singapore and South Korea have one-tier board structures, making independent directors in these jurisdictions also comparable to American independent directors, at least in this one aspect of their forms.

A second aspect of this thicker conception of the form of independent directors is the legal nature of their positions. In the US, mandatory law requires independent directors to com-

---

dismiss directors (and statutory auditors): Arts. 329 and 339, Companies Act; see also Gilson and Milhaupt, 'Choice as Regulatory Reform', 343, 348.

81) Goto, 'The Outline for the Companies Act Reform in Japan and Its Implications', 17–19; Chapter 4 (Japan) at II.1; Chapter 12 at IV.1.

82) B. E. Aronson, 'Japanese Corporate Governance Reform: A Comparative Perspective', *Hastings Business Law Journal*, 11 (2015), 85, 98–102. That foreign investors fail to understand this is a frequent lament amongst Japan insiders. In a provocative article, Matsunaka argues that the *kansayaku* have evolved over time to resemble directors so much that they have effectively lost their independent identity, leading to an 'identity crisis'. M. Matsunaka, '監査役のアイデンティティ・クライシス' [The Kansayaku's Identity Crisis], 商事法務, 1957 (2012), 4. See also シンポジウム　監査役制度の正しい理解のために [Panel Discussion on Correctly Understanding the *Kansayaku* Regime], '各界から見た日本のコーポレート・ガバナンスと監査役制度' [The *Kansayaku* Regime and Corporate Governance in Japan from the Perspectives of Diff erent Interest Groups], 月刊監査役, 613 (2013), 4, which featured representatives from the University of Tokyo, *Keidanren*, ISS, Tokyo Stock Exchange, Toyota and the professional association representing *kansayaku*. However, *kansayaku* are distinct from American independent directors for multiple reasons, including their inability to vote at board meetings and participate in decisions regarding the appointment and removal of managers. See Chapter 4 (Japan) at III.2.a.

83) See Chapter 4 (Japan) generally, which adopts the conventional approach that statutory auditors are *not* independent directors.

84) See Chapter 4 (Japan) at II.1.a.

85) See Chapter 7 (Taiwan) at II.3.

pose a majority of board members and all board-committee members in listed companie s.[86] In Asia's leading economies, Japan represents the other extreme as it is the only leading Asian economy in which mandatory law does not require *any* independent directors in listed companies.[87] In contrast, South Korean company law mandates that all large listed companies have a majority of independent directors on their boards.[88] India and Taiwan's regulatory approaches have evolved in a similar way over time: they both first introduced the independent director on a 'comply or explain' basis; and later implemented mandatory law for a minimum number/proportion of 'independent directors' after optional law did not achieve the level of independence the government desired.[89] Singapore evolved in the opposite direction: it first introduced minimal mandatory requirements for the number of independent directors; and later implemented a UK-style 'comply or explain' code to increase the number of 'independent directors' to a level that the government desired.[90]

Finally, the thickest conception of the form of the independent director may include the personal characteristics that the typical independent director in a jurisdiction brings to the position. Again, there appears to be significant differences between independent directors in the US and Asia's leading economies based on this thickest conception of form. In the US, the vast majority of independent directors are corporate executives from other companies.[91] In China, however, historically almost half of all directors on the boards of listed companies have been university professors – a trend which is also prevalent, but less pronounced, in South Korea, Taiwan and India.[92] For China, Singapore and South Korea, the formal and informal connections that independent directors have with the government tend to be more pronounced than in other jurisdictions, but for different reasons in each jurisdiction.[93] In Japan, independent directors tend to be lifetime employees and to have connections with other companies in *keiretsu* - affiliated firms.[94] In Singapore, informal connections that in-

---

86) § 303A.01, § 303A.04–06 NYSE Listed Company Manual; § IM-5605-1, § IM-5605-4, § IM-5605-5, § IM-5605-6, § IM-5605-7 NASDAQ Stock Market Rules.

87) However, Japan recently strengthened its promotion of independent directors by changing its purely optional regulation of independent directors to a UK-style 'comply or explain' regime, which requires companies to explain if they have no independent directors. See Chapter 4 (Japan) at II.1.c.

88) See Chapter 5 (South Korea) at III.2.a.

89) See Chapter 7 (Taiwan) at II.1; Chapter 10 (India) at V.3.

90) See Chapter 9 (Singapore) at II.4 and IV.2.

91) R. J. Gilson and R. Kraakman, 'Reinventing the Outside Director: An Agenda for Institutional Investors', *Stanford Law Review*, 43 (1991), 863, 872; S. Ferris et al., 'Too Busy to Mind the Business? Monitoring by Directors with Multiple Board Appointments', *Journal of Finance*, 58 (2003), 1087.

92) See Chapter 5 (South Korea) at IV.4; Chapter 7 (Taiwan) at II.2.b; Chapter 10 (India) at IV.2.

93) See Chapter 6 (China) at II.3; Chapter 9 (Singapore) at III.3; Chapter 5 (South Korea) at IV.4.

94) Lawley, 'Panacea or Placebo?', 105, 135.

dependent directors in family firms have with family controllers tend to be a defining characteristic in such firms – which also likely plays an important role in most other leading Asian economies as family controlled corporations make up a large portion of listed firms in most jurisdictions (with the notable exception of Japan).[95]

The proportion of the board of listed companies that is composed of independent directors is also a critically important aspect of the thickest conception of the form of independent directors. Today, the typical board of a listed company in the US is composed entirely of 'independent directors', except for the CEO.[96] As suggested above, due to the diversity in definitions for independence and varieties of positions held by directors who may be considered to be 'independent directors', statistics reporting the number of 'independent directors' in Asia's leading economies vary considerably depending on the criteria used by the surveyor for identifying which directors should be counted as being 'independent directors'. For example, in China, the ISS survey, which appears to have counted supervisory board members as independent directors, reported that almost 70 per cent of boards in China had a majority of independent directors;[97] another survey by the Asian Corporate Governance Association, which appears to only count members of the management board designated as independent directors, reported that approximately 20 per cent of boards in China had a majority of independent directors.[98] Even in the face of this uncertainty, however, there are no statistics suggesting that any of Asia's leading economies have approached US-levels of having (or even labelling) the entire board, except for the CEO, as independent directors. At least on a self-reporting basis (i.e., without definitional differences being scrutinised) and if the supervisory board members are not considered to be 'independent directors', it appears that the level of board independence varies widely across Asia's leading economies. On this basis, the typical board of a large listed company in India, Singapore and South Korea tends to report having a majority of 'independent directors'; in China and Hong Kong the typical board reports having one-third to half 'independent directors'; and in Japan and Taiwan the typical board reports having one or two 'independent directors'.[99] In sum, there is a significant difference in the forms that 'independent directors' take in the US and Asia's leading economies. This difference is seen in the thinnest conception of

---

95) S. Claessens et al., 'The Separation of Ownership and Control in East Asian Corporations', *Journal of Financial Economics*, 58 (2000), 81, 102–103; Chapter 9 (Singapore) at III.2.
96) Velikonja, 'The Political Economy of Board Independence', 857.
97) Gopal, 'Japan: A Closer Look at Governance Reforms'.
98) ACGA and KPMG, *Balancing Rules and Flexibility* (2014), available at www.accaglobal.com.
99) *Ibid.*; Gopal, 'Japan: A Closer Look at Governance Reforms'.

form, as the American form focuses on independence from management; whereas, the form that has emerged in Asia's leading economies focuses on independence from management *and* significant shareholders. Magnifying this difference is the fact that the very nature of the positions that independent directors in Asia's leading economies occupy are in some jurisdictions fundamentally different than in the US. Moreover, the use of (or even complete reliance on, in the case of Japan) non-mandatory regulation of independent directors in many of Asia's leading economies is distinct from the reliance on mandatory regulation in the US. Finally, the unique and diverse characteristics and skills of independent directors and the smaller proportion of independent directors on boards further distinguish the form (and, as explained below, also the function) of the 'independent director' in Asia's leading economies from the US.

Perhaps more interesting is that there are important similarities and differences in the forms of the 'independent director' *within* Asia. The most salient intra-Asia similarity is that all of Asia's leading economies have gravitated towards a concept of the independent director designed to be independent from management *and* significant shareholders – which is clearly distinct from the American concept.[100] Despite this core similarity, what has been almost entirely overlooked are the diverse varieties of forms of the 'independent director' in Asia, at least based on a thicker conception of form. In jurisdictions that mandate one-tier boards (i.e., Hong Kong, India, Singapore and South Korea) the positions occupied by independent directors are broadly comparable to the American form, at least in this aspect. However, in jurisdictions that permit non-one-tier boards (Japan, China, and Taiwan until 2018) the distinct nature of these positions complicates any direct comparison. There is also intra-Asia diversity in the non-mandatory (Japan), mandatory (China and South Korea) and hybrid mandatory/non-mandatory (Hong Kong, India, Singapore and Taiwan) approaches that exist in terms of implementing and regulating independent directors. Finally, there are similarities in the prominent characteristics and skills of independent directors among some of Asia's leading jurisdictions (e.g., in China, India, South Korea and Taiwan academics make up a sizable portion of independent directors), but not others – further highlighting varieties in the thicker conception of the form of independent directors in Asia's leading economies.

---

100) As Puchniak and Lan confirm empirically in Chapter 9 (Singapore) at II.2, the trend towards an 'un-American' form of the independent director is a global phenomenon that has been largely overlooked.

4 The Functions of Independent Directors in Asia: Diverse Expectations Revealed

There is an obvious link between the form that independent directors take and the function that they perform. As such, the significant differences between the forms of independent directors in Asia's leading economies and the US suggest that there are likely to be differences in their functions. Similarly, the diversity in the forms of independent directors among Asia's leading economies suggests that there is also likely to be functional diversity among independent directors within Asia. It cannot be assumed, however, that merely because independent directors have the same form that they will perform the same function, or that independent directors that have different forms will perform different functions. Indeed, as explained below, the unique and diverse contexts in each of Asia's leading economies suggest that the relationship between form and function is complex and highly jurisdiction-specific.

It is also important to remain cognisant of the difference between the function that independent directors are expected to perform and how independent directors *actually* function in practice. Although these two aspects of functionality are distinct, they are also interrelated. How independent directors are expected to function, may influence how they actually function and vice versa. For analytical purposes, however, it expected functions and then the actual functions of independent directors in Asia's leading economies and the US. As explained above, since the genesis of the American independent director in the 1970s, the primary expected function of independent directors in the US has been clear: to monitor management on behalf of dispersed shareholders, who are hindered by collective action problems from monitoring management themselves.[101] By contrast, the primary expected function of independent directors in most of Asia's leading economies is to monitor controlling shareholders on behalf of minority shareholders, in order to mitigate the risk of the former extracting private benefits of control from the company.[102]

---

101) See Chapter 1 at III.2.

102) 'Private benefits of control (i.e., benefits that the controlling shareholder receives as a result of their controlling power, which are not provided to the minority shareholders). A common example of private benefits of control is when a controlling shareholder causes the company to sell a piece of its property, at below market value, to a company the controlling shareholder wholly owns. In such a case, the private benefit that the controlling shareholder receives increases proportionally as the percentage of the controlling shareholder's equity stake in the company decreases. In this common example, the controlling shareholder can be seen to have used her controlling power to extract a financial benefit from the company that was greater than the proportion of her equity stake.' Puchniak, 'Multiple Faces of Shareholder Power in Asia', 527. See also R. J. Gilson and J. N. Gordon,

In China, India, Hong Kong, South Korea and Taiwan, the expectation that independent directors would primarily act as monitors of controlling shareholders is evident in the policy discussions and academic commentaries surrounding the adoption of independent directors in each jurisdiction.[103] This expectation is also evident in the inaugural definitions that these jurisdictions adopted for 'independence' which, as explained above, all generally provide that independent directors should be independent from significant shareholders.[104] Thus, although there are claims that some of these jurisdictions were inspired by the US concept of the independent director,[105] this inspiration appears to have had little or no influence on the actual details of the policy discussions and/or legislative drafting in terms of the function that independent directors were (and are) expected to actually perform in these jurisdictions.

In this context, Japan and Singapore are outliers among Asia's leading economies as independent directors in both countries have *not* historically been expected to play almost any role in monitoring controlling shareholders. This is clear in the policy discussions and academic commentaries surrounding the adoption of independent directors in both countries.[106] Also, as explained above, notably in both countries the inaugural definitions for 'independence' did *not* require independence from significant shareholders.[107] In fact, in Singapore, the policy committee and regulatory authority made it explicitly clear that the primary expected function of independent directors was to act as managerial-monitors – but not monitors of controlling shareholders.[108]

The policy debates surrounding the adoption of independent directors in Singapore suggest that another important reason for their adoption was to send a signal to international investors that Singapore has 'good' corporate governance.[109] It appears that in several of Asia's leading economies there was (and still is) an expectation among government officials and companies that the adoption of independent directors will function as an important signal of 'good' corporate governance to domestic and international investors.[110] For rea-

---

'Controlling Controlling Shareholders', *University of Pennsylvania Law Review*, 152 (2004), 785.
103) See Chapter 5 (South Korea) at III.1 and III.2.b; Chapter 6 (China) at II.1; Chapter 7 (Taiwan) at III.3.a; Chapter 8 (Hong Kong) at II.2 and II.4; Chapter 10 (India) at V.1 and V.2.
104) See Chapter 5 (South Korea) at III.2.b; Chapter 6 (China) at III.3; Chapter 7 (Taiwan) at II.1; Chapter 8 (Hong Kong) at II.2; Chapter 10 (India) at V.2.
105) See Chapter 7 (Taiwan) at I.
106) See Chapter 4 (Japan) at III.1; Chapter 9 (Singapore) at II.3 and II.4.
107) See Chapter 4 (Japan) at III.1; Chapter 9 (Singapore) at II.3 and II.4.
108) See Chapter 9 (Singapore) at II.4.
109) See Chapter 9 (Singapore) at II.4.
110) See Chapter 4 (Japan) at III.1; Chapter 5 (South Korea) at III.1; Chapter 8 (Hong Kong) at II.4; Chapter 10 (India) at V.1.

sons explained in section III below, however, it appears that this function of independent directors was likely of greater importance in Singapore and lesser importance in Japan, at least in comparison to other leading Asian economies.

Further, some civil law jurisdictions adopted independent directors to address the specific shortcomings of the supervisory board or its local equivalent under their respective corporate law regimes. In China and Taiwan, where double boards are permitted, the primary motivation for the adoption of independent directors was to address the perceived failure of their supervisory boards.[111] In South Korea, the inaugural mandatory independent regime replaced the traditional statutory auditors with an audit committee composed primarily of independent directors in large listed companies.[112] In Japan, independent directors were expected to address the perceived failure of the board of statutory auditors to effectively monitor traditional lifetime-employee-dominated 'management boards' in large Japanese companies. Japan's inaugural independent director system encouraged companies to adopt an 'American-style' one-tier board with sub-committees, under which a board of statutory auditors was not (and is still not) permitted.[113] By contrast, in China, independent directors are expected to function as members of the management board who act as complementary monitors (and not substitute monitors) to the supervisory board – with the supervisory board still monitoring the independent directors and the other members of the management board.[114] Another important driver of the adoption and reforms of Japan's independent director system has been the government's desire to signal its effective management of Japan's economic malaise.[115] There is considerable evidence in other leading Asian economies (and the US and EU) that governments – especially in the wake of poor economic performance and/or a financial crisis – often implement legislation with the aim of encouraging independent directors to signal effective political governance.[116] Although governments in several of Asia's leading economies (and the US and EU) have implemented and reformed their independent

---

111) See Chapter 6 (China) at II.2; Chapter 7 (Taiwan) at II.1.
112) See Chapter 5 (South Korea) at III.1.b; K. S. Kim, 'Transplanting Audit Committees to Korean Soil: A Window into the Evolution of Korean Corporate Governance', *Asian-Pacific Law and Policy Journal*, 9 (2007), 163, 164.
113) See Chapter 4 (Japan) at II.1; Puchniak, 'The 2002 Reform of the Management of Large Corporations in Japan', 49–56; Gilson and Milhaupt, 'Choice as Regulatory Reform', 352–353.
114) See Chapter 6 (China) at II.2 and III.4.d; J. Zhao, 'Comparative Study of U.S. and German Corporate Governance: Suggestions on the Relationship between Independent Directors and the Supervisory Board of Listed Companies in China', *Michigan State Journal of International Law*, 18 (2010), 495, 506 –507, 507 n. 76 (observing that the functions of independent directors in this context are 'more operable and direct').
115) See Chapter 4 (Japan) at III.2.
116) See Chapter 2 at II; Chapter 5 (South Korea) at III.1; Chapter 8 (Hong Kong) at II.4; Chapter 9 (Singapore) at II.4.

director regimes with the expectation that they will function as a signal of effective political governance, for reasons explained below, this expected function appears to have been particularly salient in the evolution of Japan's independent director system.[117]

Finally, it is important to note that Japan and Singapore have recently reformed their independent director systems with the expectation that one of the functions of their independent directors will be to monitor controlling shareholders.[118] Although the reforms in both countries have been cautious and limited,[119] they suggest a movement towards Asia's other leading economies (and away from the US) as independent directors are increasingly being seen as a corporate governance mechanism which is expected to monitor controlling shareholders.[120]

In sum, it appears that the expected functions of independent directors in Asia's leading economies differ significantly from the US. The main point of divergence is that in most of Asia's leading economies the primary expected function of independent directors is to monitor controlling shareholders, whereas in the US this is not the case. Within Asia, jurisdictions that currently allow or previously allowed double boards, have expected independent directors to either complement or substitute for ineffective supervisory boards – distinguishing them from common law jurisdictions which historically have had one-tier board structures. Finally, although the expectation that independent directors will function as a signal of 'good' corporate governance and/or political effectiveness appears to exist in many of Asia's leading economies, the importance of these functions appears to vary from jurisdiction to jurisdiction in Asia (and, we suspect, elsewhere).

5 The Actual Functions of Independent Directors in Asia: Empirical Ambiguity and Contextual Idiosyncrasy

Determining whether the expected functions of independent directors are actually put into practice is extremely difficult and complex. At the most general level, the question that is often asked to determine whether independent directors have fulfilled their expected functions has been similar in most jurisdictions: do independent directors improve corporate performance? Despite the widespread adoption of 'independent directors' and a litany of empiri-

---

117) See Chapter 4 (Japan) at III.2.
118) See Chapter 4 (Japan) at II.1.c and Chapter 9 (Singapore) at IV.2.
119) See Chapter 9 (Singapore) at IV.2 (observing that the Singapore's definition of 'independence' is likely to bring about a functional rather than substantive change).
120) See Chapter 9 (Singapore) at V.

cal studies, there is a surprising absence of clear empirical evidence in the United States, the EU and Asia that independent directors actually improve corporate performance.[121]

In Asia, on balance, most of the empirical evidence has failed to find a definitive link between independent directors and corporate performance.[122] However, there are a few empirical studies in Japan,[123] Hong Kong[124] and South Korea[125] that suggest that independent directors, in certain situations, may improve corporate performance.[126] Considering that the extensive empirical research on independent directors in the US has been unable to produce clear evidence that independent directors improve corporate performance, it is unsurprising that such evidence remains elusive in Asia. Moreover, as explained above, the diversity in the form and function of 'independent directors' within Asia suggests that any interjurisdictional attempt to evaluate the impact of independent directors across Asia will be fraught with methodical problems and compromised by the interjurisdictional diversity in the form and function of independent directors.[127]

It should be noted that most of the research that considers the effectiveness of independent directors has examined their impact at the firm level – but not the jurisdictional level.[128] There has been little empirical analysis on whether adopting independent directors, which may improve the image of a jurisdiction's corporate governance, has a positive macro-

---

121) See, for example, Chapter 1 at V; Chapter 2 at II.2 and IV.2; Velikonja, 'The Political Economy of Board Independence', 855, 859–860, 868–872; S. Bhagat and B. S. Black, 'The Non-Correlation between Board Independence and Long-Term Firm Performance', *Journal of Corporation Law*, 27 (2002), 231, 239; Y. Miwa and J. M. Ramseyer, 'Who Appoints Them, What Do They Do? Evidence on Outside Directors from Japan', *Journal of Economics and Management Strategy*, 14 (2005), 299.

122) See Chapter 9 (Singapore) at II.1; Chapter 10 (India) at IV.1; see also A. K. Garg, 'Influence of Board Size and Independence on Firm Performance: A Study of Indian Companies', *Vikalpa*, 32 (2007) 39; Ibrahim and Samad, 'Corporate Governance Mechanisms and Performance of Public-Listed Family-Ownership in Malaysia'; Prabowo and Simpson, 'Independent Directors and Firm Performance in Family Controlled Firms: Evidence from Indonesia'.

123) See Chapter 4 (Japan) at III.1.

124) See Chapter 8 (Hong Kong) at III.4; A. Lei and D. Deng, 'Do Multiple Directorships Increase Firm Value? Evidence from Independent Directors in Hong Kong', *Journal of International Financial Management and Accounting*, 25(2) (2014), 121; see also F. Cheng, 'Corporate Governance in Hong Kong: An Empirical Study of the Effects of Independent Non-Executive Directors on Voluntary Corporate Disclosures and Adoption of Best Corporate Governance Practices' (City University of Hong Kong Institutional Repository, 2011) available at http://dspace.cityu.edu.hk; B. Jaggi and J. Tsui, 'Insider Trading Earnings Management and Corporate Governance: Empirical Evidence Based on Hong Kong Firms', *Journal of International Financial Management and Accounting*, 18(3) (2007), 192.

125) B. S. Black et al., 'Methods for Multicountry Studies of Corporate Governance: Evidence from the BRIKT Countries', *Journal of Econometrics*, 183 (2014), 230.

126) See Chapter 4 (Japan) at III.1; Chapter 5 (South Korea) at IV.1.

127) See II.3 and II.4 above.

128) See, for example, Bhagat and Black, 'The Non-Correlation between Board Independence and Long-Term Firm Performance', 231–274 (surveying 934 of the largest US firms from 1985 to 1995); Gordon, 'The Rise of Independent Directors in the United States', 1465–1568 (reviewing overall trends in board composition in US public companies from 1950 to 2005).

economic impact. In addition, there has been limited analysis on whether the use of regulations promoting independent directors as a signal of good political governance is actually an effective political strategy.[129]

Perhaps even more interesting are the idiosyncratic and unanticipated functions that independent directors have come to perform in Asia's leading economies. Partially as a result of pressure from the IMF following the Asian Financial Crisis, South Korea adopted mandatory legislation, which now requires the boards of all large listed companies to have a majority of independent directors.[130] There has been an increasing trend to fill these mandatory independent director positions with ex-government officials so that they can function as government lobbyists.[131] It is suggested that a reason that independent directors may be increasingly fulfilling this function in South Korea is because Korean law strictly prohibits companies from retaining professional government lobbyists – driving companies to fill the mandated 'independent director' positions with clandestine government lobbyists.[132]

In Japan, there is evidence that when the inaugural independent director system was adopted that the loose definition for independence allowed companies in *keiretsu* groups to fill 'independent director' positions with senior management from other *keiretsu* - affiliated companies. The reason suggested for this behaviour was that it allowed *keiretsu* - affiliated companies to signal 'good' corporate governance, while at the same time reinforcing their corporate group links.[133] This is the direct opposite of the role that scholars and policymakers in other jurisdictions expect independent directors to play in group companies.[134]

In Singapore, there is empirical evidence that its inaugural American-style definition of independence allowed family-controlled firms (Family Firms) to systematically appoint family friends as independent directors. This allowed Family Firms to signal their compliance with 'good' corporate governance, while effectively preserving the status quo of family controllers dominating the corporate governance in such firms.[135] However, there is qualitative evi-

---

129) See, for example, Chapter 2 at II.3; Chapter 4 (Japan) at III.2; Velikonja, 'The Political Economy of Board Independence', 855, 892–915 (arguing that reforms directed at improving board independence has displaced substantive reform following corporate crises or scandals)

130) See Chapter 5 (South Korea) at III.2.

131) See Chapter 5 (South Korea) at IV.4.

132) See Chapter 5 (South Korea) at IV.4.

133) Lawley, 'Panacea or Placebo?', 117–119, 135.

134) This was precisely the intended role for independent directors in respect of South Korea's *chaebols* (i.e., corporate groups): Chapter 5 (South Korea) at III.1.a and III.1.b; A. C. Pritchard, 'Monitoring of Corporate Groups by Independent Directors', *Journal of Korean Law*, 9 (2009), 1, 18–19 (opining that independent directors should constrain the power of controlling shareholders in South Korea's *chaebols*).

135) See Chapter 9 (Singapore) at III.2; Y. T. Mak and T. Ng, 'Independent Directors: A Well-Functioning Market', *Business Times*, 16 September 2010.

dence that suggests that these family-friendly directors have in some cases served a valuable function in Family Firms by acting as trusted mediators between family member block shareholders in family-shareholder disputes.[136] Conversely, in Singapore's Government Linked Companies, independent directors appear to play a purely managerial-monitoring role as Singapore's unique institutional architecture has purposefully limited the ability of the government to exercise its full powers as a controlling shareholder.[137] This demonstrates that even within a single jurisdiction independent directors may function differently in companies with different types of shareholders – something which there is also evidence of in India.[138]

There are more examples in this book of unique, jurisdiction-specific, functions that independent directors have come to play in each of Asia's leading economies. What these examples make clear, is that there is a litany of diverse, idiosyncratic, jurisdiction-specific functions that are carried out by 'independent directors' in Asia's leading economies. These functions would have been beyond the wildest dreams of Professor Eisenberg, the 'founding father' of the (American) independent director in the 1970s.[139] Interestingly, the actual functions that 'independent directors' in Asia's leading economies now perform are a far cry from Eisenberg's conception of independent directors as monitors of management on behalf of dispersed shareholders.[140]

III Understanding the Diverse Varieties of Independent Directors in Asia: A Taxonomy

1 Building the Foundation for a Loose Taxonomy of Independent Directors in Asia

The revelation that *none* of Asia's leading economies have adopted the American concept of the independent director in form and function calls into question some of the most influential comparative corporate governance indices and research, which assume the opposite

---

136) See Chapter 9 (Singapore) at III.2; W. Ng and J. Roberts, '"Helping the Family": The Mediating Role of Outside Directors in Ethnic Chinese Family Firms', *Human Relations*, 60 (2007), 285.
137) See Chapter 9 (Singapore) at III.3.
138) See Chapter 10 (India) at II.
139) M. A. Eisenberg, *The Structure of the Corporation: A Legal Analysis* (Little, Brown and Co., 1976).
140) See Chapter 1 at III.2; Chapter 9 (Singapore) at II.1.

to be true.[141] An awareness of the varieties in the forms and functions of independent directors *within* Asia is an important reminder that local context is central to corporate governance, which undermines a prominent movement in comparative corporate governance to develop universal theories.[142] However, it is easier to demonstrate that an American-centric (universal) understanding of the 'independent director' in Asia is flawed, than to explain why diverse (un-American) varieties of independent directors have developed. Nevertheless, understanding this development is important as it provides an avenue for improving comparative analyses of independent directors in Asia which, as explained below, has significant practical and theoretical value.

An in-depth comparative analysis of the jurisdiction-specific chapters in this book reveals that there are six principal factors that help explain the evolution of independent directors in Asia (which are ranked generally in their approximate order of importance): (1) shareholder ownership structures; (2) legal origin; (3) types of shareholders; (4) functional substitutes; (5) political economy; and (6) cultural norms. Understanding how each of these factors has shaped the development of independent directors in Asia illuminates the similarities among certain aspects in the forms and functions of independent directors in Asia, and provides meaningful avenues for comparative analyses. Conversely, examining these six factors also highlights the distinct nature of the varieties of independent directors in Asia; this helps to explain why comparisons between independent directors in the US and Asia often have limited value, and why nuanced comparisons between independent directors among certain Asian jurisdictions on particular issues may produce useful insights.

These six factors provide an explanation for the evolution of varieties of independent directors in Asia and the foundation for developing a loose taxonomy of independent directors in Asia. This taxonomy, which is described in more detail below, allows for tailored inter-jurisdictional comparisons, which focus on categories (or subcategories) of the different varieties of independent directors in multiple Asian jurisdictions that share similar forms and/or functions – thus lending themselves to more meaningful comparative analyses. Ultimately, as illustrated below, systematic identification of comparable varieties of in-

---

141) See note 27 above.
142) See, for example, Chapter 13 at II (explaining how the development of independent directors in Asia challenges the 'convergence in corporate governance' theory); D. W. Puchniak, 'The Complexity of Derivative Actions in Asia: An Inconvenient Truth' in D. W. Puchniak et al. (eds.), *The Derivative Action in Asia: A Comparative and Functional Approach* (Cambridge University Press, 2012), 124–127; D. W. Puchniak, 'The Derivative Action in Asia: A Complex Reality', *Berkeley Business Law Journal*, 9 (2013), 1, 24–28. See also, P. Legrand, 'Noted Publications: Puchniak, Dan W., Harald Baum and Michael Ewing-Chow (eds.). The Derivative Action in Asia. Cambridge, Cambridge University Press, 2012', *Journal of Comparative Law*, 7 (2012), 347.

dependent directors in Asia results in comparative research that produces more accurate and insightful results, which is one of the goals of this book.

2 The Six Principal Factors Driving the Varieties of Independent Directors in Asia

The first factor, which appears to have played the strongest role in the un-American evolution of independent directors in Asia, is the difference in the shareholder ownership structures between listed companies in the US and Asia's leading economies.[143] As explained above, the managerial-monitoring model of the independent director in the US was created to address the collective action problems which are inherent in companies with dispersed shareholders.[144] In the context of American corporate governance, the evolution of the managerial-monitoring model of the independent director makes perfect sense as public companies with dispersed shareholders have traditionally predominated in the US.[145]

However, in all of Asia's leading economies – with the notable exception of Japan[146] – most companies have a concentrated shareholder structure.[147] This reorients the primary agency problem in listed companies from managerial rent seeking to block shareholders extracting private benefits of control.[148] Most policymakers in Asia's leading economies appear to be acutely aware of this difference between corporate governance in the US and Asia, and have clearly recognised the function of the independent director as a monitor of controlling shareholders in their respective jurisdictions.[149]

The US independent director was neither intended nor designed to address agency problems arising from concentrated shareholder ownership.[150] This raises a critical question: are independent directors well-suited to function as a mechanism for monitoring significant shareholders to mitigate private benefits of control? It is difficult for an independent director to be an independent monitor of the very shareholders who can appoint and remove

---

143) Most of the jurisdictions surveyed in this book are dominated by companies with concentrated ownership. See Chapter 5 (South Korea) at II.3; Chapter 6 (China) at I and II.1; Chapter 7 (Taiwan) at II.4; Chapter 8 (Hong Kong) at II.4; Chapter 9 (Singapore) at I; Chapter 10 (India) at II.3.

144) See II.2 above.

145) However, the increased involvement of institutional investors complicates this characterisation: R. J. Gilson and J. N. Gordon, 'The Agency Costs of Agency Capitalism: Activist Investors and the Revaluation of Governance Rights', *Columbia Law Review*, 113 (2013), 863.

146) See Chapter 4 (Japan) at II.3.

147) See Chapter 5 (South Korea) at II.3; Chapter 6 (China) at II.1; Chapter 7 (Taiwan) at II.4; Chapter 8 (Hong Kong) at II.4; Chapter 9 (Singapore) at I; Chapter 10 (India) at II.

148) Kraakman et al., *The Anatomy of Corporate Law*, 307–309.

149) See note 103 above.

150) See Chapter 1 at V.

her. Ensuring that independent directors are actually independent from majority and/or controlling shareholders is a common issue raised in most of the jurisdiction-specific chapters[151] – illustrating the value of interjurisdictional comparisons of independent directors *within* Asia as a method for identifying and analysing critical issues that may improve their effectiveness.

Taiwan is the only Asian jurisdiction examined in this book that has attempted to address this problem directly by requiring mandatory cumulative voting, but it appears that this has been largely ineffective in creating meaningful independence from the controlling shareholders.[152] Given the flaws inherent in majority shareholder rule, it is curious that Taiwan has been the only jurisdiction to make a serious attempt at finding an alternative mechanism for appointing independent directors.[153]

Unfortunately, the reasons behind Taiwan's failure to effectively reform its shareholder voting system are still unclear – suggesting that future comparative research on this issue would be valuable.[154]

The second factor that appears to have driven the evolution of varieties of independent directors in Asia is the legal origins of Asia's leading economies and, perhaps more importantly, the origins of the specific provisions regulating each jurisdiction's particular independent director regime (which often appear to be distinct from the jurisdiction's general legal origin or 'legal family'). As explained above, board structure impacts significantly the forms that independent directors take and functions that they perform.[155] All of Asia's leading economies with civil law origins (i.e., China, Japan, South Korea and Taiwan) have historically permitted non-one-tier boards; whereas, all of Asia's leading economies with common law origins (i.e., Hong Kong, India and Singapore) have traditionally required (and still require) one-tier boards.[156] At first blush, this suggests that it may make sense to bifurcate comparative analyses according to the jurisdiction's civil law and common law origins.

---

151) See Chapter 6 (China) at III; Chapter 7 (Taiwan) at IV; Chapter 8 (Hong Kong) at III.2; Chapter 10 (India) at II.

152) See Chapter 7 (Taiwan) at II.3.

153) The corporate statutes of South Korea do require cumulative voting, but allow a firm to opt out of it by putting a provision in the articles of incorporation (Korean Commercial Code Art. 382-2(1)). An overwhelming majority of listed firms have opted out of cumulative voting.

154) One possible solution would be to grant a third-party *locus standi* to nominate directors: Tan, 'Corporate Governance and Independent Directors', 385–386.

155) See II.3 above.

156) See Chapter 8 (Hong Kong) at I; S. Mehrotra, 'Corporate Board Structure in the United States and India: A Comparative View', *Indian Journal of Corporate Governance*, 8 (2015), 166, 167.

However, a more in-depth analysis suggests that such an approach would be flawed. The importance of the *general* origins of a jurisdiction's legal system and/or company law are often usurped by the legal origin of the *specific* corporate governance provision and/or reform being examined. US law had a clear influence on reforms to implement one-tier boards in Japan (optional, from 2003),[157] South Korea (mandatory, from 2000)[158] and Taiwan (mandatory, from 2018).[159] Post-reform, the form and function of independent directors in these historically civil law jurisdictions became more comparable with independent directors in historically common law jurisdictions.[160] In a similar vein, as might be expected, the use of a UK-style code of corporate governance, which employs an optional 'comply or explain' approach, was first adopted in Asia's leading economies with Commonwealth origins (i.e., Hong Kong (from 2005) and Singapore (from 2001)).[161] However, in 2015, Japan – a country with a civil law legal origin and no strong historical connection to the Commonwealth – adopted a code of corporate governance based on the UK 'comply or explain' model.[162]

In sum, although the civil law and common law legal origins of Asia's leading economies are not irrelevant, classifying independent director regimes for the purpose of comparison solely along these lines would be misguided. However, it appears that there is value in tracing the origins of a *specific* provision back to its source. Such a tailored approach may provide useful grounds for comparison with the source provision (e.g., comparing the effectiveness of 'comply or explain' codes for promoting independent directors in Japan and the UK) and/ or with other jurisdictions that also trace the origin of a specific provision to the same source (e.g., comparing the effectiveness of 'comply or explain' codes for promoting independent directors in Hong Kong, India, Singapore and, now, Japan).

The third factor that appears to have driven the evolution of varieties of independent directors in Asia are the different types of shareholders that exist in Asia's leading economies.[163] In all of Asia's leading economies – with the notable exception of Japan – a significant portion of listed companies are Family Firms, where family members are the controlling shareholders.[164] There is empirical evidence from Singapore that independent directors in

---

157) See Chapter 4 (Japan) at II.1.a.
158) See Chapter 5 (South Korea) at III.1.b.
159) See Chapter 7 (Taiwan) at II.1.
160) See Chapter 4 (Japan) at II.1.a; Chapter 5 (South Korea) at II.1 and II.4; Chapter 7 (Taiwan) at IV.1.
161) See Chapter 8 (Hong Kong) at II.4; Chapter 9 (Singapore) at II.4.
162) See Chapter 4 (Japan) at II.1.c.
163) Puchniak, 'Multiple Faces of Shareholder Power in Asia', 514.
164) See Chapter 5 (South Korea) at II.3; Chapter 7 (Taiwan) at II.4; Chapter 8 (Hong Kong) at II.4; Chapter 9 (Singapore) at III.2; Chapter 10 (India) at II.

Family Firms tend to be family friends.[165] However, qualitative evidence suggests that these family friends often use their unique position as trusted non-family members to play a valuable role mediating intra-family shareholder disputes.[166] The uniqueness of the expected and/or actual function of independent directors in Family Firms may be amplified by the sometimes different incentives for family-member controlling shareholders compared to other controlling shareholders (e.g., family-controllers may want to pass on a successful business to future generations – something often particularly prized in Asian cultures – which may mitigate the risk of excessive private benefits of control).[167] This suggests that further research on the role of independent directors in Family Firms may be particularly valuable for Asia's leading economies.

A prominent feature in China, Hong Kong, India and Singapore, which distinguishes these jurisdictions from the US and other leading Asian economies, is the importance of listed companies that have the government as their controlling shareholder (Government Controlled Companies – GCCs).[168] In GCCs, there is the additional agency problem of the state trying to use its controlling shareholder power for political gain. This creates the conundrum of how 'independence' should be defined in GCCs, as excluding otherwise competent independent directors on the basis of their political affiliations would seem unworkable, and may oft en be undesirable (as shown in the Singapore chapter).[169] There is no evidence that China, Hong Kong, India or Singapore have attempted to *directly* address this unique agency problem or even consider whether independent directors should (or could) play an effective role in limiting political meddling in board decisions in GCCs. Singapore appears to have successfully addressed this agency problem indirectly by creating an institutional architecture that limits the government's power as a controlling shareholder – a model which China has considered transplanting.[170] This suggests that further com-

---

165) See Chapter 9 (Singapore) at III.2.
166) See note 136 above.
167) W. Ng and J. Roberts, '"Helping the Family": The Mediating Role of Outside Directors in Ethnic Chinese Family Firms', 285, 287, 307; Puchniak, 'Multiple Faces of Shareholder Power in Asia', 530–531. It should be noted that in many non-Asian cultures there is a strong cultural norm to pass businesses onto children. However, increasingly there are prominent examples in the US where the opposite norm seems to be emerging – with the efforts by Warren Buffett and Bill Gates to encourage wealthy individuals to pass on most of their wealth to charity (and not their children) as perhaps the most prominent example. The question is whether this cultural norm is stronger in Asia's leading economies with Family Firms and, if so, what the implications may be.
168) See Chapter 6 (China) at II.1; Chapter 8 (Hong Kong) at II.4; Chapter 9 (Singapore) at III.3; Chapter 10 (India) at II.3
169) See Chapter 9 (Singapore) at III.3.
170) C. H. Tan et al., 'State-Owned Enterprises in Singapore: Historical Insights into a Potential Model for Reform', *Columbia Journal of Asian Law*, 28 (2015) 61, 62–63.

parative research on the function that independent directors should (or could) play in jurisdictions with GCCs may produce valuable insights for several of Asia's leading economies.

Foreign shareholders are another type of shareholder that has influenced the evolution of the independent director in Asia's leading economies. Several jurisdiction-specific chapters note the desire to attract foreign investors as an impetus for adopting independent directors to signal 'good' corporate governance.[171] The influence of foreign shareholders appears to be at least partially contingent on the size and developmental state of the respective economy – with the smaller and less developed economies appearing to respond more to their influence.[172]

Finally, the use of cross-shareholding and pyramid structures appears to have a significant impact on the function of independent directors in Japan and South Korea respectively – adding an important and unique element to their respective independent director regimes. Based on a purely empirical analysis, the shareholding structure of Japan's large public companies is as dispersed as the UK and US.[173] However, as a result of stable/cross-shareholding networks, lifetime-employee manager-directors who have indirect control over large blocks of shares, have dominated the governance of most public listed companies in postwar Japan.[174] This has created a unique corporate governance environment, which suggests that the role of independent directors in Japan's empirically dispersed shareholder environment is not only clearly different from the US, but also likely distinct from Asia's other leading economies.[175] The use of pyramid shareholding structures in South Korea has created a situation where cash flow and control rights are perhaps more unbalanced than in any of Asia's other leading economies.[176] This type of shareholding may also present unique challenges for its independent directors – something that could benefit from comparative analysis with other jurisdictions that have pyramidal ownership structures.[177]

The fourth factor that has driven the evolution of the varieties of independent directors in

---

171) See Chapter 4 (Japan) at II.1.c; Chapter 5 (South Korea) at III; Chapter 8 (Hong Kong) at II.4; Chapter 9 (Singapore) at II.4 and IV.1.

172) Compare Singapore's embrace of independent directors to signal compliance with global corporate governance norms, with Japan's considerably more gradual acceptance of independent directors: Chapter 4 (Japan); Chapter 9 (Singapore).

173) Kraakman et al., *The Anatomy of Corporate Law*, 29; Puchniak, 'Multiple Faces of Shareholder Power in Asia', 523–524.

174) Lawley, 'Panacea or Placebo?', 135.

175) Gilson and Milhaupt, 'Choice as Regulatory Reform', 360–362.

176) See Chapter 5 (South Korea) at II.3; K. Kim, 'Dynamics of Shareholder Power in Korea' in J. Hill and R. Thomas (eds.), *Research Handbook on Shareholder Power* (Edward Elgar, 2015), 536–540 (a short description of unique aspects of ownership structure in South Korea).

177) Claessens et al., 'The Separation of Ownership and Control in East Asian Corporations', 81–112 (comparing shareholding structures in South Korea to other Asian jurisdictions).

Asia is the functional substitutes for independent directors that vary across Asia's leading economies and distinguish them from the US and UK. Perhaps the most discussed functional substitute in Asia's leading economies is the board of statutory auditors (*kansayaku*) in Japan. As mentioned above, it has been argued that *kansayaku* essentially fulfil the same function as independent directors – a point that has been made with some success by various interest groups as a rationale for resisting mandatory requirements for independent directors in Japan.[178] A similar argument could be made in Asia's other leading economies, which have historically permitted or required non-one-tier boards (i.e., China, South Korea and Taiwan).[179] However, for various reasons, this argument has been less persuasive in these other jurisdictions: in China, mandatory legislation requiring independent directors was implemented in 2001, despite companies having supervisory boards;[180] in South Korea, strict mandatory independent director requirements were implemented in 2000 for large listed companies, replacing statutory auditors which could have been maintained as a possible functional substitute for independent directors;[181] and in Taiwan, one-tier boards with independent directors will be mandatory for listed companies from 2018, extinguishing the option for companies to have boards of statutory auditors as a functional substitute for independent directors.[182]

Another interesting functional substitute, which was mentioned above, is Singapore's institutional architecture that is designed to constrain the government's power as a controlling shareholder in GCCs. This institutional architecture has largely succeeded in preventing the government from using its controlling shareholder power to extract private benefits or influence GCCs for short-term political gain.[183] This success helped Singapore justify its use of the American definition of independence (i.e., requiring independence from management, but not significant shareholders) despite having a highly concentrated shareholder environment – while simultaneously increasing its reputation for 'good' corporate governance.[184] It is clear that the *existence* of functional substitutes has had jurisdiction-specific effects, which magnify the diversity among the varieties of independent directors in Asia. In addi-

---

178) See note 82 above.
179) See Chapter 5 (South Korea) at II.4; Chapter 6 (China) at II.2; Chapter 7 (Taiwan) at II.1.
180) See Chapter 6 (China) at II.2.
181) See Chapter 5 (South Korea) at III.1.
182) See Chapter 7 (Taiwan) at II.1 (stating that all listed companies must appoint at least two independent directors by 31 December 2017).
183) See Chapter 9 (Singapore) at III.3. It should be noted that the classic explanation of 'private benefits of control' arguably does not fit well in the context of GCCs. For a detailed explanation of this issue see, Puchniak, 'Multiple Faces of Shareholder Power in Asia', 526–532.
184) See Chapter 9 (Singapore) at III.2.

tion, the *absence* of well-recognised functional substitutes and complements for independent directors also distinguishes independent director regimes in Asia from the US and UK. According to the (Anglo)American-cum-global norms of 'good' corporate governance, the existence of hostile takeovers, shareholder litigation and proxy contests are commonly seen as corporate governance mechanisms that complement independent directors.[185] The relative weakness or absence of these complementary corporate governance mechanisms in Asia's leading economies suggests that independent directors may be even more crucial to attain 'good' corporate governance in Asia than in the US or UK.[186]

However, evidence from this chapter demonstrates that such reasoning is likely misguided, as it erroneously assumes that the functions of independent directors in Asia and the UK–US are the same – when, as demonstrated in this chapter, they are clearly not. Although hostile takeovers, shareholder litigation and proxy contests may be seen to complement the managerial-monitoring function, which is of paramount importance for independent directors in the US and UK, the importance of managerial-monitoring in Asia's controlling-shareholder dominated corporate governance environment is not as acute. This suggests that while there may be meaningful comparative lessons to draw from certain functional substitutes based on targeted comparisons within Asia, comparing functional substitutes between Asia and the UK–US may be of limited value or even misleading.

The fifth factor that has driven the evolution of varieties of independent directors in Asia is the unique and diverse political economies that exist in Asia's leading economies. In South Korea, strict mandatory legislation requiring half of the boards of large companies to be independent was a condition of an IMF bailout – which, in the 1990s, South Korea desperately required as a result of the Asian Financial Crisis.[187] Interestingly, however, it is suggested in the Korean chapter that the Korean government was more supportive of the strict mandatory requirement 'imposed' by the IMF than what may have been assumed. Indeed, it appears that there 'were factions in the government that may have wanted to use the political capital provided by the IMF to curtail the power of the *chaebol*, which would have been unthinkable prior to the financial crisis'.[188]

In several of Asia's leading economies, there appear to be political struggles between the government, corporate lobbyists and sometimes other interest groups, situations which often have unique jurisdiction-specific effects on how each jurisdiction's independent director re-

---

185) Puchniak, 'Multiple Faces of Shareholder Power in Asia', 512, 516.
186) *Ibid.*, 515–520.
187) See Chapter 5 (South Korea) at III.1.a.
188) See Chapter 5 (South Korea) at III.1.b.

gime evolves.[189] Perhaps one of the most interesting and complex examples is the domestic politics which uniquely shaped the independent director's evolution in Japan. As described in the Japan chapter, the ambitions of political operatives and parties, the informal custom of requiring consensus on government committees and powerful business lobbies resulted in a battle over whether to require a single independent director on the boards of listed companies.[190] In the end, Japan's political economy provides valuable insight into why mandatory legislation requiring even a single independent director was unattainable and a watered-down 'comply or explain' code of corporate governance was eventually adopted.[191] Although the effects of each jurisdiction's political economy vary, there are interesting common trends that can be distilled from the jurisdiction-specific chapters. It appears that in most of Asia's leading jurisdictions (with the notable exception of South Korea), stock exchanges have been heavily involved in lobbying the government to implement more stringent independent director requirements.[192] This makes sense as exchanges may benefit from signalling to the world that they are in compliance with (Anglo)American-cum-global norms of 'good' corporate governance.[193] In addition, it appears that incumbent political parties often initiate or support proposals to strengthen independent director legislation, especially in the wake of a financial crisis.[194] This may be motivated by the fact that implementing 'independent director' requirements is normally a relatively inexpensive and straightforward way for the government to signal that it is taking action to strengthen the economy without actually fundamentally changing the system.[195] Conversely, it appears that business lobbyists in most jurisdictions tend to oppose strengthening independent director regulation as they may remove power from the corporate management and/or controlling shareholders, which are the groups represented by the lobbyists.[196]

---

189) See Chapter 4 (Japan) at II.1 and III.2; Chapter 5 (South Korea) at III.1; Chapter 8 (Hong Kong) at II.4; Chapter 9 (Singapore) at II.4.

190) See Chapter 4 (Japan) at III.2.

191) See Chapter 4 (Japan) at III.2.b.

192) See Chapter 4 (Japan) at II.1.b; Chapter 6 (China) at II.2; Chapter 7 (Taiwan) at II; Chapter 8 (Hong Kong) at II.4; Chapter 10 (India) at III.

193) See Chapter 4 (Japan) at II.1.b; Chapter 6 (China) at II.2; Chapter 7 (Taiwan) at II; Chapter 8 (Hong Kong) at II.4; Chapter 10 (India) at III.

194) Velikonja, 'The Political Economy of Board Independence', 855, 892–893, 899.

195) See Chapter 4 (Japan) at II.1.d; Chapter 6 (China) at II.2; Chapter 7 (Taiwan) at II; Chapter 8 (Hong Kong) at II.4; Chapter 9 (Singapore) at II.4; Chapter 10 (India) at III.

196) See Chapter 4 (Japan) at III.2.b; Chapter 5 (South Korea) at III.1.b (observing that, under the cover of the IMF, the Korean government was able to push through reforms that might have met with resistance from the *chaebol*). For a short description of the political environment surrounding corporate governance in Korea, see, e.g., K. Kim, 'Corporate Law and Corporate Law Scholarship in Korea: A Comparative Essay' in J. O. Haley and T. Takenaka (eds.), *Legal Innovations in Asia* (Edward Elgar, 2014), 257– 258.

The sixth factor that has driven the evolution of the varieties of independent directors in Asia is cultural norms. In Japan, the post-war insider-dominated lifetime-employee corporate culture has likely played an important role in its outlier position as the only jurisdiction with no mandatory law regulating independent directors, and in corporate Japan's long resistance to having any independent directors on corporate boards.[197] In Singapore, the cultural norm in the ethnic Chinese business community of preserving wealth for future generations appears to limit family controllers' extraction of private benefits of control – potentially providing a functional substitute for or complement to the monitoring function of independent directors in Family Firms.[198] In China, India, South Korea and Taiwan, the deep culture of respect for teachers may provide some explanation for the high percentage of professors among independent directors on corporate boards.[199]

These examples suggest that cultural norms have played a role in the evolution of independent directors in Asia and that their impact may vary across jurisdictions – making the varieties of independent directors in Asia even more diverse. There are, however, at least two cultural norms that appear to be present in all of the diverse cultures of Asia's leading economies, which may present challenges for the effectiveness of independent directors: the centrality of informal relationships in business which makes finding and identifying truly independent directors particularly difficult in Asia; and the avoidance of direct confrontation, especially with people in positions of authority and in public, which may limit the effectiveness of independent directors on boards.[200] A more systematic examination of these and other potential cultural norms on the function of independent directors in Asia appears to be a particularly rich and understudied area for future research.

3 Operationalising the Six Principal Factors to Create a Loose Taxonomy

The six principal factors discussed above provide valuable insights into why varieties of independent directors exist in Asia and what has caused them to adopt their forms and functions. In addition, an understanding of these six factors provides the foundation for developing a 'loose taxonomy' of the varieties of independent directors in Asia. Such a taxonomy allows us to classify Asia's leading economies into subsets of comparable jurisdictions

---

197) See Chapter 4 (Japan) at III.2.a, IV and V (examples of resistance to independent directors).
198) See Chapter 9 (Singapore) at III.2.
199) See Chapter 5 (South Korea) at IV.4; Chapter 6 (China) at II.3; Chapter 7 (Taiwan) at II.2.b; Chapter 10 (India) at IV.2.
200) See Chapter 7 (Taiwan) at III.2.b; Chapter 8 (Hong Kong) at III.3 and IV.

with respect to particular issues and then systematically examine these issues through targeted comparative analysis. Ultimately, we suggest that this approach will improve our understanding of independent directors in Asia and illuminate new areas for meaningful comparative research.

A few brief examples illustrate how the six factors can be operationalised under our 'loose taxonomy'. To start, let us consider how the first factor, shareholder structure, can be used to classify a subset of Asia's leading economies and illuminate useful areas for comparison within this subset. In all of Asia's leading economies, except for Japan, listed companies generally have a controlling shareholder structure. This highlights a key issue for comparison: how do independent directors, which were invented to solve the dispersed shareholding problem in the US, function in controlling shareholder dominated jurisdictions? One interesting observation is that all of the jurisdictions in this subset have departed from the American concept of the independent director by requiring independence from significant shareholders in their definitions of independence. However, all jurisdictions in this subset, except for Taiwan, still allow independent directors to be elected by majority shareholder vote. This raises intriguing questions for future research: why would these jurisdictions mandate independence from majority shareholders in their definitions of independence, but then implicitly allow majority shareholders to control the appointment and removal of these 'independent directors'? On this note, why was Taiwan unsuccessful in its attempt to remedy this apparent problem by mandating cumulative voting?

Another illustration of our 'loose taxonomy' can be found in our examination of legal origins. As explained above, Asia's leading civil law economies (i.e., China, Japan, South Korea and Taiwan) comprise a subset of jurisdictions which have allowed companies to adopt a non-one-tier board. An interesting question that arises in these jurisdictions is how independent directors, which were invented in the US to operate in a one-tier board environment, fit into non-one-tier board regimes. In addition, all of the jurisdictions in this subset have or had corporate organs (i.e., statutory auditors or supervisory boards) that perform similar functions to independent directors.[201] This raises the issue of how these jurisdictions will coordinate the functions of these two overlapping mechanisms. A more targeted use of the legal origins factor may classify subsets of jurisdictions for comparison based on the historically traceable origins of a *particular* feature within a jurisdiction's independent director regime. For example, as explained above, the fact that Japan's 'comply

---

201) Large listed firms in South Korea historically had statutory auditors, but now have an audit committee instead of statutory auditors.

or explain' regime was modelled on the UK's Code provides a rational basis for comparing Japan on this issue with the UK and also with Hong Kong and Singapore (which are the two other leading Asian jurisdictions that also currently have a UK 'comply or explain' model). This example illustrates how tracing the legal origins of particular provisions in a jurisdiction's independent director regime can reveal subsets of jurisdictions for a meaningful comparative analysis of an important issue.

Yet another example can be found in our examination of specific types of shareholders. In China, India and Singapore, the government is the controlling shareholder in a substantial portion of companies. As suggested above, a potential issue for future research is whether such jurisdictions should require independent directors in government-controlled companies to be independent from the government or ruling party. A strict policy of excluding independent directors based on political affiliation may significantly reduce the talent pool for independent directors without necessarily avoiding many meaningful conflicts of interest.[202] In all of Asia's leading economies, with the notable exception of Japan, similar issues arise as to how independence should be defined with respect to Family Firms. This subset of jurisdictions could benefit from further research on this issue as there is evidence that friends of the controlling family can perform a valuable mediating role as independent directors in Family Firms.[203]

These examples merely scratch the surface of the potential uses of the six principal factors as a way to identify salient issues for comparison in particular subsets of jurisdictions, which share common characteristics among their independent directors on particular issues. This methodological approach for comparison is diametrically opposed to the prevailing approach of assuming that independent directors are universally similar and thus universally comparable in all aspects for every issue across all jurisdictions.[204] The fact that independent directors possess unique attributes in different jurisdictions should be cause for inspiration rather than resignation: indeed, the varieties of independent directors in this book have revealed fertile areas for further study.

---

202) See Chapter 9 (Singapore) at III.3.
203) See note 136 above.
204) See II.1 above.

IV Conclusion: Implications of Varieties of Independent Directors in Asia

If there is one main point that emerges from this chapter and book, it is this: there is no single concept of the independent director in Asia. There are varieties of independent directors in Asia that take on different forms and perform different functions. This discovery has important practical and theoretical implications for at least three reasons.

First, corporate governance indices, which influence the allocation of trillions of dollars of investment capital and define entire sub-fields of corporate governance research, implicitly assume that independent directors around the world take the same form and perform the same function.[205] An in-depth comparison of the jurisdiction-specific chapters in this book demonstrates that this assumption is false. Indeed, it does not hold true even within Asia. Second, it is misleading to point to the rise of the independent director in Asia as evidence of corporate governance convergence towards the American (or Anglo-American) corporate governance model. This chapter demonstrates that much of the 'convergence' that has occurred with the independent director in Asia is often only skin deep. The body of comparative evidence in the jurisdiction-specific chapters reveals the significant divergence in form and function within Asia – and even more so between Asian jurisdictions and the US –UK. This should not surprise as recent developments even suggest divergence of the concept of the independent director between the US and UK.

Third, the discovery of varieties of independent directors in Asia highlights the importance of drilling-down in comparative corporate governance research beyond common labels – which may be increasingly more abundant in our internet age. This presents a serious challenge to interjurisdictional empirical research, which tends to rely heavily on labels or law on the books for its primary data. The importance of 'labels' also raises an interesting question about their strategic value as signalling devices. The fact that 'mere' labels have been able to influence important corporate governance indices and influential research suggests

---

205) See, for example, Katelouzou and Siems, 'Disappearing Paradigms'; Black et al., 'Does Corporate Governance Predict Firms' Market Values'; A. O. Santos, 'Integrated Ownership and Control in the GCC Corporate Sector' (International Monetary Fund Working Paper, 2015), available at www.imf.org; C. Aoyagi and G. Ganelli, 'Unstash the Cash! Corporate Governance Reform in Japan' (International Monetary Fund Working Paper, 2014), available at www.imf.org; Technical Committee of the International Organisation of Securities Commissions, 'Board Independence of Listed Companies: Final Report' (2007), available at www.iosco.org; Emerging Markets Committee of the International Organisation of Securities Commissions, 'Corporate Governance Practices in Emerging Markets' (2007), available at www.iosco.org; OECD, 'Corporate Governance: A Survey of OECD Countries' (OECD, 2004), available at www.oecd.org.

that more research should be devoted to why this is the case and how this may be used or abused.

If there is a second main point that emerges from this chapter and book, it is that although corporate governance is jurisdiction-specific and complex, targeted and nuanced comparative analysis can produce valuable practical and theoretical results. Producing such results, however, requires the type of in-depth jurisdiction-specific analysis that is contained in the jurisdiction-specific chapters of this book – which is diametrically opposed to the macro-empirical analysis that has increasingly driven policymakers and the academic literature in the field of comparative corporate governance.[206] A specific example of this is how we demonstrate in this chapter that legal origins do in fact matter – but in a localised way that focuses on the *specific* historically verifiable origins of *particular* legal provisions in *each specific* jurisdiction, rather than vague (and oft en inaccurate) notions of legal origins of an entire system examined at the jurisdictional level.[207] Perhaps, most importantly, the loose taxonomy of the independent director in Asia that we have created lays a foundation for exploring this critical issue more accurately and systematically in the future.

Admittedly, this chapter raises more questions for future research than definitive answers. However, hopefully the loose taxonomy of the forms, functions and issues that together define the varieties of independent directors in Asia will provide a path for further exploration of this fascinating issue for years to come.

---

206) See, for example, Gopal, 'Japan: A Closer Look at Governance Reforms'; OECD, 'Corporate Governance Factbook 2015' (OECD Publishing, 2015), available at www.oecd.org; Puchniak, 'Multiple Faces of Shareholder Power in Asia', 520 (describing GovernanceMetric International's global corporate governance ratings); M. Siems, 'Shareholder Protection around the World ("Leximetric II")', *Delaware Journal of Corporate Law*, 33 (2008), 111; Technical Committee of the International Organisation of Securities Commissions, 'Board Independence'.

207) See II.2 above.

Transplanting Audit Committees to Korean Soil:
A Window into the Evolution of Korean Corporate Governance

Kon Sik Kim*

I. INTRODUCTION

The 1997 financial crisis brought a number of changes to corporate governance in Korea.[1] Since 1997, Korea's corporate governance has taken one step closer to an Anglo-Saxon corporate governance model – at least in form. One of the most notable changes in the corporate governance scene is the rise of outside directors in listed firms. As of 2005, the number of outsiders exceeds five members (about 58 percent of the board) on average for large listed firms with assets over two trillion won.[2] Concomitant with the rise in outside directors, audit committees have been established in many large listed firms.

It was only after the financial crisis that outside directors were required for listed firms in Korea. In 1999, the corporate statutes of the Korean Commercial Code (KCC) were revised to allow a corporation to establish an audit committee in place of a corporate auditor.[3] In 2000, the government revised the Securities and Exchange Act to require large listed firms to establish an audit committee composed primarily of outside directors.[4]

The concept of an outside director was not entirely new to the business community in Korea. Beginning in the 1980s, a few academics started advocating monitoring boards com-

---

* Professor of Law, Seoul National University, Seoul, Korea. I currently serve as audit committee member at two listed firms in Korea.

1) *See generally* Hwa-Jin Kim, *Toward the "Best Practice" Model in a Globalizing Market: Recent Developments in Korean Corporate Governance*, 2 J. CORP. L. STUD. 345, 345 (2002) (arguing that "the Korean corporate governance system successfully adapts to the best practice model accepted by global standards").

2) CORPORATE GOVERNANCE SERVICE, *GIEOB JIBAI GUJO BAIGSEO* [2006 CORPORATE GOVERNANCE WHITE PAPER] 146 (2006).

3) I was on the government committee responsible for drafting provisions relating to committees including the audit committee under the KCC.

4) *Cheunggwon georai beob* [Securities & Exchange Act], Act No. 972 of 1962 (last amended by Act No. 7762, Dec. 29, 2005), arts. 191-17, 54-6; Presidential Decree No. 18757, Mar. 28, 2005, art. 84-24.

posed of outside directors within large firms. By the mid-1990s, a small number of government-owned firms were required by law to have a board dominated by outside directors.
Thus, by the time outside directors were required for listed firms, the business community
had at least a minimum understanding of their role in corporate governance.

However, the situation was quite different for audit committees. The audit committee was
introduced primarily under pressure from international institutions such as the
International Monetary Fund (IMF) and International Bank for Reconstruction and
Development (IBRD).[5] At that time, the audit committee concept was not well known even
among business lawyers, not to mention business leaders. Introducing a foreign institution
like the audit committee under outside pressure was somewhat humiliating. Thus, it was
natural that local corporate law specialists as well as the business community were generally
opposed to its implementation in their firms. Now, however, hostility toward the audit
committee seems to have substantially decreased, at least in the business community.[6] One
hundred thirty-six–approximately one fifth of the firms listed on the primary section of the
Korea Exchange have an audit committee (see Table 1). Of these 136 firms, fifty-nine firms
have adopted the audit committee voluntarily.

TABLE 1: *Adoption of the Audit Committee by Firms Listed on the Primary Section of Korea
Exchange[7]*

Year	Listed Firms	Firms with AC	Mandatory	Voluntary
2004	666	132	74	57
2005	662	136	77	59

The audit committee is expected to play a more significant role under Korea's accounting
and audit systems, which have been strengthened under the influence of the Sarbanes-Oxley
Act. Despite the rapid spread of the audit committee in Korea, however, substantial mis-
understanding and confusion persists even among experts in Korea over the roles and functions of the committee in firm operations. Audit committee practices are not yet well established and some of the basics are still in dispute. In other words, the process of con-

---

5) International institutions first suggested that the audit committee be required for all listed firms in
   Korea. The lack of experts that were qualified to serve on the audit committee was a primary factor in
   limiting the rule's coverage.
6) Corporate law specialists still appear generally opposed to the audit committee.
7) CORPORATE GOVERNANCE SERVICE, *supra* note 2, at 184.

vergence has started, but is not yet complete.

In this paper I examine some issues raised in the process of transplanting the audit commit-tee to Korean corporations. The audit committee serves as an ideal window to glimpse the larger picture of corporate governance in Korea, which is currently undergoing a rapid and dynamic evolution. In Part II, I highlight the status of the audit committee in Korea in order to provide some background information. In Part III, I address issues related to organizing the audit committee. In Part IV, I discuss issues in operating the audit committee. In Part V, I focus on the perils of too much action, which may be unique to the audit committee in Korea.

II. CORPORATE AUDITORS AND THE AUDIT COMMITTEE

A. Development of Corporate Auditors

If the number of investors involved is small and the business is relatively simple, the invest-ors themselves may be able to supervise corporate managers. However, this is not a feasible option for a large corporation with numerous investors. Such a firm will need a pro-fessional supervisor working on behalf of investors.

The structure of management supervision may be divided into two major types: the American model with its outsider-dominated board and the German model with its super-visory board (*Aufsichtsrat*).[8] A principal difference between the two models is the separa-tion of supervision and management functions. The supervisory board function in Germany is formally separate from the management function, which belongs to the management board (*Vorstand*). The board in the United States is in charge of management - at least in principle. As the ratio of outsiders to managers increases in the board of directors, the American model in effect becomes similar to the German model.[9]

The corporate auditor in Korea does not quite fit into either of the two models. The corpo-

---

8) *See generally* Klaus J. Hopt, *The German Two-Tier Board: Experience, Theories, Reforms, in* COMPARATIVE CORPORATE GOVERNANCE THE STATE OF THE ART AND EMERGING RESEARCH 227 (Klaus J. Hopt et. al. eds., 1997) (offering a historical and functional discussion of the German supervisory board).

9) Of course, differences still exist between the two models. Perhaps the most important of such differ-ences is labor representation on the German supervisory board.

rate auditor, like many other institutions in Korea, is not Korea's own creation, but is a concept imported from Japan. The corporate auditor concept was introduced in a draft of the Japanese Commercial Code prepared by Hermann Rösler, a German legal counsel hired by the *Meiji* government.[10] Although his draft was never formally implemented, the concept of a corporate auditor took root in the Japanese Code and still remains, despite numerous revisions over the last one hundred years. In designing a supervisory structure, Rösler basically followed the German model by separating corporate auditors from the management function. However, he added an interesting twist. Unlike members of the German supervisory board, a corporate auditor was not given the power to appoint directors. Instead, shareholders appointed directors at the general shareholders meeting ("GSM"). Apparently, Rösler was afraid that the corporate auditor would become too powerful and would be prone to abuse its power to appoint and dismiss directors. Thus, given that it is difficult to expect that a supervisory organ could play an adequate supervisory role with no power to replace those under its supervision, it is hardly surprising that the corporate auditor was criticized for its lack of power right from the beginning.

When the Japanese Code was extensively revised in 1950, the American-style board of directors was introduced. Nonetheless, the corporate auditor remained largely intact. The corporate auditor's power was reduced to accounting matters as the newly introduced board assumed the role of supervising the execution of directors' duties. Even the new board of directors was soon reduced to a nominal organ in reality, primarily because there was virtually no independent director on the board. Given the absence of meaningful supervision of management, it was perhaps inevitable that corporate crimes such as accounting fraud were allowed to occur.

In theory, the lack of supervision could be remedied in two different ways. The first option was to introduce outside directors to the board, similar to the American model. The second option was to somehow strengthen the position of the corporate auditor. As recently as 2003, Japan essentially adopted the second option in its numerous reform attempts. For instance, the power of the corporate auditor was expanded to cover management affairs. Large firms were required to have at least three statutory auditors on the board of corporate auditors. Large firms were also required to appoint outside corporate auditors as well as fulltime corporate auditors. Despite various attempts to expand the role of corporate auditors, their overall level of performance does not seem to have improved in any mean-

---

10) *See generally* Hideaki Kubori, *Iinkaito setchi kaisha eno kitai to mondaiten* [*Expectation and Problems of the Companies with Committees*], 136 HO NO SHIHAI 83 (2005).

ingful fashion in Japan.[11] It is not clear why the institution of corporate auditor failed to achieve its proposed function in Japan. It might be at least partly due to the corporate auditor's lack of power to replace directors.[12]

In 2003, the Japanese Code was amended to allow firms to adopt the American-style board dominated by outside directors performing monitoring functions.[13] A firm adopting the American-style board is required to have an audit committee instead of corporate auditors. One may wonder why it took such a long time for Japan to escape from the grip of the concept of corporate auditors.[14]

Corporate auditors in Korea were not any more effective than their Japanese counterparts. Legislators in Korea enacted a special provision to strengthen the independence of corporate auditors. In an effort to limit the influence of controlling shareholders, the KCC prevents large shareholders from voting in excess of the 3 percent ceiling when appointing a corporate auditor.[15] In practice, however, this provision has failed to significantly contribute to the independence of corporate auditors.

In the past, one could generally classify corporate auditors into three categories: (1) sinecures, (2) executives, and (3) meddlers. A sinecure auditor is appointed just to comply with the statutory requirement and is someone who does virtually nothing as corporate auditor. In many cases, this person is someone the controlling shareholder needs to treat well, such as his in-law or a former bureaucrat. This type of corporate auditor normally works part time.[16] An executive corporate auditor is a corporate auditor in name only and in effect performs an executive function. Executive auditors are often found in small- and me-

---

11) Shigeru Morimoto, *Iinkaito setchi kaisha seido no rinen to kino (ge) [Goals and Functions of the Committee-based Corporation System (III)], 1668 SHOJI HOMU* [COMMERCIAL LAW MATTERS] 14 (2003).

12) *Id.* at 19.

13) *See, e.g.,* Ronald J. Gilson & Curtis J. Milhaupt, *Choice As Regulatory Reform: The Case of Japanese Corporate Governance,* 53 AM. J. COMP. L. 343, 353-54 (2005) (providing a theoretical analysis of the 2002 amendment).

14) A leading commentator still emphasizes that the replacement of corporate auditors by the audit committee does not necessarily reflect a negative judgment on corporate auditors. Shigeru Morimoto, *Iinkaito setchi kaisha seido no rinen to kino (jo) [Goals and Functions of the Committee-based Corporation System (I)], 1666 SHOJI HOMU* [COMMERCIAL LAW MATTERS] 6 (2003).

15) Sang beob [Commercial Code], Act No. 1000 of 1962 (last amended by Act No. 6545, Dec. 29, 2001) art. 409(2).

16) As of 1995, the average number of corporate auditors in a listed firm was 1.51 - more than half of them worked part-time. For example, Samsung Company had only two part-time corporate auditors: one was a retired Supreme Court judge and the other was the head of the group Chairman's office. Kon Sik Kim, Chaebol and Corporate Governance in Korea 151 (1995) (unpublished Ph.D. dissertation, University of Washington) (on file with author). During the last decade, the ratio of part timers has decreased. As of 2005, only one in four firms adopting the corporate auditor system has part timers. CORPORATE GOVERNANCE SERVICE, *supra* note 2, at 180.

dium-sized firms that cannot afford to have sinecure auditors. Meddlers are rather rare and found mostly in government-controlled corporations. Elected not by the CEO, but by the government, this type of corporate auditor tends to feel independent of the CEO. He sometimes tries to maximize his influence as against his competitor, the CEO, meddling in day-to-day operational matters.

B. The Audit Committee Versus the Corporate Auditor

Given the lethargy of corporate auditors in Korea, the Korean government's decision to introduce the audit committee is understandable. Although the audit committee was introduced in Japan as an alternative to the corporate auditor, the audit committee is mandatory for large listed firms in Korea. True, the Korean government's decision to require an audit committee may be criticized for limiting a firm's freedom to choose an appropriate organizational structure.[17] However, if the audit committee is generally more effective when compared to the corporate auditor, such a mandatory approach may be acceptable. Corporate law specialists in Korea have questioned the value of the audit committee as compared to the corporate auditor. These critics emphasize the following three points. First, commentators argue that the audit committee is not free from self-audit. According to this line of reasoning, it is unrealistic to expect the audit committee to be fair and active in monitoring corporate management because the audit committee members have already participated in the decision-making process of the board, as directors. Widely cited in the existing academic literature on the audit committee,[18] this argument may sound plausible as an abstract proposition. However, the self-audit critique is not supported by corporate realities.[19] For example, items covered in a board meeting are only a small part of the business operations subject to audit. In addition, corporate auditors are not significantly better than the audit committee on this self-audit issue. Although a corporate auditor has no vote, she is required to attend board meetings and is expected to express her views.[20] If she fails to indicate any reservations on an issue at a board meeting, it would be awkward for her to take any negative measures later on. Moreover, participation of the audit

---

17) An overwhelming majority of firms respond that they want such freedom.
18) *See, e.g.*, CHUL-SONG LEE, *HOESABEOB GANGUI* [LECTURES ON CORPORATE LAW] 670 (13th ed. 2006).
19) The self-audit concern does not seem to have many supporters in Japan. *See* Morimoto, *supra* note 14, at 19.
20) Sang beob [Commercial Code], *supra* note 15, art. 391-2(1).

committee members in the management decision-making in board meetings may prove more beneficial as they can try to block a problematic decision beforehand.

Second, some critics point to the subordinate nature of the audit committee as a sub-committee of the board. Under the KCC, the board is authorized to appoint audit committee members.[21] This seems to be the point that made commentators most uncomfortable. From their perspective, it was unrealistic to expect the audit committee - a mere committee of the board - to properly audit the work of the board, its superior organ.[22] Again, this view may appear logical on the surface, but not persuasive in practice. As long as the audit committee is composed of independent and competent outside directors, it may not matter much that the board formally appoints the audit committee. Additionally, some critics believe that a resolution of the audit committee, like other committee resolutions, may be overturned by the full board.[23] This view does not take account of differences between the audit committee and other board committees. Unlike other board committees, the audit committee's authority derives from specific provisions in the KCC, not from the board of directors. Accordingly, the board can not overturn a decision by the audit committee because such decisions are outside of the scope of the board's statutory authority.[24]

The third argument against the audit committee is based on a more practical consideration. How can the audit committee, which is primarily composed of outside directors working part-time, carry out increased responsibilities? This concern, however, is also applicable to corporate auditors because a corporate auditor does not generally need to be employed full time.[25] On the other hand, an outside director does not have to be a part-timer either. If the workload of the audit committee is heavy enough to justify a full-time position, the firm may choose to appoint a full-time director. Indeed, many financial institutions have a full-time member on the audit committee. One cannot say this practice is good or bad as a matter of principle. The answer depends upon the weight of responsibility in each case. This point will be discussed in greater detail later.

---

21) *Id.* arts. 393-2(1), 415-2(1).

22) This is the reason why the Securities and Exchange Act was revised to require that the GSM intervene in electing the audit committee members. *See Cheunggwon georai beob* [Securities and Exchange Act], *supra* note 4, art. 191-11(1).

23) *Sang beob* [Commercial Code], *supra* note 15, art. 393-2(4)(ii).

24) The government bill to revise the Commercial Code has a provision explicitly indicating that a decision by the audit committee is not to be overturned by the full board.

25) As of 1995, only about half of the corporate auditors of listed firms worked full time. *See* Morimoto, *supra* note 14. The Securities and Exchange Actnow requires a large listed firm to have at least one corporate auditor working full time. *Cheunggwon georai beob* [Securities and Exchange Act], *supra* note 4, art. 191-12(1).

As the discussion above shows, concerns about the audit committee appear rather formalistic and devoid of analysis based on reality. On the one hand, this may be partly due to a prevalent tendency in Korean legal scholarship to concentrate on formal logical consistency. On the other hand, local scholars may have advanced these negative arguments to disguise their blind hostility to yet another unfamiliar foreign institution.

III. ISSUES WITH ORGANIZING THE AUDIT COMMITTEE

A. Audit Committee Appointment

Although the KCC does not explicitly empower specific body to elect audit committee members, there has been no dispute that the board has the power to select and dismiss members of the audit committee, as it has for other committees of the board.[26] Some commentators have expressed concern that the audit committee would not be independent if the board elects the members. Under the KCC, a corporate auditor is appointed at the GSM, taking into account that the 3 percent ceiling applies to large shareholders in voting.[27] This difference was cited as yet another ground for the superiority of corporate auditors over the audit committee.[28]

The Securities and Exchange Act was revised to apply the 3 percent limit to a resolution appointing audit committee members.[29] This added requirement causes much confusion in corporate practice.[30] In order to apply this 3 percent limit, many companies make a separate resolution at the GSM for an outside director who will serve as a member of the audit committee. In such companies, it is the shareholders at the GSM, not the board, who actually selects audit committee members. This practice will not cause any material problems for a firm that has opted out of cumulative voting. However, in a small number of firms subject to cumulative voting, it may generate a significant difference. When appointing or-

---

26) The board is explicitly authorized to establish a board committee. Sangbeob [Commercial Code], supra note 15, art. 393-2. Additionally, the KCC treats the audit committee as a board committee. *Id.* art. 415-2(1).

27) *Sang beob* [Commercial Code], *supra* note 15, art. 409(2).

28) Lee, *supra* note 18, at 670.

29) *Cheunggwon georae beop* [Securities and Exchange Act], *supra* note 4, arts. 191-17(2), 54-6(6).

30) Kon Sik Kim, *Beobjeog sigag eseo bon gamsawiwonhoi* [*The Audit Committee Viewed from a Legal Perspective*], 13 BFL 35, 38-39 (2006).

dinary directors and the audit committee members at the same time, some firms split the appointment resolutions in two in order to minimize the effect of cumulative voting.[31]

B. Financial Experts

Influenced by the Sarbanes-Oxley Act, the Securities and Exchange Act requires the audit committee of a listed firm to include at least one expert in accounting or finance.[32] The Presidential Decree enforcing the Securities and Exchange Act sets forth five categories of experts that meet this requirement.[33] Perhaps the most problematic category is that of former employees of the government and the Financial Supervisory Service[34] with at least five years of experience in activities related to finance, accounting, or supervisory activities covering finance or accounting. It is not clear what kind of employees can qualify as such an expert. Moreover, it is highly doubtful whether this category of experts has any of the necessary qualities for serving on an audit committee. It is widely suspected that this category has been inserted to help former regulators land decent second jobs in the private sector. Indeed, in many financial institutions, former officials of the Financial Supervisory Service serve as full-time members of audit committees.[35]

C. Full-time Versus Part-time Members

Under current law, at least two-thirds of audit committee members must be outsiders.[36] In a growing number of large listed firms, the audit committee is composed solely of outside directors. In most financial institutions, an audit committee member works on a full-time basis. In practice, such a full-time member is treated as a non-outsider. This interpretation is based upon the Securities and Exchange Act, which defines an outside director as a director not engaged in "regular activity."[37] The Korean term for regular activity, *sangmu*, which

---

31) Judgment Mar. 14, 2006, *Daijeon jibang beobwon* [Daijeon District Court], 2006 Gahab 242.
32) *Cheunggwon georai beob* [Securities and Exchange Act], *supra* note 4, arts. 191-17(2), 54-6(2)(ii).
33) Presidential Decree No. 18757, *supra* note 4, art. 37-7(2).
34) The Financial Supervisory Service is the non-governmental operating arm of the country's principal regulator, the Financial Supervisory Commission.
35) Although the Securities and Exchange Act explicitly mentions accounting or finance, audit experience may be of more relevance to the audit committee. In reality, however, it is difficult to invite such an expert, as most candidates, affiliated with big accounting firms, hesitate to become outside directors for conflict-of-interest reasons.
36) *Sang beob* [Commercial Code], *supra* note 15, art. 415-2(2); *Cheunggwon georai beob* [Securities and Exchange Act], *supra* note 4, arts. 191-17, 54-6(2)(i).
37) *Cheunggwon georai beob* [Securities and Exchange Act], *supra* note 4, art. 2(19).

may also be translated as ordinary or daily activity, is normally used for full-time directors. The dividing line between outsiders and insiders, however, should be the nature of their work, not the length of hours worked.

Is it desirable to have a full-time audit committee members? Those who support the idea of a full-time member point to the increased work load of the audit committee. Indeed, it is acknowledged that in a fair number of Japanese firms a member of the audit committee works full time.[38] A full-time audit committee member may also face problems. First, if a member of the audit committee works full-time, his independence from management may likely be compromised. Compared to directors with other careers, the full-time member may be anxious to maintain his position and therefore more vulnerable to pressure from management. Second, an information gap may arise between the fulltime member and the part-time members, whereby the part-time members depend on the information provided by the full-time member. Finally, it may be more difficult to find a qualified person who is willing to work full-time. In large listed firms at least, outside directors are selected from those who have been highly successful in their own careers. For these people, working full-time on an audit committee may not be attractive as a career option.

IV. ISSUES WITH OPERATING THE AUDIT COMMITTEE

A. Audit Committee Powers

Under the KCC, the audit committee, like a corporate auditor, shall "audit the execution of director's duties."[39] In Korea, this audit committee function is generally referred to as the operation audit. Although the operation audit should cover accounting matters as well, the audit on accounting matters is separately called the accounting audit. In support of the supervisory function, the KCC grants the audit committee a wide range of powers to:

(1) request a business report from directors and to investigate the corporate operational matters and financial status;[40]

---

38) *KAISEI KAISHAHO SEMINA* [SEMINAR ON COMPANY LAW REFORM] 292 (Kenjiro Egashira et al. eds., 2006) (remark by Shigeru Morimoto).
39) *Sang beob* [Commercial Code], *supra* note 15, arts. 412(1), 415-2(6).

(2) attend board meetings and express opinions;[41]

(3) request that the board of directors call a GSM;[42]

(4) request a business report from a subsidiary of the firm and, in certain circumstances, to investigate the subsidiary's operational matters and financial status;[43]

(5) review directors' proposals and documents to be submitted at a GSM and to comment on their compliance with the law and the articles of incorporation;[44]

(6) report to the board of directors if it is found that a director has violated, or is likely to violate, the law or articles of incorporation;[45]

(7) enjoin a director from violating the law or articles of incorporation if such violation would irreparably harm the corporation;[46]

(8) file a suit against a director on behalf of the corporation;[47] and

(9) audit financial statements and to submit an audit report.[48]

B. The Operation Audit

As discussed earlier, the power and duty of the audit committee in Korea is much broader than its counterpart in the Unites States. While the audit committee in the United States is primarily concerned with accounting matters, its Korean counterpart is additionally required to audit "the execution of the directors' duties." The execution of directors' duties may be interpreted as covering almost every aspect of business operations. Critics wonder how the audit committee, primarily composed of part-time outsiders, can implement such enormous tasks. This issue will be discussed later.

A question arises over how to distinguish between the audit committee's audit and the board's supervision functions. Under the KCC, the execution of directors' duties is subject to supervision of the board.[49] The difference between the terms "audit" and "supervision" does not necessarily help clarify the different functions of the two different organs. A clue to our inquiry may be found in the different powers of the board and the audit committee,

---

40) *Id.* art. 412(2).
41) *Id.* art. 391-2(2).
42) *Id.* art. 412-3(1).
43) *Id.* art. 412-4.
44) *Id.* art. 413.
45) *Id.* art. 391-2(2).
46) *Id.* art. 402.
47) *Id.* art. 394.
48) *Id.* art. 447-4.
49) *Id.* art. 393(2).

as regards to the CEO, a "representative director" under the KCC parlance.

As a matter of law, the board is the decision-making body on management issues and the CEO is the officer in charge of executing decisions made by the board. Although the audit committee has various powers that may be exercised to restrain the CEO, it has no power to appoint or dismiss the CEO. It is natural that the board should have the power to appoint and dismiss the CEO when he fails to carry out the board's decisions.[50] Exercising this power, the board would be given the power to supervise every aspect of the CEO's performance. The core of the audit committee's powers may be its power to file a lawsuit on behalf of the corporation for damages incurred by a CEO's violation of his fiduciary duties and to enjoin a CEO's illegal behavior. Thus, the primary purpose of the operation audit should be to ensure the firm's compliance with the law (including the articles of incorporation) and the fiduciary duties of officers and directors.

C. The Legality and Soundness of Corporate Action

There has long been a debate among commentators as to whether the power of a corporate auditor is limited to the legality of a corporate action or whether power extends to its soundness. As legality and soundness are not mutually exclusive concepts, this kind of dispute may prove unproductive. Since the statutory powers of the corporate auditor are focused on the laws and fiduciary duties, an audit should concentrate on the legality of corporate decisions. But if a decision made by the CEO is found to be grossly inadequate, it may constitute a violation of his fiduciary duty of care, which amounts to illegality. However, the line between legality and soundness is often vague. Therefore, the corporate auditor is not completely excluded from inquiring into the soundness of any management action. The same issue arises for an audit committee as well. The distinction between legality and soundness becomes even less relevant given the fact that the audit committee consists of directors, who are members of the board in charge of business decision-making. On the soundness-related power of the audit committee, two points should be mentioned. First, the operation audit by the audit committee is subject to limits engendered by the business judgment rule, which has been functionally adopted by the courts in Korea.[51] As

---

50) The KCC expressly allows the GSM, rather than the board, to appoint a representative directors if such a mechanism is set forth in the articles of incorporation. *Id.* art. 389(1).

51) *See generally* Hwa-Jin Kim & Tehyok Daniel Yi, *Directors' Liabilities and the Business Judgment Rule in Korea*, Apr. 15, 2004, http://ssrn.com/abstract=530442 (providing analysis of the business judgment rule in Korea).

long as management or the board has reached a decision based on a careful review of relevant information, the audit committee should refrain from making further inquiries. Second, the audit committee needs to prudently exercise the power to look into the soundness of corporate decisions. The audit committee is not obligated to review every substantial business decision in advance. Such a review would also not be in accordance with best practice since the costs of such an intervention would far outweigh the benefits. Most CEOs are bound to exercise their best efforts in order to enhance corporate performance. If corporate performance falls short of the board's expectations due to a serious blunder committed by management, the board may in theory replace the management.

D. Accounting Audit

Although not expressly provided by the KCC, the CEO is ultimately responsible for the accuracy of accounting information.[52] However, the CEO may not be eager or competent to provide accurate figures. A CEO may even try to distort such figures for various reasons. In a large firm with numerous shareholders, this problem is addressed by external audits. The KCC requires the audit committee or a corporate auditor to audit the financial statements.[53] The KCC, however, is silent as to how the audit committee should carry out its audit responsibility. The KCC merely requires that certain items be included in the audit report that the audit committee is required to submit within four weeks of the end of the business year.[54] For example, the report must include whether the:

- accounting records of the company are deficient or whether the balance sheet or the income statement is not in accord with the accounting records;
- balance sheet and income statement accurately present the state of the assets and profits (or losses) in accordance with the laws and the articles of incorporation; and
- detailed statements supplementing the balance sheet and the income statement are deficient or are not in accord with the accounting records, the balance sheet or the income statement.

For a firm of any size, it is not an easy task to assess these matters within four weeks. This

---

52) Under the KCC, the financial statements prepared by representative directors are subject to approval by the board. *Sang beop* [Commercial Code], *supra* note 15, art. 447.
53) *Id.* art. 447-4.
54) *Id.* art. 447-4(2).

is by no means a task that a few part-time members of the audit committee can personally carry out. This problem may in theory be approached in two different, but not mutually exclusive, ways. The first is to appoint full-timers to the audit committee, a solution favored by many commentators. As mentioned earlier, however, a full-timer may be less independent, and it may be more difficult to find a qualified candidate. Moreover, as the size of a firm grows, even fulltimers will have difficulty in performing the audit work.

The second approach is to rely on supporters from outside the firm as well as those in-house. As mentioned earlier, a corporation with assets of seven billion won (approximately seven million dollars) or more is subject to outside audit.[55] In this kind of corporation, the outside auditor, an accounting firm in most cases, is better qualified than the audit committee to assure the accuracy of accounting information. It is unclear, however, to what extent the audit committee can rely on an audit report prepared by an outside auditor. In practice, it is invariably the chairman of the audit committee or a corporate auditor who reads the audit report at the general shareholders' meeting. A model audit report widely used in practice uses language that suggests the audit committee itself undertakes the audit work. In practice, however, the audit committee rarely engages in any audit activities personally. The audit committee chair performs his duty by reading a short audit report prepared by the internal audit department. So the question arises as to whether or not, and to what extent, the internal audit department is subject to the control of the audit committee. This issue will be discussed later.

E. Outside Audit

During the last decade, a series of reforms have been made to improve the quality of outside audit. Many of the prescriptions of the Sarbanes-Oxley Act have been imported to Korea almost verbatim. Under the current laws, the audit committee has the power to approve the appointment of an outside auditor,[56] and to approve the non-audit services of the outside auditor.[57] In practice, the audit committee routinely approves the accounting firm recommended by management. In a few firms under professional management, however, the audit committee starts playing a more active role, exercising the power on pro-

---

55) *Jusig hoesaui oebugamsa e gwanhan beobryul* [Act on External Audit of Stock Companies], Act No. 3297 of 1980 (last amended by Act No. 7524, May 31, 2005) art. 2.

56) *See id.* art. 4(2).

57) *Gongin hoegesabeob* [Certified Accountant Act], Act No. 5255 of 1997 (last amended by Act No. 7796, Dec. 29, 2005) art. 14(3).

posals and interviews with accounting firms.

The audit committee is required to make sure that the outside auditor does her job properly. However, many audit committee members are often too busy or ill-equipped to take the initiative. Even when they have the motivation to be more active, they often do not know exactly what they are supposed to do. A small but growing number of audit committees have become more active in communicating with audit firms by holding closed sessions with outside auditors on a regular basis.

F. Audit Committee Supporting Staff

The audit function requires substantial expertise and efforts on the part of the audit committee. It is simply unrealistic to expect the audit committee to carry out all its responsibilities by itself. Although the audit committee may in principle rely on outside experts, it is undesirable for the audit committee to depend exclusively on external sources. Thus, the audit committee has basically two options. Either the audit committee uses its own in-house team of audit experts, independent from the CEO or it relies on an internal audit department of the firm.

Of the two options, the in-house team approach seems more popular among commentators. It may appear reasonable in theory, but may not work well in practice. In addition to cost concerns, it may not be easy to recruit good people for positions separate from the regular corporate hierarchy. For such people, prospects for promotion within the firm are limited. Moreover, as lateral hiring among firms is still infrequent in Korea, such people may have a hard time landing a job in other firms.

Even if the audit committee manages to find competent people, they may not function effectively. Regarded as outsiders by the firm's inside directors and officers, they may be soon alienated from the rest of the organization.[58] In the United States, it is known to be highly unusual for the audit committee to have a separate staff.[59]

Then, only the internal audit department option remains. Indeed, the audit committee is known to utilize the audit department in most cases. A principal weakness of the internal audit department option may be the lack of independence of the internal auditors from the

---

58) I know of only one case where the audit committee hired a high-level assistant from outside the company. However, this person left after only one year.

59) NATIONAL COMM'N ON FRAUDULENT FINANCIAL REPORTING, REPORT OF THE NATIONAL COMMISSION ON FRAUDULENT FINANCIAL REPORTING 43 (1987), *available at* http://www.coso.org/Publications/NCFFR.pdf.

CEO. Many argue that the audit committee, not the CEO, should take charge of the internal audit department.[60] But this is not acceptable, as internal audit constitutes an element of internal control, one of the CEO's management responsibilities. If the audit committee undermines the internal audit department's control, the CEO will have to organize his own audit team again.

Although there are some instances (mostly government-owned corporations) where a corporate auditor is in charge of internal audit, it is general practice that the internal audit department is formally under the control of the CEO. In a growing number of firms, the audit committee is granted the power to issue an order to the internal audit department and to provide input into the appointment and dismissal process. Such powers will not be enough to make the internal audit department a neutral organ. If necessary, the audit committee should hire outside experts for advice or investigation.[61]

G. Internal Control and the Audit Committee

Recently, in connection with monitoring by the board or the audit committee, the concept of internal control has attracted attention in Korea. Internal control was first discussed in the context of financial institutions.[62] Now, internal control is becoming important in industrial corporations as well. The concept of internal control, however, is not well understood in the boardroom. An internal control examination manual issued by the Financial Supervisory Service, the executive arm of the Financial Supervisory Commission (FSC), defines internal control as "a series of processes continuously implemented by all members of the firm for the purpose of protecting corporate assets, securing the accuracy and reliability of accounting materials, promoting efficiency in operation, and complying with business policies and laws and regulations." Internal control, from this standpoint, constitutes an essential element of management to which the board and the CEO are accountable. The audit committee is only responsible for assuring that the internal control system established by management is adequate and for making suggestions for change. If the internal control system is adequate, the audit committee should be entitled to rely on it unless other special circumstances exist.

---

60) At least one large listed firm is known to have the internal audit function under the exclusive control of the audit committee.
61) *Sangbeob* [Commercial Code], *supra* note 15, art. 415-2(5).
62) *See Eunhyaing beob* [Banking Act], Act No. 911 of 1950 (last amended by Act No. 7428, Mar. 31, 2005, art. 23-3; *Cheunggwon georai beob* [Securities and Exchange Act], *supra* note 4, art. 54-4.

The problem is how to introduce the concept of internal control into Korean law. As discussed earlier, Korean law is generally silent on internal control of non-financial corporations.[63] A few statutes, however, deal with certain aspects of internal control. For example, a regulation promulgated by the FSC under the Securities and Exchange Act requires the audit committee to attach a statement on the operational status of the "internal monitoring mechanism" to the annual report.[64] Although monitoring constitutes only a part of internal control under the famous COSO (Committee of Sponsoring Organizations) report,[65] it is reasonable to interpret the Korean term for internal monitoring as internal control. An important concept like internal control, however, should be squarely set forth in the statutes, not in an administrative regulation. In any event, audit committees have so far not paid much attention to this requirement, and this requirement is generally satisfied in a cursory fashion.[66] A more recent and conspicuous development may be the internal accounting control system required under the Outside Audit Act.[67] Influenced by the Sarbanes-Oxley Act, the internal accounting control system is defined as "a process continuously implemented by all members of the firm, including the board and managers, as an internal control mechanism for assuring reasonable confidence in the reliability of the financial statements of the firm."[68] It is accepted that the internal accounting control system constitutes a core component of the internal control under the COSO report. The Outside Audit Act explicitly provides that it is the CEO's responsibility to establish an internal accounting control system.[69] The Outside Audit Act requires an internal accounting control officer, a position generally held by the CFO, to submit an operation report to the audit committee, which is required to evaluate the operation report and present its findings to the board.[70] Large listed companies seem more serious about this new requirement and some have consulted one of the Big Four accounting firms as to how to satisfy the evaluation requirement. The audit committee and the outside auditor of the company are required to include an opinion on in-

---

63) Of course, that does not necessarily mean that the concept of internal control is not applicable to an industrial corporation. Regardless of the statutory basis, the CEO and the board have the duty to establish an adequate internal control system.

64) Korea Financial Supervisory Commission, Regulation on the Issuance of Securities and Disclosure, art. 72(3)(i)(F).

65) COMM. OF SPONSORING ORG. OF THE TREADWAY COMM'N, INTERNAL CONTROL AN INTEGRATED FRAMEWORK (1992).

66) In my experience, it seems that even many of those corporate employees who are responsible for the annual report are not well aware of this requirement.

67) *Jusig hoesaui oebugamsa e gwanhan beobryul* [Act on Outside Audit of Stock Companies], *supra* note 55, art. 2-2(3).

68) *Id.* art. 2-2(1).

69) *Id.* art. 2-2(3).

70) *Id.* arts. 2-2(4); 2-2(5).

ternal accounting control.[71] Some commentators in Korea question how the audit committee should prepare its own report on internal accounting control. Sole reliance on a draft report prepared by the internal audit department may be inadequate because the audit department is a part of the system being evaluated. Therefore, it may be necessary for the audit committee to hire an expert, at least once every three or four years.

H. Dangers of an Overly Active Audit Committee

In the United States, attention has been given to making the audit committee more independent and active. The report of the Blue Ribbon Committee[72] is a prime example this, and has been widely studied in Korea. The Sarbanes-Oxley Act included measures to make audit committees more independent and active, increasing the workload of audit committee members. Still, the audit committee in Korea also needs to be encouraged to play a more active role. Lacking technical competence and faced with non-cooperative management, audit committee members are likely to remain passive.

At the same time, however, one should note that there is a possibility for too much action on the part of audit committee members and an overly active audit committee can lead to counter-productivity. As explained earlier, the power and duty of the audit committee is extensive, covering almost every aspect of business operation. However, Korean statutes are not clear as to the details of what the audit committee should do to carry out its duties. The audit committee enjoys a considerable amount of discretion as long as it does not violate the Korean equivalent of fiduciary duty. As a matter of principle, too much, as well as too little, action may result in liability.

However, because it is highly unrealistic to expect a court to hold an audit committee member liable for too much action,[73] it is safer for the audit committee to be active, rather than passive. Some audit committee members may want to do more because they have no other things to do or are more interested in expanding their influence. True, there is a low risk of excessive activism on the part of the audit committee in Korea. Nonetheless, the risk does exist. Popularity of arguments in favor of a full-time member or in-house supporting

---

71) As in the United States, accounting firms in Korea are known to charge substantial fees for this additional service.

72) BLUE RIBBON COMMITTEE ON IMPROVING THE EFFECTIVENESS OF CORPORATE AUDIT COMMITTEES, REPORT AND RECOMMENDATIONS (1999), *reprinted in* 54 BUS. LAW. 1067, 1067 (1999) (including recommendations for improving the independence, effectiveness, and accountability of audit committees).

73) It is also difficult to imagine a case where the audit committee's liability for too much action is justified.

staff may be evidence of such a risk. As outside directors gain more power against management, such risk may become more real.

Equipped with the power to conduct an operation audit, an overly active audit committee may slow down, if not cripple, corporate decisionmaking. If the audit committee is involved in too many corporate decisions, the burden of its members will increase, which discourages qualified candidates with other commitments from serving on audit committees. How then do we go about discouraging too much action on the part of the audit committee? I have two suggestions. First, it may be helpful to define the activities of the audit committee according to best-practice standards. The best practice standards will in effect serve as the maximum limit of the audit committee action and require audit committee members to justify their activities not supported by the best practice. Second, and more importantly, the courts should take an active role in overseeing audit committee members. Currently, an outside director that fails to perform his fiduciary duties (as a member of the audit committee) may be held liable for damages under the KCC.[74] Such a case may arise when an outside director has failed to take some appropriate action, not when he has taken any action. In order to seek damages caused by his non-action, the plaintiff must prove the existence of a duty to act. An audit committee member certainly has a duty to act. As mentioned earlier, however, it is not clear what he should actually do to avoid legal liability. Ultimately, the courts will make a decision on the merits of each case. The line will be drawn somewhere between the two poles—the pole of inaction and the pole of best practice. The court needs to be cautious, as its decision will critically affect the audit committee practice now emerging in Korea. It seems wiser for the court to start with a relatively lenient standard. My suggestion is that if the audit committee has paid some attention to internal control, they should be exempt from legal liability at a minimum. Given a small number of qualified candidates, applying too high a standard will deter relatively competent candidates from serving on the audit committees and will likely lead to excessive auditing.

---

74) *See Sang beob* [Commercial Code], *supra* note 15, arts. 415-2(6), 414.

V. CONCLUSION

Under current statutes in Korea, the audit committee enjoys a special status, with powers over operational, as well as accounting matters. In reality, however, the audit committee does not play a significant role. It is overshadowed by the board in operation auditing, and by outside auditors in accounting auditing. In conducting the operation audit, the line between the board and the audit committee is not clear. The corporate auditor is given the power of the operation audit because legislators were concerned that the board may not properly perform the monitoring function. In a small but growing number of large listed firms, the board has taken a more active role in monitoring, primarily due to the increase of outside directors on the board. If the board is properly engaged, the role of the audit committee may be adjusted to concentrate on accounting matters. In addition, for firms that are required to perform an outside audit, the audit committee should be allowed to rely on the work of outside auditors. This change would make the audit committee in Korea function like the audit committee in the United States.

Finally, a few remarks on the significance of the Korean experience with the audit committee are in order. Corporate governance scholars have widely held that despite globalization, formal convergence will not take place in the near future, if ever.[75] Developments in Korea may be pointed out as a prime example of counter-evidence to this wellknown proposition. Outside directors and the audit committee were virtually unheard of within Korea's business circles until the early 1990s. In less than a decade, however, they are now becoming increasingly visible throughout the business community.

Formal convergence is not limited to the corporate organizational structure. The Korean government has just prepared a bill to revise its corporate statutes. The bill includes many of the changes made in the new Japanese Corporate Code. Principles that are intended to protect creditor interests will be substantially diminished, if not completely abandoned. The securities that a corporation may issue will be substantially expanded. In short, Korean statutes will become more like their American counterparts.

This kind of formal convergence seems to be occurring in other developed countries as well. Japan is a good example, and the European Union and its member countries also seem to be moving in the same direction, albeit far more slowly. Arguably, this convergence is occurring only in form, but not in substance. Both outside directors and the audit com-

---

75) *See* Ronald J. Gilson, *Globalizing Corporate Governance: Convergence of Form or Function*, 49 AM. J. COMP. L. 329, 337-39 (2001).

mittee in Korea behave differently than their American counterparts. This is hardly surprising given that the people and the business environments (the legal profession, social norms, cultures, job markets, etc.) are different between the two countries.

Difference in substance should not be overemphasized, however. For example, outside directors and the audit committee were much less important in corporate governance in the United States thirty years ago. Many firms in the United States may still fall far short of best practice standards. True, the establishment of a well functioning board and an audit committee may not be as easy as manufacturing cars or electronic appliances. As time passes, however, the role of outside directors and the audit committee in Korea may grow to become as important as in the United States. From a long-term perspective, even convergence in substance may not be as difficult as it first appears.

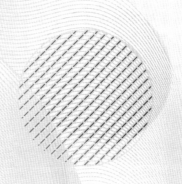

III. Conflict of interest and fiduciary duties

Revamping Fiduciary Duties in Korea: Does Law Matter in Corporate Governance?

Kon Sik Kim*

Joongi Kim †

I. Introduction[1]

Within the framework of whether convergence of corporate governance models will occur or whether a path dependence of differences will prevail, a provocative debate in comparative corporate governance discourse concerns whether law, social norms, market pressure or other factors matter more in terms of corporate governance reform. Korea offers an interesting example to examine this debate. A general consensus has emerged among policy makers and scholars that Korea's corporate governance needs to make the transition to a more capital markets-oriented system.[2] The question remains what type of role should law play in achieving this transformation. The role of law will be examined through the fiduciary duty of directors, the core principle of common law systems.

Several conflicting views exist on this subject. Economists such as La Porta, Lopez-de-Silane, Shleifer and Vishny ("LLSV") have in fact empirically advocated that deep capital markets cannot develop without investor protections.[3] They therefore stress the importance of legal

* Professor of Law, Seoul National University, College of Law, konsikim@snu.ac.kr

† Associate Professor of Law, Yonsei University, Graduate School of International Studies, kimjg@yonse-i.ac.kr

1) An abridged version of the paper was first presented for a conference sponsored by the Center for International Political Economy and Columbia Law School titled "Global Markets, Domestic Institutions: Corporate Law and Governance in a New Era of Cross-Border Deals" on April 5-6, 2002. The authors would like to like to express their thanks to Jeong Min Lee for her assistance in preparing this article.

2) Simon Johnson et al., *Corporate Governance in the Asian Financial Crisis*, 58 J. FIN. ECON. 141 (2000); KFSC ("Korea Financial Supervisory Commission") and KFSS ("Korea Financial Supervisory Service"). *Financial Reform and Supervision in Korea 2000*. Seoul.

3) Rafael La Portaet al., *Investor Protection and Corporate Governance*, 58 J. FIN.ECON. 3(2000); Rafael La Porta et al., *Law and Finance*, 106 J. POL. ECON. 1113 (1998); Rafael La Porta et al., *Legal Determinants of External Finance*,52 J. FIN. 1131(1997).

reforms.[4] In contrast, some legal scholars instead are more skeptical of the impact of corporate law. These skeptics emphasize that market pressure plays a more significant role.[5] In the case of Fischel and Bradley, they go so far as to provide that legal means such as fiduciary duties and derivative actions are overrated in terms of their utility.[6] Eisenberg and Cooter even suggests that management's behavior can be better restrained not through legal norms but more through social norms.[7] Coffee in turn recently concludes the importance of private action through self-regulation must be emphasized relative to legal change.[8]

This paper considers that these various positions are not as conflicting as they appear. It will argue that in the early stages of corporate governance reform the law, as shown through the fiduciary duty of directors, plays a critical role. Social norms, private action through self-regulation and market-based pressure undoubtedly are important as well but this paper presumes that the foundation of corporate governance reform begins with law-based discipline. Dispersed ownership and developed capital markets-oriented system as a whole have had difficulty in developing without an effective corporate governance system.[9] The most important concept in terms of legal protections remains the fiduciary duty for directors. It provides the means to minimize the potential for expropriation and the conflict between managers and shareholders. During the Asian financial crisis in late 1998, Korea indeed amended its Commercial Code to explicitly establish a "fiduciary duty" for directors.[10] According to the intentions of the Ministry of Justice, which was in charge of drafting the

---

4) For a legal scholar that emphasizes the importance of legal infrastructure see Bernard Black, *The Legal and Institutional Preconditions for Strong Securities Markets*,48 UCLA L. REV.781 (2001).

5) FRANK H. EASTERBROOK AND DAINEL R. FISCHEL. THE ECONOMIC STRUCTURE OF CORPORATE LAW(1991).

6) Daniel R. Fischeland Michael Bradley, *The Role of Liability Rules and Derivative Suit in Corporate Law: A Theoretical and Empirical Analysis*,71 CORNELL L. REV. 261(1986).

7) Melvin A. Eisenberg, *Corporate Law and Social Norms*, 99 COLUM. L. REV. 1253 (1999); Robert Cooter and Melvin A. Eisenberg, *Norms and Corporate Law; Fairness, Character, and Efficiency in Firms*, 149 U. PA. L. REV. 1717 (2001).

8) John Coffee, *The Rise of Dispersed Ownership: The Roles of Law and the State in the Separation of Ownership and Control*, 111 Yale L. J. 1 (2001).

9) Coffee suggests that private action through self-regulation also is critical. Coffee. "The Rise of Dispersed Ownership."Cheffins finds that the U.K.'s stock markets were able to develop even though shareholder protections based upon corporate law were greatly lacking. Brian Cheffins, *Does Law Matter? The Separation of Ownership and Control*, 30 J. LEGAL STUD. 459 (2001).

10) Article 382-3 of the Commercial Code, which is titled "The Fiduciary Duty of Directors," provides that "directors must carry out their official duties in a faithful manner on behalf of the corporation according to the law and the articles of incorporation." In contrast, officers and controlling shareholders are not subject to an explicit fiduciary duty. Bernard Black et al., Corporate Governance in Korea *at the Millennium*, 26 J. Corp. L. 537(2001) (suggesting the adoption of an explicit duty for directors to deal with all shareholders in a fair and equitable manner and to ensure equal treatment to all shareholders of the same class).

revisions to the Commercial Code, this new provision was meant to establish an Anglo-American style fiduciary duty.[11] The primary purpose of the duty was of course to help minimize the acute conflict of interests that arise out of the controlling shareholder's domination of corporate decision-making in Korea. While legislatively transplanting a concept such as a fiduciary duty might be relatively simple, many obstacles must be overcome before such concepts effectively function within a country's corporate governance system. The ultimate challenge is how to make fiduciary duty-type protections effective.[12]

Through the application of the fiduciary duty of directors, this paper will seek to highlight the importance of a comprehensive legal infrastructure to bring about corporate governance reform. As a result, it will describe why such a legal infrastructure is critical in the initial stages for a country to develop an effective fiduciary duty and how such a legal infrastructure can be developed to embark on the road to deeper, liquid securities markets. It will show that Korea is finally beginning to formulate a more effective corporate governance structure following the recent establishment of such a comprehensive legal infrastructure based upon fiduciary duty.

This paper will start in Part II by exploring the nature of the agency problem that exists in Korean corporations. It will discuss the controlling shareholder's disproportionate influence and the complicated ownership structure of conglomerates. The various means to reduce the agency costs through such factors as the role of the state, social norms, organizational structure, market pressure and legal structure that existed in the past will be reviewed. It will also provide a more in-depth review of the legal limitations affecting the effective application of the fiduciary duty of directors. Part III seeks to explain what had to be done to make the fiduciary duty of directors function more effectively. It reviews the significance of Korea's recent establishment of an explicit fiduciary duty for directors. It highlights elements necessary for strengthening fiduciary duties including effective private enforcement mechanisms such as class actions, the possibility of disgorgement of ill-gotten gains, and the role of the judiciary and attorneys. Part IV will show how the basic legal infrastructure was critical in effectively shaping the contours of the fiduciary duty in Korea

---

11) Ministry of Justice, *Gaejung sangbop* (*hwesapyun*)[Revised Commercial Code (Corporation Section)], Haesul [Commentaries; in Korean], 1999, 46. In the case of Japan, the U.S. occupation forces brought about the inclusion of an explicit fiduciary provision in Japan's Commercial Code, presently Article 254-3, in 1950. Although Korea's modern Commercial Code largely followed s modern Commercial Code largely followed Japan's Commercial Code when it was established in 1962, for some reason, this explicit fiduciary duty provision was not included at the time.
12) Daniel Berkowitz et al., *Economic Development, Legality and the Transplant Effect*, EUR. ECON. REV. (2002 forthcoming).

and spur corporate governance reform through several recently decided landmark cases. Part V summarizes these findings in a conclusion.

II. The Nature of the Agency Problem in Korean Firms

1. Disproportionate Control by Family Clans

While the emphasis might be different in some countries, the main goal of the corporate law is to minimize the potential for expropriation by insiders. According to the classic hypothesis of Berle and Means, as the ownership of large corporations becomes more dispersed, most shareholders lose their ability to act as controlling owners and instead managers with marginal ownership stakes begin to dominate the corporation.[13] They emphasized that under a governance structure with divided ownership and control it was necessary to establish appropriate monitoring mechanisms to ensure that managers did not neglect the interests of shareholders. In many other countries, especially those that follow a civil law tradition, in contrast, ownership and control has not separated and blockholders have remained in control.

At first, the governance structure of Korea's largest firms, the *chaebol*, resembled this latter and more prevalent type of blockholder model and controlling shareholders maintained considerably concentrated ownership positions.[14] Controlling shareholders therefore remained significant shareholders sharing similar concerns with other shareholders. Therefore the larger their share ownership, the more their interests were aligned with the corporation's and other shareholders. In the past, therefore, the agency problem was not as pronounced and the checks and balances to monitor it were not as needed or well developed. Over time, however, the ownership structure has changed. Founder-owners and their family maintained their control over management, but their ownership positions as represented through their cash flow rights dramatically declined. (Chart 1) Personal ownership stakes including family interests fell to less than 5% in most *chaebol*. Despite these dwindling eco-

---

13) ADOLPH BERLE AND GARDINER MEANS, THE MODERN CORPORATION AND PRIVATE PROPERTY (1968 rev.).

14) This paper focuses on the large family-controlled conglomerates called *chaebol* that dominate Korea's economy.

nomic stakes in terms of cash flow rights, they could maintain firm control over voting rights through cross ownership structures or pyramidal schemes.[15] Controlling shareholders dominated approximately 40% of the total voting rights through these types of cross shareholding structures. With the relative portion controlled through cross shareholding further increasing following the financial crisis, the disparity between the controlling family's cash flow rights and its voting control has widened.[16]

The ownership structure in major Korean firms has further altered with the rise in institutional ownership, particularly by foreign investors. Foreign institutional investors for instance now own close to 30% of the stock market.[17] In terms of corporate governance, unfortunately, a considerable number of domestic institutional investors are direct affiliates of *chaebol* or rely upon them for business, and therefore remain captive and passive.[18] Foreign investors in contrast are marginally more willing to take action but are restricted for other reasons such as the complications of a proxy process that operates through custodians.[19] As a result, this complex ownership structure aggravates the agency problem and the conflicts of interest between the controlling shareholder and non-controlling shareholders because it ultimately grants the controlling shareholders ruling power that far exceeds their cash flow rights based upon their personal ownership. This structure thereby leaves these controlling shareholders, who usually hold the title of "Chairman," open to the potential of favoring their personal interests over the interests of the non-controlling shareholders.[20] Controlling shareholders were never held accountable and ruled unchallenged like emperors within their *chaebol* empires irrespective of their performance and regardless of their potential for expropriation.[21] Korea's agency problem was particularly severe because of the sig-

---

15) Korea Fair Trade Commission; Rafael La Porta, et al., *Corporate Ownership Around the World*, 54 J. FIN. 471 (1999).

16) Hasung Jang, *An Analysis of the Effects of Corporate Restructuring after the Economic Crisis*, Korea University, mimeographed (2000).

17) At Korea's premier companies such as Samsung Electronics, SK Telecom, Hyundai Motors, Kookmin Bank, foreigners own majority positions.

18) In a powerful example of the influence of the chaebol that occurred in the spring of 2001, during the proxy process of obtaining votes for an outside director candidate proposed by minority shareholders at one of Korea's leading companies, a host of institutional investors who had initially disclosed publicly that they would support this candidate abruptly reversed their positions buckling under pressure from the chaebol and their affiliates. Hasung Jang and Joongi Kim, *Nascent Stage of Corporate Governance in an Emerging Market: Regulatory Change, Shareholder Activism and Samsung Electronics*, 10 CORP. GOVERNANCE: AN INT'L REV. 84 (2002).

19) Jooyoung Kim and Joongi Kim, *Shareholder Activism in Korea: How PSPD Used Legal Measures to Improve Corporate Governance*, 1 J. KOREAN L. 51 (2001).

20) These conflicts are explained in greater detail in subsection 5.

21) This state of affairs was compounded because a strong perception existed that many of the chaebol became "too big to fail"and the government often times needlessly prolonged their impending collapses

nificantly large gap between cash flow rights and voting rights; it became a country with
in effect "dispersed ownership" but still maintained a weak degree of investor protections.

2. Role of the State

During the early stages of Korea's economic development, agency costs were largely restrained through the state's control.[22] The state dominated private firms through their total
control of financing, credit, foreign exchange, licenses and approvals and protectionist trade
policies. With debt-to-equity ratios exceeding 500%, firms were completely reliant upon
debt financing from banks that were in turn owned and controlled by the state. Through
its industrial policy, the state encouraged conglomerates to use their affiliates to expand into
new business areas.

Shareholders were protected indirectly and almost residually because firms led by managers
that were considered incompetent or unscrupulous generally had difficulty in receiving government support. Given that the state's priority was economic growth and high employment, the potential expropriation of shareholders was not a primary concern and firms were
given considerable discretion as long as they performed.

In recent years, however, the state's role has noticeably diminished. Starting from the early
1980s with the privatization of commercial banks, and since the late 1980s, with the start
of a dramatic process of democratization and decentralization of power, the role of the state
has receded. Without a specific basis in the law, the state is now increasingly hesitant to
interfere with business activities, at least overtly. The capital markets have also rapidly expanded growing over 94 times in terms of market capitalization from 1980 to 2001.
Furthermore, with the onset of the financial crisis, the role of commercial banks has dramatically declined with corporate debt-to-equity ratios dropping below 200%.[23] Although
the government still maintains some controls through financing, foreign exchange and approval and licensing, overall its power has diminished considerably.[24]

---

despite clear signs of mismanagement and abuse.

22) WON-HYUK LIM ET AL., ECONOMIC CRISIS AND CORPORATE RESTRUCTURING IN KOREA,
Cambridge University Press (forthcoming).

23) OECD Economic Surveys. p. 132 (September, 2001).

24) With the government's recent bailout of a host of commercial banks and financial institutions, although
foreign strategic investors are being sought, the state's influence has still increased in the short term.
Housing and Commercial Bank, Kookmin Bank, Korea Exchange Bank, Korea First Bank, Hanmi Bank
and Hana Bank are among the leading banks now primarily controlled by foreign concerns.

3. Internal Governance Structure

The various types of agency problem discussed above may be structurally monitored through a range of internal control mechanisms. The internal mechanisms include traditional norms that directly seek to restrain a manager such as their fiduciary duty, shareholders' meetings, board of directors and audit committees, and various market pressures. This section will discuss the internal corporate governance mechanisms, while the external market factors and fiduciary duties will be covered in subsequent sections.

Like in other countries, corporations in Korea are composed of various organs such as the general shareholders' meeting, the board of directors, representative directors and statutory internal auditors. These organs are supposed to act as checks and balances against each other to prevent conflicts. If each corporate organ performs its assigned function properly, the agency problem or potential for expropriation would be far more tolerable. Until recently, however, this entire internal corporate institutional structure as a whole failed to adequately work, primarily due to the exorbitant dominance of controlling shareholders. For instance, shareholders' meetings were mere formalities in the past, and only recently have become far more serious fora for discussion.[25]

Previously, the board of directors of even the largest companies was composed of those loyal to the controlling shareholder, which all but compromised their ability to act as monitors. In the first place, formal board meetings were never held. If a board meeting was convened no discussions or objections occurred. Controlling shareholders could further their own interests because they completely dominated the decision-making process of the corporation.

To rectify this situation, the government has undertaken several notable structural reforms such as the requirement that publicly held listed companies must appoint outside directors and certain larger companies must also establish audit committees instead of a statutory auditor.[26] If truly independent outside directors also are on a board, it will be an added

---

25) Joongi Kim, *Recent Amendments to the Korean Commercial Code and Their Effects on International Competition*, 21 U. PENN. J. INT'L ECON. L. 273 (2000).

26) The Listing Rules of the Korea Stock Exchange first required that listed companies had to have at least one outside director beginning in February 1998 and in January 2000 the Securities Exchange Act was amended to require that at least 25% of the board must consist of outside directors. Companies with more than 2 trillion won not only must have board with at least 50% outside directors nominated by an outside director nominating committee but they must also have audit committees. The number of outside directors stands at 1418 as of 2000. *Saoeisa Tongye* (Statistics of Outside Directors), Korea Listed Companies Association.

restraint against controlling shareholders from blatantly pursuing their own self-interest. Outside directors can thus act as additional monitors of the controlling shareholder just by being on the board, and an audit committee consisting solely of outside directors can be theoretically more effective in reducing the potential for conflict of interest transactions than a statutory auditor, a position usually occupied by senior managers just before they retire.

From this perspective the recent reforms mandating the appointment of outside directors and audit committees are positive developments. In practice, however, it is not a simple task to successfully strengthen internal governance just by such reforms. The most important factors are of course the independence and competency of the persons involved. Unfortunately, recent statistics show that the controlling shareholders themselves have been selecting the outside directors in over 70% of the time.[27] While large companies have to elect their outside directors through outside director nominating committees, invariably those chosen are based on the preferences of the controlling shareholder and management. In fact, until recently shareholders could not even make a shareholder proposal to nominate a candidate for the outside director nominating committee to consider. Audit committees are in turn composed of the same outside directors.

Because of these limitations, many observers are skeptical of the efficacy of the outside director and audit committee system. The perception toward outside directors has been recently sullied by several scandals involving outside directors.[28] Yet, the negative criticism of these systems appears substantially based upon excessive expectations. While not readily apparent as of yet, the benefits of these reforms will no doubt increase as outside directors become more comfortable and knowledgeable about their role as fiduciaries. In several isolated but significant cases, outside directors of leading companies have recently played a critical role in safeguarding internal corporate governance, a promising sign that is emboldening other outsider directors to become more active as well.[29]

---

27) *Saoeisa Tongye* (Statistics of Outside Directors), Korea Listed Companies Association.
28) *Outside Director System in Need of Mending*, CHOSUN ILBO (Seoul), (Aug. 25, 2000). In one case, outside directors received preferential loans from the company to purchase non-tendered shares following a rights issue leading to 'in the money options.'
29) For example, the outside directors of Hyundai Heavy Industries forced the company to file a suit against a Hyundai Group affiliate for indemnification based upon a guaranty after HHI was forced to make substantial payments based on a put option on the affiliate's behalf. The Seoul District Court ruled in favor of Hyundai Heavy Industries. Seoul District Court, Judgment No. 2000 ka hap 54623 (Jan. 25, 2002).

4. The Market as a Controlling Mechanism

The private interests of the controlling shareholder can be also minimized through stronger market-based controls such as a more open product market, labor market for managers, market for corporate control and capital market.[30] This type of market-based pressure can also serve as yet another way to reduce the agency problems with respect to the dominant controlling shareholders in Korea. The only market that has been functioning even to a limited degree, however, has been the product market.[31] Heavily dependent on exports, Korean firms have long faced pressure from competition in international markets. In the future, as Korea's domestic market continues to liberalize, domestic-oriented corporations will also be subject to similar pressures. Overall, at this point, all of these various market mechanisms have been relatively underdeveloped in Korea, largely by design of economic policy makers who sought to protect firms. It is widely agreed that controlling shareholders in Korea have been, and still are, relatively free from these market pressures.[32]

A flexible labor market for managers for instance has yet to evolve in Korea. For such lateral movement to occur where professional managers transfer between different companies, business practices must first become more transparent and accountable. Otherwise, personal loyalty will always be preferred over managerial competence and the long-standing practice of recruiting managers from within a corporation changes will continue. The more top management can hide and is held unaccountable the more difficult it will be for them to recruit outsiders. With increased accountability, however, competent managers will have less incentive to condone expropriation committed by controlling shareholders if they have to sacrifice themselves and assume potential risk, especially if they have other employment options. Thus, managerial transparency and accountability must be established, for the management labor market to develop.

Recently, the merger and acquisition market has received considerable attention in Korea. The conflicts concerning controlling shareholders and inside managers for instance could both be substantially marginalized if the external corporate control market itself could act as an effective source of discipline, especially given the low cash flow rights held by control-

---

30) See, e.g., Melvin A. Eisenberg, *The Modernization of Corporation Law: An Essay for Bill Cary*, 37 U. MIAMI L. REV. 187, 203-04 (1998).
31) Companies with substantial exports have faced considerable pressure from the international markets.As market liberalization continues, the pressure on more domestic companies will increase as well.
32) Kim, *Recent Amendments, supra* note 25, 277-278.

ling shareholders. Admittedly replacing controlling shareholders through mergers and acquisitions might not be the most efficient way, but an active merger and acquisition market clearly can contribute to the reduction of agency costs. Hostile mergers and acquisitions as a whole could be attempted where the controlling shareholder's ownership stake is relatively small and the potential value differs substantially from the market stock price. In the past, hostile mergers or acquisitions were distant events in faraway countries but now hostile takeovers are becoming a more familiar concept in the Korean business community.

While Korean companies remain considerably undervalued below their potential, controlling shareholders still retain their ruling power. Following past history, there still has yet to be a hostile takeover since the end of the financial crisis. Controlling shareholders can rely on a host of defensive measures. Restrictions on the repurchase of shares for instance have largely been eliminated.[33] A more critical obstacle is perhaps the lack of information. While substantial improvement has been made, accounting information still is not widely trusted. So a merger or acquisition often falters because unexpected information such as vast contingent liabilities surface during the due diligence process. Acquiring a company without access to an accurate financial status results in indeterminable and unacceptable risks. At the same time, although considerable progress has been achieved, many observers and policymakers remain skeptical of the efficacies of hostile tender offers. Public hostility toward such attempts also remains.[34] At present, for instance, large *chaebol* and foreign investors remain the only viable sources of carrying out such acquisitions. Since the financial crisis up until October 2001, among the seven tender offers made, six were carried out by foreign companies.[35]

The product market, labor market for managers, and corporate control market may indirectly restrain controlling shareholders, but the capital market may be the best way to monitor the controlling shareholder. The Korean legal community has so far not devoted serious attention to the relationship between agency problems and the capital market. In countries where the capital market functions more adequately, however, it is considered that the agency problems are less severe. Corporations that have controlling shareholders with poor reputations or that have disproportionate voting rights are not highly appreciated by

---

33) Article 189-2, Securities Exchange Act.
34) For an opposite assessment, see Hwa-Jin Kim, *Toward the 'Best Practice' Model in a Globalizing Market: Recent Development in Korean Corporate Governance*, Y.B. L. and Legal Practice in East Asia, vol. 5. London: Sweet & Maxwell (2002).
35) Bokki Hong, *Recent Events Surrounding Tender Offers and Several Problems Concerning the Current Securities Laws*, HYUN-DAE-SANG-SA-BUP-RON-JIP(in Korean) 241 (2001); Hwa-Jin Kim, M&A AND CORPORATE CONTROL(in Korean), 3rd ed. *Bakyoungsa*, Seoul, Korea (1999).

investors. Accordingly, the share price of such corporations will tend to fall and their credit rating will be lower.

In the past when banks generously offered indirect financing to corporations with collateral security or political connections, a fall in share prices or credit ratings was not necessarily a serious problem. As corporations increasingly rely on the capital market, however, minimizing financing costs by maintaining investor confidence is becoming more important. In the United States, for instance, the practice of appointing outside directors and seeking audits by independent outside accounting firms emerged, not because of any statutory requirement, but because of the voluntary decisions on the part of the corporations themselves to secure investor confidence. As a result, one reason why controlling shareholders abuse tends to be more limited in the United States is not only because of its strong legal protection of minority shareholders, but also because the problem has been diminished through the pressure of its well-developed capital market. While minimal as of yet, such tendencies are beginning to appear in Korea as well. A classic example may be the recent splintering of the giant Hyundai Group. The loss of confidence it suffered in the market can be traced to several critical business decisions and the melodramatic succession fight carried out by two of the founder's sons.[36]

In the end, Korean companies are paying far more attention to share prices than in the past. With a favorable industrial policy based upon generous credit coming to an end, costs associated with direct financing are becoming critical for a Korean firm. Accordingly, Korean corporations are gradually beginning to face pressure to restrain controlling shareholder expropriation and to improve their ownership structures. Yet, controlling shareholders of course have little incentive to be sensitive to share prices because their interests are not as aligned; they do not have any intentions to sell their shares to seek a profit and they cannot hold stock options.[37]

5. Limitations Affecting the Effective Application of Fiduciary Duty-type Obligations

As mentioned previously, while the need to minimize the conflicts of interests of controlling shareholders has increased, the internal controls in Korean companies and the external

---

36) Don Kirk, *As Korean Heirs Feud, An Empire Is Withering; Changes and Frail Finances Doom the Old Hyundai*, NEW YORK TIMES, Apr. 26, 2001, at A1.

37) Controlling shareholders and their related parties cannot own stock options. Art. 189-4, Para. 1, Securities Exchange Act; Art. 84-6, Para 1, Implementing Decree.

controls based on market pressures remained weak. Therefore, the role of fiduciary duties as explained below is even more important in the case of Korea. This section will describe how fiduciary-type duties were applied in Korea and will review the limitations and problems that brought about the recent adoption of an explicit fiduciary duty.

5.1 Duty of Care asa Good Manager: Functional Equivalent of Fiduciary Duties

Under Korean law, the relationship between the corporation and a director constitutes a contract of mandate (Korean Commercial Code, "KCC," Art. 382 II). This means that by reference the mandate provisions under the Civil Code (Arts. 680-692) apply and like a mandatary in a mandate contract, a director always has a "duty of care of a good manager" ("good manager duty") (Civil Code, Art. 681). Considerable dispute existed among commentators as to the meaning of this good manager duty, particularly as to how it compares with the fiduciary duties of directors under U.S. law.[38]

A number of scholars, for instance, argued that this good manager duty encompassed only the fiduciary duty of care as provided under U.S. law, and therefore Korea had to follow Japan's example in explicitly adopting a duty of loyalty provision in its Commercial Code.[39] This view seems to originate, at least partly, from the literal similarity between the expression "the duty of care of a good manager" and "the fiduciary duty of care." The concept of the good manager duty itself does derive from the Civil Code of Japan (Art. 644). Yet, the legislative history at the time shows that the Japanese drafters did not necessarily intend to exclude the duty of loyalty aspect by choosing the word "care."[40] Given the open-ended nature of the good manager duty, a persuasive reason does not exist as to why it should be interpreted as only covering the duty of care standard as applied in the United States.

A better view seems that the good manager duty may be interpreted as a functional equivalent of the fiduciary duties imposed on directors under the U.S. corporate law. Those who support the opposite view even acknowledge that directors have the duty of loyalty even in the absence of an explicit provision.[41] Therefore, in practical terms the two views do not

---

38) A similar debate has been raised in Japan.

39) See Jae Yeol Kwon, "Toward Fostering Management Accountability: Finding Korea's Own Path by Reference to American Law and Experience" (Unpublished J.S.D. Dissertation, Georgetown University), 300-05. 1994.

40) Hamada M. 1987. *Simpan chushaku kaishaho*(New Edition of Commentaries on Corporate Law)(in Japanese)vol. 6: 32-34.

41) Tong Yoon Chung, *HOESABOP*(Corporate Law), 6th revised ed., 208; Bopmunsa, Seoul, Korea: 427-428. 2000.

differ significantly. While the controversy arguably has been more a matter of academic interest and at a conceptual level the merits of distinguishing between the good manager duty and the fiduciary duty are questionable, it is still necessary to review the significance of the recent regulatory change.[42]

It cannot be denied that the concept of the good manager duty is much less developed in Korea than the concept of fiduciary duty under Anglo-American law. This underdeveloped state may be due to several factors, but the inherent inadequacy of the concept, however, is not a reason. This does not mean elaborating or clarifying the good manager duty according to the American model is meaningless. In the end, it is important to note that the KCC already did have a statutory concept in terms of fiduciary duty that had the potential to grow into an equivalent of its American counterpart but for some reason it did not. During the midst of the Asian financial crisis in late 1998, Korea indeed amended its Commercial Code to explicitly establish a "fiduciary duty" for directors.[43] According to the Ministry of Justice, which was in charge of drafting the revisions to the Commercial Code, this new provision was intended to establish an Anglo-American style fiduciary duty.[44] The primary goal of the duty was of course to help minimize the acute conflict of interests that arose out of the management's domination of corporate decision-making. In any case, the new Article 382-3 has now brought this rather unproductive academic dispute to an end. Under the explicit concept of fiduciary duty, the Commercial Code now offers a solid basis upon which to develop an effective jurisprudence to monitor both directors and the controlling shareholders. Perhaps, the ultimate significance is probably that it enhanced the awareness of the importance of the concept among the judiciary, managers, practitioners and investors alike.

---

42) Fora in-depth analysis on this issue, see Kwon, 300-05; Christopher Heftel, *Corporate Governance in Japan: The Position of Shareholders in Publicly Held Corporations,* 5 HAWAII L. REV.135, 182(1983)(stating that "[t]he duty of care of a good manager under the civil law is a lesser standard than the American concept of fiduciary duty").

43) Article 382-3 of the Commercial Code, which is titled "The Fiduciary Duty of Directors,"provides that "directors must carry out their official duties in a faithful manner on behalf of the corporation according to the law and the articles of incorporation." In contrast, officers and controlling shareholders are not subject to an explicit fiduciary duty. Black et al. "Corporate Governance in Korea at the Millennium."(suggesting the adoption of an explicit duty for directors to deal with all shareholders in a fair and equitable manner and to ensure equal treatment to all shareholders of the same class).

44) Revised Commercial Code (Corporation Section), Commentaries, 46. In the case of Japan, the U.S. occupation forces brought about the inclusion of an explicit fiduciary provision in Japan's Commercial Code, presently Article 254-3, in 1950. Although Korea's modern Commercial Code largely followed Japan's Commercial Code when it was established in 1962, for some reason, this explicit fiduciary duty provision was not included at the time.

5.2 Provisions Related to Fiduciary Duties

Before the recent establishment of an explicit fiduciary duty, several existing provisions provided a basis for a U.S.-style fiduciary duty for Korean corporate directors. The KCC, like the laws of other countries, had provisions designed to restrain management misconduct with respect to the following different situations: (1) self-dealing, and (2) competition with the corporation. If a director violated the duty of a good manager or a more specific duty regarding (1) or (2) above, then the director was liable to the corporation for any damages (Art. 399(1)). If the director failed to fulfill the director's duty intentionally or by gross negligence, then the director was liable even to third parties (Art. 401(1)). The following subsection provides a short description of the first two fiduciary rules and discusses some defects of the present statutes.

a. Self-Dealing

Directors who seek to execute transactions with the corporation on their own behalf or on behalf of a third person must obtain board approval (Art. 398). Although the KCC does not expressly provide so, it is generally agreed that this requirement only applies to those transactions that pose a conflict of interest between the director and the corporation. For instance, a director is not required to seek board approval to perform an existing obligation to the corporation. The courts have held that transactions effected without the approval of the board are null and void.[45] The courts have further found, however, that when a director acting on behalf of the corporation and a third party enters into a questionable transaction without the board's approval, the corporation may not claim that the unapproved transaction was invalid against the third party unless it proves that the third party was, or had a reason to be, aware of the absence of board approval at the time of the transaction.[46]

b. Competition with the Corporation

A director who intends to enter into a transaction that falls within the same line of business as the corporation must obtain approval of the board (Art. 397(1)). A director who desires to become a director of another corporation engaged in the same line of business must obtain board approval as well. A transaction executed without the required board approval is still valid regardless of whether the opposing party knew or not. If the director

---

45) Supreme Court, Judgment No. 80 Ta 828 (July. 22, 1980).
46) Supreme Court, Judgment No. 173 Ta 955 (Jan. 15, 1974).

acts on his own behalf, then the corporation may treat the transaction as though it was executed on behalf of the corporation. If the director acts on behalf of a third person, then the corporation may still demand any benefit resulting from such transaction. The unscrupulous and avaricious director ultimately may be liable to the corporation for any damage caused by the director's conduct and may eventually be removed.

The KCC fails to adopt the so-called corporate opportunity doctrine, at least explicitly. This does not mean that directors can claim corporate opportunities at will without any accountability. Seizing corporate opportunities violate general fiduciary duties even though preventing them in practice through the fiduciary duty provision might be difficult. For directors of companies that have failed to prevent this opportunity they are only potentially liable for their inaction, but it may be difficult to consider their inaction a breach of a fiduciary duty. Furthermore, it is unclear whether the directors that succeeded in obtaining this corporate opportunity could be responsible to any one else. According to the traditional view, for instance, it may be difficult for the company to prove that it incurred damages. Second, the problem of seizing corporate opportunities can be partially resolved through Article 397 that covers non-competition. Yet, Article 397, which seeks to prohibit competition with the corporation, is quite limited compared with that of the "corporate opportunity" doctrine in the United States that precludes corporate fiduciaries from usurping corporate opportunities. Although U.S. courts are not in complete agreement as to what constitutes a corporate opportunity, the two major tests are the so-called "interest or expectancy" test and the so-called "line of business" test. Under the interest test, corporate opportunities may be defined as "opportunities in which the corporation has a right, property interest, or expectancy, or which in justice should belong to the corporation."[47] Under the line of business test, a business opportunity will be deemed to be a corporate opportunity if it is closely associated with, or essential to, the corporation's existing business activities. In contrast, considering that the KCC does not have a separate provision concerning corporate opportunities, the line of business concept needs to be interpreted liberally in Korea. A business opportunity is not required to be identical to the corporation's existing line of business. It may constitute a corporate opportunity if it shares significant, common elements such as marketing, for example, with any existing corporate business.[48]

---

47) HARRY HENN, HANDBOOK OF THE LAW OF CORPORATIONS AND OTHER BUSINESS ENTERPRISES, 2nd ed., 462 (1970).

48) According to Dean Clark, a business of making and selling contact lens wetting solution may be held to constitute a corporate opportunity of a corporation engaged in producing cold medicines since "the methods of marketing and distributing the products - through drug stores, for example - overlapped enough to permit significant economies of scale if the businesses were to be combined." ROBERT C.

In terms of allocating business opportunities, it leaves substantial room for uncertainty or abuse, especially in the group context. As mentioned earlier, in the case of Korea, each chaebol is engaged in a wide variety of business activities. It may not be always easy to determine which member firm should be allowed to pursue a new business project. Controlling shareholders will be naturally inclined to allocate more promising projects to subsidiaries in which they own higher personal interests.[49]

III. The Importance of Legal Infrastructure Surrounding Fiduciary Duties: Does Law Still Matters

With the declining the role of the state, lack of market-based pressure, the increased need to develop its capital markets and other factors, the need for corporate governance reform in Korea became critical. This section describes the various governance reform measures that were adopted to develop the legal infrastructure in Korea. It begins with a discussion of the legal changes and then describes the actual implementation and enforcement process, which are ultimately as important as the norms of the law itself. This section will then discuss the various ways that are still needed to improve the legal structure.

1. Inadequate Restraint of Controlling Shareholders

1.1 Lack of the Concept of Controlling Shareholders

Korean corporate law itself lacked the concept of a "controlling shareholder." The provisions related to self-dealing, competition with the corporation, and liability to the corporation for instance only applied to such statutory organs as the "director" or "statutory auditor."[50] Given the dominant influence of controlling shareholders in Korean corpo-

---

CLARK, CORPORATE LAW: Little, Brown ad Co., 228 (1986).

49) Conscious of this possibility of abuse in the parent-subsidiary context, Dean Clark makes a bold proposal. Under his proposed rule, all business opportunities that may be exploited by either a parent or its partially owned subsidiary should be deemed to belong to the subsidiary. The parent may legally take an opportunity if it clearly demonstrates that "the opportunity would have a substantially higher value if taken and developed by the parent company than if taken and developed by the subsidiary." Dean Clark suggests that the same rule should apply to "a family of corporations in which one or more partially owned subsidiaries exist," and to a group of firms like "*chaebol*." This rule is easy to apply and would be effective in reducing the conflict of interest problem. Moreover, it would encourage large conglomerates to avoid establishing partially owned subsidiaries, thus leading to a more simplified ownership structure. Clark, 258-61.

50) Article 398 concerning self-dealing, Article 397 regarding competition with the corporation, and Article

rations, this remained a serious flaw because controlling shareholders remained outside the formal legal framework. In larger *chaebol*, for instance, they merely assumed non-statutory titles such as "chairperson" instead of a formal statutory position such as a representative director or ordinary director.

It is conceivable that the controlling shareholder could have been indirectly restrained from abusing their managerial control if liability was imposed instead on the individual directors of the various affiliated corporations. Not only would this appear too harsh for directors, but this also remained an ineffective deterrent. It should be remembered that directors remained salaried employees without much choice or incentive but to be loyal subordinates that followed dictates and are ready to take the blame themselves on behalf of the controlling shareholder. The more effective and equitable method of course would be to impose liability directly upon the controlling shareholder. Surprisingly, for an extensive period of time, this important loophole failed to attract the attention of academics, practitioners or policy makers.

1.2. Regulatory Reforms to the KCC

This legal loophole involving controlling shareholders reached new heights during the financial crisis. Aside from the general backwardness of Korean corporate governance, one of the reasons cited for the depths of the crisis itself was the lack of means to hold the controlling shareholders accountable. Controlling shareholder accountability was thus identified as one of the five policy objectives in the corporate sector reform.[51] As a result, at last, in 1998, the KCC established Article 401-2, with the intent to encompass the controlling shareholder into the legal framework. While the term "controlling shareholder" was not used because the drafters thought that the concept was too open-ended and general, the revised KCC focused not on the 'position' held by a person but on their 'conduct.' Persons who were found to have participated in the business conduct of the corporation were subject to the same liabilities as those imposed on directors. At the same time, controlling shareholders would be liable if they did not exercise their control.

The new KCC classifies the business conduct of participants into the following three categories (Article 401-2(1)): (1) any person who has given, by using their influence over a particular corporation, instructions to a director regarding the business conduct of the corporation (Category A); (2) any person who has directly engaged in the business of a particular

---

399 relating to liability to the corporation all address misconduct by "directors."
51) Ministry of Justice Report.

corporation under a director's name (Category B); and, (3) any person not a director that has engaged in the business of a particular corporation by using a title that could reasonably be considered as carrying the authority to engage in the business of that corporation, such as honorary chairperson, chairperson, president, vice president, executive director (*chonmu*), executive (or managing) director (*sangmu*) and director. (Category C). While these categories are not limited to controlling shareholders, they were designed to encompass the various ways that controlling shareholders participate in the management of business.

For the purposes of applying the liability provisions in Articles 399 and 401 of the KCC and the provisions dealing with derivative suits in Article 403, any person who falls within any of those three categories as discussed above is regarded as a director. In other words, anyone who participates in the conduct of business may, even if they are not a director, be held liable to third parties as well as the corporation. Minority shareholders in particular may hold such participants accountable by way of a derivative suit. Furthermore, a participant in the conduct of business that is found liable will be jointly and severally liable with all other directors.

Among these categories by far the most important one is Category A. Category A concerns cases where a person participates in the management of an affiliated corporation by directly instructing the directors of that affiliate or by indirectly instructing them through such entities as a chairperson's (controlling shareholder's) office.[52] Such persons will assume the same liability as that of a director. Category A requires that the participant must have influence and have given instructions. Influence can derive from share ownership but it may also be based upon other sources. Banks or large business customers or suppliers in a dominant position for instance may be deemed to have "influence".[53]

Despite their progress, various limitations exist for Article 401-2. First, to impose liability on a party for the business conduct of a corporation, it needs to be established that the participant committed an act that affected the corporation. To impose liability on a controlling shareholder, for instance, the plaintiff must establish the presence of a controlling

---

52) Although drafted mainly with individuals in mind, Article 401-2 should be construed as applying to persons where the controlling shareholder is a juridical person (i.e. a controlling corporation). CHEOL SONG LEE, *HOESABOP GANGEUI*[Corporate Law lectures], 9th ed., 246, 603-609. (2001).

53) If the creditor bank exercised its influence over the corporation to dispose of the corporation's property to a third party under terms unfavorable to the corporation, the creditor bank may be held liable under Category A. CHEOL SONG LEE, 607. Some scholars view that even government officials exercise such influence. CHEOL SONG LEE, 607. It is questionable, however, if officials may be held liable as a participant for its conduct carried out to implement a government policy, although it may be liable under the National Compensation Law.

shareholder's instructions. It is nevertheless difficult to establish the presence of instructions because chairpersons will rarely give specific instructions. A senior manager's capability is often determined by their ability to read the controlling shareholder's implicit preferences and voluntarily act in pursuit of those interests accordingly, shielding the controlling shareholder from having to make an instruction and potentially assume liability. For this reason, it is argued that Category A only has symbolic meaning and little deterrence effect.[54] From another perspective, Article 401-2 thus creates a perverse incentive for the controlling shareholders not to openly participate in the management of business of their corporations.

Another limitation of Article 401-2 is that because of its narrow scope it cannot properly cover self-dealing and acts that compete with the company. Article 401-2 only provides for the types of conduct that will lead to liability as a director. The participants in the conduct of business are regarded as directors only for the purposes of applying Article 399 (liability to a corporation), Article 401 (liability to a third party) and Article 403 (derivative suit) of KCC. Accordingly, participants are not regarded as directors for the purposes of applying other provisions in KCC. For example, dealings between a controlling shareholder and a corporation do not fall within the definition of self-dealing by a director unless the controlling shareholder is also a director of the corporation. Therefore, advance approval from the board of directors does not have to be obtained for such transactions. The controlling shareholder would be held liable under Category A, only if one could establish that the controlling shareholder gave instructions to the corporation. Article 397, which prohibits directors from putting themselves in a position where they compete with the corporation, also does not apply to controlling shareholders. It is also difficult to hold the controlling shareholders liable under Article 401-2 because the controlling shareholders' competition with the corporation by nature is carried out without any instructions.

Despite the limitations mentioned above, overall, Article 401-2 is a significant attempt to fill the legal gap governing the conduct of controlling shareholders. It is meaningful that a controlling shareholder that should be responsible for a business decision can now be held accountable. Furthermore, the new provision has increased awareness that the controlling shareholder may now be held liable for their participation in business conduct. Recently, at the insistence of the government, most of the chieftains of *chaebol* have become directors of the flagship companies of their group. The government has even induced controlling shareholders to assume the positions of representative directors of the group's affili-

---

54) Kiuon Tsche, *Reform of KCC for Recovering from the Current Economic Crisis (Part 2)*, POPRYUL *SHINMUN*(Legal Times)(Seoul), Apr. 16 1998, at 14.

ated corporations.[55] Thus, the need to impose liability on the heads of *chaebol* as a controlling shareholder has marginally reduced. Yet, controlling shareholders have not been elected as directors of all the affiliated companies. Thus it is still necessary to control their actions and the scope of Article 401-2 still remains too narrow.

1.3. Two Possibilities

a. De facto Director

Article 401-2 is commonly interpreted as incorporating a narrow version of the concept of *de facto* director. But as mentioned previously, even if one carries out the role of a director the plaintiff must prove the existence of a relevant instruction to hold them accountable. This critical problem could be resolved if the *de facto* director concept is expanded differently and used as a supporting legal principle to hold the controlling shareholder liable. A person who has participated regularly in the conduct of a business, for instance, could be regarded as a *de facto* director, and then various types of duties and liabilities applicable to directors could be imposed. If such an expansive *de facto* director concept was adopted, then as long as it could be demonstrated that a controlling shareholder on a regular basis gave instructions to a director, then specific instructions for an individual act would not have to be shown to find accountability. Moreover, unlike Article 402-1, all the various provisions related to fiduciary duties such as self-dealing could be applied through the application of a *de facto* director concept. This type of interpretation would not necessarily require statutory change but could be achieved by including in the interpretation of a director "those that carry out a role like a *de facto* director." The potential for such judicial interpretation remains, but the adoption of Article 401-2 in some regards has ironically reduced the chances that the courts would reach such a flexible interpretation.

b. Fiduciary Duty for Controlling Shareholders

Another means of resolving the controlling shareholder problem is to recognize a fiduciary duty of the controlling shareholder. The KCC does not have an explicit provision that may be interpreted as imposing such a fiduciary duty on controlling shareholders. Explicitly adopting a fiduciary duty of a controlling shareholder for instance could allow the courts to play a more active role regarding potential expropriation. A growing number of corporate law scholars now advocate explicitly recognizing such a duty.[56]

---

55) *HANKOOK ILBO*(Seoul), 6 March1998, p.8.
56) For example, DONG-YOON CHUNG, 208.

It can also be argued that the courts should recognize such a duty despite the absence of such a statutory provision. Most notably, the highest civil court of Germany (*die Bundesgerichtshof*) in 1988 reversed its long-standing position and issued a decision recognizing fiduciary duties for a controlling shareholder despite the absence of such a statutory provision under German law.[57] Even before this decision came out, several leading scholars in Korea argued that controlling shareholders, like directors, are subject to fiduciary duties.[58]

2. Approval of the Board of Directors for Breaches of Fiduciary Duty

As with legal systems in other countries, under Korean law, directors can carry out conflicts of interest such as self-dealing if they obtain board approval. Without this approval, unlike in the U.S., regardless of the fairness of the transaction, the transaction will in principle be invalid. Under the Commercial Code, transactions that involve a conflict of interest must receive approval of the board of directors or else the transaction does not become effective. Of course, for the board of directors to give the appropriate approval they must be properly informed of the situation and they must be disinterested themselves. To be properly informed, directors should have an affirmative duty to disclose to the board when they have a conflict of interest. While this disclosure duty is critical to the fiduciary duty of directors under Anglo-American law, it is not explicitly provided for in the KCC. Because uninformed board of director approval should be considered as ineffective, this type of disclosure duty should be naturally inferred in the case of Korea as well. Furthermore, it should be stipulated in the law to avoid any disputes.

In terms of the board being disinterested, a broad definition of disinterestedness is essential. Inside directors and executive officers for instance are considered interested even if they do not have a personal stake in the decision. In Korea, however, a much narrower definition has been used that would allow the directors to vote as long as they do not have direct personal interests involved. Hence, where a controlling shareholder makes a deal with the company, all the directors, excluding the controlling shareholder if they are also directors, must participate in a board vote, but the approval is meaningless exercise because they are captive persons. The neutrality of directors is paramount. From this perspective, the new requirement for outside directors raises hope that a more independent board can make

---

57) BGHZ 103, 184. For a comment on this famous decision, see Marcus Lutter, *Die Treupflicht des Aktionärs*, 153 *ZEITSCHRIFT FÜR DAS GESAMTE HANDELS-UND WIRTSCHAFTSRECHT* 446(1989).
58) KIUON TSCHE, *SHIN HOESABOPRON*[A New Treatise on Corporation Law], 3rd ed. *Bakyoungsa*, Seoul, Korea: 341. (1987).

decisions. In the United States, for instance, a given transaction will be considered fair only when approval is obtained from disinterested directors and shareholders, which are in turn interpreted expansively. Therefore, companies have an incentive to select directors without any potential to be considered "interested."[59]

The KCC does allow individual companies to adopt stricter provisions in their articles of incorporation. Therefore, companies can adopt a provision in the articles of incorporation to require that approval from outside directors must be obtained as has been done by some firms. If management covets the trust of the capital market, then they will voluntarily adopt such provisions. The fact that such provisions can be seldom found illustrates how in the end managers still do not pay as much attention to share prices.

3. Legal Remedies for Breaches of Fiduciary Duty

In Korea, the remedies against directors who violate the fiduciary duty are weak and many restrictions exist. The legal remedies to rectify violations involving fiduciary duties are limited to compensatory damages, declaring the transaction invalid or, more fundamentally, termination of the director. This contrasts sharply with the U.S. where breaches are reviewed under equity and remedies are considered flexibly.

One critical area of reform is that shareholders should be able to claim remedies such as the repatriation of the ill-gotten gains of a director. It would be a considerable deterrent if any profits obtained as a result of a breach of their fiduciary duty could be repatriated. Under Korean law, however, this type of remedy has been recognized only for violations against establishing a competing business.[60] An even more progressive solution of course would be to consider punitive damages, especially given how difficult it is to discover and prove breaches of fiduciary duties.[61]

---

59) Ministry of Justice Report.
60) Japan's newly proposed trust law explicitly includes a provision that would allow repatriation of profits obtained in violation of trustee's fiduciary duties. Art. 22, 27.
61) Robert Cooter and Bradley Freedman, *The Fiduciary Relationship: Its Economic Character and Legal Consequences*, 66 N.Y.U.L. REV. 1045-1075. (1991).

4. Fiduciary Duty Toward Whom?

The good manager duty of directors and the fiduciary duty of directors originally were both duties established toward the corporation. Generally, the interests of the corporation have been equated with the interests of the shareholders. Under Anglo-American law, because the fiduciary duty was a concept based on equity, as long as the 'relationship of trust and confidence' existed between parties, the courts recognized the fiduciary duty even when no statutory or contract provision concerning such duty existed. Korea, however, does not share such an equity tradition. Technically, under Korean law, directors only have a contractual relationship with the corporation and not with shareholders. Without a contractual relationship, the only way for a director's fiduciary duty to be placed toward shareholders would be to have an explicit statutory provision.

Therefore, it should be stipulated in the KCC that directors and controlling shareholders both have a fiduciary duty toward shareholders. The exact contours that should exist for a fiduciary duty toward shareholders are unclear. A Ministry of Justice report describes that shareholders should be treated "fairly."[62] The question can be raised as to whether it should include creditors, employees and other stakeholders, but this will not be explored in this paper.

5. Lack of Private or Public Enforcement

According to one assessment, "[s]hareholder suits are the primary mechanism for enforcing the fiduciary duties of corporate managers."[63] Compensation for injuries to the corporation must be filed based upon a shareholder derivative action whereas compensation claims for harm against the shareholders are by direct actions. The shareholder's derivative suit was adopted in KCC in 1962.[64] It was deemed to be a crucial remedy for minority shareholders

---

62) Ministry of Justice Report.
63) Reinier Kraakman, Hyun Park and Steven Shavell. *When Are Shareholder Suits In Shareholder Interests?*, 82 GEO. L.J. 1733, (1994); *Contra*, Fischeland Bradley, *The Role of Liability Rules and Derivative Suit in Corporate Law*.
64) According to the prevailing view, a shareholder is allowed to assert a claim not only regarding the liability caused by a director's illegal act or breach of the fiduciary duty, but also the director's ordinary contract liability arising from a contract the director entered into with the company. For non-listed companies, shareholders must hold at least one percent of the total issued shares and there is no holding period requirement (Art.403(1)). The shareholder needs to satisfy this ownership requirement only at the time of filing a suit. For listed companies, the Securities Exchange Act imposes a much lower

that suffered from abuses by the management. In reality, however, this remedy failed to operate and no known derivative suits were recorded until 1997, in stark contrast to countries such as the U.S. Therefore, enforcement of breaches of fiduciary duty have been virtually non-existent. In 1998 and 1999, only 8 cases occurred against companies associated with the largest chaebol conglomerates.

A primary cause of the absence of such suits was the five-percent shareholding requirement imposed on a plaintiff shareholder. For instance, given that the average market capitalization of listed company in Korea was 62.3 billion won ($ 69 million) in 1997 this meant that shareholders had to gather a total amount of shares worth over 3.1 billion won ($ 3.5 million) in order to launch a derivative action, making it all but impossible given the collective action problems. In the 1998 revision, the five-percent limit was reduced to just one percent. And, the Securities Exchange Act was amended to apply a more lenient shareholding requirement for listed firms(Art.191-13(1)). Now, a shareholder of a listed firm may file a derivative suit, if they hold 0.01 percent of the shares for six months. Despite these reforms, unlike in Japan, the number of derivative actions still remains small.[65]

Furthermore, Korea has finally enacted a provision entitling plaintiff shareholders to seek reasonable compensation from the company for their litigation costs. (Art. 405; SEA, Art. 191-13, Sec. 6). No one disputes that the litigation costs include attorney fees. And it will be up to the court to determine the reasonable amount of attorney fees that the company should pay to the successful plaintiff. It is questionable, however, whether Korean judges will be as generous as their U.S. counterparts in respecting a contingent fee agreement. It is thus a little premature to predict whether or not harmed shareholders and consequently their attorneys now have enough incentive to file a derivative suit.

Another critical problem has been whether through a derivative suit or a direct action shareholders must pursue their claims individually or through an opt-in system of amalgamating plaintiffs. In other words, Korea still does not allow U.S.-style class actions, a critical flaw in its enforcement regime.[66] While the government plans to allow class actions start-

---

threshold of 0.01 percent, but instead requires a six month holding period(Art.191-13(1)).Those who maybe named as defendants are limited to the directors, statutory auditors, promoters, liquidators, and, since 1998, so-called *de facto* directors. Where a shareholder wins, they can demand that the firm reimburse them for reasonable legal expenses as well as the litigation costs (Art.405(1)). Contrary to normal cases where Korea follows the loser-pays rule, in a derivative action, a losing shareholder is not liable to the company for the loss caused to the company by the action, unless they acted in bad faith(Art.405(2)).

65) Mark D. West, *The Pricing Of Shareholder Derivative Actions In Japan And The United States*, 88 NW. U. L. REV. 1436 (1994).

66) As in Japan, this lack of litigation might better be attributed to institutional limitations rather than cul-

ing from early 2002, pressure from business groups are currently restricting the plans to certain types of securities fraud and do not include breaches for fiduciary duty.[67)]

In terms of public enforcement, regulators and prosecutors have rarely found managers liable for breaching their fiduciary duties. Even when they have sought to hold managers accountable prosecutors have not necessarily been consistent in their application. For instance, in two recent cases, representative directors of two medium-sized companies were indicted and then found guilty of embezzling company funds for issuing private placements of bonds with warrants to themselves at extraordinary discounts.[68)] In contrast, in a factually near identical case, the directors of a leading *chaebol* company were not indicted even though they also issued a private placement of bonds with warrants to the chairman's son and daughters, giving them over $ 100 million in gains in the process.[69)]

One of the most promising developments can be found in the recent activities of the Korea Deposit Insurance Corporation (KDIC).[70)] In the wake of the financial crisis, KDIC began to seek those accountable much like the U.S. Federal Deposit Insurance Corporation following the savings and loans crisis. In 1999, KDIC filed civil liability actions against 222 executives from 53 financial institutions for a total of 263.1 billion won ($ 202 million), and in 2000 civil actions were filed against 1,287 executives from 157 financial institutions for a total of 5 trillion won ($ 3.85 billion). In 1999 they also filed 1,560 injunctions to freeze 274.7 billion won ($ 211 billion), and in 2000, 1,812 injunctions to freeze 670 billion won ($ 515 million) in assets of allegedly liable former executives. These are among the most far-reaching legal actions ever taken to hold corporate executives accountable for their decisions and unprecedented by a public sector-based institution, particularly in its scope and severity.

6. Role of Judges and Other Legal Practitioners

Ultimately, judges and other practitioners play a critical role in enforcing and applying fiduciary duty. Given the multifarious ways in which managers can bilk shareholders, it is vital that the courts are able to hold them accountable with a flexible and general concept such

---

tural disinclinations. John O. Haley, *The Myth of the Reluctant Litigant*, 4 J. JAPANESE STUD. 359 (1978).

67) "Hearing on Establishing Securites Related Class Actions." Ministry of Justice (November 2, 2001).

68) Seoul District Court (Judgment of Aug. 30, 2001); Busan High Court (Judgment of May 2001).

69) Jang and Kim, *supra* note 18, 91.

70) Korea Deposit Insurance Corportaion 2000 Annual Report.

as fiduciary duty. In the case of the common law tradition, the courts developed it out of a need to devise a way to resolve disputes equitably. The question is why continental courts did not develop a similar jurisprudence of fiduciary duties. Some theorize that continental courts with their sophisticated legal codes tended to downplay the role of courts making law.[71] In countries such as France for instance they had a tradition of distrusting the courts. Ultimately, the differences between continental courts and common-law courts are not as wide as is commonly thought.[72] Even in France, judges played a considerable role and were active in developing jurisprudence while Korean judges themselves in general are not necessarily hesitant to exercise discretion.[73]

Yet, Korean courts have been passive in applying fiduciary duties. For instance, a basic remedy for breaches of fiduciary duty is to nullify the relevant transaction. In practice, nullification decisions must also consider the need for a stable marketplace. Korean courts, however, have showed a tendency to over-emphasize the concerns surrounding "stability of the marketplace." Their failure to nullify the new issues and private placements of convertible bonds in several recent cases such as Hanwha Merchant Bank and Samsung Electronics are classic examples.[74] In these cases, the courts were excessively cautious about nullifying the disputed securities even though stability of the marketplace should not have been a consideration because the shares were not even transferred to third parties.[75]

In the case of the Samsung Electronics, for instance, shareholders claimed that a private placement of bonds with warrants of over several million dollars was issued to the children of the controlling shareholder at a considerable discount of the market rate.[76] While citing the unnecessary nature of the transaction and the private benefits to the controlling shareholders family, the court refused to nullify the disputed securities out of consideration of the "stability of the marketplace,"which should not even have been a consideration given that the converted shares were still held by the family members.

Several reasons can be cited for the apparent passiveness of Korean courts with regard to carving out the boundaries of fiduciaries duties and providing the necessary remedy to damaged shareholders. The first is that given the sheer lack of legal actions there has not

---

71) UGO MATTEI COMPARATIVE LAW AND ECONOMICS, University of Michigan Press. P81-83 (1997).
72) Ibid.
73) MATTEI, *supra* note 71, 85. Examples include *"astreinte"* under French Law and the "general power of injunctions" under Italian law.
74) Kim, *Recent Amendments*, *supra* note 25, 315; Jang and Kim, *supra* note 18, 91.
75) Seoul High Court, Judgment No. 68 Na 4608 (June 23, 2000).
76) Jang and Kim, *supra* note 18, 91.

been enough opportunity for precedents to develop. Second, the enormous workload makes judges reluctant to enter unfamiliar territory and apply uncertain concepts such as fiduciary duties and instead leads them to be far more conservative. Third, attorneys must take the lead in unraveling sophisticated business decision made by directors and raise claims for violations of fiduciary duties but thus far Korean attorneys have not displayed this type of ability. The attorneys that represent shareholders are still few in number and lack experience. In reality, therefore, a leading public interest group that advocates minority shareholders rights has brought the only significant shareholder actions.[77]

IV. Recent Landmark Cases On the Heels of Legal Reform

The recent legal reforms that were adopted in Korea directly led to several landmark cases that are critically shaping corporate governance. Several shareholder derivative actions have sent shockwaves throughout the Korean business community by holding managers liable for breaches of fiduciary duties. The following cases demonstrate the importance of legal infrastructure in developing critical corporate governance concepts such as fiduciary duties.

1. The Prologue: Korea First Bank

The historic litigation involving Korea First Bank (KFB) illustrates the multiple layers of legal problems that have thwarted shareholders from holding directors accountable for fiduciary duty violations. It illustrates the importance of legal reforms. In 1997, a group of shareholder activist attracted 52 minority shareholders of KFB and gained widespread public attention by filing the first reported shareholder derivative suit in Korean history.[78] The Seoul District Court eventually found the KFB directors liable for 40 billion won ($ 44.4million) plus interest.

The Court held that the directors not only violated their "duty as a good manager" but also their "fiduciary duty" toward the bank. In its own terms, the court first stressed the basics of the business judgment rule. Managers deserve discretion in making business decisions

---

77) Kim and Kim, *supra* note 19, 51.
78) Seoul District Court, Judgment No. 97 Kahap 39907 (July 24, 1998). Kim, *Recent Amendments*, *supra* note 25, 321. Wollschlager, C.F. 1997. in "Historical Trends of Civil Litigation in Japan, Arizona, Sweden, and Germany: Japanese Legal Culture in the Light of Judicial Statistics." In *Economic Success and Legal System*, ed. Baum, H. Berlin/New York (supporting the traditional argument that the Japanese are non-litigious by nature).

and by nature need to take risks. The court found that as long as they were within the bounds of a business person's rational choice and they faithfully fulfilled their duty, managers would not be held responsible for decisions that subsequently led to losses. The court held that a fiduciary duty breach will be found "when based on the relevant facts, the decision making process and from the perspective of an average business person, a director makes a mistake that cannot be passed over lightly and that exceeds their scope of discretion." (emphasis added)(p. 9). The court stated that any directors that did not disagree with such decisions would also be found liable in such a case.

In their defense, the KFB directors claimed that their questionable loan decisions to the Hanbo Group deserved to be protected as fully informed business judgments. They further argued that all the necessary board approvals were obtained and that they honestly anticipated that the Hanbo Group would be a rewarding client in the future. Some directors even suggested that they should not be held liable because they were merely following the dictates of the President of the bank. Hanbo of course later imploded following a string of critically poor business decisions coupled with commitments into markets with excess supply.

Yet the facts overwhelmingly proved that the KFB directors were liable for breaching their fiduciary duty. Not only did they receive bribes in return for the questionable loans, but also they also made over 1 trillion won ($ 1.2 billion) in loans that were largely unsecured. Among the other critical facts that the court cited were that the directors were fully informed of Hanbo's dire situation and potential risk of default and still failed to take any appropriate protective measures, that they disregarded continuous warnings by their own loan officers and that they all approved these decision without any objections.

For the first time, managers in Korea came to realize that they had a fiduciary duty and that they could be held liable for breaching it. The decision is noteworthy in the following respects. First, the case would not have made possible without the lowering of the minimum shareholder ownership requirement to 0.5%. Second, overwhelmingly evidence showed that the directors violated their fiduciary duty. Such cases with such egregious facts and blatant intentional malfeasance are a rarity themselves. Third, the case was brought by leading a shareholder activist group and would not have been possible without their involvement.[79] Fourth, the case was made possible only because shareholder had access to evidence brought forth by the criminal prosecution following the sensational collapse of the Hanbo Group in early 1997.[80] Such extraordinary criminal investigations are rare in themselves and it would

---

79) Kim and Kim, *supra* note 25.

have been virtually impossible for shareholders to acquire the requisite evidence otherwise. The decision sent shockwaves throughout the cozy Korean business community. As testimony to the historical impact of the case, for the first time Korean companies started to subscribe to directors and officers liability insurance ("D&O"). The number of companies with D&O insurance dramatically increased from one case in 1996, to five cases in 1997, 105 cases in 1998 and 320 cases by 1999.[81] For the first time, the insurance market was able to sell a liability product to corporate managers based on the perception of potential legal risk and accountability.

2. The Path-Breaking Decision against Samsung Electronics

An even more path-breaking judgment was rendered against Samsung Electronics (SE) on December 27, 2001.[82] In this case, minority shareholders won a derivative action against Gun-Hee Lee, the Samsung Group chairman and controlling shareholder, and various managers of SE, Korea's flagship company. The controlling shareholder and nine directors were found liable for approximately $ 75 million. The critical claims of the case in terms of fiduciary duties involved the acquisition of an ailing affiliated company called E-Chon Electric, and the discount sales of stocks to another affiliated company.[83]

The district court's finding with regard to SE's acquisition of E-Chon Electric bears a striking resemblance to *Smith v. Van Gorkom* and for the first time established a critical standard regarding the limitations of the business judgment rule.[84] The court found that SE's managers were liable for acquiring the ailing E-Chon Electricity because during the process they did not even engage in any substantive review regarding the financial or operational status of the company and decided to acquire it in less than an hour despite the lack of any urgency. SE furthermore continued to participate in several equity issuances even after the company became defunct and ultimately SE suffered over 190billion won ($ 146 mil-

---

80) The ensuing criminal investigation revealed that KFB directors received bribes in return for favorable loan decisions and the disclosures eventually brought down eight senior politicians, aides to then President Young Sam Kim, and also led to the arrest of the President Kim's own son.

81) Financial Supervisory Service, on file with authors.

82) Suwon District Court, Judgment No. 98 Gahap 22553 (Dec. 27, 2001).

83) Another claim involved Gun-Hee Lee's bribery of a former Korean President. Such illicit "political contributions" that Lee gave were common corporate practice in the past but the court held that these acts that were carried out "on behalf of the interests of the company" actually harmed the company, and now no one now questions the criminality of the act. Another claim for improper support for another affiliated company was denied.

84) *Smith v. Van Gorkom*, 488 A.2d 858 (1985).

lion) in losses. In the other claim, SE sold an affiliated company's shares that it had acquired 8 months ago at a 74% discount to another related company without any particular reason.[85] This sale in effect therefore siphoned off SE's assets to support another company. The most problematic part of the case, however, concerns the court's finding to deny liability for Gun-Hee Lee because he did not participate in the relevant board meetings. The court held that a director's failure to attend board meetings alone did not automatically constitute a breach of duty. It stated that a director would not be liable for a board's decision unless the director "did not participate when the director knew or could have known that the decision in question was being made." Proving that a director knew or should have known of an improper board decision will usually be difficult to establish, as in this case where the court found that there was insufficient evidence. Yet, Chairmen Lee was the controlling shareholder and a director and arguably had a duty to try to know of such significant information and if he tried he clearly could have known. Absent such a finding, directors will have a perverse incentive not to attend board meetings where controversial decisions are being made to avoid liability. Therefore, the interpretation of the "could have known" standard must be expanded. The court instead held that if a company carries out an illegal act without a board decision the directors would not be liable unless they were aware of the act and failed to try to prevent it. The court dismissed the plaintiff's claim in this regard because they could not provide such proof of knowledge. It is possible that the SE directors did not know of the particular transaction but this lack of knowledge should not automatically exculpate them from liability, particularly the representative director. At the very least, the court should have justified its decision for instance by finding that the size of the transaction in question did not reach the level that would have prompted the directors to seek board approval.

From another perspective it could be argued that despite the finding of a lack of an informed decision that the board's decision in question still failed to meet the standards under the business judgment rule. SE's discounted sale of stock to other Samsung Group affiliated companies in particular should arguably not have been reviewed under a duty of care standard. This interpretation is possible because SE's acquisition of E-Chon could also be considered a conflict of interest because another Samsung Group affiliate already owned a substantial share of E-Chon.[86]

---

85) SEC followed the valuation method for unlisted stock as provided under the Inheritance and Gift Tax Law, but the court held it should have been calculated based on the total asset value. The court focused its attention on the correct valuation of the stock and did not sufficiently consider that the transaction was with an affiliated company.

Despite these problems, the SE decision was far more significant than the KFB case. The KFB decision involved a defunct bank whereas SE is Korea's flagship company. The SE court made it clear that even managers of the largest and most profitable companies can still be held liable for decisions made against shareholder interests. Therefore, regardless of the ultimate outcome of this case, which is currently on appeal, it sent a powerful message to the securities market and to foreign investors. As expected, manager groups in Korea have vigorously protested and campaigned against the ramifications of the court's assessment of liability. Yet, most of their reactions stem from a lack of understanding of the basic condition that have to be met to receive protection under the business judgment rule. SE's managers in term do deserve some sympathy because in many regards they were just following standard corporate procedure as had developed in Korea's modern history. The transactions in question were standard staple for almost all Korean corporations in the past. But, even among the most ardent critics, it would be difficult to argue that such practices are compatible with Korea's recent efforts to improve its corporate governance and develop its financial markets.

V. Concluding Remarks: Revamping Fiduciary Duties

In recent years, the potential for expropriation has increasingly become a critical problem in Korean corporations. The rapid decline of the role of the state and an increasingly dispersed ownership structure without the requisite internal corporate governance protections or market-based pressures has led to many corporate ills which in the worst cases have taken the form of spectacular corporate failures and contributed to the depths of the 1997 financial crisis. The recent collapses of over a dozen of Korea's largest *chaebol*, including the spectacular failures of the Daewoo Group and the splintering of the Hyundai Group, testify to the fragility of the Korean firms.[87]

Despite the considerable barriers, Korea has achieved considerable formal convergence toward a shareholder-centered governance model. Under these circumstances, Korea for instance made an effort to strengthen the fiduciary duty of directors. Following the 1997 financial crisis, Korea's corporate governance system has made a dramatic shift toward a cap-

---

86) Furthermore, the court did not discuss the magnitude of the E-Chon acquisition in relation to the size of most of SEC's transactions or whether there was a urgency.

87) Since 1997, as many as 12 of the top 30 chaebol conglomerates have collapsed. OECD Economic surveys, p.131.

ital markets-oriented system. In line with the vast legal changes, the thirty largest chaebol's capital market-based equity financing rose from 69 trillion won in 1997 to 155 trillion won by 2000 and their debt to equity ratio falling from 519% in 1997 to 171% by 2000. It cannot be denied that the corporate governance spectrum has become quite diverse, with professional managers finally taking the helm in many leading companies.

While it is beyond the scope of this paper, many theories have been expounded as to why these changes occurred. One prevailing view holds that external factors in terms of the financial crisis acted as a mixed blessing because through the subsequent demands of the IMF and IBRD it forced significant reform. Japan's corporate governance system in comparison has lagged behind Korea's in terms of its shareholder-oriented emphasis because they managed to escape the acute ills of the Asian contagion. The primary concern in Korea is that absent an external impetus and following the rebound of the economy the momentum for reform is subsiding too quickly.

It would also be naïve to assume that these reforms toward a more shareholder-oriented model have immediately effectuated a substantive change in corporate governance practice. For instance, for the largest *chaebol* conglomerates, functionally the controlling shareholders still retain their unchallenged authority as they did in the past.[88] As testimony to a state of affairs where actual practice lags behind the intentions of recent corporate governance reforms, Korean companies still remain markedly undervalued in terms of their earnings and assets relative to other companies.[89]

In the end, despite some more pessimistic views about the role of law, this paper argues that the significance of these changes with regard to corporate governance reform must not be overlooked. It sought to show how corporate law minimizes the ills of the controlling shareholder pursuing the private benefits of control. Legal reforms still play an important function in teaching managers and the public at large of the harms of pursuing private interests. They also contribute in building a social norm that it is improper to engage in or assist in enlarging these private benefits of control. While these social norms still remain weak, they will gradually act as another informal means of disciplining managerial decisions.

---

88) It is probably premature to term Korea's corporate governance as world class. Hwa Jin Kim, *Toward the 'Best Practice' Model in a Globalizing Market*(arguing that "the Korean corporate governance system successfully adapts to the best practice model accepted by global standards"). Bernard Black et al., *Corporate Governance in Korea at the Millenium.*

89) Amar Gill, Saints and Sinners: *Who's Go Religion?*, Credit Lyonnais Report C.G. Watch, (April 2001); *The Opacity Index*. PricewaterhouseCoopers (January 2001).

Yet, this does not mean that this revamped fiduciary duty does not have its limitations. Of course, enforcement remains equally important and efforts to improve actual implementation and enforcement must continue. Even if the legal means to properly enforce fiduciary duties are established and controlling shareholders refrain from conflicts of interests, this does not mean that Korea can immediately follow a capital markets-oriented structure. Such a capital markets-oriented structure will truly arrive when managers no longer passively refrain from directly infringing shareholder rights but when they actively seek to pursue maximization of shareholder value. The fiduciary duty provision alone does not provide the incentive for managers to pursue this type of affirmative strategy.

For these purposes, managers must be provided with the proper impetus to lead them toward this direction. Managers must feel pressured by capital markets, particularly to enhance share prices. One of the biggest differences between Korean controlling shareholders and top managers from countries with advanced capital markets remains their interest in share prices. Controlling shareholders are probably less interested in share prices because it is far more beneficial to maximize their interests through means that are unrelated to share prices.

Fiduciary duties seek exactly to reduce the private benefits of control. Once the private benefits of control are minimized, controlling shareholders have less need to maintain control. Once managers pursue the interests of shareholders based on pressure from the capital markets then the significance of the fiduciary duty provision diminishes. In the end, one can construe the significance of fiduciary duty as a necessary pillar toward corporate governance reform and toward the transition to a capital markets-oriented system.

Table 1. Top 30 Chaebol Intra-Conglomerate Shareholding (1983-2000)

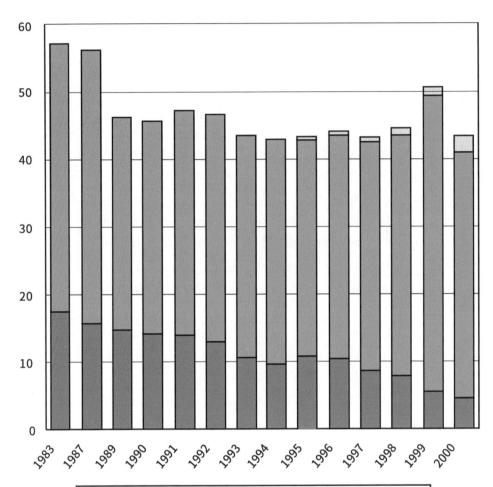

Table 2. KFTC's Fines Against Top 4 Chaebols for
Improper Intra-Conglomerate Transactions (1998-2000)

(unit: $ million)

		Hyundai	Samsung	Daewoo	LG	SK	Total per Investigation
1st KFTC Investigation (1998)	Improper Internal Transactions	593	554	325	813	812	3,097
	Fine	17	8.8	6.8	7.9	14.7	56
2nd KFTC Investigation (1998)	Improper Internal Transactions	268	154	32	52.5	642	1,148
	Fine	7	2.3	3.4	1.7	1.5	16
3rd KFTC Investigation (1999)	Improper Internal Transactions	3,149	4,177	307	845	1,009	9,487
	Fine	18.6	26.8	10	4.3	0.9	61
Special KFTC Investigation (1999)	Improper Internal Transactions	331	20.8	--	9.9	69	432
	Fine	2.9	0.3	--	0.1	0.6	4
4th KFTC Investigation (2000)	Improper Internal Transactions	435	255	--	388	22	1,923
	Fine	11	7.7	--	9.5	6	34
Total per Group	Improper Internal Transactions	4,776	5,160	665	2,108	2,553	10,618
	Fine	56.9	45.9	20.6	23.1	23.6	170

Source: Korea Fair Trade Commission

Establishing a New Stock Market for Shareholder Value Oriented Firms in Korea

Stephen J. Choi* and Kon Sik Kim**

I. INTRODUCTION

Regulators seeking to strengthen and promote Korea's capital markets face several challenges in the upcoming century. Although the trading volume and number of listed companies on the Korea Stock Exchange ("KSE") have grown rapidly over the past decade, the Composite Stock Price Index ("KOSPI") of total stock market value has, in fact, fallen. Individual investors inside Korea often choose to invest primarily in savings deposits, rather than place their money in the equity of listed companies.[1] Korean investors may have good reasons for avoiding equity investments. Many of the largest Korean-listed companies are members of conglomerate groups ("*chaebol*"). Although the Chairmen and founding families of *chaebol* often own a dwindling minority ownership stake, they typically maintain firm control over all member firms through cross shareholding arrangements,[2] and the private benefits of control are large in Korea.[3]

* Professor, University of California, Berkeley, Boalt Hall School of Law.
** Professor, Seoul National University School of Law. Thanks for helpful comments from Andrew Guzman, Un Kyung Park, and the participants of the Second Asia Corporate Governance Conference Program (Seoul, Korea 2002) sponsored by the Asian Institute of Corporate Governance (and Jack Coffee, our conference commentator).

1) Bank of Korea, *Financial Assets and Liabilities Outstanding [2000]*, available online at <htrp://vww.bo-kor.kr/bokis/bokis/m_matrixcode=D&icurrent=00000186&i-lan=eng>(visited Sept 21, 2002) (In 2000, stocks accounted for less than seven percent of the financial assets held by individual Koreans, while deposits at banks and other financial institutions accounted for more than fifty percent.).

2) See Daehong T. Jaang, et al, *Cross Sbarebolding and Corporate Financial Policy: the Case of Korea 2*, AICG Working Paper (2002), available online at <http://biz.korea.ac.kr/~aicg/paper._2nd/Cross_shareholding_and_corporate_financial.pdf> (visited Sept 20, 2002).

3) See Yoo Cheong-mo, *Corporations Urged to Raise Governance, Transparency Experiments Still Underway with Outside Director, Class Action Suit, Corporate Split, Holding Company Systems*, Korea Herald (May 29, 2002) ("In a controversial deal, LG Chemical sold 19.75 million shares in LG Petrochemical to the family of LG Group Chairman Koo Bon-Moo for 5,500 won per share prior to the firm's listing in 1999 and bought back 6.32 million shares for 15,000 won apiece April 25 this year, bringing at least 60

As a means of improving capital market liquidity, and in response to the 1997 Asian economic crisis, regulators in Korea moved to strengthen corporate governance protection for minority investors. There is reason for at least limited optimism on the effectiveness of such reforms. Legal reform can have an impact on investors and financial markets. The passage of the federal securities laws and the establishment of the SEC during the Great Depression in the United States helped to restore confidence in the markets; as some commentators have put it, the "law matters."[4]

The observation that the law matters is only a starting point, however. The more salient issue is how to generate good law. While changing the formal legal regime may have some impact, overall legality depends not only on formal laws but also on public institutions, private actors, and the background norms that support the law.[5] Indeed, the law itself may have only marginal significance. Culture, for example, may play a larger role in determining the extent to which controlling shareholders and managers expropriate value from minority investors.[6]

Norms and institutions, of course, are not impervious to change. Commentators, for example, have called for student exchanges and the establishment of US-style business and law schools in other countries, as a means of altering the background environment in which laws operate.[7] However, such methods, even if effective, may take years to generate any noticeable effect. The challenge this paper addresses is how to implement effective reform to protect investors within Korea, leading to a stronger, more vibrant capital market in a shorter time frame.

The question of how to protect investors is particularly salient in Korea. Although the post-1997 crisis reforms have generally enjoyed public support, governmental interest in undertaking further reforms now seems on the wane. Meanwhile, the voice of the business establishment denouncing the reform efforts is gaining in power, blocking or compromising serious reform proposals.[8]

---

billion won in capital gains to the owner family.").

4) See John C. Coffee, Jr., *Privatization and Corporate Governance: The Lessons from Securities Market Failure*, 25 J Corp L 1, 1-2 (1999) (coining the term "law matters").

5) See Bernard S. Black, *The Legal and Institutional Preconditions for Strong Securities Markets*, 48 UCLA L Rev 781, 790-803, 807-15 (2001).

6) See Amir N. Licht, Chanan Goldschmidt, and Shalom H. Schwartz, *Culture, Law, and Finance: Cultural Dinensions of Corporate Governance Laws*, SSRN Working Paper (2001), available online at <hrtp://papers.ssrn.com/sol3/papers.cfm.abstract_id=277613> (visited Sept 20, 2002).

7) Black, 48 UCLA L Rev at 848 (cited in note 5).

8) See Yoo Cheong-mo, *Cbaebol Callfor an End to State Meddling in Corporate Governance*, Korea Herald (Apr 21, 2000).

Rather than pursue conventional (and we contend often ineffective) efforts at reform, we propose a different course. We believe that introducing more competition in the provision of investor protection may prove to be a more effective route toward reform. Competition among regulators will provide an incentive to regulators interested in expanding the scope of their regulatory authority and generating listing fees to tailor their regulations toward what issuers-and indirectly, investors-desire. Shifting toward a more competitive regulatory system may require the expenditure of scarce political capital; nevertheless, once the shift has occurred, a system of regulatory competition is self-supporting, providing strong incentives for regulatory innovation into the future.

Of course, the mere fact that competition is effective at generating change is not enough to favor a competitive system. Change may lead regulatory systems to a "race to the bottom" as regimes compete with one another to cater to opportunistic managers.[9] Once placed under competitive pressures, regulators may also ignore external effects on third parties, as well as the benefits of market-wide standardization. While we do not think the dangers are great, we are mindful of the risks.[10] In addition, a shift toward a more competitive regulatory system may generate substantial opposition from large political and business groups that benefit from the present regulatory regime.

Our proposal in Korea therefore is to start small. We focus on the possibility of introducing more competition by giving firms greater choice within the existing regulatory regime. As an initial, obtainable goal, we propose taking an approach similar to that pursued by the Brazilian Stock Exchange ("Bovespa") to establish a new voluntary section for firms on the KSE satisfying global corporate governance standards. We also explore a second option to introduce competition by allowing some firms to opt out of domestic regulation in favor of the regulatory regime of a foreign country. Such an approach would allow firms the ability to choose for themselves - within limits - the level of investor protection they desire through a listing on a foreign exchange. Firms with large, entrenched controlling shareholders or managers and a dispersed pool of minority investors will probably not take advantage of the ability to opt into a higher level of corporate governance, because controlling shareholders will not voluntarily forsake their private benefits of control. Moreover, dispersed shareholders already receive compensation for the expected expropriation of private

---

9) See Lucian Arye Bebchuk, *Federalism and the Corporation: The Desirable Limits on State Competition in Corporate Law*, 105 Harv L Rev 1435, 1445 (1992) (summarizing the "race to the bottom" theory espoused by William Cary and others).

10) Empirical evidence from state competition for corporate charters provides some support for the alternative "race to the top" hypothesis. For a review of the empirical literature, see Roberta Romano, *Empowering Investors: A Market Approach to Securities Regulation*, 107 Yale LJ 2359, 2383-88 (1998).

benefits in the form of a discounted share price at purchase. Instead, our suggested reforms will primarily assist newer companies seeking to raise funds from the public capital markets.[11] Indirectly, the creation of a new investor-protection environment with accompanying norms and institutions will impact the rest of Korea's capital markets.

In the discussion that follows, part II provides an overview of the potential benefits from protecting minority investors and the empirical evidence of the efficacy of such protection. Part III surveys potential reform options and details our proposal to expand the choices available to companies within the KSE.

II. PROTECTING MINORITY INVESTORS IN KOREA

The KSE handled 473 million shares of daily trading volume in 2001-up from only 14 million shares of daily trading volume in 1991.[12] Since 1997, the KSE trading system has been fully computerized, thus enabling greater trading activity.[13] Despite the increase in trading volume and activity on the KSE, many Korean individual investors continue to avoid the Korean equity markets. When at least partially protected from the risk of opportunistic managers and controlling shareholders, minority investors may gain confidence in the market, leading them to invest more funds. Section A of this part discusses the theoretical need for regulation to protect minority investors. Section B then canvasses aspects of Korea's investor protection regime.

A. THE THEORY OF INVESTOR PROTECTION

Information on a firm's confidential projects, cash flows, capital expenditures, and similar items are often known (at least for a time) solely by the firm's managers and controlling shareholders. Managers and controlling shareholders with an informational advantage may attempt to sell overvalued securities to the market or engage in insider trading.

Faced with the prospect of losing money due to either lack of information or managerial

---

11) Nonetheless, even among more established firms, a small, yet growing, number of firms under professional management may be interested in moving into a more advanced section of the KSE.

12) Compare <http://www.kse.or.kr/eng/stat/pasr/daily(1991).txt> (listing daily trading volume data for 1991), with <http://www.kse.or.kr/eng/srar/pasr/daily(2001).txt> (listing daily trading volume data for 2001) (visited Sept 20, 2002).

13) See Korea Stock Exchange, *KSE Fact Book 2000* 13, available online at <http://www.kse.or.kr/eng/intr/intr-bookol.htm>(visited Sept 20, 2002).

opportunism, investors may adjust their behavior. In particular, securities investors may choose to either exit the capital markets, decreasing liquidity, or demand a discount as compensation for the risks they face. Where investors are rational and informed on the magnitude of expropriation risk they face, they will on average accurately discount securities prices to take this risk into account. Entrepreneurs that suffer an unduly high discount, due to the risks facing uninformed investors in the market, may then have an incentive at the time they sell their securities to implement contract-based forms of investor protection. A higher level of investor protection results in a reduction in the discount demanded by investors, thereby providing greater offering proceeds for entrepreneurs.[14]

Despite the possibility of a contractual response, regulations may be better suited to help alleviate the problem of asymmetric information facing investors. Regulations may involve greater economies of scale, thus assisting in the detection of violations of disclosure provisions or opportunistic acts of self-dealing. Not all investors, moreover, are sophisticated. Less sophisticated investors may fail to discount properly for all the informational and opportunism risks. Benefits may also exist from standardization - for example, in disclosure - that individual firms may ignore in their decision on which investor protection measures to provide through contract. Disclosure may also generate positive externalities that benefit unrelated third parties. When one firm discloses information on its production, for example, the disclosures provide benefits for competing firms not internalized by the disclosing firm.

Weighed against the positive benefits of regulation, however, are the possible negative consequences of relying too heavily on mandatory regulation. Once regulations become mandatory, the possibility exists for regulatory capture.[15] Moreover, regulators may have an incentive to maximize the size and importance of their own agency at the expense of social welfare. More perniciously, regulators - to the extent they are insulated from market pressures - have few incentives to innovate and develop regulations designed to meet the needs of an ever-changing marketplace. At the very least, without the discipline of the market, regulators may make mistakes and not necessarily generate regulations designed to maximize social welfare.

---

14) See Bernard S. Black, Hasung Jang, and Woochan Kim, *Does Corporate Governance Matter?: Evidence from the Korean Market*, KDI Working Paper No 02-04 (2002), available online at <http://www.kdischool.ac.kr/library/w2002.htm> (visited Sept 16, 2002) (providing evidence that greater corporate governance protection for firms listed on the KSE result in a higher measure of valuation).

15) For a public choice critique of the SEC in the United States, see Jonathan R. Macey, *Administrative Agency Obsolescence and Interest Group Fornation: A Case Study of the SEC at Sixty*, 15 Cardozo L Rev 909, 913-14 (1994).

B. EVIDENCE FROM KOREA

In recent years, scholars have produced a number of cross-country empirical studies assessing the value of legal regimes that provide strong protection of minority investors. Compared with countries of common law origin (such as the United States and the United Kingdom), La Porta, Lopez-de-Silanes, Shleifer, and Vishny ("LLSV") provide evidence across a series of articles that the relatively weak investor protection of Korea (and other civil law countries) correlates with more concentrated ownership, a smaller external financing market, and reduced stock market valuations.[16] One initial criticism of the LLSV studies is that the various indices they use as a proxy for the level of minority investor protection are flawed. LLSV's direct measure of the level of formal legal protection for minority equity investors, for example, turns in part on the presence (or absence) of the right to mail in a proxy vote, the availability of (optional) cumulative voting, and the presence of preemptive rights to purchase new issues for preexisting shareholders. Significantly, LLSV ignore the presence of antitakeover laws or the permissibility of the use of private antitakeover techniques, including poison pills.[17] It is also unclear how many large publicly-held companies actually adopt cumulative voting policies when optional.

Focusing more directly on the legal environment within Korea, nonetheless, provides corroborative evidence that the Korean investor protection regime indeed is lagging behind other countries, most notably the United States. Prior to the 1997 crisis, the Korean corporate governance regime differed from the United States along a number of dimensions.[18] First, the ownership structure in Korea was markedly different. For most large business firms, a control block was typically in the hands of the founding family, which dominated the internal decisionmaking process. With no independent directors, the board of directors of Korean firms often acted as a mere formality. While Korean law provided for a statutory

---

16) See Rafael La Porta, et al, *Legal Determinants of External Finance*, 52 J Fin 1131 (1997); Rafael La Porta, et al, *Law and Finance*, 106 J Pol Econ 1113 (1998); Rafael La Porta, Florencio Lopez-de-Silanes, and Andrei Shleifer, *Corporate Ownership Around the World*, 54 J Fin 471 (1999); Rafael La Porra, et al, *Investor Protection and Corporate Valuation*, NBER Working Paper No W7403 (1999), available online at <http://papers.ssrn.com/sol3/papers.cfn.abstractid=227583> (visited Sept 20, 2002).

17) See also John C. Coffee, Jr., *The Rise of Dispersed Ownership: The Roles of Law and the State in the Separation of Ownership and Control*, 111 Yale LJ 1; 4 n 6 (2001) ("By no means is it here implied that [LLSV's measured] rights are unimportant, but they seem to supply only partial and sometimes easily outflanked safeguards, which have little to do with the protection of control and the entitlement to a control premium.").

18) See Kon Sik Kim, *Chaebol and Corporate Governance in Korea* (1995) (unpublished PhD dissertation, University of Washington) (on file with the University of Washington library).

auditor expected to restrain the misconduct of management, such auditors were largely ineffective. Second, fiduciary duty rules in Korea were neither well established nor well utilized due to barriers to derivative suits. Disgruntled shareholders could file a derivative action only if they owned at least 5 percent of the shares.[19] Coupled with a lack of class action suits in Korea, the large threshold share ownership requirement severely curtailed the ability of shareholders to enforce their rights against management. Third, the market for corporate control was largely absent in the Korean marketplace, leaving controlling shareholders largely free from market pressures.

While the corporate governance regime in Korea had come under some pressure for reform prior to 1997, it was the 1997 crisis that dramatically changed the existing corporate governance environment. A consequence of the crisis was a sudden rise of foreign investors. Today, more than 30 percent of the shares of listed firms are in the hands of sophisticated and demanding foreign investors who tend to concentrate on a small number of blue chip companies. Also, domestic investors, both individual and institutional, have become far more conscious of the concept of shareholder value. Although the founding families of the *cbaebol* companies still enjoy effective control through complicated cross-ownership, controlling shareholders are now much more subject to pressures from other shareholders.

The most striking of the post-1997 reforms is a series of statutory reforms enacted to strengthen shareholder rights. The reforms were largely due to pressure from the International Monetary Fund and the World Bank. We point out some of the most conspicuous changes.[20] First, outside directors are required for listed firms. For large listed firms, an audit committee is required, instead of a nominal statutory auditor. The burdensome 5 percent threshold share ownership requirement for bringing a derivative suit or exercising other shareholder-related rights has been substantially moderated. For example, the share ownership required for derivative suits is now down to 1 percent, and 0.01 percent for KSE-listed firms.[21] Board approval and public disclosure are required for certain related party transactions involving large listed firms.[22] Intra-group guarantees are pro-

---

19) The 5 percent threshold requirement, moreover, was applicable to other shareholder rights.

20) For a more extensive survey of the reforms, see Hwa-Jin Kim, *Toward the "Best Practice" Model in a Globalizing Market: Recent Developments in Korean Corporate Governance*, SSRN Working Paper (2001), available online at <http://papers.ssrn.com/sol3/papers.cfinabstract._id=282051> (visited Sept 20, 2002) (describing changes in Korean corporate governance and Korean governance adaptation to global standards by analyzing data from 2000 and 2001).

21) Securities and Exchange Act, art 191-13, § 1 (S Korea), available online at <http://www.moleg.go.kr/mlawinfo/english/htms/html/lawl9.html> (visited Sept 20, 2002); Commercial Act, art 403, § 1 (S Korea), available online at <http://www.moleg.go.kr/mlawinfo/english/htms/html/law08.html> (visited Sept 20, 2002).

22) Securities and Exchange Act, art 191-19 (cited in note 21).

hibited and existing guarantees have been eliminated for certain large business groups.[23] Accounting standards were revised to bring them into substantial compliance with International Accounting Standards. Large *chaebol* groups are now required to prepare "combined" financial statements covering all the member companies in the group.[24] Listed firms are required to file quarterly reports in addition to annual and biannual reports.[25] Despite these formal legal changes, substantial doubt exists as to whether the reforms will result in a major increase in protection for minority investors in Korea.[26] The reforms have done little to shore up the confidence of the international investment community. Moreover, evidence exists that political pressures - primarily from the *chaebol* - are working to undo the reforms.[27] Given the rapid decline of willpower in the current government and the heightened voice of the united business community, it now seems that further statutory change strengthening shareholder rights is unlikely.

III. REFORM OPTIONS FOR KOREA

With unlimited political resolve, a country interested in reforming its corporate governance system - defined broadly to include not only formal laws but institutions and norms - enjoys the luxury of being able to make several attempts at legal reform. Moreover, the country may attempt to implement reforms incrementally. But political resolve, unfortunately, is limited. As we move away from the 1997 crisis, the impetus for reform will most likely decline even further. Given the reality of limited political capital for reform, we pose the question of what types of reform may prove efficacious over the long term in Korea.

Most commentators take a traditional approach toward reform in Korea, advocating top-down changes in corporate governance regulations applying to all firms.[28] As we dis-

---

23) Monopoly Regulation and Fair Trade Act, art 10-2 (S Korea), available online at <http://www.moleg.go.kr/mawinfo/english/htms/html/lawlO.html> (visited Sept 20, 2002).

24) Act on External Audit of Stock Companies, art 1-2 (S Korea), available online at <http://www.moleg.go.kr/mlawinfo/english/hrms/html/lawO9.html> (visited Sept 20, 2002).

25) Securities and Exchange Act, art 186-3 (cited in note 21).

26) See Yoo Cheong-mo, *Poll Says Conglomerates' Boards Swayed by Owners*, Korea Herald (Jan 16, 2002) ("According to a poll of 171 fund managers in Korea by the Seoul-based Hangil Research, 92.4 percent said that the chaebol's board members are incapable of making independent decisions under the influence of the largest shareholders or top executives.").

27) See Yoo, *Chaebol Call for an End to State Meddling in Corporate Governance*, Korea Herald (cited in note 8) (reporting on Chaebol resistance to corporate governance reforms in Korea).

28) See Bernard Black, et al, *Corporate Governance in Korea at the Millennium: Enhancing International Competitiveness*, 26 J Corp L 537, 560-608 (2001) (proposing a number of reforms to Korea's Commercial Code focusing on strengthening the role of the board of directors, and the ability of share-

cuss in section A, however, we remain skeptical of this approach within Korea. At the opposite extreme, one could imagine simply allowing the market to determine the level of investor protection, possibly through private contract. While we discuss this possibility in section B, we remain cautious of such a radical change within Korea's political and economic framework. Instead, section C presents our proposal for encouraging limited choice within the context of the Korea Stock Exchange.

A. ToP-DOWN GOVERNMENT REGULATION

In attempting top-down corporate governance reforms, Korea is not alone. Many countries throughout the 1990s instituted reforms affecting governance within firms. Despite the success of the United States capital markets (and economy) and the belief held by many that the US system of strong investor protection is at least partially responsible for such success, major questions exist as to whether importing US-style laws will provide similar results for other countries. Formal legal rules represent only a part (and perhaps not even the most important part) of the overall investor protection regime. Without effective public institutions, including an unbiased judiciary and regulatory enforcement officials, and similarly effective private institutions, including reputational intermediaries able to protect the interests of unsophisticated investors in the market, formal legal rules may offer little real protection for investors.[29]

Evidence exists supporting the view that mere formal changes in the law often prove ineffective in transforming practices within a country. In large part due to efforts on the part of the SEC, for example, many countries adopted formal prohibitions against insider trading in the 1980s and 1990s.[30] Despite the presence of a formal ban on insider trading, however, few countries have ever engaged in enforcement of this ban.[31] At the end of 1998, 103 countries had stock markets, 87 of those countries prohibited insider trading, but enforcement had taken place at least 32 once in only 38 countries.[32]

---

holders to approve certain transactions, among other measures).

29) For a discussion of laws and institutions (arguably) important for the development of strong securities markets, see Black, 48 UCLA L Rev 781 (cited in note 5).

30) See Harvey L. Pitt and David B. Hardison, Gaines *Without Frontiers: Trends in the International Response to Insider Trading*, 55 L & Contemp Probs 199, 204-06 (1992).

31) See Utpal Bhattacharya and Hazem Daouk, *The World Price of Insider Trading*, 57 J Fin 75, 75 (2002) (prior to 1990, only nine of thirty-four countries with prohibitions on insider trading ever engaged in an enforcement action).

32) Id. See also Katharina Pistor, Martin Raiser, and Stanislav Gelfer, *Law and Finance in Transition Economies* 2, EBRD Working Paper No 48 (2000), available online at <http://www.ebrd.com/pubs/

Korea's experience fits well with these propositions. For example, fiduciary rules in the Korean Commercial Code, although not as comprehensive as their US counterparts, were first adopted forty years ago in 1962. Nonetheless, until recently enforcement of the rules was rare due to, among other reasons, the 5 percent share ownership requirement to initiate a derivative suit. The operation of the board of directors in Korea serves as another example. Before the economic crisis, the board was a mere formality except in a small number of joint venture firms or government-owned enterprises. Directors were widely regarded as executives in the corporate hierarchy and not as members of an organ in charge of monitoring corporate decisionmaking. Large companies, such as Samsung Electronics, had up to sixty directors, yet board meetings often took place only on the books.

Of course, new legal rules often have an impact on the underlying norms and institutions within a country. Within the United States, the passage of federal securities laws during the 1930s dramatically changed how companies offer securities and provide information to the marketplace. Of significance is the fact that the passage of federal securities laws closely followed the stock market crash of 1929 and occurred while the public held a widespread belief that fraud and market manipulation led to the crash.[33]

Despite the effectiveness of some scandal-driven law reform, two problems exist with relying on scandals as a catalyst for reform. First, lawmakers in the wake of a scandal may overreact in implementing new far-reaching regulatory reform. Once reforms are in place, it may take decades to remove the legal changes. For example, the United States only recently removed barriers under Glass-Steagall, which kept the businesses of commercial banks and securities firms separate.[34] Second, when scandals are absent, the political capital for reform may diminish rapidly. Relying solely on lawmakers to generate new investor protection measures may therefore result in either too strident new regulations, or too few changes to the regulatory regime.

The Korean experience with corporate governance reform fits the pattern of scandal-driven reform. After the Asian economic crisis, numerous corporate governance reforms took place. Now, several years after the reforms, the prospect of future reform efforts appears dim at best. Rather than wait for another scandal, regulators may wish to consider reforms to the *process* of how regulations are created, in order to provide an ongoing and persistent

---

econ/workingp/48.pdf> (visited Sept 22, 2002) ("legal environment" is much more important than formal legal protection).

33) See generally Stuart Banner, *What Causes New Securities Regulation?: 300 Years of Evidence*, 75 Wash U L Q 849, 850 (1997) (observing that significant legal changes often occur following major scandals).

34) See Michael Schroeder, *Clinton Signs Financial-Services Bill, But Cautions About Privacy Shortfalls*, Wall St J A41 (Nov 15, 1999).

level of impetus for reforms that benefit investors.

B. PRIVATE CONTRACT

Where regulation fails to provide necessary investor protection measures, market partic-ipants may turn to substitute mechanisms of protecting the interests of minority investors. The market, of course, will not choose to adopt all possible types of protection. Some forms of protection, for example, are simply not cost-effective. It may be the case that forcing a full-blown audit of a corporation's business on a daily basis may deter hidden forms of self-dealing and fraud-but the costs of conducting such a daily audit far outweigh the ex-pected benefits from doing so. When protective measures are cost-effective, participants in the market will have strong incentives to adopt such measures. When investors are pro-tected, they will pay more for securities up front, raising the value of the offering proceeds for the initial promoters.

What are the possible substitute mechanisms available in Korea? Companies may use con-tractual means to protect investors. A firm, for example, may adopt provisions in its articles of incorporation. Provisions may require a majority of outside directors on the board of di-rectors or the approval of outside directors for self-dealing transactions involving control-ling shareholders. Nevertheless, some residual uncertainty exists as to what extent Korea's Commercial Code in fact gives firms the ability to bind themselves through the corporate charter.

Even without resorting to private contract, firms seeking to protect minority investors may attempt to associate with market-based reputational intermediaries. Investors, of course, may not have the ability to distinguish among different intermediaries, allowing lower level intermediaries to free ride off the reputation of higher quality intermediaries.[35] Free riding in turn, may lead higher quality intermediaries to reduce their own investment in quality. On the other hand, many high quality intermediaries are well known to Korean investors. It is unclear, for example, the extent to which investors will fail to distinguish between the Goldman Sachses and Morgan Stanleys of the market and lesser-known firms.

Firms may also choose to engage in voluntary disclosures to benefit their investors. Empirical studies show that companies that list on securities exchanges in more than one country tend to disclose a significant amount of information voluntarily.[36]

---

35) See Black, 48 UCLA L Rev at 787-88 (cited in note 5).
36) See Gary K. Meek, Clare B. Roberts, and Sidney J. Gray, *Factors Influencing Voluntary Annual Report*

Private contract nevertheless has its limits. Private actors may ignore the external impact of their decisions on other parties not related through contract to the actors. Firms choosing the level of information to disclose to the market, for example, may ignore the positive benefit from such disclosures to third parties who value more accurate securities prices. Dispersed shareholders are at risk that managers may engage in a "mid-stream" shift, changing the level of investor protection well after investors have put money into a firm. The government may also enjoy a comparative advantage in providing some forms of investor protection. Governments may employ criminal penalties, while private parties may not. Regulatory agencies may also enjoy economies of scale in enforcing existing regulations. But the fact that governments enjoy a comparative advantage does not necessarily lead to the conclusion that government regulation must be mandatory. As suggested in the next section, regulators could achieve the same comparative advantage by creating an optional high corporate governance section of the stock exchange.[37]

Lastly, private contract may bind market participants. Nevertheless, purely private contract cannot bind the government itself from engaging in expropriating activities. For example, Russia, through its tax regime, has frequently engaged in confiscatory behavior.[38]

C. EXPANDING CHOICE

Private contract is not the only means to generate choice. A regime where investors are able to choose from among different regulatory regimes in competition with one another is possible. Corporations in the United States, for example, choose their own state of incorporation. Evidence from the state competition for corporate charters inside the US provides some support for the notion that competition may lead to a race to the top, benefiting investors.[39] Expanding choice through regulatory competition may also benefit Korean investors, and thereby the liquidity of the Korean capital markets. Where the choice is provided through regulatory competition, issuers and investors will enjoy both the bene-

Disclosures By U.S., U.K. and Continental European Multinational Corporations, 26 J Intl Bus Stud 555, 566 (1995) ("Listing status is important in explaining voluntary strategic and financial, but not non-financial, disclosures.").

37) For a discussion of "self-tailored" liability, see Stephen Choi, *Market Lessons for Gatekeepers*, 92 Nw U L Rev 916, 951-58 (1998).

38) See Bernard Black, Reinier Kraakman, and Anna Tarassova, *Russian Privatization and Corporate Governance: What Went Wrong?*, 52 Stan L Rev 1731, 1758 (2000).

39) For evidence on the possibility of a race to the top, see Romano, 107 Yale LJ at 2383-88 (cited in note 10). For sources providing an exposition of the race to the top argument, see Bebchuk, 105 Harv L Rev at 1445-46 (cited in note 9).

fits of government-supplied investor protection as well as the responsiveness and innovation that come from competition.[40]

Two considerations, nevertheless, give us pause in recommending too great a level of choice for the Korean situation. First, government officials within Korea are accustomed to a large degree of intervention in the financial markets, leading to potential resistance to moving toward a full choice regime. Second, while evidence exists that choice may generally work well for state competition for corporate charters in the US, Korea may pose a different situation. Investors within Korea may lack the same level of sophistication as US investors. At the very least, Korean investors run the risk of confusion to the extent companies with different regimes are allowed to trade concurrently on the KSE. Multiple regimes may also undermine the ability of investors in Korea to compare companies with one another. Managers may also abuse the ability to shift regimes, thereby removing the few investor protection measures Korea presently provides.

Korea therefore faces a dilemma. While a full-blown regulatory competition choice regime may prove politically infeasible (at least today) and pose a number of problems, the present top-down approach to regulation is equally problematic. Without resorting completely to a full choice regime, we contend that more limited moves to increase the choice available to Korean issuers may obtain many of the benefits from regulatory competition without incurring the risks related to regulatory competition and the political costs of shifting toward such a regime. Success in providing for limited competition may then eventually lead Korea to increasing the amount of choice.

Little choice exists today for Korean companies seeking to adopt different types of protection for investors. While some countries allow firms to incorporate in foreign countries, Korea does not. Under the Commercial Code, a firm incorporated in a foreign jurisdiction is subject to all the provisions of the Code if it has its head office or main operations in Korea.[41] We propose two alternative methods of increasing choice in regulatory protection. First, we discuss the possibility of the KSE implementing a new market specifically for companies that opt into a higher level of disclosure and investor protection. Second, we discuss the possibility of a new KSE market for firms that may elect to follow the regulatory regime of another country.

---

40) For an argument that issuers and investors should enjoy choice in the form of securities regulation that applies to their securities transactions, see Stephen J. Choi and Andrew T. Guzman, *Portable Reciprocity: Rethinking the International Reach of Securities Regulation*, 71 S Cal L Rev 903, 906-08 (1998).

41) See Commercial Act, art 617 (cited in note 21).

1. Establishing a High Corporate Governance Market

Some ability to opt into a greater level of investor protection already exists for Korean companies. A Korean firm, for example, may enter into an agreement with a foreign securities exchange to become listed on the exchange. Korean firms listing on the New York Stock Exchange ("NYSE"), for example, must meet certain listing requirements, including a minimum number of shareholders and average trading volume, and quantitative requirements relating to earnings, cash flow, and global market capitalization. In addition, the NYSE provides a variety of corporate governance related listing requirements. Firms that list on the NYSE are also exposed to US federal securities regulations, including both antifraud and mandatory disclosure provisions. Listing on the NYSE, along with other global securities exchanges, therefore demonstrates the management's commitment to transparency.

Significantly, however, exchanges will often waive many of their listing requirements for qualifying foreign issuers.[42] Regulators will also make exceptions for foreign issuers, which are not available for domestic issuers within the securities regulatory regime. Even where foreign securities exchanges and regulators attempt to implement stringent investor protection, enforcement problems exist. Where the officers and assets of a listed company are located in a different country from an exchange, the exchange (and regulatory authorities such as the SEC) may have a difficult time obtaining information and seeking enforcement. Evidence nevertheless exists that foreign firms that seek to obtain an exchange listing (or a listing on NASDAQ) inside the United States come disproportionately from countries with weak investor protection.[43] Listing on a US exchange, therefore, may provide substitute forms of investor protection to fill the void left by the laws of the issuer's home country.

Despite the possibility of listing on an established foreign securities exchange, establishing a high corporate governance standard market within Korea will provide several advantages for domestic Korean companies and investors. First, companies face higher transaction costs when listing overseas. Domestic investors already may be aware of a company in ways that foreign investors are not. Language translation problems and the need to deal with foreign counsel also increase the costs of listing securities overseas. More firms, therefore, may se-

---

42) Roberta S. Karmel, *The Future of Corporate Governance Listing Requirements*, 54 SMU L Rev 325, 333 (2001).

43) See William A. Reese, Jr. and Michael S. Weisbach, *Protection of Minority Shareholder Interests, Crosslistings in the United States, and Subsequent Equity Offerings*, SSRN Working Paper (2000), available online at <http://papers.ssrn.com/sol3/papers.cfin abstract-id=194670> (visited Sept 16, 2002).

lect into a Korean high corporate governance standard market than would list on a foreign securities exchange. Second, the KSE may provide investor protection and enforcement at a lower cost due to the local proximity of Korean companies. Lastly, the KSE may tailor its provision of investor protection specifically for Korean investors and, moreover, employ corporate governance devices not presently required on overseas exchanges.

The concept of establishing a new high corporate governance market is not new. Other securities exchanges have taken the route of actively providing investor protection as a selling point of their market. The Neuer Markt in Germany, a subsidiary of the Deutsche Boerse, adopted disclosure and accounting standards on par with US standards, rather than the laxer German standards.[44] Over a three-year period, these stringent forms of investor protection allowed the Neuer Markt to grow from 2 to 302 listed companies.[45] The value of high corporate governance listing standards, moreover, is not lost on companies listed on the Neuer Markt. After a wave of bankruptcies and insider trading scandals involving listed companies, several of the top companies listed on the Neuer Markt demanded tougher listing requirements.[46] Based on private contract between the Deutsche Boerse and listing companies, the stringent listing requirements of the Neuer Markt are being duplicated in growth stock markets located in Amsterdam, Brussels, Paris and Milan.[47]

Similarly, the Bovespa in Brazil established a new section, the Novo Mercado, for firms with a corporate governance structure that provides strong minority investor protection. As with the Neuer Markt, the Novo Mercado targets smaller companies that otherwise would have few options to raise capital (aside from development banks).[48] Such companies include high technology startups as well as closely held preexisting companies. The Novo Mercado makes both stringent minority investor protection and US accounting standards part of its listing requirements. Firms listed on the Novo Mercado, for example, must only issue voting shares and give minority shareholders the right to appoint members of the supervisory board.[49] The Novo Mercado requires companies to have at least 25 percent of their equity

---

44) See Vanessa Fuhrmans, *Playing By the Rules: How Neuer Markt Gets Respect*, Wall St J C1 (Aug 21, 2000) (noting that the successful Neuer Markt portrays itself as "[t]he most regulated market" in Europe). The Neuer Markt was closed down and merged into the Frankfurt Stock Exchange in September 2002, during the last stage of editing for this article.

45) See id. Although the Neuer Markt's market capitalization grew rapidly, it has recently experienced both scandals and a large drop in market capitalization.

46) See Neal E. Boudette and Alfred Kueppers, *Frustrated Neuer Markt Members Push for Tightening Listing Rules*, Wall St J C12 (July 11, 2001).

47) See Fuhrmans, *Playing By the Rules*, Wall St J at C1 (cited in note 44).

48) See Craig Karmin, *Brazil Prepares Launch of Market to Encourage Foreign Investment Through Good Governance*, Wall St J C16 (Dec 14,2000).

49) See id.

publicly-traded. After an initial public offering, controlling shareholders must also agree to a six-month lockup period. To date, the Novo Mercado has signed only two listed companies.[50] On the one hand, this small number may indicate that higher corporate governance standards may fail to attract firms to an otherwise illiquid market. Nonetheless, even where higher corporate governance standards fail to jumpstart a market such as the Novo Mercado, such standards may work in countries with larger overall capital markets such as in the case of Germany and the Neuer Markt.[51]

Following the lead of the Neuer Markt and the Novo Mercado, a new section of the Korea Stock Exchange could set itself up as a leader in investor protection. Without elaborating on the details here, a high corporate governance section of the KSE could provide for compliance with US accounting standards or further reconciliation with the International Accounting Standards. In addition, minority investor protection could potentially be required of listed firms, and more significantly enforced under the threat of de-listing.[52] Significantly, the KSE's optional higher standards would be imposed through private contract, and only on firms that voluntarily choose to list on the new market. Implementing higher corporate governance standards through private contract reduces the need to obtain the cooperation of the various regulatory agencies that implement other aspects of private company law in Korea.

Not all firms in Korea, of course, will take advantage of a new high corporate governance market. In particular, preexisting firms where managers and controlling shareholders already enjoy high levels of private benefits will almost certainly avoid the high corporate governance market, at least initially. But where a firm has a large value project that requires additional outside capital, managers may choose to opt for higher corporate governance standards to reduce their cost of capital. This will occur to the extent the managers gain more, as shareholders, from the ability to pursue the new project than they lose in reduced private benefits. Firms lacking such high value new projects will choose not to adopt the new standards.

The failure on the part of some firms, particularly those firms with a large preexisting base of minority shareholders, to take advantage of a new high corporate governance market is not a large problem for our proposal. Minority investors are not directly harmed to the ex-

---

50) See the current list of Novo Mercado companies on the Bovespa web site at <http://www.bovespa.com.br/fra.cialistnmi.htm> (visited Sept 20, 2002).
51) Furthermore, the Novo Mercado experiment is still too new to critique fairly.
52) Minority investor protection could potentially include provisions for a majority of outside directors, independent audit, compensation and nomination committees, cumulative voting, and more elaborate and strengthened fiduciary rules.

tent they already paid a large discount when they initially purchased their shares. To the extent investors did not anticipate the creation of a high corporate governance market, they would have discounted the shares for the very likely possibility that managers would expropriate large levels of private benefits. Indeed, the ability of companies with a large contingent of preexisting minority shareholders to ignore a new high corporate governance market is precisely what gives our proposal feasibility. Once large, entrenched business interests are not forced into our regime, they will have less reason to oppose establishing such a market.

In comparison, we predict that many firms without a large base of preexisting minority shareholders will elect into a new high corporate governance market. Firms about to go public for the first time, for example, will receive a lower discount on their shares-and correspondingly larger offering proceeds-to the extent they elect into types of protection that investors value. Moreover, the provision of a standardized set of investor-protection measures through a new market on the KSE alleviates many of the concerns raised by those opposed to regulatory competition. Because only one high corporate governance option is offered, investors may easily identify those firms adopting such a level of investor protection based on their listing on the new market. Investors, as well, will have the ability to compare disclosures across firms on the new market, relying on standardization enforced through the higher listing requirements.

The KSE and government regulators behind the KSE may also take into account positive external benefits from disclosure requirements imposed in the new market. While easy to state as an abstract matter, it is more difficult to determine precisely what information investors would not want disclosed given the private costs, but that third parties in the market would find significant. Roberta Romano has put forth the argument that even if such information exists, the mandatory disclosure regime as administered by the SEC in the US fails to take such third-party externalities into account.[53] Nevertheless, there is the potential for the KSE to force firms to make such disclosures in the new market. Of course, some firms on the margin may find that the additional cost of disclosure outweighs the private benefit from protecting investors, and will choose therefore to remain outside the new market. Given the present low level of corporate governance protection for investors in Korea, the benefit to investors from the new market will likely be significantly positive and few firms that opt into the market will therefore be on the margin. Additionally, because

---

53) See Roberta Romano, *The Need for Competition in International Securities Regulation*, 2 Theoretical Inquiries L 387, 446-64 (2001).

the option offered only increases the amount of investor protection, the danger of managerial opportunism resulting in a further "race to the bottom" is absent.

Other firms, in addition to firms going public, may voluntarily select into the new high corporate governance market. Firms that already maintain a culture of managers looking out for investors may select into the high corporate governance market, because the already low private benefit levels of the managers are unlikely to be affected. We predict that at least some current well-established firms under professional managers, such as banks, POSCO, and recently-privatized firms like Korea Telecom, may elect initially into the new market.

Over time, the growth of a high governance market will then place competitive pressure on non-listed firms along a number of dimensions. First, firms listed on the new market will have strong incentives to maximize share value. One method of doing so is to hire professional managers focused on maximizing share value. The demand for professional managers will in turn affect the norms within business schools in Korea as well as standards of conduct for managers generally, in a much faster way than simply importing US-style business schools into Korea. Spillover effects on managers at firms choosing not to list on the KSE new market are therefore possible, as managers migrate across different firms and the general management culture shifts in Korea. Firms initially resistant to the new market may then eventually opt into the market.

Second, domestic investors in new high corporate governance firms will come to expect a certain level of investor protection. In addition, foreign investors are more likely to invest in firms that provide more credible investor protection. Such investors may avoid firms that choose not to list on the new market, reducing the liquidity of such firms and thereby further depressing the share price of non-listing firms. For example, foreign investors sold off the shares of companies in the LG Group, resulting in a large decline in the share prices of the companies, after the controlling family of the LG Group engaged in an internal stock deal that netted the family $46 million.[54] Investor-oriented institutions already present to a limited degree - including US-style business schools, sophisticated investment banks, and law firms - will also find an increased demand for their services, leading to a growth in these institutions within Korea and a change in the business norms toward investor-protection goals.

To the extent the new market also provides more effective avenues for shareholder activism,

---

54) See, for example, Yoo Cheong-mo, *LG Group's Owner Family Draws Bitter Criticisms for Dubious Stock Transactions*, Korea Herald (Apr 26, 2002).

shareholder groups may form to collectivize the interests of shareholders. Once such groups achieve economies of scale, they may then focus attention on firms that choose not to list on the exchange. Already in Korea the People's Solidarity for Participatory Democracy ("PSPD"),[55] a shareholder activist group, has initiated fiduciary duty-related lawsuits,[56] pushed for the appointment of outside directors,[57] and openly questioned management decisions at shareholder meetings.[58]

Third, if the migration to the new section turns out to affect the stock price favorably, firms remaining in the old section of the KSE will feel strong pressure from investors to move to the high corporate governance section, thereby accelerating changes in corporate governance practices.

A possibility exists that present business establishments (including in particular the *cbaebol*) - although not directly threatened under the Articles choice-based proposal - may nonetheless resist an experiment that may lead other firms in Korea to adopt a higher corporate governance regime. Moreover, despite the various benefits associated with implementing a new high corporate governance section of the KSE, we do not foresee the KSE voluntarily implementing such a market without government approval. Although the growing competition among global stock markets for capital will ultimately change the incentives placed on the KSE, presently the KSE enjoys a near monopoly over Korean investors seeking to put money into equity investments. Within such a monopoly position, the KSE has few incentives to pursue change. Moreover, officials in charge of the KSE today may care little about the competitive environment the KSE may encounter in the near future to the extent the impact primarily falls on future officials at the KSE.

Korea's Ministry of Finance and Economy ("MOFE") may therefore have a role in establishing the new KSE market and setting standards for listing on the market. As with all forms of mandatory regulation, the initiation of a new high corporate governance market may run into problems related to industry capture and non-responsiveness over time on the part of regulators, among others. Significantly, however, we envision the MOFE's role as important only at the start of the new market.[59] Once the new market gains scale and investor sup-

---

55) See Jooyoung Kim and Joongi Kim, *Shareholder Activism in Korea: A Review of How PSPD Has Used Legal Measures to Strengtben Korean Corporate Governance*, 1 J Korean L 51, 53 (2001) (describing the PSPD's shareholder-oriented activities).

56) See Yoo Cheong-mo, *Activist Group Seeking Court Injunction to Have Samsung Chairman Pay Damages*, Korea Herald (Jan 11, 2002).

57) See Kim and Kim, 1 J Korean L at 59 (cited in note 55).

58) See Kim Ji-hyun, *PSPD to Sit in on Korea Exchange Bank Shareholders' Meeting*, Korea Herald (Feb 5, 2002).

59) The MOFE could, of course, maintain some regulatory role. As the new market gains scale and market

port, further changes to the new market's listing standards will derive from private initiatives. In particular, we recommend giving the KSE direct incentives to ensure the listing standards on the new market continue to cater to the interests of investors. One possible structural reform would be to make the new market a for-profit subsidiary of the KSE; presently the KSE is a non-profit membership organization.[60] Alternatively, the MOFE could have the KSE sell off the new high corporate governance part of the KSE as a separate for-profit entity, demutualizing the KSE in part.[61]

Politically, efforts toward demutualization may prove difficult in Korea. The MOFE may be reluctant to accept a proposal directly compromising its authority. Nevertheless, even without any explicit domestic effort to alter the incentives of officials in the new KSE market, the growing globalization of the world capital markets will eventually generate a large amount of background competitive pressure. Short-sighted KSE officials may resist initiating a new high corporate governance market. Nonetheless, future KSE officials, once the market is in place and faced with growing capital market competition, will have the incentive and ability to cater to the preferences of investors in the global competitive marketplace while avoiding the political backlash from entrenched business interests unwilling to part with their present level of private benefits of control. Such changes, moreover, take time. If the MOFE promotes these reforms today, the KSE will be better positioned in the near future to engage in such competition.

In the upcoming global competition between securities markets, relatively smaller countries may have an advantage in providing protection that investors value. Delaware "won" the competition for corporate charters perhaps in part because of its small size. A small state may focus on maximizing the value of its rules for corporations without fearing the political impact on other constituencies.[62] Also, the fact that incorporation fees represent a large proportion of Delaware's total fiscal intake helps make credible the implicit promise on the part of Delaware lawmakers to adjust continually the corporate law rules to maximize corporate welfare. Korea may adopt a similar tactic. Through a high corporate governance ex-

---

volume, regulators may move, for example, to make it easier for shareholders to force firms into the new marker. One possible reform, for example, would be to give shareholders the unilateral right (voting as a majority) to opt into the new market.

60) See Korean Stock Exchange, Articles of Incorporation (2001), available online at <http://www.kse.or.kr /upload/rule/regOll.doc> (visited Sept 20, 2002).

61) For a discussion of the recent trend toward demutualization of securities exchanges, see Roberta S. Karmel, *Turning Seats Into Shares: Causes and Implications of Demutualization of Stock and Futures Exchanges*, 53 Hastings LJ 367 (2002).

62) SeeJonathan RL Macey and Geoffrey P. Miller, *Toward an Interest Group Theory of Delaware Corporate Law*, 65 Tex L Rev 469,490 (1987).

change with credible enforcement built up over time, the KSE may provide a welcome avenue for both investors and firms seeking to raise capital.

2. A Dual-Listed Section of the KSE

While establishing a high corporate governance section of the KSE will provide choice and competition in the provision of investor protection in Korea, the amount of competition is limited. Within Korea, the competition will be between the traditional KSE section and the new high corporate governance section. Where the standard setters for the new high corporate governance section of the KSE do not capture entirely the benefit from establishing new forms of investor protection, or at the very least are not separate from the regulators of the traditional section of the KSE, the level of competition may be small (at least absent global financial market competition).[63] As an alternative reform, we therefore suggest creating a new market within the KSE specifically designated for firms that choose to follow the listing standards and accounting disclosures of select, alternative foreign regimes.

We imagine that such a system would entail providing automatic listing on the new dual-listed section of the KSE for any company that lists on any one of several approved exchanges. The Korean government, for example, could approve the NYSE, NASDAQ, and the London Stock Exchange ("LSE"), among others, as eligible markets for firms seeking automatic dual-listing status. Within the dual-listed section of the KSE, Korean investors may then benefit from more stringent investor protection, generated through competition among the regimes of foreign markets, without having to leave the domestic Korean equity market. While radical, the KSE would not be alone in following such a free-riding approach toward regulatory competition. Since 2000, the Israeli government has allowed firms that list in the US securities markets to gain automatic dual-listing privileges on the Tel Aviv Stock Exchange.[64] Firms that dual list in the US and the Tel Aviv Stock Exchange are exempted from any additional listing or maintenance requirements as well as listing fees.[65] Along a similar vein, the SEC for the past decade has allowed Canadian firms to raise capital inside the United States while following primarily the disclosure (but not the antifraud) rules of

---

63) As discussed above, however, global competition from other securities exchanges may nevertheless place large competitive pressures on the KSE. Providing for a separate high corporate governance section of the KSE may provide an effective vehicle for meeting this global competition.

64) See Tel Aviv Stock Exchange ("TASE"), *The Dual-Listing Law: A New Era on the TASE*, available online at <http://www.tase.co.il/shows/dual/duallistfinal.pdf> (visited Sept 20, 2002). Amir Licht, on the other hand, has argued that the ability to obtain listing on the TASE automatically with a listing on a US securities market may lead to a race to the bottom. See Amir N. Licht, *David's Dilenmna: A Case Study of Securities Regulation in a Small Open Market*, 2 Theoretical Inquiries L 673, 702-03 (2001).

65) See TASE, *The Dual Listing Law: A New Era on the TASE* (cited in note 64).

Canada under the multijurisdictional disclosure system.[66]

Providing for a degree of choice within the new dual-listed section of the KSE will then generate competitive pressures on the traditional portion of the KSE to provide investor protection that firms and investors jointly desire. As with the high corporate governance section, competition will have an effect only if those in charge of establishing investor protection within the KSE are affected directly. For example, to the extent volume is drawn off of the traditional KSE and the role for regulators on the KSE is correspondingly diminished, KSE officials will have at least some incentive to modify their provision of investor protection to better suit the needs of investors.

Several criticisms are possible against our KSE dual-listed section proposal. First, a greater possibility for investor confusion may result. In particular, unsophisticated investors lacking good information may fail to price accurately the selection of a particular regime. To reduce the possibility of investor confusion, regulators may wish to restrict access to only more sophisticated investors. Much like Rule 144A in the United States, the MOFE could establish that the free market section is only accessible to sophisticated investors. As with Rule 144A, regulators may use brightline numerical criteria based on wealth, income, and invested assets, to determine which investors qualify as sophisticated. But in contrast to the US securities laws, Korean regulators may also wish to establish that securities purchased in the free market section may not be resold to unsophisticated investors, even with the passage of time from the initial offering by the issuer.

We are agnostic, however, on the need to restrict access to the dual-listed market only to sophisticated investors. Simply placing the dual-listed status firms in a separate and readily-identifiable section of the KSE helps reduce the possibility of investor confusion. Where the firm trades in an efficient market, moreover, the value of a selected regulatory regime will become incorporated in the market price, indirectly protecting the interests of unsophisticated investors. Regulators may also reduce the risk facing unsophisticated investors by limiting the choice of alternative regulatory regimes, for example, to the NYSE, NASDAQ, and the LSE.

Second, one could question the value of regulatory protection provided by a foreign source. The NYSE, for example, may lack the information necessary to enforce its listing requirements against a Korean company. Moreover, obtaining judgment against Korean nationals

---

66) See Mulrjurisdictional Disclosure and Modifications to the Current Registration and Reporting System for Canadian Issuers, Exchange Act Release No 33-6902, [1991 Transfer Binder] Fed Sec L Rep (CCH) 84,812 (June 21, 1991).

and assets located in Korea may be difficult for both the NYSE and the SEC. United States regulatory officials, as well, may not care about the impact of their actions on Korean investors, focusing primarily on the welfare of US investors. The NYSE itself has instituted a lower level of listing requirements for foreign firms, perhaps in recognition of the difficulties in obtaining the compliance of foreign firms with more stringent requirements.[67] Several responses are possible to the problem of enforcement. Korean companies will have an incentive to select only those regimes that are able to enforce their laws against Korean companies. Firms that actively opt into the dual-listed market and select a regime where enforcement is weak will face a large discount from investors. Moreover, Korea and the KSE do not have to remain passive with regard to enforcement even in the new dual-listed market. Regulators in Korea may work with specific countries to provide information and other assistance to reduce the cost of enforcement for foreign regulators. Korea may also choose to enforce certain applicable laws of another country. To the extent the US allows for class actions, for example, Korea may allow Korean investors to pursue class actions against firms that opt to adopt US standards.[68]

The lack of norms and institutions geared toward investor protection may limit the effectiveness of the KSE and the Korean government in providing more stringent enforcement of investor protection norms, even for firms on the new dual-listed market that opt into a foreign regime with a higher level of investor protection. Institutions, nevertheless, may cross international borders. Several prominent US investment banks-including Goldman Sachs and Morgan Stanley-have offices in Seoul. Firms that use the dual-listed market in the KSE to opt into US-style protection will provide a natural clientele for US-based investment banks and attorneys familiar with the operation of US listing standards and securities regulation. Providing a new, optional market removes many of the pressures against reform from entrenched business interests, leaving newer firms the ability to opt for stronger investor protection and thereby profit from the corresponding reduced cost of capital. New norms and institutions may then generate around this core group of firms opting into the dual-listed market.

---

67) The NYSE, for example, allows foreign issuers to either meet the NYSE's domestic firm quantitative listing requirements or separate foreign issuer quantitative listing requirements. See <http://www.nyse.com/listed/intnlstandards.html> (visited Sept 20, 2002).

68) Although its chances of eventually passing into law are not high, a bill for introducing class action in certain securities disputes is now pending in Korea's National Assembly.

IV. CONCLUSION

Prior to the Asian economic crisis of 1997, Korea experienced rapid growth in many sectors in its economy. Korea's government played an active role in this growth, providing subsidies and guaranteed financing for favored business sectors, particularly heavy industry and chemical manufacturing. One consequence of the Korean government's heavy-handed intervention into the market was the shift by many large *chaebol* companies into often ill-advised debt financing. Ultimately, the large levels of debt, and in particular foreign debt, put the cbaebol companies in a precarious financial state and accelerated the foreign exchange depletion leading to the 1997 crisis.

Throughout the buildup of debt financing, the needs of minority equity shareholders in Korean companies were often simply ignored. Founding families of the cbaebol companies enjoyed absolute control of their connected business empires through interlocking share positions. Of course, where minority investors were able to demand a discount in the share price, they were not directly harmed from the high private benefits. Nevertheless, the lack of protection for minority equity investors made it more difficult for new startup companies to obtain financing. Moreover, in today's post-Asian economic crisis world, even the *cbaebol* companies can no longer look exclusively to debt financing.

Changing the level of a country's investor protection, however, is not an easy assignment. Top-down reform may prove ineffective and the impetus for change may gradually dissipate. Not only may deep-rooted norms and institutional barriers exist, but also-perhaps more significantly-specific interest groups in society may actively push against change. Controlling founders of cbaebol, for example, will not easily relinquish their private benefits of control.

Rather than press for reforms that affect all Korean companies, therefore, we choose to start out on a smaller scale, recommending that the KSE establish a new section of the market for firms that choose to opt into a higher level of protection for investors compared to the present Korean regime. Modest efforts at introducing some amount of choice, and thereby competition, in the provision of regulatory protection within the Korean Stock Exchange may provide the most promising and feasible first step toward improving investor protection.

Establishing a new section of the KSE has the added benefit of potentially increasing the amount of competitive pressure placed on regulators of the remaining sections of the KSE.

Significantly, explicit moves to increase the incentives of the KSE to develop value-maximizing investor protection devices may not be necessary. Even without explicit incentives, competition will eventually arrive in Korea through the growing integration of the global capital markets. To the extent Korean investors are increasingly able to invest their funds overseas, the KSE will lose volume if it does not provide the types of protection that investors desire. Establishing a separate high corporate governance section allows the KSE the freedom to engage in competition for investors' dollars without facing the political constraints imposed by preexisting controlling blocks in companies with high levels of private benefits.

Competition may also occur to the extent Korea establishes a new dual-listed market in the KSE on which issuers may automatically list after complying with the listing standards of one of a group of select foreign securities exchanges. The new dual-listed market thus enables Korean investors to invest in domestic securities, while benefiting from regulatory competition between different global securities exchanges. Moreover, the KSE may supplement the enforcement of foreign exchange listing provisions within Korea to increase the value to Korean investors of having a Korean firm select the protection provided in a foreign jurisdiction.

Ultimately, we care most about establishing a competitive environment that provides some degree of ongoing choice and competition in the forms of investor protection provided through the KSE. With the limited political capital remaining after the Asian economic crisis, directing current reform efforts toward the realistic goal of establishing a limited competitive regulatory system may generate more valuable future reforms. A competitive regulatory system, once established, will provide the impetus for the development of institutions and norms in support of a strong investor protection regime.

Controlling the Controlling Shareholders: Conduct, Structure, and Market*

Kon Sik Kim and Seung Wook Jeong

The Conflict of Interest between Controlling Shareholders and General Shareholders

In a modern capitalist society, as the separation of ownership and control is in progress, it is rising as an important task to resolve the conflict of interest between professional managers and shareholders. The problems and the costs of such conflicts of interest are termed "agency problems" and "agency costs". It is an essential task for the corporate law of any jurisdiction to solve agency problems between managers and the shareholders. The Korean Commercial Code ("KCC") sets out a number of provisions designed for preventing the abuse of power of the directors who are in charge of the management of corporations. However, unlike in the United States and United Kingdom, ownership and control in most corporations have not yet been completely separated. Accordingly, although the conflict of interest between the professional managers and shareholders is becoming a problem of growing importance, it is not yet seen as a serious problem. The more imperative task is to reduce the agency costs between controlling shareholders and general shareholders.

Where the ownership of shares is concentrated in the hands of the controlling shareholders and the general shareholders' shareholding is negligible, each party's interest would, in most cases, be consistent with the other party's interest. Accordingly, agency problems could be ignored. In the past, family members of the head of a corporation owned most of the shares of the corporation. Therefore, there was hardly any recognition of the issue of controlling the conduct of the controlling shareholders. However, as the scale of corporations became larger, accompanied by economic growth, shareholding of the family members of

* A slightly longer Korean version of this paper will appear as a chapter of a book to be published later this year. The authors wish to express their deep gratitude to Mr. Hee-Ju Kim for his assistance in preparing this English version.

the heads of corporations has been decreasing rapidly. Nevertheless, those controlling share-holders still firmly maintain the right to management of all the corporations belonging to their business groups, by relying on mutual share ownership among the affiliated corporations of the business groups. Unlike the professional managers who must retire some day, the controlling shareholders' children succeed to their parents' management control. Accordingly, the agency problems between the controlling shareholders and general share-holders are much more serious.

The head of the controlling family (hereinafter referred to as "the controlling shareholder") has been exercising management control, usually under the title of "chairman of the busi-ness group", with the help of organs such as a chairman's office or the planning and coor-dination office. The fact that the chairman within his group enjoys a status often compared to that of an emperor has long been the subject of public criticism. Imposing legal liability on the controlling shareholder, however, was not necessarily easy, even where he had ac-tively participated in the corporate decision-making process.[1] Under the pre-1998 KCC, which recognized only the representative director or the directors as the management organ of a corporation, it was generally believed to be difficult, if not impossible, to hold the chairman liable unless he also formally served as director.

The economic crisis of 1997 provided a momentum to remedy the flaws in the control of the controlling shareholder. As the conglomerates' excessive reliance on debt financing, gen-erous mutual guarantees (*sangho pojung*) for their affiliated corporations, and reckless launching of new, unrelated businesses were subject to public criticism, the consensus that called for imposing liability on the controlling shareholder ultimately responsible for all these wrongs has gained force. This is the background of the enactment of the new Article 401-2 in December 1998 amendment to the KCC. Article 401-2 authorizes the imposition of liability on any person who has participated in the conduct of business of a corporation, even wherethat person is not a director of the corporation.

Article 401-2 should be positively assessed as an attempt to meet the challenge of holding the controlling shareholder liable. It enables the corporation (its shareholders, more realisti-cally) to impose legal liability on those exercising the management control by catching those participants in the conduct of business,[2] who are often called "*de facto* directors".

---

1) For details, see Kon Sik Kim, "*Chaebol and the protection of Minor Shareholders*" in "*Chaebol in Korea: who owns them and how are they controlled?*", (POSCO Management Institute, 1995)(in Korean), 201 onwards.

2) The KCC does not use the terms, "participants in the conduct of business", but uses the terms "persons who give instructions to conduct business" in a title. Nevertheless, in this article, as a matter of con-venience, the terms, "participants in the conduct of business" will be used as an expression referring to

Nevertheless, the problems of conflict of interest between the controlling shareholders and general shareholders have been only partially addressed by Article 401-2. The purpose of this article is to examine the scope and limits of Article 401-2. To properly achieve this purpose, we need to conduct a comprehensive examination of the agency problems between the controlling shareholders and general shareholders.

First, we will analyze and construe Article 401-2 in the course of discussing the scope and limits of liability of the persons participating in the conduct of business. As complementary measures to the regulatory approach focusing on the "conduct" of the controlling shareholder, we will discuss the measures of reforming the corporate structure, and of enhancing the roles of the capital market.

Liability of the Participants in the Conduct of Business: Control of the Controlling Shareholder' Conduct

Legislative Intent of Article 401-2: Accordance of Powers and Responsibilities

One of the most basic principles of legal liability is to accord powers with responsibilities. It would be unjust to impose liability on a person who does not have the corresponding powers. Nevertheless, the accordance of powers and responsibilities had not been achieved under the KCC prior to its amendment in December 1998. This is because in many cases, the decision making of corporations had, in practice, been carried out in different ways from those anticipated by the KCC. The KCC assumes that important management decisions are to be made, in principle, by the board of directors. However, in practice, the board of directors of a corporation has simply rubber stamped what was already decided by the controlling shareholder at his discretion. Especially in *chaebol*, a large business conglomerate controlled by a family, the "intent" of its chairman, who is the controlling shareholder of the business group, is delivered directly or indirectly to the group's individual affiliated corporations. In the past, the chairman's office or the office of planning and coordination of the group served as an informal messenger for the chairman. The boards of directors of those affiliates would invariably follow the decisions made by the chairman, and did

the actors of the three types of conduct under Article 401-2 of KCC.

not dare challenge the chairman's decisions even where those decisions would not coincide with the interest of their corporations.

There are two ways of restraining the controlling shareholder from abusing his management control: one is to impose liability on the directors of the relevant affiliated corporation. It may seem unfair, however, to hold those directors liable without sanctioning the controlling shareholder who is ultimately responsible for the wrongful decision. Furthermore, this is not a desirable option considering its effectiveness, as the individual directors, who are basically employees receiving salaries from their corporation, do not have sufficient financial means to account for the losses suffered by their corporation or its shareholders. There are a number of ways for the chairman to help his loyal subordinates who have taken the blame for the chairman. Therefore, it would be far more effective as well as fair to impose liability on the controlling shareholder. Where the controlling shareholder only held a legally meaningless position of the chairman of the business group, and did not serve as a director of any of the group's affiliated corporations, it was not easy to impose liability on the controlling shareholder under the KCC prior to the 1998 amendment.[3] The pre-1998 KCC did not recognize the controlling shareholder as a corporate organ. Article 401-2, which has been adopted to deal with the liability of the participants in the conduct of business, can be seen as a provision to solve these problems.

Conduct or Position?

Article 401-2 has not adopted the concept of "controlling shareholder", nor has it adopted the concept of "*de facto* director". Instead of adopting these general concepts, Article 401-2 sets out the types of conduct which amount to participation in the conduct of business. There is no doubt, however, that Article 401-2 has been drafted with the controlling shareholder in mind. Why, then, did Article 401-2 not employ the term "controlling shareholder"? The drafters seem to have thought that the concept of "controlling shareholder" is too open-ended a concept. To reduce ambiguity, they focused not on the "position" held by the controlling shareholders but on their "conduct". Pursuant to Article 401-2, a person is liable, whether or not he or she is a controlling shareholder, if that person has engaged in the conduct of business of a corporation; and the controlling shareholder is not liable,

---

3) It is not unquestionable whether it was absolutely impossible to impose liability on the controlling shareholders under the KCC prior to the amendment. However, this issue will not be dealt with in this article.

if he has not in any way affected in the corporate decision-making.

Two Methods of Imposing Liability

Article 401-2 imposes the same liabilities as those imposed on directors on any person who has participated in the conduct of business. Article 401-2 is commonly interpreted as having adopted the concept of "*de facto* director". One may identify, however, two distinct methods of imposing director's liabilities: one is to impose director's duties and liabilities on a person, if that person has satisfied certain requirements ("Method 1"). A perfect example of the Method 1 would be "shadow directors" under the Company Act 1985 of the United Kingdom. Under section 741(2) of the Company Act, shadow directors are persons "in accordance with whose directions or instructions the directors of the company are accustomed to act". Once a person has been qualified as a shadow director, substantially the same duties and liabilities as those imposed on the directors will be imposed on that person. Accordingly, such person will not be liable simply because he or she is a shadow director, but because he or she has, as a shadow director, breached the director's duties. In other words, the conduct that is required for a person to be recognised as a shareholder is one thing, and the conduct that leads to the imposition of liability is another.

Another method of imposing director's liability on a person is to impose liability on the basis of that person's particular conduct ("Method 2"). This is the very method that has been adopted by Article 401-2: it imposes the director's liability on a person where that person directly or indirectly participates in the conduct of business of a corporation. Under Article 401-2, the conduct that is required for a person to be recognised as a participant in the conduct of business is the same as that which leads to the imposition of director's liability. In other words, a person assumes duties as a director by means of his participation in the conduct of business. Where that person's conduct of participating in the business management constitutes breach of the director's duties, he becomes liable as a director.[4]

---

4) From this point of view, it is difficult to agree with the opinion that because the participants in the conduct of business are not corporate organs, they cannot be liable for negligence in discharging their duties. Tae Ro Lee and Cheol Song Lee, *Hoesabop kangui*(*Lectures on Corporation Law*)(7th ed. 1999), 586-587.

Three Types of Conduct

The KCC

The KCC as amended in 1988 classifies participants in the conduct of business into the following three categories (Article 401-2(1)):

(1) any person who has given, by using his or her influence over a particular corporation, instructions to any director regarding the conduct of business of that corporation ("Category (i)");

(2) any person who has directly conducted the business of a particular corporation in a director's name ("Category (ii)"); and

(3) any person who is not a director, but has conducted the business of a particular corporation by using a title that could reasonably be considered as carrying the authority to conduct the business of that corporation, such as honorary chairman, chairman, president, vice president, executive director (*chonmu*), executive (or managing) director (*sangmu*), and director, etc. ("Category (iii)")

Category (i) deals with the situation where a person has been indirectly involved in the conduct of business. Categories (ii) and (iii) deal with the cases where a person has been directly involved in the conduct of business. Persons who fall within any of these categories, especially those within the scope of Category (iii), are not necessarily confined to the controlling shareholder. There is no doubt, however, that all of these three categories apply to the controlling shareholder. The three categories have been prepared to accommodate the various forms in which the controlling shareholder participates in the management of business. We will examine each of these three categories below.

Category (i)

Any person who has given, by using his or her influence over a particular corporation, instructions to any director regarding the conduct of the business of that corporation

A. Requirements under Category (i)

Category (i) deals with the cases where a controlling shareholder participates in the management of any affiliated corporation, by directly instructing the directors of that affiliated corporation, or indirectly through such organs as the chairman's office. Like the other categories, Category (i) does not require a participant in the conduct of business to be a controlling shareholder, but employs the concept of "influence". Accordingly, "influence" and "instructions" would be essential elements under Category (i).

B. Influence

The reason "influence" is adopted as a requirement under Category (i) is that a person's instructions to the directors of a particular affiliated corporation may not be respected unless that person has influence over the corporation. The most typical source of such influence would be shareholding. Accordingly, where a controlling shareholder instructs the directors of a particular affiliated corporation, the controlling shareholder will, as a participant in the management of that corporation, assume the same liability as that of a director. As the KCC fails to specify the sources of influence, the controlling shareholder will still fall within the scope of Category (i), even if his or her influence over the relevant affiliated corporation is based upon a source other than his or her shareholding. Creditors of a corporation such as banks, or business customers in a dominant position (for example, a car manufacturer that purchases parts from a parts supplier), may also have "influence" over the corporation.[5] Care must be taken, however, with respect to those creditors or business customers whose powers are based upon contracts. This is because those creditors or business customers cannot be prevented from exercising their contractual rights against the corporation. Accordingly, even where the corporation suffers losses from the exercise of their contractual rights, the corporation has no option but to accept. For example, where a bank demands that the corporation repay the loan, refusing to extend the term of the loan, and, as a result, the corporation is forced into bankruptcy, the creditor bank would not be held liable to the debtor corporation for its bankruptcy, at least under Article 401-2. However, if the creditor bank has exercised its influence over the corporation to dispose of

---

5) Tae Ro Lee and Cheol Song Lee, supra note 4, 584. Some scholars take a view that even the government officials exercise influence. Tae Ro Lee and Cheol Song Lee, supra note 4, 585. It is questionable, however, whether the government may be held liable as a participant in the conduct of business for its conduct carried out to implement a government policy, although it may be liable under the National Compensation Law.

any of its property to a third party under terms unfavorable to the corporation, the creditor bank may be held liable under Category (i).

C. Instructions

In order for Category (i) to apply, "instructions" of a person having influence over a particular corporation, such as a controlling shareholder, must be established. Accordingly, the controlling shareholder will not be held liable unless he or she has given instructions to any director of the corporation. Instructions do not have to be express, but can be implied by acquiescence. In most cases, however, it would be difficult to establish instructions. In practice, it would be rather unusual for the chairperson of an established business group to be pressed to give specific instructions. A manager who, unable to read the chairperson's inner thoughts, has to seek the chairperson's instructions for every single matter may be regarded as unqualified to serve as a director. It is quite natural that the chairperson would prefer a manager who makes delicate decisions on his own. Therefore, even when the corporation commits a blunder under pressure from the controlling shareholder it would not be easy to impose liability on the controlling shareholder by establishing his instructions. This is a limitation of Category (i).

D. Applicability to Controlling Corporations

Although Article 401-2 seems to have been drafted mainly with individuals in mind, it is not to be construed as applying only to natural persons.[6] It is not an easy question whether Category (i) is applicable to cases where the controlling shareholder is a juridical person (i.e. a controlling corporation). We believe that Category (i) is applicable to corporations as well as individuals. First of all, Category (i) does not expressly rule out juridical persons from the scope of its application. More important, given the widespread practice of parent-subsidiary relationships in business circles, we need to impose liability on parent corporations for their unreasonable instructions by means of Category (i). Recently, the Anti-monopoly and Fair Trade Act was changed to expand the scope of holding companies authorized under the Act (Art. 8). Thus, there is a greater need for encompassing corporations in Category (i).

In the context of parent and subsidiary corporations, a number of delicate problems may arise out of the application of Category (i): in what circumstances can a controlling corporation, not its directors, be considered as having given instructions?; (ii) to what extent can

---

6) Tae Ro Lee and Cheol Song Lee, supra note 4, at 585.

a holding corporation legitimately give instructions?; (iii) where the controlling corporation is held liable, will its representative director or controlling shareholder be also held liable? Answers to these questions may vary depending on one's perspective of the relationship between parent and subsidiary corporations. This topic will be reserved for a future discussion.

Category (ii)

> Any person who has directly or indirectly conducted the business of a corporation in director's name

Category (ii) deals with cases where a controlling shareholder conducts the business of a corporation by using the director's seal in his possession, instead of giving instructions to the directors of the corporation. Category (ii) only requires that a person has acted in director's name, and does not require any particular status or position of that person. Accordingly, at a glance, what is contemplated by Category (ii) would seem to be cases of ostensible agency.[7] It should be noted, however, that not everyone who conducts business in the director's name could achieve his objective. The corporation could probably deny the effect of any act of someone without valid authority. The reason such act could remain valid is that the corporation honors such act. Under what circumstances will the corporation honor the acts of someone without formal authority? Although this point is not expressly covered by Category (ii), the corporation would probably accept only those acts executed by a controlling shareholder, or at least someone in a special relationship with the controlling shareholder.

The reason Category (ii) requires the business of a corporation to be carried out "in director's name" is probably that it is impossible to distinguish the acts revertible to the corporation without such a requirement.

Category (iii)

> Any person who is not a director, but has conducted the business of a corporation by using a title that could reasonably be considered as carrying the authority to conduct the business of that corporation

---

7) Some scholars actually take this view. Tae Ro Lee and Cheol Song Lee, supra note 4, at 587.

Category (iii) imposes liability not only on a controlling shareholder who holds the title of "chairman" or "honorable chairman", but also on the head of the office of planning and coordination, for example, who acts in the interest of the controlling shareholder. While Category (ii) requires the use of "director's name", Category (iii) requires the "use of title". In this sense, some scholars call the persons within the scope of Category (iii) "apparent directors".[8] Unlike the concept of apparent representative directors under article 395 of the KCC, the requirement of "use of title" is not a provision for the protection of the third party's reliance on the title. This requirement is perhaps based upon the rationale that only the acts of a person with the title as described in Category (iii) can influence the relevant corporation. Accordingly, the terms "use of title" should not be narrowly interpreted, but should be given wide interpretation to include any act of a person who may, in practice, influence the corporation.

Category (iii) applies to every case in which any person who is not a director, including a controlling shareholder, has conducted the business of a corporation by using a title that may create a reasonable impression that the person has the authority to conduct the business of the corporation. Accordingly, executive directors, usually called "*chonmu*" or "*sangmu*", may be subject to the application of Category (iii).

In the past, in many *chaebols*, there were people directly accountable to the chairman. They usually carried titles such as chief secretary of the chairman's office or head of the planning and coordination office. Would Category (iii) apply to cases where any of these people has inflicted loss on a particular affiliate corporation by conducting the business of a corporation in pursuit of the chairman's private interest? If the requirement, "use of title", is to be given narrow interpretation, it would be difficult to apply Category (iii) to those cases. This is because the chief secretary of the chairman's office or the head of the planning and coordination office, a mere agent or employee of the chairman and not an officer of the affiliate corporation, does not normally have the "authority to conduct business". As previously discussed, however, if the terms, "use of title", are expansively interpreted, there would not be any problem with applying Category (iii) to a person who has actually conducted the corporation's business.

What constitutes an act of "conducting business"? It would be difficult to consider an act of merely delivering the chairman's instructions as an act of "conducting business". Recently, in most business groups, positions on a group level such as "chief secretary of the chairman's office" have been abolished and absorbed by the group's individual affiliated

---

8)   Tae Ro Lee and Cheol Song Lee, at 587.

corporations. Therefore, in the future, there will not be many cases where Category (iii) applies to persons who hold such positions.

Effect of Application

For the purposes of applying the liability provisions in Articles 399 and 401 of the KCC and the provisions dealing with derivative suits in Article 403 of the KCC, any person who falls within any of the three categories discussed above is regarded as a director. In other words, any participant in the conduct of business may, even if he or she is not a director, be held liable for the compensation of damages to third parties as well as the corporation. Minority shareholders may call such participant to account by way of a derivative suit. Where a director and the participant in the conduct of business are liable, they are jointly and severally liable. (Article 401-2(2))

Limits of Art. 401-2

Requirement of an "act"

In order to impose liability on a participant in the conduct of the business of a corporation, it needs to be established that the participant has done an "act" affecting the relevant corporation. Even a controlling shareholder cannot be held liable in the absence of an act on his part. Accordingly, the provisions in Article 401-2 do not have the function of promoting the active participation of controlling shareholders in the management of the business of their corporations, but they may be able to restrain abuses of power by the controlling shareholders.

Difficulties in Establishing the Requirements

In order to impose liability on a controlling shareholder under Article 401-2, the plaintiff must establish that the controlling shareholder gave instructions or conducted business. However, as previously pointed out, since an instruction under Category (i) is normally given in secret, it is difficult to expect the shareholders outside the corporation or the corporation's creditors to establish the requirements under Article 401-2. Furthermore, where a manager has voluntarily done an act in pursuit of the controlling shareholder's interest upon his or her own perception of the controlling shareholder's inner thoughts, there are no instructions from the controlling shareholder. Accordingly, it would be basically impossible to impose liability on the controlling shareholder. For this reason, it is argued that the provisions in Category (i) would have only a symbolic meaning and little deterrent effect.[9] Unlike Category (i), Categories (ii) and (iii) require the establishment of the person's "conduct of business". Therefore, it would be relatively easy to establish the requirements under Categories (ii) and (iii). Nevertheless, it is still questionable in how many cases the controlling shareholder directly conducts the business of affiliated corporations.

Reaction from Business Groups

In the past, the heads of *chaebol* hardly stood at the front line of management of the groups' affiliated corporations. Recently, however, they have been induced by the government to voluntarily appoint themselves the representative directors of the groups' affiliated corporations.[10] Accordingly, the necessity for imposing liability on the heads of *chaebol* has been reduced. Furthermore, it is well known in the economic circles that as a result of the amendment to the KCC, the controlling shareholder may now be held liable for their participation in the conduct of business. Accordingly, it is anticipated that the controlling shareholder will take a relatively cautious attitude towards participating in the conduct of business. As a result, it is more difficult to establish the controlling shareholder' instructions or conduct of business.

Limit of the Scope of the Application of Article 401-2

As previously discussed, the doctrine of "*de facto* director" has been much discussed as a supporting legal principle to hold the controlling shareholder liable. According to this doctrine, a person who has participated regularly in the conduct of business is regarded as a *de facto* director, and various types of duties and liabilities applicable to directors are imposed on that person. Article 401-2, instead of adopting the doctrine of practical director, goes no further than providing for the types of conduct that lead to the imposition of director's liability. Article 401-2 regards the participants in the conduct of business as directors only for the purposes of applying Articles 399 (liability to a corporation), 401 (liability to a third party) and 403 (derivative suit) of the KCC. Accordingly, Article 401-2 does not regard those participants as directors for the purposes of applying other provisions of the KCC. For example, dealings between a controlling shareholder and a corporation do not fall within the definition of "self-dealing by a director", unless the controlling shareholder is al-

---

9) Kiuon Tsche, "Reform of KCC for Recovering from the Current Economic Crisis (Part 2)" *Popryul shinmun*(Legal Times), 16 April 1998, at 14.
10) *Hankook Ilbo*, 6 March 1998, at 8.

so a director of the corporation. Therefore, there is no need to obtain approval for such dealings in advance from the board of directors.[11] Also, the provisions of Article 397 that prohibit a director from putting himself in a position where he competes with the corporation do not apply to controlling shareholders.[12]

Evaluation

Article 401-2 deserves to be appreciated as an attempt to fill the gap caused by the lack of regulations governing the conduct of the controlling shareholders. The defect originating from the discordance of the controlling shareholder's powers and liabilities has now been rectified to some extent. Nevertheless, as previously pointed out, Article 401-2 is still unsatisfactory in various aspects as a means of solving the agency problems between the controlling shareholder and general shareholders.

Structural Improvement

Solutions for Agency Problems

As previously discussed, Article 401-2 basically takes an approach whereby it controls the controlling shareholder's conduct of participating in the conduct of business. Although Article 401-2 has the effect of restraining the controlling shareholder's abuse of power, it has an inherent limitation as a means of addressing the agency problems. This is because the agency costs arising from the conflict of interest between the controlling shareholder and general shareholders cannot be satisfactorily resolved simply by restraining the controlling shareholder's irregular conduct. Such limitations exist even if the controlling shareholder is made subject to fiduciary duties. Accordingly, in order to effectively tackle the agency problems between the controlling shareholders and general shareholders, it is necessary to take a further step from merely controlling the control-

---

11) It will be possible, of course, to hold the controlling shareholder liable for damages by applying Category 1, if one can establish that the controlling shareholder has given instructions to the corporation.
12) In that case, it is also difficult to hold the controlling shareholders liable by using Article 401-2. This is because the controlling shareholders' competition with the corporation is, by nature, carried out without any instructions to their corporations.

ling shareholder's outward conduct *ex post facto*, and to seek for a more fundamental solution. One of the fundamental measures to solve the agency problems would be to improve the "structure" of corporations in order to ameliorate the conflict of interest between the controlling shareholders and general shareholders. We will briefly discuss below several proposals for such structural improvement.

Simplification of Ownership Structure

The phenomenon of conflict of interest between the controlling shareholders and general shareholders is more conspicuous in conglomerates than in individual corporations. Where there is a wide difference in the controlling shareholder's shareholding among the affiliated corporations of a conglomerate, it is natural for the controlling shareholder to maximize his personal interest by favoring one corporation over another. For example, a controlling shareholder is highly likely to shift wealth from one corporation where his shareholding is relatively small ("CorporationA") to another corporation where his shareholding is large ("Corporation B").[13] In that case, general shareholders of the Corporation A would suffer a loss. As the transfer of assets between affiliated corporations may take various forms, it is extremely difficult to prevent such transfers. If the ownership structure of a conglomerate is simplified and one holding company at the top is made to control several wholly owned subsidiaries, the conflict of interest would largely disappear. It would be unrealistic, however, to require all the conglomerates to transform into such a neat pyramid structure. Even so, it is still necessary to improve the present situation where even a controlling shareholder with an actual shareholding of less than 10 percent can exercise absolute control by maintaining the complicated ownership structure through the widespread use of inter-company shareholdings.

It would be best for the laws not to intervene in the ownership structure of corporations, and to leave it up to individual corporations. This is because there is no single ownership structure that fits every corporation. The United States has simplified the ownership structure of corporations by enacting the Public Utility Holding Corporation Act 1935, as the

---

13) Kon Sik Kim, supra note 1, at 205. For example, let us assume a situation where the controlling shareholder controls Corporation A and Corporation B by holding 10% of Corporation A's shares and 50% of Corporation B's shares. If Corporation A sells its real estate to Corporation B for 500 million Won, although the market value of the real estate is 1 billion Won, Corporation A will suffer a loss of 500 million Won, and Corporation B will make a profit of 500 million Won. If the share price of each Corporation exactly reflects the value of its assets, the controlling shareholder will ultimately make a profit of 200 million Won. (500 million X 0.5 − 500 million X 0.1 = 200 million)

complicated holding corporation structure in the electricity and gas industries had caused serious troubles. However, this was an extremely exceptional case. It would be worthwhile to consider methods of inducing rather than forcing corporations to simplify their ownership structures by making them pay for maintaining the complicated ownership structures. For example, if a corporation with a complicated ownership structure is discriminated against in its credit rating, the corporation will be under strong pressure to voluntarily simplify its structure.

Accordance of Incentives

Agency costs arise from the alienation of the controlling shareholder's interest from the general shareholders' interest. Accordingly, a more fundamental solution to this problem will be to accord the controlling shareholders' interest with that of the general shareholders to the maximum extent. It is obvious that as the controlling shareholder's shareholding increases, the conflict of interest between the controlling shareholder and other general shareholders decreases. This may not work for every corporation, however, because as the size of the corporation becomes larger, the shareholder's shareholding inevitably decreases. If the controlling shareholder can enjoy a greater profit as the corporation makes more profit, the controlling shareholder's incentive to pursue his private interest at the cost of other shareholders' interest would decrease. As a means of achieving this result, one could induce the managers who are large shareholders to make efforts to improve the outcome of management, by providing the managers with such incentives as stock options. Under the current Securities Transaction Law, there are restrictions on corporations which may issue stock options, on persons who may be provided with stock options, and on the limit up to which stock options can be provided (Art. 189-4).[14] The problem is that the largest shareholders, major shareholders, and even the persons in a special relationship with them, are excluded from the persons who may be provided with stock options (Art. 84-6(1), Enforcement Ordinance of the Securities Transaction Law). This exclusion seems to be intended to prevent the abuse of stock options by the controlling shareholders. Undoubtedly, stock options have been introduced with professional managers in mind. If the share of a controlling shareholder in charge of management is modest, say, five percent, the person will behave

---

14) In principle, stock options may only be provided to listed corporations and corporations registered with the Korea Securities Dealers Association. (Article 84-6(5) of the Enforcement Ordinance of the Securities Transaction Law), and may be given within the limit of 15% of the total number of shares.

more like a professional manager. In this respect, it seems unwise to exclude controlling shareholders from the persons who may be provided with stock options under the Securities Transaction Law.

Improving the Outside Director System

A controlling shareholder may seek his own interest at the cost of the corporation and the remaining shareholders only where the controlling shareholder is in complete control of the decision making process. If an independent person, apart from the controlling shareholder's subordinates and supporters, participates in the board of directors as an outside director, it would not be easy for the controlling shareholder to bluntly pursue his own interest. From this point of view, it is necessary to further improve the outside director system. A considerable part of the agency costs would be eliminated if outside directors who are really independent actively serve as monitors, examining transactions which carry conflict of interest risks.

Control Through the Capital Market

Agency problems arising from the presence of controlling shareholders will be far less serious if the controlling shareholder is subject to the pressures of the capital market. Accordingly, in order to reduce the agency costs, we also need to work for an environment in which the controlling shareholder's conduct can be adequately controlled through the capital market. The product market, management labor market, corporate control market, and capital market may restrain the controlling shareholder's conduct. It is widely agreed that controlling shareholders are relatively free from the pressure of such markets in Korea. Only the product market is serving as some restraint on them.[15]

The management labor market cannot function properly unless the persistent practice of recruiting high-level managers internally from among the employees changes dramatically. If the top management has something to hide, it is difficult for them to recruit outsiders. Thus, unless management transparency is established, the management labor market will not be developed. Even if the management labor market is developed, however, it is ques-

---

15) Corporations heavily dependent on exports have long been under pressure from competition in the international market. In the future, as the opening of market makes progress, other domestic corporations will also be subject to similar market pressures.

tionable whether professional managers will actively try to restrain the controlling share-holders' self-serving conduct.

The corporate control market is the market that has so far been receiving the most attention. Hostile takeovers, regarded as irrelevant to Korea in the past, are now becoming a more familiar phenomenon in the Korean business community. Especially since the coun-try's economy was under the control of the International Monetary Fund ("IMF"), objection to hostile takeovers seems to have been diluted to a considerable degree. There is no doubt that the corporate control market performs the function of reducing agency costs. However, one cannot say that replacement of the controlling shareholders and top management through takeovers is an ideal solution for agency problems. Hostile takeovers are only fea-sible where the controlling shareholder's shareholding is relatively low, and it will normally be carried out where there is a substantial difference between the potential value of the cor-poration and its market share price.

Now, it is the capital market that we should pay more attention to. The legal community in Korea has so far not paid serious attention to the relationship between agency problems and the capital market. However, in other countries where the capital market adequately performs its function, agency problems are less serious. A corporation whose controlling shareholder has a bad reputation or which has an abnormal ownership structure cannot be highly appreciated by investors. Accordingly, the share price of such corporations falls, and its credit rating is lowered. In the past, when it was easy for corporations in Korea to ob-tain loans from banks as long as the corporation had security or political connections, a fall in its share price or credit rating was not necessarily a serious problem. As the corpo-rations' reliance on the capital market has increased, however, they now have to be con-cerned about gaining investors' confidence. Otherwise, the financing costs will increase. Today, with the closing of the era of rapid economic growth, corporations can no longer afford heavy financing costs. Accordingly, most corporations are under pressure to restrain their unreasonable conduct and to improve their ownership structures. Examples showing the force of the capital market are numerous. In the United States, the practice of appoint-ing outside directors and audits by independent CPAs emerged not because of any specific law but because of voluntary decisions on the part of corporations themselves in order to instill investors' confidence. One reason why controlling the conduct of the controlling shareholders does not attract much attention in the United States is not only that the legal mechanisms for such conduct have been in good order, but also that the seriousness of the problem has been diminished through a well-developed capital market.

Conclusion

The Korean economy has so far been heavily dominated by two kinds of concentration: the concentration of economic power in the hands of a small number of conglomerates and the concentration of stock ownership in the hands of a small number of controlling shareholders. The size of shareholdings that these controlling shareholders directly maintain is not substantial, less than ten percent in many cases. Nevertheless, by means of wide-spread inter-company share ownership, they continue to exercise unrestrained power. It is widely believed that Korea's economic crisis is partly, if not primarily, due to controlling shareholders'irrational business decisions to over-expand their business empires, relying on short-term debt financing. Some people go on to criticize the concentration of deci-sion-making power in the hands of controlling shareholders. It may not be justified, how-ever, to attack *chaebol* for the undemocratic nature of their decision-making process. Democracy values procedure more than result. In business, however, what counts is result rather than procedure. Most investors may be willing to put up with dictatorial manage-ment as long as they achieve a good outcome. The problem arises when the dictatorial chairman keeps exercising unchallenged control despite serious mistakes. A corporation which is not managed properly will eventually be flagging. It is not desirable to let improp-er management continue until it finally leads to the collapse of the corporation. Accordingly, it is necessary to provide a remedy to correct mismanagement at an early stage. Article 401-2 could be positively evaluated as a device to impose liability on the controlling shareholders for their participation in management. It should be noted, however, that Article 401-2 has inherent limits in terms of its ability to solve the agency problems of the controlling shareholders. Controlling shareholders'abuse of power in pursuit of their person-al interests is merely a part of the agency problems. As previously discussed, it is not an easy task to restrain the controlling shareholders from seeking their personal interests at the expense of minority shareholders. The more difficult task, however, is to induce them to devote their best efforts for shareholder value. For this to be achieved, it is necessary to make efforts to improve the corporate structure, and to consider methods of providing the large shareholders in charge of management with such incentives as stock options. Furthermore, efforts should be made to provide an environment in which the markets, es-pecially the capital market, are able to adequately perform their functions. This is because a substantial part of the agency problems between the controlling shareholders and general shareholders would be solved if the capital market performs its function adequately.

Related Party Transactions in East Asia

KON SIK KIM

Acknowledgments: This chapter was funded by the 2019 Research Fund of the Seoul National University Asia-Pacific Law Institute, donated by the Seoul National University Law Foundation. I express my deep gratitude to those participants in the two authors' workshops held in Oxford and Frankfurt, Luca Enriques and Peter Muelbert in particular, and Tomotaka Fujita and Xing-Xing Li for giving me useful information on Related Party Transactions (RPTs) in Japan and China, respectively. This chapter was completed during the period when I was visiting NUS as Visiting Research Professor in 2018. I want to thank Tan Cheng Han and Dan Puchniak for their generous support.

I Introduction

RPTs exist in most countries, including developing countries as well as those already developed. RPTs may take place on an ad hoc basis, or routinely. Routine RPTs are commonly found in a corporate group structure and pose tougher regulatory challenges than ad hoc RPTs do. The degree of prevalence of RPTs and the shape of their regulation vary country by country, reflecting differences in their corporate governance environment. Stated reversely, a glimpse into the actual regulation of RPTs may shed light on essential features of the corporate governance ecosystem of a particular jurisdiction.

The purpose of this chapter is to examine, from a comparative perspective, the status of RPTs and their regulation in three East Asian countries, namely Japan, South Korea (henceforth to be referred as Korea), and China. Why do we focus on these three countries? Firstly, they are the three largest economies in East Asia, together accounting for more than 20 percent of the world's GDP. They are closely intertwined with each other, historically, culturally, and economically. They have all inherited a Confucian legacy, although to somewhat different degrees. Their legal systems, in general, all belong to the so-called civil law family. More significantly from the perspective of corporate governance, they each experienced a period of government-led economic growth in the twentieth century. Despite these commonalities, however, the realities of corporate governance vary substantially between them. Corporate governance is stakeholder (employee)-oriented in Japan, (controlling) shareholder-centered in Korea, and state-led in China. This variation does not seem to be attributable to disparate levels of economic development. Also, although the overall corporate governance landscape is changing, each jurisdiction is evolving differently. This chapter focuses on RPTs – primarily on routine RPTs involving large listed firms – which will serve as a convenient window through which to view the complex world of corporate governance in the three aforementioned countries.

This chapter proceeds as follows. Part II sets out the theoretical framework which serves as a basis for the ensuing discussion. It addresses basic perspectives and conventional strategies employed to deal with RPTs. Part III entails a brief survey of the current status of RPTs and the regulatory structure in each jurisdiction. It first presents basic RPT-related data, and goes on to outline substantive constraints, procedural constraints. and disclosure requirements applicable to RPTs. Based on this survey, Part IV attempts to make some general observations from

a comparative perspective. Part V offers a conclusion.

II Theoretical Framework

A Model Related Party Transactions

Figure 11.1 shows a simplified example of RPTs between Firm A and Firm B, both belonging to Corporate Group X. Firm A and Firm B both are under the control of O, its controlling shareholder, who may be a natural person or a corporation. Let us suppose that O's ownership stake in Firm B is larger than in Firm A. In reality, O may engage in transactions with Firm A or Firm B. Such transactions can also be classified as RPTs, which may be called "vertical" RPTs as opposed to "horizontal" RPTs between Firm A and Firm B. As explained later, vertical RPTs outnumber horizontal RPTs in Japan and China and are quite common in Korea as well.

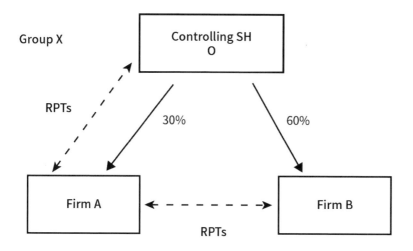

Figure 11.1 A simplified example of Related Party Transactions in a business group

B Related Party Transactions and Industrial Organization

Routine RPTs normally take place in a group context. Group structure is a form of industrial organization. Routine RPTs, therefore, are closely related to the industrial organization of each jurisdiction. The existing regulation on RPTs may well shape the pattern of industrial organization in the future. Conversely, the current state of industrial organization might affect the form and the intensity of regulation, both in the books and in reality. From the perspective of industrial organization, a primary function of RPTs is to replace market transactions. According to Ronald Coase, firm boundaries are determined in consideration of transaction costs.[1] Based on their assessment of transaction costs, managers decide either to produce goods and services internally ("self-supply") or to procure them from the markets ("outsourcing").

Figure 11.2 illustrates the principal types of organizing economic activity in each business firm. Type 1 refers to vertical integration into a stand-alone firm, which produces all the necessary parts and components for its end products in-house. In a modern developed economy, however, firms that stick with such a pure form of self-supply are few in number, among large listed firms at least.[2]

---

1) Ronald H. Coase, *The nature of the firm*, 4 ECONOMETRICA N.S. 386–404 (1937).
2) The larger the firm becomes, the larger the internal costs, i.e., a complicated decisionmaking process,

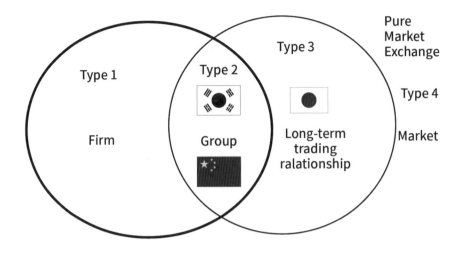

Figure 11.2 Types of organizing economic activity

What stands in sharp contrast with Type 1 is Type 4, which represents pure outsourcing. Outsourcing has its own merits and demerits. A primary advantage of outsourcing comes from the division of labor. If outsourcing is widely practiced, a number of specialized intermediate input suppliers will emerge, generating increased efficiency. Outsourcing, however, is often difficult to realize, mainly for two reasons. The first is the underdevelopment of markets.[3] This is often a serious problem in developing countries. The second obstacle for outsourcing is high market transaction costs. A car manufacturer, for example, is vulnerable to the strategic behavior of its parts suppliers, and vice versa.[4]

Types 2 and 3 may be perceived as two hybrid options available to a business firm when neither self-supply nor outsourcing is feasible. Of more relevance for our purposes is Type 2, which involves a vertically integrated group structure combined with routine intragroup RPTs.[5] Type 2 may be viewed as a means to achieve self-supply as intragroup RPTs can minimize transaction costs and the risk of opportunism.[6] Formally, they may not be quali-

---

information dissemination costs, etc.

3) Motoshige Ito, *Interfirm Relations and Long-Term Continuous Trading*, in BUSINESS ENTERPRISES IN JAPAN (Kenichi Imai & Ryutaro Komiya, eds., 1994), 113.

4) For a succinct discussion of this problem, see, e.g., Benjamin Klein, *Vertical Integration as Organizational Ownership: The Fisher Body-General Motors Relationship Revisited*, THE NATURE OF THE FIRM (Oliver E. Williamson & Sidney G. Winter, eds., 1993), 213–26.

5) Intragroup RPTs can be found in a business group composed of firms in unrelated industries. For example, a firm in financially distress may depend on its cash-rich affiliates for financing. Such RPTs normally take place on an ad hoc basis.

6) For a discussion on benefits of RPTs, see Sang Yop Kang, *Rethinking Self-Dealing and the Fairness Standard: A Law and Economics Framework for Internal Transactions in Corporate Groups*, 11

fied as pure self-supply since Firm A and Firm B are legally separate from each other with a distinct group of shareholders. From a functional perspective, however, intragroup RPTs are different from pure outsourcing as both Firm A and Firm B belong to the same corporate group (X) and are both subject to O's control.[7]

Vertically integrated groups are common in an emerging market economy with under-developed markets. All three countries under review started developing their economies based, at least partly, on the vertically integrated group structure. Japan started parting with this structure when business conglomerates (called *zaibatsu*) were disbanded during the Allied occupation of Japan after World War II. As discussed later, however, Korean and Chinese firms still rely on vertical integration to a larger extent and, as a consequence, engage more heavily in intragroup RPTs, although both of them, China in particular, are now increasingly dependent on outsourcing to other market participants.

Type 3 illustrates a long-term trading relationship with unaffiliated firms, another alternative way of organizing business activity.[8] Type 3 differs from Type 4 in that a car manufacturer, for example, can minimize opportunistic behavior on the part of its parts suppliers while securing a smooth collaboration with them. Type 3 arrangements are common in advanced economies manufacturing complicated products.[9] In this regard, Japan is a prime example. Type 3 arrangements are found in Korean *chaebols* as well. *Chaebol* firms maintain a long-term trading relationship with external firms, often called "cooperative firms".[10]

C Rationale for Regulating Related Party Transactions

As mentioned earlier, intragroup routine RPTs may bring greater benefits in developing countries. RPTs, even those conducted routinely among member firms, may entail substantial costs, however. The most serious problem with RPTs is the risk of so-called "tunneling".[11] Depending on how price terms are determined, wealth may be transferred

---

VIRGINIA LAW & BUSINESS REVIEW 95, 107–09 (2016).

7) If Firm A's decision-making is undertaken to pursue its own interest, not the interest of Group X or its controlling shareholder O, it will become closer to outsourcing. If the reverse is true, it will approach self-supply.

8) On the long-term trading relationship, *see, e.g.,* Ito, *supra* note 3, at 105–15.

9) For a paper pointing out the existence of, and issues involved in, yet another alternative way of organizing economic activity, *see* Ronald Gilson et al., *Contracting for Innovation: Vertical Disintegration and Interfirm Collaboration,* 109 COLUMBIA LAW REVIEW 431 (2009) (suggesting "that the change in the boundary of the firm has given rise to a new form of contracting between firms – what we call contracting for innovation.").

10) Unlike in Japan, the long-term relationship between Korean firms does not normally involve equity investments.

from Firm A to Firm B. Wealth transfers can be divided into two groups in theory. The first is the type of wealth transfer which may be potentially in the long-term interest of Firm A. A prime example of such type of wealth transfer is one undertaken to prop up an ailing affiliate (propping). The second type of wealth transfer is undertaken primarily to serve O's personal interest at the expense of Firm A. It is sometimes difficult to distinguish between the two types of wealth transfer as an RPT may have a dual motive. The second type of unjustified wealth transfer is widely and better known as tunneling.

Minimizing tunneling is commonly presented as the rationale behind regulating RPTs. RPTs, and intragroup routine RPTs in particular, have a deleterious side effect. As an area of the economy dominated by RPTs expands, market opportunities for stand-alone firms are bound to shrink. This very issue is now attracting much attention from the general public in Korea. As discussed later, part of Korea's RPT regulation purports to address this concern. The goal of RPT regulations in most jurisdictions, however, is to minimize the risk of tunneling without undermining the potential benefits of RPTs.

D Overview of Regulatory Framework

1 Laws Applicable to Related Party Transactions

RPTs attract attention from many different areas of law. These include corporate law, capital market law, criminal law, tax law and, in the case of Korea, fair trade law. An egregious incident of tunneling may lead to a criminal sanction in many jurisdictions. In Korea, for example, it is not unusual for the head of a business group to be indicted on a charge of breach of trust, a charge normally invoked for tunneling. Such instances are not confined to Korea and similar cases have been found in European countries including France and Italy as well.[12] This chapter, however, primarily focuses on corporate and capital market law.

---

11) For a seminal work on tunneling, see Simon Johnson et. al., *Tunneling*, 90 AMERICAN ECONOMIC REVIEW 22 (2000). Tunneling can be divided into three types, namely cashflow tunneling, asset tunneling and equity tunneling. Vladimir Atanasov et al., *Law and Tunneling*, 37 JOURNAL OF CORPORATION LAW 1 (2011). This chapter focuses on asset tunneling.

12) Simeon Djankov et al., *The Law and Economics of Self-Dealing*, 88 JOURNAL OF FINANCIAL ECONOMICS 430, 437 (2008) ("most countries impose severe criminal sanctions when the transaction has been approved in violation of the law"). This so-called "criminalization of corporate law" is observed in the United States as well. See Lisa M. Fairfax, *The Criminalization of Corporate Law*, 2 JOURNAL OF BUSINESS & TECHNOLOGY LAW 1 (2007) and articles included in the same Issue.

2 Regulatory Options

A variety of regulatory approaches are being employed to deal with RPTs, with four types attracting most attention from policy makers. Listing them in order of restrictiveness, these are: outright prohibition; substantive constraints; procedural constraints; and disclosure requirements.[13]

The most radical measure against tunneling is to prohibit RPTs altogether and, as a consequence, to have Firm B rely on either pure self-supply or outsourcing. No major industrial jurisdiction, however, is known to adopt such a drastic solution because RPTs, as mentioned earlier, may bring substantial benefits depending on the circumstances. A notable exception is prohibiting credit extension to certain related parties. Corporate statutes in Korea and China have such provisions (Korean Commercial Code Art. 542–9(1), Chinese Company Act Art. 115, respectively). This chapter mainly addresses the other three types of regulation.

The term "substantive constraints" is intended to refer to regulatory measures purporting to secure the fairness of an RPT. When controlling tunneling, what matters most is the fairness of the contract terms. If substantive constraints such as fiduciary duties work properly, we may not need other regulatory measures such as board approval or disclosure. But substantive constraints too often fail, for reasons discussed later. So, policy makers impose procedural constraints in addition to substantive constraints. Procedures, however, often fall short of guaranteeing the fairness of the transaction. Another regulatory option gaining popularity recently is to require the disclosure of relevant information on RPTs. Although these three approaches are conceptually distinct from each other, there are some overlaps. For example, some jurisdictions require firms to seek and disclose an opinion of an outside expert on the fairness of an RPT, which involves all three elements. Many advanced jurisdictions, in one way or another, rely on all three different approaches in controlling the tunneling risk arising from RPTs.

3 Substantive Constraints: Fairness and the Arm's Length Test

a Fairness in Process and Substance   Decision makers of a firm involved in an RPT owe an equivalent of fiduciary duties under corporate statutes. They can discharge their fiduciary

---

13) Luca Enriques, *Related Party Transactions: Policy Options and Real-World Challenges(With a Critique of the European Commission Proposal)*, 16 EUROPEAN BUSINESS ORGANIZATION LAW REVIEW 1, 13 –25 (2015).

duties by satisfying the fairness standard. Fairness is required not only for the substance of the transaction but also for the process. This point is most conspicuously embodied in the entire fairness standard adopted by state courts of Delaware. The ultimate reason for requiring procedural fairness, however, is to ensure fairness in substance. This point has been emphasized by the Delaware Court of Chancery in the famous *Trados* decision.[14] The court held that the entire fairness standard was met as long as the price was fair even if the directors were not disinterested and the process was unfair. Thus, the critical question is of substantive fairness, which seems pertinent to RPTs because it is a crucial concept in terms of restraining tunneling arising from RPTs.

b Limitations of the Arm's Length Test The concept of substantive fairness is bound to remain abstract. What is most widely accepted as supporting fairness appears to be the arm's length test. The arm's length test is straightforward and easy to understand. It does have limitations, however. The first limitation relates to market price, which is almost universally accepted as satisfying the arm's length test. In many intragroup RPTs, however, the relevant market price is often not available.[15] Services and parts involved often have idiosyncratic features. Consequently, judges exercise much discretion in determining the hypothetical market price. Moreover, under the arm's length test, the end result of the judge's exercise of discretion will likely point to a "range" of price (e.g., US$ 40 to 42), rather than a definite price (US$ 41).[16] Thus, the controlling shareholder O can still extract substantial profits through RPTs without deviating from the fairness range.[17]

The second limitation relates to its insufficient attention to the "need" for the transaction involved. Suppose Firm A purchases real estate from Firm B in an effort to rescue Firm B from financial distress. Can we say that the RPT is fair as long as the price remains in the fairness range? If we understand the arm's length test narrowly, we may well conclude that Firm A does not suffer any loss as long as the price does not deviate substantially from the range of fair market price. Can we still say that the RPT is fair even if Firm A does not really need the real estate for its business or if the RPT has the effect of reducing Firm A's investment in more promising business projects?

The third, and more fundamental, defect of the arm's length test is that it may lead to in-

---

14) *In re Trados Incorporated Shareholder Litigation*, 73 A.3d 17 (Del. Ch. 2013).
15) Kang, *supra* note 6, at 134.
16) Id., at 133–34.
17) It seems partly due to this regulatory black hole that the practice of so-called "funneling of business" to members of the controlling family persists in Korea despite statutory restrictions on RPTs.

efficient results if narrowly construed. The arm's length test may be construed as not taking into account the potential benefits of maintaining a long-term relationship between the trading affiliates. If Firm A and Firm B keep engaging in a range of RPTs, it may make less sense to examine RPTs on an individual transaction basis.[18] In jurisdictions populated by business groups, there is a strong demand from the business community for the deployment of an all-encompassing, rather than individual, perspective.

c Efficacy of Shareholder Lawsuits   It is widely acknowledged that the role of shareholder lawsuits is crucial in enforcing substantive constraints such as the fairness requirement. If access to shareholder lawsuits is somehow limited or the plaintiff shareholder is not given an effective means to secure evidence, substantive constraints will remain no more than "a cake in the picture."

4 Procedural Constraints

a. Board Approval   It is now standard practice to impose on a firm engaging in an RPT a procedural constraint such as approval by a corporate organ. The most common corporate organ authorized to approve RPTs is the board of directors. In some jurisdictions, the general meeting of shareholders (GMS) is empowered to exercise such power for material RPTs, alone or in addition to the board of directors. As a regulatory option, board approval has its own advantages and disadvantages. The most obvious advantage is that it is less cumbersome to have a board meeting than a GMS. Moreover, directors are supposed to be better informed and better qualified than the average shareholder. On the other hand, directors may be lacking in terms of motivation and independence which are essential to properly perform their screening function. The degree of independence required by law (as well as actual independence) differs from country to country.[19] In an effort to enhance independence, the board may delegate its power to a special committee composed solely of disinterested directors. It is now increasingly popular for the board or the special committee to obtain an opinion from a thirdparty expert on the fairness of the RPT involved.[20]

---

18) Kang, *supra* note 6, at 135–36.
19) Dan W. Puchniak & Kon Sik Kim, *Varieties of Independent Directors in Asia: Divergent Convergence*, in INDEPENDENT DIRECTORS IN ASIA: A HISTORICAL, CONTEXTUAL AND COMPARATIVE APPROACH, (Dan W. Puchniak, et al., eds., 2017) 89, 102–10(discussing different requirements for independence in various Asian jurisdictions).
20) Although formally having no binding force in most cases, the third-party opinion has some deterrent effect as it is to be disclosed by the firms to the general public.

b GMS Approval   The greatest merit of GMS approval may be that the shareholders, who are the ultimate stakeholders, participate in decision-making. There are some concerns about GMS approval, however. Shareholders often have neither the necessary expertise nor incentive. This problem may be somewhat mitigated with the increase of holdings of institutional investors. Another concern is the cost of holding a GMS, which may be non-negligible in a large listed firm. In the case of a material RPT, the potential benefit may outweigh the cost. The cost may be further reduced if we allow the GMS to give comprehensive approval for a group of routine intragroup RPTs.

c Effect of Approval   A more delicate, and often ignored, issue is the effect of the existence or absence of required approval. This varies depending on the jurisdiction. In Delaware, for example, the RPT remains valid if its fairness can be demonstrated (Delaware Code Title 8 §144(a)(3)). In Japan and Korea, however, the absence of approval renders the RPT involved null and void.[21]

The existence of approval does not necessarily immunize managers involved in RPTs. In Delaware, for example, the plaintiff can still, in principle, challenge the fairness of the approved RPT, although the burden of proof is shifted to the plaintiff if the RPT is approved by disinterested directors (or shareholders).[22] Thus, in Delaware, approval constitutes a part of the fairness inquiry and approval by disinterested decision-makers is difficult, if not impossible, to override in practice.[23] In contrast, the courts in the United Kingdom place more weight on such approval, and do not delve into the fairness of the transaction as long as there is approval.[24]

A principal virtue of the approval requirement is helping the court to avoid, or minimize, the burden of fairness inquiry. Moreover, the approval requirement allows Firm A to block an RPT which is fair in terms of the price, but irrelevant for its core business.

---

21) KENJIRO EGASHIRA, LAWS OF STOCK CORPORATIONS (7th ed. 2017) 448 (in Japanese); KON SIK KIM, ET AL. , CORPORATE LAW (3d ed. 2018) 424 (in Korean).

22) *See, e.g., Kahn v. Lynch Communication Sys., Inc.*, 638 A.2d 1110, 1117 (Del. 1994). In a recent decision, the Delaware Supreme Court held that the business judgment rule, rather than an entire fairness review, can be applied when both an independent special committee is involved and a majority of the minority shareholders approves the transaction involved. *Kahn v. M&F Worldwide Corp.*, 88 A.3d 635, 642–44 (Del. 2014).

23) *Weinberger v. UOP, Inc.*, 457 A.2d 701, 709 n7 (Del. 1983): "[F]airness in this context can be equated to conduct by a theoretical, wholly independent, board of directors acting upon the matter before them."

24) Luca Enriques, et al., *Related-Party Transactions*, in THE ANATOMY OF CORPORATE LAW (Reinier Kraakman, et al., eds., 3d ed. 2017), 161 note 114.

5 Disclosure Requirements

Recently, disclosure has been gaining more popularity as a regulatory measure against RPTs. Disclosure of RPT-related information can be made on two different fronts: disclosure of information to the firm's decision-making organs such as the board or the GMS (internal disclosure); and disclosure to investors outside the firm (external disclosure). External disclosure is found in corporate disclosure materials such as annual statements filed with the regulators or reports to stock exchanges.[25] Accounting principles also impose disclose requirements on RPTs.

Disclosure has distinct merits as a regulatory measure. It is the least intrusive in the sense that it does not directly impede RPTs in advance. Although firms must bear some cost to produce relevant information, this is affordable in most cases. If disclosure is exempted for smaller transactions, the cost can be further reduced. Ease of enforcement is another advantage. An absence of disclosure, or inadequate disclosure, may be relatively easy to identify and sanction.

Disclosure may not necessarily bring desired results, however. If directors are not truly independent, they may not be eager to delve into the information disclosed to them. If market participants such as institutional investors, analysts and business media are not aggressive enough, disclosure may fall short of generating the desired market pressure.

E Players in Enforcement

The violation of RPT rules mentioned earlier may in principle entail a variety of sanctions such as invalidation of the transaction, damages, tax, criminal punishment, and civil penalty. Such sanctions can be invoked only when enforcement mechanisms function adequately. Depending on the capacity and incentives of players involved in the enforcement, the regulation in action may vary widely. Principal players include courts, regulatory agencies, prosecutors, and stock exchanges.

1 Courts

RPT regulation is ultimately enforced in courts. The quality and mindset of judges is thus crucial.[26] In order to deal properly with such an abstract notion as fairness, judges need

---

25) Internal disclosure may be classified as ex-ante control, while external disclosure, together with substantive constraints, as ex-post control.

to be afforded substantial discretion as is the case in the Delaware Court of Chancery. Granting discretion can achieve desired results when the judges are equipped with competence, independence and inventiveness, which cannot necessarily be taken for granted in every jurisdiction.

2 Prosecutors

In jurisdictions where shareholder remedies are not well developed, criminal prosecution often serves as an alternative. As mentioned earlier, prosecutors play a role in restraining abusive RPTs in Korea and such a phenomenon is not confined to Korea. The criminalization of corporate misbehavior, however, is not advisable for the following reasons. First, criminal prosecution can restrain only the most egregious type of tunneling. Second, prosecutors have limited resources and often lack business expertise. Third, prosecutors may be more susceptible to political pressure, and thus often reach decisions politically palatable to those in power.

3 Regulators

Regulators may serve as an alternative to prosecutors. Indeed, capital market regulators often play a leading role. In this regard, the China Securities Regulatory Commission (CSRC) is a prime example. Regulators may prove superior to prosecutors for the following reasons. First, they tend to be technically better qualified to deal with RPTs. Second, they can move proactively and develop and implement a set of sophisticated rules. Third, as their mandate is more limited than prosecutors, they have a greater incentive to actively tackle RPTs. Regulators may have some shortcomings though. First, they may be even more vulnerable than prosecutors to political pressure. Second, they may be susceptible to lobbying efforts of the business community.

The pros and cons of mobilizing regulators may differ depending on the country. The extent to which a country relies on regulators in dealing with RPTs can be determined by the various conditions of the particular country. For instance, a country with a low incidence of shareholder lawsuits may need to rely more on regulators.

---

26) For a recent paper highlighting the importance of judges in regulating RPTs, *see* Ronald Gilson, *A Model Company Act and a Model Company Court*, http://ssrn.com/abstract=2750256 (accessed March 26, 2018).

4 Market Institutions

In addition to official players discussed above, market institutions can also play a role in restraining RPTs. Stock exchanges, institutional investors, investment banks, analysts,[27] accounting firms, business media,[28] and proxy advisors can all play a role to some degree. As the concept of fairness is open-ended, formal regulation alone may not be enough to bring desired results. These market institutions may be more effective in reducing unfair RPTs as they can put pressure directly on the managers involved. In a country with a sophisticated market infrastructure, formal enforcement players may perform a less conspicuous role.[29]

III Related Party Transactions and Their Regulations

A Ownership Structure and Industrial Organization: two Factors Affecting the Incidence of Related Party Transactions

The incidence of RPTs depends on a range of factors, two of which are worthy of attention: ownership structure and industrial organization. For the former, controlling shareholders may have more incentive to engage in RPTs than professional managers primarily because they are better insulated from threats from both inside and outside the firm. If the controlling shareholder, as is often the case, chooses to form a business group, the need for intragroup RPTs grows.

The incidence of RPTs is also closely related to industrial organization. As mentioned earlier, if markets are so well-developed that firms can easily procure intermediate goods and services on the market, the firms may have less reason to engage in intragroup RPTs. It is not easy, however, to collect data on these factors and the incidence of RPTs in the three jurisdictions. Before we embark on reviewing the regulation of RPTs, let us take a look at these points in each country.

---

27) Yan-Leung Cheung, et al., *Buy high, sell low: How listed firms price asset transfers*, 33 JOURNAL OF BANKING & FINANCE 914, 922 (2009) ("Only firms with an audit committee on their board and firms with a large analyst following conclude related party transactions at more favorable prices.").

28) For a discussion on the role of media, see Alexander Dyck, et al., *The Corporate Governance Role of the Media: Evidence From Russia*, 63 JOURNAL OF FINANCE 1093, 1097 (2008).

29) Vladimir Atanasov, et al., *Law and Tunneling*, 37 JOURNAL OF CORPORATION LAW 1, 24 (2011) (emphasizing the role of market infrastructure in restraining tunneling in the United States).

1 Japan

a Ownership Structure: Stable Shareholders and Employee-Managers   Japan is one of the few countries in the world with a dispersed share ownership structure. As is the case in the United States and the United Kingdom, there is no controlling shareholder in most of its large listed firms. In the absence of controlling shareholders, such firms are typically run by professional managers. These managers are predominantly selected from white collar employees who have spent their whole business careers with the firm. For example, in 1997 Toyota's board was composed of fifty-six directors who were all "inside" directors.[30] These managers can be called "employee-managers".

Rarely holding a sizable number of shares, these employee-managers can secure their "management independence" with the help of so-called "stable shareholders" – i.e., shareholders who hold shares primarily to maintain a trade relationship with the company. The company often serves as a stable shareholder for its own stable shareholders. According to the conventional view, this mutual shareholding structure (*kabushiki mochiai*) has been a hallmark of Japanese corporate governance and a bulwark against pressures from the capital market.[31]

This situation started to change after the bubble burst in the early 1990s. The subsequent changes in shareholder profile started with banks. In an effort to meet regulatory capital requirements, they started selling shares of borrower firms, abandoning the role as stable shareholders. Instead, the holdings of foreign investors soared, particularly in larger listed firms. As of 2016, foreign investors as a group hold 30 percent or more in 42.8 percent of the firms composing the JPX-NIKKEI Index 400.[32] In most of these firms, however, the control of employee-managers seems to have remained despite the changes in ownership structure. Most of these employee-managers lack the incentive or sufficient power to engage

---

30) Takuji Saito, *Determinative Factors in Introducing Outside Directors in Japanese Firms and its Effect*, in CORPORATE GOVERNANCE IN JAPAN (Hideaki Miyajima, ed., 2011), 181, 184 (in Japanese). Except for one former bureaucrat from the Ministry of Trade and Industry, all of them joined the firm straight out of college.

31) This kind of mutual shareholding structure is supposed to help cement a stable long-term trading relationship. Recent studies by Japanese scholars find that Japanese firms are now much less interested in holding shares of their trading partners. *See, e.g.*, Zenichi Shishido, *Reality and transformation of "Japanese trade practices"*, Shojihomu No. 2142 (August 25, 2017): 4, 10 (in Japanese). For a paper which disputed the conventional view, *see* Yoshiro Miwa & J. Mark Ramseyer, *Rethinking Relationship-Specific Investments: Subcontracting in the Japanese Automobile Industry*, 98 MICHIGAN LAW REVIEW 2636, 2655 (2000).

32) Tokyo Stock Exchange, White Paper on Corporate Governance of Firms Listed on Tokyo Stock Exchange (2017) at 5 (in Japanese).

in RPTs.

Although share ownership is dispersed in most listed firms, there are controlling share-holders in some firms. As of 2016, 17.9 percent of the firms listed in the Tokyo Stock Exchange had controlling shareholders, the majority of whom were listed firms themselves.[33] The pyramidal ownership structure commonly found in Korean groups is relatively rare in the Japanese economy.[34]

b Industrial Organization: Long-Term Relationships with Suppliers   As mentioned earlier, Japanese firms tend to trade with outside suppliers, rather than engage in intragroup RPTs. To secure stable supply and cooperative behavior, they maintain long-term trading relation-ships with these suppliers.[35] Such business arrangements generate little risk of tunneling, as the firms are trading with outsiders.[36]

c. Incidence of Related Party Transactions   It is difficult to find reliable data on the fre-quency of RPTs in Japan. Professor Takahito Kato of the University of Tokyo argues that the risk of tunneling arising from RPTs may be negligible.[37] He cites an empirical study showing that a subsidiary does not necessarily suffer loss when both the parent and the subsidiary are listed.[38] He further states that as a matter of theory, the management of a listed parent will have less incentive to exploit its subsidiary as they may not achieve any personal gain from such exploitation.[39] This lower risk of tunneling may be a reason why Japan has been hesitant about directly regulating RPTs.

2 Korea

a. Ownership Structure: Chaebol and Controlling Minority Shareholders   Corporate governance in Korea centers on *chaebols*, which are family-controlled business conglomerates that domi-

---

33) 7% of those firms have individual controlling shareholders, id., at 8.

34) Takahito Kato, *A memorandum on agency problems between controlling and minority shareholders*, 11 TOKYO UNIVERSITY LAW SCHOOL LAW REVIEW 222, 224 (2016) (in Japanese).

35) For a short account of the long-term trading relationship in Japan, *see* Ito, *supra* note3, at 105–15. This kind of long-term trading relationship emerged since Japanese firms had been forced to abandon the holding company structure after the World War II.

36) This type of industrial organization is made possible probably because markets in Japan are relatively better developed than in Korea and China.

37) Kato, *supra* note 34, at 226–28.

38) Hideaki Miyajima, et al., *An Economic Analysis of the Listing of Parent and Subsidiary – Is the conflict of interest really serious?*, in CORPORATE GOVERNANCE IN JAPAN (Hideaki Miyajima, ed., 2011) 289, 332–33 (in Japanese).

39) Kato, *supra* note 34, at 228 (adds that as an individual controlling shareholder is generally presumed to serve as director, his or her conduct can be restrained by the exiting fiduciary duty regime).

nate the national economy. The ownership structure of a *chaebol* is often characterized as a controlling minority shareholder (CMS) structure.[40] The CMS is a patriarch with the title of "chairman," who effectively controls all the member firms by means of extensive inter-company shareholdings. Composed of numerous pyramidal and circular holdings, a *chaebol*'s actual ownership structure used to be extremely complicated. Under the tacit encouragement of the government, many *chaebols* have been converted into a holding company structure. As most of these holding companies hold only about 30 percent of the shares of their subsidiaries, the dominance of CMS remains intact even in a simplified ownership structure.

Korea's CMS structure exhibits three principal features. First, the CMS's cash-flow rights are extremely low in larger groups, although the figure for smaller business groups is substantially higher.[41] Second, the CMS can still secure absolute control by means of acquiring holdings of other member firms. In other words, these member firms are a functional equivalent of stable shareholders in Japan. Third, despite recurring criticism on the growing disparity between the CMS's cash-flow right and the control right, the CMS structure has remained stable over the last two decades.

b Industrial Organization: Prevalence of Corporate Groups and Related Party Transactions   In the 1960s, Korean firms started expanding by exporting low-tech manufacturing goods to developed countries. As domestic markets were woefully underdeveloped, the exporting manufacturers had to set up new firms and have them supply core parts for their end products.[42] By means of vertical integration, the export industry was able to avoid inefficiency from the "hold-up" problem and enhance competitiveness in the global market.[43] Leading exporters soon grew into giant conglomerates while intragroup RPTs have been commonly undertaken for purely business purposes and, sometimes, for tunneling purposes.[44] The prevalence of RPTs may be attributable, at least partly, to the backward state of markets. Or, viewed from a different angle, pervasive intragroup RPTs may have been a fac-

---

40) Kon Sik Kim, *Dynamics of shareholder power in Korea*, in RESEARCH HANDBOOK ON SHAREHOLDER POWER (Randall S. Thomas & Jennifer G. Hill, eds., 2015) 535, 536–37.

41) In an extreme case, the founder-controlling shareholder of Lotte Group controls the whole group with only 0.1% of the cash-flow right. Kang, *supra* note 6, at 123.

42) Setting up a new firm, the controlling shareholder made relatively lucrative affiliates invest their surplus funds, leading to a complicated ownership structure.

43) For a view emphasizing the counter-productiveness of vertical integration in Korean *chaebol*, see, e.g., SEA-JIN CHANG, FINANCIAL CRISIS AND TRANSFORMATION OF KOREAN BUSINESS GROUPS. THE RISE AND FALL OF CHAEBOLS (2003), 112–17.

44) Cross-subsidization among group firms may be regarded as a mixture of the two purposes.

tor impeding market development in Korea, taking away business opportunities for small- and mediumsized firms including start-ups. This is a reason why, as discussed later, RPTs have been subject to regulation under the Act relating to Monopoly Regulation and Fair Trade (Fair Trade Act or FTA) in Korea.

c Incidence of Related Party Transactions   *Chaebol* firms actively engage in intragroup RPTs. As of 2015, RPTs on average accounted for 11.7 percent of the total sales in forty-seven large business groups, down from 13.2 percent in 2011.[45] In 36.7 percent of the firms, the figure amounted to 30 percent or higher.[46]

Tables 11.1 and 11.2 reveal that as the share ownership of the CMS family (heirs of the CMS in particular) goes up, the percentage of intragroup RPTs in the firm's sales figure rises.[47] It is generally believed that these intragroup RPTs are often abused for tunneling purposes.[48] In a typical scenario, Firm A routinely purchases goods and services from Firm B, paying above-market prices. For example, Hyundai Motors funneled all its car delivery service contracts to an affiliate called Hyundai Glovis, almost wholly owned by ChungMong-koo, Chairman of the Hyundai Motor Group, and his son.[49] This is a prime example of RPTs being beneficial only to a firm owned by the heirs of the controlling family.[50] RPTs have been a well-known means of transferring wealth to *chaebol* heirs to help them inherit their family business.

---

45) Korea Fair Trade Commission, *Analysis of internal transactions in large corporate groups in 2015,* www.ftc.go.kr/solution/skin/doc.html?fn=bf82cc5fdc843c725c6b7c1d88eab7c6fd0b397bce01aa307d6dccb5c 78b8e6f&rs=/fileupload/data/result//news/report/2016/(accessed January 7, 2018), at 6 (in Korean)

46) Id., at 3, 12 (The percentage is higher in firms in service industries. In the business facilities management and business support services, the percentage is as high as 51.9%).

47) Id., at 18, 20.

48) For a short description of some high-profile instances of tunneling, *see* Sang Yop Kang, *"Generous Thieves": The Puzzle of Controlling Shareholder Arrangements in Bad-Law Jurisdictions,* 21 STANFORD JOURNAL OF LAW & FINANCE 57, 77–80 (2015). For a paper showing an adverse effect of routine RPTs on firm market value in poorly governed firms, see Bernard Black, et. al., *How corporate governance affect firm value? Evidence on a self-dealing channel from a natural experiment in Korea,* 51 JOURNAL OF BANKING AND FINANCE 131–50 (2015).

49) Black, et al., *supra* note 48, at 144.

50) Sunwoo Hwang & Woochan Kim, "When Heirs Become Major Shareholders: Evidence on Pyramiding Financed by Related-Party Sales" (unpublished paper, January 2016) (demonstrating that "related-party sales are used as a means to financially support the firms in which heirs become major shareholders, and allow them to control other member firms in the group through pyramiding").

Table 11.1 Percentage of Intragroup Related Party Transactions by CMS Family Holdings as of 2015

CMS family holdings	0~20%	20~30%	30~50%	50~100%	100%
Intragroup RPTs	12.2%	9.0%	11.3%	16.5%	34.6%

Table 11.2 Percentage of Intragroup Related Party Transactions by Holdings of the Heirs of CMS as of 2015

Holdings of the heirs of CMS	0~20%	20~30%	30~50%	50~100%	100%
Intragroup RPTs	11.7%	12.5%	23.1%	25.5%	59.4%

3 China

a Ownership Structure: Corporatization and the Rise of Corporate Groups   Until the late 1970s, when China started to embrace market elements into its economy, all business activities were undertaken by the State. In 1993, the State decided to turn these state-run enterprises into corporations, called state-owned enterprises (SOEs). This policy measure was taken to enhance the performance of SOEs by preventing bureaucrats from interfering with operational decisions. After this process called "corporatization," distinct from "privatization," a number of large SOEs in the form of joint stock company under the Company Act were listed in the newly-established Shanghai and Shenzhen stock exchanges. Although the number of privately-owned enterprises (POEs) has grown during the last four decades, SOEs still dominate the national economy and account for the majority of large listed firms.[51]

Ownership in the listed firms generally remains concentrated. As of 2008, more than 95 percent of the listed firms had "ultimate controlling shareholders" holding at least 10 percent of shares.[52] Another conspicuous feature of the ownership structure in China is the prevalence of the pyramidal structure.[53] Based on pyramidal holdings, Chinese firms gen-

---

51) QIAO LIU, CORPORATE CHINA 2.0 (2016), 7 ("Out of 98 mainland companies on the 2015 *Fortune* Global 500 list, only 10 companies are private.").
52) Id., at 118.
53) Id., at 121.

erally operate in group structures. As corporatization progressed, the number of corporate groups grew exponentially. Like corporatization, corporate groups are a product of government policy. It was in the mid-1980s that the Chinese government decided to start fostering business groups: a decision based on an expectation that these would contribute to new technology, stable financial performance, and international competitiveness.[54] As few POEs were in operation at that time, SOEs were chosen to be transformed into groups. In 1991, fifty-seven large SOEs were converted into corporate groups and the number of corporate groups exceeded 7,000 in the early 1990s.[55]

The rise of corporate groups was also partly due to a peculiar feature of the initial public offering (IPO) of SOEs in the 1990s. The Chinese government encouraged cash-stricken SOEs to undertake IPOs in overseas capital markets.[56] In order to whet the appetite of foreign investors, these SOEs often set up a subsidiary with attractive assets separated from the original firm and listed this subsidiary only. This kind of SOE split-up took place in domestic stock markets as well in order to meet the strict listing requirements of the Shanghai or Shenzhen stock exchanges. The resulting parent and subsidiary firms naturally kept on operating as one enterprise in the form of a corporate group and as a consequence engaged in intragroup RPTs to manufacture end products.

Group structures are not confined to SOEs alone, however. Many POEs including household names such as *Alibaba*, *Wanda* and *Wahaha* now also operate as corporate group. Given the external financial constraints, they voluntarily adopted a group structure to foster internal capital markets.[57]

b Industrial Organization Vertical integration was pervasive in China even before the reform and opening-up policy started in the late 1970s. "Chinese managers often preferred to make, rather than buy, inputs because they wanted to reduce the dependence on potentially unreliable suppliers."[58] Attempts were made to reverse this tendency even in the 1950s, but

---

54) Jia He, et al., *Business Groups in China*, 22 JOURNAL OF CORPORATE FINANCE 166, 168 (2013). It was also partly due to the fact that Japanese and Korean economies, which served as role models for China, had grown based on the group structure, *see* Benjamin L. Liebman & Curtis J. Milhaupt, *Introduction: The Institutional Implications of China's Economic Development*, in REGULATING THE VISIBLE HAND? (Benjamin L. Liebman & Curtis Milhaupt, eds., 2016), xvi–vii.

55) Jia He, et al., *supra* note 54, at 168.

56) The Chinese government no longer encourages overseas listing. Instead, in recent years, re-listing on Chinese exchanges of overseas listed firms is in vogue.

57) Liu, supra note 51, at 121.

58) Yifan Zhang, Essays on Industrial Organization in China's Manufacturing Sector (PhD diss., University of Pittsburgh, 2005), 16. SOEs even founded their own schools and hospitals.

these largely failed. Vertical disintegration started only in the late 1970s with the growth of market forces resulting from market reforms.[59] As SOEs "purchased more and more intermediate inputs through markets," vertical disintegration occurred in twenty-seven out of thirty-one industrial sectors.[60]

c Incidence of Related Party Transactions Despite the increasing specialization of Chinese firms, it is generally believed that RPTs are still widespread even among listed firms. Table 11.3 shows that more than 80 percent of listed firms engage in RPTs and this proportion has been rapidly increasing.[61]

Table 11.3 Popularity of Related Party Transactions in Listed Firms

	Percentage of listed firms	Total amount of RPTs (100M yuan)
2002	85.2	5846
2003	89.5	9073
2004	92.9	28976
2005	90.3	37006
2006	98.2	45907
2007	82.0	120808

Although Chinese firms engage in various types of RPTs, three types are particularly noteworthy: the provision of security; the sale of goods; and the extension of credit.[62] In terms of percentage, the provision of security is by far the largest, ranging from 55 to 62 percent during the period of 2007 to 2010. Prior to 2006, however, credit extension took up the largest portion as low or no interest lending between affiliate firms was commonplace.[63]

---

59) Id., at 4.

60) Id., at 16–17. Zhang argues that "[t]he comparative advantage of vertical integration declined gradually and almost disappeared in the 1980s" (id. at 17). A recent study shows that vertical integration has a negative impact on productivity, in contrast to recent studies based on US firms, Hongyi Li, et al., *Vertical integration and firm productivity*, 26 JOURNAL OF ECONOMICS & MANAGEMENT STRATEGY 403 (2017).

61) KAI ZHONG, A STUDY OF LEGAL ISSUES OF RELATED PARTY TRANSACTIONS UNDER THE COMPANY ACT (Beijing, 2015), 29 (in Chinese). According to a more recent survey, the percentage of listed firms engaging in RPTs is 81.15% in 2013, 92.69% in 2014, and 91.90% in 2015, Bin Wang, et al., *On the regulation of disclosure of RPTs in listed firms*, CHINESE SECURITIES (No. 8, 2016) 31, 32 (in Chinese).

62) Id., at 30–1.

63) As of the end of 2005, 374 firms among 1,308 listed firms were engaging in financial transactions with

In 2003, the CSRC decided to prohibit listed firms from lending to affiliates and ordered them to get rid of existing credits.[64]

RPTs between parent and subsidiary firms account for the largest percentage of RPTs: 41.4 percent on average. Meanwhile, RPTs between affiliate firms under the common control come next at 24.41 percent on average.[65] Unlike in Korea, RPTs involving individual shareholders and managers are believed to be negligible.[66] Nevertheless, tunneling is still perceived as a serious problem in China.[67] A Chinese legal scholar asserts that although tunneling in unlisted firms remains widespread due to inadequate regulation, tunneling in listed firms is in decline.[68] Anecdotal evidence showing otherwise abounds, however.[69]

B Substantive Constraints

1 Japan

The Japanese Company Code (JCC) has no special provision directly targeting controlling shareholders. It is generally accepted in Japan that a controlling shareholder does not owe fiduciary duties to the firm or its fellow shareholders.[70] Although no provision directly addresses the behavior of controlling shareholders, they may still be held liable as a de facto director or based on the general tort provision in the Civil Code (Art. 709).[71] In practice, however, it is difficult to hold a controlling firm liable for damages to the firm based on

---

their affiliates, and loans to their affiliates accounted for 8.6% of the total assets, Guohua Jiang, et al., *Tunneling through Non-Operational Fund Occupancy: An investigation based on officially identified activities*, 32 JOURNAL OF CORPORATE FINANCE 295, 296 (2015).

64) Notice relating to some issues on financial transactions between listed firms and their affiliates and listed firms' provision of security. For a short account of this notice, *see, e.g.*, Nicholas Calcina Howson, "*Quack Corporate Governance*" *as Traditional Chinese Medicine – the Securities Regulation Cannibalization of China's Corporate Law and a State Regulator's Battle Against State Political Economic Power*, 2 SEATTLE UNIVERSITY LAW REVIEW 667, 681–82 (2014).

65) Zhong, *supra* note 61, at 31.

66) RPTs between listed firms and individual shareholders (and their family) amount to 0.01% on average. Ibid.

67) Id., at 56.

68) Id., at 57.

69) *E.g.*, Jiangang He, *Profit shifting, media monitoring and corporate governance: a study of the wuliangye case*, MANAGEMENT WORLD (No. 10, 2008) 141; China Securities Regulatory Commission, *CSRC strengthens the sanction on information disclosure violation by listed firms (July 31, 2015)* , www.csrc.gov.cn/pub/newsite/zjhxwfb/xwdd/201507/t20150731_282052.html (accessed February 8, 2018), in Chinese.

70) Kato, *supra* note 34, at 233. In the process of the 2014 amendment of the JCC, a proposal was made to provide for the fiduciary duty of a controlling shareholder, but was rejected, partly due to the criticism that the concept is too ambiguous to be applicable in a court decision, id., at 225.

71) Id., at 224, 228. According to him, however, it will be difficult to regard a corporate controller as de-facto director because a legal person is not allowed to serve as director under the JCC (Art. 331(1)(i)).

the theory of de facto director.[72]

As for the substance of an RPT, the fairness standard is applicable. Fairness is generally deemed to have been established when an RPT meets the so-called arm's length test.[73] The scope of transaction that is governed by the arm's length test, however, is not clearly delineated.[74] Taking a strict view, fairness is to be established on an individual basis even when the firm engages in a range of RPTs with its affiliates. So, in principle, even when the RPTs as a whole are deemed to be fair, a particular RPT may still be held to be unfair. The opposite conclusion may come about if a more flexible view is taken, which would allow the establishment of fairness to be verified on an overall basis.

In the process of preparing an amendment to the JCC in 2014, a proposal was made to introduce the duty of the parent corporation to compensate for the "disadvantage" arising from a transaction between the parent and the subsidiary.[75] The proposal purported to adopt a global, rather than an individual, approach in calculating the amount of disadvantage.[76] Faced with opposition from the business community, however, the Japanese government dropped the proposed provision when it submitted the bill to the Diet.

At around the same time, adopting a rather broad approach, a district court decided in favor of the director of a subsidiary which participated in the Cash Management System run by its parent. Acknowledging the possibility of the subsidiary benefiting from the CMS on a long-term basis, the court stated that the decision of the director to participate in the CMS was not to be regarded as unreasonable even when the subsidiary was not likely to borrow funds from the CMS in the near future.[77] This decision may be construed as a sign of the rising popularity of the flexible view in Japan. According to a conventional view, however, directors of a controlled firm are still not allowed to sacrifice the firm's interest for the interest of the controlling firm or the group as a whole.[78]

---

72) Id., at 228 n. 25.
73) Egashira, *supra* note 21, at 447–48.
74) Koji Funatsu, "Pursuit of the Group Interest and the Provision on "the Parent's Liability"," *Shojihomu No. 1959* (March 5, 2012): 4, 5–6 (in Japanese).
75) Kato, *supra* note 34, at 225.
76) Id., at 230–31.
77) Yokohama District Court, February 28, 2012, Judgment 2010Wa1651. For a comment on this decision, *see* Yoh Ohta & Daisuke Morimoto, "An Analysis of the Yokohama District Court Decision in the Shareholder Derivative Suit involving Nissan Car Body (I)," *Shojihomu No. 1977* (September 25, 2012): 16 (in Japanese); Yoh Ohta & Daisuke Morimoto, "An Analysis of the Yokohama District Court Decision in the Shareholder Derivative Suit involving Nissan Car Body (II)", *Shojihomu No. 1978* (October 5, 2012): 73 (in Japanese).
78) Egashira, *supra* note 21, at 54.

2 Korea

a Controlling Shareholders   As is the case in Japan, the majority of commentators are of the opinion that a controlling shareholder does not owe fiduciary duties to the firm or its fellow shareholders in Korea. Corporate law rules are contained in the Korean Commercial Code (KCC). The KCC has a few provisions applicable to controlling shareholders. The most relevant of these is Article 401–2, which holds a person with "influence over the firm" liable to the company if they give "an order" to its directors as a result of which the firm suffers loss (Art. 401–2(i)). There is no dispute that this provision was put in place primarily as a means to hold controlling shareholders liable. Although only a few relevant cases have been reported so far, the court seems to have been quite cautious in acknowledging the existence of an order. As yet, no court has held a controlling shareholder liable under this special provision.

b Group Context   Both the fairness standard and the arm's length test are generally accepted in Korea as well. Court decisions elaborating on the arm's length test are rare, however. Most commentators are of the opinion that directors of a controlled firm are not allowed to sacrifice the firm's interest for the interest of the controlling firm or the group as a whole. Group-oriented behavior, however, still remains prevalent in Korea, generating myriads of intragroup RPTs. An individual RPT which is inconsistent with a firm's immediate interest may serve the long-term interest of the group as a whole. Particularly relevant in this context are RPTs entered into to prop up an ailing affiliate. The Supreme Court acknowledges the possibility of allowing such an RPT, but takes a highly cautious attitude toward propping up transactions.[79)]

---

79) In a case on the criminal liability for a series of RPTs conducted to prop up its ailing affiliates, the Supreme Court held those managers including the controlling shareholder liable, pointing to such factors as lack of reasonable and objective standard in selecting supporting firms among the group firms and lack of countervailing benefits to those supporting firms who bore a substantial financial burden as a result of the propping up transactions, Supreme Court Decision No. 2013Do5214 (September 26, 2013). In a more recent case on the same issue, however, the Supreme Court held the defendants not guilty for breach of trust, stating that the defendants are lacking in criminal intent when certain requirements are satisfied, Supreme Court Decision No. 2015Do12633 (November 9, 2017). The requirements mentioned in the decision are hard to meet. They include the following factors: the existence of the common interest among affiliate firms; propping up transactions undertaken to promote the common interest; reasonableness of the size of propping up transactions and the selection of the firm benefitting from propping up transactions; propriety and lawfulness of propping up transactions; and, objective possibility of the supporting firm receiving commensurate compensation.

c Fair Trade Act A set of idiosyncratic provisions targeting RPTs are laid out in the Fair Trade Act. The first provision adopted in 1996 is Article 23(1)(vii), which aims to regulate acts of "unfair assistance" by preventing business firms from dealing with their affiliates or other firms on "fairly preferential terms." Whether a price involved in an RPT is preferential or not is to be determined in comparison with the so-called "normal price" which is a price that would be reached in an arm's length transaction.[80] The Supreme Court holds that the burden of proving the normal price falls on the Fair Trade Commission (FTC), and applies a strict evidentiary requirement, which the FTC has often failed to satisfy.[81] Due to this heavy evidentiary burden, the provision has been ineffective in restraining intragroup RPTs. It has been particularly inadequate in dealing with the so-called "funneling of business" (*ilgam molajugi*) to a related party, a practice met with severe public disapproval. Business funneling involves awarding contracts to a related party, normally a firm owned by an heir apparent of the controlling shareholder. In 2013, a new provision was included in the FTA to specifically address business funneling (Art. 23–2(1)(iv)). A virtuous feature of the new provision lies in the fact that it can be applicable even when the terms are not "fairly preferential" to the related party. The provision is based on the premise that funneling a substantial amount of business can by itself be beneficial to the related party even when the terms do not deviate from the market price. The Korean government, however, included a number of exceptions to this rule, presumably taking into consideration the reality that many business groups depend heavily on intragroup RPTs.[82]

3 China

a Article 21 of the Company Act The Company Act of China (CCA) contains certain provisions potentially applicable to RPTs. The most relevant example may be Article 21, which provides that the controlling shareholder, de facto controller, directors, supervisors and senior officers of a company may not cause damage to the company by taking advantage of their "affiliation relation" with the company, and that those who cause damage to the company shall be liable for compensation of the damage.[83] "Affiliation relation" is broadly de-

---

80) Supreme Court Decision, No. 2009Du20366 (November 13, 2014).
81) In addition, the FTC is required to prove "a potential harm to the fair trade."
82) For example, the FTA exempts RPTs with a related listed firm if the controlling family holds less than 30% of the shares of the firm or if the RPTs account for less than 30% of the listed firm's revenue. In most *chaebol* firms, the controlling family managed to avoid this provision by lowering their holdings below the 30% line.
83) The controlling shareholder and de-facto controller are defined in Article 216. The concept of controlling shareholder is based on either of the two elements: ownership of a majority of shares or influence on the resolutions of the GMS (Art. 216(ii)). The "de facto controller" is defined as a per-

fined to include relations with firms under the direct or indirect control of the controlling shareholder or de facto controller (CCA Art. 216(iv)). The judicial interpretation of the Supreme Court proclaims that the court will support a lawsuit filed by a company or its shareholders against a shareholder who damaged the corporate interest by using RPTs (Judicial Interpretation (3), Art. 12).

It appears that shareholders, in theory, can file a derivative lawsuit against those involved in abusive RPTs under Article 21. Shareholder derivative suits, however, are rare and almost all of them involve limited liability companies, rather than stock corporations.[84] Even when a derivative suit is filed, Chinese courts are extremely reluctant to interfere with the substance of a board decision.[85]

b Other Company Provisions   Another general provision potentially applicable to RPTs is Article 20(1), which provides that shareholders shall not harm "the interest of the firm or other shareholders" by abusing their so-called "shareholder rights." Shareholders who have violated this provision shall be liable to the firm or other shareholders in accordance with the law (Art. 20(2)). A critical defect of this provision is that it requires the abuse of "shareholder rights." The shareholder rights most likely to be involved in an RPT may be voting rights. It is difficult to establish an abuse of voting rights, however. For an RPT not involving a shareholder resolution, it would be even more difficult to prove an abuse of shareholder rights, unless the concept of shareholder rights is liberally construed.

The CCA includes a provision on general concepts equivalent to fiduciary duties in the United States. Article 147(1) provides that "directors, statutory auditors and senior executives" owe the duty of loyalty and the duty of diligence to the company. These duties are generally regarded as a functional equivalent of fiduciary duties under American law. Although this provision does not explicitly mention controlling shareholders, a growing number of leading scholars are of the opinion that controlling shareholders owe fiduciary duties to general shareholders as well as to the firm.[86]

---

son who despite her non-shareholder status is capable of actually controlling the conduct of the company "through investment relations, agreements or other arrangements" (Art. 216(iii)).

84) Donald C. Clarke & Nicholas Howson, *Pathway to minority shareholder protection: derivative actions in the People's Republic of China*, in THE DERIVATIVE ACTION IN ASIA (Dan W. Puchniack et al, eds. 2012), 243, 275–78.

85) Jianbo Lou, *Ordinary Corporate Conduct Standard vs. Business Judgment Rule, in German and Asian Perspectives on Company Law*, eds. Holger Fleischer, et.al. (Tuebingen, 2016), 83, 103; Zhong, *supra* note 60, at 185.

86) JUNHAI LIU, MODERN COMPANY LAW(I) (3rd ed. 2015), 340–43 (in Chinese); Xudong Zhao ed., CORPORATE LAW (4th ed. 2015), 235–36 (in Chinese).

c Administrative Rules A regulation issued by the CSRC contains some provisions on the fairness of RPTs. The "Administrative Rules on IPO and Listing of Shares" require that the issuer firm does not engage in RPTs that are "conspicuously unfair" (Art. 19).[87]

C Procedural Constraints

1 Japan

a Narrow Scope of the Basic Self-Dealing Rule Under the JCC, a director of a company with a board of directors[88] who desires to enter into a transaction with the company is required to obtain approval of the board of directors in advance (Art. 365(1)). As this provision is aimed at directors only, it is generally regarded as inapplicable, in principle, to related parties such as controlling shareholders who do not formally serve as a director. If the size of an RPT is substantial, however, the board of directors may be required to approve the RPT based on its general statutory power (Art. 362(4) (i)). Even in such a case, securing board approval itself may not necessarily be an onerous hurdle as there are relatively fewer independent directors in Japan.[89]

b Role of Directors, Statutory Auditors and Disinterested Parties Prior to a reform in 2014, there was no special regulation on RPTs other than the disclosure provision under the Company Accounting Rules, which requires an RPT between the controlling shareholder and the controlled firm to be disclosed in the notes of non-consolidated financial statements of the controlled firm (Arts. 98(1)(xv), 112(1)). The 2014 reform strengthened procedural constraints as well as disclosure by introducing provisions making it more difficult for a related party to engage in tunneling activities. First, the directors of the controlled company are required to state in the business report that they have taken precautions to ensure that RPTs disclosed in the notes of non-consolidated financial statements do not damage the controlled company's interest (Company Code Enforcement Rules Art. 118(v)). Second, the statutory auditor is required to audit the business report and to state in the audit report his or her opinion on the RPTs covered by the business report (Company Code Enforcement Rules Art. 129(1)(ii)).[90] Third, the Listing Rules of the Tokyo Stock Exchange

---

87) CSRC Regulation No. 32 (May 17, 2006). It further requires the issuer firm to conduct RPTs at fair prices and not to manipulate its profits by means of RPTs (Art. 32).
88) The JCC allows a stock corporation to choose among a wide range of governance structures. Larger firms tend to have the board of directors.
89) As of 2016, in about 80% of the overall listed firms, the portion of independent outside directors' accounts for less than one third of the board members. Tokyo Stock Exchange, *supra* note 32, at 77.

require the executive organ to seek the opinion of a disinterested party when entering into a material RPT (Rules 441–2(1)).

c A Recent Supreme Court Decision on a Management Buyout Transaction Like their American counterparts, Japanese courts are now paying more attention to procedural aspects of RPTs. This phenomenon is conspicuous in court decisions on management buyout (MBO) transactions, a prime example of conflict of interest transactions. In a recent decision on a two-step MBO composed of a tender offer and an ensuing squeeze out, the Supreme Court of Japan stated that it would not delve into the fairness of the price in the squeeze out transaction as long as the tender offer is undertaken "in accordance with a procedure that is generally accepted as fair," and the squeeze out price is equal to the tender offer price.[91] Undertaking the MBO transaction, the majority shareholders, in an effort to neutralize the conflict of interest involved, took such measures as appointing an independent third party committee and obtaining an expert opinion. The Court accepted the procedure as fair without scrutinizing the actual effect of those measures in detail.[92]

2 Korea

a. Expansion of the Scope of the Basic Self-Dealing Rule In terms of corporate statutes, Korea's approval requirements appear to be the most extensive of the three countries. Under the pre-2011 KCC, the basic self-dealing rule was similar to its Japanese counterpart, requiring board approval only for transactions between the firm and a director. The 2011 amendment substantially expanded the scope of related parties to include "major shareholders" and firms in which the "majority" of shares were under the control of major shareholders (Art. 398).[93] This latter category is not as comprehensive as it first appears because the majority test is too high to cover large affiliated firms in reality. As the controlling shareholder often holds less than 50 percent of shares of the firms in his or her business empire, many significant intragroup RPTs remain outside the reach of the revised provision. This defect is somewhat remedied by a special provision applicable to listed firms

---

90) The same provision applies to the audit and supervisory committee and the audit committee (Enforcement Rules Arts. 130–2(1)(ii), 131(1)(i)).

91) Supreme Court Decision, *Kinyu-shoji hanrei* No. 1497 (July 1, 2016): 8 (in Japanese).

92) For a critical comment on this decision, *see, e.g.*, Manabu Matsunaka, "The supreme court decision on JCOM and the fair price in a two-step acquisition involving a structural conflict of interest", *Shojihomu No. 2114* (October 25, 2016): 4 (in Japanese).

93) A major shareholder is broadly defined to include shareholders with 10% shares or with influence over material business matters. KCC Art. 542–8(2)(vi). The 2011 amendment heightened the voting requirement to a two-thirds majority.

(Art. 542–9), which expands the scope of affiliates to include all the member firms of a business group under the FTA (KCC Enforcement Decree Arts. 35(5), 35(4)(ii)(B)). This provision may potentially cover even routine intragroup RPTs conducted by a listed firm. In order to minimize the burden of listed firms, the KCC allows a special exception, according to which the firm does not have to obtain board approval for each and every RPT, as long as it has obtained a comprehensive approval for routine RPTs, normally on an annual basis (Art. 542–9(5)). This exception is widely utilized in the business community, and the general practice thereof goes like this: The listed firm prepares a document which indicates the monetary sum total of RPTs with each affiliate and submits this document to the board of directors for approval, normally at the beginning of the business year. The document typically indicates only the sum total of RPTs, and does not contain details of their trade terms. In practice, the board of directors almost invariably gives a comprehensive approval without considering the fairness of the terms. As yet, no case of rejection has been reported.

b Independence of Directors Approving Related Party Transactions   The independence of directors is an essential condition for effective board monitoring. In this regard, the situation in Korea does not warrant much optimism. According to the dominant view, even an executive director is entitled to vote on an RPT with his or her boss as long as the former has no personal interest in the RPT involved. This weakness may be somewhat ameliorated by the involvement of outside directors. In Korea, a large listed firm is required to fill a majority of board seats with outsiders (KCC Art. 542–8). Many firms, however, manage to fill these seats with nominally independent, but actually pliant, directors. It is thus not surprising that examples of outside directors voting "no" are extremely rare.[94]

3 China

The CCA prohibits directors and senior executive officers from dealing with a firm without obtaining approval of the GMS (Art. 148(1)(iv)). The provision does not cover other related parties such as the controlling shareholder or affiliate firms.[95] RPTs are thus rather thinly

---

94) A low objection rate does not necessarily mean inaction on the part of the outside directors as they are customarily given an opportunity to let management know their negative view informally in advance, Kyung-Hoon Chun, *Korea's Mandatory Independent Directors: Expected and Unexpected Roles*, in INDEPENDENT DIRECTORS IN ASIA: A HISTORICAL, CONTEXTUAL AND COMPARATIVE APPROACH (Dan W. Puchniak, et al., eds., 2017) 176, 200–01.
95) There are other provisions applicable to RPTs. The CCA, for example, requires approval of the GMS for providing security for shareholders or de-facto controllers (Art. 16(1)). This special rule for provision of

regulated under the CCA. This regulatory lacuna is filled by government regulations and exchange rules. As exchange rules are tightly controlled by the CSRC, they are functionally indistinguishable from government regulations.

Perhaps the most prominent feature of the CSRC's regulation of RPTs is the veto power granted to independent directors.[96] The CSRC requires a listed firm to fill more than one-third of seats (two at least) on the board with independent directors, one of whom needs to be an accounting professional[97] and to approve certain large RPTs before board approval is secured.[98] At times, these independent directors may hesitate to block an RPT involving the controlling shareholder as they are normally appointed at the behest of the controlling shareholder. There is some empirical evidence, however, suggesting that a positive role is played by these independent directors.[99]

This procedural requirement is further specified in the stock exchange listing rules and the guidelines promulgated under the listing rules. The Listing Rules of the Shanghai Stock Exchange, for example, contain a chapter on RPTs (Ch. 10). More systematic and detailed is a special guideline for RPTs (the RPT Guideline)[100] enacted by the Shanghai Stock Exchange. The RPT Guideline is composed of sixty-three provisions, which include comprehensive rules on every aspect of RPTs, covering substance, procedure and disclosure. For example, the RPT Guideline has a set of detailed rules on the definition of a related party (Arts. 7–11). The related party is broadly defined to include a natural or legal person or other organization "that has such a special relationship with the listed company as would

---

security may be justified by the fact that the transaction was so widespread.

96) In addition, the CSRC, together with the State Economy and Trade Commission, promulgated in 2002 "the Principles of Corporate Governance for Listed Firms", which provide for general rules on RPTs.

97) CSRC, *Guidelines for Introducing Independent Directors to the Board of Directors of Listed Companies (2001)*, www.csrc.gov.cn/pub/csrc_en/newsfacts/release/200708/t20070810_69191.html (accessed March, 27, 2018). On the enforcement of this requirement, *see* Donald C. Clarke, *The Independent Director in Chinese Corporate Governance*, 31 DELAWARE JOURNAL OF CORPORATE LAW 126, 197–201 (2006).

98) Id., at Para. 5(1). Moreover, independent directors have power to issue an independent opinion report on material corporate matters including "events that the independent directors consider to be detrimental to the interests of minority shareholders." (id., Para. 6(1)).

99) Agnes W. Y. Lo, et al., *Can Corporate Governance Deter Management from Manipulating Earnings? Evidence from Related-Party Sales Transactions in China*, 16 JOURNAL OF CORPORATE FINANCE 225, 226 (2010) (finding that firms with high percentages of independent directors tend to "have a smaller magnitude of manipulated transfer prices"); Juan Ma & Tarun Khanna, *Independent Directors' Dissent on Boards: Evidence from Listed Companies in China*, HARVARD BUSINESS SCHOOL WORKING PAPER 13–089 (October 24, 2013), 19–20 (finding that independent directors are more likely to dissent after the departure of the board chair who appointed them). On the role of minority-appointed directors to control RPTs, *see* Alessio M. Pacces, *Controlling the Corporate Controller's Misbehaviour*, 11 JOURNAL OF CORPORATE LAW STUDIES 177 (2011).

100) Guidelines on the implementation of RPTs of Firms listed on the Shanghai Stock Exchange.

make the listed company tilted towards her or its interests in accordance with the principle that essence is more important than form" (Arts. 8(v), 10(v)).

The RPT Guideline divides RPTs into three groups and applies different regulations for each category of RPT. Regulations on the largest RPTs amounting to RMB 30 million or more and 5 percent or more of the net assets of the firm ("the largest RPTs") are strictest and include procedural rules (Art. 20). For the largest RPTs, both prior approval of independent directors and approval of the board of directors are required (Art. 25(1)).[101] Reports or opinions to be submitted to the board of directors include: an audit or appraisal report prepared by a securities firm (Art. 20(i)); and the opinion of the audit committee or a special RPT committee (Art. 25(2)). The largest RPTs need to be approved by the GMS as well (Art. 20). In addition, the board of statutory auditors[102] is required to monitor the process of deliberation, voting, disclosure and implementation regarding RPTs and to present its opinion in the annual report (Art. 28). The RPT Guideline has a separate chapter for routine RPTs to minimize the compliance burden on firms (Chapter 8, Arts. 42–7).[103] Finally, caution is advised regarding the efficacy of the approval requirement. The approval requirement can take effect only when the proposal to engage in an RPT is submitted to the board or the GMS for approval. There is no guarantee, however, that such a formal procedure is adopted in reality. Indeed, a recent study on fraud cases involving firms listed in Hong Kong and Singapore seems to support this suspicion.[104] Although potentially applicable to Japan and Korea as well, this statement is presumably more relevant to China.[105]

D Disclosure

1 Japan

a Accounting Rules Regarding the disclosure of RPTs, basic rules are contained in the Company Accounting Rules promulgated under the JCC. The Accounting Rules require certain larger firms to disclose substantial RPTs with their controlling shareholders in the

---

101) The related directors are not allowed to vote at the board meeting (Art. 26(1)).
102) This should be distinguished from the audit committee composed of directors.
103) The Guideline allows the firm to get a comprehensive approval for multiple routine RPTs on an annual basis.
104) Wai Yee Wan, et al., *Managing the Risks of Corporate Fraud: the Evidence from Hong Kong And Singapore*, https://ssrn.com/abstract=3165829(accessed June 11, 2018), at 23 ("almost half (45.2%) of the fraud cases in the sample involve either misappropriation of assets or problematic RPTs which were not disclosed to the boards and/or shareholders nor properly approved by the boards and/or shareholders").
105) Id., at 7 ("a significant proportion of fraud firms in each of Hong Kong and Singapore are overseas mainland Chinese enterprises").

notes of their non-consolidated financial statements (Company Accounting Rules 98(1)(xv), 112(1)). In reality, however, the disclosure of RPTs is often implemented inadequately, such as by not including contract terms.[106]

b Company Code Enforcement Rules   The rules related to RPTs were substantially strengthened in 2014. According to the revised Company Code Enforcement Rules (Art. 118(v)), matters to be disclosed in the business report include the following: directors' opinion as to whether the RPTs involved adversely affect the interest of the controlled firm; and the opinion of outside directors if it contradicts the board's judgment. The Enforcement Rules (Art. 129(1)(vi)) further require the statutory auditors (and other equivalent organs) to audit the business report, and to state their opinion on the RPTs with its controlling shareholders in the audit report.

c Exchange Rules   As is the case in China, stock exchanges, and particularly the Tokyo Stock Exchange (TSE), play an increasingly conspicuous role in regulating RPTs. The TSE has recently enacted a set of detailed rules on RPTs with controlling shareholders.[107] First, a listed firm with a controlling shareholder is required to adopt its own special guideline on RPTs: "the guideline on measures to protect minority shareholders in conducting transactions with controlling shareholders" (RPT Guideline; TSE Listing Rules Art. 204(12)(i), Implementation Rules Art. 211(4)(1)). Second, the board of directors is required to obtain an opinion from an independent third party before reaching its decision on a material RPT (TSE Listing Rules Art. 441–2(1)). Third, the firm is required to make the necessary and sufficient disclosure for a material RPT (TSE Listing Rules Art. 441–2(2)). Fourth, the firm is required to disclose its compliance with the RPT Guideline, as well as the measures it has taken to ensure fairness and to avoid a conflict of interest (TSE Listing Rules Art. 411(1), Implementation Rules Art. 412(6)).

Actual RPT guidelines announced by listed firms often adopt an arm's length test as the standard to be applied to an RPT.[108] They also provide for procedures to be adopted. In some cases, they require an opinion of an outside director or outside expert independent from the parent company. The approval of a majority of minority shareholders (MOM),

---

106) Masao Yanaga, *Related party transactions and procedural safeguards*, in A PATH OF ENTERPRISE LAW (FESTSCHRIFT FOR COMMEMORATING PROFESSOR KENJIRO EGASHIRA'S SEVENTIETH BIRTHDAY), (Etsuro Kuronuma & Tomotaka Fujita eds., 2017]), 319–23 (in Japanese).

107) Kato, *supra* note 34, at 230.

108) Ibid.

however, is rarely, if ever, required in reality. In addition, although RPTs are disclosed, detailed information on their terms is generally not disclosed.[109] Thus, even the enhanced disclosure under the TSE Listing Rules falls short of equipping a potential plaintiff shareholder with adequate information.

The task of controlling RPTs is largely assigned to internal corporate organs such as directors and statutory auditors. In that sense, one can say that the primary purpose of the TSE rules is not so much to provide investors with detailed information on RPTs but rather to ensure the fairness of the terms.

2 Korea

a Korean Commercial Code and the Capital Market Act   As mentioned earlier, the KCC requires material RPTs to be approved by the board of directors and to be reported to the GMS (Art. 542–9(3)(4); Enforcement Decree Art. 35(8)). A more detailed disclosure rule exists in the Capital Market Act,[110] which requires the annual report to include "contents of transactions with large shareholders or directors and employees" (Enforcement Decree Art. 168(3)(vi)). This rule, however, is not particularly effective in reality. Disclosure under this rule is to be made only when the annual report is prepared. Moreover, details of RPTs which should form the basis of the fairness decision are often not fully disclosed. These defects may in theory be remedied by the rules of the stock exchange. The Korea Exchange, the country's only stock exchange, however, has no specific rules on RPTs.

b Fair Trade Act What is expected to fill this regulatory vacuum is the FTA, which requires firms belonging to large business groups to disclose large RPTs following the board decision (Art. 11–2(1)). As such, disclosure is to be made within one day of the board decision (FTC Rules on Board Decision and Disclosure of Large RPTs Art. 6(1)), so this can be a source of timely information. The FTC Rules do require the terms of the RPT to be disclosed, but the level of required disclosure is not specified (FTC Rules on Board Decision and Disclosure of Large RPTs Art. 6(1)). In practice, disclosure is often neglected[111] or when it is made, the scope of disclosed information is generally quite limited.

---

109) Yanaga, *supra* note 106, at 320.
110) Its full title is "the Act regarding Financial Investment and Capital Market."
111) The sanction for non-compliance is only an administrative fine (FTC Rules on Board Decision and Disclosure of Large RPTs Art. 11).

3 China

a Administrative Regulations   For the disclosure of RPTs of a listed firm, China has a set of detailed rules. First of all, the Code of Corporate Governance for Listed Companies proclaimed by the CSRC and National Economic and Trade Commission in 2002 encompasses basic provisions on consultation in writing and disclosure (Arts. 12 to 14). More concrete rules are scattered across several regulations issued by the CSRC. For example, the Rules on Implementing Disclosure at Listed Firms contain a set of rules on the disclosure of RPTs for the secondary market (Arts. 48, 59, 63, and 71(3)).[112]

In practice, however, RPT-related disclosure is often inadequate or delayed.[113] The CSRC, from time to time, imposes sanctions for violation of disclosure rules.[114] The extent of sanctions seems relatively mild, especially when imposed on controlling shareholders and managers involved.[115]

b Stock Exchange Rules and the Related Party Transactions Guideline   More comprehensive disclosure rules on RPTs, however, are found in the listing rules of stock exchanges. The RPT Guideline, mentioned earlier, includes detailed rules on disclosure of RPTs. It divides RPTs into three groups and deals with each type differently. For example, in the case of an RPT with a related natural person, a timely disclosure is required if the amount involved reaches or exceeds RMB 300,000 (Art. 18). In the case of an RPT with a related firm, disclosure is required only when it reaches or exceeds RMB 3 million and accounts for 0.5 percent or more of the net assets (Art. 19). For an RPT which satisfies the size requirement of RMB 30 million and 5 percent of the net assets, the listed firm must also provide an audit and appraisal report prepared by a securities firm, and shall acquire GMS approval (Art. 20). These requirements do not apply to routine RPTs, however. Instead, the RPT Guideline prescribes the firm to disclose certain matters including pricing policy regarding RPTs and the reasons behind conducting RPTs (Art. 38).

Sanctions for violating RPT-related disclosure rules appear lenient, however. According to an unofficial hand count, only eleven cases of sanctions for such a violation were reported

---

112) Disclosure rules applicable to RPTs relating to the primary market are contained in the Administrative Rules on the Issuance of Securities by Listed Companies (Arts. 44 and 53).

113) BIN WANG, ET AL., *supra* note 61, at 32.

114) Sanctions are imposed in accordance with the Securities Act Arts. 192, 193, and 223. As of 2014, out of 24 cases of the CSRC's disclosure-related administrative sanctions, seven cases relate to RPTs, ibid.

115) Id., at 34. Since 2015, the CSRC is imposing higher civil penalties for violation of RPT disclosure rules.

by the Shanghai Stock Exchange during the period between 2016 and February 2018.[116] The harshest sanction imposed by the Exchange was public censure, and this was imposed only once in that period.

IV General Observations

It is admittedly an ambitious task to discuss in one chapter the law and realities of RPTs in these three jurisdictions. Given the paucity of available data, it may be premature to embark on a comparative analysis of the three different RPT systems. Nevertheless, dispensing altogether with a comparative analysis would render this chapter insipid. We will thus attempt a comparative analysis of sorts, focusing on three aspects of RPT regulation, albeit in a highly subjective and cursory manner.

A Evolution of RPT Regulations

1 Hypothetical Framework

The three jurisdictions all have a basic self-dealing provision in their corporate statutes. Primarily aimed at directors and officers, the self-dealing provision falls short of dealing with intragroup RPTs properly. In all three countries, various reform measures have been taken to improve control of RPTs. The initiation of such reform is presumed to depend on the balance between two conflicting forces: the pressure for reform on the one hand, and the powerful resistance from the business community on the other.

The driving force behind reform may comprise various factors, two of which will be addressed here: prevalence of tunneling; and pressure from the capital market. It is indisputable that the prevalence of tunneling will intensify pressure for reform. The role of the capital market here may need some explanation, however. Widespread intragroup RPTs with the potential for tunneling do not fit well with a vibrant capital market. Foreign investors, in particular, will view RPTs with suspicion. A countervailing force against reform may vary depending on: the power of controlling shareholders as a whole; and the importance of intragroup RPTs as a way of organizing business activity.[117]

---

116) Shanghai Stock Exchange, www.sse.com.cn/disclosure/credibility/supervision/measures (accessed February 8, 2017).
117) This will again depend on the feasibility of market transactions.

a Japan   In view of the hypothetical framework described above, the recent reforms of RPT regulation in Japan are puzzling to explain. Regarding the pressure for reform, RPTs were not so widespread nor was tunneling regarded as a serious issue in Japan, in contrast to Korea and China. On the other hand, the resistance does not appear to be strong either. As mentioned earlier, most of the controlling shareholders are publicly held firms, who presumably have less incentive to engage in tunneling in comparison with individual controllers. Moreover, intragroup, routine RPTs are less significant in the Japanese industrial organization than in Korea and China. An additional relevant factor is pressure from the capital market. Since the late 1990s, foreign investors have been steadily expanding their holdings to such a level that, as of 2016, 30 percent or more of the shares in 42.8 percent of the firms composing the JPX-NIKKEI 400 were owned by foreign investors.[118] In recent years, Japan has been under pressure from foreign investors to improve its corporate governance.[119] Nevertheless, faced with opposition from the business community in the process of the 2014 revision of the JCC, Japan decided not to adopt a mandatory outside director requirement.[120] Viewed cynically, it was presumably easier for the business community to accept RPT reform focusing on disclosure rather than a mandatory outside director requirement.

b Korea   Korea's current RPT regulatory regime may be regarded as a product of compromise between a loosely knit group of reformers and the business community dominated by *chaebols*. A public outcry over rampant tunneling was a factor driving reform measures on intragroup RPTs. On the other hand, as many *chaebol* firms were heavily dependent on intragroup RPTs, they made strenuous efforts to tone down reforms. As a consequence, Korea has ended up with a set of seemingly rigorous rules, which are porous in reality. Unsurprisingly, scandals involving abusive RPTs continue to emerge.

Increasingly concerned about dwindling market opportunities for smaller firms, the general public is putting pressure on the newly installed reformist government to implement further reform. The road to successful reform, however, is not without obstacles. As long as an alternative way of industrial organization (such as Japanese-style long-term trading relationships or pure market exchange) remains unacceptable to *chaebol* firms, even the reformist government may hesitate to further strengthen restrictions (entailing costs and uncertainty)

---

118) Tokyo Stock Exchange, *supra* note 32, at 6.
119) Gen Goto, et al., *Japan's Gradual Reception of Independent Directors*, INDEPENDENT DIRECTORS IN ASIA: A HISTORICAL, CONTEXTUAL AND COMPARATIVE APPROACH (Dan W. Puchniak, et al., eds, 2017), 135, 147–50.
120) Id., at 160–71.

on routine intragroup RPTs.

c China   From an early stage, the Chinese government was mindful of the risk of tunneling accompanied with RPTs. On the other hand, there has been little resistance from controlling shareholders. Many large listed firms are SOEs and those who run them on a daily basis are bureaucrat-managers who commonly rotate between their positions in the Chinese government (including the Chinese Communist Party) and the SOE. As their terms of office are limited, they have less incentive to resist reform measures initiated by the Government. Although the controlling shareholders of POEs are private individuals by definition, they may not be nearly as influential as their counterparts in countries like Korea when it comes to opposing a government.

From the perspective of industrial organization, intragroup RPTs are becoming less important as it is now increasingly possible for firms to trade with external firms on the market.

2 Summary

Table 11.4 below encapsulates the relative importance of various factors at work in each of the three jurisdictions.

Table 11.4 Pressure for Reform and Strength of Resistance in the Three Countries

	Japan	Korea	China
Prevalence of RPTs	weak	strong	moderate
Capital market pressure	strong	moderate	weak
Power of controlling SHs	weak	strong	weak
Importance of RPTs	weak	strong	moderate

B Features of the Regulation of Related Party Transactions

1 Japan

As discussed above, substantial differences exist in RPT regulations between the three countries. For Japan, RPTs have been much less prevalent compared to the other two jurisdictions. Significant RPTs are mostly those between parents and subsidiaries, i.e. vertical

RPTs. Having started to pay more attention to RPTs only recently, Japan has chosen to focus on strengthening procedural and disclosure requirements. As substantive constraints remain largely unchanged, courts are not likely to play a significant role. This may have been due to the persistent concern on the part of Japanese policy makers (as well as the business community) about proliferating shareholder lawsuits. Instead, the reformers chose to rely more on outside directors, statutory auditors and third-party experts in ensuring the fairness of an RPT. The majority of minority (MOM) approach, which is gaining support from policymakers as well as scholars in many jurisdictions, has not yet been seriously considered.

As for enforcement, Japan relies heavily on the stock exchanges in actually regulating RPTs. This is in line with an approach taken by the UK, Hong Kong and, more relevantly, China.

2 Korea

Of the three jurisdictions, it is probably in Korea that RPTs are most common and where RPTs attract most attention from the policy makers and the public. As far as statutory law is concerned, Korean regulation may appear to be the strictest. In addition to the fairly broad RPT provisions under the KCC, there are further provisions in the FTA as well. These rules, however, have largely failed to eradicate abusive RPTs in Korea's economy due to the shortcomings in enforcement mentioned earlier. This regulatory gap is being filled by criminal prosecution. Prosecutors often bring criminal charges against *chaebol* chairmen involved in egregious RPTs, asserting a breach of trust under criminal statutes. The criminal sanction approach may bring immediate results, but it should not be heavily depended upon because it has many limitations.

In theory, a more active role could be expected of the Korea Exchange, which is equipped with the necessary expertise and resources. The Korea Exchange, however, has failed entirely to respond to such expectations, unlike its counterparts in China and Japan. The Korea Exchange's inaction is presumably due to its relatively subordinate political status when it comes to dealing with big business.

3 China

The Chinese government brought in RPT regulations to prevent bureaucrat-managers stealing from SOEs. The basic approaches taken by China are similar to those in Japan. China tends to focus on procedure and disclosure. This may be partly attributable to the fact that courts still play a relatively passive role in China. Like Japan, China has also chosen to rely more on stock exchanges than on courts. Some differences exist, however. In China, the CSRC, the capital market regulator, is actively involved in matters of general corporate governance.[121]

4 Overall Evaluation

Table 11.5 below summarizes our initial evaluation of the three features of RPT regulation in each jurisdiction according to law in action as well as in the books.

Table 11.5 Evaluation of the Three Features of Related Party Transaction Regulation

	Japan	Korea	China
Substance	moderate	moderate	weak
Procedure	strong	moderate	moderate
Disclosure	moderate	weak	moderate

Table 11.5 is largely consistent with the evaluation prepared by the World Bank in its Doing Business Report (DBR) of 2018.[122] The DBR evaluates the quality of the RPT regulation of 190 countries, employing the so-called "extent of conflict of interest regulation index", which is in essence equivalent to the "RPT Index."[123] The RPT Index is composed of three categories: disclosure; director liability; and shareholder lawsuits.[124] Although similar in substance, these categories do not exactly correspond to those adopted in this chapter, the first is meant to cover "procedure" as well, and the second and third together are functionally the same as "substantive constraints."

Table 11.6 below presents the RPT Index scores for the three jurisdictions. China's scores should be given particular attention, as it scores very low on substantive constraints, and director liability in particular. This is in line with the evaluation shown in Table 11.5. On the other hand, China scores 10, the highest possible score, for disclosure. Although China admittedly applies a set of strict procedural and disclosure rules to listed firms, this score appears too high especially when compared with the corresponding score for Japan.

---

121) For a view in favor of the proactive role of the CSRC, *see*, *e.g.*, Howson, *supra* note 64.
122) World Bank Group, "Doing Business 2018. Reforming to Create Jobs", www.doingbusiness.org/%7E/media/WBG /DoingBusiness/Documents/Annual-Reports/English/DB2018-Full-Report.pdf (accessed March 27, 2018).
123) Dan W. Puchniak & Umakanth Varottil, "Related Party Transactions in Commonwealth Asia: Complexity Revealed", Chapter 12 in this volume.
124) DBR 91–94.

Table 11.6 RPT Index Scores in the Doing Business Report

DBR 2018	This chapter	Japan	Korea	China
Director liability	Substantive	6	6	1
Ease of shareholder suits	constraints	8	8	4
Disclosure	Procedure Disclosure	7	7	10
RPT Index score		7	7	5

C Potential Consequences of Strengthening Related Party Transaction Regulations

If RPTs are more tightly regulated, it will become costlier for business groups to continue to engage in intragroup RPTs. Business groups would then have to change their mode of business activity. This is not a serious issue in Japan as firms rely primarily on long-term trading relationships on the market. In China, firms have already started expanding their market transactions. The challenge will likely be most daunting for Korean *chaebols*. In principle, they will be left with four options. The first option is to deal more with outside firms on the market. Firms already depend increasingly on external firms, called "cooperative firms." If they cannot find appropriate firms on the market, they may choose to turn their affiliate trading partners into wholly-owned subsidiaries to eliminate any room for dispute. This is their second option. It will require an enormous amount of funds, however. They will then likely be forced to sell some member firms to secure funds for maintaining control over their core firms, ending up with a less sprawling business empire. The third option is not an easy one either: instead of giving up some of their non-core firms, they may let the holding company (in a statutory or functional sense) issue new shares or bonds or secure bank loans to secure funds for turning the member firms into wholly-owned subsidiaries. This option will inevitably lead to a weakening of control on the part of controlling families. None of these three options would be easy to swallow from their perspective. Accordingly, they may opt for the fourth option, which is to block or dilute any attempts at reform.

If any of the first three options are pursued, any room for tunneling will largely evaporate. This would further decrease the incentive of controlling shareholders to keep control of their business empires within the family, especially when they are not sure about their superior business acumen. Will they eventually part with control as their counterparts did in the past in the United States or the United Kingdom? This will be one of the most fascinating developments for corporate governance scholars to monitor.

Table 11.7 below outlines the potential impact of further RPT reforms on business firms in each jurisdiction.

V Concluding Remarks

The incidence of RPTs may be affected by the existing share ownership structure and industrial organization. Indeed, it will be difficult to strengthen regulations on RPTs as long as this economic environment remains unchanged. Reining in RPTs alone may lead to counterproductive results. Current as well as past attempts to revamp RPT regulations in most jurisdictions aim or have aimed to minimize tunneling without impeding legitimate transactions.

As we have seen, considerable differences exist in RPT regulation between the three East Asian countries under review. Such disparity is attributable to differences in the salience of RPTs, in the economic and political environment, and in the institutional infrastructure of each jurisdiction. Another relevant factor may be the extent of each country's need to develop capital markets. A country's need to promote its capital market may vary depending, partly at least, on the type of its principal industries. The three countries all started their economic development with relatively low-tech, and thus low-risk, manufacturing industries. They could all safely depend heavily on bank loans for business capital. The three countries, and certainly their leading firms, have been moving into higher-tech and higher-risk industries, requiring risk capital in the capital market. It will still take more time, however, to clarify whether the financing behavior of leading firms can be changed and the impact such change would have on the extent to which each country relies on RPTs.

IV. Shareholder remedies

Declining Relevance of Lawsuits on the Validity of Shareholder Resolution in Korea

A Comparative Essay

Kon-Sik Kim / Moon-Hee Choi

I. Introduction

Over the past few decades, a convergence in corporate law has been in progress between civil law and common law jurisdictions. Proliferation of outside directors, adoption (or promotion) of shareholder derivative suits and emphasis on internal control may be presented as prime examples in corporate governance. In corporate finance, a permissive attitude toward stock repurchases and share issuance to a third party is becoming a new norm. In the midst of this tide toward convergence, a notable exception is lawsuits contesting the validity of shareholder resolutions ("SR lawsuits"). It is well known that SR lawsuits play only a trivial role in the US.[1] In contrast, they serve as an important remedy in civil law jurisdictions. The rules on SR lawsuits, however, vary widely even among civil law countries such as Korea, Japan and Germany.[2] Although those rules are not identical among European jurisdictions,[3] disparity appears greater between Europe and East Asia. The disparity lies not just in the contents of the relevant rules, but also in the role of such lawsuits in corporate governance in reality.

The purpose of this paper is to examine the law and reality of SR lawsuits in Korea in comparison with German law and from a broader comparative perspective. This paper shall first set the stage for our discussion of SR lawsuits in Korea, presenting some background

---

1) M. GELTER, Why do Shareholder Derivative Suits Remain Rare in Continental Europe?, 37 Brooklyn Journal of International Law (2012) 883; H. FLEISCHER, Entwicklungslinien des aktienrechtlichen Beschlussmängelrechts: Rechtsvergleichung – Dogmengeschichte – Reformvorschläge, in: Fleischer / Kalss / Vogt (eds.), Aktuelle Entwicklungen im deutschen, österreichischen und schweizerischen Gesellschafts- und Kapitalmarktrecht (Tübingen 2013) 84.

2) FLEISCHER, supra note 1, 84

3) FLEISCHER, supra note 1, 69 et seq.

information about Korean company law in general (II.). Secondly, it will provide a short sketch on historical development of the rules of SR lawsuits (III.), before setting out the law and reality of SR lawsuits in Korea (IV. and V.). Fourthly, based on the information provided in the previous sections, we will then discuss some of the salient features of Korean law on SR lawsuits in comparison with German law (VI.). Finally, we will conclude with a few remarks about the declining relevance of SR lawsuits in Korea (VII.).

II. Some Background Information

1. Korean Commercial Code

Unlike most advanced jurisdictions, Korea still does not have an independent code of company law. The statutes related to companies are contained mostly in the third book of the Commercial Code ("KCC") (Arts. 288–542-13 KCC), which was enacted in 1962 and came into effect in 1963. The KCC provides for five types of companies, which all have a legal personality: general partnership companies; limited partnership companies; limited liability companies; limited companies; and joint stock companies ("corporations") (Art. 170 KCC). These five types of companies differ mainly in the scope of the member's liability for company debt. The KCC has a set of special provisions for listed firms as well. In an idiosyncrasy of the Korean system, corporate finance matters are covered by a different piece of legislation called the Financial Investment Business and Capital Markets Act.

2. Overwhelming Popularity of Corporation as a Form of Business

Among these five types of companies, the corporation is by far the most popular form of business, accounting for about 92 percent of all the companies in Korea. Table 1 shows the number of corporations by paid-in capital as registered in the official commercial registry. According to Table 1, slightly over 800,000 corporations exist as of January 2015.[4] Of these corporations, about 1,900 firms are listed in Korea Exchange, the only stock exchange in Korea.

---

4) Only about half of these corporations are reported to be actually in operation.

Table 1: Number of Corporations (as of January 2015)[5]

Paid-in Capital (Korean Won)	Firms	Percentage
More than 500 billion	88	0.01%
100 billion to 500 billion	356	0.04%
50 billion to 100 billion	417	0.05%
10 billion to 50 billion	2,697	0.34%
5 billion to 10 billion	3,078	0.38%
1 billion to 5 billion	27,323	3.41%
100 million to 1 billion	250,832	31.26%
50 million to 100 million	125,429	15.63%
10 million to 50 million	284,373	35.44%
10 million or less	107,725	13.43%
Others	30	0.004%
Total	802,348	100%

As the overwhelming majority of companies have adopted the form of corporation, it is not surprising that most of these corporations are small in size. Table 1 reveals that less than five percent of them have a paid-in capital of 1 million US-dollars or more. These small corporations often ignore the formalities of the general shareholders meeting ("GSM"), giving rise to SR lawsuits. Additionally, the prevalence of smaller firms in turn makes it more difficult to strengthen the requirements for the GSM.

3. Major Corporate Organs and the General Shareholders Meeting

In principle, the KCC requires every corporation to have the following three organs: (i) the GSM; (ii) the board of directors and representative directors; and (iii) statutory auditors. Korea has adopted a one-tier board that is composed solely of directors appointed at the GSM.[6] While the board of directors is empowered to make decisions regarding management of the firm, it is the representative directors that are in charge of implementing those decisions. A functional equivalent of the chief executive officer in the US., the representa-

---

5) Commercial Registration Statistics.
6) Large listed corporations are required to appoint a majority (not less than three) of external members to the board (Art. 542-8 para. 1 KCC).

tive director is generally appointed by the board (Art. 389 para. 1 KCC) and is authorized to represent the firm as against third parties (Arts. 389 para. 3, 209 para. 1 KCC). A statutory auditor is an organ originally derived from the German supervisory board (*Aufsichtsrat*), but in contrast to its German prototype, it is not equipped with the power to appoint directors.[7]

The KCC now allows a corporation to employ an alternative structure. A corporation can have statutory officers instead of representative directors (Art. 408-2 KCC), or an audit committee instead of statutory auditors (Art. 415-2 KCC). The KCC allows a small corporation to dispense with the board of directors (Art. 383 paras. 1, 4 KCC), but requires a large listed corporation to establish an audit committee (Art. 542-11 para. 1 KCC).

The most significant corporate organ when dealing with SR lawsuits is the GSM. The power of the GSM under the KCC is quite extensive, more extensive than that of, say, Delaware law. Under the KCC, the GSM may decide on such matters as are specified in the KCC or in the articles of incorporation (Art. 361 KCC). The KCC explicitly subjects a broad range of matters to the resolution at the GSM. For example, the GSM is authorized to appoint directors, determine CEO remuneration (Art. 388 KCC), declare dividends (Art. 462 para. 2 KCC), and select audit committee members in some listed firms (Art. 542 para. 1 KCC). In addition, the KCC explicitly indicates that the firm may empower the GSM to decide on matters such as issuance of new shares (Art. 416 KCC) and the appointment of representative directors (Art. 389 para. 1 KCC) by inserting an appropriate provision in the articles of incorporation. It is also widely agreed that even in the absence of such an explicit reference in the KCC, the firm can choose to expand the GSM's scope of authority by so providing in the articles of incorporation.[8]

Of these various powers of the GSM, the power to appoint directors may be the most crucial from a corporate governance perspective.[9] Selection (or dismissal) of directors has often been a subject of dispute in a majority of SR lawsuits in Korea.

---

7) K. KIM, Transplanting Audit Committees to Korean Soil: A Window into the Evolution of Korean Corporate Governance, 9 Asian-Pacific Law & Policy Journal (2007) 163.

8) Supreme Court, 10 May 2007, 2005 Da 4284.

9) The power to appoint directors may be more important in Korea than in Germany because Korea, unlike Germany, has a one-tier board without co-determination.

III. Historical Development of the Rules on SR Lawsuits

1. General

During the period when Korea was under Japanese control, Japanese codes were applicable in Korea. The Japanese Commercial Code ("JCC"), which contained company statutes, was one of such codes applied in Korea. Although Korea was liberated from Japan in 1945 and the government was established in 1948, it took almost two decades for Korea to enact its own commercial code, the KCC. The KCC and its provisions regarding SR lawsuits, however, were strongly influenced by the JCC.[10] The JCC of 1899[11] and the rules on SR lawsuits were in turn developed under the heavy influence of the German commercial code of the day (*Allgemeines Deutsches Handelsgesetzbuch* (ADHGB) of 1861) and its successive codes, such as the new German commercial code (*Handelsgesetzbuch* (HGB)) of 1897 and the Corporation Code (*Aktiengesetz* (AktG) of 1937). Accordingly, a short description of historical developments in Germany and Japan is in order.

2. Development in Germany

The ADHGB of 1861 had no provision on SR lawsuits. Rules on SR lawsuits were formed by court decisions and scholarly articles.[12] SR lawsuits were first recognized by a court decision in 1873[13] and introduced into the ADHGB of 1884, which provided that "a shareholder resolution in violation of law or the company contract can be rescinded by means of a lawsuit" (§ 190a ADHGB). This provision on rescission lawsuits, without much modification, was inherited by the HGB of 1897 (§§ 271–273 HGB).[14] It was around the turn of the 20th century that discussion started as to whether lawsuits for nullification of a resolution ("nullity lawsuits") should be allowed. Commentators, however, could not reach a

---

10) K. KIM, Codification in East Asia: Commercial Law, in: Wang (ed.), Codification in East Asia (Cham 2014) 61–79.
11) This code is often called the new Commercial Code in contrast to the old Commercial Code of 1898 replaced by it.
12) FLEISCHER, *supra* note 1, 101.
13) ROHG, 22 April 1873, Rep. 120/73, ROHGE 9, 273 et seq.; ROHG, 23 October 1874, Rep. 736/74, ROHGE 14, 354, 356.
14) FLEISCHER, *supra* note 1, 109–111.

consensus on how to distinguish between rescission and nullity lawsuits as grounds for a claim. It was the AktG of 1937 that formally adopted the provisions on nullity lawsuits (mm^3 195, 196 AktG),[15] completing the skeleton of German law on SR lawsuits. These rules remained largely the same in the AktG of 1965.

3. *Development in Japan*

The JCC of 1899 had a provision for SR lawsuits (Art. 163 JCC),[16] which was modelled on the ADHGB of 1884.[17] The Japanese provision differed from its German counterpart in that the ground for rescission was limited to a violation of the law or the articles of incorporation in "the procedure employed in convening a GSM or in passing a resolution,"[18] i.e., procedural defects. Although the wording of the first draft was quite similar to that of § 190a ADHGB of 1884, it was changed to cover only procedural defects later in the legislative process. The reason for this change is not entirely clear, but is presumed to be the promotion of legal certainty regarding the firm's legal relations.[19]

The JCC of 1899 was criticized for its failure to cover procedural issues involved in SR lawsuits. Under the influence of the HGB (§§ 271–273 HGB), the JCC was revised in 1911 to provide for relevant procedural issues, such as consolidation of lawsuits, exclusive jurisdiction and public notice. It was the revision of the JCC in 1938 that formed the basic structure of Japanese law on SR lawsuits. Following the AktG of 1937, the JCC of 1938 adopted a provision for a nullity lawsuit. The dividing line between rescission and nullity lawsuits, however, was drawn differently from that of German law and will be discussed in detail later. Other changes, also made in the 1938 revision, include the introduction of so-called discretionary dismissal, which will also be covered in detail later.

In 1981, the JCC formally adopted a new type of lawsuit, the lawsuit for confirming non-existence of a shareholder resolution ("non-existence lawsuit"), which had been generally recognized by the courts and commentators even in the absence of an explicit provision. The structure of Japanese law on SR lawsuits basically remains intact now under the new Company Act ("JCA"), which was enacted as an independent code in 2005.

---

15) The lawsuit for nullification was a subject for discussion at the Meeting of German Jurists in 1926.

16) Although it was indicated as a lawsuit for nullification, it was to be filed to seek rescission, not nullification of a resolution. The term was later changed to a lawsuit for rescission in the JCC of 1938.

17) S. IWAHARA, *Kabunushi Sokai Ketsugi o Arasou Sosho no Kozo* (1) [Structure of Lawsuits Attacking Resolutions of the General Shareholders Meeting (1)], 96 Hogaku Kyokai Zassi (1979) 678 (in Japanese).

18) IWAHARA, *supra* note 17, 678–679.

19) T. ISHII, *Kabunushi Sokai no Kenkyu* [A Study of the General Shareholders Meeting] (Tokyo 1958) 209 –210 (in Japanese).

4. Development in Korea

As mentioned earlier, the KCC of 1963 was drafted under the strong influence of the JCC of 1950. For some unknown reason, however, the core provisions on SR lawsuits under the KCC of 1963 were virtually identical to those of JCC of 1938. Although the KCC has been revised several times since 1963, the provisions on SR lawsuits have been changed only twice, in 1984 and in 1995. In 1984, the KCC was revised to grant an additional standing to statutory auditors to file a rescission lawsuit (Art. 376 para. 1 KCC). Also, following the JCC of 1981, the KCC explicitly adopted a non-existence lawsuit (Art. 380 para. 1 KCC). The revision of 1995 made two changes regarding SR lawsuits. First, a judgment in favor of the plaintiff was changed to have retroactive effect as well (Arts. 376 para. 2, 380, and 190 KCC). Second, violation of the articles of incorporation was changed from a ground for nullification into a ground for rescission (Art. 376 para. 1 KCC).

Table 2: History of SR Lawsuits

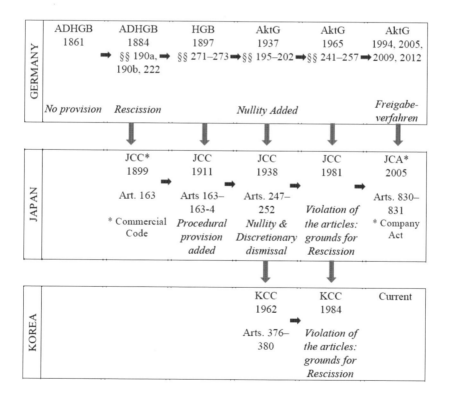

Although Korea and Japan have recently followed different routes in company law legislation, the current provisions on SR lawsuits under the KCC (Arts. 376–381 KCC) are still quite similar to those of the JCA (Arts. 830, 831 JCA). Table 2 shows the history of the SR Lawsuits in Germany, Japan, and Korea.

IV. SR Lawsuits in Korea: Law

1. General

The KCC provides for four types of SR lawsuits: (i) lawsuits to rescind a resolution ("rescission lawsuit"); (ii) lawsuits to confirm nullity of a resolution ("nullity lawsuit"); (iii) lawsuits to confirm non-existence of a resolution ("non-existence lawsuit"); and (iv) lawsuits to set aside an unfair resolution ("unfairness lawsuit"). The last category, unfairness lawsuits, is a product of a peculiar feature of the KCC. The KCC prohibits a shareholder with special interests in a resolution from voting at the GSM (Art. 368 para. 3 KCC). The interested shareholder may file a lawsuit to rescind or change the resolution involved if the following two conditions are satisfied (Art. 381 para. 1 KCC): (i) if the resolution passed without the shareholder's participation turns out to be grossly unfair to that shareholder, and (ii) the shareholder could have blocked it had the shareholder been allowed to vote. The unfairness lawsuit was originally imported from the JCC of 1938. Although Japan abolished the unfairness lawsuit in 1981, the KCC still retains it. As it is rarely used in practice,[20] we will focus on the remaining three types of SR lawsuits in this paper.

The three types of SR lawsuits can be differentiated by type of defect. Defects may be divided into procedure defects and substance defects. The former refers to defects in the procedure of the GSM, while the latter refers to defects in the substance of the resolution involved. Prior to 1995, a substance defect could justify a nullity lawsuit. Since the revision of 1995,[21] however, a substance defect involving violation of the articles of incorporation, rather than law, may generate a rescission lawsuit. On the other hand, if a procedure defect is so extreme as to render a resolution non-existent in effect, a nonexistence lawsuit may be filed.

---

20) Of 128 Supreme Court decisions issued during the ten year period from 2005 to 2004 (until October 16), none were unfairness lawsuits.
21) This revision was an attempt to reflect a change in the JCC.

2. Rescission Lawsuits

a) Grounds for Rescission

The KCC recognizes two grounds for rescinding a shareholder resolution: (i) where the procedure employed in convening a GMS or in passing a resolution is in violation of laws, decrees or the articles of incorporation, or is grossly unfair (Art. 376 para. 1 KCC; procedure defect); and (ii) where the substance of a resolution is in violation of the articles of incorporation (Art. 376 para. 1 KCC).[22] Examples of the procedure defect (ground (i)) include the absence of a board resolution calling for the convening of a GSM,[23] and the participation of a non-shareholder in the resolution.[24] An example of the ground (ii) exists when directors are appointed in excess of the number specified in the articles of incorporation.

b) Limitations

Rescission lawsuits are subject to various limitations while non-existence and nullity lawsuits are not. First, the standing is limited to shareholders, directors and statutory auditors (Art. 376 para. 1 KCC).[25] Second, a rescission lawsuit may be filed within two months from the date of the resolution (Art. 376 para. 1 KCC). Third, even when there is a procedure defect, the court can, at its discretion, dismiss the plaintiff's claim based on various factors such as the content of the resolution and the status of the corporation (Art. 379 KCC). This discretionary dismissal will be discussed later in detail.[26] Finally, although non-existence or nullity of a resolution may be asserted without necessarily requiring a lawsuit, rescission can be claimed only by way of a rescission lawsuit.

---

22) The ground (ii) was added to the grounds for a rescission lawsuit based on the view that it may be more reasonable to allow the shareholders to give up on a lawsuit as the articles of incorporation may be changed by the shareholders.
23) Supreme Court, 28 April 1987, 1986 DaKa 533.
24) Supreme Court, 23 August 1983, 1983 Do 748.
25) As discussed in detail later, the standing requirement is much more broadly construed than in Germany.
26) VI.3.c).

3. Nullity Lawsuits

a) Grounds for Nullity

Under the KCC, a ground for nullity exists when the substance of a resolution is in violation of laws or decrees. Although the ground for nullity appears quite comprehensive, such lawsuits are rarely filed in practice. Commentators generally agree that grounds for a nullity lawsuit exist in any of the following resolutions: (i) a resolution in violation of the principle of equal treatment of shareholders; (ii) a resolution on matters not within the scope of authority of the GSM; and (iii) a resolution constituting an abuse of majority power.[27]

b) Comparison with the Rescission Lawsuit

A nullity lawsuit is also subject to a set of procedural exceptions applicable to rescission lawsuit (Art. 380 KCC) as discussed later. Thus, for example, a judgment of nullity is binding not only on the plaintiff but also on third parties (Arts. 380, 190 KCC). There are some differences, however, between the two types of lawsuits.[28] First, nullity of a resolution does not necessarily need to be claimed by means of a lawsuit. Second, there is no limitation on the standing of the plaintiff in a nullity lawsuit. Any party with a legitimate interest in the resolution involved may bring a nullity lawsuit. Thus, a creditor may be entitled to sue depending on the circumstances.[29] Third, there is no two-month statute of limitation for a nullity lawsuit. Fourth, a nullity lawsuit is not subject to discretionary dismissal.

4. Non-existence Lawsuit

a) Grounds for Non-existence

A ground for non-existence lawsuit exists where a gross procedural defect effectively renders the resolution non-existent. Examples of gross procedural defects include: (i) a GSM convened by an unauthorized person in the absence of the board's resolution; and (ii) a resolution passed at a meeting mostly composed of non-shareholders.[30]

---

27) K. KIM, *Hoesabop* [Corporate Law] (Seoul 2015) 321 (in Korean).
28) The same differences exist between a non-existence lawsuit and a rescission lawsuit.
29) Supreme Court, 27 October 1980, 1979 Da 2267. Such a case, however, is rare.
30) Supreme Court, 31 January 1968, 1967 Da 2011.

b) Comparison With Nullity Lawsuits

Non-existence lawsuits are treated just like nullity lawsuits under the KCC. The special pro-visions applicable to nullity lawsuits also apply to nonexistence lawsuits (Art. 380 KCC). Also, non-existence of a resolution can be claimed not necessarily by means of a lawsuit.

c) Comparison With Rescission Lawsuits

The distinction between rescission and non-existence lawsuits is very important as rescission lawsuits are subject to various limitations while nonexistence lawsuits are not. A limitation that often becomes critical in practice is the two-month statute of limitation. So when a shareholder wants to dispute the validity of a resolution after two months, the only option available is to claim non-existence. Thus, differentiating between rescission and non-ex-istence is crucial in such cases.

As mentioned above, non-existence is recognized when the procedural defect involved is so extreme as to render the resolution non-existent in effect. The degree of seriousness of the defect required for a non-existence lawsuit, however, is not necessarily clear. A resolution will certainly be deemed nonexistent when only the minutes were prepared without actually holding a meeting, or when only non-shareholders attended the GSM. Distinction between non-existence and rescission becomes less obvious when a substantial number of share-holders have participated in the resolution. In a case where sixty percent of the shareholders were not given notice of the GSM, the Supreme Court confirmed non-existence of the resolution.[31]

5. Procedural Provisions

A corporate law dispute differs from a general private lawsuit in that the former potentially involves far more interested parties than the latter. As for lawsuits involving certain corpo-rate law matters, the KCC provides for a set of exceptions to the rules of general civil procedure. These rules are applicable to all kinds of SR lawsuits. They relate to such mat-ters as exclusive jurisdiction (Arts. 376 para. 2, 186 KCC), public notice of the lawsuit (Arts. 376 para. 2, 187 KCC), consolidation of lawsuits (Arts. 376 para. 2, 188 KCC), effect

---

31) Supreme Court, 13 July 1993, 1992 Da 40952. In a case where only forty one percent of the share-holders were not notified, non-existence was not recognized. Supreme Court, 26 January 1993, 1992 Da 11008.

of the judgment (Arts. 376(2), 190 KCC), liability of the losing plaintiff (Arts. 376 para. 2, 191 KCC) and security deposit (Art. 377 para. 1 KCC).

What attracts most attention among these exceptions may be the effect of the judgment. A judgment in favor of the plaintiff is binding not only on the plaintiff but also on third parties (Arts. 376 para. 2, 190 KCC). A judgment against the plaintiff, however, does not bind a third party. A judgment in favor of the plaintiff takes effect retrospectively as well as prospectively. Thus, a legal relationship formed on the basis of the defective resolution must be dissolved in principle as a consequence of the judgment.

V. SR Lawsuits in Korea: Reality

1. Some Statistics

We will set forth here some basic statistics about the reality of SR lawsuits in Korea. Table 3 shows the number of decisions resulting from SR lawsuits from 1990 to 2014.[32] It only covers decisions of the Supreme Court, the five high courts and the seven district courts in the Seoul metropolitan area.[33] According to Table 3, the number of such decisions has been generally on the increase, especially since 1997/1998, the beginning of the financial crisis in Korea. The increase is most conspicuous in the number of district court decisions.

Table 3: Number of SR Lawsuits (1990–2014)

Year	Supreme Court	High Courts	Seven District Courts
2014	10	5	12
2013	7	34	44
2012	8	23	64
2011	7	32	57
2010	14	30	68
2009	24	32	46
2008	9	44	52

---

32) The decisions were handpicked by means of the internal decision search system of the Supreme Court of Korea. The figures for 2014 reflect only those announced until October 16 for the Supreme Court decisions and until September 20 for lower court decisions.
33) It is presumed that a majority of SR lawsuits in Korea are taking place in these courts.

2007	14	22	58
2006	22	19	57
2005	13	33	57
2004	17	36	45
2003	11	27	37
2002	7	20	47
2001	4	21	31
2000	4	17	29
1999	5	16	28
1998	7	16	22
1997	5	11	20
1996	5	12	11
1995	3	8	13
1994	7	11	15
1993	18	7	11
1992	9	22	11
1991	7	12	13
1990	1	13	12
Total	**238**	**523**	**860**

2. Relative Importance of SR Lawsuits

SR lawsuit decisions, however, account for only a small percentage of the private law deci-sions as a whole. In 2013, they amount to less than 0.1% (10)[34] of the total private law decisions (10,576)[35] produced by the Seoul Central District Court, the largest district court in Korea. Focusing solely on the Supreme Court decisions, the percentage is slightly higher, 7 out of 4,691 decisions (0.15%).[36]

Although the number of SR lawsuit decisions still remains modest, it is far larger than that of derivative suit decisions, as illustrated by Table 4. Table 4 shows the numbers of de-rivative suit decisions and SR lawsuit decisions announced by the Seoul Central District Court during the period from 1995 to 2013. According to Table 4, SR lawsuit decisions (253) outnumber derivative suit decisions (38) by more than six times.[37]

---

34) See Table 4.
35) They include only decisions issued by a panel of judges.
36) The figure covers only those Supreme Court decisions arising from a decision made by a panel (not a single judge) of a district court.

Table 4: Number of SR Lawsuits vs. Derivative Suits in Seoul District Court (1995–2013)

Year	Derivative Suits	SR Lawsuits
1995	-	3
1996	-	6
1997	-	8
1998	1	11
1999	-	15
2000	-	13
2001	-	13
2002	4	16
2003	-	13
2004	4	14
2005	3	16
2006	6	16
2007	6	21
2008	2	23
2009	1	13
2010	3	16
2011	5	22
2012	2	21
2013	1	10
Total	38	253

3. Number of SR Lawsuits by Type of Lawsuits

Let's now move to the number of SR lawsuits by type of SR lawsuit. During the period from 2005 to 2014 (until October 16), the Supreme Court handed down 128 decisions.[38] To classify them according to case name, there were 64 non-existence cases, 34 rescission cases, and 29 nullity cases.[39] The case name is normally determined by the plaintiff filing a complaint with the court and serves to help the court and the parties identify the case.

---

37) They are more than three times as many as derivative suit decisions made by all the district courts during the same period.
38) The result obtained from a personal survey of the court database by one of the authors.
39) One case is not classified as any of three types of lawsuits.

As it is rarely changed during the litigation, it often fails to coincide with the final claim of the plaintiff. That is exactly the case with the nullity lawsuits – of those decisions classified as nullity lawsuits on the base of case name, we have found only one real nullity lawsuit.[40] The rest would properly be reclassified either as rescission or non-existence lawsuits.

4. Prevalence of Non-existence Lawsuits

According to the statistics mentioned earlier, non-existence lawsuits are commonplace in Korea, accounting for a majority of SR lawsuits. This may strike one as a little strange given that they are only allowed for extremely serious defects. This naturally raises the question of why there are so many non-existence lawsuits in Korea? We suspect that at least three factors may contribute to the prevalence of non-existence lawsuits. First, as mentioned earlier, even small firms prefer to take the corporate form in Korea. These often fail to respect formalities of the GSM, with many dispensing with cumbersome meetings altogether. Second, the identity of eligible shareholders is often in dispute because of the peculiarities of Korean corporate law. In principle, under the KCC, only those who appear as shareholders in the official list of shareholders can vote (Art. 337 para. 1 KCC). In some exceptional instances, however, the court grants voting rights to real shareholders, rather than nominal shareholders. A typical instance exists when one holds shares in the name of a different person who agrees to such an arrangement.[41] If the corporation is aware of this "borrowed-name holding" arrangement and can

easily prove it, which is often the case in a close corporation, the corporation is required not to let the nominal shareholder vote.[42] Third, as the two-month statute of limitation applies to a rescission lawsuit, the plaintiff has no other option than to file a non-existence lawsuit if the two month statute of limitation has expired. Thus the plaintiff may have a strong incentive to characterize a procedural defect as a ground for nonexistence.

5. Who Files an SR Lawsuit?

SR lawsuits are mostly filed by shareholders (or those who claim to be shareholders). Although directors and statutory auditors have standing to sue under the KCC, they rarely

---

40) Supreme Court, 24 September 2014, 2013 Da 71821 (a decision holding a resolution null and void when the resolution exceeds the scope of the court approval on calling the special GSM).
41) This borrowed-name holding has been widely practiced primarily for tax purposes.
42) Supreme Court, 8 September 1998, 1996 Da 45818.

file an SR lawsuit except in an unusual situation where they were dismissed or an opponent has appointed new directors or statutory auditors at the GSM.[43] Unlike in Germany, however, there is no evidence of professional shareholders who specialize in filing SR lawsuits in expectation of settlement payments from the firm. This may be primarily due to the fact that an SR lawsuit under Korean law is not as great a threat. We will come back to this point later.

6. Matters Disputed in SR Lawsuits

Table 5 shows the items disputed in SR lawsuits. According to Table 5, by far the most popular subject of SR lawsuits is appointment and dismissal of directors and statutory auditors. The firms involved in such lawsuits are mostly closely held corporations, *de facto* partnerships among a few business partners who serve as board members.[44] When their relationship turns sour, the majority shareholder often attempts to evict his or her business partner/s from the board.

Table 5: Items Disputed in SR Lawsuits[45]

Items disputed in SR lawsuits	Number
Appointment/Dismissal of directors/statutory auditors	56
Amendment of articles of incorporation	13
Agendas in the ordinary general meeting – ex) approval of financial statements; dividend; approval of directors'/statutory auditors' compensation	5
Reduction of legal capital/decrease of no. of shares	5
Fundamental changes – mergers; divisions; sales of assets	5
Dissolution/Liquidation/Continuation	4
Stock option	2
Total	**90**

---

43) In such situations, they are also likely to be shareholders at the same time.
44) According to the disclosures made by the Korea Stock Exchange during the one year from 15 March 2014 to 14 March 2015, there were 10 SR lawsuits involving appointment or dismissal of directors or statutory auditors in listed firms.
45) Some important cases of the Supreme Court of Korea.

VI. Comparative Analysis

1. Dividing line Between Rescission and Nullity Lawsuits

a) General

Although the rules on SR lawsuits under the KCC largely originated from German law, the division of SR lawsuits differs widely in Korea and Germany. Both jurisdictions have rescission and nullity lawsuits. As mentioned earlier, the KCC recognizes yet another category, non-existence lawsuits, while the AktG does not formally recognize a non-existence lawsuit as a separate category.[46] Functionally, however, these non-existence lawsuits do not differ greatly from nullity lawsuits. Both nullity and non-existence can be claimed by anybody, anytime, and not necessarily by means of a separate lawsuit.

On the other hand, a disgruntled shareholder in Germany may file a nullity lawsuit to attack a resolution with a certain procedural defect. A procedural defect specified as a ground for nullity under the AktG (Art. 241 no. 1 KCC) is broad enough to cover some of the gross procedural defects regarded as grounds for non-existence in Korea. Thus, this difference with respect to nonexistence lawsuits does not matter much in practice. Of much more importance is the dividing line between rescission and nullity lawsuits. While the dividing line between the two types of lawsuit is straightforward in Korea, the German situation is much more diffuse.

b) Differences

In Korea, division between revocation and nullity lawsuits depends on the nature of defect involved. While a procedural defect, except in extreme cases, constitutes a ground for rescission, a defect of substance, except for those that violate the articles of incorporation, constitutes a ground for nullity. In contrast, Germany adopts a more pragmatic approach. In Germany, violation of law or the articles of incorporation constitutes a ground for rescission in principle (§ 243 para. 1 AktG). As the AktG does not limit grounds for rescission to procedural defects, defects of substance also constitute grounds for rescission, al-

---

46) Although there is some dispute as to whether or not the category of non-existence should be recognized, Germany does not formally adopt non-existence lawsuits. J. KOCH, in: Hüffer, Aktiengesetz, 11th ed. 2014, § 241 marg. no. 3.

though the AktG specifies a set of grounds for nullity (§§ 241, 250, 253 AktG).

These statutory grounds for nullity include procedural as well as defects of substance. The procedural defects specified as grounds for nullity under the AktG are two-fold: (i) violation of law in convening the GSM ("convening defect"), and (ii) violation of law in recording the resolution ("recording defect") (§ 241 nos. 1, 2 AktG). Both of these procedural defects appear rather technical from a Korean perspective. As the KCC does not recognize recording defects, we will focus on convening defects from a comparative perspective.

Convening defects specified in the AktG are as follows: (i) absence of a lawful resolution of the management board to convene the GSM, or lack of proper authority of the person who has actually convened the GSM; (ii) failure to indicate in the notice of the GSM the firm's business name, domicile, or time and place of the GMS; (iii) absence of the notice of the GSM. These convening defects would also constitute a ground for rescission in Korea except in extreme situations. For example, if the notice was not given to a majority of shareholders, who could not attend the GSM as a consequence, the resolution passed at the GSM would be regarded as non-existent.[47]

Let us now turn to defects of substance. Unlike in Korea, a defect of substance constitutes a ground for rescission in principle in Germany (§ 243 para. 1 AktG). As an exception to this rule, the AktG provides for the following two categories of substance defects constituting ground for nullity (§ 241 nos. 3, 4 AktG): (i) when a resolution "is not compatible with the nature of the company or by its terms violates provisions which exist exclusively or primarily for the protection of the company's creditors or otherwise in the public interest", and (ii) when a resolution "by its terms is unethical".[48] Of these two categories, the first category (i) seems more relevant in practice. It is noteworthy that the law covered by the first category does not include provisions intended to protect the interests of shareholders. So in Germany, violation of the principle of shareholder equality (§ 53a AktG), abuse of majority power, and violation of the fiduciary duty of shareholders, for instance, can only generate rescission lawsuits.[49] Table 6 illustrates the division among the three types of SR lawsuits in Korea.

---

47) Supreme Court, 13 July 1993, 1992 Da 40952.
48) English translation based on Norton Rose Fulbright, German Stock Corporation Act.
49) KOCH, *supra* note 46, § 243 marg. nos. 5, 21; K. LANGENBUCHER, Aktien- und Kapitalmarktrecht (3rd ed. Munich 2015) 207.

Table 6: Grounds for Rescission vs. Nullity

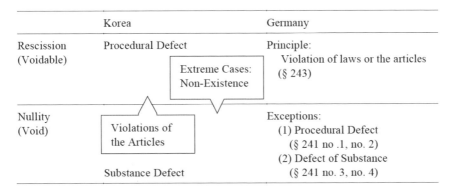

	Korea	Germany
Rescission (Voidable)	Procedural Defect	Principle: Violation of laws or the articles (§ 243)
	Extreme Cases: Non-Existence	
Nullity (Void)	Violations of the Articles	Exceptions: (1) Procedural Defect (§ 241 no .1, no. 2) (2) Defect of Substance (§ 241 no. 3, no. 4)
	Substance Defect	

c) History

From its beginning, the law diverged from its German source. When the JCC of 1899 first introduced a rescission lawsuit,[50] the Japanese legislators decided to restrict its grounds to procedural defects. It is not clear why Japanese legislators chose to deviate from the German model in that respect.[51] One reason given for limiting the ground for a rescission lawsuit to a procedural defect was the need to promote stability in corporate legal relations.[52] Nullity lawsuits were first adopted in the JCC of 1938 (Art. 252 JCC).[53] The legislators, however, did not follow the AktG of 1937 on differentiating between rescission and nullity lawsuits.

d) Two Observations

Regarding the dividing line between rescission and nullity lawsuits, we would like to make two observations, one for each country. Beginning with Korea: distinguishing nullity and revocation lawsuits based on the nature of defect as in Korea and Japan is certainly straightforward and easy to implement, although only a few countries have adopted this approach.[54] One weakness of this approach lies in its lack of flexibility: while a procedural

---

50) To be precise, it was called a lawsuit for announcing nullity under the JCC of 1899.
51) ISHII, *supra* note 19, 209.
52) ISHII, *supra* note 19, 210.
53) Even before the JCC of 1938, however, it was generally agreed that a lawsuit could be filed, as a lawsuit under the general civil procedure, to confirm the nullity of a resolution with a substance defect.
54) A notable example of such countries is Netherland. W. HALLSTEIN, Die Aktienrechte der Gegenwart (Berlin 1931) 280. The Current Dutch Civil Code (*Burgerlijk Wetboek*) §§ 2:14 (null and void resolutions); 2:15 (voidable resolutions).

defect is less problematic in terms of rigidity, it may lead to a non-existence lawsuit if it is regarded as too serious. On the other hand, rigidity may matter in the case of a defect of substance. If the defect of substance involved is not material, it may be better to treat it as a ground for rescission, which is subject to requirements such as the statute of limitation and discretionary dismissal. Such a change was already made with the 1995 reforms to the KCC that treated violation of the articles of incorporation as a ground for rescission. It may be better for Korea to follow the German approach in this respect by treating a defect of substance as a ground for rescission, if the alleged legal violation relates to the interest of minority shareholders, rather than that of third parties or the general public. Under this new approach, violation of the principle of equality of shareholders, for example, could constitute a ground for rescission, rather than nullity. As the equality principle purports to protect the interests of minority shareholders, these should have the option of not blocking a resolution that allegedly violates that principle.[55] Indeed, a lower court decision does seem to have adopted a similar logic.

The case involves a shareholder resolution to approve a statutory auditor's taking office of a conflicting position. The KCC explicitly prohibits a statutory auditor from serving concurrently as a director or employee of the firm or its subsidiary (Art. 411 KCC). This provision is generally presumed to be mandatory, meaning that it cannot be avoided by an approval of the GSM or the board of directors. On the other hand, the GSM's authority under the KCC extends only to such matters as provided in the KCC or in the articles of incorporation (Art. 361 KCC). The plaintiff asserted that a resolution approving a statutory auditor's appointment to a conflicting position was in violation of the latter provision, which constituted grounds for nullity suit. The court, however, rejected the plaintiff's claim, holding that "a resolution in violation of a certain provision is null and void only when the violated provision is material enough to be characterized as mandatory. Art. 361 KCC is not mandatory."[56]

Let us now turn to Germany. As mentioned earlier, the AktG specifies two types of procedural defects, i.e., convening and recording defects, as grounds for nullity. Although at least some of these procedural defects appear quite technical, they can, in contrast to Korea, still give rise to nullity lawsuits. Moreover, unlike the case of rescission lawsuits, the AktG does not provide for an exception based on negligibility.

---

55) This seems generally in line with what A. HUECK and T. ISHII proposed several decades ago.
56) Daejeon District Court (Cheonan Branch), 13 June 2013, 2014 KaHap 10056; translated from Korean by the authors.

Rigidity arising from the AktG's emphasis on procedure may not create much difficulty in Germany as German corporations are generally much larger than most corporations in Korea and are in a better position to comply with formalities. But even in Germany, a majority view argues that the negligibility exception should be permitted for a nullity lawsuit.[57] This may be justified from the perspective that a blocking remedy like SR lawsuits should be used sparingly – a view reflected already in the AktG as well. The AktG acknowledges that some procedural defects may be remedied with the passage of time or a sepcific event (e.g., registration) (§ 242 AktG). So, in reality, the difference between the two countries may not be as great as it first appear.

2. Effect of Pending SR Lawsuits

What is potentially more important is the difference in effect of a pending SR lawsuit in Korea and Germany. Under German law, important resolutions regarding restructuring (*Umwandlung*), share issuance and change in the articles of incorporation become effective only after the registration with the commercial registry (e.g., § 181 para. 3 AktG).[58] If a lawsuit is filed with respect to a resolution yet to be registered, the court in charge of registration may, and often does, suspend the registration until the judgment becomes finalized (§§ 381, 21 FamFG[59]). As an SR lawsuit has a potential to block implementation of the relevant shareholder resolution, a plaintiff may file an SR lawsuit merely to hinder its progress, i.e. with intent to realize its nuisance value, thus making corporations naturally concerned about a potential SR lawsuit.[60]

The German legislature attempted to ameliorate this problem by adopting a new provision in the AktG in 2005,[61] which allows the court to go ahead with the required registration even in the middle of a lawsuit (§ 246a AktG). This procedure, widely called a release procedure (*Freigabeverfahren*), was evaluated as inadequate to deter "predatory shareholders" (*räuberische Aktionäre*) from filing abusive SR lawsuits.[62] As a consequence, the provision

---

57) H. FLEISCHER, Bagatellfehler im aktienrechtlichen Beschlussmängelrecht, ZIP 2014, 149.
58) M. LUTTER, Die Eintragung anfechtbarer Hauptversammlungsbeschlüsse im Handelsregister, NJW 1969, 1873.
59) Gesetz über das Verfahren im Familiensachen und in den Angelegenheiten der freiwilligen Gerichtsbarkeit (BGBl. I 2008, 2586).
60) M. WINTER, Die Anfechtung eintragungsbedürftiger Strukturbeschlüsse de lege lata und de lege ferenda, in: Habersack et al. (eds.), Festschrift für Peter Ulmer zum 70. Geburtstag am 2. Januar 2003 (Berlin 2003) 699.
61) Gesetz zur Unternehmensintegrität und Modernisierung des Anfechtungsrechts (UMAG), 22.9.2005, BGBl. I 2005, 2802.

was again revised in 2009 to enhance the possibility of securing such a release from the court.[63]

In contrast, Korean law does not generally require notarization or registration as a prerequisite to a resolution taking effect. Korean law does require certain matters to be registered, and when such a matter is determined by a shareholder resolution, the firm is required to submit the minutes of the GSM,[64] which must in turn be notarized.[65] There is however no dispute about the resolution being effective, even without the minutes or notarization.[66] Should a plaintiff wish to suspend the effect of a particular resolution, the plaintiff may, and often does, seek a provisional injunction from the court. This injunction affords the court a broad discretion and an excuse for declining a claim deemed to be abusive is often easily found.

3. Dealing with Abusive or Inefficient Lawsuits

a) General

A powerful blocking remedy, an SR lawsuit has great potential for abuse. Indeed, the abuse of SR lawsuits and its reduction have been a hot research topic in Germany. In contrast, however, such abuse is much less serious in Korea. Even in the absence of abusive intent on the part of the plaintiff, it may be unwise as a practical matter to invalidate a resolution depending on the circumstances. In a large listed firm, it takes substantial resources to hold the GSM. Once a resolution is passed, it may serve as the base for a wide range of legal relationships involving numerous parties. Subsequent invalidation of a resolution may undermine legal certainty, and makes less sense given the firm could secure the same resolution at a new GSM. This is not to denigrate the value of SR lawsuit as a remedy for minority shareholders – only to highlight the importance of finding a balance between the two conflicting considerations: protection of minority shareholders and minimizing abuse of SR lawsuits.

In this regard, two features of Korean law on SR lawsuits are worthy of attention: (i) broad

---

62) T. BAUMS / D. GAJEK / A. KEINATH, Fortschritte bei Klagen gegen Hauptversammlungsbeschlüsse? Eine empirische Studie, ZIP 2007, 1629; RegE ARUG, BT-Drucks. 16/11642, 20, 40.
63) Regarding the impact of the revision on abusive SR lawsuits, see, e.g. T. BAUMS / F. DRINHAUSEN / A. KEINATH, Anfechtungsklagen und Freigabeverfahren. Eine empirische Studie, ZIP 2011, 2329; W. BAYER/T. HOFFMANN, "Berufskläger" in der aktuellen rechtspolitischen Diskussion, ZIP 2013, 1193.
64) Art. 91 Commercial Registration Act; Art. 130 Commercial Registration Rules.
65) Art. 66–2(1) Notary Public Act.
66) Supreme Court, 28 June 2007, 2006 Da 62362.

standing and (ii) discretionary dismissal. While broad standing purports to facilitate SR law-suits[67], discretionary dismissal serves as a means to weed out abusive or inefficient lawsuits. These two features shall be examined individually.

b) Standing requirement for plaintiff

The standing requirement for plaintiff is quite broadly interpreted in Korea to enhance access to SR lawsuits as a remedy for minority shareholders. First of all, there is no minimum shareholder requirement, meaning even a shareholder with just one share can file an SR lawsuit. That shareholder is also entitled to sue, when she voted in favor of the relevant resolution, when she failed to attend the GSM,[68] when she has bought the shares after the relevant GSM, or when she is not directly affected by the procedural defect.[69]

Historically, the JCC of 1911 imposed additional restrictions on the plaintiff shareholder following the lead of the ADHGB of 1884 (§ 190a ADHGB) and the HGB of 1897 (§ 271 para. 3 HGB). In the revision of 1938, however, the JCC eliminated these restrictions (Art. 241 JCC) and adopted discretionary dismissal (Art. 251 JCC) instead.

In contrast, the standing requirement under German law is much narrower than under Korean law. The AktG grants standing to a shareholder with a single share, but with some restrictions (§ 245 nos. 1–3 AktG). For example, the shareholder has no standing if she acquired the shares after the publication of the agenda, or if she attended the GSM but did not vote against the resolution according to the minutes.

Recently, proposals have been made to further restrain the plaintiff's standing by imposing a minimum holding requirement.[70] These proposals, which have been made to address concerns about abusive lawsuits have not been adopted, rightly in our opinion.

c) Discretionary Dismissal

The KCC has a unique and potentially powerful weapon against abusive SR lawsuits. Under the KCC, the court can dismiss the plaintiff's claim, if it finds rescission to be inappropriate, considering "the content of resolution, the current status of the firm and other relevant factors" (Art. 379 KCC). It is generally agreed that the provision applies only to

---

67) Korean law imposes relatively modest court costs on the plaintiff of an SR lawsuit, which amount to about 200 US dollars. Art 2 para. 1 no. 2, para. 4 Act on Stamp Duty for Civil Litigation and Others, Art. 15 para. 2 Rules on Stamp Duty for Civil Litigation and Others. This low court costs may serve as another factor facilitation SR lawsuits.

68) Supreme Court, 27 March 1979, 1979 Da 19.

69) Supreme Court, 12 May 1998, 1998 Da 4569.

70) FLEISCHER, *supra* note 1, 129–130.

a rescission lawsuit based on a procedural defect, although this is not explicitly stated in the KCC. The court can *ex officio* dismiss the claim at its discretion, a practice that is quite often seen in practice: of 59 district court decisions dealing with the issue (during 1994–2014), the court granted discretionary dismissal in 19 decisions.[71]

The provision on discretionary dismissal was modelled after the JCC of 1938 (Art. 251 JCC). Although the current JCA still maintains a provision on discretionary dismissal, (Art. 831 para. 2 JCA) it is different in substance from its Korean counterpart. Japanese law allows the court to grant discretionary dismissal when two requirements are satisfied: (i) materiality of a procedure defect and (ii) causal relationship between the defect and the resolution involved.

The requirements under Korean law are less strict. The critical test is whether or not rescission of the resolution is appropriate. Inappropriateness of rescission is not necessarily equated with abuse. It is instead a forwardlooking approach. So even if there is a material defect which affected the resolution, the court can still find rescission inappropriate and dismiss the suit based on "the content of resolution, the current status of the firm and other relevant factors." These relevant factors include interests of shareholders or of the firm,[72] transactional safety[73] and possibility of financial crisis.[74] Materiality of defect[75] and causal relationship between the defect and the resolution[76] are often considered, but not necessarily regarded as essential, unlike under the JCA.

The following case illustrates the forward looking attitude of the court well:[77] The case involved a corporation needing to amend its articles of incorporation to comply with government policy. Minority shareholders opposed to the firm's proposal to amend the articles of incorporation, making other unrelated demands. The firm excluded the minority shareholders from the meeting hall and passed the resolution to change the articles. The court held in favor of the firm, finding the discretionary dismissal justified even when the defect affected the result of the resolution.[78]

The permissive attitude of Korean courts toward discretionary dismissal does not seem to

---

71) Discretionary dismissal, however, is rarely disputed in the Supreme Court. We could find only four such cases.
72) Supreme Court, 8 September 1987, 1986 DaKa 2971; Supreme Court, 11 July 2003, 2001 Da 45584.
73) Supreme Court 27 April 2004, 2003 Da 29616; Supreme Court, 11 July 2003, 2001 Da 45584.
74) Seoul High Court. 8 August, 1998 Na 5267.
75) Supreme Court, 11 July 2003, 2001 Da 45584.
76) Supreme Court, 27 April, 2003 Da 29616.
77) Supreme Court, 8 September 1987, 1986 DaKa 2971.
78) For a decision following a similar line of reasoning, see Supreme Court, 10 October 2003, 2001 Da 56225.

be in accord with German law. Scholars and the court in Germany are of the view that rescission should not occur where the provision claimed to have been violated is not significant to the shareholder.[79] This socalled *Relevanztheorie* was partly adopted in the revised AktG in 2005. Under the AktG (§ 243 para. 4 AktG), a rescission lawsuit based on a procedural defect involving incorrect, incomplete or refused information can only be recognized if a reasonable shareholder would have regarded the information as essential to exercise his rights.

d) Plaintiff's Liability and Security Deposit

Another means of limiting abusive lawsuits is to hold the unsuccessful plaintiff liable for the damages. Under the KCC, a plaintiff acting in bad faith or gross negligence is liable for damages to the firm (Arts. 376 para. 2, 191 KCC), although this liability is rarely recognized in practice. Even if the firm manages to win the case, the plaintiff may be judgment proof. To protect itself against a judgment proof plaintiff, the company may request the court order the plaintiff shareholder to deposit a security with the court (Art. 377 KCC). This order requires the company to show prima facie evidence of bad faith on the part of the plaintiff. Bad faith is not necessarily interpreted as filing an ill-founded claim, but as knowingly putting the firm in difficult situation. In reality, the court rarely orders the plaintiff to deposit security.[80]

4. SR Lawsuits as a Shareholder Remedy

The SR lawsuit is a powerful shareholder remedy, enabling a shareholder to block a corporate action which the shareholder does not like. It can be an inadequate and even wasteful remedy especially when the firm can simply produce the same resolution by holding another GSM. In Korea however, SR lawsuits have been serving as a major shareholder remedy in the absence of other effective remedies. Attracting much attention from academics as well as practitioners, SR lawsuits have been widely invoked and long comprised a substantial portion of corporate law disputes in court. But with the rise of other remedies, such as derivative suits and dissenting shareholders' appraisal remedy, SR lawsuits have lost some of their luster in corporate governance.

---

79) W. ZÖLLNER, in: Kölner Kommentar zum Aktiengesetz, 1st ed. 1985, § 243 marg. no. 94; BGHZ 149, 158 (164 et seq.); 153, 32 (36 et seq.); 160, 385 (391 et seq.).
80) We could find only two such cases, including Seoul Central District Court, 24 October 2011, 2011 KaHap 3638.

This is by no means surprising given that an SR lawsuit often falls short of an adequate remedy, generating a less than ideal solutions to an underlying dispute. In many cases, an SR lawsuit arises from a dispute among partners in a closely-held firm.[81] When partners fall out with each other, the majority shareholder often tries to alienate a minority shareholder from the company's affairs. In such an awkward situation, an SR lawsuit may be an only remedy available to the minority shareholder to potentially nullify a major corporate action. This does not however resolve the underlying discord, and the plaintiff's minority status remains unchanged.

We do not mean to downplay the significance of SR lawsuits, however. Although not perfect, they are still powerful as a blocking remedy. Moreover, they constitute a convenient remedy for a disgruntled shareholder thanks to the relaxed standing requirements discussed earlier. As long as the burdensome shareholding requirements for derivative suits[82] and the strict stance of the court on such suits remain unchanged, a minority shareholder will be likely to resort to an SR lawsuit.

VII. Concluding Remarks

Unlike in Anglo-Saxon countries, SR lawsuits serve as an important shareholder remedy in practice in civil law jurisdictions such as Germany and Korea. Although originally modelled after German law, provisions on SR lawsuits under the KCC are quite different from their current counterparts under the AktG. As discussed earlier, however, the difference between the two countries, from a functional perspective, is not as substantial as it may first appear. Also, the role of SR lawsuits in corporate governance seems to be on the decline, albeit slowly, in both countries. Convergence of the practice of SR lawsuits in the two countries may be due to the widely shared view that it may not be wise from a policy perspective to block a shareholder resolution purely on procedural grounds. Such developments may be more justified if accompanied by the strengthening of other shareholder protection mechanisms such as shareholder derivative suits. If such change continues, however, the corporate governance terrain of the two countries may further approach that of Anglo-Saxon countries.

---

81) An SR lawsuit may be invoked even in a listed firm when there is a dispute between the controlling shareholder and a group of activist or employee shareholders over a major business decision.
82) One percent for non-listed firms and 0.01% for listed firms (Arts. 402, 542-6 para. 6 KCC).

Invigorating Shareholder Derivative Actions in Korea

Hyeok-Joon Rho & Kon-Sik Kim*

I. INTRODUCTION

The primary purpose of shareholder derivative actions is to compensate a corporation for losses caused by its directors' wrongdoings, thereby protecting its investors. Based on the empirical data on the shareholders' stock price gains from derivative actions, however, criticisms have been raised in the United States that the benefits of derivative actions appear to be insignificant at best.[1] But the compensation of the injured is not the only mission of derivative actions: to hold one accountable to those harmed by one's misdeeds provides a powerful disincentive for others to conduct themselves in a similar fashion.[2] From this 'general deterrent effect', the investing public can benefit, even though a particular corporation's stock price declines due to excessive litigation expenses.[3]

The positive deterrent effect on management may justify the legislature's efforts to encourage derivative actions because the economic incentive of shareholders may not be so strong as to bring a sufficient number of derivative actions. But frequent lawsuits against directors may deter not only management abuses, but also creative and efficient business activities. Thus, all countries which have a derivative action mechanism seek two goals that seem difficult to reconcile: encouraging legitimate or value-increasing lawsuits while discouraging

* Associate Professor Hyeok-Joon Rho(hjoon@snu.ac.kr) and Professor Kon-Sik Kim(konsikim@snu.ac.kr) are members of the faculty of Seoul National University School of Law. The authors would like to thank Professors Dan W. Puchniak, Alexander Loke and John M. Leitner for helpful comments and suggestions.

1) See, for example, D. Fischel and M. Bradley, 'The Role of Liability Rules and the Derivative Suit in Corporate Law: A Theoretical and Empirical Analysis' (1986) 71 *Cornell Law Review* 261 at 277-283; R. Romano, 'The Shareholder Suit: Litigation Without Foundation?', (1991) 7 *Journal of Law, Economics and Organization* 55.

2) J. Cox, 'The Social Meaning of Shareholder Suits' (1999) 65 *Brooklyn Law Review* 3 at 8.

3) J. Coffee, 'Understanding the Plaintiff's Attorney: the Implications of Economic Theory for Private Enforcement of Law Through Class and Derivative Actions' (1986) 86 *Columbia Law Review* 669 at 673.

frivolous or value-decreasing ones.

Since its enactment in 1962, the Korean Commercial Code (hereinafter, the 'KCC') has had detailed provisions on derivative actions. In reality, however, the emphasis at the time was on suppressing frivolous lawsuits, and derivative actions were rarely filed. But in the wake of the financial crisis late in the 1990s, the Korean government, mindful of the importance of investor protection in developing the capital market, revised corporate statutes to facilitate derivative actions. Derivative actions have become relatively more common since then. It does not necessarily follow, however, that the current mechanism is efficient and optimal. This essay will analyze derivative actions in Korea from the perspective of two apparently conflicting goals and will suggest a better regulation scheme. Because the Korean legislation is rooted in derivative actions of the United States, a comparison of the two countries will be made where necessary. This chapter proceeds as follows. It begins with a survey of statutes and statistics on derivative actions in Korea and a discussion of incentive structure (Section II). The next three sections explore three major issues in Korean derivative action practices: standing for plaintiffs, entrepreneurial lawyers, and regulation of frivolous actions (Sections III-V). In consideration of the importance of the courts' role in derivative action practice,[4] a brief analysis of new trends in case law will follow (Section VI). The final section provides a conclusion (Section VII).

II. BASICS OF DERIVATIVE ACTIONS: LAW AND REALITY IN KOREA

A. Background: The Shareholding Structure and the Legal Institutions for Shareholder Protection in Korea

1. The Shareholding Structure

Group affiliation and controlling shareholders are thought to be typical features of many listed corporations in East Asia.[5] In Korean *chaebols*, or large business conglomerates,

---

4) For a general explanation of the importance of judiciary role, see J. Coffee, 'The Mandatory/Enabling Balance in Corporate Law: An Essay on the Judicial Role' (1989) 89 *Columbia Law Review* 1618.
5) S. Prowse, 'The Structure of Corporate Ownership in Japan' (1992) 47 *Journal of Finance* 1121; R. La Porta et al., 'Corporate Ownership around the World' (1999) 54 *Journal of Finance* 471; S. Claessens et al., 'The Separation of Ownership and Control in East Asian Corporations' (2000) 58 *Journal of*

member firms are managed under the ultimate control of the controlling family. A recent research study shows that family ownership in *chaebol* firms, on average, amounts to 25.1 percent, compared to 53.5 percent in non-*chaebol* firms.[6] In the case of Samsung Group, the largest Korean *chaebol*, the average shareholding ratio of the controlling shareholders is estimated to be 13.52 percent, according to the annual report.[7] In Korea, it is common for the controlling family to maintain control of the whole group with substantially less than majority ownership. As is well-known, the extensive use of cross-shareholdings and stock pyramids makes it possible for the controlling family to secure control of the member firms even with modest cash flow rights.

This so-called 'Controlling Minority Shareholder'('CMS') structure can generate serious agency problems that threaten minority shareholders' interests.[8] Consequently, the Korean government adopted a unique approach to address agency problems caused by the CMS structure of *chaebol*. The Monopoly Regulation and Fair Trade Act imposed a ceiling on the equity investment by certain *chaebol*-affiliated companies. This regulation was designed to limit excessive use of reciprocal or pyramidal shareholding arrangements. In response, large *chaebol* firms strongly criticized this regulation on the grounds that it obstructed their investments. Under persistent pressure from the business community, the government ultimately abolished this controversial provision in 2009.[9] Thus, in the absence of the last statutory obstacle to the CMS structure, it has now become more important to develop legal mechanisms or remedies for protecting minority shareholders.

2. Legal Institutions for Shareholder Protection: Shareholder Direct Suits and Class Actions in Korea

In Korea, as in other countries, there are various mechanisms for investor protection: a listed company should maintain a minimum number of outside directors on its board[10]; most

---

Financial Economics 81.

6) Euysung Kim, 'The Impact of family ownership and capital structures on productivity performance of Korean Manufacturing firms: corporate governance and the 'chaebol problem' *Hill Governance Center Working Paper* No. 05-02 (2005) pp.14-15.

7) Jinho Chang and Hyun-Han Shin, 'Family Ownership and Performance in Korean Conglomerates' (2007) 15 *Pacific-Basin Fin. J.* 329 at 334. Further, they estimate that the ratio of controlling shareholders is as little as 1.14 percent, according to the combined financial statements.

8) L. Bebchuk et al., 'Stock Pyramids, Cross-Ownership and Dual Class Equity: The Mechanisms and Agency Costs of Separating Control from Cash-Flow Rights' in Randall K. Morck (ed.), *Concentrated Corporate Ownership*, National Bureau of Economic Research (USA: The University of Chicago Press, 2000).

9) Art. 10 of the Act was abolished as of March 25, 2009.

10) According to Sec. 1 of Art. 542-8 of the KCC, the number of outside directors shall be not less than 1/4 of the total number of directors in a listed company (with the exception of certain types of listed

listed companies should have full-time auditors or an audit committee[11]; and directors may be subject to criminal or administrative charges where applicable.[12] In addition to these general mechanisms, the need for effective shareholder suits has long been discussed in Korea. There are two kinds of shareholder suits: direct and derivative. Direct shareholder suits can be distinguished between individual and class suits. Like derivative suits, direct suits may be filed to seek remedy from wrongdoing directors. In contrast to derivative actions, however, they may result in direct recovery for investors because the fruits of successful litigation go to the investors, not to the corporation.

Despite their potential advantage, however, direct shareholder suits have little significance in Korea. First, under the KCC, it is unclear whether or when a shareholder may bring a 'direct' suit for her own damage. According to the jurisprudence in Korea, two types of damage to a shareholder exist: damage *directly* resulting from a director's wrongdoings (e.g., an incorrect representation by a director which leads to further investment by a shareholder); or damage to a corporation by a director's wrongdoing (e.g., a misappropriation of corporate funds) that would cast a negative effect on its stock price and eventually cause its shareholders *indirector* reflective damages. According to Korean jurisprudence, a shareholder may bring a direct suit against a director when she has suffered direct damages. However, the availability of a direct suit for *indirect* or reflective damages has been an issue for debate. The Supreme Court has weighed in on this debate by plainly denying the availability of a direct suit by a shareholder where *indirect* damage was involved.[13]

The Supreme Court seems to believe that a derivative action is more appropriate for indirect damage. There are several arguments supporting this logic: (1) if a direct suit for reflective or indirect damage is allowed, a director may be obliged to pay damages to the shareholders as well as the corporation (i.e., there will be a risk of 'double recovery'); (2) as indirect damage is derived from direct damage to the corporation, the best solution is

---

companies, like a newly-listed one or a bankrupt one). Further, a listed company whose total assets are not less than 2 trillion Korean Won shall appoint three or more outside directors, and the number of outside directors shall account for not less than half of the total directors.

11) According to Sec 1 of Art. 542-10 of the KCC, a listed company whose total assets are not less than 100 billion Korean Won shall appoint one or more full-time auditor(s). In addition, under the Art. 542-11 of the KCC, a listed company whose total assets are not less than 2 trillion Korean Won shall constitute an audit committee. An audit committee shall have three or more members, and at least 2/3 of the audit committee members shall be outside directors (Sec 2 of the Art. 415-2 of the KCC).

12) See, for example, chapter 7 (Art. 622-637) of the KCC, which stipulates criminal charges of wrongdoing directors.

13) The Supreme Court 91Da36093 (Jan. 26, 1993); The Supreme Court 2003Da29661 (Oct. 24, 2003). For details and comments on 91Da36093, see Kon-Sik Kim, 'Corporate Legal Personality and Corporate Loss in Korean Law', in *Festschrift fuer Klaus J. Hopt zum 70 Geburtstag am 24 August 2010: Unternehmen, Markt und Verantwortung* (Walter de Gruyter, 2010), pp.3115-3134.

to let the corporation recover its direct damage through a corporate or derivative suit; and (3) when the corporation or the responsible director is financially insolvent, a direct suit by the shareholders based upon indirect damage may lead to unfair results.[14]

The concern for overcompensation, however, is baseless because the defendant director will be exempt from liability to the extent that she has already paid the plaintiff shareholder. Moreover, a derivative action is not always an effective remedy for shareholders. As the actual recovery of a successful derivative action belongs to the corporation rather than to the individual shareholder, the efforts of the plaintiff shareholder—especially in a closely-held corporation in which a dominant shareholder influences the management—may not remedy the situation. Specifically, the fruits of a successful derivative action may be delivered to the hands of the dominant shareholder who is responsible for the wrongdoing in the first place.[15]

Admittedly, there are some cases in which a derivative action provides better protection for shareholders than a direct suit. However, the Supreme Court's unconditional preference for derivative actions should be reconsidered. At least in a closely-held company, where the possibility of a derivative action is not likely to discourage the directors from disloyal behaviour, a direct suit should be allowed.

Second, although a direct suit often proves effective only when it is initiated in the form of a class action, according to Korea's Securities Class Action Act (the 'SCAA'), which was adopted in December 2003, class actions are only available in a limited number of causes of action. The causes of action for damages under the SCAA are limited to the recovery of damages arising from false statements in the registration statements; business prospectuses; annual, semi-annual, and quarterly reports; insider trading; stock price manipulation; unfair trading; and poor audits by the auditor (Art. 3 of the SCAA). The Securities Class Action maybe approved by the courts if the following requirements are met: (1) the number of members in the class that is harmed is 50 persons or more, (2) the sum of the securities held by the class members is not less than 1/10,000 of the total number of the outstanding securities of the defendant corporation, (3) major questions of law or fact are common to all the class members; and (4) the class action suit is an appropriate and efficient method for the members in the class to exercise their rights or protect their interests (Art. 12 of the SCAA). The SCAA mandates that both the plaintiff and defendant appoint

---

14) It is two-fold: if the corporation is financially distressed, a direct suit against an unfaithful director by shareholders may hurt creditors because the claim against the director constitutes an asset of the corporation; if the unfaithful director is financially distressed, a direct suit may hurt other shareholders who have failed to sue.

15) See Kon-Sik Kim, above n. 13; American Law Institute, Principles of Corporate Governance: Analysis and Recommendations (Proposed Final Draft) (1992), pp. 606-607 pointed to this problem as well.

legal counsel to represent them in the suit(Sec. 1 of Art. 5 of the SCAA). A person who has been engaged in three or more securities class actions as a lead plaintiff or a legal counsel during the preceding three years may not become a lead plaintiff or a legal counsel, unless the courts determine otherwise (Sec. 3 of Art. 11 of the SCAA).

The SCAA came into effect on January 1, 2005,[16] but only one securities class action has been filed and approved by the court as of May 2010.[17] Even that action was settled soon after it was filed, and no class action has yet been tried on its merit. Why? While introducing a US-style class action remedy, the Korean government added several provisions for the purpose of restricting frivolous or abusive actions; the shareholding requirement in a class and the limitation of causes of action are not found even in the PSLTRA in the United States. Further, the limitation on the number of class actions which the same legal counsel can handle has an obvious chilling effect on the emergence of specialized class actions attorneys and law firms. The cost of litigating a class action is also believed to be substantial.[18] The rareness of class actions in Korea seems attributable to such excessive restrictions, and the situation may remain unchanged under current provisions in the SCAA.

As shown above, shareholder protection mechanisms other than derivative actions, that is, shareholder direct suits (individual and class), are given a limited role to play in Korea. Thus, for the protection of minority shareholders, the role of shareholder derivative action is crucial.

B. Overview of the Structure of a Derivative Action

According to Art. 403 of the KCC, a derivative action is a lawsuit brought on behalf of a corporation by its shareholder(s) against the director(s) or auditor(s) of the corporation.[19] While a derivative action may be brought against the auditor as well as the director, this

---

16) However, for companies whose total assets, as of the end of the fiscal year immediately prior to January 1, 2005, amount to less than 2 trillion Korean Won, the law applied starting on January 1, 2007 (with the exception of damages arising out of stock price manipulation and insider trading).

17) The Suwon District Court 2009 KaHap 8829. In this case, the lead plaintiffs (the Seoul Investment Co. et al.) sought 2,026,208,915 Won (or about US$ 1.85 million) against the defendants (Jinsung TEC and its directors) on the grounds that the defendant company hid losses from option investments and made a false disclosure in the quarterly report. The class action was filed on April 13, 2009 and approved by the court in Jan. 2010. A settlement was made in May 2010, according to which the defendant company was to pay 1,371,696,201 Won and distribute 199,664 shares to the class members.

18) Ok-Rial Song, 'Improving Corporate Governance Through Litigation: Derivative Suits and Class Actions in Korea', in H. Kanda, Kon-Sik Kim and C. Milhaupt (ed.), *Transforming Corporate Governance in East Asia*(New York: Routledge, 2008), p.103.

19) For a comparative analysis on derivative actions under the United States, Japanese, and Korean statutes, see Ok-Rial Song, *ibid.*, at pp.94-98.

chapter focuses on the responsibility of directors because in reality, plaintiff shareholders target directors in most cases. In a derivative action, the plaintiff shareholders exercise the rights of the corporation. In principle, the right of a corporation should be exercised by the management, specifically by the board or the CEO. Under the KCC, however, the corporation's right to sue its director is to be exercised by the auditors or audit committee. Further, in consideration of situations in which even the auditors or the audit committee hesitate to sue a fellow director with whom they have worked on the board, the lawmakers adopted the derivative action. Thus, the shareholders (i.e., the class most seriously affected by breach of fiduciary duties) are provided with a strong monitoring tool over the directors. How can a shareholder exercise this power?

The basic requirements and procedure under the current KCC for bringing a derivative action are as follows:[20] (1) when a corporation fails to sue a wrongdoing director, a shareholder (or group of shareholders) with a minimum amount of shares (as stipulated by the KCC) may bring a derivative action on behalf of the corporation; (2) before bringing a derivative action, the plaintiff shareholder must demand that the corporation (the auditors or the audit committee, to be more specific) initiates the action in question on its own; (3) the corporation, not the plaintiff shareholder, receives any remedy that flows from the successful derivative action; and (4) the plaintiff shareholder in a successful derivative action is entitled to reimbursement for a reasonable amount of their litigation and other expenses.[21]

C. Some Statistics and Features

Even though the derivative action provisions were adopted in the KCC over forty years ago, one can find only a limited number of derivative actions in Korea. According to the statistics shown in the appendix, only around fifty-five cases have been brought to the district courts since the well-known 'Korea First Bank Case'.[22] In twenty-one cases, the shareholder plaintiffs prevailed fully or partially. In twenty-five cases, the claims were rejected or dis-

---

20) Art. 403 of the KCC.
21) Art. 405 of the KCC.
22) This was the first lawsuit of its kind in Korea, in which the defendant directors were found to be responsible in a derivative action. The Supreme Court 2000Da9086 (Mar. 15, 2002); The Seoul High Court 98Na45982 (Jan. 4, 2000); The Seoul District Court 97GaHap39907 (Jul. 24, 1998). For details of this case, see Kon-Sik Kim & Joongi Kim, 'Revamping Fiduciary Duties in Korea: Does Law Matter in Corporate Governance?', in C. Milhaupt (ed), *Global Markets, Domestic Institutions: Corporate Law and Governance in a New Era of Cross-Border Deals*, (New York: Columbia University Press, 2003), pp. 389-391.

missed by the courts.[23] In nine cases, the lawsuits are still pending or the plaintiff has withdrawn their derivative action. Settlements between directors and plaintiff shareholders are quite rare, which is a phenomenon quite different from US practice. Although D&O insurance is often provided to directors of larger listed firms, unlike the United States, its role has so far been insignificant in Korea.

The type of corporation involved in a derivative action varies. About twenty-seven derivative actions were filed on behalf of unlisted companies, as compared to twenty-eight actions for listed companies. Those listed companies include firms belonging to big conglomerates commonly called *chaebol*, such as Samsung, LG, and Hyundai Motors.

Three features of derivative action practice in Korea are noteworthy. First, as the statistics above show, derivative actions in Korea are not nearly as common as in the United States and Japan. The number of lawsuits does not always reflect the actual level of corporate governance enforcement because a derivative action may not be brought if the firm is well-managed. However, unremitting corporate scandals show that corporate governance is nonetheless far from adequate in Korea. To explain the infrequency of derivative actions, some commentators have pointed to Korea's small number of lawyers, judicial unfamiliarity with derivative suits, and the affiliation of many institutional investors with *chaebols*.[24] Although these factors may sound persuasive, this paper will focus on the incentive structure of the current system, which appears to discourage legitimate lawsuits as well as abusive ones.

Second, one particular NGO has played a dominant role in initiating derivative actions in Korea. Many derivative actions have been brought by a single NGO, the Solidarity for Economic Reform (hereinafter, the 'SER'),[25] which has initiated nine derivative actions.[26] Institutional investors are not keen on being active players. Faced with wrongdoing directors, they prefer selling their shares to filing lawsuits against the directors. Also, many of the institutional investors are affiliated with business groups and may well hesitate to cause a stir by suing directors of other firms, since such an action may invite a similar attack on

---

23) Under civil litigation jurisprudence in Korea, only the cases satisfying the prerequisites for trial (such as appropriate jurisdiction, competence of parties, etc.) may be tried on their merits; otherwise, they will be dismissed with a brief judgment.

24) B. Black et al., Shareholder Suits and Outside Director Liability: the Case of Korea, *ECGI Working Paper* No. 47/2005 (2005), p.22; C. Milhaupt, 'Nonprofit Organizations as Investor Protection: Economic Theory and Evidence from East Asia', (2004) 29 *Yale Journal of International Law* 169 at 188-191.

25) For the role of nonprofit organizations, see C. Milhaupt, *ibid.* The SER succeeded a department on economic reform in the People's Solidarity for a Participatory Democracy in 2006.

26) The list of the corporations includes the Korea First Bank, Samsung Electronics Co., Ltd., LG Corp., Cheil Industries, Inc., Daesang Corp., Hyundai Motor Company, and Shinsegae Corp.

managers of their affiliate firms. Public institutional investors are not active, either. For example, the National Pension Fund, a giant public fund for social security in Korea that invested around 50 trillion Won (or about US$45 billion[27])) in stocks as of 2009, is also passive in filing lawsuits. Although the role of SER should not be slighted, it tends to focus on big corporations due to its limited resources. Thus, for smaller corporations, where a risk of management abuse may be more serious, a derivative action still remains a foreign idea.

Third, derivative actions frequently follow criminal prosecutions or bankruptcy proceedings. This is because it is difficult for the plaintiff shareholders to secure evidence through statutory procedures.

These features maybe explained through an examination of the incentive structure that plaintiff shareholders face when deciding whether to pursue a derivative action. In theory, a shareholder will compare the expected benefits and costs before bringing a derivative action.[28]) Where the chance of winning becomes higher, more lawsuits will be filed. In the absence of a US-style discovery process, the verification of facts in a criminal or bankruptcy proceeding would increase the chances of winning a derivative action. Thus, derivative actions are often filed after a director has been convicted in a criminal proceeding or the corporation has gone bankrupt.

Also, the more shares an investor holds the greater the incentive to pursue corporate claims against a wrongdoing director. It is highly unusual, however, for a majority shareholder to start a derivative action[29]) and institutional investors in Korea have been reluctant to file derivative actions—which helps account for the scarcity of shareholder suits. Furthermore, a unique judicial doctrine on limiting directors' liability developed by the Korean courts

---

27) For the past five years, 1 Dollar was worth between 900 and 1,500 Korean Won in general. Hereinafter, for the sake of convenience, the exchange rate is assumed as 1 Dollar=1,100 Korean Won.

28) The expected benefit would be 'α x (p x M),'where 'α,' 'p,' and 'M' refer to chances of winning, his/her shareholding ratio, and the amount of corporate recovery, respectively. The expected cost would be 'E $-\alpha$ x R,'where 'E' and 'R' refer to the litigation expenses and the reimbursed litigation expenses. Thus, a derivative action would be filed under the condition 'α x (p x M) E $-\alpha$ x R.'Admittedly, this formula is too simple, leaving out such immeasurable elements as cultural and psychological factors that might also influence derivative action practices. But it sheds some light on what elements should be considered in designing an ideal system for derivative actions. In addition, the approach emphasizing cultural elements or values faces strong criticisms. See M. West, 'The Pricing of Shareholder Derivative Actions in Japan and the United States', (1994) 88 *Northwestern University Law Review* 1436 at 1439-1441; M. Ramseyer, 'Takeovers in Japan: Opportunism, Ideology and Corporate Control', (1987) 35 *UCLA Law Review* at 39-40.

29) S/he is likely to be connected with the directors. Even if a majority shareholder is not connected with the directors, s/he normally can use his/her power to replace the wrongdoing directors and/or have the company sue.

may negatively impact the incentive for shareholders to pursue a derivative action by reducing the potential economic benefits of derivative litigation.

III. STANDING FOR PLAINTIFFS

A. General Shareholding Requirement Under the KCC

Only a shareholder of the corporation is authorized to serve as the plaintiff in a derivative action. Unlike in the United States and in Japan, the KCC does not allow every shareholder to sue; instead, it requires the plaintiff to hold a certain number of shares. According to the pre-1998 KCC, the statutory minimum was 5 percent of the outstanding shares. Under this prohibitively high threshold requirement, no derivative action was brought. After the financial crisis, Korea substantially lowered the minimum shareholding ratio, first for listed companies, then for non-listed companies.[30] The KCC has not given up the minimum shareholding requirement, although the statutory minimum differs depending on whether the corporation is listed or not.[31] In an unlisted company, a shareholder (or shareholders) holding 1 percent or more of the outstanding shares may bring a derivative action (Sec. 1 of Art. 403 of the KCC). For a listed company, however, the statutory minimum is as low as 0.01 percent, but the plaintiff needs to have held the shares for at least the last six months (Sec. 6 of Art. 542-6 of the KCC). By putting a special provision in the articles of incorporation, the KCC allows a listed company to reduce the minimum shareholding ratio or period (Sec. 7 of Art. 542-6 of the KCC).

The minimum shareholding requirement may not be as strict as it first appears. Once the plaintiff meets the statutory threshold, the sale of her shares afterwards will not jeopardize her standing as long as she holds at least one share (Sec. 5 of Art. 403). Moreover, unlike in US law, the KCC does not have a contemporaneous share ownership requirement. A

---

30) In 1998, the KCC reduced the shareholding requirement from 5 percent to 1 percent (Sec. 1 of the Art.). For listed companies, the Securities and Exchange Act was revised in 1997 to reduce the shareholding requirement from 5 percent to 1 percent (0.5 percent for large listed companies); in Feb. 1998 to 0.05 percent; and in May 1998 to 0.01 percent. The 0.01 percent threshold for listed companies was codified in Art. 542-6 of the KCC after the repeal of the Securities and Exchange Act.

31) Under Sec. 1 of Art. 542-2, a listed company is defined as a company whose shares are traded in a securities market stipulated in the Presidential Decree (e.g., the Korea Exchange).

shareholder who has purchased the shares at a decreased price after the wrongdoing of directors may also file a derivative action in Korea. However, one cannot ignore the chilling effect of the minimum shareholding requirement. Without the help of institutional investors, it is very difficult, if not impossible, to bring a derivative action.[32] It is by no means clear that the minimum shareholding requirement has anything to do with the merit of a lawsuit. Given the importance of the deterrent effect of derivative actions, Korea needs to reconsider the minimum shareholding requirement.

What if a qualified plaintiff shareholder wants to sell all or part of their shares in the midst of a derivative action? Under an amendment made to the KCC in 1998(Sec. 5 of Art. 403), the sale of shares by the plaintiff does not bar them from continuing to pursue a derivative action as long as the plaintiff still owns at least one share. However, this amendment has been criticised on the basis that a plaintiff who no longer has a significant financial interests in the corporation is not the right person to maintain a derivate action. This being said, the minimum shareholding requirement itself is unreasonable and, from the perspective of encouraging legitimate monitoring of corporate management by shareholders, it seems absurd to reject a derivative action merely because the plaintiff has sold some of their shares. Furthermore, the constitutional property rights of the plaintiff shareholder, which include free disposal of their belongings, would be better protected by allowing them to sell all or part of their shares whenever they desire.

Does a derivative action become automatically invalid when the plaintiff shareholder has sold all of their shares? While the KCC does not address such a situation, a new shareholder who has purchased the shares shall succeed the status of the plaintiff in the derivative action. In a case where a shareholder plaintiff had filed a lawsuit for cancellation of the new share issuance and then sold all of his shares, the Supreme Court approved the succession of litigation by the new shareholder.[33]

---

32) Joongi Kim, 'Recent Amendments to the Korean Commercial Code and Their Effects on International Competition', (2000) 21 *University of Pennsylvania Journal of International Economic Law* 273 at 282.
33) The Supreme Court 2000Da42786 (Feb. 26, 2003).

B. Double Derivative Action

1. Concept of a Double Derivative Action and a Recent Supreme Court Case

A double derivative action means a derivative action brought by shareholders of the parent company against directors of its subsidiary. As opposed to a single or normal derivative action, it is the shareholder's (i.e., parent's) shareholder that initiates the derivative action. Whether the parent company's shareholders also have standing in a derivative action against the subsidiary's directors has long been discussed in Korea and was finally dealt with by the Supreme Court.

In that case, shareholders of the parent company (corporation 'A') brought a derivative action on behalf of its subsidiary (corporation 'B'). Around 80.55 percent of outstanding shares in B were held by A. The defendant, B's representative director accused of misappropriation, argued that the plaintiffs failed to satisfy the standing requirement because they were not the shareholders of B.[34]

The Seoul High Court[35] held in favour of the concept of the double derivative action, citing several rationales. First, the possibility of double derivative actions would provide a positive *ex ante* deterrent against wrongdoing by directors (e.g., to reduce disloyal behaviour on the part of directors of subsidiaries). Second, damages incurred by a subsidiary are also detrimental to its parent. Third, alternatives to double derivative actions (e.g., a derivative action against directors of the parent corporation for their failure to prevent the unfaithful behaviour of the directors of the subsidiary or to sue the directors of the subsidiary directly) are inadequate.

The decision, however, was overruled by the Supreme Court.[36] Interpreting narrowly and strictly the provisions of the KCC, the Supreme Court stated that the plaintiff(s) in a derivative action should be shareholders of the corporation involved, not shareholders of its parent corporation. The Court added that although the parent company controls the subsidiary, the parent and subsidiary should not be regarded as a single entity.

---

34) For details of this case, see Kon-Sik Kim, 'The Role of Judges in Corporate Governance: The Korean Experience', in H. Kanda, Kon-Sik Kim and C. Milhaupt (2008), above, n.18, pp. 126-128.
35) The Seoul High Court 2002Na13746 (Aug. 22, 2003).
36) The Supreme Court 2003Da49221 (Set. 23, 2004).

2. Analysis: Why Are Double Derivative Actions Necessary in Korea?

According to the Supreme Court decision, the double derivative action is not permitted in Korea. However, recently attempts have been made by some members of the Ministry of Justice to provide for double derivative actions by revising the KCC. In 2006, the Ministry of Justice released a draft KCC reform bill that covered a wide range of issues.[37] It included a new provision (Art. 406-2) explicitly allowing double derivative actions which stated that 'shareholder(s) holding one percent or more of a corporation may file a derivative action to seek the liability of directors of its subsidiary company.' However, this provision was later deleted from the government's final reform bill (hereinafter, the 'Reform Bill') delivered to the National Assembly in 2007.[38] The Ministry of Justice seemed to have succumbed to pressure from the business community.

Double derivative actions should be allowed. As was properly pointed out by the Seoul High Court above, the possibility of bringing a double derivative action has *ex ante* positive deterrent effects for improving corporate governance. Moreover, under the current legal regime, the interests of shareholders in parent companies are inadequately protected. In theory, they may file a lawsuit against the parent's directors for their failure to sue the subsidiary's directors.[39] However, it would be extremely difficult to succeed in such a cause of action.[40] Since the parent's directors may well try to justify their decision not to sue based on their 'business judgment', it would be very difficult to prove that such a failure to act amounted to negligence or intentional wrongdoing on the part of the parent's directors.

Double derivative actions are particularly crucial in circumstances where the holding company structure is widely adopted in the business community, as in Korea. The government's failure to adopt double derivative actions in the Reform Bill shows that the government is still not sufficiently free from the pressure of big businesses.

---

37) Ministry of Justice Doc. No. 2006-106 (dated on Oct. 4, 2006).
38) The KCC Reform Bill No. 177463 (dated on Sep. 21, 2007).
39) The Seoul District Court Southern Branch Decision 2003GaHap1749 (Sep. 19, 2003) acknowledged the possibility of such lawsuits.
40) In the decision No. 2003GaHap1749, the court eventually dismissed the claim by mentioning that the plaintiff failed to prove misconduct by directors.

IV. ENTREPRENEURIAL LAWYERS: FEES AND INCENTIVES

A. Lack of Shareholders' Incentives and the Role of Entrepreneurial Lawyers in Derivative Actions

Even when a minority shareholder has enough shares to meet the minimum shareholder requirement to file a derivative action, they may choose not to pursue a legitimate claim because of an absence of economic incentives. Indeed, normally shareholders have little economic incentive to file a derivative action because if they prevail the recovery will go to the corporation (and not to them personally). The shareholder will benefit from the recovery only on a pro-rata basis according to the value of their shares. One can imagine only two potential candidates who would likely have a sufficient economic motive to initiative in a derivative action: institutional investors and professional lawyers. It is true that institutional investors with sizable holdings may overcome collective action problems. However, as mentioned earlier, institutional investors in Korea have so far been rather passive, opting to stick to the 'Wall Street rule'. The more promising candidates seem to be plaintiff lawyers who are seeking attorney fees in a successful derivative action. The aggressive practices of entrepreneurial lawyers in shareholder lawsuits in the United States are now well-known. Strengthening the incentives of such professional lawyers to push forward with derivative actions, however, may prove risky because their interests are not always the same as those of shareholders. Unlike shareholders, entrepreneurial lawyers may pay little attention to the firm's long-term value when they make a decision to sue and to settle; their interests lie insecuring generous attorney fees.[41] As such, although there is the inherent risk of over incentivising lawyers, offering sufficient incentives to the lawyers is an indispensable component of reforming derivative actions in Korea.

The role of entrepreneurial lawyers in Korea can be approached from two angles: (1) who will pay the plaintiff lawyers; and (2) how much will the plaintiff lawyers be paid? Litigation expense in Korea is a broad concept which includes stamp taxes paid at the time of filing a lawsuit and the security required by the court.[42] However, some of these ex-

---

41) See J. Coffee (1986), above, n. 3, p.680.

42) The litigation expenses over a derivative action generally include stamp taxes (Sec. 4 of Art.2 of the Act on the Stamps Attached for Civil Litigation, etc.; Art. 15 of the Supreme Court Rule on the Stamps Attached for Civil Litigation, etc.) and the security ordered by the court (Sec. 7 of Art. 403 of the KCC,

penses—such as the stamp taxes—are merely nominal. For the sake of simplicity, the term 'litigation expenses' is employed here to refer solely to attorney fees. For public-minded lawyers affiliated with an NGO like SER, who are pursuing their own social or political agendas, attorney fees may not be their primary concern. As such, activist lawyers are limited in number and it may not be wise to rely solely on such lawyers to bring derivative actions. It is thus crucial to provide entrepreneurial lawyers with an appropriate incentive in the form of competitive attorney fees.

B. Who Will Pay the Plaintiff's Lawyers?

Under the general principle of Korean civil litigation, the losing party is obliged to pay the other party's litigation expenses.[43] However, the loser does not have to pay all of the attorney fees that the other party actually paid. A special rule promulgated by the Supreme Court (i.e., the Supreme Court Rule on the Range of Attorney Fees in Calculating Litigation Expenses—hereinafter the 'Attorney Fees Rule'), stipulates the amount of the attorney fees to be paid by the loser.[44] The Attorney Fees Rule calculates the fee based on the amount pursued in the lawsuit.[45] The purpose of the rule is to protect the loser from excessive attorney fees.

In addition to this general principle, the KCC provides a special provision on reimbursement for successful plaintiff shareholders. Section1 of Art. 405 of the KCC states that '⋯ the plaintiff shareholder who has won a derivative action shall be entitled to reimbursement for a reasonable amount of litigation expenses and other expenses that were paid in connection with the action.' This provision is based on the idea that the litigation expense for a successful derivative action shall be shared by all the shareholders.[46] Under this provision, it is clear that a corporation is obliged to reimburse only if the plaintiff shareholder has won.[47] Whereas the general loser-pay rule is concerned with reimbursement from the defendant director, this special provision provides for reimbursement from the corporation itself.

The legislation assumes that the shareholder plaintiff, *after* having paid fees to their lawyer,

---

Art. 176 of the KCC).

43) Art. 98 of the Civil Procedure Act.

44) Sec. 1 of Art 109 of the Civil Procedure Act.

45) Art. 3 of the Attorney Fees Rule.

46) See Ok-Rial Song, above, n. 18, p. 97.

47) According to Sec. 2 of Art. 405, the corporation which has paid its reimbursement obligation is entitled to re-reimbursement from the defendant director.

seeks reimbursement from the corporation or defendant director. However, according to the practice that has evolved in derivative litigation, this is not what actually happens. To the contrary, 'reimbursement' occurs *prior to* the plaintiff's lawyer being paid. In other words, the plaintiff shareholder merely transfers the 'reimbursement' payment from the company or defendant director to their lawyer after they have received it.

Such a practice was acknowledged by a District Court decision. The issue in that case involved the interpretation of the specific language used in Sec. 1 of Art. 405 above: '... litigation expenses and other expenses *that were paid* in connection with the action'[emphasis added]. The literal interpretation of the words 'that were paid' would require actual payment of attorney fees by the plaintiff shareholder as a prerequisite for reimbursement. However, as long as the amount of attorney fees can be determined, there is no reason to force the plaintiff shareholder to pay attorney fees prior to seeking reimbursement. To force the successful plaintiff to pay attorney fees from their own funds and then to reimburse themis just a meaningless repetition of process. The District Court made it clear that the actual payment of attorney fees is not be a prerequisite for reimbursement.[48]

Another issue related to the reimbursement of the shareholder plaintiff's legal expenses involves whether the plaintiff's lawyer may directly file a lawsuit against the corporation or the defendant director for their attorney's fees. No case law exists on this question. Due to the fact that it is the lawyer who has an ultimate interest in the shareholder plaintiff's attorney fees, the plaintiff's lawyer should be allowed to demand that the corporation or defendant director pay such fees.

In derivative actions, the plaintiff shareholder's lawyer normally works for a nominal retainer combined with a large contingency fee and they expect to get paid by the corporation or defendant director.[49] As such, if the derivative action turns out to be unsuccessful the plaintiff shareholder's lawyer normally gets nothing. Even when they win, their reward may not be as generous as in the United States. In a successful derivative action, the plaintiff's lawyer will get their fees from the defendant director in accordance with the Attorney Fees Rule and/or from the corporation under Sec. 1 of Art. 405 of the KCC. If the director

---

48) The Seoul Central District Court 2007 GaHap 43745 (Jun. 20, 2008). The case was based upon Sec. 6 of Art. 191-13 of the Securities and Exchange Act, but the same jurisprudence on the timing of reimbursement would be applied where Sec. 1 of Art. 405 of the KCC is concerned.

49) The non-refundable retainer for general civil litigations is around 5 million Won (or about US$ 4,500) in Korea. While the fee arrangements for the 55 derivative actions are not publicly available, it is known that the lawyers commenced a derivative action with a retainer of less than 3 million Won in many cases. For example, in the derivative action against directors of Samsung Electronics, the law firm named 'Si-Min' undertook the lawsuit without any retainer (refer to 2007GaHap43745 case above).

has no substantial assets, the claim for attorney fees will be of little value. The insolvency of directors has so far not been a serious problem in practice and is unlikely to become one if D&O insurance becomes more widely available. More significantly in terms of the lawyer's incentive, is the reimbursement from the corporation. Under the current law, there are some obstacles to full reimbursement of attorney fees, which will be addressed in the next section.

C. How Much Will Plaintiff Lawyers Be Paid?

Even if the plaintiff prevails in a derivative action, in at least two cases, the plaintiff's lawyers may not fully receive their legal fees: (1) when there is a limitation on the amount of contingency fees; and (2) when there is a limitation on the amount of director's liability. In such cases, the lawyer's economic gain from the lawsuit will be reduced, and the prospect of reduced economic gains will negatively affect the incentive of entrepreneurial lawyers in general. What are the rationales behind these limitations, and what are the possible alternatives to them?

1. Limitation on Contingency Fees

In most derivative actions, the strongest incentive for plaintiff lawyers is to secure large contingency fees.[50] Although there is no Supreme Court case on contingency fees in a derivative action, there exists a lower court case on this issue.[51] The case was filed by shareholders of Samsung Electronics Co., Ltd. (hereinafter, 'Samsung Electronics') against Samsung Electronics. The plaintiff shareholders had succeeded in a derivative action against directors of Samsung Electronics. Subsequently, they filed another lawsuit seeking reimbursement for attorney fees from the corporation in accordance with the agreement between the plaintiff shareholders and their lawyer (hereinafter, the 'Agreement'). According to the Agreement, the plaintiff shareholders were obliged to pay 5 percent of the amount recovered in the derivative action. This obligation was due, according to the Agreement, when the plaintiff shareholders were reimbursed by Samsung Electronics.

As a result of the Court in the derivative action having ordered the directors to pay

---

50) The contingency fee arrangement would become more important for lawyers because in deciding fee structure for derivative actions, plaintiffs seem to prefer small retainers combined with a large contingency fee. The same trend has appeared in Japan. See M. West, 'Why Shareholders Sue: The Evidence from Japan', (2001) 30 *Journal of Legal Studies* 351 at 368-369.

51) The Seoul Central District Court 2007GaHap43745 (Jun. 20, 2008).

24,109,245,204Won (or about US$ 22million) to Samsung Electronics,[52] the shareholder plaintiffs claimed 1,205,462,260Won (or about US$ 1.1million), which was 5 percent of the corporate recovery, to pay the attorney fees in accordance with the Agreement. The Seoul Central District Court explicitly stated that the 'attorney fees in a derivative action reimbursable under Sec. 6 of Art. 191-13 of the Securities Exchange Act shall be objectively decided in consideration of various factors related to the appropriateness of attorney fees. Starting from the amount already agreed upon between the lawyer and the plaintiff shareholders, the Court would also consider the amount of the claim, the number of parties, the difficulties of the case, the complexity of the process, preliminary measures taken before the commencement of the lawsuit and the amount of corporate recovery.' According to this principle, the Court concluded that the contingency fee of 5 percent in the Agreement was excessive and that only 720 million Won (or about US$ 650,000), which was 3 percent of the corporate recovery, would be fair and reasonable. Samsung Electronics appealed this decision, but the case was later settled.[53]

The quantum of permissible contingency fees is a controversial issue. One may argue that the contingency fee would be economically justified as long as the fee is not more than the corporate recovery.[54] In this view, a contingency fee agreement that distributes to a lawyer a portion of the net gain from the derivative action, as in the Agreement in the case above, should be upheld. However, excessive attorney fees may lead to more frivolous derivative actions initiated just for the benefit of entrepreneurial lawyers. Further, under the black letter law in Korea, a contingency fee agreement is subject to court review. Thus, why should contingency fee agreements in the context of derivative actions be free from court intervention, while those in other actions (i.e., a lawsuit by the corporation against its director) are subject to court review?

A lawyer specializing in derivative actions might be compared to a bounty hunter. The idea of law enforcement by private individuals seeking their own profits, however, still seems foreign to Koreans. Thus, entrepreneurial lawyers should take into account the possibility of the contingency fee arrangement being changed by the court. This possibility will negatively affect lawyer incentives. Here, we want to emphasize one point. The court should

---

52) The Supreme Court 2003Da69638 (Oct. 28, 2005).
53) The case no. 2008Na66469 at the Seoul High Court was settled on Dec. 16, 2009.
54) See R. Kraakman et al., 'When Are Shareholder Suits in Shareholder Interests', (1994) 82 *The Georgetown Law Journal* 1733 at 1766. ('⋯ plaintiff's attorneys should receive fee awards only if positive corporate value remains after subtracting all litigation costs from adjusted corporate recoveries⋯ courts could set the size of fees either as a percentage of the adjusted corporate recovery or, following the lodestar formula, as a reasonable return on plaintiff's investment in litigation').

acknowledge the unique nature of derivative actions in deciding on the contingency fee issue. Compared with other types of litigation, the plaintiff lawyers in a derivative action play a central role,[55] orchestrating the whole procedure from the beginning to the end. They are normally not paid until after the successful resolution of the derivative action, which may well take several years. Without their active involvement, derivative actions can hardly achieve their prescribed function of disciplining wrongdoing directors. Thus, the court needs to be more open to more generous fee agreements when reviewing contingency fees in derivative actions.

2. Limitation of Directors' Liability

The magnitude of the contingency fee is usually based upon the amount finally approved by the courts. Thus, if the amount of directors' liability is reduced, the amount of attorney contingency fees will be reduced as well, and the lawyer's incentive will be weakened. The new KCC of 2011 allows companies to limit directors' liability in their articles of incorporation.[56] If companies, as expected, choose to adopt such a provision in their articles, entrepreneurial lawyers will likely become much more hesitant to initiate a derivative action.

More importantly, the courts have recently developed a unique theory to limit the liability of directors.[57] At present, the court often exercises its discretion in reducing the liability of directors substantially (by as high as 80 percent in one case) based on mitigating factors such as the prior contribution of the defendant director to the firm's success. The court justifies its wide discretion based on the age-old good faith principle under the Civil Code. In the presence of Sec. 1 of Art. 400, which allows partial or full exemption of directors' liability only with the unanimous consent of the shareholders, such an extension of the good faith principle is questionable. Moreover, the court has been inconsistent and unpredictable in exercising its new power. For example, in one decision, the Court reduced the liability of directors even where the directors' personal gains from their misconduct were far more than the harm done to the corporation.[58]

---

55) Yoon, Young-Shin, 'Attorney's Fees in the Shareholder's Derivative Suit (*in Korean*)', (2001) *Commercial Law Review* 195 at 209.

56) According to Sec. 2 of Art. 400 of the new KCC of 2011, a corporation may set a limit of director's liability, by the articles of incorporation, equivalent to six times the annual salary of a director (three times in the case of an outside director). The limitation would not apply when a director's actions, intentionally or with gross negligence, have resulted in damage to the corporation.

57) The Seoul Southern District Court 2003GaHap1176 (Aug. 17, 2006); The Supreme Court 2002Na60467, 60474 (Dec. 10, 2004); The Seoul Central District Court 2008GaHap47867 (Feb. 8, 2010).

58) In the aforementioned 2003GaHap1176 case, the defendant directors of LG Chem. obtained personal

V. REGULATION OF FRIVOLOUS ACTIONS

A. Demand Requirement

1. Introduction

According to Art. 403 of the KCC, minority shareholders are required to demand that the corporation sue the directors before they file a derivative action. More specifically, a derivative action can be filed if the corporation fails to sue within thirty days from the date the corporation received the demand notice. When the demand requirement might result in irreparable losses to the corporation, minority shareholders may immediately file a derivative action without waiting for thirty days. Examples of irreparable losses include the imminent application of the statute of limitations and the director's attempt to dispose of all of their property.

The demand requirement aims to provide the corporation with an opportunity to exercise its own right to sue before a third party (e.g., minority shareholders). In the United States, the demand requirement plays an important role in limiting frivolous lawsuits. Having received the demand from shareholders, the board often authorizes a special litigation committee to decide whether to file a lawsuit against the director. A decision by the committee not to sue blocks the derivative action by shareholders in most cases.[59] The demand requirement under the KCC, however, operates quite differently in reality. If derivative actions become more common, devices for stemming frivolous lawsuits will become more important. What kind of measures should Korea take? Should Korea follow the US model represented by the independent special committee or the UK model relying on the role of the court? Before exploring these matters, two controversial issues on the demand requirement in Korea need to be addressed: (1) the effect of the corporation's decision not to sue; and (2) the fate of a derivative action that has not gone through the demand process.

---

gains through wrongful transactions, but the court allowed limitation of liabilities for such directors. (The plaintiff shareholders argued that the limitation of liabilities would be unreasonable because the directors resold the shares in LG Petrochemical Co. Ltd. later, thereby obtaining huge financial gains. But the court denied their argument by stating that the transaction made afterwards shall not be considered in limiting director's liabilities).

59) For example, see American Law Institute, Principles of Corporate Governance: Analysis and Recommendations, Vol. 2 (1994), pp.107-170.

2. Corporation's Decision Not to Sue

It is clear that shareholders may not file a derivative action once the corporation files its own lawsuit against the director. However, are shareholders allowed to file a derivative action despite the corporation's decision not to sue? The KCC does not provide any support for the concept of the special litigation committee. It is the auditor or the audit committee who has the authority to make a decision to sue directors. Article 403 of the KCC is silent on the effect of the auditor's decision not to sue.

Indeed, not all lawsuits against a director are beneficial to a corporation. There are many legitimate reasons why a corporation may choose not to initiate a lawsuit against its own directors. One may argue that the court should respect the corporation's decision not to sue by dismissing a derivative action filed in defiance of the decision made by a disinterested committee. Given the strict position of the current KCC on director's liability,[60] Art. 403 will not be interpreted as providing a corporation with any power to block a derivative action(e.g., by using a special litigation committee).[61]

3. A Derivative Action Filed Without Going Through the Demand Process

In Korea, the demand requirement is classified as a prerequisite for filing a lawsuit. A derivative action filed without having satisfied the demand requirement will be dismissed without deciding on the merit. Many lower courts have followed the traditional approach and dismissed derivative actions that had not gone through the demand process.[62]

In some cases, however, the court has adopted a different approach in interpreting the demand requirement more liberally. In one case decided by the Seoul District Court,[63] the plaintiff shareholders did demand that the corporation file a lawsuit, but then they brought a derivative action before the thirty-day period had expired. The Seoul District Court, however, did not dismiss the lawsuit. It clarified that the defect in the demand process (i.e., non-observance of the waiting period) would be cured where the corporation failed to file its own lawsuit against the director after the derivative action had been commenced. This decision was later supported by the Supreme Court.[64]

---

60) Under Sec. 1of Art. 400 of the KCC, a unanimous consent from shareholders is required to exempt directors of their liabilities toward the corporation.

61) Kon-Sik Kim, 'Activation of Shareholders' Derivative Suits (*in Korean*)', (1996) 37 *Seoul Law Journal* 164 at 179.

62) The Changwon District Court 2001GaHap4231 (Sep. 6, 2002); The Seoul Central District Court 2004GaDan232721 (Dec. 17, 2004); The Daejeon District Court 2006GaHap4186 (Jul. 3, 2006).

63) The Seoul District Court 97GaHap39907 (Dec. 26, 1997).

Also in the 2005GaHap97694 case,[65] the plaintiff did not demand anything of the corporation before the commencement of the derivative action. The Seoul District Court ruled that the absence of the demand process was cured because the plaintiff shareholders had called for the corporation to hold the direct or responsible after the commencement of the derivative action, but the corporation did not take any actions to do so. This line of jurisprudence has been followed by other lower court cases, such as 2003Na5360.[66]

There is skepticism about this new approach taken by the courts. It is argued that because the demand requirement is supposed to benefit the corporation, the corporation should be given a substantial opportunity to file its own lawsuit. If the courts, based on the passage of thirty days after the commencement of derivative action, approve the derivative action without an actual demand, the demand requirement cannot function as initially designed. However, such criticism might limit the availability of the derivative action based upon minor procedural problems. Especially when the corporation did not show any intention to file its own lawsuit, it would be unreasonable to dismiss a derivative action and then to force minority shareholders to bring another action satisfying the demand requirement. Thus, the more facilitative interpretation taken in some of the recent lower court decisions seems to be a move in the right direction.

4 Analysis

Under Korean law, the demand requirement seems to play an insignificant role in limiting frivolous lawsuits. In an environment where the threat of frivolous lawsuits is negligible, weak measures to prevent anti-frivolous actions may prove to be inconsequential. However, as the number of derivative actions is growing, Korea needs to develop a rational and effective system for limiting value-decreasing derivative actions.

The best way to regulate frivolous lawsuits is to prohibit any frivolous or abusive lawsuit from being filed. However, *ex ante* it is difficult to determine whether or not initiating a lawsuit against a company's director will increase corporate value. Theoretically, there are three candidates who might exercise such decision-making authority: (1) the shareholders; (2) the special litigation committee; and (3) the courts. Korean jurisprudence pays full respect to the decision-making power of shareholders. Conversely, the decision-making power

---

64) The Supreme Court 2000Da9086 (Mar. 15, 2002).

65) The Seoul Central District Court 2005GaHap97694 (Nov. 30, 2006).

66) The Seoul High Court 2003Na5360 (Jun. 27, 2003). As in the 2005GaHap97694 case, the plaintiff shareholders made a demand of the corporation after the commencement of the derivative action. Based upon the same logic as the decision No. 2005GaHap97694, the Seoul High Court declared that the absence of the demand process had been cured.

of the special litigation committee or a court—with respect to whether the lawsuit would contribute to corporate value—does not influence the fate of derivative actions. Is it reasonable to give such authority exclusively to shareholders? Further, as explained above, the KCC has a minimum shareholding requirement to file a derivative action. However, is there any proof that the shareholders satisfying the shareholding requirement are the best gate-keepers for the derivative action?

One may consider the special litigation committee in the US system as a viable alternative. Compared with minority shareholders, an independent committee may have more specialized

knowledge anda level of independence to increase the chance ofreachinga decision in the interests of the shareholdersas a whole. In order to adopt such a system in Korea, however, the independence of the committee willhave tobe secured. Whenboard members tend tobe beholden to the influence of controlling shareholders, as is often witnessed in Korean business practice, the control of derivative actions by the committee may only benefit wrong-doing directors.

What about the role of the courts in controlling frivolous or abusive suits? In the UK, a member of a company who brings a derivative action must apply to the court for permission to continue the action.[67] There are some reasons to be skeptical about the competence of non-specialist courts to deal with such complex economic issues. However, an early intervention by the courts might make some sense, especially when frivolous lawsuits are rampant and no other independent entity could effectively control them.

B. Limiting Collusive Settlement

As in other countries,[68] the KCC requires the approval of the court in order to validate a settlement in derivative actions.[69] The court's intervention on settlement agreements results from the public character of derivative actions.

In the United States, most derivative actions result in settlements, not judgments on their merits,[70] and the phenomenon of collusive settlements has been intensively discussed. For

---

67) Art. 261 of the Companies Act 2006.
68) See J. Cox (1999), above, n. 2, p.12. In the United States, like the Korean courts, 'The court would review the fairness, reasonableness, and adequacy of the settlements.'
69) Sec. 6 of Art. 403 of the KCC.
70) See J. Cox (1999), above, n. 2, p.11. J. Coffee (1986), above, n. 3, at p.673 explains 'only a very small percentage of derivative actions (apparently less than one percent) result in litigated plaintiff victories.'

both the plaintiff (and their lawyer) and defendant, a settlement would eliminate the risk of the final judgment. Further, defendant directors normally prefer settlements because the agreed-upon amount can be covered by D&O insurance. In terms of the plaintiff's lawyer, an early settlement is an attractive option considering there sources they must invest in such complex litigation. Under this structure, the plaintiff's lawyer might file an abusive action with a view to reaching an early settlement and in turn, an easy and lucrative contingency fee. US courts tend to approve such settlement agreements, including attorney's fees clauses, without seriously modifying conditions upon which the parties agreed.[71]

However, in Korea, settlements in the midst of derivative actions are rare. What accounts for the difference between the two countries? The inactive D&O insurance market in Korea helps explain part of this phenomenon. Directors are more likely to scrutinize the conditions of settlements in cases where the funds for the settlement come from their own pockets rather than form insurance companies. Another reason for the dearth of settlements in Korea may be that unlike the United States—where most derivative actions are led by entrepreneurial lawyers seeking economic gains—many derivative actions in Korea are motivated by the political agendas of civic activist groups seeking 'economic justice'. A compromise through a settlement agreement could be viewed as a deviation from its original purpose. Under current Korean practice, the additional regulation of derivative action settlements seems to be unnecessary. However, in the future, if derivative actions become more common, abusive actions led by entrepreneurial lawyers expecting collusive settlements might become problematic. If this happens, the limitation of collusive settlements should be made with two policy considerations in mind. First, the regulation of collusive settlements must be coordinated with other legislation for limiting frivolous lawsuits. Such potentially collusive settlements might be regulated by various methods, including the limitation of attorney fees for a settled case or active court intervention. These proposed tools for regulating potentially collusive settlements are distinctive from current legislative efforts against frivolous lawsuits. For example, the strict requirement for standing does not eliminate the necessity for regulating socially undesirable settlements. The purpose of implementing strict procedures for filing derivative suits and the regulation of collusive settlements overlap —both seek to get rid of frivolous derivative actions which decrease corporate value. Thus, it might be safely argued that strict regulation of collusive settlements is not required because the existing legislation already discourages most frivolous lawsuits.

---

71) See J. Cox (1999), above, n. 2, pp.11-12.

Secondly, the general jurisprudence on the limitation of attorney's fees should also be taken into account. Most collusive settlements occur in lawsuits controlled by entrepreneurial lawyers. Thus, the problem is unlikely to be serious when, in general, lawyers' fees are strictly regulated by the court. As noted in the contingency fee discussion, case law in Korea has already developed jurisprudence limiting the validity of attorneys' fee arrangements in general civil litigation. The adoption of any additional regulations specifically targeting contingency fees in the context of derivative action settlements must be justified by showing that the current position generally taken by the courts is insufficient.

VI. A NEW TREND IN CASE LAW: DIGRESSION FROM THE PASSIVE ROLE MODEL?

Among various instruments for better corporate governance, the derivative action is the one that is most likely influenced by the court's attitude. Besides the legislation itself, the courts could encourage or discourage derivative actions through the interpretation of statutes. Traditionally, civil law judges were believed to be less active than their common-law colleagues in their role of making rules.[72] In several recent cases, however, the Korean courts have adopted quite a flexible interpretation of derivative action statutes. It would be hasty to make a conclusive remark with such a small sample size, but the rise of this new trend is noteworthy.

Case law on derivative actions, as already reviewed, cover various issues in derivative actions, including standing for plaintiffs, attorneys' fees, and the litigation process. In general, the courts have adopted a literal interpretation by sticking to the letter of the statute; among others, the representative example is found in double derivative action cases where the Supreme Court limited the standing according to the literal meaning of the KCC provision. For certain issues on derivative actions, however, the courts have applied a more generous standard. Contrary to the explicit expression under the KCC, many lower courts have refused to dismiss derivative actions that failed to satisfy the demand requirement; a lower court adopted a favourable interpretation for shareholders on the reimbursement timing issue despite the relevant provision of the KCC; the Supreme Court adopted a lenient

---

72) See Kon-Sik Kim (2008), above, n. 34, p.132. But the differences between continental courts and common law courts are not as wide as is commonly thought. See K. Pistor et al., 'The Evolution of Corporate Law: A Cross-Country Comparison', (2002) 23 *University of Pennsylvania Journal of International Economic Law* 791.

interpretation on another procedural issue in the Korea First Bank Case.[73] What are the common features of the cases in which the plaintiffs succeeded in persuading the courts to adopt a more generous interpretation than that of the literal meaning? The technical characteristics of those issues are noteworthy. For example, failure to satisfy procedural requirements often results from ignorance of complicated litigation rules or minor technical errors, such as a miscalculation of a time period. As the plaintiff should prove their case on its merits even after such technical problems are solved, the courts might feel less burdened in curing technical defects. Also, the courts might consider the legislative intention of the recent reform in the KCC (i.e., alleviating the strict requirements for filing derivative actions).

However, the digression from the formalistic interpretation does not always benefit plaintiffs and their lawyers. In particular, the limitations on directors' liability and contingency fees would negatively influence the incentives of shareholders and their lawyers. It is very difficult to find a consistent logic on when the courts benefited defendant directors by deviating from the letter of the statute. The courts might have been too conservative and cautious on issues like the amount of liabilities that constitute the final result of a lawsuit (as opposed to technical issues), thereby benefiting defendant directors.

VII. CONCLUDING REMARKS

Among various elements influencing the derivative action system, this chapter explored major procedural and incentive issues believed to be crucial for a mature understanding of Korean practice. Since the late 1990s, several derivative actions were filed, and most corporate managers are now aware of the threat of lawsuits by shareholders. This trend may be attributable to the reform of the KCC on the derivative action procedure as well as the change of social surroundings in Korea. That being said, the number of shareholder actions is still limited compared to the United States and Japan. In order to enhance the deterrent effect that would positively influence Korean corporate governance, the government may need to activate derivative actions by providing minority shareholders and entrepreneurial

---

73) In that case, the Korea First Bank participated in the derivative action that had been filed by minority shareholders, and later, the shares held by the plaintiff were cancelled in the process of restructuring led by the government. The defendant director argued that the lawsuit should be dismissed because the plaintiff shareholders, by losing all of their shares, failed to satisfy the shareholding requirement. The Supreme Court applied a generous interpretation: while the original lawsuit by minority shareholders would be dismissed, the Bank could proceed with the derivative action.

lawyers with more incentives. On the other hand, the current system for discouraging friv-olous lawsuits, which currently depends too much on the minimum shareholding require-ment, should also be reexamined.

From the perspective of encouraging legitimate lawsuits, most derivative actions in Korea have been filed by unusual plaintiff lawyers in exceptional cases; the lawsuits were often ini-tiated by NGO-related lawyers and were often by-products of criminal or bankruptcy proceedings. Put another way, Korean directors are unlikely to be sued as long as they avoid such unusual or exceptional situations. Radical reforms intended to address this issue, including the introduction of a US-style discovery process, would invite more lawsuits, but it is not clear whether such reforms would lead to an ideal derivative actions practice with-out causing overall confusion in the corporate litigation system. This chapter has focused on more practical issues and has suggested regulatory alternatives: double derivative actions should be allowed; the courts should adopt a more generous interpretation of the re-imbursement requirement and contingency fee arrangements; and the demand requirement as a prerequisite for derivative actions should not be strictly imposed.

In terms of discouraging frivolous lawsuits, the primary device stipulated in the KCC is the minimum shareholding ratio. Once the threshold is passed, however, no one can pro-hibit a derivative action from being filed or processed. However, it is not certain that a shareholder with sufficient shares is always in the best position to measure the impact of the lawsuit on shareholder value. Particularly when the number of derivative actions reaches an intolerable level, the Korean government may have to consider allowing an in-terruption of the derivative action process by independent third parties like the special committee or the court.

[Appendix1: Derivative Actions in Korea for 1997. 1. 1. ‒2010. 5. 30.]

| Year | Filing of Derivative Actions | Status of Derivative Action | | | |
		Final Decision for Plaintiffs	Final Decision for Defendant	Pending	Withdrawn
1997	2	2	-	-	--
1998	4	2	2	-	--
1999	4	-	4	-	--
2000	2(1)*	-	1	-	1(0)
2001	2	-	2	-	-
2002	4	2	1	-	1
2003	6	4	2	-	-
2004	9	6	2	1	-
2005	9(8)*	4	4	1(0)	-
2006	8	-	7	1	-
2007	-	-	-	-	-
2008	3	1	-	2	-
2009	-	-	-	-	-
2010	2	-	-	2	-
Total	55(53)*	21	25	7(6)	2(1)

[Source: Jooyoung Kim, Survey on Derivative Actions and Analysis on Court Decisions (*in Korean*), 34 CG Review 09/10(2007); the database of the Supreme Court of Korea (www.scourt.go.kr); the database of the Korea Exchange (www.krx.co.kr); the personal archive of Prof. Moon-Hee CHOI of Kangwon National Univ. School of Law].

* In 2000 and 2005, there were two cases that could not be traced despite the report of lawsuit by local daily journals.

The Demand on Directors Requirement and the Business Judgment Rule in the Shareholder Derivative Suit: An Alternative Framework

Kon Sik Kim*

I. INTRODUCTION

The shareholder derivative action is generally regarded as a useful and necessary device by which shareholders of corporations may deter and remedy abuses of corporate power.[1] Nevertheless, the derivative action has been viewed by many with suspicion. This suspicion has manifested itself in a number of restrictions which hinder the ability of shareholders to bring derivative actions.[2] Among the restrictions are the demand rule and the business judgment rule. The demand rule requires shareholders to seek redress or action from the board of directors prior to commencing a derivative action. The business judgment rule adds a degree of finality to the decision of the board of directors on whether to commence legal action against alleged corporate wrongdoers by blocking derivative suits absent allegations that the board of directors failed or were unable to exercise sound business judgments.[3] The finality of the director's decision has been strengthened by recent decisions[4] which en-

---

* Currently practicing law in Seoul, South Korea; LL.B. and LL.M., Seoul National University; article written while Mr. Kon Sik Kim was an LL.M. candidate at Harvard.
1) See Dykstra, *The Revival of the Derivative Suit*, 116 U. PA. L. REV. 74, 77-82 (1967).
2) Examples of restrictions that have been placed on the derivative suit include: the security for expenses requirement, *e.g.*, N.Y. BUS. CORP. LAW 627 (McKinney Supp. 1980), the contemporaneous ownership requirement, e.g., FED. R. CIV. P. 23.1, and the demand rule. *Id.*
3) *See, e.g.*, Ash v. IBM, 353 F.2d 491, 493 (3d Cir. 1965), *cert. denied*, 384 U.S. 927 (1966). What constitutes a failure to exercise sound business judgment or an inability to do so is unclear. *Id.* But it would seem reasonably certain that allegations that the individual directors were personally involved in the wrongdoing or that they demonstrated bad faith would defeat the protection of the business judgment rule. *Id.*
4) The first of the decisions was Burks v. Lasker, 441 U.S. 471 (1979), which held that state law should determine whether a group of disinterested directors may block a shareholder derivative action. *Id.* at 486. The effect of the *Burks* decision was that a special litigation committee, which was used by the defendants in the case, *Id.* at 474-75, would be permitted if not prohibited by state law. This effect was given further substance by the decisions of Abbey v. Control Data Corp., 603 F.2d 724 (8th Cir. 1979), *cert.* denied, 444 U.S. 1017 (1980), and Maldonado v. Flynn, 485 F. Supp. 274 (S.D.N.Y. 1980), both of

able a "special litigation committee" to exercise the veto power otherwise vested in the board of directors.[5] The litigation committee may consist of even a minority of the total board[6] and may consist of outside consultants.[7] The primary substantive restraint on the committee is that it be able to act in a detached and disinterested manner.[8]

First, this article will suggest that the restrictions on the shareholder derivative suit, particularly the nearly absolute power of the board of directors to block such suits, are largely unnecessary and confusing. Second, it will be demonstrated that the board of directors can easily abuse its power under current doctrines. Last, this article will suggest alternatives which may be more effective and desirable.

This article will concentrate on shareholder derivative actions in federal courts. The discussion will focus on derivative claims against corporate insiders; suits involving third parties are beyond the scope of this article. In addition, the discussion will be limited to the context of the publicly held corporation and the term "corporation," as used in this article, should be interpreted as publicly held corporation.

II. PRESENT PRACTICE

A. The "Demand on Directors" Requirement

1. The Rule

The "demand" rule requires shareholders who wish to bring a shareholder derivative action to first request the board of directors to take appropriate action before the shareholders commence the derivative action.[9] Although not expressly mandated, the demand rule is

---

which upheld the power of a special litigation committee to discontinue a derivative suit under Delaware law. 603 F.2d at 730; 485 F. Supp. at 279-80.

5) See, e.g., 485 F. Supp. at 279.

6) The necessary make-up of the litigation committee has not been clearly addressed in the decisions. The district court in the *Burks* decision held that a minority of the board could still block a derivative action. Lasker v. Burks, 404 F. Supp. 1172, 1178-80 (S.D.N.Y. 1975). Nevertheless, implicit in the court's opinion is the requirement that the litigation committee, at a minimum, constitute a statutory quorum of the entire board. *Id.* at 1175. See also Lasker v. Burks, 441 U.S. at 474-75.

7) See, e.g., Lasker v. Burks, 404 F. Supp. 1172, 1175 (S.D.N.Y. 1975) (litigation committee retained a former Chief Judge of the New York Court of Appeals).

8) See, Abbey v. Control Data Corp., 603 F.2d at 729-30; Maldonado v. Flynn, 485 F. Supp. at 278-79.

9) See Dykstra, *supra* note 1, at 97.

currently traced to the requirement of rule 23.1 of the Federal Rules of Civil Procedure that the shareholder-plaintiff allege "with particularity the efforts... made... to obtain the action [desired] from the directors."[10] It is reasoned that the directors of a corporation should be given an opportunity to exercise the power vested in them before permitting shareholders to bring an action on the part of the corporation.[11] The rationale for the demand rule has its limits, but the courts often disagree as to when those limits have been reached.[12] Nevertheless, courts have generally concurred that when the shareholder can demonstrate that making a demand on the directors would be futile the failure to make such a demand will be excused.[13] Futility may be shown by showing that a majority of the board of directors are controlled or dominated by the alleged wrongdoers,[14] there is a substantial and persuasive conflict of interest among the directors,[15] when a majority of the board of directors actually participated or acquiesced in the alleged wrongdoing,[16] or when the board has unequivocally expressed its opposition to the suit or the board's intention to take no action

---

10) FED. R. CIV. P. 23.1. Many states have similar requirements. *See, e.g.,* N.Y. BUS. CORP. LAW § 626(c) (McKinney 1963); COLO. R. CIV. P. 23.1.

11) Note, *The Demand and Standing Requirements in Shareholder Derivative Actions*, 44 U. CHI. L. REV. 168, 171 (1976) and cases cited therein.

12) Requirements, such as that in FED. R. CIV. P. 23.1, generally contain no standards for determining when a failure to make a demand on a board of directors prior to commencing a derivative action should be excused. As a result, the determination has been left to the sound discretion of the court. 3B MOORE's FEDERAL PRACTICE 23.1.19 (2d ed. 1980) (hereinafter cited as MOORE'S). Although the courts can generally agree as to the proper standard to be used and the broad circumstances that satisfy that standard, *see* notes 13-17 *infra* and accompanying text, they often differ on the specific application of those principles. *Compare* Liboff v. Wolfson, 437

13) *See, e.g.,* Nussbacher v. Continental Ill. Nat'l. Bank & Trust Co., 518 F.2d 873, 877 (7th Cir. 1975), *cert. denied,* 424 U.S. 928 (1976); In re Kauffman Mut. Fund Actions, 479 F.2d 257, 263 (1st Cir.), *cert. de-nied,* 414 U.S. 857 (1973) (by implication); Liboff v. Wolfson, 437 F.2d 121, 122 (5th Cir. 1971). In ad-dition to the word "futile" courts have often used such terms as "useless," "unavailing," or "an idle ceremony." 7A C. WRIGHT & A. MILLER, FEDERAL PRACTICE AND PROCEDURE § 1831 at 379-80 (1972) [hereinafter cited as WRIGHT & MILLER].

14) *See* Note *supra* note 11, at 173-74 and cases cited therein. The courts have differed as to the facts which must be alleged in order to demonstrate sufficient control to excuse a failure to make a demand. Compare Doctor v. Harrington, 196 U.S. 579, 588 (1905) (by implication) with *In re* Kauffman Mut. Fund Actions, 479 F.2d 257, 263-64 (1st Cir.), *cert denied,* 414 U.S. 857 (1973). The majority position appears to be that unsupported allegations of control by the wrongdoer are insufficient to excuse demand. *See* Note supra note 11, at 174.

15) *See, e.g.,* Landy v. F.D.I.C., 486 F.2d 139, 148-150 (3d Cir. 1973), *cert. denied,* 416 U.S. 960 (1974) (implicitly adopting the conflict of interest excuse but finding so much conflict present under the facts of the case). The *Landy* case illustrates the limits of the conflict of interest excuse. A shareholder rely-ing on the conflict excuse must show a very substantial conflict of the type which precludes the exercise of independent objective business judgment. *Id.* at 149.

16) The inference of futility has been strongest where it has been shown that a majority of the board ac-tually participated in the alleged wrongful conduct. The inference becomes less when the allegations are merely that a majority of the board acquiesced in the conduct. Accordingly, the courts are split over whether allegations of acquiescence are sufficient to excuse demand with the majority concluding in the negative. Note *supra* note 11, at 175-80.

on behalf of the shareholder's complaint.[17)

2. Analysis

The conditions which have been found to excuse a shareholder's failure to request the board to take action prior to the shareholder commencing a derivative suit present, on the surface, a theoretically sound basis on which to determine the applicability of the demand rule. Nevertheless, serious practical difficulties exist in the application of the standards articulated by the courts.

When the alleged wrongdoer owns a controlling percentage of the corporation's stock, the existence of a control relationship between the wrongdoer and the board of directors sufficient to excuse noncompliance with the demand rule is not difficult to establish.[18) But control may exist in far more subtle forms as well. For example, a wrongdoer or group of wrongdoers may be in a position to exercise control pressure over the board of directors by virtue of family or other personal ties with the board members.[19) The shareholder confronted with such a more subtle control relationship may find it extremely difficult to prove the existence of that relationship. At the same time, the courts are confronted with the equally difficult task of determining how much control must be shown to excuse noncompliance with the demand rule.[20)

Similar difficulties exist in determining when the board has adopted the necessary unequivocal opposition to taking the action requested by the shareholders. Clearly, the fact that the board had adopted such a position with regard to another suit in another jurisdiction involving the same issues could be evidence of futility.[21) However, when the board has never formally adopted a position or when a considerable amount of time has

---

17) *Id.* at 180-82.

18) *See, e.g.*, Dopp v. American Elec. Labs, Inc., 55 F.R.D. 151, 153 (S.D.N.Y. 1972).

19) There is empiricial evidence that in large American corporations many corporate directors, who appear to be independent, are tied economically or psychologically to the other corporate officers, particularly the chief executive officer. *See* M. EISENBERG, THE STRUCTURE OF THE CORPORATION 146 (1976); [hereinafter cited as EISENBERG]; Note, *The Business Judgment Rule in Derivative Suits Against Directors*, 65 CORNELL L. REV. 600, 619-22 (1980).

20) The term "control" receives a variety of definitions depending on the context in which it is used. It would appear that in the context of a shareholder derivative action the "control" alleged must be sufficiently great as to make the board incapable of doing its' duty. *See In re* Kauffman Mut. Fund Actions, 479 F.2d 257, 263 (1st Cir.), *cert. denied*, 414 U.S. 857 (1973). When this level is reached, however, is the subject of a diversity of opinion. See Abbe v. Goss, 411 F. Supp. 923, 924-25 (S.D.N.Y. 1972) (44% ownership sufficient to demonstrate control); Levitan v. Stout, 97 F. Supp. 105, 114 (W.D. Ky. 1951) (concluding that 40% is not sufficient to satisfy the control exception).

21) *See* Nussbacher v. Continental Ill. Nat'l Bank & Trust Co., 518 F.2d 873, 878-79 (7th Cir. 1975), *cert. denied*, 424 U.S. 928 (1976)

elapsed since adoption of the position it may be reasonable to conclude the board is not opposed to the action, particularly when new directors have been elected in the meantime.

The ambiguity in application of the "futility" standards makes it very difficult for the complaining shareholders to determine when demand is required. Although the shareholders could avoid potential difficulties later in the litigation by complying with the demand rule at the outset, it is more likely that the shareholders will attempt to name a majority of the board as defendants and thereby avoid the demand rule.[22] Of course, the shareholders would have to have facts to sustain their allegations during any pretrial dismissal motions. Allegations, however, that the directors violated their fiduciary duty to the corporation by passively acquiescing in an illegal transaction should usually be sufficient to give the shareholders their day in court.[23] Regardless of the final outcome, however, it is clear that the ambiguity in "futility criteria" is likely to add to the time and expense of making the initial determination of whether demand should have been made on the directors.

B. Effect of the Board's Refusal to Sue: The Business Judgment Rule

1. General Application

Assuming that the shareholder complies with the demand rule, or has his noncompliance excused, he must then prove that the express or implied refusal of the board to sue was not a valid exercise of the director's business judgment. As stated in *Ash v. LB.M., Inc.*,[24] a shareholder derivative suit:

> can be maintained only if the stockholder shall allege and prove that the directors of the corporation are personally involved or interested in the alleged

---

22) *See* Phillips v. Bradford, 62 F.R.D. 681, 688 (S.D.N.Y. 1974). Some courts have held that a failure to make a demand will not be excused when a majority of the board has been named as defendants and there are no allegations that the directors named as defendants actually participated in the wrongful conduct or possessed a conflict of interest or bias. *See* Jones v. Equitable Life Assurance Soc'y, 409 F. Supp. 370, 372-74 (S.D.N.Y. 1975). *See also* Dent, *Shareholder Litigation: The Death of the Derivative Suit?*, 75 Nw. U.L. REV. 96 (1980); Note *supra* note 19, at 630 n. 147.

23) Passively acquiescing in an illegal transaction is likely to run afoul of provisions such as that in New York's corporation law which impose on the directors the duty to perform his obligations "in good faith and with that degree of care which an ordinarily prudent person in a like position would use under similar circumstances." N.Y. BUS. CORP. LAW § 717 (McKinney Supp. 1980). *See also* Dyson, *The Director's Liability for Negligence*, 40 IND. L.J. 341 (1965).

24) 353 F.2d 491 (3d Cir. 1965), *cert. denied*, 384 U.S. 927 (1966).

wrongdoing in a way calculated to impair their exercise of business judgment on behalf of the corporation, or that their refusal to sue reflects bad faith or breach of trust in some other way.[25]

Under the business judgment doctrine adopted in *Ash*, directors would apparently be permitted to refuse to assert even meritorious claims when they can show sound business reasons for their actions.[26]

The instances when it has been found that a wrongful refusal to sue has occurred are remarkably similar to those where noncompliance with the demand rule has been excused. A shareholder derivative action can be maintained when it is shown that the directors were unable to exercise sound business judgment because of a conflict of interest or because the alleged wrongdoers exercised control over the directors.[27] In addition, courts have sustained a derivative suit when the directors have participated in an unlawful transaction.[28] The burden of proving that the decision of the board of directors not to sue was not a legitimate exercise of business judgment is often extremely difficult to satisfy.[29] The business

---

25) *Id.* at 493. States are generally in accord with the Ash doctrine. *See,* 13 W. FLETCHER, CYCLOPEDIA OF THE LAW OF PRIVATE CORPORATIONS § 5822, at 144-45 (rev. perm. ed. 1980) [hereinafter cited as FLETCHER]. The *Ash* doctrine arises from the notion that corporate involvement in litigation is generally entrusted to the control of the board of directors. As stated in United Copper Sec. Co. v. Amalgamated Copper Co., 244 U.S. 261 (1917), "whether or not a corporation shall seek to enforce in the courts a cause of action for damages is, like other business questions, ordinarily a matter of internal management and is left to the discretion of directors..." *Id.* at 263.

26) *E.g.,* Ashwander v. Tennessee Valley Auth., 297 U.S. 288, 343 (1935). The exercise of business judgment in deciding not to bring a claim against accused wrongdoers should not be confused with ratifying the accuseds' wrongful conduct. The court, in Gall v. Exxon, 418 F. Supp. 508 (S.D.N.Y. 1976), clearly drew the distinction when it said:

> The decision not to bring suit with regard to past conduct which may have been illegal is not itself a violation of law and does not result in a continuation of the alleged violation of law. Rather, it is a decision ... that pursuit of a cause of action ... is not in the best interest of the corporation. Such a determination, ... must be made by the corporate directors in the exercise of their sound business judgment. The conclusive effect of such a judgment cannot be affected by the allegedly illegal nature of the initial action which purportedly gives rise to the cause of action.

Id. at 518. Because the business judgment rule and ratification are distinct doctrines, the merits of a shareholder's claim are not solely determinative of whether a refusal to bring suit has been made in bad faith and most courts refuse to consider the merits of a shareholder's claim in deciding whether the board has acted in good faith. *See* Note *supra* note 11, at 195 and cases cited therein. Nevertheless, at least one court has permitted a derivative action to proceed over board objection where the claims of the shareholders were clearly meritorious. Epstein v. Schenk, 35 N.Y.S. 2d 969, 981 (Supp. Ct. 1939).

27) *See* Ash v. IBM, 353 F.2d 491, 493 (3d Cir. 1965), *cert. denied,* 384 U.S. 927 (1966); Swanson v. Traer, 249 F.2d 854, 858 (7th Cir. 1957). *But see* Issner v. Aldrich, 254 F. Supp. 696, 702 (D. Del. 1966).

28) *See* Swanson v. Traer, 249 F.2d 854, 858 (7th Cir. 1957).

29) Under current practice, the plaintiff shareholder bears the burden of proving that the board's decision not to sue was in bad faith or otherwise "wrongful." Ash v. IBM, 353 F.2d 491, 493 (3d Cir. 1965),

judgment rule, therefore, represents a significant barrier to the maintenance of a shareholder derivative suit. This barrier becomes even more significant in light of the difficult to apply standards heretofore articulated by the courts.[30]

2. Recent Variation in the Application of the Business Judgment Rule

a. The Variation

Because of the difficulties in satisfying the burden of proof and because of the strong policy favoring director control of corporate activity, the business judgment rule has always been a formidable obstacle to pressing a shareholder derivative suit. The obstacle, however, was not insurmountable. In an effort to further insulate themselves and the corporation from shareholder derivative actions, corporate boards of directors are relying increasingly on the business judgment rule, not only as a defense to such suits, but as a device to block shareholder derivative suits altogether.

The directors accomplish this variation in the use of the business judgment rule by appointing a "special committee" to review the request of the shareholders that legal action be taken to remedy an alleged wrongdoing.[31] Typically, the special committee will decide that it is not in the best interests of the corporation to press the claim.[32] When the shareholders

---

cert. denied, 384 U.S. 927 (1966). By placing the burden of proof on the shareholder the limited immunity afforded the directors by the business judgment rule is significantly expanded. Directors reviewing allegd wrongful conduct, protected as they are by the business judgment rule, may be tempted to conduct only a cursory investigation or even deliberately overlook past wrongdoing by their colleagues, particularly when the wrongful conduct is not likely to recur. The strong economic, psychological, emotional and personal ties that can arise between directors, especially when their control and leadership are challenged, must not be underestimated. See M. EISENBERG, supra note 19, at 146; Note, supra note 19, at 619-22. These factors have caused some to argue that "complaining shareholders should be allowed to maintain a derivative action where the corporate claim is clear, the costs of litigation are relatively small in relation to the probable recovery, and a lawsuit would not overly disrupt the commercial relations of the corporation." Note, supra note 11, at 196. Although some change in the business judgment rule is necessary, the change suggested above goes too far. Determining whether a shareholder's claim is "clear" and whether the claim would "overly disrupt" corporate functions would not only pose a Herculean task for the courts but would embroil them in many intricate business judgments. See Note supra note 19, at 627. Such participation by the courts in making business judgments would eviscerate both the policy and effect of the business judgment rule. At the same time, because not all shareholder challenges to a board's decision not to sue will be grounded on the merits of the claim, there is no guarantee that the abuses giving rise to the suggested change would be eliminated.

30) See notes 18-22 supra and accompanying text.
31) See notes 4-8 supra and accompanying text.
32) The board of directors is likely to believe, at the time the committee is formed, that a favorable determination will be forthcoming. This belief is not unjustified given the numerous biases that may exist in even technically disinterested directors. See notes 19, 29 supra. At the same time, it must be conceded that a truly disinterested litigation committee is not precluded from commencing suit. Moreover, it must be recognized that there may be many instances where it is legitimately in the best interests of the corporation to forego meritorious claims. Maldonado v. Flynn, 485 F. Supp. 274, 285 (S.D.N.Y. 1980).

either initiate an action on their own or continue an action already commenced, the board may request counsel for the corporation or defendant to move for dismissal alleging that the decision not to sue was taken as an exercise of sound business judgment which may not be circumvented by a shareholder action.[33] This device has met with a great deal of success.[34] To be successful, however, the special committee appointed by the board of directors must be comprised of "disinterested" and "impartial" board members.[35] Often the committee will hire very reputable and obstensibly objective outside consultants to add to the committee's credibility as a detached and disinterested body.[36] Of course, the committee must be able to offer some business reason to justify its conclusion that no legal action should be taken.[37] Business justifications, however, have not been difficult to formulate.[38]

b. Analysis

The special committee approach to shareholder derivative suits has the advantage of facilitating investigation into the merits of the shareholders' claim.[39] This advantage is negated, however, by the potential for abuse that is inherent in the scheme.

Because the special committee so often includes outside consultants and, by requirement, directors not named as defendants in the proposed action, it is likely to be all but impossible for the shareholders to prove that the directors were less than detached and disinterested investigators. It is particularly difficult to prove bias in light of the fact that the board minutes or committee reports are not likely to contain evidence of bias or bad faith even if it does exist. As a corollary, it is likely that the committee will spend as much time carefully drafting its findings so as to appear to be rational and objective as it does actually investigating the claim. Together, the difficulty of proof and the carefully drawn reports make it extremely unlikely that a special committee's determination not to sue will be over-

---

33) *E.g.*, Maldonado v. Flynn, 485 F. Supp. 274, 277-78 (S.D.N.Y. 1980).

34) *See, e.g.*, Lewis v. Anderson,.615 F.2d 778 (9th Cir. 1979); Abbey v. Control Data Corp., 603 F.2d 724 (8th Cir. 1979), *cert. denied*, 444 U.S. 1017 (1980); Cramer v. General Tel. & Elec. Corp., 582 F.2d 259 (3d Cir. 1978), *cert. denied*, 439 U.S. 1129 (1979); Rosengarten v. International Tel. & Tel. Corp., 466 F. Supp. 817 (S.D.N.Y. 1979); Siegel v. Merrick, 84 F.R.D. 106 (S.D.N.Y. 1979).

35) *See* Abbey v. Control Data Corp., 603 F.2d 724, 729-30 (8th Cir. 1979), *cert. denied*, 44 U.S. 1017 (1980); Maldonado v. Flynn, 485 F. Supp. 274, 278-79 (S.D.N.Y. 1980).

36) *See* note 7 *supra*.

37) *See, e.g.*, Maldonado v. Flynn, 485 F. Supp. 274, 284-85 (S.D.N.Y. 1980).

38) *Id.* at 284 n.35. *See also* Rosengarten v. International Tel. & Tel. Corp., 466 F. Supp. 817, 821-22 (S.D.N.Y. 1979).

39) By appointing a rather small, specialized committee the costs and time involved in investigating the allegations can be lessened over what they would be if the entire board participated. Moreover, by comprising the committee of outside consultants and disinterested or uninvolved directors a more objective and complete investigation may be possible. *Bee see* notes 19, 29 *supra*.

turned even when that determination intentionally favors the defendants.

Perhaps a more fundamental weakness in the special committee scheme is the questionable validity of the premise that there can ever be a "detached and disinterested" committee comprised of directors whose friends, colleagues and business associates are to be investigated. This concern was succinctly stated by the lower court ruling in *Burks v. Lasker*:[40]

> It is asking too much of human nature to expect that the disinterested directors will view with the necessary objectivity the actions of their colleagues in a situation where an adverse decision would be likely to result in considerable expense and liability for the individuals concerned.[41]

III. AN ALTERNATIVE FRAMEWORK

Present practice in the area of shareholder derivative suits has resulted in substantial confusion over the power of a board of directors to terminate a shareholder derivative suit. Moreover, present practice creates a significant potential for abuse of the business judgment rule by a board of directors. Accordingly, an alternative framework for shareholder derivative actions is required.

A. Strict Enforcement of the Demand Rule

Much of the confusion as to the applicability of the demand rule could be eliminated by adopting a stricter enforcement of the rule. Under the stricter enforcement, a shareholder would be required in nearly every case to make a demand on the board of directors before instituting a shareholder derivative action. The mere unlikelihood that the directors will refuse to take the requested action would not be sufficient to constitute futility. Rather, demand would be required unless there was no reasonable basis for believing that the board could objectively assess the shareholder's claim. An example of that is when the entire board is alleged to be involved in the wrongdoing and the facts make such allegations reasonable.[42]

The strict enforcement of the demand rule is supported by policy and reason. It has long

---

40) 567 F.2d 1208 (2d Cir. 1978), *rev'd*, 441 U.S. 471 (1979).
41) *Id.* at 1212. *See also* Maher v. Zapata Corp., 490 F. Supp. 348, 354 (S.D. Tex. 1980).
42) *See* Note *supra* note 11, at 181-82. This suggestion necessarily means that when it is possible to form a special litigation committee the demand requirement must be satisfied.

been the policy of state corporation statutes to vest ultimate managerial decisionmaking in the board of directors.[43] This decisionmaking responsibility necessarily includes the decision of whether to embroil the corporation in a controversy which may be costly, time consuming and adverse to the corporation's public image. Accordingly, it is appropriate that prior to commencement of a derivative action by the shareholders, the board is given an opportunity to review the merits of the underlying allegations and discuss the appropriate action to take. This review and discussion process may promote judicial economy by encouraging informal and expedited resolution of the dispute.[44] Finally, shareholders often lack the resources and competence to press the claim adequately in a protracted law suit. Moreover, even when the shareholders are in a position to press their claims aggressively, the demand requirement does not pose a significant obstacle to the shareholder action.[45] Therefore, a strict enforcement of the demand rule is justified.

B. Limiting the Business Judgment Rule

The desirability of strict enforcement of the demand rule notwithstanding, the shareholder derivative suit represents a necessary and effective device for policing corporate activity. Under present practice, however, the board of directors are in a position to eliminate the shareholder derivative suit as a check on the exercise of corporate power. The power of the board to block a shareholder derivative action is neither necessary nor desirable as a means of protecting the legitimate oversight of corporate action by the board of directors. Accordingly, the decision, even of a disinterested litigation committee, not to pursue a shareholder's claim upon demand should not be binding on the shareholders.[46]

---

43) See, e.g., N.Y. BUS. CORP. LAW § 701 (McKinney Supp. 1980); ILL. REV. STAT. ch. 32, § 157.33 (1977). The notion that the power of managing the corporation should be vested in the board of directors has been criticized on the ground that it does not reflect corporate realities. In large publicly held corporations, the corporate officers, not the directors, actually manage the affairs of the corporation. Eisenberg suggests that the corporation statutes should be amended to confer on the board a monitoring, rather than management, function. EISENBERG, *supra* note 19, at 164-68. Even under the Eisenberg proposal, however, the prosecution of claims against corporate insiders would likely be within the monitoring duties of the board.

44) See, e.g., Lerman v. ITB Management Corp., 58 F.R.D. 153, 157-58 (D. Mass. 1973); Barr v. Wackman, 36 N.Y.2d 371, 378-79, 368 N.Y.S.2d 497, 505 (1975).

45) *See* Note *supra* note 11, at 172.

46) One commentator has suggested a middle-ground approach to the effect that a decision not to sue would not be binding if a majority of the board are implicated in the ailged wrongdoing. See Dent, *supra* note 22, at 110. A distinction based on the number of directors implicated in the wrongdoing, however, would be undesirable for two reasons. First, such a rule would inevitably encourage sham pleading as shareholders attempt to avoid the binding effect of a board decision by implicating a majority of the board. *See* Note *supra* note 19, at 630 n. 147. Second, there is no reason to believe any

1. The Demand Rule and the Business Judgment Rule

At first glance, making the decision of a disinterested litigation committee nonbinding on the shareholders would appear to be inconsistent with the more strict enforcement of the demand rule advocated above. Closer examination of the relationship between the demand rule and the business judgment rule, however, reveals that no inconsistency exists.

The primary purpose of the demand rule is to afford the board of directors of a corporation an opportunity to review the merits of a shareholder's claim before the derivative action is commenced. The question then arises whether it is necessary, in order to protect the directors' ability to manage the corporation, for the decision of the board not to press the claim to be binding on the shareholders.

The rationale for permitting the decision of a disinterested special litigation committee to be binding on the shareholders is twofold. First, it is argued that the board of directors, by virtue of their expertise and continuing oversight of the affairs of the corporation, are in a better position to evaluate the merits of the shareholders' claims in the light of the best long-range interests of the corporation.[47] Second, it is argued that permitting the board to block a shareholder derivative action is both necessary and desirable to prevent vexatious "strike suits."[48] Neither of these arguments is persuasive.

a. The "Best Interests" Argument

The decision of a special litigation committee not to bring an action against corporate personnel accused by the shareholders of wrongdoing will generally arise from a consideration of some combination of the following five factors:

- the unfavorable prospects for the success of litigation regardless of the actual merits;[49]

"structural bias" that may exist will be diminished as the number of directors implicated decreases. *Id.* at 629.

47) A shareholder derivative action will generally be sought by a minority of the corporate shareholders. This minority is likely to have fairly narrow interests. The board, on the other hand, is answerable primarily to the majority shareholders and is thus more likely to analyze all factors weighing on the wisdom of commencing a derivative action. *See* Note *supra* note 11, at 171-72. These factors will likely include relatively long-term factors such as corporate image and morale. *See* text accompanying notes 52-53 *infra*.

48) Strike suits are those suits which have as their principle aim the recovery of large attorney's fees, rather than the furtherance of corporate well-being. *See* note 86 *infra* and accompanying text. Although the prevention of strike suits is related to protecting the best interests of the corporation, the goal presents its own problems and is worthy of separate consideration.

49) *See* Maldonado v. Flynn, 485 F. Supp. 274, 284 n. 35 (S.D.N.Y. 1980); Gall v. Exxon Corp., F. Supp.

- the costs of conducting the litigation;[50]

- the potential for disruption of corporate management and business;[51]

- the potential for undermining managerial and employee morale;[52] or

- the potential for negative impacts on the public's perception of the corporation.[53]

In order for the "best interests" argument to be persuasive it must be shown that the board of directors is in the best position to assess the factors mentioned above. Moreover, and perhaps more important, it must be shown that the best interests of the corporation will be protected only if the board's evaluation of the five factors is binding on the shareholders.

(1) Likelihood of Success and the Cost of Litigation

The likelihood that potential litigation will be successful and the cost involved in vigorously pressing a claim are legitimate factors to be considered by a board of directors when it considers whether the corporation should commence an action. Nevertheless, it is not appropriate for the board to be able to block a shareholder's suit on the basis of the success and cost factors.[54]

The great majority of the costs involved in a shareholder derivative action will be borne by the shareholders whether they be minority or majority shareholders. It is to be expected, therefore, that the board will carefully evaluate the likely costs and potential for success before commencing a derivative action. Moreover, because most counsel undertake shareholder derivative actions on a contingent fee basis,[55] the attorneys for the shareholders are likely to be convinced that the action will succeed before they initiate a costly and time consuming derivative action.[56] Therefore, the board of directors is not the only body that

---

508, 514 n. 13 (S.D.N.Y. 1976).

50) *Id.*

51) *Id.*

52) *Id.* Also within this category would be the risk that the corporation would be unable to attract or retain competent directors.

53) *See* Maldonado v. Flynn, 485 F. Supp. 274, 284 n. 35 (S.D.N.Y. 1980).

54) *See* Dent, *supra* note 22, at 129 (suggesting that factors relevant to determining whether the corporation ought to bring a suit may not be equally relevant in determining whether shareholders ought to be barred from bringing a derivative suit).

55) It is not unusual for derivative actions to be initiated by counsel in anticipation of recovery of substantial fees. *See* R. POSNER, ECONOMIC ANALYSIS OF LAW 450 (2d ed. 1977); N. LATTIN, THE LAW OF CORPORATIONS § 114, at 448 (2d ed. 1971). Regardless of the overall merits of the contingent fee, the fact remains that frequently the stakes for individual shareholders are too small to motivate them to bring suit.

56) Derivative actions tend to be complex, time consuming and expensive. Counsel, who is not likely to be paid unless the case is won or settled favorably, is likely to balance carefully the prospects for success

is in a position to adequately and objectively evaluate the costs that will be involved with a shareholder derivative action or the chances that such an action will succeed.

Although the corporation is usually a passive participant in a shareholder derivative action,[57] there are certain costs that may be incurred by the corporation as a result of a shareholder derivative action.[58] By virtue of the equitable relief that may be requested, the corporation may be required to file an appearance and answer on behalf of the corporation.[59] In addition, when the interests of the corporation are threatened by a derivative action, the board may be inclined to employ counsel to represent the interests of the corporation.[60] In many cases legal fees for the corporation will not be substantial.[61] Moreover, the impact of the legal fees and other expenses to the corporation in derivative suits[62] are more likely to be the greatest in unsuccessful litigation.[63] Since, as has been argued, shareholders are not prone to commence law suits with little chance of success,[64] the costs to the corporation derived from a derivative action are not sufficient to justify adopting a rule that would permit a board effectively to eliminate outside policing by the shareholders.

(2) The Remaining Factors

The remaining factors often cited to justify a board of directors' decision to drop or refuse

---

in the litigation, the costs involved and the anticipated return should the case succeed. *See Developments in the Law, Class Actions*, 89 HARV. L. REV. 1318, 1622 n. 180 (1976). *See also* S. Wallace, *Facts and Fallacies of Directors' and Officers' Liability, in Protecting the Corporate Officer and Director from Liability*, 25 CORP. LAW & PRAC. COURSE HANDBOOK SER. 121, 126 (W. Carroll ed. 1969).

57) The corporation is made a party to the suit so that the court may draft the decree in a manner that will provide the corporation with a recovery. See 13 FLETCHER, *supra* note 25, § 5997, at 507.

58) *Id.* at 508.

59) *See* Garlen v. Green Mansions, Inc., 9 A.D.2d 760, 193 N.Y.S.2d 116, 117 (1959). Under the *Garlen* decision the appearance must be by independent counsel. *Id.*, 193 N.Y.S.2d at 117.

60) *See* 13 FLETCHER, *supra* note 25, § 5997, at 507.

61) *Id.*

62) In addition to legal fees, the corporation may be required to indemnify the defendant directors should they prevail in the litigation. *See, e.g.,* N.Y. BUS. CORP. LAW § 724 (McKinney 1963); CAL. CORP. CODE § 317(d) (Deering Supp. 1980); DEL. CODE ANN. tit. 8, § 145 (1974). The burden imposed by the indemnification requirement may be significantly lessened by obtaining insurance. *See, e.g.,* N.Y. BUS. CORP. LAW § 727(a) (West Supp. 1980). One might be tempted to argue that the risk of indemnification expenses should be a factor favoring the board's power to block a derivative suit. This argument is undermined, however, in the light of the fact that a corporation may insure against the risk. Moreover, insofar as the indemnification statutes do not distinguish between direct actions against directors and derivative actions, there is little reason to enable the board to avoid the risk of indemnifying its directors in derivative suits when it would be unable to in direct actions. *See generally* Note, *Distinguishing Between Direct and Derivative Shareholder Suits*, 110 U. PA. L. REV. 1147 (1962).

63) In other words, if the derivative action is unsuccessful and the directors prevail not only will the corporation be faced with paying attorney's fees for both sides, but it may also have to absorb the indemnification expense if it is not insured.

64) *See* notes 55-56 *supra* and accompanying text.

to press a shareholder claim-disruption of corporate affairs, the destruction of employee morale and adverse publicity-are equally unpersuasive.

At the threshold is the fact that the potential for disruption of corporate affairs, the destruction of corporate morale, and the public's reaction are difficult to measure. The very terms "disruption," "morale," and "public reaction" are vague and easily abused.[65] By contrast, the benefits of a successful shareholder derivative suit are substantial and concrete.[66] Moreover, although the potential for abuse exists,[67] the shareholders are likely to have a lesser motive to abuse the derivative suit than a board of directors is likely to have to block even valid claims.[68]

Even if the factors discussed above could be isolated, measured, and evaluated, it remains true that Congress has expressly approved the derivative action as a means of curbing corporate abuses in the securities markets.[69] It would seem appropriate, therefore, to adopt rules which encourage shareholder policing of the corporation's activities rather than discourage it.

(3) An Alternative to the Power of a Board of Directors to Block a Shareholder Derivative Suit

Given the great potential for abuse of the power of a special litigation committee to block a shareholder derivative suit, an alternative policing mechanism for the derivative action is necessary; that mechanism could be the courts. The courts could prevent shareholder derivative suits that are clearly contrary to the best interests of a corporation by utilizing the "adequacy of representation" requirement of rule 23.1 of the Federal Rules of Civil Procedure[70] and exercising the broad discretion given to the courts to award attorney's fees

---

65) *See Developments, supra* note 56, at 1494-95.
66) Although somewhat dated, Judge Rifkind's analysis in Brendle v. Smith, 46 F. Supp. 522 (S.D.N.Y. 1942), continues to reflect the advantages of the derivative action. He said:

> Despite the numerous abuses which have developed in conjunction with [derivative] suits they have accomplished much in policing the corporate system especially in protecting corporate ownership as against corporate management. They have educated corporate directors in the principles of fiduciary responsibility...discouraged membership on boards by persons not truly interested in the corporation...[T]he minority effect of such actions has... prevented diversion of large amounts [of money] from stockholders to managements and outsiders... [and has provided] an arsenal of authorities to support... cautioning [directors] who may be disposed to risk evasion of the high standard the courts have imposed [on them].

Id. at 525-26. *See also* Dykstra, *supra* note 1, at 77-78.
67) 46 F. Supp. at 525. The "strike suit" may be one such abuse. *See* note 86 *infra* and accompanying text.
68) *See generally* notes 19, 29 *supra* and accompanying text.
69) *See* Securities Exchange Act of 1934, § 16(b), 15 U.S.C. § 78p(b) (1976), which authorizes derivative suits to recover short-swing profits earned by corporate "insiders" notwithstanding the decision of a board of directors not to sue.
70) FED. R. CIV. P. 23.1.

in derivative actions.[71]

Rule 23.1 of the Federal Rules of Civil Procedure provides that "[t]he derivative action may not be maintained if it appears that the plaintiff does not fairly and adequately represent the interest of the shareholders or members similarly situated in enforcing the right of the corporation or association."[72] Like the parallel requirement in the class action, the adequate representation requirement is designed to prevent a conflict of interest among the plaintiff-shareholders purportedly being represented in the action.[73] Clearly, the adequate representation requirement was not intended to be nor must it be interpreted in a manner that would permit the objection of a minority of shareholders to amount to inadequate representation.[74] Nevertheless, rule 23.1 requires that the plaintiff-shareholder represent the interests of shareholders other than himself.[75] A derivative action which is clearly shown to be contrary to the best interests of a corporation must also be contrary to the interests of the shareholders of the corporation, particularly when significant negative pressures on corporate profits can be expected.[76] Accordingly, a court would be justified in dismissing such a derivative action under rule 23.1.[77]

---

71) *See* 7A WRIGHT & MILLER § 1841 (1972).

72) FED. R. CIV. P. 23.1.

73) *See* 7A WRIGHT & MILLER § 1833, at 393.

74) Arguably, whenever there is a disagreement' among the shareholders over whether a derivative action should be commenced a conflict of interest exists. Such a conflict, however, cannot be sufficient to demonstrate inadequacy of representation. *Id.* at 394. Otherwise, virtually all derivative actions would have to be dismissed. A more cogent reading of 23.1 is that the plaintiff is required only to be an adequate representative for those similarly situated, namely minority shareholders. *Id.*

75) *See* Kuzmickey v. Dunmore Corp., 420 F. Supp. 226, 231 (D.C. Pa. 1976).

76) The shareholder, who commences the action may have an interest in the outcome of the derivative claim based on principle. The shareholder's attorney, of course, will be expecting a significant fee. Although arguably ethical management is in the best interests of the corporation over the long-term, neither the shareholder's interest in principle nor his attorney's interest in fees are likely to be deemed consistent with the interests of the remaining shareholders or the corporation.

77) That argument receives considerable support from an analogous situation in the context of class action suits. Many of the factors used in determining whether a plaintiff adequately represents the other members of the class in a class action under Federal Rule of Civil Procedure 23 would also appear to be applicable in derivative actions under rule 23.1. See 7A WRIGHT & MILLER § 1833, at 393 (1972). There may be instances where the very process of litigation could adversely affect the overall interests of the other class members. *See generally* Development *supra* note 56, at 1493-95. For example, if the class members are joined in an ongoing business relationship, the costs of litigation, the risk of classwide liability, and adverse publicity may seriously undermine that relationship. *Id.* at 1494. There is a strong possibility that a significant conflict of interest can arise in such an instance. It is the responsibility of the court to determine whether the class action should be permitted to continue. *Id.* at 1495. The court has a similar task in the derivative suit and through proper execution of that responsibility it may protect the corporation from undesirable litigation. In making its determination, however, the court must balance the benefits to be derived from litigation against the likelihood that the corporation will be adversely affected. Insofar as it is unusual for a derivative action to be contrary to the long-term best interests of the corporation, the burden of proving the undesirability of the litigation should be with the corporation.

The court may also control the number of derivative suits brought contrary to the best interests of the corporation by the careful exercise of its discretion to award attorney's fees to a successful plaintiff-shareholder.[78] The courts have always considered the benefits obtained by the corporation as a result of the derivative suit as one of the factors relevant in determining the amount, if any, of attorney's fees that should be awarded.[79] When the derivative action has been shown to be clearly contrary to the best interests of the corporation the court would be justified in denying attorney's fees even to a successful plaintiff. Denying attorney's fees to plaintiffs in a derivative suit that is harmful to the best interests of the corporation would be a potent deterrent to such suits, particularly since the prospect of large attorney's fees is often a major incentive for bringing such actions.[80]

Court policing of the derivative action necessarily will require the court to engage in making at least a limited business judgment on the desirability of permitting the derivative action to continue. The traditional model of litigation,[81] however, calls for the judge to act as a somewhat passive umpire settling disputes between two adverse parties.[82] Thus, there will be those who will argue that it is inappropriate for a judge to intrude into matters concerning corporate management. These arguments, however, are not persuasive.

The traditional model of litigation has been significantly altered with the advent of so called public law litigation.[83] Judges have been increasingly thrust into matters requiring the analysis of business policy in order to reach a resolution of a conflict. The California General Corporation Law,[84] for example, indicates that the judge may be required to consider whether a derivative suit is consistent with the best interests of the corporation when determining whether the plaintiff-shareholder should be required to furnish security.[85]

---

78) *See* 7A WRIGHT & MILLER § 1841 (1972).

79) *See, e.g.,* Newmark v. RKO General, Inc., 332 F. Supp. 161, 163-64 (S.D.N.Y. 1971). Among the other factors considered by the courts are: (1) the amount of the recovery, (2) the novelty and complexity of the legal issues, (3) the skill with which the services were performed, (4) the quality of the attorney, (5) the contingent nature of the attorney's retention and (6) the number of hours reasonably spent by the attorney in preparing the case. *Id.*

80) *See* note 55 *supra* and text accompanying note 87 *infra.*

81) *See generally* Chayes, *The Role of the Judge in the Public Law Litigation,* 89 HARV. L. REV. 1281 (1976).

82) *Id.* at 1286.

83) *Id.* at 1284.

84) CAL. CORP. CODE §§ 1-2319 (Deering Supp. 1980).

85) *Id.* at § 800(c)(1). Section 800(d) inidicates that the court, in ruling on a motion under § 800(c)(1), must "consider such evidence ... as may be material . . .to the ground or grounds upon which the motion is based." *Id.* at § 800(d). Such a consideration must necessarily entail some evaluation of the business factors offered by both sides. *Cf.* Findley v. Garrett, 109 Cal. App. 2d, 166, 177, 240 P.2d 421, 427-28 (1952) (although business judgment of directors will be given great consideration, even absent allegations of fraud or bad faith, the court must consider, on the facts alleged, whether the best inter-

Indeed, the debate seems to have already shifted from whether to assume the role of business analyst to how to perform the role successfully.

Courts are not necessarily ill-equiped to deal with matters requiring analysis of business policy. Hearings, off-the-bench research, special masters, expert witnesses and consultants are all available to insure that the court is well informed when making its decision. Accordingly, the court should assume a more aggressive posture in policing the shareholder derivative action.

b. Preventing "Strike Suits"

It has often been argued that a board of directors must be able to terminate shareholder derivative suits in order to prevent "strike suits." Much of the persuasiveness of this argument turns on the definition of strike suits that is employed.

One law dictionary defines a strike suit as a "shareholder derivative action begun with hope of winning large attorney fees or private settlements, and no intention of benefiting the corporation on behalf of which suit is theoretically brought."[86] This definition is overly broad and raises the spectre of evils that may not exist.

Although to some it may appear undesirable to permit derivative suits that are motivated largely out of a desire to attain large attorney's fees, the motive of the suit is not always indicative of the merits of the claim or of the desirability of letting the claim go forward. The prospects of large individual recoveries in a shareholder derivative suit are not often bright. Accordingly, the prospect of lucrative fees may serve as a major and legitimate incentive for attorneys to represent shareholders in derivative actions.[87] At the same time, the motive of the attorney is not necessarily indicative of the motive of the shareholders. To the extent that a meritorious derivative action helps correct and deter corporate wrongdoing, the longterm interests of the corporation and society must be furthered. Therefore, insofar as the derivative suit is a socially beneficial private enforcement mechanism, the motives and incentives on the part of either the shareholders or their attorneys for bringing a meritorious claim should be irrelevant.

When a group of shareholders attempt to obtain some personal gain at the expense of the

---

ests of the corporation would be clearly compromised by a refusal to prosecute a claim). *See also* Cramer v. General Tel. & Elec. Corp., 582 F.2d 259, 275 (3d Cir. 1978); Note supra, note 11, at 196. The position advocated in this article advocates no greater involvement by the court than was evident in *Findley*. However, this article does advocate altering the analysis from whether the refusal to prosecute the derivative action is so clearly contrary to the interests of the corporation to whether prosecution would be contrary to the best interests of the corporation.

86) BLACK'S LAW DICTIONARY 1276 (5th ed. 1979).
87) *See* note 19 *supra*.

judicial system and their corporation, the derivative suit ceases to be a useful and desirable private enforcement mechansim. A more appropriate definition of a strike suit, therefore, would be a suit commenced for the purpose of obtaining a private settlement or to annoy or embarrass the defendants. Whether or not a derivative action is a strike suit is likely often to be determined with reference to the merits of the claim. The element of shareholder intent, however, is never totally eliminated. It would be patently inappropriate to permit a special litigation committee to make the subjective determination that a derivative claim should be dismissed because it was intended to "embarrass or annoy" the defendants, particularly in light of the fact that all litigation is likely to annoy and embarrass the defendants to some extent.

(1) Alternative Means of Preventing Strike Suits

There are alternative measures for preventing strike suits that would not have the potential for abuse or the adverse effect on the derivative action that permitting a board of directors to block a derivative action would have.

Discouraging private settlements, which profit the shareholders but do little to benefit the corporation in the way of correcting the alleged wrongful practice, is essential if the strike suit is to be eliminated. Theoretically, such a settlement is precluded by operation of Federal Rule of Civil Procedure 23.1.[88] Rule 23.1, however, is not always as effective as it could be. For example, the proposed dismissal or compromise might not reveal the private payment.[89] Moreover, the settlement may not become public because the plaintiff did not go through customary dismissal procedures to end the suit.[90] The lack of standards for the approval or rejection of a proposed dismissal or compromise might also impede application of rule 23.1.[91]

Illicit private settlements might be more effectively deterred by establishing a rule which makes the shareholder a constructive trustee on behalf of the corporation of any funds received as a result of a private settlement in a derivative suit.[92] These funds could then be

---

88) Rule 23.1 provides that "[t]he action shall not be dismissed or compromised without the approval of the court, and notice of the proposed dismissal or compromise shall be given to shareholders or members in such manner as the court directs." FED. R. Civ. P. 23.1. It has been suggested that the adverse effects arising from private settlement of derivative suits was one of the major catalysts for adopting rule 23.1. Haudek, *The Settlement and Dismissal of Stockholders' Actions-Part II: The Settlement,* 23 SW. L. J. 765, 816 (1969) [hereinafter cited as Haudek Part II].
89) *See* Haudek Part II, *supra* note 88, at 816.
90) *See* Haudek, *The Settlement and Dismissal of Stockholders' Actions-Part I,* 22 SW. L. J. 767, 776-79 (1968).
91) *See generally* Haudek, *supra* note 90, at 770, 783.
92) *See* Haudek Part II, *supra* note 88, at 816-17.

recovered at the suit of the corporation.[93] Moreover, recovery of the funds would not be conditioned upon the corporation showing that it had been injured or suffered loss,[94] nor would it be necessary that the plaintiff actually have commenced, as opposed to merely threatening to commence, a derivative action.[95] The effective implementation of the constructive trust approach would require the cooperation and participation of the other shareholders. Cooperation could be enhanced by developing some form of reward for shareholders who discover and disclose illicit private settlements.

Strike suits could be further discouraged by enacting and vigorously enforcing statutes that enable victorious defendants to recover their litigation expenses. Under current law the prevailing party in an action may not recover attorney's fees unless expressly permitted by statute.[96] This practice provides the plaintiff in a derivative action a great advantage by enabling him to seek a substantial private settlement without the risk of incurring double litigation expenses.[97] Conversely, the defendant in a derivative action is likely to be encouraged to settle privately in order to avoid the risk of substantial litigation costs.[98] By enabling a successful defendant to recoup litigation expenses from the plaintiff, commencing strike suits would become far more risky.[99] Accordingly, strike suits would likely decrease in number.[100]

Finally, strike suits may be discouraged by requiring security deposits from derivative suit plaintiffs[101] and by requiring such plaintiffs to be shareholders of record at commencement of the action and throughout the proceedings.[102] Although it is a relatively simple task to

---

93) *Id.*

94) *Id.* at 817.

95) *Id.* at 818.

96) *See generally* 6 MOORE 54.70[l]. An exception is made when a party has acted in bad faith, vexatiously, wantonly or for an oppressive reason. *Id.* at 54.77[2] and n.17, at 1709.

97) The fact that attorneys generally undertake derivative suits on a contingency fee basis should have some deterrent impact on frivolous suits. *See* notes 55-56 *supra* and accompanying text. Nevertheless, plaintiffs are likely to have fewer costs involved in litigating the claim. *See* Berlack, *Stockholders' Suits: A Possible Substitute*, 35 MICH. L. REV. 597, 603 (1937). By enabling a defendant to recover its attorney's fees, the risks to the plaintiff are increased and it becomes less likely that a frivolous or nonmeritorious derivative action will be commenced. *See* POSNER, *supra* note 55, at 452-53.

98) Because of the indemnification expense involved, *see* note 62 *supra*, the corporation will also be encouraged to settle even when the individual director would prefer to put on a defense.

99) *See* note 97 *supra.*

100) *Id.* It has been suggested that a shareholder or a corporation may have a tort action against a strike suitor based on malicious use of process or abuse of process. *See* M. SCHAEFTLER, THE LIABILITIES OF OFFICE: INDEMNIFICATION AND INSURANCE OF CORPORATE OFFICERS AND DIRECTORS 18 (1976). Although such an action theoretically provides some deterrance to strike suits, in practice it may be undermined by the difficult burden of establishing "malice," "willfulness," or the "absence of probable cause." *Id.* at 18-19.

101) *See* Dykstra, *supra* note 1, at 88-94.

102) *Id.* at 94. Both the security requirement and the contemporaneous holdings requirement have been at-

avoid security statutes[103] and the contemporaneous holdings requirement,[104] these two devices have prevented strike suits.[105]

IV. CONCLUSION

Permitting an even obstensibly "disinterested" litigation committee, acting under the authorization of a board of directors, to block a shareholder derivative action is unnecessary either as a means of adequately protecting the board of directors' role as chief managing body of the corporation or as a means of protecting against undesirable strike suits. At the same time, the litigation committee approach is difficult to police and easily abused.

By removing from the board of directors or its offspring-the litigation committee-the power to block derivative suits, much of the potential for the abuse of the business judgment rule would be eliminated. Moreover, directors, knowing that they can no longer block shareholder derivative suits, may be more inclined to examine a shareholder's complaint carefully and arrive objectively at a proper course of conduct. Finally, strict enforcement of the demand rule could lead to more efficient judicial handling of shareholder derivative claims. Of course the alternatives that this article proposes would not eliminate all of the problems now associated with the shareholder derivative suit. For example, corporate control of a derivative action may give rise to abuses heretofore less common.[106] Moreover, strike suits may be somewhat more prone to arise under the alternative deterrent devices proposed by this article, particularly if the active commitment of the court and nonplaintiff shareholders

tacked as being unsupportable. *See* N. LATTIN, LAW OF CORPORATIONS § 106, at 422-23 (2d ed. 1971) (discussing the contemporary holdings requirement); Hornstein, *New Aspects of Stockholders' Derivative Suits*, 47 COLUM. L. REV. 1, 4 (1947) (discussing security requirements).

103) A security statute could be avoided by simply filing the action in a state which lacks a security statute or by bringing the action under federal law. See A. FREY, J. CHOPER, N. LEECH & C. MORRIS, CASES AND MATERIALS ON CORPORATIONS 706 (2d ed. 1977).

104) The extent to which the contemporaneous holding requirement can be avoided may turn in large measure on the construction given to the requirement by the courts. See Dykstra, *supra* note 1, at 94-97.

105) It should be apparent to the reader that the security and contemporaneous holdings requirement should not be used as the primary deterrent to derivative actions. Rather, they are useful only as supplements to the award of attorney's fees and those devices intended to curb private settlement.

106) Directors, their power to block derivative suits removed, still possess ways of protecting their colleagues when the directors assume control of the litigation. For example, directors can ordinarily settle or dismiss an action without court approval. See Haudek, *supra* note 90, at 772 and cases cited therein. Although a settlement approved by a board controlled by by the defendants is subject to judicial scrutiny, *see* Wolf v. Barkes, 348 F.2d 994, 996 (2d Cir.), *cert. denied*, 382 U.S. 941 (1965), the protection afforded is illusory since control is easily avoided by use of the litigation committee and difficult to prove even in the absence of a litigation committee.

is not forthcoming.

New abuses will require new safeguards to curb those abuses.[107] Until the necessary safeguards arise, however, the social and commercial benefits that can be realized from an effective shareholder derivative suit process would seem to far outweigh the potential for abuse that exists in a system where a board can effectively obstruct shareholder attempts to eliminate corporate wrongdoing.

---

107) For example, the ability of directors to protect their colleagues through settling the claim or having it dismissed may be lessened by permitting shareholders to bring suit against such directors for breach of fiduciary duty. *See* Note, *supra* note 11, at 176 n.60. In light of the broad discretion given to directors with respect to litigation, however, *see* Maldonado v. Flynn,. 485 F. Supp. 274, 280-81, 284-85 (S.D.N.Y. 1980), the chances for success in such an action are minimal. A more effective approach would be to encourage shareholder intervention in the action under rule 24(a)(2) of the Federal Rules of Civil Procedure. FED. R. Civ. P. 24(a)(2). Rule 24 permits intervention whenever there is a substantial possibility that the representation may prove inadequate. 7A WRIGHT & MILLER § 1909, at 520-21 (1972). Although representation in corporate litigation by directors is generally presumed to be adequate vis-a-vis the shareholders, *Id.* at 525-27, this presumption is easily rebutted. One commentatory has opined that "intervention will be allowed, if there is even a hint of collusion between the purported representative and those to whom he is formally opposed in the litigation, or if for any other reason is appears that the representative is not making a diligent effort to protect those whom he represents." *Id.* at 529-30. Shareholder intervention would limit the board's power to dismiss or settle the claim, *see* Haudek *supra* note 90, at 773, and would more adequately assure full and adequate representation.

Corporate Legal Personality and Corporate Loss in Korean Law

Kon Sik Kim

I. Introduction

Stock corporations in Korea generally share common characteristics with business corporations in other jurisdictions, such as legal personality, limited liability, and "centralized management under a board structure.[1] Although corporate legal personality, strictly speaking, does not necessarily entail limited liability or centralized management, the term will be employed here broadly to incorporate the other two corporate traits. A fiction brought in to simplify complicated legal relationships involving a corporation, the concept of legal personality, if strictly applied, may engender inappropriate or even unjust consequences. A familiar example of such injustice arises when a controlling shareholder dominating the corporate decision-making process tries to hide behind the "corporate veil" to avoid corporate creditors. Courts of most industrialized jurisdictions address this problem by invoking a kind of "piercing the corporate veil" doctrine.[2] Korea is no exception. It is now well established in Korea that the court can pierce the corporate veil to enable corporate creditors to reach the controlling shareholder behind it in certain circumstances.[3]

In other contexts, however, the corporate form is still firmly respected. The most conspicuous examples may be court decisions involving one-person corporations. In 1983, the Supreme Court in a full chamber decision held that shareholder-managers who misappropriated corporate funds were liable for the crime of breach of trust, despite the fact that they together held all the shares of the firm.[4] The rationale behind this decision was simple – the corporation is a separate legal entity, distinct from its shareholders.

The court's separate-entity rationale may engender unnecessary hurdles in various contexts.

---

1) *Reinier Kraakman et. al.* The Anatomy of Corporate Law 5 (2d ed. 2009).
2) *Reinier Kraakman et. al.* supra note 1, 139.
3) *Chul-Song Lee Hoisabeop Gangui* (Lectures on Corporate Law), 46–47 (16th ed. 2009) (in Korean).
4) Supreme Court, Judgment of December 13, 1983 (No. 83Do2330).

Recent decisions on leveraged buyouts (LBOs) are a prime example. Also, decisions on issuance of equity securities at an unfairly low price have stimulated reexamination of the concept of legal personality by corporate law scholars. These decisions not only raise intriguing theoretical issues but also have the potential to significantly influence economic activities in Korea. Indeed, a famous decision involving a firm called Everland, a de facto holding company of Samsung Group, was closely covered by the local media, as it affects the succession of management control in the largest business group in Korea.[5]

These cases reveal changing facets of economic reality in Korea and, at the same time, the current status of corporate legal personality in Korean jurisprudence. The purpose of this paper is to examine the proper role of the concept of corporate legal personality, and the related notion of corporate loss, on the basis of the analysis of these cases.

The paper proceeds as follows: Part II describes the relevant court decisions. Part III is an analysis of these court decisions from functional and comparative perspectives. Based on the analysis, Part IV attempts to redefine the role of legal personality and corporate loss in corporate law.

II. Recent Court Decisions

1. Corporate Law's Task and Two Types of Problems

Although there is still some dispute as to whose interests the corporation should serve, it is now widely agreed that shareholder interests should be given priority, if not exclusive attention, at least in financially sound firms.[6] One can safely say that a primary task of corporate law is to promote shareholder interests. This should be done in two ways: first, by restraining management decisions that harm shareholder interests, and second, by refraining from unduly hindering management decisions that promote shareholder interests.

Korean corporate law at the moment is faced with challenges on both of these fronts. A shareholder who suffers loss from a particular management action may have no effective remedy. This will be called the Type I problem. On the other hand, even when a transaction does not damage the interests of corporate stakeholders (such as shareholders and

---

5) This decision attracted global attention as well. Economist, June 6, 2009, at 63.
6) For a more cautious account, see, e.g., *Reinier Kraakman et. al.* supra note 1, 28–29.

creditors), the court sometimes proscribes it, focusing on corporate loss. This will be called the Type II problem.

Both the Type I and Type II problems seem to have the same origin, namely, the notion that a corporation has a separate legal personality. They both center on the concept of corporate loss. The Type I problem involves share-holder's remedies, whereas the Type II problem relates to creditor interests. Court decisions dealing with the two types of issues will be discussed in the following sections.

2. Type I Problem: Corporate Loss and Shareholder's Remedies

The Type I problem arises when shareholders are given no effective remedy for their loss. In some cases, even when shareholders are the ones who suffer ultimate loss, the corporation, not individual shareholders, is given legal remedies based on the concept of corporate loss. Corporate loss involved in the Type I problem can be divided into two kinds of loss: positive and negative. Positive loss occurs when the corporation's value decreases as a result of management misconduct, while negative loss occurs when a particular act of management obstructs an increase in the corporation's value. This section will introduce two leading cases, one involving each kind of loss.

Before we start, a brief explanation on yet another division of loss is in order. This division applies to shareholder loss only. Shareholder loss may be divided into direct and indirect losses. Indirect loss refers to the loss caused to shareholders as a consequence of corporate loss. For example, if a director's misconduct causes a decline in corporate value, its shareholders suffer indirect loss as a result. Direct loss, on the other hand, refers to the loss of shareholders unrelated to corporate loss.

a) *Hanra Venture Capital* Decision: Positive Loss

The Type I problem is related to indirect loss. Commentators are in dispute as to whether or not an individual shareholder can sue directors to recover an indirect loss. A leading case on this issue was decided in 1993.[7] A venture capital firm called *Hanra* purchased 30 percent of the shares of *Daeil Precision Manufacturing* ("*Daeil*") in April 1989. *Daeil*'s majority shareholder ("X"), owning more than 60 percent, was running *Daeil* as a representative director (the functional equivalent of a chief executive officer). In June 1989, X misappropriated corporate funds, and *Daeil* went bankrupt as a result. *Hanra* sued X for dam-

---

7) Supreme Court, Judgment of January 26, 1993 (No. 91Da36093).

ages under Article 401 of the Commercial Code, which allows a third party to sue a director directly if the third party's loss is caused by the director's intentional or grossly negligent failure to perform his or her fiduciary duty. The Supreme Court dismissed *Hanra's* claim, ruling that the shareholders were not entitled to sue the wrongdoing director for indirect loss under Article 401. The court did not provide any justification for this ruling, and went on to deny X's liability under the general tort provision in the Civil Code (Article 750).

Corporate loss involved in *Hanra* was positive loss. When negative loss is involved, the issue becomes more difficult conceptually. A leading decision on negative loss was made in the *Everland* decision mentioned earlier.

b) *Everland* Decision: Negative Loss

The *Everland* case involved issuance of equity securities to a third party at an excessively low price. A de facto holding company of *Samsung Group*, *Everland* owned an amusement park and real estate and held, directly and indirectly, shares in major member firms of *Samsung Group*. A majority of *Everland's* shares were held by Mr. *Kun-Hee Lee*, the group chairman, and several major affiliates of the group. In October 1996, *Everland's* board decided to issue convertible bonds (CBs) in the amount of 10 billion won.[8] Originally, CBs were issued to the existing shareholders, and the board reserved the right to assign unsubscribed CBs to a third party.[9] The conversion price was 7,700 won per share, which the court later found grossly unfair. Surprisingly, all but one shareholder declined the opportunity to purchase these cheap securities.[10] The board promptly assigned the unsubscribed CBs to the four siblings of Chairman *Lee*, including Mr. *Jae-Yong Lee*, his heir apparent. The younger Mr. *Lee* and his sisters converted the CBs into shares amounting to about 64 percent of total shares.[11] These shares enabled him to secure effective control of Everland, and eventually of the entire Samsung Group.

Despite the significance of this transaction, it was virtually ignored by the local media until June 2000, when a group of law professors filed a charge with the prosecutors' office against

---

8) During the last 15 years, US$1 has been mostly valued at somewhere between 800 and 1,300 won.
9) Unless otherwise provided for in the articles of incorporation, shareholders have preemptive rights for shares, convertible bonds and bonds with warrant (Commercial Code Articles 418, 513(3), and 516-2(4)). The model articles of incorporation generally adopted by listed firms include provisions enabling the board of directors to issue those securities within certain limits to a third party. It is not clear whether *Everland*, a non-listed firm, had such provisions in its articles of incorporation.
10) The exceptional shareholder was *Cheil Sugar Manufacturing*, a former affiliate of *Samsung Group* now under control of Chairman Lee's nephew. *Cheil Sugar* duly subscribed to about 3 percent of the CBs.
11) Curiously, the relative size of these shares was not even mentioned in the Supreme Court opinion.

those involved in the transaction. After some foot-dragging, the prosecutor's office managed to indict two senior officers of *Everland* just before the expiry of the period for prosecution. Both the district court and the high court found the officers guilty of breach of trust. In May 2009, the Supreme Court, in a split (6 to 5) full chamber decision, reversed the lower court decision.[12] Although widely criticized by the general public, this decision in effect saved *Samsung Group*, and the *Lee* family, from a state of limbo. The decision involved various issues; this discussion will focus on one: corporate loss in share issuance. Although the company actually issued CBs, the term "shares" will be employed here for the sake of convenience, as applicable provisions are essentially identical.

It is not in dispute that a board enjoys wide discretion in setting the price in a rights offering – or that, as long as the issue price is not lower than the par value, the corporation does not suffer a loss even when the issue price is substantially lower than the market price. Dispute does exist, however, as to whether the corporation suffers loss when it issues shares to a third party at an unfairly low price ("unfair share issuance"). After the lower court pronounced the managers guilty, some scholars strongly criticized the decision, arguing that it was the shareholders, not the corporation, who suffered loss. They asserted that corporate loss could not arise from a so-called equity transaction, a corporate act of issuing or acquiring its own equity securities.[13] This view is based on the conceptual distinction between the corporation and its shareholders. According to this view, share issuance can theoretically incur no loss to the firm because the shareholders' equity is bound to increase regardless of the level of the issue price.

This view, however, could persuade only one Supreme Court judge in *Everland*. It was rejected both by the majority opinion and by the dissenting opinion. Both the majority and the dissenting judges recognized the existence of corporate loss in unfair share issuance. The majority found a basis of corporate loss in the corporate statutes. Under the Commercial Code, a third party is required to pay to the firm an amount equal to the gap between the issue price and the fair price, if the third party, in collusion with directors, subscribed to the shares at an excessively low price (Article 424-2(1)). The Code also provides that the third party's liability does not affect the directors' liability for damages to the corporation and the shareholders (Article 424-2(3)). The Commercial Code thus acknowledges the possibility of corporate loss in unfair share issuance.

---

12) Supreme Court, Judgment of May 29, 2009 (No. 2007Do4949).
13) See, e.g., *Chul-Song Lee* Equity Transactions and Criminal Liability of Officers, *Ingwon Gwa Jeongeui* (Human Rights and Justice) Vol. 359, 96 (2006) (in Korean).

According to the majority, corporate loss is to be determined by multiplying the number of newly issued shares by the gap between the fair price and the actual issue price. They noted that corporate loss is different from the combined loss of individual shareholders arising from the dilution of the value of their shares. The majority stated that the two losses differ in some respects including the method of calculation.

The majority and dissenting opinions differed only as to the characterization of the issuance. The majority opinion regarded the issuance as a rights offering and held that its nature did not change even when most of the shareholders failed to subscribe and the unsubscribed shares were allocated to the controlling family. On the contrary, the dissenting judges emphasized that the issuance was in effect a private offering designed to hand over the control of the group to the younger Mr. *Lee*.

3. Type II Problem: Corporate Loss and Creditors

The Type II problem arises when a particular corporate activity is proscribed despite the absence of shareholders' loss. If the activity harms the interests of creditors, the court may be justified in prohibiting such activity. The court, however, sometimes prohibits a certain transaction without regard to its impact on creditor interests, relying instead on the notion of corporate loss. A classic example is decisions involving the one-person firm.

a) One-Person Firm Decisions

The first reported opinion of the Supreme Court on the one-person firm came out in 1974.[14] The case involved a one-person corporation whose shareholder disposed of an important corporate asset without securing shareholder resolution.[15] The court pronounced the accused shareholder not guilty of breach of trust. It denied the shareholder's intent to inflict loss on the corporation on the grounds that the corporate loss is identical to the shareholder's loss in a one-person firm.

This reasoning was explicitly rejected, however, in a full bench decision of the Supreme Court in 1983.[16] The case involved two shareholder-directors, who in collusion misappropriated corporate funds to settle their personal debts. Although the prosecutor's office indicted them for breach of trust, the lower court held them not guilty, basically following

---

14) Supreme Court, Judgment of April 23, 1974 (No. 73Do2611).
15) This decision predated the Supreme Court decision holding that a formal shareholder meeting is not required in a one-person firm. Supreme Court, Judgment of April 13, 1976 (No. 74Da1755).
16) Supreme Court, Judgment of December 13, 1983 (No. 83Do2330).

the reasoning of the 1974 decision. The Supreme Court, however, reversed the lower court decision, emphasizing that the shareholder and the corporation are separate legal entities even in a one-person firm. This reasoning has been faithfully followed in subsequent decisions.[17]

b) Decisions on Leveraged Buyouts

This kind of formalistic thinking proves especially cumbersome in the context of LBOs. Generally, an LBO is a set of transactions designed to acquire a target company with funds borrowed from financial institutions. A distinctive feature of the LBO is that the acquirer uses the target's assets as security for debt financing. Although LBOs may take various forms in reality, use of the target's assets constitutes a core element. LBO transactions started gaining popularity in Korea after the economic crisis in the late 1990s. A recent decision of the Supreme Court, however, was a cold shower for the LBO industry.[18]

The target involved in this simple LBO was *Shinhan* Co.("*Shinhan*"), which was in a bankruptcy proceeding. Believing that he could turn the company around, the defendant decided to acquire *Shinhan*. In 2001, to acquire *Shinhan*, the defendant incorporated a paper company ("S") with 300 million won. On June 4, S borrowed from *Dongyang Hyundai Merchant Banking* Co. ("*Dongyang*") 35 billion won for the takeover. S promised *Dongyang* to put up as security for the loan the newly issued shares of *Shinhan* it planned to acquire. S further promised that after it took over *Shinhan*, it would replace the shares with *Shinhan*'s real estate. On June 7, S acquired 66.2 percent of the newly issued shares of *Shinhan* for 26 billion won, and the defendant took office as representative director. From July 3 to 9, 2001, in exchange for the *Shinhan* shares returned from *Dongyang*, S made *Shinhan* offer its real estate as security. S also acquired from *Shinhan*'s creditors existing *Shinhan* shares and bankruptcy claims against *Shinhan*. *Shinhan* spent 16.1 billion won to repay its bankruptcy obligations. The defendant failed to pay any compensation for *Shinhan*'s credit support. The prosecutor's office indicted the defendant on a charge of breach of trust.

The Seoul High Court rejected the prosecutor's claim of breach of trust, denying the defendant's intention to inflict loss on *Shinhan*.[19] The court's reasoning went as follows: His decision to put up *Shinhan*'s real estate as security was to secure the funds S needed for the acquisition of *Shinhan*, and it did not necessarily impose a risk of real loss on *Shinhan*.

---

17) For example, Supreme Court, Judgment of May 23, 1989 (No. 89Do570); Supreme Court, Judgment of August 23, 1996 (No. 96Do1525).
18) Supreme Court, Judgment of November 9, 2006 (No. 2004Do7027).
19) Seoul High Court, Judgment of October 6, 2004 (No. 2003No3322).

As a result of the transaction, *Shinhan*'s ability to service the debt improved, which reduced *Shinhan*'s risk of losing the real estate. The court found that the whole transaction was in *Shinhan*'s interest.

The Supreme Court, however, reversed the lower court decision, employing a formalistic approach based on the one-person corporation decision. According to the court, a corporation and its shareholders are separate entities, and a shareholder's action to inflict a loss on a corporation constitutes a breach of trust even when the corporation is wholly owned by the shareholder. The same logic applies to a director who acts with the understanding of the single shareholder.

Generally, the target corporation runs the risk of losing its assets if the debtor-purchaser fails to repay the loan. The Supreme Court emphasized that using the target's assets as security is justified only if the purchaser properly compensates the target for its risk. If the debtor-purchaser provides additional security to the creditor, the target's risk of losing the real estate will decrease. The Supreme Court, however, held that a target's management cannot avoid criminal liability just by providing additional security.[20] Thus, the debtor-purchaser must pay a proper consideration to the target to avoid criminal liability.

The Supreme Court in *Shinhan* briefly noted that the potential interests of shareholders and creditors should be protected. It did not, however, discuss how these interests had been affected by the LBO. Even admitting that *Shinhan* repaid part of its debt with the money paid in by S, the court did not take account of the fact that the creditors were repaid in reality. Nor did the court take account of the fact that *Shinhan*'s financial position improved as a result of the LBO. Ignoring these factors relating to the actual interests of shareholders and creditors, the court focused on the possibility of loss to *Shinhan*.

This decision of the Supreme Court sent a shock wave through the entire financial industry. It did not, however, sound the death knell for LBOs. It just made LBO professionals more cautious and led them to try a different type of LBO, which involves merger with the target instead of formal credit support by the target, to achieve essentially the same economic effect. This merger-type LBO has also been subject to the court's review. A leading case was decided by the Busan High Court in 2009.[21]

The relevant facts of this complicated case may be summarized as follows: A member firm of *Dongyang Group, Dongyang Major Co.* ("*Dongyang*") wanted to acquire *Hanil Synthetic Fiber Co.* ("*Hanil*"), which had lots of cash but was in reorganization proceedings. Learning

---

20) Supreme Court, Judgment of February 28, 2008 (No. 2007Do5987).
21) Busan High Court, Judgment of June 25, 2009 (No. 2009No184).

that *Shinhan* now prevents the target from putting up its assets as security for the acquirer's loan, *Dongyang* decided to employ a different type of LBO. *Dongyang* first established a special purpose company ("SPC"). The SPC borrowed 470 billion won and acquired 91.5 percent of the shares of *Hanil*. *Dongyang* merged first with the SPC and then with *Hanil*. After the mergers, Dongyang paid back its debt with the funds (180 billion won) originally held by *Hanil*.

The prosecutor's office indicted the directors of *Hanil* on a charge of breach of trust on the grounds that this transaction was similar in effect to the LBO transaction proscribed in *Shinhan*. The prosecutor's office focused on the fact that the assets (funds) of the target (*Hanil*) were used to finance the acquisition. The district court rejected the prosecutor's claim. The court stated that if the merger was carried out legally, the surviving corporation's decision to pay back its debt with the target's funds was within the realm of legitimate business judgment.[22] The prosecutor's office appealed this decision to the high court. Confirming the lower court decision, the Busan High Court stated that the transaction in this case was different from a security-type LBO as the funds had been raised without putting up *Hanil*'s assets as security.[23] The high court also emphasized that the merger was without defect in process as well as in substance.

III. Analysis of the Decisions

1. Influence of Corporate Legal Personality

The decisions described in Part II illustrate the conspicuous role of the corporate legal entity in Korean jurisprudence. The court's strong tendency to rely on corporate legal personality may be called "entity absolutism." Prime examples demonstrating entity absolutism are decisions on the oneperson corporation. *Shinhan* is merely a logical extension of entity absolutism.

---

22) The district court, however, left room for intervention. It conceded that merging with a nominal SPC with no assets may constitute a breach of trust, as in such cases the target in effect takes over the debt of the acquirer without receiving adequate consideration.

23) Unlike the district court, the high court did not mention the room for intervention in the case of merging with a nominal SPC.

Dealing with the third-party liability of directors, *Hanra* also exuded a strong flavor of entity absolutism. Denying recovery to the shareholder plaintiff, the court in *Hanra* based its conclusion on the existence of corporate loss. If corporate loss is recognized, went the reasoning, a shareholder is not allowed to recover his or her loss individually.

This kind of entity absolutism showed signs of decline in *Everland.* Generally, however, it still remains a dominant discourse in corporate law in Korea. This is problematic from a functional perspective, as entity absolutism may sometimes impede an efficient transaction or an effective remedy for shareholders. From a comparative perspective, entity absolutism is not so prevalent in other developed countries such as the United States, Germany, and Japan.

2. Functional Analysis

a) Type I Problem

Entity absolutism sometimes prevents the court from providing an effective remedy to shareholders (Type I problem) and hinders an efficient transaction (Type II problem). The Type I problem relates to shareholders' remedies. In a corporate context, a remedy may be discussed at two different levels. First, who has the power to initiate and control the process, individual shareholders or the firm? Second, who is entitled to recovery when the process is successfully completed, individual shareholders or the firm? The two questions are related but conceptually distinct.

From the perspective of an entity absolutist, the concept of corporate loss determines the answer to these questions. If corporate loss is recognized, the corporate decision-making process will govern. In Korean law, a statutory auditor, rather than the board, is authorized to control the firm's suit against directors (Commercial Code, Article 394(1)). If the statutory auditor refuses to sue directors, anyone holding at least 1 percent of the shares of the firm can file a derivative suit (Article 403(1)). Even if the shareholders win in the derivative suit, the recovery goes to the corporation. On the other hand, if corporate loss is not recognized, shareholders who suffer loss can initiate their own suit against responsible directors. If they succeed in the suit, the recovery goes to them.

In *Hanra*, it was not in dispute that *Hanra*, the plaintiff shareholder, suffered economic injury as a result of the defendant director's misconduct. The Supreme Court, however, did not allow *Hanra* to sue the director on the grounds that the case involved corporate, not shareholder, loss. The short opinion of the court did not provide any substantive support for its conclusion.

One may try to justify the court's ruling in two different ways. First, the decision may be justified from the perspective of creditors. If the shareholder recovers directly from the director, the interests of creditors may be jeopardized. The opinion, however, was silent as to whether creditors were involved and whether *Hanra*'s recovery might compromise the interests of creditors.

Second, one may also point out that the plaintiff shareholder was not without remedy as it could file a derivative suit instead. If a plaintiff shareholder cannot satisfy the statutory shareholding requirement (1 percent for a nonlisted firm like *Daeil*), a derivative suit ceases to be an option. This requirement could not have been a problem for *Hanra*, a 30 percent shareholder. It is not clear, however, whether *Hanra* could file a derivative suit afterward. Even if *Hanra* filed and won the derivative suit, the recovery would belong to the firm, which was still dominated by the wrongdoing director.

The Supreme Court in *Hanra* closed its eyes to these concerns. Blinded by the existence of corporate loss, the court did not consider the shareholders. In *Everland*, however, the Supreme Court became more flexible in dealing with unfair share issuance. If the corporation and its shareholders are distinct from each other, it is not easy to recognize corporate loss in unfair share issuance. Share issuance, an equity transaction, is different from normal business transactions. Issuing shares, the corporation does not give up any assets in return for the funds received from investors. This is why the concurring opinion denied corporate loss in *Everland*. Both the majority and dissenting opinions, however, recognized corporate loss in unfair share issuance. Neither provided any grounds for its conclusion. On the other hand, the majority opinion implied that the corporation should take account of the market price or inherent price when it sets an issue price in a non-rights offering. In other words, the majority opinion implicitly acknowledged that the directors have a duty to set the issue price properly in a private offering. The majority's focus on the duty of directors is noteworthy. Although corporate loss was not obvious conceptually in unfair share issuance – shareholders' equity increased, after all, as a result of the issuance in this case – the majority recognized corporate loss, presumably on the basis of breach of director's duty. The focus on the duty of directors, rather than on the abstract legal personality, is functionally more desirable because the duty concept can better induce the court to consider the interests of the real stakeholders behind the corporate entity.

b) Type II Problem

The Korean courts have been generally pragmatic in dealing with one-person corporations. According to the Supreme Court, one-person corporations do not need to hold a formal shareholder meeting,[24] nor do they have to prepare the minutes of the meeting.[25] With the consent of the shareholder, they can even skip the requirement for board approval.[26] In contrast to the flexibility demonstrated in this line of decisions, the Supreme Court has maintained a strict attitude toward appropriation of corporate assets by the shareholder. In a one-person corporation, the shareholder's appropriation of corporate assets does not hurt the shareholder's interests. If there is a creditor, his or her interests may be harmed. Although creditors were presumed to exist in most cases, the court did not explicitly address their presence. Once the court finds corporate loss, it does not seem to feel the need to examine the interests of the stakeholders behind the corporate legal personality, i.e., shareholders and creditors. The problem with this formalistic reasoning is that it may be applied regardless of whether creditor interests are involved.

This problem has been well illustrated in recent LBO decisions in Korea. In *Shinhan*, the acquirer secured only 66.2 percent of the shares. Thus, one may try to justify the ruling in *Shinhan* on the grounds that the transaction only furthered the majority shareholder's sale of his shares.[27] The reasoning of the Supreme Court in *Shinhan*, however, does not support this view. A primary reason for the court's holding in *Shinhan* was that the target corporation did not get any consideration in return for its credit support service – putting up its assets as security for the acquirer's loan. Thus, in order to eliminate the risk of criminal liability, the acquirer should provide some consideration to the target. Given the strict attitude of the court in recent decisions, the acquirer may feel pressure even when it holds all the shares of the target. True, a safer alternative is available to potential acquirers. As *Dongyang* illustrated, an acquirer may achieve essentially the same result by adopting a merger-type LBO. This, however, takes more time and money. The entity absolutism of the court thus leads to increased costs in LBOs.

The Supreme Court's emphasis on the consideration given to the target seems to stem from its obsession with the notion of corporate loss. Reaching its conclusion, the Supreme Court

---

24) Supreme Court, Judgment of April 13, 1976 (No. 74Da1755).
25) Supreme Court, Judgment of December 10, 2004 (No. 2004Da25123).
26) Supreme Court, Judgment of March 31, 1992 (No. 91Da16310).
27) Indeed, LBO transactions carried out with the consent of the 100 percent shareholder are believed to have been subject to no criminal proceedings.

turned a blind eye to the potential benefits of LBO. LBO is admittedly a highly controversial transaction. It may transform a financially sound corporation into a highly leveraged firm. To service the swollen debt after LBO, management may have to sell or close some divisions, abruptly forcing many employees to leave the firm. In the process, a small number of insiders and bankers make lots of money. On the other hand, LBO has a number of positive functions as well. It may be in the interests of the existing shareholders. And if, as in *Shinhan*, LBO is employed as a means of restructuring a troubled firm, it may be in accord with the interests of creditors as well. In LBOs, it is not unusual for existing creditors to get more money than they could otherwise get. Moreover, the acquirer may be more competent and financially solid than the old management.

The court in Dongyang sanctioned merger-type LBOs. A significant difference between the two types of LBO is that the merger type triggers a statutory mechanism for creditor protection under the Commercial Code (i.e., prepayment or offering collateral). From a functional perspective, as long as creditors are similarly protected, even a security-type LBO should not constitute a breach of trust. To provide the same level of protection, the acquirer must get the prior consent of individual creditors, which may not be feasible in reality. A more realistic alternative may be to disallow only those LBOs highly likely to jeopardize the interests of creditors. This alternative is in line with the general practice of corporate governance. As long as the firm remains solvent, management is allowed to engage in a wide range of transactions, regardless of their impact on creditors. Categorically excluding LBOs from this scope of normal transactions may not be justified.

3. Comparative Analysis

A corporation is regarded as a separate legal person in most developed countries. The actual degree of separateness seems to vary from country to country. A recent trend seems to interpret the concept of legal personality in such a manner that it does not lead to functionally unjustifiable results. The following survey shows how the issues discussed in Part II are treated in three other industrial jurisdictions: Japan, Germany, and the United States.

a) Director's Liability to Shareholders

A shareholder like Hanra is in a better position to recover its individual loss in other developed jurisdictions. Courts in the United States, Delaware courts in particular, seem most willing to allow individual shareholders to sue directors directly. In the past, Delaware courts allowed such a shareholder suit only when the plaintiff shareholder suffered a "special injury" – an injury "separate and distinct" from that suffered by other shareholders.[28] If interpreted strictly, the special injury doctrine would severely limit a shareholder lawsuit. The special injury doctrine, however, was abandoned in 2004 in *Tooley v. Donaldson, Lufkin & Jenrette, Inc.*[29] In *Tooley*, the court modified the special injury doctrine by adopting the following formula: whether a shareholder's claim is derivative or direct "must turn *solely* on the following questions: (1) who suffered the alleged harm (the corporation or the suing shareholders); and (2) who would receive the benefit of any recovery or other remedy (the corporation or the stockholders individually)?"[30] Under the *Tooley* formula, a shareholder can file a direct action even when "all stockholders are equally affected" or when the stockholder's injury is not "separate and distinct from that suffered by other stockholders."[31] As shown later, the flexibility of Delaware courts has been further demonstrated in cases dealing with unfair share issuance.[32]

Japanese courts are more willing to accommodate lawsuits filed by shareholders like *Hanra*. Like Korea, Japan has a provision in the Corporate Code specifically dealing with the director's liability to third parties (Article 429(1)). It has long been in dispute whether or not this provision allows shareholders to sue directors directly for their indirect damages. Mindful of the dangers of ignoring the distinction between corporate and individual loss, many scholars support the view that such a shareholder should rely on a derivative suit, not an individual suit. In a number of decisions, however, the courts have allowed individual shareholders to sue directors directly for indirect loss, especially in the context of a close corporation dominated by a controlling shareholder.[33] This pragmatic approach of the court is now gaining support from scholars.[34]

In Germany, shareholder initiative is well respected, but shareholder recovery is not. The shareholder's derivative suit was introduced in the corporate statute in 2005 (Aktiengesetz, Article 148). Before it was introduced, a 10 percent shareholder could force a corporation to file a lawsuit against a director who had inflicted loss on the corporation (pre-2005

---

28) *Kenneth B. Davis* The Forgotten Derivative Suit, 61 Vanderbilt Law Review 387, 442 (2008).
29) 845 A.2d 1031 (Del. 2004).
30) Id. at 1033.
31) Id. at 1038-39.
32) In a close corporation setting, courts in other states have allowed a shareholder to file a direct suit where the corporation suffers loss. *Robert B. Thompson* The Shareholder's Cause of Action for Oppression, 48 Business Lawyer 699, 735 (1993).
33) *Yuji Ito,* Loss of the Corporation and the Shareholder's Claim for Damages (1), 123 *Hogaku Kyokai Zassi* (Journal of the Jurisprudence Association) 1759 (2006) (in Japanese).
34) *Kenjiro Egashira Kabushiki Kaishaho* (Laws of Stock Corporations) 466 (3d ed. 2009) (in Japanese).

Aktiengesetz, Article 147(1)). A shareholder who could not overcome this 10 percent hurdle could instead resort to an individual lawsuit based on tort provisions in the Civil Code.[35] The shareholder's suit was limited in an important respect – if the shareholder wins, the recovery goes to the corporation, not to the plaintiff shareholder.[36]

b) Unfair Share Issuance

In the United States, it is not questioned that unfair share issuance brings injury to the corporation. The question is whether or not a shareholder can sue to recover his or her own loss. The courts have been generally reluctant to allow such shareholder suits. This negative attitude has changed in a recent decision of the Delaware Supreme Court, *Gentile v. Rossette*.[37] *Gentile* involved the controlling shareholder of a corporation, Rossette, who succeeded in favorably changing the conversion ratio for the corporation's debt to him. This change is similar in effect to unfair share issuance. Minority shareholders could not file a derivative suit as the corporation no longer existed after a merger. They instead filed direct suit against Rossette for breach of fiduciary duty. The Delaware Chancery Court held in favor of Rossette, finding that the shareholders' claim was solely derivative.

The Delaware Supreme Court, however, reversed, holding that the shareholders' claim was both direct and derivative. Stating that unfair share issuance normally results in only indirect loss to shareholders, the court admitted that there are instances in which loss can be viewed as direct as well as indirect. A prime example is when shares are issued to controlling shareholders. In such a case, the court emphasized, "the public shareholders are harmed, uniquely and individually, to the same extent that the controlling shareholder is (correspondingly) benefited." In this situation, the shareholders can file a suit directly against the controlling shareholder.[38] In a more recent decision, the Delaware Supreme Court has further extended the scope of direct suits, recognizing direct loss when shares were unfairly issued to a non-controlling shareholder holding 35.9 percent.[39] In Japan, the majority of commentators support the view that corporate loss arises from unfair share issuance.[40] The Supreme Court also acknowledges that the shareholders suffer loss as a re-

---

35) *Uwe Hüffer* Aktiengesetz §93 Rn. 19 (8th ed. 2008).
36) Id. The shareholder can sue regardless of whether the corporation has a claim against the defendant. BGH, Judgment of March 20, 1995, (BGHZ 129, 136).
37) 906 A.2d 91 (Del. 2006).
38) Id. at 100.
39) *Loral Space & Communications Inc. v. Highland Crusader Offshore Partners, L.P.*, 2009 WL 2185494 (Del.Supr.).
40) *Egashira* supra note 34, at 711. A few scholars, however, argue that unfair share issuance results in loss only to the shareholders. *Tomotaka Fujita* Corporate Finance of Stock Corporations (2), 265 *Hogaku*

sult of unfair share issuance.[41] The shareholder's claim was based on the directors' liability to third parties. It can be based on torts as well.[42] Thus, both the corporation and the shareholders are deemed to suffer loss as a result of unfair share issuance.

In Germany, the situation is a little more complicated as share issuance normally requires a resolution at the shareholders' meeting, and shareholders are required to fix the minimum threshold for an issue price if shares are to be issued at a price over the statutory minimum issue price (Aktiengesetz, Article 182(1), (3)). Although there is some dispute, a number of commentators recognize the duty of the management board (*Vorstand*) to aim for a higher issue price when the shareholders' meeting fails to specify the issue price.[43] In the case of unfair share issuance, members of the management board are liable for the corporate loss (Aktiengesetz, Article 93(2)).[44] Commentators are not in agreement, however, as to whether or not an individual shareholder has an individual claim based on torts.

c) One-Person Corporations

It seems that there is not much discussion on one-person corporations in the three jurisdictions. In Japan, a recent decision of the Tokyo District Court on the one-person corporation is noteworthy.[45] The case involved a financially distressed corporation ("X") operating amusement parks. X was wholly owned by the defendant, who served as representative director. The defendant wasted X's assets by, for example, paying unjustified consulting fees to several people close to him. X sued the defendant for damages, arguing his breach of fiduciary duties. The defendant argued that fiduciary duties were not breached as no conflict existed between the corporation and its sole shareholder. The court held in favor of X, emphasizing that the corporation is a legal entity separate from its shareholders. Although the parties exchanged arguments on the interests of creditors, the court did not mention creditor interests in reaching its conclusion.

In Germany, the one-person firm is discussed in the context of a limited liability company (*Gesellschaft mit beschränkter Haftung* or GmbH), not a stock corporation (*Aktiengesellschaft* or AG). In 2001, a decision called *Bremer Vulkan*[46] attracted much attention in the

---

Kyoshitsu (Law Classroom) 72, 79 (2002) (in Japanese).

41) Supreme Court, Judgment of September 9, 1997 (*Hanrei Jiho* 1618–138).
42) Chiba District Court, Judgment of August 28, 1996 (*Hanrei Jiho* 1591–113).
43) *Hüffer* supra note 35, § 182 Rn. 25.
44) Ibid.; *Andreas Cahn* Ansprüche und Klagemöglichkeiten der Aktionäre wegen Pflichtverletzungen der Verwaltung beim genehmigten Kapital, ZHR 164, 137–138 (2000).
45) Tokyo District Court, Judgment of July 18, 2008 (*Hanrei Taimuzu* No. 1290, 200).
46) BGH NJW 2001, 3622.

German legal community. The case involved a corporation that took away funds from its wholly owned subsidiary (GmbH). The subsidiary's creditor sued the chairman of the parent's management board for damages based on tort provisions of the Civil Code (BGB) (Articles 823(2)). The German Federal Court of Justice (*Bundesgerichtshof*) held the parent liable, based on the concept of "existencedestroying liability" (*Existenzvernichtungshaftung*).[47] According to this concept, the sole owner of a limited liability company is liable to the company's creditors if he or she abusively takes away the company's assets and this leads to or worsens the insolvent status of the company. In this reasoning, what is important is the fact that an associate's act destroys the company's existence, not the size of his or her ownership interest. Thus, in later decisions, the existence-destroying liability has been imposed on associates with less than 100 percent ownership.[48] In 2007, the German Federal Court of Justice substantially modified its stance on existence-destroying liability in its decision called *Trihotel*.[49] First, the statutory ground for the liability was changed to Article 826 of BGB, a provision on tort liability for an intentional act in violation of public policy. Second, *Trihotel* allows the company, and not its creditors, to sue. Even under *Trihotel*, however, the liability arises only when the defendant's act leads to or worsens the insolvent status of the company.

d) Leveraged Buyouts

Of the three countries, Germany seems to be most hostile to LBOs. The credit support by the target firm may constitute a breach of trust under the Criminal Code (Article 266).[50] If the LBO leads the target to insolvency, the existence-destroying liability may attach to the acquirer. There are yet two other obstacles if the target is a stock corporation. LBO may be claimed to violate two provisions: one prohibiting the firm from returning paid-in capital to the shareholders (Aktiengesetz, Article 57), and another prohibiting the firm from financially assisting share purchase (Aktiengesetz, Article 71a). These provisions have recently been revised to facilitate LBOs.

The first provision has been interpreted as covering the act of offering the firm's assets as security for a shareholder's loan.[51] This provision was revised in 2008 to expand the scope

---

47) The chairman of the parent corporation was later convicted of breach of trust. BGH NJW 2004, 2867.
48) BGH, Judgment of February 25, 2002 (BB 2002, 1012); BGH, Judgment of December 13, 2004 (ZIP 2005, 1174).
49) BGH, Judgment of July 16, 2007 (NJW 2007, 2689). For a short comment on this decision, see, e.g., *Barbara Dauner-Lieb* Die Existenzvernichtungshaftung als deliktische Innenhaftung gemäß § 826 BGB, ZGR 2008, 34.
50) *Beisel/Klumpp* Der Unternehmenskauf, 13 Kap. Rn. 13 (5. Aufl. 2006).

of exception. Under the revised Article 57(1), if the firm is given the fully valuable claim for repayment (*vollwertigen Rückgewähranspruch*), its act of offering its assets as security is not per se illegal. If, as is the case in most LBOs, a special purpose vehicle used in LBO has no significant assets other than the target's shares, the firm's claim may be deemed not fully valuable.[52]

The second provision, on financial assistance, prohibits the firm from granting loans or credit support to a third party acquiring its shares (Aktiengesetz, Article 71a(1)). This provision has been generally construed as blocking the target's grant of credit support for LBO.[53] Commentators believe, however, that the acquirer may avoid these two hurdles by adopting a merger-type LBO.[54] The merger-type LBO is thus preferred in practice although its legality has not yet been confirmed by the court.[55] Even in Germany, the two provisions are "a hindrance rather than an insurmountable hurdle."[56]

In the United States, fraudulent conveyance laws protect creditor interests in the context of LBOs. When the target's assets are offered as security without receiving adequate consideration and the target thereby becomes insolvent or nearly insolvent, the credit support transaction becomes voidable.[57]

IV. Instrumental Nature of the Concepts of Corporate Legal Personality and Corporate Loss

From a functional perspective, corporate legal personality is a concept devised to simplify complicated legal relationships arising from a corporate enterprise. Legal personality helps partition a business firm from other assets owned by the firm's owners. If strictly interpreted, this technique may sometimes lead to inappropriate results. The strictness of legal personality was first moderated in situations justifying piercing the corporate veil. The veil-piercing doctrine was developed primarily to address abuse by a controlling shareholder

---

51) *Hüffer* supra note 35, § 57 Rn. 12; *Bodo Rieger* Kapitalgesellschaftsrechtliche Grenzen der Finanzierung von Unternehmensübernahmen durch Finanzinvestoren, ZGR 2008, 233, 236–237.
52) *Rieger* supra note 51, 238–239.
53) For a contrary view, id. at 239–242.
54) Id. at 246–249.
55) *Robert Freitag* "Financial Assistance" durch die Aktiengesellschaft nach der Reform der Kapitalrichtlinie – (k)ein Freifahrtschein für LBOs?, AG 2007, 159.
56) *Eilis Ferran* Regulation of Private Equity Backed Leveraged Buyout Activity in Europe, 25 (2007) (a paper available on the website of the Social Science Research Network: http://ssrn.com/abstract=989748).
57) *Lee B. Shepard* Beyond Moody: A Re-examination of Unreasonably Small Capital, 57 Hastings Law Journal 891, 893 (2006).

harming the interests of creditors.

Regarding the relationship between the corporation and management, the court decisions discussed in Part II show that the concept of corporate personality is still strictly respected in Korea. In all these decisions, the concept of corporate loss, a corollary of the corporate personality, played a critical role. Once corporate loss was recognized, the court paid no attention to shareholder or creditor interests, and moved on to its conclusion – holding managers guilty of a breach or blocking the plaintiff shareholder's individual claim.

Existence of corporate loss triggers the corporate initiative: the corporation (to be precise, a statutory auditor or the audit committee under Korean law), not individual shareholders, makes a decision on lawsuits against managers. As a matter of policy, this may be more efficient because the statutory auditor or audit committee may be equipped with more information and resources. If the corporate organ fails to sue, shareholders are allowed, and expected, to play a role by filing a derivative suit. The shareholder's role, however, is limited to initiation and control of the litigation process. If the shareholder wins, the recovery goes to the corporation. The "asset partitioning" between the firm and the shareholders thus remains intact in the context of a shareholder lawsuit.

In cases like *Hanra*, however, the corporate recovery is not sufficient to make shareholders whole. In such cases, the presence of corporate loss should not prevent individual shareholders from seeking remedies individually. One way of achieving this result is to acknowledge that the conduct of management gave rise to shareholder loss as well as corporate loss. This is exactly the approach adopted by the courts in the United States and Japan in decisions on unfair share issuance. No one disputes that unfair share issuance harms shareholder interests. The problem is whether or not corporate loss is recognized. Part III shows that the courts in all the reference countries and Korea recognize corporate loss in such cases. If the corporate remedy is not adequate to protect the shareholders, the shareholder loss should be recognized as well to support individual recovery as in the United States and Japan. In other words, corporate loss should not necessarily preclude shareholder loss.

On the other hand, corporate loss should not be recognized when there is no harm to the shareholders and creditors – stakeholders of the corporation. Thus, corporate loss is not recognized in a rights offering – which does not negatively affect the relative status of shareholders and promotes the interests of creditors – even when the shares are issued at a below-market price. If we apply the same reasoning to LBOs, corporate loss should not be recognized when neither the interests of shareholders nor those of creditors is compromised. Corporate loss, in a sense, is not a starting point, but an end result of inquiry.

A more relevant inquiry in pursuing director's liabilities is whether or not a director violated his or her fiduciary duty. In the United States, directors have a duty to shareholders as well as the corporation. When a director is found to have violated this duty, it is easy to allow shareholders to sue this director. In Korea, however, it is generally believed that directors have a duty to the corporation only. The Supreme Court in a full chamber decision denied that there is any relation between directors and shareholders, stating that "directors are not in a position of directly handling the business of shareholders."[58]

As a practical matter, however, it is not impossible to support a shareholder's suit against directors under Korean law. Although directors have a duty to the corporation only, this duty can be interpreted as incorporating a duty to promote the interests of shareholders. In unfair share issuance, for example, the board of directors is found to have violated this duty to promote shareholder interests. If this duty is found to be violated, one must decide which is better positioned to seek remedies. Normally, it is better to rely on the corporate machinery, so corporate loss is recognized and the corporate recovery process begins. In other cases where the recovery should go to shareholders directly, shareholders should be allowed to sue and recover personally. In Korea, although directors owe no duty to shareholders directly, the Commercial Code (Article 401(1)) authorizes shareholders to sue directors for their individual damages.

Corporate legal personality is understood as an instrument devised to simplify complicated legal relationships arising from a business enterprise. Its instrumental nature leads to a proposition that it may, and should, be suppressed to reach a just outcome in certain situations. Corporate veil piercing is a prime example. And entity absolutism, still persistent in Korea, seems to be in retreat in other developed jurisdictions. True, this kind of exceptional solution will inevitably generate some uncertainty. Such uncertainty, however, is not particularly burdensome and can be reduced to a manageable level.

---

58) Supreme Court, Judgment of June 17, 2004 (No. 2003Do7645).

The Role of Judges in Corporate Governance: Korean Experience*

Kon Sik Kim (Seoul National University)

I. INTRODUCTION

In comparative corporate governance discourse, a debate is still under way among researchers in different parts of the world as to whether (and the extent to which) law matters in improving corporate governance.[1] It seems now generally agreed, however, that law in practice matters far more than law on the books.[2] What makes law in practice approach law on the books is enforcement. Although enforcement is now being discussed widely, the concept of enforcement seems to differ depending on commentators. Although the focus has been traditionally placed on enforcement of law (hard law, to be precise), the term "enforcement" is now often broadly defined as a process of generating a desirable behavior on the part of market participants.

In this broad sense of the word, enforcement may depend on various elements of society. Not only formal elements such as government agencies, SROs, outside directors and private lawsuits but also informal elements such as market pressures, mass media and NGOs all affect corporate governance practice in one way or another. Although enforcement consists of various factors, law enforcement occupies a central, if not dominant, position. And in conventional law enforcement, judges play a crucial role, although their exact role differs depending on the country.[3]

As for Korea, law did not matter much in corporate governance prior to the financial crisis

---

* I express my gratitude to Hideki Kanda, Joo-Young Kim and Curtis Milhaupt for valuable comments.

1) For a short description of this discourse, see, e.g., Kon Sik Kim & Joongi Kim, Revamping Fiduciary Duties in Korea: Does Law Matter in Corporate Governance?, in: Curtis Milhaupt ed., *Global Markets, Local Institutions* at 373 (Columbia University Press 2003).

2) Regarding the relationship between corporate governance and enforcement, see, e.g., Erik Berglöf & Stijn Claessens, "Enforcement and Corporate Governance" (September 2004). *World Bank Policy Research Working Paper* No. 3409. Available at SSRN: http://ssrn.com/abstract=625286.

3) On the role of judiciary in corporate law, see, e.g., John C. Coffee, Jr., The Mandatory/Enabling Balance in Corporate Law: An Essay on the Judicial Role, 89 *Columbia Law Review* 1618 (1989).

in 1997. Lawsuits filed in relation to corporate governance disputes ("corporate governance lawsuits") were rare, if not totally absent. The judge's role was insignificant on the corporate governance stage. Since the crisis, however, the situation has changed dramatically. Corporate governance lawsuits are rapidly on the rise. The increase of such lawsuits may be attributable to various factors. First, the corporate statutes have been revised to make it easier to file a shareholder derivative suit. Second, shareholder activists, especially those affiliated with People's Solidarity for Participatory Democracy ("PSPD"), have been relying heavily on lawsuits in achieving its objectives.[4] PSPD has been taking a variety of legal measures, civil as well as criminal, against managers of chaebol, family-controlled conglomerates in Korea. Third, since the crisis, the share of foreign investors in the stock market has gone up tremendously. As of the end of 2006, they account for 37.3 percent (in terms of the market capitalization) of the shares listed in the prime section of the Korea Exchange.[5] In blue chip firms, however, their share is even higher: for example, 83% in Kookmin Bank (the largest commercial bank in Korea), 62% in POSCO and 49% in Samsung Electronics.[6] Foreign investors tend to be less patient than their domestic counterparts and some of them are less inhibited about filing lawsuits.

With the increase of lawsuits, the role of judges is becoming crucial in corporate governance practice in Korea. Their decisions may not only determine the outcome of a particular corporate governance dispute but also shape (or distort) the actual picture of corporate governance. For the last decade, the judiciary has been faced with various corporate governance disputes. Dealing with these disputes, judges show a somewhat "schizophrenic" attitude. They sometimes adopt a highly formalistic approach, sticking with the letters of a statutory provision, while in other cases they would liberally digress from the statutes to reach an outcome not explicitly supported by the statutes. The purpose of this paper is to examine the role of judges in Korea's corporate governance on the basis of these decisions showing different attitudes in judicial decision-making.

This paper proceeds as follows: Part II will survey the status of corporate governance lawsuits. It will discuss factors causing the increase of such lawsuits and cover diverse types of such lawsuits. Part III introduces a sample of corporate governance lawsuits which appear contradictory to each other in judicial reasoning. Part IV attempts to present a few

---

4) For a survey of the role of NGOs in corporate governance in Asia, see Curtis J. Milhaupt, "Nonprofit Organizations as Investor Protection: Economic Theory, and Evidence from East Asia," 29 Yale Journal of International Law, 169(2004)

5) Financial Supervisory Service, Report on the Securities Transactions by Foreign Investors for December 2006, 2 (2007)(in Korean).

6) http://stock.naver.com/sise/sise_foreign_hold.nhn(last visited January 16, 2006).

perspectives from which one may explain these apparently inconsistent decisions. Part V is a conclusion.

II. RISE OF CORPORATE GOVERNANCE LAWSUITS

Lawsuits related to Shareholder Resolution

Under Korean law, shareholder lawsuits may arise in various contexts of corporate governance. For example, a shareholder may sue to vacate a shareholder resolution for violation of law or the articles of incorporation, or to nullify a merger or issuance of shares. Minority shareholders holding a certain number of shares may file a lawsuit to seek dismissal of a director for violation of law or illicit behavior (Art. 385 II) or a derivative suit against a wrongdoing director for damages (Art. 403).

Prior to the financial crisis, shareholder lawsuits were largely confined to those seeking to invalidate a shareholder resolution.[7] As such lawsuits have long been addressed by the Commercial Code (Arts. 376-381), lawyers are generally familiar with them. The prevalence of such lawsuits in Korea may be primarily due to the following two factors. First, unlike shareholder derivative suits, even a shareholder holding one share is qualified to file this kind of lawsuit. Second, the general shareholders meeting ("GSM"), in smaller firms in particular, is often conducted in disregard of formal procedures under the corporate statutes. As long as there are no disputes among shareholders, no one pays much attention to this kind of technical flaws. Once a feud between business partners arises, these flaws may be picked up as a pretext for attack.

This lawsuit invalidating a shareholder resolution is indeed a powerful weapon against majority shareholders. This remedy, however, is not without limits. First, it may not address the real complaint of discontented shareholders. Such a lawsuit is often a product of a long, ruptured relationship, not just a one-time misconduct. Invalidating a particular move by majority shareholders does not help restore the broken relationship. Second, more sig-

---

7) The situation is similar in other civil law countries as well. For Italy, see, Luca Enriques, Do Corporate Law Judges Matter? Some Evidence from Milan, 3 *European Business Organization Law Review* 765, 784-86 (2002) For Germany, see Katharina Pistor & Chenggang Xu, Fiduciary Duty in Transitional Civil Law Jurisdiction: Lessons from the Incomplete Law Theory, in, Curtis Milhaupt ed., *Global Markets, Local Institutions*(Columbia University Press 2003).

nificantly, this remedy is of limited relevance in corporate governance disputes. The limit derives from the limited power of the GSM as a corporate organ. Under Korean law, the jurisdiction of the GSM is broader than in the United States. For example, dividends are declared by the GSM, not the board of directors, under Korean law. Still, the power of the GSM is largely limited to fundamental changes such as mergers and amendments to the articles of incorporation. The division of power between the GSM and the board is not as strict as in the United States as the power of the GSM may be liberally expanded by the articles of incorporation. It may not be a practical option, however, to further expand the power of the GSM, because it will then hinder timely and flexible corporate decision-making. Thus, material business decisions are mostly being made in the boardroom. From the corporate governance perspective, it is thus more important to restrain the behavior of the board and individual directors, than the GSM.

Lawsuits aimed at the Board and Directors

Korea does have a statutory framework designed for restraining abuse by directors. First of all, the corporate statutes recognize a Korean version of fiduciary duties, i.e., the "duty of care of a good manager" ("good manager duty") (Civil Code, Art. 681) and the duty of loyalty (Art. 382-3) introduced in 1998. Academics still dispute the conceptual relationship between the two duties. It is now well accepted, however, that the two duties can be interpreted as a functional equivalent of the fiduciary duties imposed on directors under the U.S. corporate law.[8]

The two statutory duties, however, failed to grow into an equivalent of their American counterpart. This is largely due to the inadequacy of shareholders' derivative suits under Korean law. Although the shareholder's derivative suit was adopted in KCC in 1962, no derivative suits were recorded until 1997. The absence of derivative suits did not signify the absence of wrongs against shareholders. A primary cause of the absence of such suits was the five-percent shareholding requirement imposed on a plaintiff shareholder. For a large listed firm, this shareholding requirement served as a virtually insurmountable hurdle.

---

8) This paragraph is partly based on Kon Sik Kim & Joongi Kim, Revamping Fiduciary Duties in Korea: Does Law Matter in Corporate Governance?, in: Curtis Milhaupt ed., *Global Markets, Local Institutions* 373, 381 (Columbia University Press 2003)

Inadequacy of Criminal Sanction

This does not necessarily mean that management abuse was completely beyond control. Tunneling activities by managers may constitute a breach of trust, a crime under the criminal code in Korea (Art. 355(2)). Unlucky managers, those of bankrupt firms in particular, have often been indicted and convicted for a breach of trust. Examples of criminal sanctions against top executives abound, including recent scandals involving SK, Hyundai, Doosan and Samsung. This approach of imposing criminal sanctions on wrongdoing corporate managers does have merits, as it is familiar, powerful and flexible. It has its own shortcomings as well. First, prosecutors may be more susceptible to public pressure. Although they no longer receive the cue from the Blue House, the office of the president, they are not entirely free from political considerations. Indeed, prosecutors have been exercising much discretion in indicting managers. In a recent case, for example, the CEO of a medium-sized company was indicted and then found guilty of breach of trust for acquiring private placements of bonds with warrants at a substantial discount.[9] In contrast, in a nearly identical case involving Samsung Group, a leading *chaebol* in Korea, prosecutors showed a different attitude. Samsung Everland, a non-listed real estate developer and a *de facto* holding company of Samsung Group, issued convertible bonds by private offering to Chairman Lee's son and daughters. This transaction was severely criticized as the young children of the chairman allegedly gained an enormous windfall profit in the process. In 2000, a group of law professors filed a charge against the top executives with the prosecutor's office, but the prosecutor's office refused to indict them. Then, in 2005, more than four years after the charge had been filed, the prosecutor's office changed its mind and indicted the two representative directors. The defendants were convicted at the trial court.[10] Second, as breach of trust is subject to a criminal punishment, the scope of misconduct covered by it should be limited to highly reprehensible behavior. Indeed, a breach of duty, a central element of the crime of breach of trust, is rather vague and amenable to a quite liberal interpretation.[11] In a recent Supreme Court decision, a CEO who engaged in an LBO transaction was convicted for breach of trust.[12]

---

9) Supreme Court, Judgment No. 2001Do3191 (September 28, 2001).
10) Seoul Central District Court, Judgment No. 2003 Kohap 1300 (October 4, 2005).
11) Punishing managerial misconduct with the crime of breach of trust is heavily criticized by commentators. Chul-Song Lee, Officers' Criminal Responsibility for the Issuance of Convertible Bonds at an Unfair Price, *Human Rights and Justice* No. 359, 96 (2006)(in Korean).

Third, the level of criminal sanction imposed on wrongdoing managers is regarded as relatively low in Korea. This is well illustrated in a recent criminal case involving yet another *chaebol*. Several members of its controlling family were found to have long engaged in usurping tens of million dollars from firms under their control.[13] Under the criminal statutes, the defendants could be sentenced to from a minimum of 5 years to life.[14] Unlike other white collar criminals in a similar situation, however, they were not even arrested even though the facts were not disputed. They were all convicted, but could get away with a suspended sentence.[15] Finally, even if the wrongdoing controlling shareholder is sent to prison, he is normally released from prison after a few months and resumes his position eventually. The government would feel strong pressure from the business community and the media to put him back at the helm of the ship by staying the sentence or granting amnesty.

Corporate Governance Reform after the Crisis

From this analysis, we can see that criminal sanctions should not be allowed to take the front seat in corporate governance. Since the financial crisis, the government has made efforts to facilitate shareholder suits. Through a series of revisions, the shareholding requirement for a derivative suit has been substantially alleviated. For a large listed firm, the shareholding threshold has been lowered to as low as 0.01 percent of the shares (Securities Exchange Act Art.191-13(1)). If the firm is really large, it may still not be easy to clear this hurdle. In such case, the only realistic option is to form an alliance with a foreign institutional investor.

Attorney fees are known to be a critical element in shareholder lawsuits. Now, there is a possibility that plaintiff's lawyers may be compensated for their services. Korea has finally enacted a provision entitling plaintiff shareholders to seek reasonable compensation from

---

12) Supreme Court, Judgment No. 2004 Do 7027 (November 9, 2006).

13) The whole scheme was disclosed to the public by a disgruntled family member who had been ousted from the chairman's office.

14) Act relating to the Heightened Punishment for Certain Economic Crimes, Art. 3(1)(i); Criminal Code, Art. 355.

15) This incident has led to yet another controversy. A few days after this decision, the chief justice of the Supreme Court severely criticized the overly lenient attitude of judges at a dinner with senior judges. He was reported to have said, "if a thief steals one hundred million Won, you will surely send him to prison for a few years at least. If a person who stole from his company tens of billion Won is set free with a suspended sentence, how would the general public react?" http://www.e-goodnews.co.kr/sub_read. html?uid=43965&section=section3(last visited January 16, 2007).

the company for their litigation costs (Art. 405; SEA, Art. 191-13 (6)), which include attorney fees. It will be up to the court to determine the "reasonable" amount of attorney fees that the company should pay to the successful plaintiff. It is not entirely clear, however, whether Korean judges will be as generous as their U.S. counterparts in determining attorney fees. In Korea, it is still a foreign idea to give an incentive to private individuals to file a lawsuit in the interest of others.

Rise of Lawsuits against Managers

Given the cumbersome shareholding requirement and the lack of incentive to sue, it is somewhat surprising to observe shareholders' derivative suits in Korea at all. So far, PSPD and a small number of public-minded lawyers have been behind these few lawsuits. These lawsuits have sent shockwaves throughout the Korean business community by holding managers liable for breaches of fiduciary duties. The first landmark decision is the decision involving Korea First Bank.[16] The case is based on KFB's questionable loans to the Hanbo Group, which went under after making a string of overly optimistic investments. At the time of the loan decisions, Hanbo was regarded as "unqualified" under KFB's own internal loan standards. Moreover, KFB's top executives received bribes from the chairman of Hanbo. A group of shareholders organized by PSPD filed, for the first time in Korea, a shareholder derivative suit against directors for damages. Although the defendant directors argued that their decision was basically a business judgment, the district court rejected this argument by saying that "a director made a mistake that cannot be passed over lightly and that exceeded their scope of discretion."[17]

The Korea First Bank Decision attracted much attention from the mass media, partly because the directors were held liable for as much as 40 billion Won (roughly 40 million Dollars), an exorbitant sum of money for salaried managers.[18] Less spectacular, but more influential, are the lawsuits filed by Korea Deposit Insurance Corporation (KDIC) against responsible managers of bankrupt financial institutions and debtor firms. Since the financial crisis, KDIC, like the U.S. Federal Deposit Insurance Corporation following the savings and loans crisis, has been suing those responsible managers. As of the end of 2005, KDIC filed civil liability actions against 9,144 executives of 489 financial institutions for more than 1.6

---

16) For details of this famous decision, see Kim & Kim, supra note1, at 389-391.
17) Seoul District Court, Judgment No. 97 Kahap 39907 (July 24, 1998).
18) The amount was later reduced to one billion Won on appeal.

trillion won in total. Also, KDIC has demanded that financial institutions file lawsuits against 698 managers of 132 distressed firms.[19] The litigation activities of KDIC will not continue indefinitely, however. KDIC may exercise its broad litigation power only in exceptional circumstances where public funds are injected to a distressed financial institution (Deposit Protection Act, Art. 21-2).

Duty of Care

In the KFB case, it was the duty of care that was violated. But the case involves a conflict-of-interest aspect as defendant directors were found to have received a bribe from Chairman Chung of Hanbo. Indeed, cases where a director is held liable purely on the grounds of the duty of care are rare, as Korean courts recognize a version of the business judgment rule.[20] It is not clear, however, to what extent this business judgment rule reaches. As shown later, there are cases where related party transactions are at issue. In theory, it may be treated as a duty of care case for those directors who are not "specially interested" in the transaction in question. Then the court could apply the business judgment rule to the directors' decision to approve the transaction. Holding the directors liable for damages, the court made no distinction between the two duties, nor did it discuss the business judgment rule. In one recent case, outside as well as inside directors were held liable for approving an unfair related party transaction.[21]

The duty to monitor, a subset of the duty of care, is growing increasingly relevant, especially for outside directors.[22] Primarily under the influence of the Sarbanes-Oxley Act, the concept of internal control is now being discussed and has been adopted in the statutes. Enforced strictly, this concept may lead to an increase in cases regarding the duty of care. It is not clear, however, how the court will react to this concept.

---

19) Korea Deposit Insurance Corporation, Annual Report(2006). 81-83.
20) Regarding the business judgment rule in Korea, see, e.g., Hwa-Jin Kim & Tehyok Daniel Yi, "Directors' Liabilities and the Business Judgment Rule in Korea" (April 15, 2004). Available at SSRN: http://ssrn.com/abstract=530442 or DOI:10.2139/ssrn.530442.
21) Seoul Southern District Court Judgment No. 2003 Kahap 1176 (August 17, 2006).
22) The director's duty to monitor is now well recognized by the court. Supreme Court, Judgment No. 84 Daka 1954 (June 25, 1985); Supreme Court, Judgment No. 2002 Da 60467, 60474 (December 10, 2004).

Duty of Loyalty

In Korea's corporate governance practice, the duty of loyalty should be far more relevant. Except for a small number of former government-owned firms privatized during the last decade (e.g., KT, POSCO, KB and KT&G), even the largest firms in Korea generally have controlling shareholders. Although the cash-flow rights of controlling families have been on the decline, below 5 percent in some business groups, the controlling family enjoys effective control over all the group companies by means of complicated circular and pyramid share-holding schemes.[23] As Table 1 at the end of this paper shows, there is a wide gap between the controlling shareholder's voting rights and cash-flow rights. In other words, the so-called voting power multiplier (VPM: voting rights over cash-flow rights) is high for controlling shareholders. According to Table 1, VPM for 14 business groups with more than 5 trillion Won in assets is as high as 7.47.[24]

The dwindling cash-flow right of the controlling family, coupled with its effective control over group firms, provides a strong incentive to engage in "tunneling" activities to the detriment of minority shareholders. Related party transactions among affiliated companies are rampant and not effectively regulated. An endless stream of scandals involving controlling families demonstrates the inefficacy of the corporate statutes in restraining abuse.

Korea's corporate statutes have many holes in regulating conflict-of-interest transactions arising from the *chaebol* structure. For example, the statutes do not explicitly recognize the concept of controlling shareholders *per se*, nor do they cover corporate opportunities.[25] But the statutes are bound to be incomplete in this area, as there are so many different ways of tunneling.[26] It is up to the judges to fill these holes by way of statutory interpretation. As discussed later, however, Korean judges do not seem to be enthusiastic about playing this crucial role.

---

23) In 2006, the Fair Trade Commission's attempt to revise the Anti-monopoly and Fair Trade Act to regulate practices of circular share ownership holding ended in failure due to all-out opposition by the big business.

24) Fair Trade Commission, Ownership Structure of Large Business Groups 11 (2006)(press release in Korean).

25) The proposed government bill to amend the Commercial Code attempts to include a provision on corporate opportunities.

26) Katharina Pistor & Chenggang Xu, Fiduciary Duty in Transitional Civil Law Jurisdiction: Lessons from the Incomplete Law Theory, in, Curtis Milhaupt ed., *Global Markets, Local Institutions* (Columbia University Press 2003).

Since the financial crisis, the statutes have been strengthened as regards related party transactions. Related party transactions encompass a wide variety of transactions, including sale of assets or issuance of securities to affiliates of the controlling shareholders. What has come into the spotlight in recent years is the sale of shares of a non-listed firm. Under the revised statutes, these transactions are now subject to board approval and disclosure requirements. The board approval requirement turned out not to be as effective as expected in filtering out shady transactions.

Under the corporate statutes, a director "specially interested" in a transaction in question is not allowed to vote on a board resolution (Commercial Code, Arts. 391(3), 368(4)). The concept of "special interest", however, seems rather narrowly construed by commentators. For example, suppose Firm A is selling a major asset to Firm B, an affiliated firm under the control of the same controlling shareholder, C. The sales transaction is now required to be approved by the board in both firms (STA Art.191-19(2); Fair Trade Act Art.11-2). Although C is excluded from voting in Firm A's board meeting, other inside directors may, and do, vote unless they serve on Firm B's board at the same time. It is not difficult to predict how these insiders, mostly longtime subordinates of C, would vote on this matter. True, listed firms are now required to have outside directors, up to 50% of the board in large listed firms. However, since such transactions are normally presented as legitimate transactions on fair terms, passive outsiders would not dare ask awkward questions in the board meeting. It is thus no wonder that controversial related party transactions, which later caused lawsuits, were formally approved by the board.[27]

As a matter of principle, shareholders may still sue directors for damages if they can prove loss to the firm incurred by a particular transaction. In reality, however, it is difficult to obtain information to prove the unfairness of the transaction. Even if a shareholder has all the information, it still must meet the burdensome shareholding requirement. Once a derivative suit is filed, however, the court may make its own judgment as to the fairness of the transaction. In a few recent cases involving a sale of unlisted shares, the court has examined in detail the fairness of the price.

---

27) For a recent decision holding outside as well as inside directors liable for an unfair related party transaction, see, Seoul Southern District Court, Judgment No. 2003 Kahap 1176 (August 17, 2006).

Lawsuits Arising from Control Disputes

Prior to the financial crisis, the controlling family normally enjoyed almost absolute control even in the largest firms in Korea. Together with shareholdings of affiliate firms, the controlling family could normally secure more than 50% of the voting rights. Consequently, a hostile takeover attempt was quite rare. Things have changed somewhat after the crisis, however. As Table 1 above shows, the voting power of the controlling shareholders fell below 50% in many *chaebol*, even below 30% in some *chaebol*. As the figures in Table 1 refer to the group average, the actual percentage for individual firms, large firms in particular, may be even lower.

A vacuum created by the dwindling holding of controlling shareholders has been filled by institutional investors, especially foreign investors. As mentioned earlier, foreign investors now occupy more than 37% of the Korea Exchange. As their investment concentrates on blue-chip firms, their share is now hovering over 50% in top firms such as Samsung Electronics and POSCO. As a result, the controlling family's control is no longer as secure as before.

An immediate consequence of this change is a small, but growing number of instances where the controlling shareholders are challenged by shareholders. Challenge against the controlling family may take the form of a formal tender offer. Formal tender offers, however, are rarely employed even in a hostile takeover context. Proxy contests are more common. Proxy contests have been initiated not only by foreign investors such as Tiger Fund, Sovereign, and Carl Icahn, but also by domestic investors. In connection with the proxy contest, interested parties often file various lawsuits, including lawsuits seeking preliminary injunction. Disgruntled shareholders may, for instance, attempt to gain access to the books and accounts of the firm, or to block the firm's issuance of equity securities to a white knight. On the other hand, management may seek to prevent the raiders from voting shares acquired in violation of the five percent rule under the Securities Transaction Act, which requires an investor to report to the financial regulator when its shareholding reaches five percent in a certain company (Art. 200-2).

These new types of corporate governance lawsuits pose a challenge to judges, who are not well versed in policy implications of control disputes. Korea does not have a developed set of statutory rules applicable to takeovers, except for tender offer provisions included in the Securities Transaction Act. Thus, judges are the ones expected to make rules in this area.

Defensive measures available to management under the current corporate statutes are quite limited. Dual class voting shares are not allowed.[28] More importantly, poison pills, a widely popular and powerful weapon against hostile takeovers in the U.S. and increasingly in Japan, are not available, largely due to strict statutory provisions on securities. Pyramidal and circular shareholding patterns commonly observed in almost every *chaebol* may be regarded as a functional substitute for poison pills. It is difficult to predict how long controlling families can afford to maintain these complicated ownership structures. With the increase of challenges against the controlling family, however, we will observe more and more corporate governance lawsuits of various types.

III. RECENT CORPORATE GOVERNANCE LAWSUITS

As shown above, corporate governance lawsuits become more common and diverse in the corporate governance scene of post-crisis Korea. Dealing with these lawsuits, judges seem to adopt somewhat inconsistent attitudes depending on circumstances. In some cases, the court employs a rather formalistic approach, sticking to the letter of the statutes. In other cases, however, the court liberally exercises discretion in statutory interpretation to reach a preferred outcome, not explicitly supported by the statutes. This kind of inconsistency in case law may be unavoidable to a certain extent, and observed in other jurisdictions as well. It seems notable, however, that decisions issued during a relatively short period of time show such contrasting perspectives. This Part will illustrate the contrast by presenting a selected group of leading court decisions.

Decisions Adopting a Formalistic Approach

Civil law judges are still generally believed to be more formalistic in their mindset than their common law colleagues. It is not difficult to find in the corporate governance area decisions based on a formalistic reasoning. Here, only two of them will be discussed.[29]

---

28) Non-voting preferred shares may be issued up to a certain limit.
29) Other examples of corporate governance decisions adopting a formalistic reasoning include Seoul Central District Court, Judgment No. 2006 Kahap 3203 (November 2, 2006)(rejecting a preliminary injunction for gaining access to the shareholder register by a corporate governance fund); Daejon District Court, Judgment No. 2006 Kahap 242 (March 14, 2006)(rejecting a preliminary injunction sought by foreign funds).

[Samsung Electronics CB Case]

A prime example showing Korean judges' formalistic mindset in the corporate governance area is the famous Samsung Electronics Convertible Bond Case.[30] On March 24,1997, Samsung Electronics, the flagship company of the Samsung group and by far the largest listed firm in Korea, issued by private offering convertible bonds(CBs) in the amount of 60 billion Won: 15 billion Won to Samsung Corporation, a member firm of Samsung Group, and 45 billion Won to the 29-year old son of Chairman Lee of the Samsung group. The terms and conditions were as follows:

Due date: March 24, 2002

Conversion price: 50,000 Won

Conversion period: from September 25, 1997 to March 24, 2002

Interest rate: 7%

On September 29, 1997, Lee Jr. exercised his conversion right and acquired about 900 thousand common shares, 0.9% of the total shares of SE. PSPD filed a lawsuit to invalidate the CB issuance, arguing, among other things, that the conversion price of 50,000 Won was unduly low, given the fact that the share price at the time of issuance was 56,700 Won and that the conversion price of CBs issued two months later was 123,635 Won.[31] Although the Seoul High Court admitted that the conversion price was relatively low, it refused to invalidate the CBs, stating:[32]

"This fact may justify a shareholder's claim for injunctive relief prior to the issuance of the CBs, a claim against directors for damages, or a claim against the purchasers of the CBs in question for additional payment. It by no means justifies, however, invalidation of the CBs already issued."

The formalistic attitude of the court is well illustrated in the following passage:

"The current Commercial Code does not require an advance notice or public announcement

---

30) For a translation of the lower court decision, see 1 Journal of Korean Law 157(2001). Disputes regarding related party transactions involving Samsung Electronics are discussed in Hasung Jang & Joongi Kim, "Nascent Stages of Corporate Governance in an Emerging Market: Regulatory Change, Shareholder Activism and Samsung Electronics," 10 *Corporate Governance: An International Review* 94, 95-103 (2002).

31) Although this case involved other interesting legal issues, only the conversion price issue will be discussed here.

32) Seoul High Court, Judgment No. 98 Na 4608 (June 23, 2000).

to the shareholders concerning the total amount of CBs, issue price, terms of conversion, conditions for the shares to be issued as a result of conversion, and conversion period at the time of issuance. It may be acknowledged that such a legal deficiency should be remedied. But even when the board of directors has deprived a shareholder of an opportunity to exercise his right to enjoin by secretly and promptly issuing CBs without making an advance public announcement of such matters, the issuance of the CBs should not be held illegal."

The Supreme Court upheld the lower court decision basically on the same grounds. The Supreme Court also stated that even the CBs suspected to be issued for purposes of pre-arranged inheritance, gift or control transfer can not be invalidated without other grounds. Emphasizing the so-called "stability of the marketplace", the Supreme Court stated that issuance of CBs may be invalidated only on limited grounds such as material violation of law or material impact on shareholders interests. Upon learning that the CBs were issued, PSPD sought a preliminary injunction enjoining the listing of the CBs on the stock exchange. The preliminary injunction was granted. The Supreme Court, however, did not place much value on the injunction, stating that it can not block a sale outside the exchange. The Supreme Court did not discuss whether Lee Jr. had sold the converted shares to a third party. On a similar note, stating that shareholders may recover damages instead by filing a shareholder derivative suit, the court did not go into whether or not the plaintiff shareholder can satisfy the shareholding requirement for a derivative suit.

[Double Derivative Suit Case]

Another example showing the judiciary's formalistic approach to statutory interpretation is a recent decision by the Supreme Court denying the so-called double derivative suit. The facts of the case are summarized as follows: Y, the defendant, is the representative director of Company A, who was alleged to have misappropriated A's fund. X, the plaintiff, is a minority shareholder of Company B, the 80% shareholder of Company A. Although X is not formally a shareholder of Company A, he filed a derivative suit against Y. The most significant issue involved was whether or not a shareholder of the parent company has a standing to file a derivative suit against directors of the subsidiary company. In other words, the issue was whether or not to recognize a double derivative suit. This issue was of the first impression in Korea. The Seoul High Court surprised the legal profession by holding in favor of X.

The criticism on the double derivative suit is two-fold. The first criticism is based on a literal interpretation of the statutes. Under the statutes, a derivative suit may be brought by shareholders holding a certain percentage of shares (Article 403 of the Commercial Code, Article 191-13 of the Securities Exchange Act). One may argue that shareholders of the parent are not counted as shareholders of the subsidiary. The second criticism is based on a practical consideration that shareholders of the parent have alternative remedies. According to this line of reasoning, the parent's shareholder may first demand that the parent's board of directors take action against the subsidiary's directors. If the board refuses to act, the shareholders can file a regular derivative action against the parent's directors for violating the duty of care to protect the parent's investment in the subsidiary.

The Seoul High Court, however, allowed a double derivative suit on the following practical grounds. First, it may be very difficult to appraise the indirect loss of the parent company caused by the act of the subsidiary's director. Second, if a double derivative suit is not permitted, managers controlling both the parent and the subsidiary may shield themselves from legal liability by having a director of the subsidiary commit an illicit act. Third, a double derivative suit would not only have a deterrent effect on the subsidiary's directors but also help the parent reduce its damages.

It is noteworthy that the court emphasized "the necessity of a double derivative suit" in interpreting "shareholders" under Article 403 of the Commercial Code as including "shareholder of a corporate shareholder." The Supreme Court, however, rejected this flexible interpretation of the High Court. Turning a blind eye to the effect of the decision, the Supreme Court simply stated that the double derivative suit is not allowed, as the shareholders under Art. 403 refer to those of the company involved, not its parent.

Although the case involved a relatively small firm, it was closely watched by big business and PSPD. Many firms in Korea now have subsidiaries. If a subsidiary enters into a dubious transaction with an affiliate, minority shareholders of the parent company have no effective remedy under the current law.[33] In relation to recent corporate scandals, PSPD is reported to have given up on a double derivative suit as they were not sure of the legality of such suits under the current law. The bill to revise the corporate statutes prepared by the Ministry of Justice first included a provision which explicitly allows a shareholder of a parent company to file a derivative suit against directors of its subsidiary (Art. 406-2). This provision was heavily criticized by the Federation of Korean Industries, a main trade association for *chaebol*. PSPD, on the other hand, was also critical of this provision, arguing for further relaxing the requirements.[34] The Ministry of Justice eventually dropped the provi-

---

33) They may file a criminal complaint against the managers involved.
34) The provision does not cover directors of a subsidiary's subsidiary. Moreover, a firm is counted as a

sion in its final draft.

Decisions Adopting a Liberal Approach

Despite the popular perception that civil law judges are relatively passive in statutory interpretation, Korean judges sometimes digress from the letters of the statutes to reach a conclusion they find appropriate. Two examples will be discussed here.

[Samsung Electronics Derivative Suit]

The first example again relates to Samsung Electronics. In 1998, PSPD filed a shareholder derivative suit against directors of Samsung Electronics including Chairman Lee and his top executives. Although this case deals with many interesting issues, only an issue related to damages will be discussed here. In December 1994, Samsung Electronics sold to an affiliated company the shares of another affiliate it had acquired 8 months ago. The sale price was 2,600 Won per share, 74% discount from the purchase price, 10,000 Won per share. Samsung Electronics followed a widespread practice of retaining a reputable accounting firm to determine the value based on a valuation formula for unlisted stock under the Inheritance and Gift Tax Law. The formula is a combination of the net asset value and the profit value. The accounting firm came up with 2,361 Won per share (50% X 4,723 Won + 50% X 0 Won). The accounting firm reached the final figure, 2,597 Won, by adding 10% control premium. But the Suwon District Court held that the tax law formula should not govern as the context is different, and that the fair value should have been calculated based on the net asset value only. The court calculated its own net asset value to be 5,733 Won. Finding no factors justifying the low sales price as opposed to the net asset value, the court held that the directors had violated the duty of care and had to pay more than 62 billion Won for damages. The Seoul High Court upheld the district court decision, but reduced the damages by as much as 80% based on various mitigating factors.[35] The High Court decision was upheld in 2005 by the Supreme Court. The Supreme Court based the reduction of damages on "the ideal of equitable allocation of losses." As mitigating factors considered in reducing the damages, the court enumerated not only factors related to the conduct causing the damages but also general factors such as the degree of the director's past con-

---

subsidiary under the Commercial Code only when the parent holds more than 50 percent (Art. 342-2 (1)).

35) Seoul High Court, Judgment No. 2002 Na 6595 (November 20, 2003).

tribution to the firm.

This decision is particularly noteworthy because it appears inconsistent with Article 400 of the Commercial Code, which requires the consent of all the shareholders to reduce the liability of directors. Although Article 400 has been widely criticized as unduly restrictive, the courts have been reluctant to moderate its rigidity. In one recent case, the Supreme Court even held that the consent of shareholders holding 96% of the shares is not sufficient.[36] Prior to this decision, it had been generally believed that there was no other way to reduce the liability. The judges could thus achieve by way of interpretation what even the 96% shareholders could not achieve. In the process, they showed how flexible and creative even the civil law judges could be in reaching a favored conclusion which appears to contradict the explicit letter of the statutes.

[Preliminary Injunction Related to the Shareholders Meeting of SK]

The court's creativity is also revealed in our second case, which derived from a well publicized dispute between SK and Sovereign, a Dubai-based private fund run by two New Zealanders.[37] The controversy started when Sovereign bought in early 2003 about 15% shares of SK Corp., a *de facto* holding company of the SK Group. At the time of the purchase the SK Group was in trouble as Chairman Chey, the controlling shareholder of the SK Group, was indicted for accounting and share transfer scandals. In June 2003, the Seoul Central District Court sentenced Chairman Chey to three years imprisonment for, among other things, a criminal breach of trust and accounting fraud.[38]

After the purchase Sovereign began a campaign to neutralize Chairman Chey and enhance SK's transparency. In March 2004, it vigorously waged a failed proxy fight against the management. Sovereign nominated five candidates, all respectable Korean nationals. In an effort to boost the public image of SK, Chairman Chey presented his own slate of distinguished outsiders. At the general shareholders meeting ("GSM"), Chairman Chey managed to defeat Sovereign by a narrow margin, filling all five slots of the board with his nominees.

In connection with the GSM, Sovereign also submitted a proposal to include in the articles of incorporation a provision excluding from the board those sentenced to imprisonment, a provision obviously aimed at Chairman Chey. Although this proposal garnered slightly

---

36) Supreme Court, Judgment No. 2003Da69638 (October 28, 2005).
37) The whole saga is narrated and discussed in Chapter 7 of *Law and Capitalism* by Curtis J. Milhaupt and Katharina Pistor (2007).
38) Seoul Central District Court, Judgment No. 2003 Kohap 237, 311 (June 13, 2003).

more than 50% of the votes, it was not passed because the Commercial Code requires a two-thirds majority (Art. 434).

In October 2004, Sovereign requested that SK Corp. call an extraordinary GSM exclusively to deal with essentially the same charter amendment issue.[39] When SK Corp's board rejected Sovereign's request, Sovereign filed a petition for the court's approval of an extraordinary GSM. In December 2004, the Seoul District Court rejected Sovereign's petition. Under the statutes, a shareholder holding at least 1.5% of the shares for the last six months is qualified to call a GSM with the court's approval(SEA Art. 191-13(5)). Commentators generally agree that the court must approve the request unless the minority shareholder's exercise of this right amounts to "an abuse of right." Holding that there was no abuse of right, the court still refused to approve Sovereign's petition.

The court stated that in approving the shareholder's request, it should consider the necessity of an extraordinary GSM from a paternalistic perspective based on various factors such as the possibility of passing a resolution or impact on the national economy. The court mentioned many different factors. The court stated, for example, that "because continuous instability in management control might lead to the departure of investors and the decline in the investment value, given the nature of SK Corp's business, requiring long-term investment and business plan, a benefit from stabilizing management control at least until the GSM next year is not insignificant." The court also noted that in exercising shareholder rights, a corporate, as opposed to individual, shareholder is "more likely to sacrifice the interests of the corporation for its own firm interest." The court even mentioned that "it is not impossible for SK Corp to voluntarily propose to make a similar change to the articles of incorporation at the annual GSM to be held in March 2005."

At the March 2005 GSM, Chairman Chey was reelected to the board, receiving 55.3% of the votes. In May 2005, the Seoul High Court upheld the lower court's ruling denying Sovereign's petition. Unlike the lower court, the High Court chose to adopt a simpler reasoning, holding that Sovereign's request to call the GSM constituted an "abuse of right." An abuse of right is normally recognized in extreme situations. The High Court set forth the two requirements(subjective and objective) for the abuse. Subjectively, one must exercise his right solely to inflict harm on the opposite party without any benefit to himself. Objectively, the exercise of the right must be in violation of public policy. In actual reasoning, however, the High Court flatly ignored the subjective requirement, concentrating exclusively on whether or not the exercise of the right was in conflict with the original purpose or func-

---

39) This time, Sovereign attempted to exclude from the board those who are indicted.

tion served by the minority shareholder's right to call an extraordinary GSM.

Like the lower court, the High Court enumerated various factors to support its holding. The court noted that such an amendment was not in the interest of the firm and the shareholders as it would exclude even a competent director who has been sentenced to imprisonment for a traffic accident. Outside directors with serious criminal records are not allowed to sit on the board under the STA (Arts. 191-12(3)(iii), 54-5(4)(i)). From the court's perspective, as SK Corp had already seven outside directors, it appeared unreasonable to impose a strict qualification requirement on remaining three inside directors.

Not long after the decision, Sovereign sold its SK holdings, achieving a profit of almost one billion dollars. Sovereign has been widely depicted by the media as a prime example of greedy foreign investor.

Conflicting Decisions Concerning the Sale of Treasury Shares

Formalistic and liberalistic decisions discussed above relate to different corporate law issues. In one example, however, different judges took conflicting attitudes on the same issue. The issue relates to the sale of treasury shares in the presence of takeover threats.

[SK Case]

The first case again derives from the SK Corp's fight against Sovereign. As a defensive measure against Sovereign's challenge to Chairman Chey, SK Corp came up with a plan to sell treasury shares carrying 10.4% of the votes to a group of friendly banks, which promised to vote the shares in favor of Chairman Chey at the March 2004 GSM. Sovereign sued to enjoin SK Corp from selling the shares. Although the Commercial Code provides for shareholders' preemptive rights for newly issued shares (Art. 418(1)), it is silent on the sale of treasury shares. Sovereign, however, argued that the company should not favor a particular group of outsiders to the exclusion of the existing shareholders in selling the shares. Rejecting Sovereign's argument, the Seoul District Court allowed the sale to go forward.[40] According to the court, an adverse impact of the proposed sale on Sovereign's position is not enough to block the sale. The court implied such a sale may be blocked in a situation where keeping management is not in the interest of general shareholders. In the absence of any evidence suggestive of such a situation, the court stated that "the decision by SK Corp's board, which was made to defend its management control against Sovereign's take-

---

40) Seoul District Court, Judgment No. 2003 Kahap 4154 (Dec. 23, 2003).

over attempt, should be held legal."

[Daelim Trading Case]

In 2006, however, a different court manifested a contrary attitude on the same issue. The case involves Daelim-Trading ("Daelim"), a listed firm largely owned by two factions of the same family. The facts can be summarized as follows. As of the end of 2004, Factions A and B controlled 34.11%, and 29.98%, respectively. The dispute arose in 2003 as a member of Faction B was ousted from management dominated by Faction A. In 2005, Faction A had Daelim sell a large block of treasury shares to Faction A, and issue new shares to the exiting shareholders. At the end of these transactions, Faction A could control 47.49% of the vote while Faction B's share (including shares of their allies) amounted to 30.24%. When Faction A called the GSM for dividing the company, Faction B filed a petition for preliminary injunction, enjoining Faction A from voting the shares acquired from Daelim. Contrary to the Seoul Central District Court above, the Seoul Western District Court granted the preliminary injunction[41] and then held the sales transaction invalid.[42]

Until this decision, the SK ruling discussed above was the only decision on the sale of treasury shares. A few years ago, there was a ruling on the issuance of shares. When there was a fight for control of Hyundai Elevator, a de-facto holding company of Hyundai Group, Hyundai Elevator attempted to issue a large number of shares to the general public.[43] Its primary purpose was to dilute the share of KCC, the raider. At the request of KCC, the court enjoined Hyundai Elevator from conducting the offering.[44]

Although the Commercial Code explicitly provides for a lawsuit for invalidating issuance of shares (Art. 429), it is silent as to the invalidation of the sale of treasury shares. Central to the reasoning of the court is the fact that the sale of treasury shares is functionally similar to the issuance of shares. A leading corporate law expert criticizes this decision for exceeding the scope of interpretation.[45] The sale of treasury shares, his argument goes, is not different from the sale of company assets and so the company should be free to sell those treasury shares to a particular shareholder.

---

41) Seoul Western District Court, Judgment No. 2006 Kahap 393 (March 24, 2006).
42) Seoul Western District Court, Judgment No. 2005 Kahap 8262 (June 29, 2006).
43) Under the articles of incorporation, the shareholders do not have the preemptive right if shares are issued by public offering.
44) Suwon District Court (Yeoju Branch), Judgment No. 2003 Kahap 369 (December 12, 2003).
45) Chul-Song Lee, Validity of the Unfair Sale of Treasury Shares, 7 *Korean Journal of Securities Law* 1 (2006)(in Korean).

IV. UNDERSTANDING THE DECISIONS

Traditionally, civil law judges were believed to be less active than their common law colleagues in their role of making rules. It is now widely agreed that the differences between continental courts and common-law courts are not as wide as is commonly thought.[46] The sample of decisions described in Part III is certainly too small to warrant a definitive conclusion on this issue. Judges' attitudes revealed in the cases are somewhat confusing. In some decisions, judges were quite flexible in interpreting statutes to reach a conclusion they want. Judges would invoke general and flexible concepts such as "equity" or "good faith," and make an inquiry into the "purpose or function" of a legal provision. In other decisions, judges adopted a formalistic attitude, turning a blind eye to the practical consequences of their reasoning. How do we understand these conflicting attitudes of judges? One may try three possible explanations: favorable, neutral, and cynical ones.

Favorable Explanation

One may argue that judges' vacillation between formalism and liberalism in statutory interpretation represents their efforts to reach the right conclusion. In other words, as judges primarily care about results, they are ready to sacrifice consistency to achieve a just result in each case. Indeed, for the judiciary, this explanation may be most favorable, as it assumes the judges to be both capable and acting in good faith.

This kind of judicial attitude, however, is not acceptable. If the judge adopts a formalistic approach in a particular decision, it will be difficult to know the real reasons for the conclusion. An answer that the conclusion is mandated by the statutes does not suffice alone. As the judge is generally capable of finding a way to avoid the statutes, she should disclose the reason why she did not try to digress from the literal interpretation of the statutes.

---

46) Katharina Pistor, Yoram Keinan, Jan Kleinheisterkamp & Mark D. West, The Evolution of Corporate Law: A Cross-Country Comparison,23 University of Pennsylvania Journal of International Economic Law 791, 799 n.27 (2002) ("civil law courts have at times played a much more proactive role in shaping the contents of legal rules than the general principle that 'judges interpret, but do not make the law' may suggest.").

Neutral Explanation

One may try a more neutral explanation. Inconsistent decisions mentioned earlier may reflect different ways of thinking on the part of Korean judges. Like other parts of Korean society, the judiciary is also in transition. The mindset of judges varies depending on individuals. Some judges are more conservative in the sense that they place much weight on the letter of the statutes. Other judges are more liberal in the sense that they emphasize potential consequences of a decision.

A conservative tendency of Korean judges may be attributable to their upbringing. Law school training in Korea still emphasizes deductive reasoning unrelated to sophisticated policy considerations. Their heavy caseload also makes judges reluctant to tread on unfamiliar territory, experimenting with novel concepts or theories. It may be far more tempting to a busy judge to stick to a formalistic approach.[47]

Cynical Explanation: An Entrapment Theory?

One may also explain these cases from a more cynical perspective. It may be interesting to examine these cases from the perspective of who won and who lost. Start with formalistic decisions. In the Samsung CB case, Samsung Electronics won, and PSPD lost. In the double derivative suit case, the decision was favorable to chaebol firms with numerous subsidiaries, and detrimental to shareholder activist lawyers. Turn to the liberalistic decisions. In Samsung Electronics derivative suit case, the court's decision to reduce the amount of damages was beneficial to Samsung's top executives. The SK GSM decision was obviously favorable to SK Corp, and detrimental to Sovereign, a foreign shareholder.

In the SK Treasury Share ruling, the court, adopting a formalistic approach, refused to grant an injunctive remedy to a foreign fund challenging the controlling shareholder of a major *chaebol*. On the other hand, in the Daelim Trading case, which derived from a family feud among domestic shareholders, the court granted a remedy, based on a flexible reasoning emphasizing the practical effect of the decision.

By now, one may hardly fail to notice a trend in this group of decisions. Regardless of the type of reasoning adopted, those related to big business won, while activist shareholders and

---

47) Likewise, judges in the U.S. are believed to rely on heuristics (simplistic rule-like tests) to simplify their decision-making process. Hillary Sale, Judging Heuristics, 35 U.C. *Davis Law Review* 903 (2002).

foreign investors lost. True, given the small size of sample, one must not place too much weight on this rather cynical observation. One may point to other decisions which may contradict this observation. Indeed, shareholder activists have recorded a victory in a small number of lawsuits against *chaebol*, in which judges reached a result favoring minority shareholders based on a substantive analysis. The decisions discussed in Part III may be more important, however, in terms of number and significance. They are by no means aberrations, but mainstream decisions carefully written by elite judges.

It is difficult to find a proper word for this kind of pro-*chaebol*, anti-shareholder activist, and anti-foreign investor attitudes. Let's use the adjective, "conservative" for the sake of simplicity. A cynical observer may try to explain the "conservative" tendency of Korean judges, elite judges in particular, as follows. First, elite judges may be close to business executives working for *chaebol* and lawyers representing these *chaebol* clients. They may be tied to each other by common educational, professional and social backgrounds. Second, of more significance may be a career pattern of Korean judges. Most judges, including even former judges of the Supreme Court, practice after retiring from the bench, often affiliated with top law firms representing chaebol firms. One may presume that retired judges known for an anti-*chaebol* record may have a hard time landing a position with a major law firm, let alone finding *chaebol* clients. In a sense, judges, like other players of Korean society, may not be immune to *chaebol* interests.

What exacerbates this pro-*chaebol* mindset is a growing antipathy against foreign investors, and the activism of foreign funds, to be more precise. Recently, the local media, business dailies in particular, has been attacking foreign funds on various grounds such as seeking short-term profits and threatening management control.[48] It is now becoming increasingly awkward even for an academic to take sides with foreign investors in public. It may be difficult to expect the judiciary to ignore this pressure in making a decision.

Evaluation

It is not clear which of the three explanations is most persuasive. All three may have at least some truth. Regardless of the explanations, one may feel rather uncomfortable after reading the decisions discussed in Part III. It must be emphasized, however, that the picture of case law in the corporate governance area may change in the future in accordance with Korea's changing corporate governance environment.

---

48) Foreign investors suffering from image or even legal problems are numerous, including Sovereign, Tiger Fund, Hermes, LoneStar, Newbridge Capital and Carl Icahn.

V. CONCLUDING REMARKS

The more discretion courts are allowed discretion, the more likely it becomes that courts
will abuse their discretion. An obvious solution for this kind of abuse may be enacting
more detailed statutory rules. The solution may not be technically feasible, however. As
there are numerous ways in which a conflict of interest develops between managers and
shareholders, a flexible and general concept such as fiduciary duty is essential for addressing
such conflicts. As for conflict-of-interest transactions, it may be better, if not inevitable, to
leave law "incomplete".[49]

In Korea, relying on judges may not be as bad as in other countries. First, the judiciary
is relatively clean, compared with other sectors of Korean society. True, a corruption scandal involving judges is exposed from time to time, and the general public's perception of
judges is not necessarily favorable. It may be safely said, however, that a judge would not
change her holding in return for an outright bribe.[50] Second, most judges are quite
capable.[51] In terms of integrity and competence, it may be difficult to find those who are
better qualified than judges.

This does not mean, however, that judges are perfect. Although they would not accept a
cash bribe from the parties, they may be prone to a more subtle form of pressure. It is still
a widespread practice in Korea that parties select counsel based on the strength of social
ties between the presiding judge and counsel. Also, career judges with no business experience may often lack sophistication on business matters. This may not be a serious defect,
however, in the long run. Fast learners, judges will quickly achieve a level of expertise as
they are exposed to more cases.

It may not be realistic to expect Korean judges to become as flexible as their common law
colleagues in a short period of time. So even in the presence of fiduciary duties in the corporate statutes, it may make sense to put more concrete provisions in the statutes. The provision on *de facto* directors (KCC Art. 401-2) is a prime example. Along this line of reasoning, the draft new Commercial Code includes a new provision on double derivative suits

---

49) Katharina Pistor & Chenggang Xu, Fiduciary Duty in Transitional Civil Law Jurisdiction: Lessons from
the Incomplete Law Theory, in, Curtis Milhaupt ed., *Global Markets, Local Institutions* (Columbia
University Press 2003).

50) Luca Enriques, Do Corporate Law Judges Matter? Some Evidence from Milan, 3 *European Business
Organization Law Review* 765 (2002).

51) Each year, only around top 10-20% of the graduates from the Judicial Research and Training Institute
are normally invited to join the bench.

(Art. 406-2) and expands the scope of self-dealing transactions under Art. 398.

Admittedly, the role of judges in restraining management behavior seeking private benefits of control is still limited. It may be particularly relevant in Korea to activate market pressure on owner-managers. Market pressure may turn out to be more effective because it tends to restrain even an undesirable behavior not formally constituting a violation of fiduciary duty. So far, pressure from the market for corporate control has been minimal, if not totally absent, in Korea. If cross or pyramidal share ownership schemes are crumbling, threats of hostile takeovers will loom large. Then, Korea may need to consider introducing a Korean version of poison pill. In such case, the role of judges will become even more crucial. It is not clear whether Korean judges are well prepared to take up such a delicate role. Indeed, as the new draft Commercial Code gives management more freedom on finance matters such as dividends and types of securities, judges are expected to play a more active role in minimizing management abuses. It will be fascinating to observe how the role of Korean judges evolves in the coming years.

Table 1: Cash-flow and Voting Rights of 14 Largest Business Groups (2006)

	Cash-flow	Voting	Voting/Ownership
Samsung	4.20	29.00	6.91
Hyundai Motors	6.28	38.51	6.13
SK	2.21	36.32	16.42
LG	5.58	38.08	6.83
Lotte	9.94	47.85	4.81
GS	18.58	51.98	2.80
Hanwha	4.02	50.39	12.53
Doosan	4.63	53.82	11.62
Kumho-Asiana	13.45	50.96	3.79
Dongbu	16.43	55.53	3.38
Hyundai	4.65	21.50	4.62
CJ	13.18	48.24	3.66
Dalim	12.33	43.32	3.51
Hite Beer	15.22	46.13	3.03
Average	6.36	37.65	7.47

Source: Fair Trade Commission

논문출처목록

I. General issues

1. Kon Sik Kim, Codification in East Asia: Commercial Law, Codification in East Asia (Wen-Yeu Wang ed.), Springer International Publishing, 61-79, 2014.2

2. Kon Sik Kim, Corporate Law and Corporate Law Scholarship in Korea: A Comparative Essay, Legal Innovations in Asia (John O. Haley & Toshiko Takenaka eds.), Edward Elgar, 243-258, 2014.10

3. Kon Sik Kim, Corporate Governance in Korea, 8 Journal of Comparative Business and Capital Market Law 21-37, 1986.10

4. Kon Sik Kim, Intermediary Risk in the Indirect Holding System: A Comment From the Perspective of a Civil Law Jurist, 12 Duke Journal of International and Comparative Law 335-339, 2002.10

II. Shareholders and corporate organs

1. Kon Sik Kim, Dynamics of shareholder power in Korea, Research Handbook on Shareholder Power (Randall S. Thomas & Jennifer G. Hill eds.), Edward Elgar, 535-551, 2015.8

2. Dan Puchniak & Kon Sik Kim, Varieties of Independent Directors in Asia: Divergent Convergence, in Dan W. Puchniak et. al., Independent Directors in Asia: A Historical, Contextual and Comparative Approach 89-132, Cambridge University Press, 2017.11

3. Kon Sik Kim, Transplanting Audit Committees to Korean Soil: A Window into the Evolution of Korean Corporate Governance, 9 Asian Pacific Law & Policy Journal 163-184, 2007.12

III. Conflict of interest and fiduciary duties

1. Kon Sik Kim & Joongi Kim, Revamping Fiduciary Duties in Korea: Does Law Matter to Corporate Governance, in Curtis Milhaupt ed., Global Markets, Domestic Institutions, Columbia University Press, 373-399, 2003.8

2. Stephen J. Choi & Kon Sik Kim, Establishing a New Stock Market for Shareholder Value Oriented Firms in Korea, 3 Chicago Journal of International Law (University of Chicago Law School) 277-300, 2002.12

3. Kon Sik Kim & Seung-Wook Jeong, Controlling the Controlling Shareholders: Conduct, Structure and Market, Recent Transformations in Korea Law and Society (Dae-Kyu Yoon ed.), Seoul National University Press, 153-170, 2000.6

4. Kon Sik Kim, Related Party Transactions in East Asia, in Luca Enriques and Tobias Tröger, eds., The Law and Finance of Related Party Transactions (Cambridge University Press) 285-326, 2019.6

IV. Shareholder remedies

1. Kon Sik Kim & Moon-Hee Choi, Declining Relevance of Lawsuits on the Validity of Shareholder Resolution in Korea – A Comparative Essay, German and Asian Perspectives on Company Law, in Holger Fleischer et al. eds., German and Asian Perspectives on Company Law, 217-241, Mohr Siebeck, 2016.12

2. Hyeok-Joon Rho & Kon Sik Kim, Invigorating Shareholder Derivative Actions in South Korea, The Derivative Action in Asia (Dan W. Puchiniak et al. eds.), Cambridge University Press, 189-217, 2012.7

3. Kon Sik Kim, the Demand on Directors Requirement and the Business Judgment Rule in the Shareholders Derivative Suit, 6 Journal of Corporation Law 511-529, 1981.10

4. Kon Sik Kim, Corporate Legal Personality and Corporate Loss in Korean Law, Festschrift für Klaus J. Hopt zum 70. Geburtstag am 24. August 2010: Unternehmen, Markt und Verantwortung, Walter de Gruyter, 3115-3134, 2010.8

5. Kon Sik Kim, The Role of Judges in Corporate Governance: the Korean Experience, Transforming Corporate Governance in East Asia (Hideki Kanda et al., eds.), Routledge, 116-138, 2008.7

〈대담〉

김건식 교수 정년기념 대담

일   시 : 2019. 12. 8. (일) 15:00∼18:00

장   소 : 김건식 교수 서초동 자택

대 담 자 : 노혁준(서울대학교 법학전문대학원 교수)

　　　　　송옥렬(서울대학교 법학전문대학원 교수)

　　　　　안수현(한국외국어대학교 법학전문대학원 교수)

　　　　　윤영신(중앙대학교 법학전문대학원 교수)

　　　　　천경훈(서울대학교 법학전문대학원 교수)

　　　　　최문희(강원대학교 법학전문대학원 교수)

녹취·정리 : 송순섭(서울대학교 법학연구소 조교)

　　　　　이정은(서울대학교 대학원 법학과 박사과정)

〈인사 및 소개〉

송옥렬 : 오늘 법학연구소에서 김건식 교수님 정년을 기념해서 선생님을 모시고 지난 이야기를 나눌 수 있는 자리를 마련하여 주셨습니다. 이 자리에는 중앙대 윤영신 교수님, 강원대 최문희 교수님, 한국외국어대 안수현 교수님이 멀리서 참석하여 주셨고, 서울대에서 노혁준, 천경훈 교수님도 참석하여 주셨습니다. 바쁘신 중에 이렇게 자리를 함께 해 주셔서 감사의 말씀을 드립니다. 그리고 저는 서울대 송옥렬입니다. 먼저 간단히 소감을 여쭙는 것으로 시작하면 어떨까 합니다. 교수로서 지난 30년이 넘는 긴 여정을 마무리하시는 소감이 어떠신지요?

〈정년 소감〉

김건식 : 지난주 수요일 오후 대학원 강의를 끝으로 마무리를 했습니다. 지난 33년 반 동안 서울대에서만 강의하며 보냈던 터라 마지막 말을 하면서 혹시 울컥하지 않을까 걱정했는데 다행히 전혀 그런 일 없이 담담하게 끝났습니다. (웃음) 연구실에 있는 책을 어떻게 옮길 것인지 아직 고민거리가 많아서 그런 것 같기도 합니다. 전부터 그랬지만 특히 최근 몇 년 동안은 일생을 교수로, 더구나 서울대에서 보낼 수 있었다는 것이 얼마나 행운이었나 하는 생각을 많이 했습니다. 사실 능력도 뛰어나지 못하고 노력도 실제로 그렇게 많이 하지 못한 처지라 일생을 좋은 곳에서 편안하게 보낼 수 있었던 것을 미안하면서도 감사하게 생각하고 있습니다.

윤영신 : 33년 반 동안 서울대에서 봉직하셨다고 말씀하셨는데요. 그러면 아주 많은 일이 있었을 것 같습니다. 그 가운데 특별히 기억에 남는 일들이 있다면 한두 가지 듣고 싶습니다.

김건식 : 사실 활동이 아주 많았다고 이야기할 순 없을 것 같은데요. 질문을 받고 생각을 해보니 특별히 '이거다' 하는 순간은 없는 것 같고 그냥 여러 가지 모멘트가 있었던 것 같아요. 그중에는 좋은 일도 있고 또 안 좋은 일도 있고 그랬습니다만, 그래도 저로서는 좋았던 순간이 더 많았던 것 아닌가 생각합니다. 돌이켜 생각해보니 서울대에서의 기간을 세 단계로 나눌 수 있는 것 같아요. 처음 1986년 2학기부터 시작했는데 그때부터 외환위기를 맞은 1997년도까지 10년 정도가 1/3을 차지하는데, 그때까지는 내실을 쌓는

단계였던 것 같습니다. 학내적으로 이런저런 일이 없지 않았지만 그래도 비교적 조용히 공부하며 지낼 수 있었습니다. 특별히 밖에서 어떤 요청도 없었고, 학내에서만 지냈으니 어떻게 보면 밖에서 별로 남들이 알아주지 않는 생활을 한 셈이죠. 독일 뮌헨대에서 1년 간, 그리고 일본 동경대에서 8개월간 미국 아닌 외국 사회를 접할 수 있었던 것도 이 기간 중의 일이었습니다.

다음으로 1997년부터 2010년까지는 그 전에 비해서 굉장히 여러 가지 활동을 하게 되었습니다. 기업지배구조 관련해서 입법에 관여하는 한편, 몇몇 회사에서 사외감사와 사외이사로 일하면서 몇 가지 잊지 못할 경험을 했었습니다. 학교 내에서는 금융법센터를 만들고, 센터 발간으로 『BFL』을 창간한 일이 기억에 남습니다. 그전에는 『Journal of Korean Law』도 제가 Founding Editor-in-Chief로 창간작업을 수행했었습니다. 각종 연구프로젝트도 2000년대 초부터 많이 했던 것 같아요. 여기 안수현 교수도 계시고, 최문희 교수도 계시지만 여러분들 도움을 받아서 여러 종류의 프로젝트를 정말 많이 했습니다. 그리고 국제적인 학술교류와 외국대학에서의 강의를 시작한 것도 이 무렵의 일입니다. 그 와중에 총장선거에도 두 차례나 깊이 관여하면서 학내정치의 세계를 접할 수 있었습니다. 연구나 강의에는 전혀 도움 되지 않았지만 세상 돌아가는 이치를 조금이나마 깨칠 수 있어서 후회는 없습니다. 그런데 2007년 로스쿨법이 통과되고 2008년 법대 학장에 취임하고부터는 거의 전적으로 로스쿨 업무에 주력하며 이 모든 일들에서 손을 놓을 수밖에 없었습니다. 지금 생각해 보면 이 기간 동안 상당히 여러 가지 일을 하며 다양한 사람을 만났었던 것 같습니다.

마지막 세 번째 단계가 2010년 6월 학장직을 마치고 퇴직하기까지의 기간인데, 그 전 단계와는 생활이 180도 바뀌었습니다. 학교에 있기 마련인 여러 가지 귀찮은 업무들로부터는 대체로 면제를 받았습니다. 그렇게 될 수 있었던 건 그 기간 동안, 말하자면 2000년대 초반부터 2010년까지 송옥렬 교수부터 천경훈 교수까지 여러 교수님들이 들어오셔서 그분들이 귀찮은 일들을 모두 맡아주셨기 때문입니다. 덕분에 나로서는 하고 싶은 일만 하고 지낼 수 있어서 늘 고맙게 생각하고 있습니다. 그런데 이런 잡무에 대한 면제는 학문적인 영역에도 파급되어서 국내에서는 발표에 대한 의뢰도 싹 사라져버렸습니다. 이젠 학회에서도 사회나 보는 신세가 되었습니다. 대신 국제교류가 활발해짐에 따라 뜻밖에 영문발표가 늘어난 것은 국내 학계에서 조기 퇴출된 덕분인 것 같습니다.

안수현 : 이제 정년을 마치시고 하고 싶으신 일도 많으실 텐데 어떤 계획을 세우고 계신지 말씀을 듣고 싶습니다.

김건식 : 사실 그런 질문은 굉장히 많이 받아왔습니다. 한 10년 전쯤에는 정년퇴직을 하면 이제 법학연구는 떠나 볼까 하는 생각도 좀 했습니다. 그래서 역사에 대해서 공부해보면 어떨까, 역사 쪽에서는 동양사, 중국사 이런 쪽을 해보면 어떨까 싶어서 중국어도 좀 배우고 중국에서 한 달간 살아보고 했습니다. 또 정치사상 같은 것을 잠시 들여다보기도 했습니다. 그런데 시간이 흐를수록 잘못하면 정년퇴직을 하고도 오래 살 가능성도 있는데 그래도 무언가 쓸모 있는 일을 해야 되지 않나 하는 생각도 들더군요. 결국 어설픈 꿈은 버리고 지금은 회사법하고 자본시장법 분야에서 그래도 내가 할 수 있는 유익한 일을 좀 하면 좋겠다고 생각하고 있습니다. 그래서 퇴직을 하고 나면 할 일로 한두 가지 생각하고 있는 것이 있긴 한데, 아직 충분히 구체화 되지 않은 단계여서 여기서 말씀드리기는 적절치 않을 것 같습니다.

〈법학으로의 입문과 유학생활〉

천경훈 : 저는 91학번으로 대학에 들어와서 처음 선생님께 상법 과목을 배웠던 기억이 나는데요. 그때는 선생님께서 외람된 말씀이지만 (웃음) 굉장히 젊으셨을 때였던 것 같아요. 선생님께서는 법대 73학번으로 입학을 하셨는데, 입학 당시에 학교 분위기나 선생님의 주요 관심사는 어떤 것이었고, 또 상법에 관심을 가지시게 된 계기는 어떤 것이었는지 듣고 싶습니다.

김건식 : 네, 말씀을 드리자면 한이 없는데요.

천경훈 : 길게 충분히 말씀해 주십시오. (모두 웃음)

김건식 : 당시 학교 분위기는 유신 시절이라 아주 암울했습니다. 1973년 가을에는 최종길 교수 변사 사건이 있었고, 또 1974년에는 민청학련 사건이 있었죠. 그 당시에는 긴급조치 시대라 데모라는 것을 생각하기가 어려울 정도로 굉장히 억눌려 지내던 시절이었습니다. 그렇게 저항을 하기 어려운 시절이었는데도 가을이면 무언가 소란스런 일이 벌어져서, 그런 일이 벌어지면 바로 학교가 휴교를 하고 그래서 수업을 리포트로 대체하던 일이 반복됐었습니다. 저도 속으로는 다른 학생들처럼 그 당시 정부에 대해서는 매우 비판적이었지만 학생운동과는 항상 거리를 두고 있었기 때문에 그런 면에서는 비겁한 생활을 했다고 볼 수가 있죠. 그런데 사실 분위기는 암울했는데도 적어도 75년까지는 캠퍼

스에 낭만이라고 할 만한 요소가 없지 않았습니다. 그래서 지금은 좀 기이하게 느껴지기도 합니다만, 남녀 대학생들이 어울리는 쌍쌍파티라든지 카니발이 학교마다 있었는데, 물론 서울대에도 있었고 법대에도 있었습니다. 그런데 80년대 들어서면서는 광주사태 영향인지, 학생운동이 프로화된 탓인지 모르겠는데, 카니발 같은 건 시대상황에 맞지 않는 퇴폐적인 것으로 보게 되고, 학교생활에서 일종의 금욕주의나 엄숙주의가 팽배해진 것이 인상 깊게 남아 있습니다.

법대 입학 당시에는 고등학생을 겨우 벗어난 처지라 유치한 지적 호기심에 사로잡혀있었습니다. 소위 의식 있는 대학생들이 애독하던 『창작과 비평』, 『문학과 지성』 이런 잡지들의 과월호까지 헌책방에서 구해서, 물론 소화도 덜된 상태로 마구 읽었던 기억이 있고요. 그때에는 문학 평론 쪽이 왠지 멋있게 보여서 당시 이름을 날리던 분들인 백낙청, 김현, 김윤식 이런 분들의 글을 즐겨 읽었습니다. 김윤식 교수님은 우리 1학년 때 교양 국어를 가르치셨죠. 그때 그분은 세상 고민을 다 하는 듯이 심각한 표정으로 앉아서 정확히 잘 이해되진 않지만 뭔가 심오하게 들리는 말씀만 하시고 그랬는데, 지금 생각해보면 그분이 그때 기껏해야 30대 후반이어서 (모두 웃음) 지금 생각하면 웃음이 나죠. 당시엔 소설도 많이 읽었습니다. 지금도 유명한 황석영 씨가 우리가 입학하자마자 대학신문에 단편소설을 발표했던 기억이 있고, 이문구 씨라고 작고한 분이시지만 만연체의 그분 소설을 찾아 읽던 기억도 있습니다. 그리고 요즘도 간혹 논의가 됩니다만, 리영희 교수의 글들이 당시에도 상당히 화제를 불러일으켜서 저도 몇 권 사서 보긴 했습니다만, 그렇게 크게 끌렸던 것 같지는 않아요. 오히려 후에 나온 그분의 자서전 비슷한 책은 아주 재밌게 읽었던 기억이 있는데, 그분의 중국이나 월남전에 대한 글은 그렇게까지 감명을 받지 못했습니다. 아마도 제가 애초부터 부르주아적 성향이 강했던 탓이 아닌가 생각됩니다.

그리고 당시에는 아마 일제시대 때부터의 영향인지 모르겠는데 문과 쪽 대학생이라면 영, 독, 불, 일 4개 국어는 해야 된다는 식의 지적 허영심 같은 것이 남아있었습니다. 당시만 해도 제가 뭐 학자가 될 생각은 없었는데, 그래도 지식인 비슷한 흉내는 내야 한다는 욕심은 있었던 것 같습니다. 그래서 1학년 1학기에는 누나 친구 중에 불어를 전공하는 분이 계셨는데, 그분한테 불어를 배웠고, 1학년 겨울방학 때는 외대 일어과 2학년 여학생에게 일본어를 두 달간 배웠습니다. 사실 1학년 때는, 법대가 문리대 바로 옆에 있었기 때문에 문리대 가기가 아주 쉬웠어요. 그래서 라틴어도 배워볼까 하는 허황된 욕심에 문리대 종교학과 신사훈 교수라는 분이 뜻있는 학생들을 상대로 하는 라틴어 강의에 참석한 적이 있습니다. 그런데 그분이 상당히 종교적인 말씀을 많이 하셔서 '이것까지는 내가 못하겠다.'고 포기를 했던 일이 있습니다. 한 마디로 치기만만한 시절이었습니다.

1학년 때부터 법학개론이 있었지만, 본격적인 법학 수업은 2학년 때부터 시작되었는데, 솔직히 큰 재미를 느끼지는 못했습니다. 자신이 별 흥미를 못 느꼈던 학문을 학생들에게 가르치는 입장이 되니 몇 마디 변명을 해야겠네요. 우선 그때는 낭만적인 시대라 교수와 학생 피차간에 학교 강의에 크게 신경을 쓰시지 않는 분위기였고 그런 강의나마 시국 때문에 제대로 이루어지질 않았습니다. 강의내용도 추상적이고, 이론적인 학설 다툼이 중심이고 현실문제와는 괴리된 경우가 많았습니다. 지금 생각해보면, 당시는 유신시대니까 법이 작용하는 영역이 굉장히 좁았죠. 그러니까 민법이나 민사소송법 정도를 빼놓고는 나머지 분야에서는 법은 존재하더라도 실제로 적용되는 상황이 아니었기 때문에, 학생들이 실제 적용되지 않는 법에 대한 흥미를 갖기가 어려운 것은 당연하게 생각됩니다. 또 당시 책 서문에는 교수들조차 판례를 구하기 어렵다는 불평을 적어놓은 경우도 있었습니다. 그러니까 학자들이 현실세계에서 일어나는 일을 접하기가 어려웠어요. 그런데 재밌는 것은 최근에 중국법을 공부하면서 보니 중국의 법서들이 딱 그런 것 같더군요. 그러니까 중국의 현실분쟁은 다루지 않고, 미국, 독일 같은 외국의 이론 소개에 주력하고 있어서 '아, 이게 결국은 법치주의가 확립되지 않은 나라들에선 어쩔 수 없는 현상이 아닌가.' 그런 생각을 했습니다. 그러니까 법치주의가 정착되지 않은 상황에서 법학이 발달한다는 것은 기대하기 어려운 것 같습니다.

상법과 인연을 맺게 된 것은 굉장히 우연한 일이에요. 4학년 1학기 때 작고하신 정희철 교수님께서 가르치시던 상법연습을 택해서 들었습니다. 그 수업은 학생들의 발표로 진행되었는데, 제가 첫 번째 발표를 맡게 되었습니다. 당시 테마가 지금도 생각이 나는데, '개업준비행위'에 관한 것이었어요. 나름대로 국내 논문도 찾아보고 그때 배웠던 일본어 지식을 동원해서 일본 상법책도 찾아보고 해서 발표를 무사히 마쳤습니다. 그랬더니 정희철 교수님이 상당히 깐깐하신 분인데 잘했다고 칭찬을 해주셨습니다. 그때 교수님께 직접 칭찬을 들은 것은 처음이었기 때문에, 그다음부터는 그분을 더 가깝게 느끼게 되었고, 설날에 세배도 가게 되었습니다. 그래서 그걸 보더라도 '칭찬이 굉장히 중요한 거다.'라는 것을 느끼는데, 저는 사실 실천을 별로 못 했습니다. 학자로서 하는 일이 아무래도 발표의 허점이랄까, 빈틈이랄까 하는 것들을 발견해서 그런 걸 지적하고 개선방안을 제시하는 것이다 보니까, 남의 발표를 들으면 '아, 잘했다.' 이런 이야기를 하기보다는, '그것은 이런 이런 부분에서 문제가 있고 이렇게 하면 좀 더 좋아지겠다.'는 식으로 말하다 보면, 칭찬을 할 기회를 놓치는 경우가 많은 것 같습니다. 저는 학생을 가르칠 기회는 거의 없을 것으로 생각됩니다만, 여러분은 앞으로 기회가 많을 테니까, 이런 점을 고려해서 칭찬을 많이 해주면 좋을 것 같습니다.

윤영신 : 선생님께서는 그럼 동숭동에서 학교를 다니신 것인가요?

김건식 : 그렇죠. 동숭동에서 2년을 다녔어요. 지금도 대학로 쪽에 가면 그 무렵의 기억이 살아나곤 합니다.

노혁준 : 학부시절까지 이야기해 주셨는데요. 선생님께서는 학부 마치시고서 바로 미국 유학을 떠나신 것으로 알고 있는데, 어떤 계기로 특히 독일이 아니라 미국으로 떠나시게 되었는지 여쭤보고 싶습니다. 그때 벌써 교수 쪽으로 생각을 하고 계셨던 것인지요?

김건식 : 사실은 대학 졸업하자마자 유학을 간 것은 아니었습니다. 나를 모르는 사람들 중에는 내가 일생동안 그냥 승승장구하면서 탄탄대로를 걸었다고 생각하는 사람들도 있습니다만, (모두 웃음) 나름대로 수많은 좌절을 겪었지요. 당시는 사법시험이 겨울에 있었는데 4학년 말에 마음먹고 본 시험에서 실패를 했습니다. 그래서 크게 의기소침한 상태에서 대학원에 진학을 했습니다. 이미 4학년 때 고도근시로 징집면제가 됐기 때문에, 굳이 군 입대를 미룰 목적으로 대학원에 진학할 필요는 없었는데, 어떤 이유에서인지 대학원에 진학을 했습니다. 당시 법대에선 송상현 선생님이 가장 젊고 활발한 분이어서 대학원에서도 학생들이 많이 따랐죠. 그런데 그분이 왜 그랬는지 모르겠는데, 절 잘 보셔서 학자가 되는 쪽으로 유도를 많이 했습니다. 그래서 송상현 선생님께 민사소송법, 회사정리법 과목들을 들었습니다. 그리고 논문 제목으로 집단소송(Class Action)이라는 걸 받아가지고 1978년도 여름에 한창 더웠을 때 하루하루를 논문작성으로 보낸 기억이 있습니다. 당시엔 컴퓨터가 있기 전이어서 먼저 노트에다가 초고를 적고 그것을 원고지에다 옮겨 쓰는 식으로 작업을 했었죠. 당시 집단소송에 대해서는 국내 자료를 찾을 수 없었습니다. 그때 마침 일본에서는 그에 대한 논의가 많이 되고 있었어요. 일본에 신도우코지(新堂幸司)라는 동경대학 민사소송법 교수가 있는데 그분이 쓴 글이 몇 개가 있었습니다. 도서관에서는 구할 수가 없어서 편지를 써 국제우편으로 좀 보내주십사 부탁했더니, 조교를 통해서 진짜 보내왔어요. 그래서 그것들을 읽었던 기억이 있고요. 지금 생각하면 당돌함에 얼굴이 달아오릅니다. 집단소송의 모국이 미국이다보니 자연히 미국 논문들을 많이 참조할 수밖에 없었습니다. 마침 1976년에 Harvard Law Review에서 집단소송을 특집으로 다룬 일이 있는데 백 페이지도 넘는 그 논문을 많이 참조했습니다. 두세 번씩 읽어도 알 듯 모를 듯해서 진땀을 흘렸던 기억이 있습니다. 그렇게 낑낑대며 논문을 작성하는 과정에서 신기하게도 재미를 느꼈습니다. 주제가 국내에 거의 알려지지 않은 것이었기 때문에 '내가 남들이 모르는 좀 첨단적인 것을 연구한다.'는 자부심에 차 있기

도 했던 것 같습니다. 당시에 저 말고도 대학원에서 논문을 쓰는 분들이 몇 분 있었는데, 주로 선배들이었습니다. 만나면 각자 자신이 쓰는 논문이 얼마나 새로운 것인지 은근히 과시하곤 했던 기억이 납니다. 하버드에서 석사학위 논문을 쓸 때에도 약간 비슷한 느낌을 가졌었는데, 시간이 흐르면서 논문을 쓸 때 그런 지적인 자부심 같은 것은 거의 느끼지 못하게 돼 버린 것 같아요.

유학할 때 미국을 택한 것은 제게는 너무 당연한 일이었습니다. 당시 대학원에는 최병조 교수님도 같이 계셨는데, 그때도 이미 독일어를 굉장히 잘하셔서 지금도 기억나는 것이, 정희철 교수님께서 수업시간에 최병조 교수님이 독일어 논문에 대해서 발표하는 것을 듣고서 "자네는 나보다 더 잘하는 것 같다."라고 말씀하셨습니다. 그런데 저는 독일어를 배운다든가 독일로 유학을 간다는 생각은 한 번도 해보지 않았어요. 한국의 법학에 대해서 무언가 약간 실망감이랄까 불만이 있었는데, 그것이 독일법의 영향을 받은 탓이 아닌가 하는 막연한 생각 때문이 아니었을까 짐작해봅니다. 그런데 나중에 독일에 가서 보니까 독일 법학이라는 것이 그렇게 답답한 것이 아니었는데 제가 잘못 생각했다는 것을 깨닫게 됐습니다. 또 당시에 형님이 미국에서 유학을 마치고 서울대 교수를 하고 계셨는데 그 영향도 컸던 것 같습니다. 하버드에서 공부하실 때 하버드 로스쿨에 오셨던 분들이 여러분이 있었는데, 그때만 해도 워낙 한국 사람 수가 적다 보니 서로 다 알고 지냈던 것 같아요. 그래서 김영무 변호사님, 이태희 변호사님, 법대 백충현 선생님을 다 잘 알게 되었습니다. 그분들께서 이야기도 많이 해주시고 해서 미국 유학에 대한 동경을 품게 되었던 것 같습니다.

최문희 : 선생님께서는 집단소송(Class Action)을 주제로 석사논문을 쓰시고 이후 연구는 주로 회사법, 증권법 쪽 글을 많이 쓰셨는데요. 미국 유학 시절에는 주로 어느 분야를 연구하셨나요? 미국에서 공부하신 시간이 나중에 선생님의 진로와 학문에 어떤 영향을 끼쳤는지 궁금합니다.

김건식 : 이것도 말씀 드리자면 한이 없는데요. 미국에는 두 차례 가게 되었습니다. 79년도에 처음 하버드에 가서 LL.M.을 마치고 잠시 한국에 들어왔다가 다시 국비장학금을 받아서 워싱턴대학(University of Washington)에서 J.D.를 하게 됐죠. 하버드 유학은 형님 친구 분인 아시아시멘트 이윤무 회장께서 학비를 대주셔서 할 수 있었습니다. 그간 별로 기회가 없었는데 이 자리를 빌려서라도 다시 한번 깊이 감사드리고 싶습니다.

하버드에서는 회사법으로 논문을 쓰게 됐는데, 로버트 클라크(Robert C. Clark) 교수는 당시 30대 중반 정도였는데, 그분께 회사법을 들었습니다. 공정거래법의 최고 권위자인 필립 아리다(Phillip E. Areeda) 교수께 Antitrust Law를 듣고, 스티븐 샤벨(Steven Shavell) 교수한테 Law & Economics, 나중에 연방항소법원 판사가 된 더글라스 긴즈버그(Douglas H. Ginsburg) 교수로부터 경제규제법을 들었습니다. 그런데 회사법을 빼놓고는 어느 것도 우리나라에 존재하지 않는 과목을 들었기 때문에 정말 힘들었습니다.

클라크 교수에게 논문지도를 부탁드리고 적당한 주제의 추천을 부탁드렸더니 그분이 금방 나온 재판관련 속보를 하나 던져줬습니다. 당시 연방법원과 델라웨어주법원에서 동시에 진행되던 분쟁에 관한 걸로 기억되는데 분쟁이 일단락된 것은 1981년의 일(Zapata Corp. v. Maldonado, 430 A.2d. 779 (Del. 1981))이니 1979년 당시에는 한창 논의가 진행 중인 상황이었습니다. 그 문건의 내용은 Special Litigation Committee, 즉 특별소송위원회에서 대표소송에 대해서 청구할 것인지 말 것인지를 결정하게 되면 법원이 그 결정을 경영판단으로 보아 그것을 존중해서 대표소송을 각하하는 최신 동향에 관한 것이었습니다. 그런 따끈따끈한 판례속보가 대학교수 연구실에 전달된다는 사실이 퍽 인상적이었습니다. 사실 대표소송이라고 하는 건 집단소송하고 유사한 것이지요. 그래서 당시 미국의 「Federal Rules of Civil Procedure」를 보면 제 기억에 23조가 아마 집단소송이고, 23.1조가 대표소송으로 되어있어서 집단소송에 관한 석사논문을 쓸 때 한번 스쳐보았던 일이 있었습니다. 그래서 이것을 하면 좀 쉽지 않을까 하는 얄팍한 속셈도 작용해서 선택하게 되었습니다. 그러니까 인생이란 정말 우연의 연속인 것 같습니다. 제가 집단소송을 주제로 석사학위 논문을 쓸 때 '그렇게 되면 나중에 대표소송을 쓰기 쉽겠다.' 이렇게 생각해본 적은 당연히 없었지요. 하지만 결과적으로 석사논문은 제가 회사법으로 전공을 정하는데 결정적 영향을 미쳤던 겁니다. 당시에 특별소송위원회는 미처 관련 논문이 나오기 전으로 그야말로 최신의 주제였습니다. 지금은 좀 생각이 달라졌습니다만 그 당시 제게는 이것이 대표소송을 피하기 위한 회사의 꼼수로만 여겨졌습니다. 우리 상법상 원고주주가 감사의 부제소결정에 전혀 구속되지 않는다는 점도 작용했겠지요. 그래서 미국의 최신 실무를 정면으로 비판한다는 치기가 다시 발동해서 이런저런 논거를 짜내느라 고심했습니다. 그에 관한 논문은 다음 해부터 나오기 시작했기 때문에 간접적으로라도 내 주장을 뒷받침할 논거를 사방으로 찾던 기억이 생생하네요. 논문초고를 클라크 교수에게 제출하고 코멘트를 기다렸는데 아무런 소식이 없었습니다. 초조한 마음으로 연구실로 찾아갔더니 클라크 교수 만면에 미소가 가득한 채 두툼한 원고의 무게를 손으로 다는 듯한 시늉을 하며 "pretty good"이란 말을 해줬습니다. 사람이 좋아 겉으로 표시는 안하지만 늘 면담을 빨리 끝내고 싶어 하는 기색이 역력했던 그분이 그렇게 긍정적인 태도를 취했던 것은 처음이었습니다. 그래도 논문의 잘못된 점을 지적해주거나 개선방향을 제시해주거나 하는 '지도'는 일체 없었습니다. 그저 미국에서는 논문을 발표하는 게 중요하다는 말씀에 용기를 얻어서 초고상태의 논문을 여기저기 보냈죠. 여기저기서 딱지도 맞았습니다만, 『The Journal of Corporation Law』에서 받아주겠다는 편지를 받고서 몸이 붕 뜨는 느낌으로 황홀했던 기억이 있습니다.

로리뷰에 논문을 발표도 하게 되었으니 학계로 가야되는 것 아닌가란 생각을 그때 조금 해 봤습니다. 그런데 학비가 떨어져 귀국을 해야 했는데 80년 말에 귀국을 하게 되었습니다. 일도 배우고 돈도 모을 겸 해서 김&장 법률사무소에 잠시 근무를 했습니다. 아까도 말씀드렸습니다만, 형님이 김영무 변호사님하고 친분이 있었기 때문에 들어갈 수 있었던 것이지요. 거기서는 각종 법률문서, 계약서, 의견서 등의 국·영문 번역을 많이 했습니다. 국내외 소송과 관련해서 통역을 했던 일도 몇 번 있었습니다. 번역은 좀 따분하긴 했습니다만, 나중에 글을 쓰고 하는 데에는 좋은 경험이 된 것으로 생각합니다.

다음에는 미국생활에서 받은 영향에 대해서 몇 말씀 드리지요. 제가 미국에 간 것이 만 24살 때로 비교적 어린 나이였고 사회경험이 전혀 없는 순진한 상태였기 때문에 창피하지만 미국영향을 아주 강하게 받았습니다. 당시 한국하고 미국은 정치, 경제, 사회 등 모든 면에서 천양지차(天壤之差)였지요. 그러니까 1979년은 박정희 시대 말기로 온 나라가 암울한 상태였는데, 갑자기 자본주의 첨단을 달리는 나라의 최고 로스쿨로 갔으니까 제가 받은 충격이 클 수밖에 없었습니다. 한국 상황에 대해서 열등감이 컸기 때문에 가서 보니까 모든 것이 다 좋게만 보였습니다.

특히 인상 깊었던 것은 한국에서는 책에서나 볼 수 있었던 '자유주의'라는 것이 현실적으로 실천이 되고 있는 것이었습니다. 저로서는 정부가 후견적으로 간섭하는 것이 너무나 자연스럽게 받아들여졌는데, 그쪽에서는 정부 권력에 대한 불신이 지나치게 느껴질 정도로 광범위하게 퍼져 있었습니다. 어린 나이였고 한국의 모든 것에 대한 자존감도 약했기 때문에 미국물이 아주 많이 들었던 것으로 생각이 됩니다. 당시 1년 반밖에 살지 않았는데, 귀국 직후 길을 가다가 사람을 툭 치고 지나가면서 불쑥 "Excuse me."라는 말이 나왔던 적도 있었고요. (웃음) 또 친구들하고 이야기할 때도 "미국에서는 이렇게 하더라."라는 말을 많이 했던 기억도 있습니다. (웃음) 얼마나 재수 없게 느꼈을지 언제 생각해도 낯이 뜨거워집니다.

학문적으로는 미국의 실용주의 학풍에 큰 영향을 받았습니다. 당시 한국의 법학계에서는 역사적인, 비교법적인 고찰을 중요시했던 것 같습니다. 논문을 쓰면 로마법, 독일법, 역사적 발전 등에 대해서 외국 문헌에 근거하여 치밀하게 서술하는 그런 식의 글들이 많았습니다. 그에 비해 미국에서의 학술 논문은 특히 회사법 분야의 경우 기능적인 분석이 많았던 것이 인상적이었습니다. 당시는 법경제학의 영향이 점점 커지고 있던 시점이었습니다. 시카고대학의 리차드 포즈너(Richard Posner) 교수가 한창 명성을 높여가던 시절이었는데 하버드에 와서 강연을 한 적이 있었습니다. 강연을 마친 후 어떤 교수가 "당신은 너무 이론적이다."라고 이야기하니까 "맞다. 난 이론적이다."라고 바로 응수하던 기억이 아직도 납니다.

또 한 가지 영향은 인접학문의 중요성을 인식하게 된 것입니다. 70년대 정도부터는 우리나라에서도 학제적인 연구(Interdisciplinary Research)란 말이 많이 유행을 했는데, 제가 보기에 법학에서 학제적인 연구는 두 가지 측면이 있는 것 같아요. 하나는 법학 내부에서의 인접 분야와의 관련, 즉 상법의 관점에서 본다면 세법, 도산법, 소송법 등과의 관련이 중요한데, 그 부분에 대해서 계속 관심을 가져야 되겠다는 생각을 하게 되었습니다. 법학 외부의 연관 분야와 관련해서는 회계나 경제학에서의 산업구조론이나, 경영학에서의 재무관리나 이런 것들에 대한 지식이 필요하다는 인식을 하게 되었습니다.

그리고 조금 다른 이야기입니다만, 제가 유학했던 70년대 말 80년대 초에는 소위 비판법학(Critical Legal Studies)이 기세를 올리던 시절이었습니다. 하버드는 비판법학의 '소굴'이라고도 볼 수 있는데, 당시 비판법학의 대표 격인 던컨 케네디(Duncan Kennedy) 교수의 '불법행위법' 강의를 청강하기도 했습니다. 사실 민주화가 되지 않았던 시절의 한국인에게는 매우 와 닿는 면이 있었습니다. 그래서 나중에 귀국해서 비판법학에 관한 논문을 번역해서 『현상과 인식』이라는 잡지에 게재하고 법학개론 시간에 소개한 일도 있습니다. 그런데 법경제학이나 비판법학은 굉장히 유익한 시야를 제공하는 것은 사실이지만, 그것이 극단에 흐르게 되면 너무 사물을 단순화하기 때문에 복잡한 현실을 담아내지 못하는 문제점이 있다고 생각합니다. 그래서 나는 이런 시각이 자칫 비상식적인 결과로 이끌 위험이 있는 것 같아 한편으로는 관심을 가지면서도 그렇게 크게 끌리지는 않았습니다. 아마 내게는 일찍부터 점진주의적, 실용주의적 성향이 있었던 것 같습니다.

이와 관련해서는 일화가 있습니다. 1980년대는 회사법 쪽에서 법경제학이 헤게모니를 잡아가는 시기였습니다. 당시 좀 극단적인 또는 순수한 법경제학자들은 강행규정이라는 것은 필요가 없다는 주장을 폈습니다. 그런데 유명한 회사법학자이자, 계약법학자인 멜빈 아이젠버그(Melvin Eisenberg) 교수가 다소 전통적인 입장에서 회사법상 강행규정을 정당화하는 논문을 발표했습니다. 그와 비슷한 시기인 1988년에 아이젠버그 교수가 『The Nature of the Common Law』라는 책을 출간했습니다. 그 책에서 그분은 판사가 재량을 가지고 마음대로 판결하는 것 같지만 사실은 그렇지 않고 사회적인 여러 요인들이 있어서 그에 따른 제약을 받는다고 주장했습니다. 여러 요인들 가운데서도 판결에 대한 학계의 평가 같은 것도 중요해서, 그런 것을 의식하다 보면 판사가 그렇게 마음대로 할 수 있는 것이 아니란 것이지요. 나는 아이젠버그 교수의 유명한 『The Structure of the Corporation: A Legal Analysis』라는 책을 번역한 일도 있어서, 1982년 그분을 뵈러 버클리 대학에 다녀온 적이 있습니다. 20년이 지난 2001년에 콜럼비아대학에서 Visiting Scholar로 연구할 때, 마침 그분이 그곳에서 회사법 강의를 하고 있었습니다. 청강을 해도 되겠냐고 인사를 했더니, 반가워하면서 패컬티 클럽에서 점심을 사줬어요. 점심을 먹으면서 제가 조심스레 이야기를 꺼냈습니다. "당신은 『The Nature of the Common Law』라는 책에서 보면 비판법학에 대해서 비판을 하고 있는 것 같다."고 말문을 열었더니 그분은 정색을 하며 자신은 평생 어떤 견해를 비판하기 위해서 글을 쓴 일이 없다고 잘라 말했습니다. 그래서 나는 "비판법학자들은 판사가 기득권층을 대변해서 거의 마음대로 판결을 내릴 수 있으니 결국은 기득권층의 이익을 보호하는 판결을 한다는 식으로 주장한다. 당신은 정면으로 비판법학을 거론하진 않지만, 판결 그 자체가 사회적인 여러 여건의 영향을 받는다는 주장을 하고 계시니, 이것은 법학, 판결의 독립성, 자족성 같은 것이 존재한다는 것을 말씀하신 셈으로 간접적으로 비판법학 주장에 반대하는 것으로 볼 수 있을 것 같다. 그리고 당신이 법경제학 쪽의 극단적인 주장에 반대하는 것이나, 비판법학 쪽의 극단적인 주장에 반대하는 것 모두, 상식에 따른 사고라는 점에서 일관성이 있는 것 같다."라고 내 생각을 설명했지요. 그랬더니, 그분이 잠시 내 눈을 빤히 쳐다보더니 껄껄 웃으며 "당신은 내가 보지 못한 것을 본 것 같습니다."라고 하더군요. (모두 웃음)

천경훈 : 지금까지 선생님께서 첫 번째 유학 가셨을 때 이야기를 주로 해주셨는데요. 그럼 두 번째 유학 가셨을 때는 어떠셨는지요? 첫 번째와 어떻게 다르셨는지, 느낀 것이나 경험하신 것을 듣고 싶습니다.

김건식 : 두 번째 유학을 갈 때에는 국비장학금을 받았습니다. 그래서 국가 도움을 받아 공부를 했는데 뭔가 국가에 도움 되는 일을 했나 하는 반성을 이따금 하곤 합니다. 왜 Ph.D.가 아닌 J.D.를 했느냐에 대해서도 질문을 많이 받았습니다. 저는 그때 순진하게도 미국법을 제대로 공부하려면 J.D.부터 해야 되는 것이 아닌가라는 생각을 했었는데, 지금은 전혀 그렇게 생각을 하지 않습니다. (웃음) 그냥 젊은 치기에 끌렸던 것 같습니다. LSAT 점수가 잘 나와서 솔직히 하버드나 예일 같은 명문대에 가고 싶었지만 그런 곳을 갈 수 있는 성적은 아니었지요. 몇몇 학교에서 입학허가를 받았는데, 시애틀에 있는 워싱턴대학이 아시아법, 특히 일본법을 제일 활발하게 하는 곳이었습니다. 저는 오래전부터 일본에 대해서 관심이 많았어요. 그래서 일본법에 대해 공부하면 좋겠다 싶어서 시애틀로 가게 되었던 것이지요. 그런데 워싱턴대학은 주립대학으로 나쁜 대학은 아니지만

그렇다고 엘리트 스쿨은 아니다 보니 학생들도 다르고 교수들도 다르고, 지적인 분위기나 이런 것은 하버드랑 비교할 수가 없었지요. 그렇지만 교수들 관심은 더 받을 수 있어서 좋았습니다. 특히 일본법 전문가인 헨더슨(Dan Fenno Henderson) 교수와 헤일리(John O. Haley) 교수로부터는 학문적으로나 인간적으로 많은 도움을 받았습니다. 회사법과 세법 전공의 커머트(Richard Kummert) 교수는 business planning이란 매우 실무적인 과목도 가르쳤는데 강의가 치밀하면서도 군더더기 없어서 나도 언젠가 저런 강의를 할 수 있으면 좋겠다는 생각을 하곤 했습니다.

천경훈 : 지금도 많은 학생들이 미국으로 유학을 떠나고 있고, 선생님께서는 아마 추천서도 받으러 올 것 같은데요. 선생님께서 유학하실 때와는 환경이나 여건이 많이 다를 것 같습니다. 요새 떠나는 학생들에게 당부말씀이 있다면 한 말씀 듣고 싶습니다.

김건식 : 환경은 엄청나게 좋아졌지요. 무엇보다도 지금은 우리나라도 정치적으로 민주화가 됐고 그래서 법치주의도 확산됐고, 경제적으로도 성장해서 두 나라 사이에 격차가 크게 줄어들었습니다. 법학 분야에서는 아직 격차가 남아 있지만 전에 비해서는 크게 줄어들었다고 볼 수 있죠. 제가 갔을 때 경험을 좀 말씀드리면, 회사법 수업을 듣는데 'tender offer'라는 말을 처음 들었습니다. 사전을 찾아봐야 되는데 'tender'라는 말도 알고 'offer'라는 말도 알아서, (모두 웃음) 무언가 좀 아는 것 같다는 생각을 했었어요. 그렇지만 제대로 알지는 못했죠. 그것이 '공개매수'를 가리키는 것이라는 것은 나중에 알게 되었는데, 그때까지 한국에선 공개매수라는 개념은 거의 가르치거나 논문에서 다룬 일이 없었던 것 같습니다. 지금은 우리나라에서도 공개매수가 실제로 일어나고 있고, 학교에서도 가르치고 있지요. 비슷한 예는 많습니다. 그래서 지금 가는 사람들은 내가 겪었던 그런 어려움은 크게 줄어들었을 것입니다.

그리고 지금도 잊을 수 없는 것은, 당시 회사법은 랑델 노스라는 큰 강의실에서 100명이 넘는 학생들과 같이 들었습니다. 클라크 교수는 매우 명쾌하게 강의를 하는 사람이긴 하지만, 말 자체가 영어로는 'mumble'이라고 그러는데 조금 웅얼웅얼하는 버릇이 있었습니다. 그래도 그분의 말씀은 그나마 좀 알아듣겠는데, 학생들하고 하는 질의응답은 도통 알아들을 수가 없었습니다. 학생들이 무슨 말을 하는지는 알아듣기가 무척 어려웠고, 몇 번 질의응답이 왔다 갔다 하면 전혀 무슨 말을 하고 있는지 모르게 되는 겁니다. 그러다 보면 '아, 내가 이 중에서는 제일 바보가 아닌가.'하는 (모두 웃음) 참담한 생각이 드는 겁니다. TOEFL은 높은 점수를 받았는데도 그런 거예요. 그런데 지금은 우리 대학에서도 수업이 착실히 이루어지고 있어서 법학지식 면에서 준비도 많이 되어 있고, 또 영어실력도 예전에 내가 갔을 때보다는 훨씬 좋아져서 어려움을 좀 덜 겪지 않을까 생각하고 있습니다.

다른 면에서는 이제 나라의 위상도 많이 올라갔기 때문에 뭔가 위축되는 면도 덜하지 않나 생각이 되고, 오히려 지금은 가면 미국의 단점이 많이 보이지 않을까도 싶습니다. 예를 들면 좀 청결하지 못하고 냄새가 난다든지 허술한 구석들이 보일지도 모르겠어요. 최근에는 한국에서 대학을 나온 이른바 토종 한국인들이 미국에 가서 공부해 미국 로스쿨에서 정식으로 교수가 되는 예가 늘고 있습니다. 우리 법대 졸업생 중에도 그런 사람들이 몇 있지요. 예전에는 상상도 할 수 없었던 일입니다. 최근에는 추천서 쓰는 횟수도 크게 줄어들었습니다만, 지금은 특별히 당부하는 것은 없고, 그저 학교에 가면 "여러 가지 강연도 많이 있고 하니까 가능하면 많이 가서 들으라."거나 또 "'백문이 불여일견'이니까 주위에 가볼 만한 곳이 있으면 구경도 많이 하고 경험도 쌓고 돌아오라."는 식의 이야기를 하고 있습니다.

윤영신 : 교수님께서는 워낙 영어를 잘하셔서, 영어를 못 알아들어서 어려움을 겪으셨을 거라고는 생각해 본 적이 없었습니다. 무언가 저희들과의 공통분모가 있는 것 같아 안도감이 듭니다. (모두 웃음)

김건식 : 참담하단 생각을 했던 적이 많이 있습니다. (웃음)

최문희 : 아까 클라크 교수님이 선생님 석사논문을 코멘트하면서 논문을 출간하라고 그러셨다는데 저는 정말 놀랐습니다. 그런 권유를 아무한테나 할 것 같지는 않거든요. 한국에서 온 25세된 학생에게 출간하라고 하는 것은 정말 대단한 일 같습니다.

김건식 : 솔직히 말하면 논문이 출간할 만하니까 적극 권하는 그런 취지는 아니었고, 그분 이야기는 미국에서는 평가를 받는 데 출간하는 것이 좋으니까 내봐도 좋겠다는 정도였지요.

최문희 : 그래도 논문 수준이 떨어지면 빈말로도 그런 말 안 할 것 같은데요.

김건식 : 나중에 하버드 로스쿨 학장이 된 클라크 교수가 1996년에 송상현 교수님께서 학장 하실 때 한 번 법대를 방문한 적이 있습니다. 그때 그분의 강연을 내가 통역했기 때문에 만난 자리에서 옛날 이야기를 했더니, 나라는 존재는 어렴풋이 기억하면서도 그 밖의

일은 하나도 기억을 하지 못하더라고요. (모두 웃음) 내가 서울대 교수가 된 것이 자랑스럽다는 말씀을 했습니다.

〈상법학 연구〉

송옥렬 : 선생님께서는 1986년에 서울대학교에 부임하신 것으로 알고 있습니다. 연구 측면에서 당시 상황이랄까요. 당시 상법학계의 상황 등은 어떠했는지요? 선생님께서 당시 어떤 생각을 하셨는지 여쭙고 싶습니다.

김건식 : 나는 정희철 교수님 후임으로 들어오게 됐는데요. 당시는 정희철 교수님 같은 1세대 상법학자들은 퇴임하시고, 2세대 분들이 남아있는 상황이었습니다. 상법분야의 최기원, 양승규, 송상현 교수님들은 모두 대학시절 스승이시고 연배도 크게 차이나서 나는 한참을 조교 비슷한 기분으로 지냈습니다.

당시에는 연구도 아직 사법시험의 영향을 많이 받고 있었던 것이 아닌가 생각이 됩니다. 주로 교과서 중심으로 연구가 이루어지고, 교과서가 본격적으로 두꺼워지던 시절이었습니다. 1970년대에 내가 공부할 때는 골격만을 설명한 얇은 교재가 대부분이었는데, 차츰 외국, 특히 독일의 학설들을 많이 도입해서, 양적으로 굉장히 팽창되어가고 있었습니다. 그런데 '성격'이라고 할까요. 그런 면에서는 크게 달라진 것은 없지 않았나 생각을 합니다. 제 생각에 중요한 것은 우리 문제를 제대로 파악해서 법을 정비하고 해석하는 일인데, 그런 의식은 좀 부족했던 것이 아닌가 싶습니다. 말하자면 문제를 중심으로 법을 연구하기보다는 기존의 법제도를 중심으로 연구를 하는 그런 풍조가 일반적이었던 것으로 생각이 됩니다. 또 당시는 졸업 정원제로 인해서 법대 정원이 대폭 늘었던 시기라, 석사학위만 있으면 서울시내에서도 교수가 되는 것이 가능했습니다. 그래서 지금에 비하면 젊은 교수들이 굉장히 많았죠. 내 73학번 법대동기인 권기범 교수만 하더라도 이미 시립대에서 교편을 잡고 있었고, 지금과 달리 30대 교수가 무수히 많았습니다.

윤영신 : 교수님께서 증권법은 서울대에서 처음으로 가르치신 거였죠?

김건식 : 네, 그렇죠. 1987년 1학기에 대학원에서 처음 개설했으니 33년 전의 일이네요.

윤영신 : 선생님께서 연구를 계속 하시면서 관심을 가지신 주제가 어떤 것이었는지 궁금

합니다. 또 그러한 관심 분야도 시간이 가면서 많이 변하셨을 거라는 생각도 드는데, 특히 IMF 금융위기의 영향이 있지 않았을까 싶기도 하고요. 그 부분에 대해서 말씀해 주시면 좋겠습니다.

김건식 : 그러면 이제 이야기가 약간 뒤로 돌아가게 되는데, 내가 워싱턴대학에서 J.D.를 마친 것이 1985년입니다. 당시에 서울대 공채가 있었는데 떨어졌습니다. 그래서 어떻게 할까 고민을 했는데, 장학금 기간이 더 남아 있었습니다. 마침 워싱턴대학에는 Ph.D. 프로그램이 있어서, 그 프로그램에 들어가게 되었습니다. 1986년 3월에는 거기서 한국법을 강의할 기회를 주었는데, 그러니까 나는 첫 강의를 미국에서 영어 강의로 시작한 셈입니다. 바로 얼마 안돼서 서울대 취직이 결정됐다는 소식을 듣고 7월 말까지 Course Work (대학원 수업과정)을 마치고 귀국을 했는데요. 그 당시에 논문 제목은 『Corporate Governance』로 정하고 들어왔습니다.

주제를 이렇게 정한 것은 1986년에 『Corporate Governance in Korea』라는 짧은 논문을 미국에서 발표한 것이 계기가 되었습니다. 그 논문은 1985년 3학년 때 있었던 비교법세미나에서 발표한 페이퍼를 발전시킨 것입니다. 발표를 준비하면서 처음으로 우리 회사법이 우리의 문제해결에 전혀 기능하지 못하고 있다는 사실을 깨닫게 되었습니다. 나중에 그 논문을 어느 한 선생님께 보내드렸었는데, 그분께서 "이거 다 아는 이야기 아니냐?"라고 말씀하셨다는데, 그 말이 맞습니다. 그런데 다 알지만 말하지 않는 이야기였거든요. 그 논문은 너무 간략한 것이었기 때문에 귀국해서 발전시켜야겠다고 마음먹었습니다. 그래서 1986년부터 강의를 하면서도 항상 머릿속에는 그 논문을 빨리 마치고 새로운 것을 연구해야 된다는 부담을 느꼈습니다. 그런데 결국 그 논문을 제출해서 학위를 받은 것은 1995년이니까, 거의 10년 정도를 끈 셈이에요. 오래 걸린 핑계를 대자면 한이 없지만 무엇보다 내 게으름을 탓해야겠지요. 다만 그 기간 동안 Corporate Governance에만 전념할 수 있었던 것이 아니고, 여러 가지로 시간을 뺏는 일이 많았는데, 특히 강의준비에 시간이 많이 들었습니다. 대학원 강의 외에 학부에서 법학개론, 상법총론, 어음·수표, 회사법 특강 등을 가르쳤는데, 모두 학부시절에 충분히 강의를 듣지 못한 과목들이어서, (모두 웃음) 자습을 해서 가르쳐야 했습니다. 강의 첫해에는 학생들보다 한 일주일 정도 앞서는 정도만으로 아는 척을 해야 되는 그런 상황이었습니다. 그리고 대학원에서 개설한 증권거래법 관련해서는 연구를 더 해서 논문을 몇 편 쓰기도 했습니다. 이런 것들은 Corporate Governance하고 직접 관련된 것은 아니었기 때문에 시간을 따로 내야 했습니다.

논문을 늦게 내서 좋은 점도 있었습니다. Corporate Governance란 것이 여러분도 다 아시다시피 여러 분야에 걸쳐 있고, 또 계속 바뀌는 테마였습니다. 그래서 당시 논문에도

'moving target'이란 표현을 썼는데, 계속 바뀌는 테마라 연구하기 어려운 면이 있다는 식의 표현을 변명 삼아 썼던 것이죠. 그래도 외환위기 전에 마쳐서 다행이지, 외환위기 후였다면 영영 마치지 못했을 것 아닌가란 생각도 듭니다. 결국 논문의 결론 내지 주된 논지는 Corporate Governance의 개선에도 회사법의 역할이 있다는 것이었습니다. 당시에는 이에 대한 논의가 국제적으로도 크게 일어나기 전이긴 했습니다만, 어떻게 보면 뻔한 이야기라고도 볼 수 있는데, 그런 식의 주장을 하는 사람은 거의 없던 때였습니다. Corporate Governance 관련해서 과연 법이란 것이 역할이 있는 것인가, 영어로는 "Does law matter?"라는 물음이 있는데, 여러분도 다 아시다시피 지도급 법학자들은 법의 역할이 별로 없다는 주장을 많이 하지요. 그런데 좀 자기 자랑을 섞어 말한다면 내 논문은 국제 학계에서 그런 논의가 성행하기 전에 나온 겁니다. 그리고 아직도 나는 법의 역할을 부정하는 견해에 대해서는 '극단론'이란 느낌을 떨칠 수 없습니다.

그리고 또 한 가지 말씀드릴 것은, 자료수집의 어려움인데 당시만 해도 소위 'Controlling Shareholder'에 관한 논문이 거의 없었습니다. 국내외 학계의 관심이 별로 그쪽에 있지 않았고, 주로 미국 쪽에서 나오는 이야기는 대개 management의 문제를 다루는 것이었고, 법도 management의 행동을 통제하는 것이어서, Controlling Shareholder의 행동을 통제하는 것에 대해서는 자료가 별로 없었어요. 그래서 여러 가능성을 살펴본 기억이 납니다. 그 중에 하나는, 예를 들면 영국법상의 'Oppression Remedy'라고도 하고, 'Unfair Prejudice Remedy'라고도 하는 제도인데, 말하자면 소수주주 억압에 대한 구제수단이지요. 그런데 당시에 브리티시 콜럼비아대학 교수였고, 지금은 캠브리지 대학에 있는 브라이언 체핀스(Brian R. Cheffins)라고 하는 교수가 'Unfair Prejudice Remedy'에 대해서 쓴 논문이 있어서 그것을 읽고 혹시 지배주주 통제수단으로 활용할 수 있는지 검토한 적이 있습니다. 그런데 사실 'Unfair Prejudice Remedy'라는 것은 주로 폐쇄회사에서 이용되는 것이거든요. 워낙 참고할 만한 것이 보이지 않으니, 그런 것까지 들춰본 것이지요. 그런데 논문을 겨우 마친 후에는 갑자기 상황이 바뀌어서 사람들이 Controlling Shareholder에 대해서 관심을 갖기 시작했습니다. 회사에서의 '대리문제'란 것이 주식 소유가 분산된 회사와 그렇지 않은 회사에서는 내용이 상당히 다르고, 그에 대처하기 위한 전략들도 다르다는 식의 논의가 있는 것은 여러분도 잘 아실 것입니다. 그런 변화를 보면서 한편으론 좀 부러웠습니다. 내가 연구할 때는 그렇게 아무것도 없고 아무도 관심을 보이지 않더니, 지금은 이 주제에 대해서 주식소유 분산은 미국, 유럽, 일본 등에 특유한 현상이고, 일반적으로는 지배주주의 행동을 어떻게 통제할 것인가가 더 문제라고 이구동성으로 외치고 있는 걸 보면 참 여러 가지 감정이 교차합니다.

노혁준 : 선생님의 여러 토픽 중에서 가장 중심이 되는 것이 기업지배구조에 관한 것이고, 1986년에 부임하신 이후 IMF 구제금융 시기까지 거치시면서 우리나라 기업지배구조 제도의 산 증인이라고 하실 수 있는데요. 그 과정에서 어느 부분이 우리 법제에서 특히 개선이 되었는지, 그리고 앞으로 더 개선되어야 될 부분이 있다면 어떤 것들이 있을지 좀 말씀해 주십시오.

김건식 : 이것은 아주 일반적으로만 말씀을 드리겠습니다. 기업지배구조에 관해서는 외환위기를 거치면서 상당한 변화가 있었던 것이 사실이죠. 법률적인 면에서 변화도 있었지만, 법률 외적인 면에서도 변화가 있었던 것 같습니다. 그렇다고 문제가 다 해결됐다고 볼 수는 없죠. 그렇지만 어느 나라도 기업지배구조가 완벽하지 않고 나름의 문제를 안고 있는 것이기 때문에, 단기적인 관점에서 접근할 문제는 아니라고 생각합니다. 지배구조라는 것은 사회 전반의 문제와 관계가 있기 때문에 학계, 특히 회사법 학계에서 감당할 몫이라는 것은 반드시 큰 것만은 아니라고 생각하고 있습니다. 너무 막연한 이야기인지 모르겠습니다만 회사법을 연구하는 우리로서는, 기능주의적 사고를 좀 더 착실하게 해나가야 하는 것이 아닌가라는 생각을 합니다. 문제를 인식하고 문제 해결에 적합한 방법이 무엇인가 하는 걸 모색하는 것이 중요한 과제라고 생각합니다.

윤영신 : IMF 외환위기 직후의 우리나라 지배구조에 관해서는 법 개정도 숨가쁘게 이루어졌고, 그 과정에서 선생님께서 일도 많이 하셨다고 말씀하셨는데요. 선생님의 연구와 관련하여 에피소드나 소감을 듣고 싶습니다. 외환위기가 아니었으면 처음에 말씀하셨던 교수로서의 삶의 단계도 달라지셨을까요?

김건식 : 그럴 거예요. 사실 이런 이야기를 하긴 미안하지만 외환위기가 저한테는 큰 행운이었어요. 왜냐하면 제가 Corporate Governance에 대해 오래 연구했잖아요. 그 이전에는 Corporate Governance라는 말도 잘 쓰지 않을 때였어요. 그런데 갑자기 그 용어가 신문지상에까지 등장하게 되어 버렸잖아요. 지배구조 전문가로서는 굉장히 운이 좋았던 거죠. 그래서 정말 속된 말로 하면 '호떡집에 불난 것'처럼 이일 저일에 관여하면서 여러 경험을 많이 했습니다.

금방 생각이 나는 것은 당시 IMF, IBRD 쪽에서 우리나라 회계 자료는 못 믿겠다고 감사위원회 도입하라고 압력을 넣던 일입니다. 회계정보를 못 믿으니 M&A 할 때 합병이나 주식매수 대신 소위 Asset Deal로 했잖아요. 말하자면, 한국 기업의 회계정보는 전혀 믿을 수가 없고, 회계정보의 신뢰도를 높이기 위해서는 감사위원회가 필요하다는 거예요.

그때는 감사위원회는 아는 사람이 거의 없었고, 나도 아는 바가 별로 없었습니다. 금융지원을 받으려면 도입을 하긴 해야 하는데 감사위원회는 사외이사로 구성된 위원회라서 사외이사까지 도입해야 했습니다. 이걸 특별법으로 도입하긴 좀 어렵고 특별법에 규정을 두더라도 상법에 근거가 있어야 된다고 해서 당시 법무부 상법개정위원회에서 감사위원회 도입을 위한 소위원회를 따로 만들었어요. 당시 상법개정위원회에는 마침 나도 제일 말석에 위원으로 참여를 했습니다. 그런데 감사위원회에 대해서는 상법개정위원회 교수들이 다 반대를 했어요. 말하자면 외부 압력으로 그런 이상한 것을 만드는데 내가 책임지지 않겠다는 식으로 다 피하니까 결국 나한테 떨어져서 내가 외부 교수 몇 분들을 모시고 소위원회를 만들어서 초안을 만들었습니다. 그 과정에서 IBRD 한국 담당자가 와서 여러 차례 만났고, 그 인연으로 나중에는 IBRD 컨설턴트로도 일하게 되었는데, 그 사람의 요구는 가능한 한 적용범위를 넓게 하라는 거였어요. 상장회사 전체를 적용대상으로 하라는 거였어요. 그래서 예나 지금이나 점진론자인 나는 그것은 너무 비현실적이라고 하면서, 그러지 말고 소수로 시작해서 성공 경험을 쌓아서 조금씩 확대하자는 식의 주장을 했습니다. 한참 실랑이를 하다가 결국은 총자산 2조원 이상 규모의 상장회사를 대상으로 하게 되었습니다. 가만히 있었으면 상장회사 전부가 될 수도 있었는데 그래도 그 정도로 막을 수 있었던 것을 다행으로 생각하고 있습니다. 상법에서는 감사위원회의 근거만 마련하면 되는 것이었는데 감사위원회 초안을 가지고 상법개정위원회에 갔더니 역시 학계위원들과 법원 대표로 나온 위원이 지금의 감사 제도가 무엇이 잘못이냐며 다 반대를 했습니다. 이분들에게 감사 제도는 대륙법계 상법에서의 자존심 같은 것이었는데 그것을 포기하고 미국식 제도를 도입하는 것은 자존심이 상하는 일이었던 것이죠. 그래서 그냥 표결을 했다면 당연히 부결이 되는 것이었지요. 그런데 당시 IMF 등으로부터 돈을 받아야하는 정부로서는 이들의 요구를 거부할 수 없었습니다. 그래서 법무부가 나서서 우리도 불만이 있지만 구제금융을 받기 위해서는 도입할 수밖에 없다고 설득하여 겨우 통과시킬 수 있었습니다. 새로운 제도도입에 관한 논의가 실제 진행되는 모습을 지켜본 것은 그때가 처음이어서 강한 인상을 받았습니다.

윤영신 : 제가 그때 선생님 소위원회 하실 때 리서치를 도와드렸었는데 지금 생각해 보면 감사위원회가 무엇인지 잘 몰랐었다는 것이 한 가지가 있고요. 또 법의 내용을 보면 감사를 대체하는 것으로 되어서, 감사가 하던 모든 것을 감사위원회가 하는 것으로 되다 보니까 감사위원회가 미국과는 다르게 이상하게 된 면이 있는 것 같습니다.

김건식 : 미국에서의 감사위원회는 외부감사가 제대로 이루어지는지 확실히 담보하는 것

이 가장 중요한 역할이죠. 그런데 그것만으로는 우리가 도저히 만족할 수 없는 상황이었습니다. 감사가 없어지면서 그런 사소한 역할로 축소되는 것에 대한 반발을 최소화하기 위해서 감사권한을 전부 감사위원회에 넘기게 된 겁니다. 하지만 감사의 권한을 현실적으로 감사위원회가 모두 수행하는 것이 바람직한가는 쉬운 이야기는 아니에요.

안수현 : 실제로 저도 많이 느끼고 있는 것 중 하나가 코스닥 상장회사임에도 불구하고 감사위원회를 둔 곳은 실제로는 감사의 기능은 거의 못 하고 있다는 느낌을 받았습니다. 회계감사는 그래도 외부감사인 이야기를 듣고서 좀 하는데, 업무감사는 거의 이루어지지 못하고 이슈가 무엇인지도 모르는 경우가 많은 것 같습니다. 미국의 회계감사는 감사위원회의 주된 일이고, 업무감사는 그렇게 부담을 안 주니까 그것을 미국하고 비교하기는 쉽지 않고, 한국에 들어온 감사위원회 제도만이라도 정착시켜야 되는데, 코스닥 상장회사들을 보면 감사위원회가 잘 작동을 하지는 못하는 것 같아 우려가 됩니다.

김건식 : 그 회사들은 그게 강제가 아닌데도 임의로 두고 있다는 거죠?

안수현 : 네, 임의로 두고 있고요. 대부분 감사위원으로 오신 분들이 이른바 권력기관에서 오신 분들이 많으신 것 같습니다. 업무감사라는 건 그냥 보고하면 되는 것으로 이해하는 경우도 많은 것 같습니다.

김건식 : 감사위원회가 미국식으로라도 작동하려면 전제조건이 사외이사 제도가 정착이 되어야 하는데 그것부터가 제대로 안 되어 있기 때문에 성공하기가 어렵지요. 그렇긴 한데 내가 항상 하는 이야기는 현실적으로 제대로 작동하지 않는다고 해서 그냥 그대로 과거의 감사로 돌아가는 것이 좋은가 하면, 그렇지는 않다고 생각합니다. 내가 늘 비유를 하는 것이, 국회의 기능이 형편없다고 해서 그걸 없애면 어떻게 되겠느냐는 말입니다. 사외이사도 그런 것이지요. 사외이사가 허수아비라는 비판이 많은데 상당 부분 맞는 말이지만, 그렇다고 그것을 없애면 대안이 뭐가 있겠습니까? 그보다 나은 대안도 별로 없거든요. 그래도 한 번 만들어놓으면 조금씩 나아질 수 있는 것 아니겠어요? 국회에 대해 지금도 비판하는 사람들이 물론 많이 있지만, 70년 전 처음 출발할 때는 더 기가 막힌 부분도 많았을 거예요. 그래도 시간이 지나면서 조금씩 나아지고 있지 않나요. 아니면 더 좋은 예는 대학일지도 몰라요. 1945년에 해방된 다음에 솔직히 대학이라고 할 수 있는 수준을 갖춘 곳이 얼마나 있었겠습니까? 그렇지만 여기저기 대학이란 간판 걸고 하다 보니 조금씩 나아져서 세계 몇 대 대학에도 이름을 올리고 하는 것 아니겠어요. 말

하자면 시작은 보잘것없더라도 길게 보고 조금씩 좋게 만들어 가는 것이 중요하지 않나 하는 겁니다. 사외이사, 감사위원회도 긴 호흡을 가지고 개선해 나가야 하는 것 아닌가 라는 생각이 듭니다.

송옥렬 : 외환위기 당시의 이야기는 늘 흥미롭습니다. 제가 얼마 전에, 선생님께서 예전에 비슷한 시기에 SK Telecom 사외감사를 하시다가 소송을 하신 일이 있다는 이야기를 들었습니다. 저희들도 잘 모르던 일인데요. 지배구조와 관련해서 큰 의미가 있는 것 같은데, 자세한 사연을 들려주시면 좋겠습니다.

김건식 : 자세한 이야기를 하려면 한이 없는데 그런 일이 있었던 건 사실입니다. 1998년 2월에 하버드에서 강의를 마치고 귀국하자마자 SK Telecom이란 회사의 사외감사로 일하게 되었습니다. 당시 SK Telecom은 SK그룹이 대주주지만 상당 부분을 KT와 타이거펀드라는 헤지펀드가 보유하고 있었습니다. 특히 이들 두 주주가 독립적인 인사의 이사회 참여를 강력히 주장해서 결국 사외이사 4명과 함께 내가 사외감사로 취임하게 되었습니다. 당시 SK Telecom은 돈을 잘 버는 이른바 캐시카우였는데 일반주주들은 회사 돈을 어려운 계열사로 빼돌리는 것 아니냐는 의심을 하고 있었습니다. 그런 의심을 뒷받침하는 일들도 없지 않아서 대주주 측과 사외이사들이 대립하는 일이 잦았습니다. 그 내용을 일일이 말씀드릴 여유는 없지만, 하여간 1998년에는 사외이사들이 한 주에 3, 4차례 만나 대책을 논의하는 일이 비일비재했습니다.

1999년 초에는 어느 정도 주주들 간의 관계가 정상화되어서 평온한 상태였는데 갑자기 회사가 대규모 신주발행을 강행하는 바람에 대주주와 사외이사 사이의 대립이 격화되었습니다. 신주발행은 규모도 컸지만 직전의 투자설명회에서는 물론이고 사외이사들에게도 사전에 전혀 알리지 않아서 사외이사들이 격분하였습니다. 사외이사들은 회사 측에 일단 이사회에서 발행이유를 설명한 후에 발행여부와 시기를 정하자고 요구했지만 회사 측은 전혀 응하지 않았지요. 그래서 사외이사들이 모여 의논한 끝에 결국 대주주 쪽에 압력을 가하는 방편으로 당시 대표이사인 손길승 회장의 해임을 구하는 임시주총소집을 사외감사인 내가 회사에 요구하게 되었습니다. 그런데 회사는 주총의 주도권을 유지하기 위해서 스스로 주총을 소집하되 그 일자를 신주발행이 끝난 후로 잡았던 것입니다. 그래서 나는 법원에 주총소집일자를 당겨야 한다는 가처분을 신청했지만 결국 받아들여지지 않았습니다.

사실 임시주총소집을 요구하고 가처분을 신청한 것은 이길 자신이 있어서라기보다는 대주주 측에 압력을 넣기 위해서였는데 우리는 당시 재벌에 다소 비판적인 DJ가 집권하고 있었고 외환위기가 완전히 가라앉지도 않은 때였던지라 언론에서도 비판적인 태도를 취할 것으로 내심 기대했었습니다. 그런데 알고 보니 우리의 기대는 순진하기 짝이 없는 것이었죠. 신문에서는 처음에는 다소 중립적인 태도를 취하는 듯하더니 나중에는 일방적으로 회사 편을 들었습니다. 사외이사들을 외국투자자의 앞잡이쯤으로 묘사하기도 했습니다. 심지어 회사 측 준비서면을 보니 나마저도 외국투자자의 앞잡이로 의심 받을 소지가 있다는 식의 표현도 있더군요. 대리인이 전부터 잘 아는 로펌이고 그 표현을 쓴 변호사가 제자일 가능성도 있었기에 내가 받은 충격은 컸습니다. 그때야 비로소 알게 된 것은 국내 언론이란 결국 광고에 의해서 움직인다는 사실이었습니다.

결국 이 분쟁은 저를 비롯한 사외임원들의 완전한 패배로 끝났습니다만 그 후의 전개는 승패를 따지기 어려운 것 같습니다. 자세히 말씀드리지는 않겠습니다만 당시 승리했던 대주주 측은 나중에 여러 문제로 고초를 겪었습니다. 만약 이때부터라도 무리한 운영을 자제했더라면 그런 고초는 피할 수 있지 않았을까 생각해봅니다. 한편 저는 이 일을 통해서 사외이사들 및 당시 타이거펀드 담당자와는 가까운 관계가 되었고 그 친분은 20년이 지난 지금까지도 유지되고 있습니다.

최문희 : 언론을 통해 어렴풋이 알던 SK Telecom 사건 전말을 듣고보니 흥미롭네요. 어려웠던 시절에 정말 용기있는 행동을 해 주셔서 저희도 같이 뿌듯합니다. 이제 마지막으로 저희 같은 후학들에게 연구와 관련하여 조언이 있으시다면 몇 말씀 부탁드립니다.

김건식 : 사실은 여러분 모두 제 제자인 셈이지만 이미 연구 면에서는 내가 어떤 조언을 할 수 있는 단계는 지난 것으로 생각합니다. 이 대담을 젊은 연구자들도 혹시 본다면, 그분들에게 한마디 하고 싶습니다. 최근에 젊은 연구자들을 만나면 제가 하는 말이 있는데요. 논문을 쓸 때 앞으로 단행본으로 만들 것을 염두에 두고 쓰라고 권고합니다. 저는 그걸 못했습니다. 저는 그냥 우연히 의뢰받은 것을 쓰거나 생각나는 것을 쓰거나 해서 그 논문들이 서로 간에 연관성이 없었습니다. 만약에 다시 연구자로 시작할 수 있다면 나중에 책을 낸다고 전제하고 미리 계획을 세워서 가령 책이 8장으로 구성된다고 하면 요번에 쓰는 건 3장, 그 다음엔 5장 이런 식으로 나눠서 쓰고, 나중에 그것을 모아서 책으로 내고 싶습니다. 아무래도 논문으로 되어 있으면 찾아서 읽기가 힘든데 책으로 만들면 찾아서 읽기가 쉬워지니까 그렇게 하는 것이 깊이도 더 생길 수 있고 좋은 것이 아닌가 해서 젊은 학자들 만나면 그런 식으로 해보라고 이야기를 합니다. 외부에서 의뢰를 받을 때에도 협상하기 따라서는 원하는 방향의 테마를 고를 수 있는 여지도 있으니까 그렇게 좀 체계적으로 연구를 해보라고 권고하고 있습니다.

〈해외 교류〉

천경훈 : 다음으로는 해외 교류 관련해서 몇 가지 말씀을 좀 나누었으면 싶은데요. 선생님께서는 다른 교수님들보다는 특히 해외 교류를 열심히 하셨고, 많은 성과도 거두신 것 같습니다. 처음 해외학자들과의 교류의 필요성을 느끼신 것은 언제부터였는지요?

김건식 : 솔직히 처음에는 해외 교류보다는 해외학자로부터 보다 효과적으로 배우려는 마음이 더 컸습니다. 아무래도 수준차가 있고, 또 외국 쪽에서 우리나라 법에 대한 관심이 없었기 때문에 쌍방적 교류라는 것을 기대하기 어려웠죠. 일본학자들하고도 일찍부터 만났지만, 학문적으로 주고받는 것은 기대할 수가 없었습니다. 외국학자들이 관심을 가지는 내용은 주로 자기 나라 사정이나 일부 선진국 사정에 관한 것인데, 그 면에서는 내가 그 사람들의 관심을 끌 만한 것을 제공할 수도 없었지요. 우리 법에 대해서는 내가 물론 비교우위가 있다고 할 수 있지만, 그 사람들이 우리 법에 대한 관심이 없었기 때문에 학문적 교류를 기대할 수가 없었는데, 차츰 시간이 흐르다 보니까 한국의 위상도 올라가고 특히 Corporate Governance의 경우에는 비교법적인 관심이 늘게 되니까 조금은 교류의 여지가 생겨났습니다.

노혁준 : 해외 교류를 위한 지원이 거의 없던 시절에 선생님께서 거의 혼자 애쓰신 것 같습니다. 학계에서도 해외 교류에는 소극적이었던 것 같구요. 말씀하신 것처럼 해외에서도 한국, 서울대의 존재가 크지 않았던 때에 해외 교류를 시작하셨는데요. 힘든 사정들이 많으셨을 것 같습니다.

김건식 : 여러 가지 힘든 것들이 있는데요. 지금도 그렇지만, 보통 교류에서 제일 먼저 신경 쓰는 것은 언어, 즉 영어지요. 영어실력이 어느 정도가 되어야 교류가 가능한데 그런 영어 실력을 갖췄는지가 제일 먼저 문제되지요. 그런데 제가 생각하기엔 영어도 물론 중요하지만, 그보다 더 중요한 것은 그 사람들이 관심을 가질만한 콘텐츠를 갖추는 것이라고 생각합니다. 그런 콘텐츠를 갖추기 위해서는 먼저 상대방이 어떤 것에 관심을 느끼고 있는지를 알아야 하고, 그것을 알려면 그 사람들의 논의 상황을 통해서 관심사항을 알아야 하는 것이지요. 그러니까 그쪽 사정을 모르고서 그냥 만나서 이야기를 할 수는 없고, 그 사람들이 무엇에 관심이 있을지를 대강 파악하고서 대화를 시작해야 하는 것이지요.

그 다음은 이야기를 재미있게 풀어나가는 능력이 중요한 것 같아요. 사실 이 두 가지,

즉 상대방이 관심 있는 내용, 또 그것을 어떻게 재밌게 풀어내느냐 하는 것이 모든 커뮤니케이션에서 기본이라고 생각을 하는데, 젊어서는 사실 누가 가르쳐 주는 사람이 없었기 때문에 그 중요성을 전혀 몰랐습니다. 특히 내가 무엇인가 발표를 하면 청중이 모두 다 그것을 듣고 싶어 하는 줄 알았어요. (모두 웃음) 그런데 지금은, 청중은 아무 관심이 없을 것으로 전제하고서 이야기를 시작합니다. 일반적으로 외국학자, 특히 일류학자들은 상대방에게 배울 것이 없는 관계는 원하지를 않습니다. 무언가 좀 얻을 것이 있다고 생각해야 만나서 이야기도 하고 그렇지, 그렇지 않으면 가능한 한 그 사람하고의 대화는 빨리 끝내려고 하지요. 나중에 어느 정도 친분이 쌓이고 하다보면 우정도 생기고 학문적으로도, 인간적으로도 배우는 것이 많이 있습니다.

안수현 : 해외학자들 중 인상적인 분들, 배울 점이라든가 혹은 에피소드 같은 것이 있으실까요?

김건식 : 사실 그런 면에서는 굉장히 운이 좋아서, 유명한 학자들을 정말 많이 만났습니다. 세계 주요 국가의 회사법이나 기업지배구조를 연구하는 사람들 중에서 중견 이상의 학자들은 대개 만나봤죠. 그래서 여러 가지로 배우고 자극을 받았고, 또 그들 중 일부와는 친해지기도 했습니다. 에피소드는 많지만 두 가지가 생각나네요. 하나는 1990년 뮌헨에 갔을 때의 일입니다. 당시 독일어로는 Betreuer라고 하는데 일종의 지도교수를 맡아주셨던 분이 세계적으로 유명한 홉트(Klaus J. Hopt) 교수입니다. 뮌헨은 워낙에 집을 구하기가 어려워서 집 구하고 이사하는 문제로 1년 내내 고생을 했습니다. 홉트 교수님이 그런 제 모습을 보고 답답해하는 거예요. 저는 그때까지 집 구하는 일을 제대로 해 본 적이 없어서 그냥 신문 보고 전화해보는 식으로 접근했는데, 그분이 저를 딱하게 보고서 이렇게 말했어요. "집을 구하는 일도 변호사가 하듯이 계획을 세우고 데이터를 수집해서 하나씩 하나씩 처리해야지. 당신같이 체계 없이 해서야 되겠습니까." (웃음) 이런 이야기를 듣고 처음엔 조금 서운하기도 했죠. '좀 더 잘 도와줄 수 있는 것 아닌가.' 이런 생각도 했는데, 그런 면에서 당시에 내가 너무 의존적이었던 것 같습니다. 나중에 생각해 보니 홉트 교수님 말씀이 다 맞다는 생각이 들어서 반성을 했죠.

다음으로 생각나는 분은 일본의 유명한 동경대 회사법 교수인 에가시라 겐지로(江頭憲治郎) 교수입니다. 그분하고도 친해져서 일본에 가면 요즘도 식사 대접을 받곤 합니다만, 그분한테는 본받을 점이 참 많이 있습니다. 그분은 주말에도 학교를 나가는데, 그 이유가 자기가 젊었을 때 집에 책상이 없어서 학교에 가서 연구를 해야만 했는데 그게 습관이 되어 그런다는 겁니다. 그 말을 듣고는 '에가시라 교수 같은 정말 일본을 대표하는 세계적인 학자도 집에 책상도 없어서 학교에 와서 연구를 한다는데, 나는 정말 얼마나 혜택받은 사람인가. 내가 무슨 불평을 할 수가 있을까.'라고 생각하게 되었습니다. 그 후로 주위 여건이 뭔가 좀 불만스럽다고 느끼는 순간이면 에가시라 교수를 떠올리며 참게 되었습니다. (모두 웃음) 또 하나 비슷한 이야기를 들었던 것이 생각나네요. 아마 세법 교수인 나카자토 미노루(中里實) 교수 이야기일 거예요. 그분은 젊었을 때 집에 잠 잘 공간이 없어서 식탁 밑에서 잤다는 거예요. 내가 상상하기로는 식탁 밑으로 발을 뻗고 잤다는 말인 것 같은데, 우리는 집이 좁아도 적어도 그렇게까지 하며 살지는 않잖아요. '나카자토 같은 뛰어난 학자도 그런 생활을 견디고 있는데 내가 무슨 불평을 할 수가 있느냐.' 항상 일본에 다녀올 때면 좀 겸허하게 살아야겠다 반성을 하곤 합니다.

윤영신 : 선생님께서는 외국에서 강의도 많이 하셨는데요. 재밌었던 일이나 인상 깊었던 일이 있으셨는지요? 우리나라와 비교해 봐도 재미있을 것 같은데요.

김건식 : 1986년 3월 첫 강의를 시작으로, 올해 1월 싱가폴국립대학 강의까지 하면 대략 6~7번 했던 것 같아요. 외국에서의 강의는 저보다 더 많이 하신 분들이 계시니까 특별히 제가 강의 경험을 자랑할 수 있는 것은 아닌데, 사용하는 언어가 영어일 뿐이지 내용 면에서는 그렇게 크게 차이가 있는 것은 아니라는 생각을 합니다. 최근에 와서 중요하게 생각하는 것은, 어떻게 하면 수강생에게 도움 되는 내용의 강의를 할 것인가 하는 문제입니다. 단순히 정보를 전달하는 걸 넘어서 무언가 자극이나 시사를 줄 수 있으면 좋겠죠. 최근에는 중국법, 일본법도 곁들인 강의도 하긴 했습니다만, 아무래도 한국법 사례를 통해서 일반적으로 적용될 수 있는 무엇인가를 가르쳐야 되는데, 그것을 어떻게 가르쳐야 할 것인가 고민을 많이 하죠.

〈교육〉

최문희 : 선생님께서는 서울대에서 33년 넘게 학생들을 가르치셨는데, 로스쿨 체제에서는 변호사시험에 치중해서 가르치기 때문에 교육철학을 겸비하는 것이 마치 도달할 수 없는 이상처럼 느껴지기도 합니다. 좀 추상적이긴 하지만, 선생님의 교육철학을 듣는 것으로 이야기를 시작하면 어떨까 합니다.

김건식 : 글쎄요. 교육철학이라고 하면 너무 거창해서 내가 뭐라고 말씀드리긴 어렵겠네

요. 내가 주로 관심을 가졌던 것을 중심으로 말씀을 드리겠습니다. 지금 생각하면 잘못한 것 같은데, 처음 교수생활을 시작할 때는 교과서에 없는 것을 가르쳐야 하는 것이 아닌가 생각해서 교과서에 안 나오는 것을 조사해서 보충해주는 식으로 강의를 했습니다. 그 후에는 갈수록 책이 워낙 두꺼워지고 내용이 많아져 오히려 중요한 것을 알기 쉽게 가르쳐서 확실하게 이해시키는 것이 더 중요하다고 생각이 들어 그것에 중점을 두었죠. 그런데 더 욕심을 부리자면, 학생들이 뭔가 다양한 측면에서 문제에 접근을 해서 좀 더 수준 높은 이해를 할 수 있도록 하면 좋겠다는 생각도 하곤 합니다. 말하자면 어떤 한 문제에 대해서 잘 배워서, 배우지 않은 다른 문제에도 응용할 수 있는 그런 능력을 기르게 해주는 것이지요. 우리가 다양하고 많은 문제들을 다 다룰 수는 없기 때문에, 일부 문제만을 가르칠 수밖에 없는데, 중요한 것은 거기에서 연마한 능력을 갖고 새로운 문제에 적용시킬 수 있도록 가르치는 것이지요. 그것은 어디까지나 욕심의 영역에 속하는데, 실제로 그것까지는 달성하지 못한 것 같다는 생각을 하지요.

그다음으로는 특히 최근에 와서 부쩍 느끼는 것인데, 어떻게 보면 이것은 강의실에서 가르칠 수 없는 것인지도 모르겠습니다. 그렇지만 중요한 것인데, 나는 그것이 바로 '공동작업을 하는 능력'이라고 생각해요. 세상에 혼자 할 수 있는 일이라는 것은 그렇게 많지 않고, 결국은 공동으로 하거나 남의 도움을 받아야 하는 일들이 많습니다. 그런데 학습능력이 뛰어난 사람일수록 남들하고 일을 같이하거나 남이 도와주고 싶게 만드는 능력은 크게 부족한 경우가 많이 있는 것 같아요. 그래서 학생들한테 그런 역량을 키우는 것이 중요하다는 식의 이야기를 많이 하는데, 자칫 시쳇말로 '꼰대'스런 이야기가 될 것 같아 조심스럽습니다.

송옥렬 : 아마 선생님께서 처음 교수가 되셨을 때와 지금은 상황도 많이 다르고, 환경도 다르고 모든 것이 다 다를 거 같은데요. 어떤 점이 가장 차이가 난다고 생각하시는지요? 요즘 학생들이라든지, 교육환경 등에 대해 말씀해 주시면 좋을 것 같습니다.

김건식 : 내 인상 중심으로 말씀드리면, 처음 강의를 시작할 때인 1980년대 후반에는 내 착각인지 모르겠습니다만 그때만 해도 내가 가장 젊은 교수였던 터라 학생들이 동질감을 느끼면서 좋게 봐주었던 것 같습니다. 법학개론을 많이 가르쳤는데 어설프기 짝이 없는 강의였습니다만, 학생들이 굉장히 집중을 하고 신기해한다는 느낌을 받았던 적이 여러 차례 있었어요. 그런데 시간이 점점 지남에 따라서 그런 식의 경험은 줄어든 것 같습니다. 도대체 무엇 때문에 그렇게 된 건지 생각해보면, 아마도 법학개론보다 상법은 아무래도 좀 더 기술적이어서 학생들의 흥미를 유발하기가 어려워서가 아닌지 모르겠습니

다. 또 솔직히 10, 20년 지나면서 아는 것은 점점 더 많아졌지만, 어쩌면 처음 시작할 때에 비해서 가르치는 열정이 줄어들어서가 아닌지도 모르겠습니다. 과거에는 열정이 있었고 학생들이 그것을 느꼈기 때문에 좋은 반응을 보여주었는데, 지금은 그런 열정이 아무래도 식다보니까 학생들도 그것을 눈치채고 따분하게 느끼는 것이 아닌가 싶기도 합니다. 그런 것을 보더라도 역시 정년이라는 것이 필요한 것이 아닌가 하는 생각을 해 봅니다. (모두 웃음) 반면에 학생들 쪽을 보면 특히 학부 학생들은 순진했다는 생각이 들어요. 지금은 로스쿨이 되었기 때문에 평면적으로 비교하기는 어렵지만, 지금 학생들은 더 똑똑하죠. 나쁘게 말하면 영악하게 된 것 같다는 느낌을 받습니다. 이렇게 막 이야기해도 되나요? (모두 웃음)

안수현 : 말씀하시니까 생각이 나는데, 제가 제일 열심히 가르쳤을 때 평가점수는 더 나쁜 것 같아요. 너무 열심히 가르치니까 학생들이 피곤해 해서요. (모두 웃음) 상법, 특히 회사법은 학생들이 접하기 어려운 내용입니다. 학부 학생이든 로스쿨생이든 사실 이해가 쉽지는 않습니다. 선생님께서 학생들을 가르치실 때 특히 신경 쓰신 부분이나 노하우를 가르쳐 주신다면 어떤 것이 있을까요?

김건식 : 노하우라고 할 것까지는 없는 것 같고요. 저는 그냥 일반적으로 이론을 위한 이론이 아니라 실제 도움이 되는 것을 가르치고 싶었습니다. 이는 법학의 성격이 실용학문이라서 그런 것도 있지만, 어떻게 보면 평생 실무경험 없이 학교에만 있었기 때문에 약간의 자격지심이 작용했던 것 같기도 합니다. 계속 학교에 있다 보면 공허한 이론에 빠지기 쉬울 것 같아서, 내가 잘 모르긴 하지만 그래도 실무 쪽을 의식해서 강의를 해야 된다고 생각했습니다. 또 다른 한편으로 실용적인 관점에서 보더라도 이론이라고 하는 것은 알면 좋지만 몰라도 그렇게 크게 문제될 것은 없습니다. 게다가 이론만 공부했는데 그 이론을 제대로 소화하지 못한 경우에는 아무짝에도 쓸 데가 없고, 오히려 해롭기까지 하죠. 그런데 실용적인 지식은 독창적인 것도 아니고 대단할 것은 없을지 모르겠지만, 쓸모가 있거든요. 아주 뛰어난 학생이 되진 못하더라도 쓸모 있는 지식을 갖추어서 밖으로 나가면 사회에서 쓸모 있는 사람이 되는 것이라고 생각해서, 가능하면 그런 쪽을 강조하려고 했습니다. 그러다 보니 시간이 흐르면서 강의내용도 좀 변화가 되었는데, 초창기에는 회사법 강의할 때 채권자 보호, 회사의 총칙, 회사의 설립 등과 같은 부분에 시간을 많이 들였지만, 점점 그 부분을 좀 덜 강조하게 되었습니다. 돌이켜보면 과거에는 그 부분 강의를 한 달가량 했던 것 같은데, 지금은 1주 반 정도로 끝나는 것 같습니다.

노혁준 : 교육 관련해서는 로스쿨 이야기를 피해가기 어려울 것 같은데요. 더구나 선생님께서는 서울대 로스쿨 초대학장으로서 지금의 로스쿨을 설계하시다시피 하셨기 때문에, 그 당시 특히 중점을 두었던 부분이 무엇이었는지 듣고 싶습니다.

김건식 : 여기 계신 분들은 대부분 기억을 하실 텐데, 당시 갑자기 로스쿨법이 통과되는 바람에 거의 패닉 상태였습니다. 서울대의 경우에도 로스쿨 인가를 받기 위해 인력 면에서의 대비는 물론이고, 물적 요건을 갖추었어야 했는데 모든 것이 제대로 마련되어 있지 않은 상태였죠. 거기다가 예산도 없어서 모금부터 해서 시설을 마련해야 하는 상황이었습니다. 당시에는 모든 사람이 이건 위기라고 생각했기 때문에 학교 내부뿐만 아니라 외부에서도 도움을 많이 받았습니다. 그 과정에서 한편으로는 서울대에 대한 외부의 시기를 실감하기도 했지만, 다른 한편으로는 서울대에 거는 기대도 많이 느꼈기 때문에 큰 책임감을 갖는 계기가 되기도 했습니다.

이와 동시에 교육 내용도 완전히 제로 베이스에서 새로 설계를 했어야 했죠. 이 작업을 할 때는 여기 계신 송교수께서 많이 도와주셔서 힘을 많이 덜 수 있었습니다. 각 과목별로 가르치는 내용이나 방법이 과거와는 좀 달라야 할 텐데 그것을 교수들한테 인식시키는 것이 상당히 어려웠습니다. 아무리 그 중요성에 대해 역설해도 뭔가 좀 벽이 있는 것 같다는 느낌을 받았어요. 개인적으로는 여기 공동저자들이 다 계시지만, 회사법도 새로운 형태의 교재가 필요하다고 생각해서 오랫동안 공동작업을 했던 일이 즐거운 기억으로 남아 있습니다. 그 당시만 해도 강의를 통해 모든 분야를 다 커버할 수 없으니까 일부에 집중해서 깊이 가르칠 필요가 있다고 생각했습니다. 일부를 깊이 가르치면 나머지는 자습을 통해 익힐 수 있겠다고 낙관적인 생각을 했었죠. 그런데 변호사시험이 예상보다 너무 중요해지다 보니, 이제는 정보전달도 소홀히 할 수 없어서, 점점 옛날 강의 방식으로 돌아가고 있는 것이 아닌가라고 생각을 해봅니다.

천경훈 : 지금 말씀하시는 과정에서 조금 언급하신 것 같습니다만, 로스쿨 도입 후 이제 10년이 지나갔는데요. 처음 제도를 설계하시고 출범하는데 결정적인 역할을 하신 선생님으로서 소회가 남다르실 것 같습니다. 지금 현상에 대한 평가, 그리고 앞으로 어떻게 발전시켜 나가야 할지에 대해서 생각을 말씀해 주십시오.

김건식 : 로스쿨 졸업하고 사회로 나가서 변호사로 활동하는 제자들을 가끔 만나는데, 만나면 참 보람을 느낍니다. 앞으로는 정보 전달 이것도 물론 중요합니다만, 이것을 넘어서 교육의 수준을 높여가는 것이 중요하다고 생각합니다. 다만, 강의가 변호사시험하

고 연결이 되어 있기 때문에 그것이 쉽지는 않죠. 서울대만을 두고 보자면, 교육만이 아니라 연구 면에서도 해야 될 일이 있으니까 법학연구 수준도 좀 높여갈 필요가 있는데, 그것도 그렇게 쉬운 일은 아닌 것 같고요. 특히 세상이 점점 국제화 되고 있어서 법학연구도 국제 수준에 어느 정도 맞추어 갈 필요가 있다고 생각이 되는데, 현실적으로 연구가 쉽지 않은 상황이어서 걱정입니다. 어떻게 보면 이런 시점에서 정년퇴직을 하는 것이 다행스러운 면도 있는 것 같아요. 남아있는 분들께서 나보다 더 뛰어난 분들이니까 이런 문제들은 잘 대처해주실 것이라 기대하고 있습니다.

〈BFL 등 실무와의 교류〉

윤영신 : 오늘 말씀해 주신 것도 그렇고 제가 선생님 뵈었을 때도 느꼈던 것이, 선생님께서는 이론을 위한 이론이 아니라 좀 더 실용적인 것을 강조하셨던 것 같습니다. 그런 면에서 『BFL(Business Finance Law)』 창간작업이 선생님께서 하신 활동 중에 중요한 부분이 아니었을까 싶습니다. 굉장히 독특한 잡지이고 아직까지도 우리나라에서 이런 유형의 잡지가 잘 없는 것 같은데, 어떻게 처음 시작하시게 된 것인지요?

김건식 : 내가 실무의 중요성을 강조했다고 말씀하시는데 사실입니다. 그런데 내가 실무를 많이 알고 있어서 강조한 것이 아니라, 잘 모르기 때문에 알아야 한다는 차원에서 중요하다고 역설한 것입니다. 『BFL』 같은 잡지가 있으면 좋겠다는 생각은 오래전부터 가지고 있었습니다. 예컨대 일본의 『상사법무(商事法務)』와 같은 잡지를 보면, 그것이 무슨 심오한 학술논문을 싣는 것은 아니지만 실무상 유용한 정보들이 많이 담겨져 있습니다. 그것을 구독하면서 우리도 이런 잡지가 있었으면 좋겠다고 늘 생각했었습니다. 일본학자들을 만날 때마다 느낀 것이지만, 이 사람들은 25세부터 학계에 몸담고 있는 그야말로 순수한 학자들인데도 실제 일어나는 문제에 대해서 굉장히 구체적으로 알고 있다는 느낌을 받았습니다. 그런데 우리는 전혀 그렇지 못했단 말이에요. 그것이 항상 부러워서 우리도 『상사법무』 같은 잡지가 있으면 좋겠다고 생각했는데, 솔직히 그것을 제가 시작한다는 것은 생각도 못 했습니다. 좀 있으면 그런 것이 나오겠지 하고 기다렸는데 아무리 기다려도 나오질 않는 거예요. 1990년대 중반에 송상현 선생님이 학장 하실 때 우리도 이런 수준 높은 잡지를 만들어야 되는 것 아니냐는 이야기가 젊은 교수들 사이에서 나온 적이 있습니다. 그런데 당시에 교수들이 원했던 것은 수준 높은 학술지였습니다. 그 당시만 해도 소위 peer review는 고사하고 원고 자체가 부족한 상황이어서, 원고의 수

준과 무관하게 무조건 학술지에 게재할 수 있던 시절이었습니다. 그래서 좀 엄격한 심사를 통해 믿을 만한 좋은 논문만을 선별해서 실을 잡지의 필요는 당연히 있었고, 같이 있었던 대부분의 교수들이 그 필요에 동감했었습니다. 그런데 저로서는 물론 그것도 좋지만 그보다 먼저 실무에서 일어나는 일을 알 수 있는 잡지를 해보면 좋겠다고 말씀드린 일이 있었습니다. 결국 두 가지 다 실현되지 못한 채로 끝나게 됐죠.

노혁준 : 『BFL』을 처음 창간했을 때는 사람들 사이에 좀 회의적인 시각도 있었던 것 같지만, 곧 100호가 나올 정도로 성공적으로 정착하였는데요. 중간에 어떤 어려움이 있었다든지, 기억에 남을 만한 일이 있었다면 듣고 싶습니다.

김건식 : 처음 시작하려고 하니까 말리는 사람이 많았습니다. 학계에 있는 분들도 그렇고 또 실무가분들도 그렇고. 괜히 고생만 한다고 말리는 분들이 많았습니다. 창간사가 다소 비장한 톤으로 되어있는 건 그 때문입니다. 그래도 제가 도움을 요청했을 때 대개 다들 도와주셨어요. 그래서 그렇게까지 어려운 부분은 없었던 것 같습니다.

그런 일을 시작한 동기와 관련해서 한 말씀을 드리고 싶네요. 얼마 전부터 유튜브에서 강연이나 인터뷰를 즐겨봅니다. 그것을 통해 알게 된 분으로 에즈라 보겔(Ezra Feivel Vogel)이라고, 하버드대학에서 일본학과 중국학을 연구하는 분이 있습니다. 굉장히 유명한 분이고, 한국에도 그분 제자들이 많이 있습니다, 임현진, 송호근 이런 분들이 아마 다 제자일 거예요. 그분이 인터뷰에서 한 이야기가 생각나는데, 자기 이야기인지 중국학을 하던 페어뱅크(John K. Fairbank) 교수 이야기를 전한 것인지 확실치 않습니다. 그분이 하버드대 교수의 사명이라고 하면서 이야기하는 것이, 하버드대학은 훌륭한 도서관에 엄청나게 많은 자료를 가지고 있고, 재정적으로도 비교할 수 없이 튼튼하니까 그곳의 교수들은 무언가 사회를 위해서, 학계를 위해서 봉사하는 일을 해야 한다는 취지였어요. 나는 서울대 교수의 사명도 그와 비슷하다고 생각합니다. 서울대가 국제적으로는 몰라도 국내 다른 대학에 비해서는 상대적으로 훨씬 좋은 환경에 있는 것만은 사실입니다. 보통 이런저런 일로 외부에 도움을 청하면 다들 도와주려고 합니다. 나도 여러 가지로 도움을 많이 받았어요. 물론 이런 일 저런 일 안 하고 개인적으로 연구만해서 논문 내는 것이 좀 더 학자적으로 보일 수 있습니다. 그런데 서울대 교수로서 내가 사회적으로 의미 있는 일을 주도하면 성공확률이 더 높은데 그런 일은 외면하고, 자기 개인적인 연구만 하는 것이 과연 좋은 것인가라는 고민을 항상 해왔습니다. 그런데 이런 일은 여러 사람의 도움을 받아야 하는 공동작업이거든요. 그렇지만 다들 각자 엄청나게 바쁘고 힘들게 사는 것을 아는데 내가 뭘 또 시작하자는 이야기를 꺼내기는 어렵습니다. 가만히 있으면 편하고 좋긴 한데, 서울대 교수의 지위를 낭비하는 것은 아닌지라는 생각이 들어서, 늘 고민을 했습니다. 이젠 그런 고민에서도 해방돼서 홀가분합니다.

최문희 : 제가 선생님 통해서 알게 된 몇몇 동경대 교수들을 만나서 이런 저런 이야기를 하던 중, 그 교수들이 한국에도 『상사법무』 같은 것이 있냐고 물어보길래 우리도 있다고 그러니까 어느 회사에서 나오는 거냐고 물어보더라고요. 회사가 아니라 서울대 금융법센터에서 김건식 선생님께서 만들어서 나온 것이라고 하니까 굉장히 놀라워 하더라고요. 어떻게 출판 비용이며, 저자 섭외 등을 회사가 아닌 학교에서 할 수 있냐고 그러더라고요. 선생님께서 앞으로도 『BFL』 창간자로도 왕성한 기여를 해 주실 거라 믿지만, 저희는 그래도 선생님께서 학교를 떠나신 후가 걱정이 되기도 합니다. 앞으로 『BFL』이 어떤 방향으로 발전해 나갔으면 좋겠다고 생각하시는지 말씀해 주시기 바랍니다.

김건식 : 저는 현실주의자라서 모든 것을 판단할 때 '이것이 없는 것보다 나은가'의 기준으로 판단하곤 합니다. 『BFL』이 지금 상태에서 하나도 변화되는 것이 없더라도, 그러니까 유지되기만 하더라도 저는 만족할 수 있다고 생각을 해요. 그런데 욕심을 부리자면 이것을 시작한 것이 16년 전인데 그때는 여러 가지로 지금보다 여건이 더 좋지가 않았을 때인데도 어떻게든 발간했는데, 계속 현상유지에 그친다면 좀 아쉬움은 있죠. 솔직히 그때의 발간 부담에 비해서 지금은 부담이 덜한 것이 사실이니까요. 그래서 질적으로 더 좋게 만드는 노력도 물론 필요하지만, 양적인 확대도 필요한 것 아닌가 간혹 생각합니다. 그런데 이건 또 부담을 늘리는 일이라 이제 내가 할 수 있는 이야기는 아닌 것 같습니다.

안수현 : 『BFL』은 대학원 수업에서 더 유용하게 활용하고 있고, 다른 기관에 가서도 『BFL』에 실린 타이틀을 이야기하면서 좀 참고하라 그러면 고마워하기도 하고, 이미 기관지로 구독을 하고 있는 경우도 있어서 굉장히 뿌듯합니다. 이렇게 『BFL』은 실무와의 교류를 위한 정말 좋은 방법의 하나인 것 같습니다. 그 외에도 실무와의 교류가 정말 중요한데, 어떤 방법으로 더 이루어질 수 있을지 저희 연구자들한테 말씀해 주시면 큰 도움이 될 것 같습니다.

김건식 : 그에 대해서는 구체적으로 더 말씀드릴 것은 없는 것 같습니다. 일반론으로는 이미 몇 차례 말씀드렸습니다만, 법학이라는 것이 실용학문적 요소가 강하니까 실무와 괴리되어서는 안 된다는 명제 자체에 대해서는 누구도 토를 달 수 없겠죠. 특히 학계에

오래 있다 보면, 자칫 실무를 소홀히 하고 자기만족에 빠져버리기가 쉽습니다. 그래서 실무가와 교류하고 다른 학자들과 소통하는 것이 반드시 필요하다고 생각합니다.

개인적으로는 젊었을 때 민사판례연구회에 참여했던 것이 큰 도움이 되었습니다. 처음으로 실무가들이 판례를 읽고 해석하는 태도를 가까이서 접할 수 있어서 너무 좋았습니다. 무식하단 소릴 들을까 봐 토론에 끼지도 못하고 그저 듣기만 하는 게 좀 부끄럽게 생각될 수도 있었지만 꾸준히 참석하며 많이 배웠습니다.

기본적으로 학자의 연구란 혼자 하는 작업이 많고, 그런 면에서는 고독한 길이라고 할 수 있죠. 그런데 크게 보면 학문 공동체라는 게 있어서 공동으로 해야 되는 일들도 있다고 생각해요. 그것을 외면하면 자칫 독단에 빠지기 쉽고, 반면에 너무 사람들하고 어울리다 보면 시간과 에너지가 많이 소모돼버리죠. 인생만사가 모두 그렇지만 이 일에서도 둘 사이의 밸런스를 맞추는 것이 중요하다는 생각을 합니다.

안수현 : 이것과 관련해서 간혹 국회하고 세미나를 하거나 어떤 단체와 협업을 하게 되면 오해받는 경우도 없지 않은 것 같습니다. 소송사건을 학회에서 이슈로 다룬다고 하면 로펌과 같이 세미나를 하는 것도 가능한 교류가 될 수 있고, 국회와의 교류도 제도 개선의 측면에서 중요할 수 있는데, 한자리하려고 그러느냐는 등 뭔가 다른 의도가 있는 것이 아닌가 하는 오해를 받는 것이지요. 이런 문제들에 대해서는 어떻게 생각하시는지요?

김건식 : 사실 어떤 단체하고 같이 활동을 할 때에는 그 단체가 원하는 쪽으로 결과물을 내는 데에 이용당할 가능성도 있지요. 그래서 학문의 중립성, 객관성하고 충돌할 위험이 있는 것이 사실이어서, 그것은 경계해야 된다고 생각합니다. 그렇다고 해서 그런 곳과는 완전히 관계를 끊고 아무것도 안 한다면 현실과 괴리될 위험이 있기 때문에, 뭐라고 이야기해야 될지 모르겠지만 항상 조심하면서 교류를 계속해 나가야 하는 거라는 생각이 듭니다.

자리 욕심 때문에 외부활동을 하는 것 아니냐는 이야기를 들으니, 얼마 전에 학교 간행물 학생기자와 한 퇴직 인터뷰가 생각나네요. 학교 외부에서도 오라는 유혹이 많으셨을 텐데 왜 30년 넘게 학계에만 계속 계셨냐는 질문을 받았어요. 그런데 생각해 보니 지난 30여 년 동안 한 번도 외부에서 무슨 자리를 해보라고 제의를 받은 적이 없어 조금 민망하더라고요. (모두 웃음) 그런데 나는 어쩌다 보니 학계에서 일생을 보냈지만 교수가, 특히 법학교수가 공직을 맡아 일을 하는 것 자체를 꼭 나쁘게 볼 것은 아니라고 생각합니다. 아예 거기로 진로를 바꿔도 좋고, 아니면 거기에서 경험하고 학교로 돌아와도 좋고요. 교수의 다양성이란 면에서는 좋은 점도 있을 거라는 생각입니다. 물론 거기 가서 어떤 일을 하느냐가 중요하겠죠.

송옥렬 : 마지막으로 추가하시고 싶은 말씀이 있으시면 부탁드리겠습니다.

김건식 : '떠날 때는 말없이'란 말을 실천하고 싶었는데 말문이 터지다 보니 너무 말을 많이 한 것 같네요. 나는 이상적인 상법학자가 되기에 여러 가지로 부족하다는 생각을 하며 살았습니다. 뒤늦게나마 좀 보완해보려고 애를 써보기도 했지만 역부족인 상태에서 퇴직을 맞게 되었습니다. 부족하기 짝이 없지만 그래도 뭔가 쓸모 있는 일을 해보려고 꿈틀거렸던 것이 내 인생인 것 같습니다. 나는 이 대담을 읽는 젊은 사람들도 너무 위만 쳐다보지 말고 각자 자기 처지에서 할 수 있는 일을 조금씩이라도 해나가며 삶의 보람을 찾으면 좋겠습니다.

나는 일생동안 다른 사람들에 비해서 너무 많은 혜택을 누렸습니다. 이 자리에서 말씀드린 것은 극히 일부에 지나지 않습니다. 도움을 주신 모든 분들을 여기서 일일이 언급할 수는 없겠지만 그래도 법대 여러분들께는 감사드리고 싶습니다. 학생시절 가르쳐주셨던 은사님들, 특히 상법분야의 정희철, 최기원, 양승규, 송상현 선생님께는 나이가 들수록 감사의 마음이 깊어지네요. 특히 생존해 계신 세 분께는 최근에 따로 찾아뵙고 큰 절을 올렸습니다. 그럴 수 있어 너무 행복했습니다. 법대에 같이 근무했던 선배, 동료, 후배 교수님들로부터도 이런 저런 도움을 많이 받았습니다. 때론 학내 대소사에 대한 생각 차이로 대립하며 사이가 서먹해진 경우도 없지 않았습니다. 돌이켜보면 인간사에 대한 지혜와 관용이 부족한 자신을 탓해야할 경우도 많은 것 같습니다. 모자란 사람을 늘 따뜻하게 대해준 법대 구성원들께 진심으로 머리 숙여 감사드리고 싶습니다. 앞으로도 간혹 마주칠 기회가 있을 텐데 잘 부탁드리겠습니다.

일동 : 긴 시간 동안 좋은 말씀해 주셔서 감사합니다.

저자 약력
서울대 법대 법학사 및 법학석사
하버드법대 LL.M.
워싱턴주립대 법대 J.D. & Ph.D.
서울대 법대 학장 겸 법학전문대학원 원장 역임
한국상사법학회 회장 역임
서울대 법학전문대학원 명예교수

주요 저서
회사법연구 I , II (2010)
기업지배구조와 법(2010)
자본시장법(제3판 2013 공저)
회사법(제4판 2020 공저)

서울대학교 법학연구소 Medvlla Iurisprudentiae

"Medvlla Iurisprudentiae"는 '법의 정수精髓 · 진수眞髓'라는 뜻으로, 서울대학교 법학전문
대학원에서 정년퇴임하시는 교수님들의 논문을 모아 간행하는 총서입니다.
법학 교육과 연구를 위해 일생을 보내고 정년퇴임하는 교수님들의 수많은 연구업적들 중
학문적으로 가장 가치있는 논문만을 엄선하여 간행하였습니다.
이 총서가 법학자의 삶을 되돌아보게 하고 후학에게 귀감이 되기를 바랍니다.

Corporate Law and Governance - Collected Papers

초판발행	2020년 5월 13일
지은이	김건식(Kon Sik Kim)
펴낸이	안종만 · 안상준
편 집	한두희
기획/마케팅	조성호
표지디자인	조아라
제 작	우인도 · 고철민
펴낸곳	(주) **박영사**
	서울특별시 종로구 새문안로3길 36, 1601
	등록 1959. 3. 11. 제300-1959-1호(倫)
전 화	02)733-6771
f a x	02)736-4818
e-mail	pys@pybook.co.kr
homepage	www.pybook.co.kr
ISBN	979-11-303-3642-8 93360

copyright©김건식, 2020, Printed in Korea

* 잘못된 책은 바꿔드립니다. 본서의 무단복제행위를 금합니다.
* 저자와 협의하여 인지첩부를 생략합니다.

정 가   37,000원